Reader's Digest

NATURE IN
NORTH AMERICA

NATURE IN
NORTH AMERICA

The Reader's Digest Association (Canada) Ltd.

NATURE IN NORTH AMERICA

PROJECT EDITORS: Richard L. Scheffel,
Alice Philomena Rutherford
PROJECT ART EDITORS: Gerald Ferguson,
Lucie Martineau
SENIOR ART EDITOR: Kenneth Chaya
EDITORS: Paula Pines,
Andrew Richmond Byers
ASSOCIATE EDITORS: David Diefendorf,
Megan A. Newman
ART ASSOCIATE: Marisa Gentile
EDITORIAL ASSISTANT: Dolores Damm
RESEARCH: Wadad Bashour
COPY PREPARATION: Joseph Marchetti
PHOTO RESEARCH: Rachel Irwin
COORDINATION: Susan Wong
PRODUCTION: Holger Lorenzen

CONSULTANTS

Drs. Lorus and Margery Milne, Dr. Peter F. Cannell, David
M. Ludlum, Dr. James E. Roche, Dr. William A. Weber

CONTRIBUTORS

WRITERS: Thomas Christopher, John Farrand, Jr.,
Peter R. Limburg, Alan Pistorius, Judy Rice
PHOTO RESEARCHER: Jacki Tolley
COPY EDITOR: Mel Minter
INDEXERS: Laura Ogar, Sydney Wolfe Cohen

CANADIAN CATALOGUING IN PUBLICATION DATA

Main entry under title:
Nature in North America

1st Canadian ed.
Includes index.
ISBN 0-88850-188-9

1. Natural history—North America—Encyclopedias.
2. Earth Sciences—North America—Encyclopedias.
I. Reader's Digest Association (Canada).

QH102.N28 1992   508.7'03   C91-090637-8

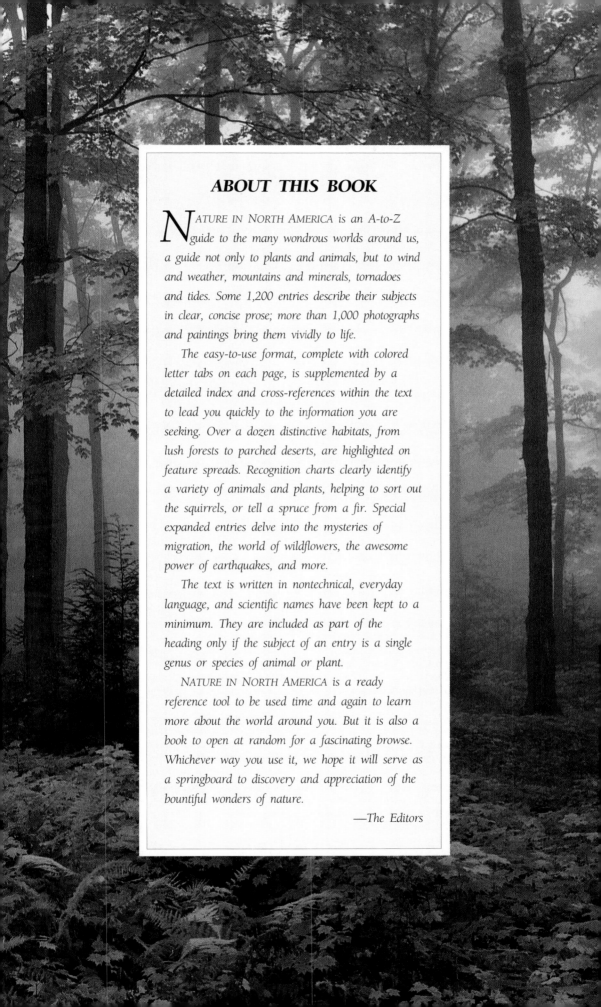

ABOUT THIS BOOK

NATURE IN NORTH AMERICA is an A-to-Z guide to the many wondrous worlds around us, a guide not only to plants and animals, but to wind and weather, mountains and minerals, tornadoes and tides. Some 1,200 entries describe their subjects in clear, concise prose; more than 1,000 photographs and paintings bring them vividly to life.

The easy-to-use format, complete with colored letter tabs on each page, is supplemented by a detailed index and cross-references within the text to lead you quickly to the information you are seeking. Over a dozen distinctive habitats, from lush forests to parched deserts, are highlighted on feature spreads. Recognition charts clearly identify a variety of animals and plants, helping to sort out the squirrels, or tell a spruce from a fir. Special expanded entries delve into the mysteries of migration, the world of wildflowers, the awesome power of earthquakes, and more.

The text is written in nontechnical, everyday language, and scientific names have been kept to a minimum. They are included as part of the heading only if the subject of an entry is a single genus or species of animal or plant.

NATURE IN NORTH AMERICA is a ready reference tool to be used time and again to learn more about the world around you. But it is also a book to open at random for a fascinating browse. Whichever way you use it, we hope it will serve as a springboard to discovery and appreciation of the bountiful wonders of nature.

—The Editors

A

Abalone shells, mottled on the outside (above), have lustrous interiors (right).

A polished agate displays swirls of color.

Abalone

Popular with collectors for their pearly, iridescent shells, abalones are also prized by gourmets for their tasty meat. Fairly common along the Pacific coast, these large marine snails creep across rocks, propelled by a large muscular foot, and feed on algae and microscopic animals. The shell is perforated with a line of small holes along one edge, permitting the expulsion of wastes and the water that is used for breathing. During their first week of life, the tiny free-swimming larvae attach to rocks and other hard objects, and there they mature into adults up to 12 inches long. Although all species are edible, many people consider the red abalone a particular delicacy.

Acacia

Found in tropical and subtropical regions all around the world, acacias are widespread members of the legume, or pea, family. Only 15 species are native to the United States, but many others have been cultivated successfully, particularly in California and Florida. Growing as either shrubs or small trees, acacias are a source of dyes, tannins, and a gum used in medicines, foods, and manufacturing. Their wood is used for everything from furniture to fence posts.

The sweet acacia, a thorny shrub or small tree, is indigenous to Texas and cultivated elsewhere. It favors dry, sandy soils and produces bright yellow heads of tiny flowers in February and March. The fragrant blossoms are used in sachets and as a perfume ingredient.

Another species, the catclaw acacia, grows in dense thickets in the deserts of the Southwest. Named for the armament of hooked spines on its branches, the catclaw is decorated with elongated spikes of creamy yellow flowers in early spring and intermittently throughout the summer. The Pima and Papago Indians made a meal, pinole, from its seeds and gathered the honey produced from its nectar.

Accipiter

Short, rounded wings and long tails distinguish the accipiters from all other hawks. Agile woodland birds that alternately flap their wings and then glide, they are sometimes called bird hawks because of their predominant prey, although they feed on insects and small mammals as well. The three species found across most of North America are the foot-long sharp-shinned hawk; the medium-size Cooper's hawk; and the northern goshawk, larger than a crow and formidable enough to kill ducks and rabbits.

Acid rain

A by-product of automobile exhaust and the combustion of coal and oil in factories and power plants, acid rain has become a serious problem in many areas. It has made many lakes uninhabitable to fish, even in areas far from the sources of pollution. It has killed or damaged trees and crops. And it has corroded masonry buildings and other man-made structures.

Acid rain is produced when nitrogen oxide and sulfur dioxide are released into the atmosphere. There they combine with water vapor to form nitric acid and sulfuric acid, resulting in rainfall that is far more acidic than normal precipitation.

Emission control devices designed to remove pollutants from smokestacks are available. But they must be more widely used if the problem is to be controlled.

Agave leaves are the source of sisal and henequen, strong fibers used to make rope.

Agaves, which thrive in the Southwest and Mexico, send up flowering stalks from clusters of tough, spearlike leaves. The sap of some species is distilled to make tequila.

Agate

Valued for their swirling bands of color, agates have long been used in mosaics and jewelry. The vivid colors for which they are prized are not always the gift of nature; even the ancients knew that these porous stones could be dyed to intensify their natural hues.

Agates are deposited slowly, layer by layer, in cavities in older rocks. Composed of almost pure silica, they are a type of quartz. Their colorful patterns are caused by minute quantities of iron and other mineral impurities that highlight the concentric bands. In North America, gemstone-quality agates have been found in Yukon, British Columbia, Manitoba, New Brunswick, Nova Scotia, Oregon, Washington, Idaho and around Lake Superior.

Agave

Sometimes known as century plants because they take so long to bloom (not a century, by any means, but often many decades), several species of agaves flourish from Virginia to California. Tolerant of hot, dry growing conditions, they are especially common in the parched deserts of the Southwest.

Most agaves consist of a dense rosette of thick, spiny-edged, spearlike leaves up to several feet long. The flowering stalk that eventually emerges from among the leaves may grow to be 20 feet tall and is topped by clusters of tubelike flowers. The blooms are pollinated by long-tongued bats that sometimes hover in the air, hummingbird style, as they lap up the nectar. Some kinds of agave die after flowering, while others bloom year after year.

In Mexico the sap and pulp of certain species are used to make the alcoholic drinks pulque, mescal, and tequila. Agaves also are cultivated for their fibers, called sisal and henequen, which are used to make thread and rope. In many areas they are also planted as ornamentals—a tribute to their dramatic beauty.

Ailanthus *Ailanthus altissima*

Featured in the novel *A Tree Grows in Brooklyn*, the ailanthus is a common sight in cities all across the country. Since it easily endures poor soils and air pollution, it thrives where few other trees can grow.

A native of the Orient imported to North America in the 19th century, the ailanthus is also known as the tree of heaven, a reference to its speedy growth (as much as 10 feet a year) to heights of 60 feet or more. Its featherlike compound leaves are up to three feet long, giving the tree a luxuriant, somewhat tropical look. But its branches are easily broken and its male flowers give off a rank odor, discouraging its use as a street tree. Condemned by many as a rampant weed, the ailanthus nevertheless manages to sprout, unbidden, wherever the wind carries its papery, single-winged seeds.

A

Air pollution, an unpleasant by-product of the industrial age, once was tolerated as a nuisance but now is recognized as a significant threat to health and the environment.

Air

The air we breathe is part of the mixture of gases—the atmosphere—that envelops the earth and sustains life. It consists of 78% nitrogen, 21% oxygen, and minute traces of a variety of other gases, including about .03% carbon dioxide. Water vapor also is present in varying amounts, depending on temperature and location. And as any city dweller can attest, air is adrift with a host of microscopic particles, ranging from soot and dust to salt and plant spores.

Scientists believe the atmosphere began to form billions of years ago as gases escaped from the earth's interior, mainly through volcanoes. This early atmosphere lacked oxygen, until green plants developed in the ocean and released that vital gas through photosynthesis.

Air pollution

Long recognized as a threat to human health and to the environment, air pollution is a worldwide problem. The contaminants that foul the air range from dust and soot to noxious fumes such as sulfur oxides and carbon monoxide. Among the major sources are emissions from motor vehicles, factories, and power plants.

An especially pernicious form of pollution—the dense, dark haze known as smog—results when smoke and other gases mix with water vapor in the air. If atmospheric conditions prevent its dispersal, the results can be disastrous. In Donora, Pennsylvania, in October 1948, for example, a slow-moving ridge of warm air hung over the town for days on end, trapping the pollutants from its many industrial smokestacks. By the time the air cleared, 20 people were dead and thousands more suffered serious illness.

In recent decades significant strides have been made in cleaning North America's dirty air. With stricter emission standards, the installation of pollution-control devices, and other measures, we all will breathe more easily. But much remains to be done before the problem is solved completely.

An adult alderfly rests on an alder leaf.

Albatross

The largest and perhaps the most highly adapted of all seabirds, albatrosses glide effortlessly over the waves on stiffly held, very long and narrow wings. Taking advantage of winds and small updrafts, they can remain aloft for hours on end with scarcely a beat of their wings. Indeed, these nomads of the open sea come ashore only to breed, usually on remote islands.

Albatrosses live mainly in southern oceans, but a few species visit North American waters. Most often seen is the black-footed albatross, which nests in the central Pacific and appears off the west coast in summer and fall. Dusky brown, with a white face, it has a wingspan of nearly 7 feet. The Laysan albatross, with a wingspan slightly shorter than that of its relative, is white with a blackish back, tail, and wings and also is seen in summer off the Pacific coast. It nests in the Hawaiian Islands. In typical albatross fashion, both species feed on fish, squid, and other marine animals, and some willingly accept scraps thrown from passing ships.

Alder

Growing both as shrubs and small trees, alders are found mainly in northern temperate regions. Tolerant of moist conditions, these members of the birch family often grow in dense thickets in swamps and along streams. Although they are of little value to wildlife, the nitrogen-fixing bacte-

A Laysan albatross, soaring gracefully above the open sea, spends most of its life in the air.

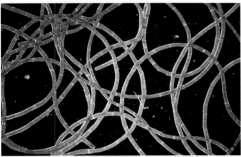

Filamentous algae (upper) and marine rockweed (lower) are two examples of this simple but varied plant group.

ria that live in nodules on their roots play an important role in enriching the soil. Because of their growth habits and their ability to add nitrogen to the soil, alders are useful in preventing erosion and helping reestablish plant growth in fire-scorched areas.

The largest North American species, the red alder, reaches heights of more than 100 feet. Reseeding quickly after fires and logging operations, it is the most important hardwood in the Pacific Northwest, where it is used for making both furniture and paper.

Alderfly

Living as adults in the vegetation near ponds and streams, alderflies are named for the trees in which they often congregate. An inch or less in length, these black or dark brown insects have long, threadlike antennae and two pairs of large smoky wings. The adults—sluggish fliers that apparently do not eat—live for only a few days and die soon after mating. The aquatic larvae, on the other hand, live for a year or more underwater, where they crawl along stones and feed actively on other small insects. They come ashore to pupate, burying themselves in the mud, and emerge the following spring for their brief life as mature alderflies.

Algae

These simplest of all plants—they have no true roots, stems, leaves, or flowers—are an extremely varied group. Algae range in size from microscopic single-celled organisms to the giant kelps, seaweeds that grow to lengths of 200 feet or more. They thrive on land, in fresh water, and in the sea and may be green, blue-green, red, or brown. All of them, however, contain green chlorophyll—the substance that enables plants, using sunlight for energy, to make their own food from carbon dioxide and water, a process called photosynthesis.

Millions of single-celled algae form the filmy green growth sometimes seen on damp, shaded tree trunks, walls, and roofs. Other microscopic algae live in both fresh and salt water, where they may drift in huge numbers—a very important food source for other forms of life. Common freshwater algae include threadlike spirogyra, found in billowing cottony masses in the quiet water of ponds and ditches, and volvox, which consists of thousands of individuals grouped in spheres the size of pinheads. Diatoms, encased in microscopic glassy shells, are among the most abundant of the marine algae. More commonly seen are the larger types known as seaweeds.

Some algae form remarkable associations with other living plants and animals. Lichens, for instance, are dual plants made up of both algae and fungi. Single-celled algae also live inside the tissue of reef-building corals and seem to play a role in the formation of the reef.

9

A baby alligator perches atop its mother's head. Only about 9 inches long at hatching, it may reach an adult size of 12 feet or more.

The amanitas are pretty—but most are poisonous.

Alligator *Alligator mississippiensis*

Kin of the dinosaurs and our continent's largest reptiles, American alligators grow up to 15 feet long and sometimes weigh more than 500 pounds. On land, they are awkward and slow, but in water they are agile swimmers. Their huge jaws and sharp teeth are used not to chew, but to catch and hold prey. Far from fussy feeders, alligators eat almost anything that walks, flies, or swims within their reach, including fish, small mammals, and waterfowl.

In spring, bellowing by the males signals the onset of the mating season. The females lay dozens of eggs in large nesting mounds, cover them with vegetation, and guard them until the offspring hatch. Their sex is determined by the incubating temperature of the eggs. If they remain below 86°F, only females develop; if their temperature rises above 93°, all hatch as males.

Alligators once were hunted to near extinction, but laws now protect them. The mighty reptiles again are lords of lowland swamps and rivers in the southeastern United States.

Alligator lizard

Five species of alligator lizards are found in the western United States, living in habitats as diverse as the humid northern forests and the dry grasslands of Arizona. Long-tailed, short-legged, and armored with bony plates beneath the skin, these foot-long reptiles look like miniature versions of their namesake. They all share one characteristic feature—a pleatlike fold of skin along each side of the body that expands after the animals eat and when the females are heavy with eggs.

Alluvial fan

Apron-shaped deposits of sand, gravel, and rock are a familiar sight at the foot of mountain slopes in arid regions. Known as alluvial fans, they are, in effect, deltas on dry land. During the torrential downpours that are characteristic of desert areas, tremendous amounts of debris are swept down normally dry streambeds. Dumped where the river slows down at the base of the mountain slope, the sediments accumulate as alluvial fans.

Alpine meadow

Perched between forests below and snowy peaks above are the high-elevation alpine meadows of the northern Rockies and other western mountains. The meadows are best known for their annual floral displays: even while the ground remains dotted with snow and ice in spring and summer, they burst into bloom with acres of glacier lilies, bear grass, alpine butter-

Alpine meadows are filled with flowers.

cups, and dozens of other wildflowers. Ptarmigans and rosy finches are among the birds that forage there for seeds and insects, while marmots and ground squirrels are two of the meadows' more conspicuous mammals.

Amanita

The ghostly white destroying angel and the greenish-yellow death cup are among the many amanita mushrooms that are poisonous. While a few kinds are edible, experts recommend that they all be avoided because of the potentially fatal consequences of a mistaken identification. Fortunately, the amanitas have a few telltale characteristics that make recognition fairly easy. Typically, the stem has a bulbous base surrounded by a fleshy cup and a collar of loose skin near its top. Some of the amanitas have brightly colored caps and make attractive accents on the forest floor. But in the case of these fungi, it is best to look and leave alone.

Amber

Glassy and golden brown, amber has been valued for its beauty since ancient times. Early Romans fashioned it into jewelry, believing that amulets of amber worn at the neck could prevent tonsilitis and goiter; the Greeks wore it as a talisman, claiming it was formed from tears shed by exotic birds.

In fact, amber is the fossilized resin of now-extinct coniferous trees that lived millions of years ago. Small insects and plants sometimes were trapped in the gummy resin and preserved there when it hardened into amber, providing a glimpse of life long ago. Most of the world's amber comes from the Baltic coast of Europe, but specimens have been uncovered in New Jersey and other neighboring eastern states.

The American copper has a metallic shine.

American copper *Lycaena phlaeas*

Only an inch across, this butterfly makes up for its lack of size with brilliance and bravado. Both of the American copper's fiery orange forewings are punctuated by blackish spots, and the lower borders of the darker hindwings are bedecked with orange and black. In western and central Canada and the northeastern United States, this unlikely aggressor may be seen chasing off other butterflies and even blitzing dogs and birds.

Ammonite

Some 200 million years ago, while dinosaurs still roamed the earth, ammonites lived in the shallow seas that covered vast areas of present-day North America. Now extinct, these mollusks had coiled, elaborately chambered shells much like those of their descendants, the nautiluses. Most species were a few inches or so in diameter, but a few were huge. One particularly large specimen unearthed from a shale bed in Wyoming was more than five feet in diameter.

A

The Change from Egg to Frog

A frog's egg laid in the water soon develops into a fishlike tadpole with gills and a long tail. In the course of its underwater life, legs appear, lungs replace the gills, and the tail gradually disappears. The mature frog then crawls out of the water to begin its life as an air-breather.

Frog eggs

Tadpole

Intermediate stage

Adult frog

The bullfrog is the baritone of amphibians.

A salamander eyes a damp hiding place.

Amphibian

Frogs, toads, and salamanders, the most familiar of the amphibians, belong to a well-named group: the word *amphibious* is derived from the Greek for "leading a double life." And that is what amphibians do. Most begin life in water, swimming and breathing like fish, and mature into four-legged, air-breathing adults.

Frogs and toads undergo the most dramatic change, or metamorphosis, from egg to adult. The eggs, deposited in water, hatch into fishlike larvae called tadpoles, with gills for breathing and long tails for swimming. In time, four legs appear, the gills are replaced by lungs, and the tail shrinks to nothing, completing the transition from life in the water to life on land.

As the tadpoles of salamanders mature, they too grow legs but keep their long tails. Some develop lungs, others breathe through their skins as adults, and still others retain their gills throughout life and never leave the water.

All amphibians are scaleless, moist skinned, and cold-blooded. In winter most hibernate underground. Then, in spring, they revive and return to the ponds and streams, where they mate and produce a new generation.

Though not so commonly seen as frogs, salamanders actually are more numerous in North America than anywhere else. They are difficult to find because most are active only by night and fond of dark, damp hiding places. But a patient search under rocks or rotting logs in the spring and summer months should turn up a few of these shy and elusive creatures.

Amphiuma

Growing to a length of 30 inches or more and equipped with legs so tiny they are barely noticeable, these brown or grayish salamanders sometimes are mistaken for snakes or eels. Unlike most of their relatives, amphiumas have strong jaws and sharp teeth that enable them to bite fiercely if provoked. They hunt for snails, crayfish, frogs, and fish by night and hide themselves in muddy burrows during the day. The females lay strings of beadlike eggs near the water's edge, then coil around them until they hatch some five months later. Amphiumas live in swamps, ponds, and drainage ditches in the Southeast, from Virginia to Florida and west to the lower Mississippi Valley.

Anchovy

Traveling in enormous schools, throngs of these silvery little fish set the water shimmering. They are closely related to herrings and sardines, and like their relatives, they are of great commercial value. Vast numbers are caught annually for use as human food and fish bait, and for processing into fish meal and fish oil. Feeding on minute plant and animal life called plankton, anchovies are also a vital link in oceanic food chains, for they serve as a major food source for larger predatory fish and seabirds.

The kinds most commonly seen in North American waters are the northern anchovy, found off the Pacific coast, and the bay anchovy of the Atlantic and the Gulf of Mexico. As short as

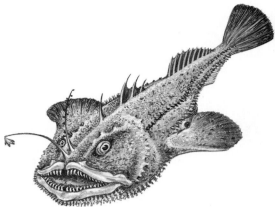

The angler uses a built-in rod and lure.

an inch and a half, and rarely exceeding six inches in length, anchovies are slender silvery fish with a faint stripe along each side. Like most anchovies, both of these American species have large eyes and very large mouths, with the upper jaw protruding beyond the tip of the lower jaw.

Anemone *Anemone*

As well known for their seed heads as for their flowers, the anemones have also been given the name of windflowers. Some say they earned this name because their delicate flowers seem to be blown open by breezes; others claim they are so called because their fluffy seeds are easily wafted away on the wind.

Members of the buttercup family, the anemones have attractive cup-shaped flowers. (The "petals" are actually showy sepals.) They include many cultivated varieties grown as ornamentals and for the florist trade.

A well-loved and widespread wild species is the dainty wood anemone, which bears solitary starlike white flowers. In early spring its lovely blooms can be admired in woodlands and meadows across most of North America. Another, the lavender pasqueflower, or prairie crocus, is so named because it blooms around Easter. Indians used to employ its crushed leaves to treat rheumatism and its flowers to stop nosebleeds. Now the floral emblem of both Manitoba and South Dakota, it has no medical uses today.

Angler

Found in oceans around the world, angler fish are notable for their unique method of capturing prey. A fleshy, often wormlike flap dangles from a spine on the angler's head and hangs in front of its face. Any fish attracted by this "bait" is quickly snapped up in the angler's huge, tooth-studded jaws. So voracious are their appetites that some of the larger anglers have been known to swallow prey almost as big as themselves.

The anglers' method of reproducing is as unusual as their feeding habits. By the time they are ready to breed, females are as much as 20 times the size of the stunted males. In some spe-

The anhinga stretches its wings to dry.

The prairie crocus, emblem of Manitoba.

cies, the males become permanently attached to their mates and serve only to fertilize their eggs.

Anhinga *Anhinga anhinga*

Because they often swim almost completely submerged, with only their heads and long, sinuous necks protruding from the water, anhingas are sometimes known as snakebirds. Their fan-shaped tails account for another, less elegant common name—the water turkey.

Large, blackish birds of southeastern swamps and marshes, anhingas are well adapted for fishing: they swim and dive easily in search of prey and impale their catch on their slender, sharply pointed bills. (They are, in fact, the only birds that do so; herons and other species with similar bills seize their prey rather than spearing it.) Anhingas then bring their catch to the surface, toss it in the air, and swallow it headfirst.

Like their relatives the cormorants, anhingas have loose plumage that does not repel water, and so are often seen perched with their wings spread out to dry. But the easiest way to find them in the trackless swamps they inhabit is to watch the sky: they can be seen soaring gracefully on outstretched wings as they circle high above the treetops.

A

Animals: Not Just Mammals

Invertebrates, animals without backbones, range from insects and snails to crabs and jellyfish.

Fish live and breathe in the water, have fins, and are as diverse as eels, rays, and salmon.

Amphibians, such as frogs, toads, and salamanders, lead two lives, first in water and then on land.

Reptiles, covered with scales or plates, include snakes, lizards, turtles, and alligators.

Birds all have wings and feathers, though not all can fly.

Mammals suckle their young on milk, and most are covered with hair or fur.

Anoles, though not true chameleons, can change color to match their surroundings.

Animal

Nearly 2 million species of animals have been identified around the world, and their diversity is astonishing; they range from microscopic, single-celled organisms such as amoebas and paramecia to creatures as complex as human beings. Regardless of their size, however, all animals share one common characteristic. Unlike plants, they cannot manufacture their own food; they must instead get their nourishment by eating plants or other animals.

Most animals share a number of other traits as well, characteristics related in part to the fact that they must actively seek food. A nervous system and sense organs, for instance, are essential for finding plants or prey. A means of locomotion enables animals to pursue or collect food—and to avoid being eaten themselves. And a digestive system extracts nutrients and energy from whatever foods they eat.

This diversity of feeding habits helps account for the tremendous variety of animal life. Cats, for example, are skilled predators equipped with muscles, claws, and teeth that would be useless to a nectar-feeding butterfly.

Despite their diversity, all animals are divided into two broad groups, those that have back-bones, the vertebrates, and those that do not, the invertebrates. Insects are by far the most numerous animals in either category, with more than 800,000 species known to science.

Animal behavior See *pp.16–17.*

Annual

The life spans of flowering plants differ dramatically. The shortest-lived are the annuals, such as corn and sunflowers, which germinate, blossom, set seed, and then die in a single growing season. The biennials, such as carrots and mullein, need two years to mature; they germinate and store food in their first year, then blossom and die in their second. Longest lived are the perennials, which survive for more than two years. Some perennials—peonies, for example—appear to die at season's end, but their underground structures survive to send up new shoots the following spring. Trees and shrubs, in contrast, have permanent woody stems that grow larger with each passing year.

Anole *Anolis carolinensis*

Able to turn from green to brown, green anoles often are mistaken for chameleons. (The true chameleons are old-world lizards.) Males supplement their color by fanning a bright red throat flap. Found in swamps and woodlands of the southeastern United States, these eight-inch climbers have special hooked toe pads used for clinging to branches and scurrying up walls. Welcomed around homes, anoles earn their keep by feeding on flies and mosquitoes.

These ants are carrying buds to their nest.

Antennae come in a variety of shapes. This male moth has featherlike antennae that are highly sensitive to the female's scent.

Ant

Thriving in almost every dry-land habitat from deserts and beaches to forests and human homes, ants are well known for their industrious ways. Whether exploring for food, toting burdens from place to place, or excavating tunnels, they seem to be constantly busy.

Like honeybees, ants are highly social insects and live in colonies that may include thousands of individuals. A colony begins when a winged, fertile female, the future queen, mates in flight with a male. The male then dies, while the female sheds her wings and, in the seclusion of a small burrow, lays her first eggs. The vast majority of her offspring are sterile females, the worker ants whose labors keep the colony going. Eventually, however, some of the eggs develop into males and young queens that mate to form new colonies. The queen does not in any sense "rule" her colony; she just keeps laying eggs, year after year, for the rest of her life, which may last as long as two decades.

Ants have a variety of lifestyles. Nomadic army ants, for instance, have no fixed colonies; they march across the land in military columns, feeding as they go. Fungus-growing ants, sometimes called parasol ants, carry pieces of leaf over their heads like umbrellas; they use the leaves to feed the fungi they cultivate as food. Dairying ants "milk" aphids for a sugary secretion called honeydew, and slave-making ants steal pupae from the nests of other species, then raise the kidnapped victims as slaves.

Most ants are harmless to humans, but a few are destructive. Carpenter ants can damage buildings by tunneling in the wood. And the imported fire ant builds unsightly nest mounds in pasturelands in the southeastern United States and attacks livestock with its powerful sting.

Antelope See *Pronghorn.*

Antelope ground squirrel

Scampering across the desert floor, these frisky little rodents curve their short tail over the back, exposing the white underside. The resemblance to the white rump patch of a fleeing pronghorn antelope accounts for their name. Although antelope ground squirrels are able to withstand the blistering heat of foothills and canyons in the southwestern United States, they sometimes retreat to their burrows or smear their heads with saliva in order to cool off. Active all year round, they spend their days hunting for fruits, seeds, and insects.

Antennae

Sometimes called feelers, antennae are the paired sense receptors protruding from the heads of a variety of creatures, such as insects, centipedes, crabs, and lobsters. They are sensitive to touch, taste, smell, and in some cases light, temperature, and moisture as well. To animals that possess them, they are as important as eyes and ears are to us. An ant's antennae, for instance, are in constant motion, tapping the ground like a blind person with a cane, pointing into the wind to receive odors, sampling food before it enters the mouth, and greeting other ants with a kind of hello.

Depending on species, antennae may look like anything from threads or strings of beads to knobs or gracefully branching feathers. They are usually equipped with thousands of tiny hairs, pegs, or pits that serve as receptors. Bedbugs use their antennae to sense warm objects. The antennae of male mosquitoes can detect the sound of a female's wing beats a quarter of a mile away, while those of moths can sense a mate's odor up to a mile away.

Some creatures use their antennae for other purposes as well. Fleas grasp each other with their antennae while mating, certain beetle larvae capture prey with them, and spiny lobsters use them as whips against would-be captors.

Courting grebes perform an intricate dance.

A sea otter uses a rock as a tool to crack open a shellfish.

Some ants tend aphids and are rewarded with honeydew secreted by the tiny insects.

Animal Behavior

To the casual observer, animals may seem to pass the time aimlessly—a bird sings from the treetops, a butterfly alights on a flower, a rabbit races across a meadow. But scientists have found that virtually all animal behavior has a purpose. The bird whose song seems so carefree is trying to attract a mate; the butterfly fluttering from flower to flower is searching for food; and the nimble rabbit is fleeing from a predator. Most animal behavior, in short, is tied directly or indirectly to life's most compelling requirement—staying alive.

Bluffing and battling

Animals often have to defend themselves against others of their own kind while competing for food, mates, and living space. The security of a home or territory is crucial for mating and rearing young, and each animal has its own way of marking its property and warning others to stay away. The male fox sprinkles urine on stones and trees that border its territory. Other foxes are well aware of these "keep out" signs, but if one should trespass, a conflict of some sort is likely to take place. Usually, though, the encounter is limited to bluffing and threatening until the intruder gives in and is sent on his way.

Defense against predators is a different mat-ter, because the fight, if it occurs, is usually a matter of life or death. Teeth, claws, acute senses, and even poisons are used by both predator and prey. Prey species may also defend themselves by running, hiding, or playing dead, or in the case of the armadillo or porcupine, presenting a platelike armor or a formidable array of sharp quills.

Animal language

Each animal species has its own language of sound, scent, or display through which it communicates with others of its kind. A male bird may repeat his song thousands of times a day to proclaim his territory or to court a female. And when not singing, birds use call notes to scold, beg for food, summon young, and keep the flock together. Sound is used by many animals: frogs croak, wolves howl, and elk bugle during the rutting season. Among insects, male mosquitoes locate females by the whirring sound of their wings. In the ocean, whales and porpoises have a sophisticated vocabulary of grunts, chirps, whistles, and clicks that scientists have spent years trying to decipher.

Some animals use scent to communicate. The feathery antennae of the male moth can detect the scent of a female more than a mile away.

Mammals such as deer and badgers use scent glands, urine, or feces to mark their territories.

Like humans, some animals use facial expressions and body language to express themselves. Cats and dogs use their mouths and ears to show anger, contentment, or hunger. Members of a wolf pack greet the leader with a ceremonial nuzzle, and he in turn reminds them of his dominance with a gentle nip on the neck. Prairie dogs greet each other with a kiss. And bees do a complicated dance to announce the discovery of a new food source.

Rites of courtship

If animals failed to mate, their species would vanish. So the sometimes bizarre and complicated behavior associated with courtship plays a vital role in survival.

In most cases, courtship is initiated by the males, many of whom go through elaborate rituals to woo their object of desire. The fiddler crab waves an oversized claw at the female, as if to say, "Here I am!" Some male spiders, midgets compared to the females and in danger of being mistaken for prey, announce themselves with intricately choreographed dances; others pluck the female's web like a bass fiddle before coming too close. Some birds, such as hummingbirds, display dazzling colors, while others, like brown thrashers, entice mates with a repertoire of melodious songs. And some of the hawks perform dramatic aerial acrobatics, with pairs locking talons as they swoop through the air.

But seductive displays of color, movement, and song are not the only courting devices. In the ocean, many creatures rely on chemical lures to attract mates. Male oysters, for instance, announce their readiness to spawn by subtly changing the flavor of the water.

Learning vs. instinct

While most animal behavior is instinctive rather than learned, many animals are undeniably able to acquire new skills through training. In the laboratory, rats have been taught to push levers, climb ladders, and negotiate mazes when rewarded with food. And such unusually intelligent animals as chimpanzees and dolphins have demonstrated an almost human ability to learn.

In the wild, many young animals learn by imitating adults. During play they copy the hunting and killing maneuvers of their parents, and so develop the strength and timing they will need later in life. Bobcat kittens, for instance, regularly play at crouching, stalking, and ambushing mock prey, as do fox cubs.

Still, clear-cut examples of learning are relatively rare in the animal world. For the most part, wild creatures are acting according to instincts or reflexes that have determined the behavior of their species for tens of generations. And such predetermined behavior, however mechanical or predictable, has served them well in the most crucial tasks of life—courtship, self-defense, communication, and ultimately, survival itself.

Salmon, the gazelles of white water, make spectacular leaps as they migrate upriver to spawn.

A

Antlers have a hairy skin called velvet that is shed when the antlers are mature.

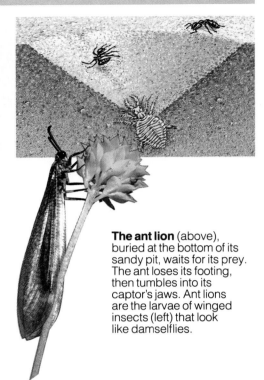

The ant lion (above), buried at the bottom of its sandy pit, waits for its prey. The ant loses its footing, then tumbles into its captor's jaws. Ant lions are the larvae of winged insects (left) that look like damselflies.

Antler

Majestically crowning the heads of deer, moose, elk, caribou, and reindeer, antlers serve both as ornaments and as weapons—primarily among males competing with each other during the mating season. Though they are sometimes used to fight off natural enemies such as wolves, their main purpose is to assert dominance, by means of threats and clashes, over other males of the same species.

Antlers first appear when the animal is one or two years old, and are shed and replaced annually. They begin growing in early summer from knobs on the skull and consist of dense connective tissue that later hardens into bone. At first they are covered by a thin, hairy skin called velvet, which allows blood to nourish the developing antlers. As the fall mating season approaches, the velvet dries out, becomes loose, and is scraped off by the animal. In late winter the antlers fall off. They begin growing again in early summer, and the cycle repeats itself.

Horns—the headgear of bison, cattle, goats, and other animals—are different from antlers. Both are bony inside, but horns have a hard outer covering similar in composition to fingernails and lack the many spikes and branches that antlers have. Also, horns are not shed but remain on the animal throughout its lifetime.

Ant lion

A wily hunter, the ant lion traps unsuspecting prey in a self-made sandy lair. By moving around in circles in dry sandy soil and throwing sand grains to the side, the little creature, also known as the doodlebug, digs a funnel-shaped pit about two inches wide and one inch deep.

Burying itself at the bottom, it lies in wait with only its long pincerlike jaws protruding. When an ant walks by, loose sand at the edge of the pit gives way and more is hurled up by the ant lion, causing the ant to lose its footing and tumble to the bottom. The ant lion then seizes its victim in its jaws, sucks out its juices, and tosses the empty carcass aside.

In all, some 60 species of these curious creatures inhabit sandy areas throughout the United States, especially in drier sections of the South. Some, rather than building sand traps, ambush their prey from behind rocks. But whatever their habits, all ant lions are the larvae of delicate flying insects that resemble damselflies.

Aphid

Seldom more than an eighth of an inch long, aphids are soft-bodied insects that suck sap from plants. They are often known as plant lice because of the damage they do to crops, not only by drinking the sap but also by spreading diseases. Ladybird beetles and their larvae are among the many insect enemies that help keep aphid numbers in check. Some kinds, however, are protected by ants, which feed on honeydew, a sweet, sticky substance excreted by the aphids.

The typical aphid's seasonal cycle begins in spring with eggs that have wintered on trees and shrubs. When the eggs hatch, only females are produced, and they in turn give birth only to females. Several generations are born over the course of the summer, with each aphid producing up to 50 daughters in her two or three weeks of life. Finally in the autumn some males are produced. They mate with females, who lay fertilized eggs that can survive the winter and so start the cycle anew the following year.

A

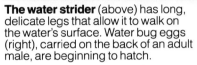

The water strider (above) has long, delicate legs that allow it to walk on the water's surface. Water bug eggs (right), carried on the back of an adult male, are beginning to hatch.

An aphid mother gives birth to her young.

Apple *Malus*

No one who smells wild apple trees in bloom can ever forget their sweet perfume. Several species of these wildlings grow throughout the southeastern part of the continent and up the Pacific Coast from northern California to Alaska. All North America's wild apples are crab apples, which are relatives of the larger, domesticated apples grown in orchards. Canada's two native species are the Pacific crab apple and the wild crab apple.

Wild apples come into flower later than the orchard trees, with blossoms ranging from shell pink to pure white, depending on the species. All bear similar fruits, however: about an inch across, they are sweetly scented, hard, and usually a glossy yellow-green. Despite their appetizing aroma, they are too sour to eat out of hand (though deer, black bears, and ruffed grouse relish them). Pioneers made cider and an orange-red jelly from wild crab apples; they also used the trees as understock on which to graft the eating apples they imported from Europe. Nowadays the wild crab apples are more often planted as ornamentals.

Aquatic insects

Ponds and streams are home to an array of aquatic insects, both immature and adult. A few, such as black fly larvae, live attached to the bottom, but most move about in one way or another. Agile water striders skitter across the surface on long, slender legs. Also seen on the surface are large groups of whirligig beetles, which give the appearance of dancing in all directions at once. Back swimmers and water boatmen use their long, oarlike legs to paddle through the water, while dragonfly nymphs dart from place to place by forcing water from their bodies in a kind of jet propulsion. And caddisfly larvae drag along their own self-made mobile homes—neatly camouflaged tubelike cases made of sticks, bits of stone, or leaves.

Like their counterparts on dry land, aquatic insects must be able to breathe, and they do so in a variety of ways. The nymphs of dragonflies, damselflies, and mayflies have gills that enable them to absorb oxygen dissolved in the water. The larvae of mosquitoes, in contrast, are snorkelers; they breathe through tiny tubes that reach up to the surface. Still others are like scuba divers, taking along their own oxygen supply; water boatmen, back swimmers, and many diving beetles carry bubbles of air next to their bodies whenever they descend to the depths.

Feeding methods are equally diverse. Among the plant eaters are water boatmen, which scrape algae from underwater surfaces. Some of the caddisfly larvae spin silken nets that strain bits of food from the passing current. And many aquatic insects are predators. Dragonfly nymphs have hinged lower jaws that snap out to snatch passing prey, and giant water bugs use their powerful front legs to seize fish and tadpoles twice their size. Thanks to these and other adaptations, aquatic insects are able to thrive in fresh water nearly everywhere.

19

A

Water lily leaves float on the pond's surface, while the roots are anchored in the mud below.

Aquatic plants

Growing in the water of ponds, swamps, and marshes, aquatic plants have developed a number of strategies for coping with their habitat. Different kinds, for example, are adapted for survival in water of different depths, thus taking advantage of every bit of living space.

Plants such as cattails, anchored in mud near the water's edge, and arrowheads, growing in the shallowest water just offshore, are the most like land plants; their roots may be wet, but their leaves are raised out of the water and exposed directly to the sun. Water lilies and pondweeds grow in somewhat deeper water; long stems permit their leaves to float on the surface, faceup to the sun. At still greater depths are plants that grow completely underwater, such as the bladderworts and water milfoil. Finally, there are plants that have lost all connection with the bottom, such as duckweeds, water hyacinths, and even a few ferns; they float freely on the surface, dangling their roots below.

The plants that live underwater typically have lacy or strap-shaped leaves—shapes that maximize the surface exposed to sunlight and which are also resilient, preventing damage from any movement of the water. Some of the emergent plants, such as many pondweeds, have bladelike leaves at or above the water's surface and lacy or straplike leaves below.

The lacy leaves and stems of underwater plants allow them to absorb oxygen, carbon dioxide, and dissolved nutrients directly from the water. Thus the roots of these plants serve mainly to anchor them in place.

Many aquatics have air pockets between the tissues of their stems and leaves, which helps keep them floating. In the case of the water hyacinth, air pockets in the swollen stem serve as pontoons that keep the entire plant afloat.

Aquatic plants also rely on water as a medium for dispersal. Some colonize by simply drifting along the surface. Others, such as water lilies, have floating seeds. Sweet flag often spreads by means of broken bits of root that grow into new plants, and waterweed does so with bits of the plant itself.

Aquifer

Layers of porous rock, such as sandstone, retain water that seeps into them from the surface. Resting on impermeable rock layers that prevent the water from flowing any deeper into the earth, these formations, known as aquifers, are capable of holding tremendous quantities of water and serve as natural underground reservoirs. Indeed, wells drilled into aquifers are the primary water source in many areas.

Arborvitae *Thuja*

Slow-growing and long-lived, arborvitaes are handsome conical evergreen trees with fanlike sprays of branchlets sheathed in scaly foliage. Some say that their name, which means tree-of-life, refers to their longevity. Others claim the name was provided by the 16th-century French explorer Jacques Cartier; while wintering in Canada, he and his crew were saved from scurvy by a vitamin-rich tea brewed from the tree.

Two species of arborvitae are native to North America. The giant arborvitae, also known as western red cedar, grows in moist soils in the mountains of the Pacific Northwest. Sometimes reaching heights of 200 feet, it has coarse, lightweight wood that is nearly impervious to insects and decay. Indians used it for making canoes, and it still is unexcelled for shingles and siding.

Smaller but extremely hardy, the eastern arborvitae, or northern white cedar, is found in swampy areas from Nova Scotia to North Carolina. Its wood is valued for poles, fence posts, and lumber, and an oil distilled from its twigs has been used for medicinal purposes.

A

Some Showy Aquatic Plants

The flowers of aquatic plants have many distinctive features that aid in identification, including color, the number of petals, and the overall shape of the blossoms.

Impressive, showy aquatic plants abound in many of our ponds, rivers, and marshes. Shown below are a few of the more common and colorful varieties.

Yellow

IRREGULAR FLOWERS
5 PETALS
Leaves lacy or threadlike and submerged

Yellow bladderwort

REGULAR FLOWERS
4 TO 6 PETALS
Leaves lance shaped, stems long and floating

Yellow waterweed

Leaves lacy and submerged

Yellow water buttercup

Flower with disk at center; leaves heart shaped or rounded

Yellow pond lily

White

REGULAR FLOWERS
3 PETALS
Flowers small and numerous

Water plantain

Flowers few and large

Arrowhead

5 PETALS
Leaves lacy and submerged

White water buttercup

MANY PETALS
Flower large; leaves floating and heart shaped

White water lily

REGULAR FLOWERS: MANY PETALS

Flower with yellow stamens at center

Banana water lily

Blue or Violet

IRREGULAR FLOWERS
Flowers in tall spikes

Pickerelweed

Flowers small, on stalks

Purple bladderwort

Flowers clustered on short stalk; whole plant floating

Water hyacinth

REGULAR FLOWERS
MANY PETALS
Flower on stalk above surface

Blue water lily

Flower with tall disk at center

American lotus

A

The armadillo uses its stout claws to dig a burrow.

The broad-leaved arrowhead has edible potatolike tubers.

Arete

The rugged beauty of the Rockies, Cascades, and other glaciated mountains is enhanced by sharp-edged ridges called aretes. They were formed by the continued erosion of adjacent cirques—steep-sided, bowllike, glacier-carved amphitheaters. Glacial erosion enlarged the abutting cirques until finally they were separated only by the narrow, knife-edged wall of rock.

Armadillo *Dasypus novemcinctus*

Looking more like a scaly lizard than a furry mammal, the nine-banded armadillo trots about in search of insects, digging them out of the ground or scraping them from leaf litter with its stout claws. The creature, 2 feet long when fully grown, has little to fear from most predators, for its body, head, and tail are encased in hard, bony plates. Its name, bestowed by the Spanish conquistadores, means "little armored one." In fact, armadillos occasionally defend themselves by curling up into armor-plated balls, but more often they flee to their burrows or dig a new one on the spot.

The young are born in spring, with each female always producing a litter of identical quadruplets. The babies are soft shelled at birth, but the bony plates quickly harden, and with eyes already open, the young can walk within hours.

Once found only west of the Mississippi, in Texas and neighboring states, armadillos in this century have greatly expanded their range. Nowadays these comical-looking creatures can be seen all the way east to Florida.

Arrowhead *Sagittaria*

Handsome aquatic plants, arrowheads are distinguished by their three-petaled white flowers borne in whorls of three. The commonest species, broad-leaved arrowhead, has extremely long, arrowhead-shaped leaves. But other kinds have leaves that are oval or even straplike, with no resemblance to arrowheads at all. The plants' potatolike tubers, once favored foods of many Indian peoples, are responsible for such alternate names as water nut and duck potato.

Arroyo

Steep-sided, flat-bottomed channels are among the characteristic landforms of arid regions, where rainfall is scant and evaporation rapid. Known in the southwestern United States as arroyos or dry washes, they are the stream beds through which water rushes briefly, often torrentially, after desert downpours, and then, usually within hours, the streams dry up again. In some areas, rain is so infrequent that the arroyos remain dry for most of the year.

Artesian well

Naturally pressurized, artesian wells can produce spectacular jets of water, much like the oil spurting from a gusher. They occur in places where a downward-sloping water-bearing rock layer (an aquifer) is sandwiched between two impermeable rock layers. Rainfall soaks into the upper end of the aquifer, resulting in tremendous water pressure at lower levels. If a well is drilled into the aquifer, this pressure causes water to flow to the surface. Whether drilled by man or flowing naturally through fissures in the earth, artesian wells and springs are important water sources over parts of the Great Plains and in many other areas.

Ash *Fraxinus*

Popular shade and timber trees, ashes of several kinds grow throughout North America. Most are tall, sturdy trees that typically bear featherlike compound leaves in opposite pairs. The

An arroyo rushes with water after a sudden desert storm. Within a short time, this sandy stream channel will once again be dry.

Quaking aspens, their leaves on flattened stems, tremble with the slightest breeze.

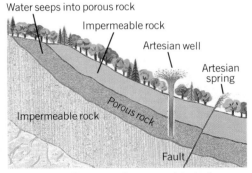

Water seeps into porous rock

Impermeable rock

Artesian well

Artesian spring

Porous rock

Impermeable rock

Fault

Artesian wells, naturally pressurized, often produce copious flows of water.

trees also produce one-seeded fruits with single, elongated, papery wings that catch the wind.

The most common and valuable of the 16 North American species is white ash. Its tough, pliant wood, ideal for baseball bats and other sporting equipment, is also used for tool handles and cabinetmaking. Herbalists and American Indians believed the tree had medicinal properties: tea made from its bark was recommended for a variety of ailments, and its seeds were valued as an appetite stimulant and fever remedy.

Blue ash, another species with both decorative and practical uses, is named for the dye derived from its inner bark. A fast-growing, long-lived tree, it can be found in the limestone soils of the Midwest. Much more familiar is green ash, which takes its name from the color of its twigs. The most widely distributed of all the ashes, green ash thrives in moist soils along streams. It is especially abundant in the Mississippi Valley, where its seeds are an important food for quail, turkey, and rodents. Another common species, the black ash, also favors damp places and is named for its dark, almost black, buds. Like some of the other ashes, its wood is often split into strips for weaving into baskets and chair seats.

Aspen

Every breeze makes the aspens come to life with quaking foliage, for their leaves, suspended on long, ribbonlike stems, are set to trembling by even the slightest movement of the air. In spring and summer the leaves shimmer with a shiny green on top and a paler gray-green on their undersides, and in the fall they have a luminous golden glow.

The aspens' bark, smooth and pale, is often marred with deep black scars—the remnants of claw marks left by passing bears. The trees also are attractive to beavers, who eat the soft inner bark and use the trunks and branches when building their dams and lodges.

Foresters classify the fast-growing aspens as "pioneer" trees, since they are among the first to return to abandoned fields and areas scorched by fire. Soft-wooded and brittle, they are of little commercial value but play an important role in anchoring the soil until other trees can reestablish themselves.

Only two species of aspens grow in North America. The quaking aspen is common all across the West and Northeast; its taller relative, bigtooth aspen, is found only in the Northeast.

23

A

New England asters shine brightly in fall.

Auks, such as these razorbills, congregate on rocky coasts, where they lay their eggs.

The aurora borealis, one of nature's most spectacular light shows, here appears as eerie curtains of greenish light.

Aster *Aster*

Taking their name from the Greek word for star, asters do indeed shine brightly, especially in the fall. Although some kinds begin to bloom as early as July or August, the brightest displays of these blue-, white-, or purple-flowered perennials come in September and October. Because the peak of bloom often occurs around the feast of St. Michael, on September 29, our ancestors used to call them Michaelmas daisies.

Asters, some of which are popular garden flowers, are found around the world, with more than 100 species native to North America. Telling one wild species from another can be a challenge even for the specialist. Adaptability is one reason for their success: some can survive even in salt marshes, while others, such as the tough-stemmed white heath aster, prefer the parched western plains.

Among the most beautiful is the New England aster, which, despite its name, flourishes from central Canada south to the Carolinas and westward beyond the Mississippi. Growing to heights of six feet or more, it is covered with masses of two-inch pink to brilliant purple flowers that are true stars of the autumn.

Atmosphere

Compared to the size of the earth, the atmosphere—the layer of air surrounding our planet—is but a thin mantle. Indeed, 99 percent of the air is concentrated within just 20 miles of the earth's surface.

Far from uniform, the atmosphere consists of concentric envelopes of air that differ in temperature and composition. The lowest layer, the troposphere, contains about 80 percent of the world's air. Ranging in thickness from 6 to 10 miles, it is the arena in which winds and clouds make up what we call weather. Air temperature in the troposphere decreases with altitude until it reaches a low of about −70°F.

Extending up for another 20 miles above the troposphere is the stratosphere, where the temperature rises again to about 32°. Here the sun's rays react with oxygen to form the ozone layer, which serves as a barrier protecting life on earth from damage by the sun's ultraviolet radiation.

Higher still is the mesosphere, also 20 miles thick, where temperatures rise and then fall again. Next, some 400 miles high, is the ionosphere, where the sun's rays bombard what little air there is, heating it to more than 1000° and producing electrically charged particles called ions. This ion layer reflects radio waves, enabling us to "bounce" signals around the world.

In an avalanche, tons of snow and ice tumble down the side of a mountain with unbridled force.

Beyond the ionosphere and extending for thousands of miles into space is the exosphere. There the air molecules are so few and far between that they rarely collide with each other; sometimes they even escape the earth's gravity altogether and drift off into outer space.

Auk

Found only in northern oceans, the 22 species of auks are stocky seabirds that stand upright like penguins. All members of the family are expert divers that use their short wings both for flying and as flippers for swimming in pursuit of fish, shrimp, and other prey.

Most auks dress in basic black and white, but during the nesting season a few sport white or yellow plumes on their heads, and puffins are decorated with large, colorful bills. Auks range in size from the 6-inch least auklet of the Bering Sea to the 19-inch thick-billed murre. The giant of the family was the flightless great auk of the North Atlantic; extinct since 1844, it stood 30 inches tall.

Auks spend most of the year at sea and come to land only to breed on rocky coasts or offshore islands. Some nest in burrows, others on rocky ledges; the marbled murrelet of the Pacific Northwest sometimes nests in trees.

With their seafaring way of life, flipperlike wings, black-and-white plumage, and erect posture, auks are the northern counterparts of the Southern Hemisphere's penguins.

Aurora borealis

Assuming a variety of forms, the sky spectaculars known as the aurora borealis may appear as an eerie grayish glow, as flashing, fanlike bands of green, or even as a dazzling array of multicolored pleats of light draped across the heavens. Also known as the northern lights, the displays are brightest and most dramatic in the far north but are sometimes visible even in the southern United States. They occur most frequently at times of heavy sunspot activity and are caused by charged particles from the sun hurtling toward the earth's magnetic poles. High in the atmosphere, these particles collide with molecules of air, releasing energy in the form of light. The same spectacular phenomenon takes place near the South Pole, where it is referred to as the aurora australis, or southern lights.

Avalanche

The sudden, thundering slide of snow and ice down a mountainside is among nature's most terrifying spectacles. Called an avalanche, it can be triggered by the vibrations from a loud noise or the melting of packed snow by spring rains. Many avalanches occur after heavy snowfalls, when a slick surface develops between the new precipitation and the older snow. In some cases the old snow begins to form dense crystals beneath the new, causing the mass of snow to sweep downhill as if on ball bearings.

The cascade of snow sweeps along rocks, soil, trees—anything in its path. Wet avalanches, formed of dense, slushy snow, are treacherous due to their enormous weight and their tendency to freeze upon impact. But dry avalanches, consisting of airborne, powdery snow, are the most devastating—sometimes racing down mountains at over 100 miles per hour.

Avalanches are a serious danger to skiers, climbers, buildings, and anything else standing in their way. In order to avert disaster, they often are triggered intentionally at opportune moments, letting the snow slide when it can do the least damage.

Avalanche lily *See Dogtooth violet.*

The white mountain aven, floral emblem of the Northwest Territories.

An American avocet stands over a downy hatchling that will soon be swimming and foraging on its own.

Avens *Geum*

Unlike their showy cousins the roses, the avens are rather modest wildflowers. Their blooms, usually an inch or so across, come in yellow, orange, or white. (The white mountain aven is the floral emblem of the Northwest Territories.) Nodding from stalks one to four feet tall, the flowers of many species mature into burrlike fruits equipped with hooks that cling to clothing and animal fur. The long-plumed avens, which produce fruits with long wispy hairs, have inspired such colorful alternative names as prairie smoke and old man's whiskers.

Though the various kinds of avens differ in the habitats they prefer and in their seasons of bloom, all share one characteristic—a thick, aromatic root. Indians and colonists boiled the root in water, then added milk and sugar to make a chocolate-flavored drink. Home-brewed ale was laced with avens root, both for the spicy zest it imparted and because it kept the beer from souring. The root was also mixed with wine to produce a cure-all tonic that, as one 19th-century herbalist put it, "restores to health the most shattered and enfeebled constitutions."

Avocet *Recurvirostra americana*

Boldly patterned in black and white, American avocets are long-legged, duck-sized shorebirds with slender, strikingly upcurved bills. They are found mainly in the western United States, where they inhabit marshes and shallow lakes, but occasionally they summer on brackish lagoons along the southern Atlantic coast.

Avocets use their upcurved bills to forage in a special way that enables them to take food other shorebirds miss. Sweeping their bills back and forth just beneath the water's surface, they catch tiny crustaceans, aquatic insects, and drifting seeds, located with their acute sense of touch.

During the breeding season avocets lay three or four eggs in a shallow depression in sand or on firm mud near the water's edge. They provide little in the way of a nest lining, but if the water level rises, the birds quickly build up the nest with sticks or any other debris they can find in order to keep the eggs from being flooded.

Often several pairs nest in loose colonies and will come to each other's defense by mobbing any predator that comes too near. Both male and female share in tending the eggs; the male does most of the incubating during the first week, and then the female takes over. The young are downy at hatching and, with their tiny webbed feet, manage to begin diving and swimming within a matter of hours.

Azalea *Rhododendron*

Found in a kaleidoscope of brilliant colors, wild azaleas, like their cultivated cousins, are prized for their showy flowers. Often among the first to bloom in spring, these beautiful shrubs add splashes of white, pink, yellow, orange, red, and even lavender to the woodland environments that they prefer.

Some of the native azaleas are known as wild honeysuckle, and their funnel-shaped flowers, with long, protruding stamens, do resemble the blossoms of that familiar vine. One pink-flowered species, the Florida pinxter, even mimics the honeysuckle's perfume. Unlike their relatives, the evergreen rhododendrons, which retain their elegant foliage all year round, most azaleas shed their leaves in winter.

The only species native to the Pacific Coast is the western azalea, a colorful shrub that flourishes from southern Oregon to southern California. Eastern North America, on the other hand, offers a wider variety of wild azaleas than any other region of the world, with a total of 18 different species.

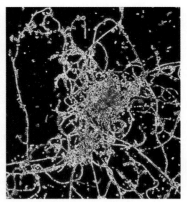

Iron bacteria appear under the microscope in tangled, threadlike chains.

The badger's sharp front claws help it to dig holes in record time. Though some have been tamed as pets, badgers can be ferocious fighters, especially when cornered in the wild.

Back swimmer

Swimming upside down in freshwater ponds and streams and using their long hind legs as oars, back swimmers look very much like tiny rowboats. They often are seen just below the surface and can remain underwater for hours on end because, like scuba divers, they carry along their own supply of oxygen—a bubble of air trapped among hairs on the body.

Although they are only half an inch long, back swimmers are fierce predators, willing to attack small fish and tadpoles as well as insect prey. Piercing their victims with their sharp beaks, they suck out the body fluids. They also can pierce a human finger if handled carelessly, causing a painful sting.

Bacteria

Probably the most widespread of living things, bacteria are also the most abundant. A spoonful of garden soil may contain 100 billion of these single-celled microscopic organisms. Able to survive almost everywhere on earth, some kinds live in the steaming water of hot springs, while others thrive on glacial ice.

Bacteria are responsible for a variety of diseases, such as cholera, tuberculosis, tetanus, and typhoid fever. In plants they cause many kinds of blights and wilts. They are, however, crucial to the existence of all other forms of life. Many benign bacteria inhabit the intestines of animals, helping to digest food and supplying essential vitamins. Others speed the process of decay, recycling nutrients and making them available once again to plants. Still others convert nitrogen from the air into a form that plants can use. Some are even used to prepare foods, including yogurt, certain cheeses, and sauerkraut. Without the ubiquitous bacteria, life as we know it could not exist on earth.

Badger *Taxidea taxus*

Found in deserts and grasslands from the Prairie Provinces through most of the central and western United States, badgers are chunky members of the weasel family. They grow to about two feet long and can weigh as much as 25 pounds. Except for short black feet and black-and-white facial markings, their fur is yellowish gray.

Active mostly by night, badgers hunt all year round, although they stay underground in their burrows during the severest winter weather. Their sturdy front claws enable them to dig rapidly—so fast, in fact, that these digging dynamos can escape predators by excavating a burrow right on the spot. Their food consists mainly of small mammals such as mice and ground squirrels, but birds and insects are also taken. It has been reported that badgers may actually form special hunting partnerships with coyotes. The coyote uses its keen sense of smell to locate an underground rodent, the badger digs the animal out, and the two then share the meal.

Mating occurs in summer or early fall, and up to five young are born the following spring on a bed of dry grass in the den where the mother has spent the winter. They are weaned in about six weeks but remain with the mother for several months before setting out on their own.

Badlands

Sharp, toothlike ridges and steep, V-shaped gullies etched into barren, semiarid hills make for "bad lands to cross." And that is exactly how Indians and fur traders long ago described the rugged, nearly impassable terrain adjoining Alberta's Red Deer River. Found in several other places on the Prairies, these moonscapes were formed by flash floods that stripped away surface soil and vegetation, then gnawed away at layers of weak, easily eroded rock. The most scenic badlands, encompassing spectacular multicolored cliffs and forbidding canyons, have been preserved in Dinosaur Provincial Park in Alberta and in Badlands National Park in South Dakota.

Bald cypress *Taxodium distichum*

Unlike most conifers, this handsome relative of California's giant redwood is deciduous: in autumn the bald cypress sheds its feathery foliage and remains bald throughout the winter. Equally unusual are its knees, twisted knobs of wood that rise from the roots and stand three or four feet above the surface of swamps, where the tree grows best. Botanists speculate that these strange protuberances may supply air to the bald cypress's waterlogged roots, or perhaps they help to stabilize it on its muddy bed.

A characteristic tree of southern wetlands, the bald cypress is typically festooned with silvery clumps of Spanish moss. Common from Florida to eastern Texas, it also ranges as far north as Delaware and up the Mississippi Valley to southern Indiana. The largest tree in swamps throughout its range, it sometimes reaches a height of 150 feet, with a diameter of 12 feet near the base of its swollen, buttressed trunk.

Not surprisingly, the wood of this swamp dweller is extraordinarily resistant to decay. Sometimes known as the "wood eternal," bald cypress is valued for uses ranging from greenhouse construction to railroad ties.

Baneberry *Actaea*

Clusters of attractive white or crimson berries crown the knee-high stalks of baneberries. But as their name suggests, the pea-sized fruits of these widespread woodland perennials are poisonous. Mice and ruffed grouse eat them with no ill effect, but they can be fatal to humans.

Pretty, too, but harmless, puffs of feathery white flowers top the plants from midsummer into fall. The blossoms make the baneberries an appealing choice for woodland gardens and shady spots in rockeries.

In many areas the white-fruited baneberries are called doll's eyes because their glossy, ivory-colored berries, each marked with a single black spot, seem to gaze up like the eyes of an old-fashioned china doll. Since they also look as if they could be strung on a thread, the plants are known as white beads and necklaceweed as well.

South Dakota's badlands, a dry, rugged wilderness, testify to the powers of erosion.

Barberry *Berberis*

Attractive throughout the year, the common barberry produces dangling clusters of yellow bell-shaped flowers in the spring. Throughout the summer it wears a cloak of dense green foliage that turns to red in fall. Then it drops its leaves to expose an array of bright red berries that remain on the shrub well into winter.

Because of its fierce armament of spines, early farmers imported barberry from Europe and planted it in hedges to protect their fields. Settlers used its yellow sap for dye and made jellies from the berries.

Ironically, this plant is now recognized as an enemy of agriculture. Because it serves as an alternate host for black stem rust, a fungal disease that attacks wheat, oats, rye, and barley, it has been the target of repeated attempts at eradication in the United States, where most grain-producing states prohibit its cultivation. Barberry does not root easily in Canadian soil.

Not all the barberries are a bane, however. The Japanese barberry, a popular ornamental, is completely immune to black stem rust.

Bark

The appearance of its bark gives each tree a distinctive signature—so much so, in fact, that experts can identify some trees by their bark alone. Unmistakable, for instance, are the mottled, flaky patterns on sycamore bark and the vertically peeling skin of the shagbark hickory.

Bark acquires its telltale textures and patterns

because trees, as they grow, become too big for their skins, causing the bark to give way under pressure. And each species has its own way of splitting, peeling, flaking, or shredding on the surface as new bark is added underneath.

Botanists distinguish between two layers of bark—the tree's visible outer skin and a soft, thin layer of inner bark. The inner bark is made up of living cells that transport sugars from one part of the tree to another; the much thicker outer bark is composed of dead cork cells that protect the delicate inner tissue. Outer bark must be waterproof to prevent dehydration and tough enough to protect the tree against insects and disease, as well as sun, wind, rain, and ice.

For some trees, especially in arid western forests, bark may also serve as fireproofing. Ponderosa pines, for instance, often go unscathed in forest fires thanks to their two-inch armor of corky bark, and the thick reddish bark of the giant sequoias is virtually impervious to flame.

Shagbark hickory   White birch

Ponderosa pine   Persimmon

Tree bark, smooth and thin on saplings, splits into distinct patterns as the trees grow.

Bark beetle

Sometimes called engraver beetles, these small black or brown cylindrical insects and their larvae dig intricately patterned networks of tunnels beneath the bark of hickories, pines, firs, and many other kinds of trees. The adults first excavate brood galleries, with the females laying eggs at intervals along their lengths. When the eggs hatch, the larvae dig tunnels that branch out in distinctive patterns. After transforming into adults, the beetles emerge from holes at the ends of their tunnels.

Some species of bark beetles live only on dead wood, while others attack living trees. Among the most destructive are the elm bark beetles, which transmit Dutch elm disease. The insects themselves do little damage, but they carry a fungus that blocks the elms' water- and sap-transporting vessels, causing the trees to die.

Barnacle

Firmly attached to piers, boats, driftwood, seaside rocks, and even whales, barnacles seem as immovable and eternal as the sea itself. Once thought to be cousins of shellfish, they actually are more closely related to lobsters and crabs. They begin life as free-swimming larvae, then glue themselves to underwater surfaces by means of a powerful self-made cement. After forming their limestone shells, barnacles remain fixed to the same spot for the rest of their lives. Only their feathery legs ever protrude from the shell; swaying in the water, they sweep food into the creature's mouth.

At low tide, clusters of goose barnacles, looking much like the heads of geese on long, leathery necks, can be seen attached to log pilings. The other familiar type, acorn barnacles, resemble tiny volcanoes and usually encrust rocks. One species of acorn barnacle, found near Puget Sound in Washington, grows to the size of a layer cake and is prized as food.

Goose barnacles (upper) and acorn barnacles (lower) encrust pilings, ship bottoms, and living creatures.

B

A great barracuda, though fast and fierce, is less of a danger to swimmers than it is to eaters.

Young barn owls, anticipating the arrival of food, peer out from a hollow tree trunk.

Barn owl *Tyto alba*

Truly creatures of the night, common barn owls spend the day sleeping in hollow trees or hidden among dense foliage. At dusk they venture out, flying silently with mothlike wing beats, to hunt for mice and voles. Aided by facial feathers arranged to channel sound into the ears, their hearing is so acute that the birds can locate and capture prey even in total darkness.

As their name implies, barn owls often nest in barns or other buildings, but they also use natural cavities. A clutch consists of anywhere from 3 to 11 eggs, depending on the availability of prey. Since incubation begins as soon as the first egg is laid, each brood includes young of several sizes. If food is scarce, it is the younger nestlings that starve, leaving the older and more aggressive offspring to perpetuate the species.

Although barn owls are usually secretive, during the breeding season they proclaim their presence with loud bill snapping during courtship flights. And, as if to announce their coming of age, the young hiss and squeal noisily just before leaving the nest to set out on their own.

Barometric pressure

We live at the bottom of an ocean of air extending many miles into the sky. And the weight of all that air pressing down on us, called barometric pressure, is constantly changing, becoming heavier or lighter depending on the density of the air above us at any given moment.

One device that is commonly used to measure atmospheric pressure is the mercury barometer. It does so by balancing the weight of the air with the weight of a column of mercury in a calibrated vertical tube. The top end of the tube is sealed, creating a vacuum, while the bottom end is open, allowing some of the mercury to spill out into a cup exposed to the pressure of the air. When atmospheric pressure rises, the mercury is forced higher into the tube; when it falls, the mercury drops. On the average, air pressure at sea level is 14.7 pounds per square inch, the equivalent of about 30 inches of mercury. A rising or falling barometer indicates impending changes in the weather. Low pressure is associated with clouds and storms, and high pressure with fair skies. Barometric pressure also decreases at higher elevations because less air is pressing down from above.

Barracuda *Sphyraena*

It would be hard to mistake a barracuda for any other fish. Torpedo-shaped, with large knifelike teeth and a protruding lower jaw, these fearsome hunters roam warm coastal seas and occasionally venture into deeper water offshore. As they skirt the shallows in search of prey, barracudas are frequently attracted by the glint of moving objects. Many fishermen, reeling in their lines, have seen the steely flash of a barracuda as it slashes at their catch. Divers and swimmers also may be startled by these insistent marauders, though attacks on humans are rare.

The Pacific barracuda and the great barracuda, the commonest species, are both fast, voracious predators. Found off the Atlantic and Gulf coasts, great barracudas are the largest of the group, occasionally reaching 6 feet in length. While they are sometimes caught for food, they often carry a toxin that has been known to cause fatal poisoning. Not all barracudas, however, are poisonous; Pacific barracudas, which range from Alaska to California, are a popular food fish on the West Coast.

Barrier island

In the shallow water along some seacoasts, waves and currents deposit long narrow ridges of sand called barrier islands. Standing as buffers between the mainland and the open sea, they are backed by quiet lagoons. Padre Island in the Gulf of Mexico and Hatteras Island, North Carolina, are well-known barrier islands. Though often anchored by vegetation, barrier islands are constantly battered by winds and water; some last only a few years, others a few thousand.

Barrier islands, such as North Carolina's Outer Banks, serve as natural breakwaters.

Basalt cliffs along the Columbia River in Washington were formed by cooling lava.

B

A big brown bat reacts to the photographer by baring its fangs. Common in western Canada and all over the United States, these creatures benefit humans by consuming large quantities of harmful insects.

Basalt

Dark and fine-grained, basalt is the most common of all volcanic rocks. It forms when lava rich in iron and magnesium oozes through fissures in the earth's crust and solidifies on the surface. The mineral content of the lava causes the rock's dark color, and rapid cooling on the earth's surface results in its fine texture. Basaltic lava may pile up in the form of volcanoes or create lateral fissure flows that flood vast areas.

Basswood *Tilia*

When our several species of basswoods come into bloom in early summer, they are enveloped in fragrance and abuzz with the humming of hundreds of honeybees. The trees, in fact, often are called bee trees, since their plentiful nectar produces an especially delicious honey.

Also known as lindens and limes, basswoods are popular ornamental and shade trees. Because they are relatively unbothered by diseases or air pollution, they are a familiar sight along city streets in many parts of the country. The trees' fibrous inner bark was traditionally used for making rope, and the soft, white, easily worked wood is excellent for carving. Animals such as rabbits and deer eat both the buds and twigs, while birds and squirrels feed on the dangling clusters of pea-sized fruits.

Bat

Most commonly seen as dark shadows fluttering across the night sky, bats are North America's only true flying mammals. They are not feathered like birds; the main parts of their wings are actually their hands, with thin membranes stretched between the bones of their fingers.

Bats generally emerge from their hiding places at twilight and, except for a few nectar-feeding species in the southwestern United States, pursue flying insects in the dark. Contrary to the expression "blind as a bat," these nocturnal mammals can see clearly, but they do not use their eyes to find prey in the dark. Instead, they rely on a system of echolocation. Bouncing high-pitched sound waves off nearby objects and then picking up the echoes with their large ears, they can determine the size and shape of the objects and how far away they are. Once a bat pinpoints the location of a flying insect, it scoops its prey out of the air with its tail membrane or wings, then crushes it with its sharp teeth.

Many bats are social, roosting in groups during the day in buildings, caves, or hollow trees. The most famous of the social bats are the millions of Mexican free-tailed bats that roost in Carlsbad Caverns in New Mexico. Other kinds, among them the migratory red bat, are solitary and likely to be found roosting alone, hanging from a branch or the bark of a tree.

31

B

A bayou where blooming water hyacinths thrive may have its surface entirely covered by the plants later on in the summer.

Alaskan brown bears dry off by the McNeil River.

Bauxite

Named for Les Baux, France, where it was first discovered, bauxite is the ore from which most aluminum is made. It comes in various forms, which may be as soft as dirt or as hard as rock, and its mottled surface is often dotted with pea-like spheres. The color also varies; depending on the presence of impurities in the ore, it can range from brown or red to pink or ivory. When wet, soft bauxite gives off a strong smell of fresh earth or clay. Composed mainly of aluminum hydroxide, bauxite deposits are found near the earth's surface and are formed by the weathering of aluminum-rich rocks. The ore is mined with earth movers and dynamite, then shipped to processing plants, where it is refined and smelted into aluminum. Though a number of states contain deposits, most of the bauxite mined in this country comes from Arkansas.

Bayberry Myrica

Shrubs or small trees that bear clusters of small grayish fruits covered with an aromatic wax, bayberries are also known as wax myrtles and candleberries. The wax can be extracted by boiling the berries in water and has long been used for making scented candles, soap, and sealing wax. The resinous, leathery leaves are sometimes brewed into a tea that herbal healers have traditionally recommended for a variety of illnesses, and the bark of some species is used in a medicine prescribed to ease swelling.

The northern bayberry, a shrubby species, is found in the northeastern states, mainly in sandy seaside areas. The southern bayberry, of-

The bearberry, with its shiny leaves and delicate, vaselike blossoms, is sometimes cultivated as a ground cover.

ten growing to tree size, ranges from New Jersey south and west to eastern Texas. The Pacific bayberry, yet another well-known species, has dense, shiny evergreen leaves and thrives along the coast from Washington to southern California. Like all the bayberries, its fruits are eaten by myrtle warblers and several other birds.

Bayou

Derived from a Choctaw Indian word meaning stream, bayou is a term applied to some sections of swampy wetland near the Gulf of Mexico, especially in Louisiana, Mississippi, and Texas. Often occupying abandoned river channels or oxbow lakes, bayous are filled with shallow, slow-moving, or even stagnant water. Bald cypress trees rise from the sluggish waters, where river otters, amphibians, alligators, and other wildlife reside. Bayou Lafourche, southwest of New Orleans, is among the most extensive of these characteristic southern swamplands.

Beardtongues belong to the snapdragon family.

Bear grass blossoms, like daytime torches, brighten an alpine meadow in Mt. Rainier National Park, Washington State.

Bear *Ursus*

Of North America's three kinds of bears—black bears; brown, or grizzly, bears; and polar bears—the most familiar and most widely distributed are black bears. Our smallest species, averaging about 300 pounds, they inhabit forests and mountainous areas across much of the continent. Despite their name, their color varies from pale cinnamon to black, often with a white patch on the chest.

The brown, or grizzly, bears once flourished throughout the western half of the continent, but today they are confined to Alaska, western Canada, and wilderness areas south of the Canadian border in the Rocky Mountains. Up to 9 feet from snout to tail and weighing more than 1,600 pounds, Alaskan brown bears are the world's largest flesh-eating land mammals.

The great white polar bears, weighing as much as 1,000 pounds, seldom venture far south of the Arctic Ocean. Accomplished swimmers, they are well adapted for hunting seals on frigid ice floes. Like all the bears, they are very dangerous when threatened or alarmed.

Bears feed on almost anything that is edible and are as fond of berries, roots, and leaves as they are of rodents, fish, and carrion. In the fall they begin to gorge on rich foods in preparation for their long winter sleep. While bears are not true hibernators, they spend the colder months sleeping in dens dug in hillsides, under trees, or in other protected spots. The females give birth to their young in these snug winter nests. The cubs—usually twins—are tiny, blind, and helpless at birth and remain with their mothers for a year or more.

Bearberry *Arctostaphylos uva-ursi*

A ground-hugging evergreen shrub with leathery, oval leaves, bearberry ranges across much of North America, forming dense carpets over barren, sandy soils. Clusters of tiny pink or white urn-shaped flowers adorn its branches in spring, and it is decorated in winter with brilliant red berries eaten by birds and bears. Though rather bland and mealy, the fruits are nourishing and were consumed by aboriginal peoples, who also mixed the dried leaves with tobacco for smoking. Recommended by herbalists for many ailments, the leaves do in fact contain an astringent that is effective in treating problems of the urinary tract.

Beardtongue *Penstemon*

Named for the tuft of colored "whiskers" on the flowers' tonguelike fifth stamen, beardtongues are attractive wildflowers found in most of North America. The trumpet-shaped blossoms may be tiny or up to two inches long; they come in a rainbow of hues, enlivening grasslands and deserts with welcome splashes of color. Some, such as mat beardtongue, are low growers, but most are upright, robust plants topped with clusters of flowers. A large and complex group, the beardtongues are hard to identify precisely, challenging even the experts.

Bear grass *Xerophyllum tenax*

Unmistakable and unforgettable, bear grass produces handsome, rounded clusters of creamy white, starlike flowers atop sturdy stalks up to six feet tall. Stands of them, swaying in the breeze, are a common sight in open woodlands and alpine meadows on many northwestern mountains. A closely related species, turkey beard, grows in dry, sandy areas, such as pine barrens, in some of the eastern states.

Tufts of long, grasslike leaves, normally tough and unpalatable, grow from the base of the plant. In spring, while still young and tender, they are eaten by bears—hence the name bear grass. Other names include basket grass and squaw grass, alluding to the fact that Indians wove the leaves into clothing and baskets.

A mother beaver, in the safety of her lodge, nurses three kits while a fourth explores on its own. Gnawed branches, rocks, grass, and other debris were cemented with mud and clay to build the lodge.

A honeybee (left) visits a clover blossom in search of nectar. As if flying on a magic carpet, a leaf-cutting bee (right) transports a leaf fragment to its nest.

Beaver *Castor canadensis*

The master builders among North American mammals, beavers were busy erecting their complex dams and lodges while early humans still lived in caves. Propped up by their scaly, paddle-shaped tails, these animal engineers use their chisellike teeth to cut down aspens, willows, and other trees. (The pointed stumps they leave behind are unmistakable signs of their presence.) The logs are then used to dam a stream, creating a shallow pond in which the beavers build a dome-shaped lodge of branches, rocks, and mud.

One family, including a pair of adults and several offspring, lives in each lodge. By day they stay inside; at dusk they leave through an underwater exit to cut down more trees, feed on the tender bark, and store branches on the bottom of the pond to serve as a winter food supply.

Growing to three to four feet in length and weighing as much as 60 pounds, beavers are our largest rodents. The hind feet are webbed for swimming underwater, where beavers may remain for as long as 15 minutes at a time. At the first sign of danger, an alarmed beaver warns its fellows by slapping the water with its tail as it dives to safety.

By the late 19th century, beavers had been trapped to near extinction for their lustrous brown fur. Now protected by law, they have made a dramatic comeback in recent years and are found all across the continent. Some people even consider them a nuisance when their dams flood roads or cropland. But many more praise beavers as water conservationists that also create living space for other animals and plants.

Bedrock

The solid rock which lies buried beneath soil, sand, or gravel (but which in some areas stands exposed at the earth's surface) is known as bedrock. While the type of rock differs from place to place, bedrock is found everywhere and helps determine the contours of the landscape.

Bedstraw *Galium*

Sweet-smelling plants that often grow in sprawling mats, bedstraws have a long and varied history of use. According to one legend, the Virgin Mary laid a thick cushion of bedstraw in the manger at Bethlehem. Early settlers prized the plant as a mattress stuffing, and herbalists have prescribed bedstraws for everything from fading freckles to eliminating kidney stones.

Many kinds of bedstraws grow throughout North America, often preferring moist woods and meadows. Most have bristly stems, produce

Bee balm blossoms look like crimson fireworks.

The beech's gray bark resembles elephant hide.

Beech leaves are thin and papery; spiny cases enclose the sweet nuts.

clusters of small white flowers, and bear whorls of four to eight lance-shaped leaves.

Cleavers, the best-known species, is named for the prickly little hooks that line its stems and fruits, catching onto anything they touch. Its roasted seeds serve as a coffee substitute, and its vitamin-rich shoots can be cooked for a nourishing vegetable. Another widespread species, yellow bedstraw, grows up to three feet tall and produces long dense heads of bright yellow flowers. Cheese makers traditionally used its leaves and stems to curdle milk, and dyes are extracted from its roots and flowers.

Bee

Of more than 3,500 kinds of bees found in North America, only the well-known honeybees and bumblebees are social insects that live and raise their young in large, rigidly organized colonies. The vast majority are solitary species that lay their eggs in nests provisioned with pollen and nectar and then leave their young to fend for themselves.

In contrast to the elaborate, multichambered wax combs of honeybees, the nests of most of the solitary bees are tunnels bored into soil, twigs, logs, and similar places. The tunnel typically is divided into a series of chambers, with a single egg laid on a pollen ball in each cell. A few parasitic species, such as cuckoo bees, deposit their eggs in the nests of others. Bumblebees, like honeybees, build multiple brood cells of wax, usually in underground chambers such as abandoned mouse nests.

Among the most useful of all insects, bees play a vital role in pollinating plants. As they fly from flower to flower gathering pollen and nectar, pollen grains stick to the hairs on their bodies and then rub off on the next flowers they visit, thus fertilizing them. The bees also actively collect pollen for use as food, both for themselves and for their young. They derive added nourishment by inserting their long, tonguelike mouthparts deep inside blossoms and sucking out nectar.

Bee balm *Monarda didyma*

In midsummer, the brilliant red blossoms of bee balm are often abuzz with bumblebees. Ruby-throated hummingbirds also come to sip the nectar deep in its clusters of tubular flowers. Growing up to five feet tall with fragrant opposite leaves, bee balm is a member of the mint family. Oswego Indians were known to brew a tea from its refreshingly scented leaves, a practice that colonists imitated when real tea became scarce at the time of the American Revolution. Still known as Oswego tea in many areas, this beautiful wildflower has a preference for moist, partly shaded soil. It flourishes throughout the eastern United States and is widely cultivated as an ornamental.

Beech *Fagus grandifolia*

Soaring to heights of 80 feet or more, with a trunk as much as 4 feet thick, the American beech is one of our most magnificent woodland trees. All too often, however, its trunk is disfigured with unsightly scars; its distinctive smooth gray bark seems to be irresistible to vandals, whose whittled initials can mar the tree's unfurrowed bole for decades.

Luckily, the beech's bark is not its only attraction. The oval leaves with sawtooth margins have a beautifully silky texture when they first open in spring and, after turning yellow in the fall, often remain on the tree throughout the winter. Its nuts, encased in spiny burs, provide food for a wide variety of wildlife, including foxes, bears, deer, and many kinds of birds. Nutritious and sweet-tasting, they also are enjoyed by humans, whether eaten raw or cooked, or ground as a coffee substitute.

Once common across much of eastern North America, the beech in earlier times was often doomed to immediate destruction. Realizing that its presence was a sign of deep, fertile soil, pioneers hacked down beech groves wherever they found them and converted the land to fields for growing crops.

B

Tortoise beetles (above) and grapevine beetles (right) are quite destructive, while ladybird beetles (below) eat pests.

Beechdrops *Epifagus virginiana*

Growing just 5 to 16 inches tall beneath their giant host, the beech tree, beechdrops are modest parasites that seem all stems and very little else. From August to October, however, dainty white tubular blossoms striped with purple appear along the upper parts of their slender brownish stalks. Along the lower stems, budlike, self-pollinating flowers produce an abundance of seeds. Although they depend upon beech roots to survive, their host is not harmed.

Beetle

Totaling about 300,000 species, beetles form the largest group of animals in the world, outnumbering all the fish, amphibians, reptiles, birds, and mammals combined. Their extraordinary success stems in part from their great adaptability. Found in nearly every habitat except oceans, they live in the soil, burrow in wood and other plant tissue, and also inhabit freshwater ponds and streams. One species is even capable of tunneling into the lead sheathing of telephone cables. Almost all can fly, though they are rather unskilled compared to other insects.

Beetles go through a complete metamorphosis: beginning life as soft-bodied larvae, usually called grubs, they pass through a pupal stage and emerge as hard-bodied adults. The larvae of some species are quite active, moving about in search of prey; others live in the soil, where they feed on roots and other plant parts.

The stiff, shieldlike front wings of adult bee-

tles protect the abdomen and the delicate hind wings, which do the flying. Thus armored, they can burrow into the ground or force their way under logs and stones without injuring their bodies or tearing their wings.

Another key to the beetles' success is their chewing mouthparts, which allow them to eat many kinds of food. Most are vegetarians, but some are predators, and still others are scavengers, feeding on everything from dung to clothing fibers. Some, such as the weevils, are very destructive, causing millions of dollars in damage each year to crops and stored foods. Others, such as the ladybird beetles, are highly beneficial, preying on aphids and other insects that are harmful to plants and man.

Bellflower *Campanula*

Nodding on slender stalks, the delicately flared blossoms of most of the bellflowers look like dainty pastel church bells. Two familiar domestic varieties, which have graced garden plots since pioneer days, are Canterbury bells and harebells, also known as bluebells of Scotland. While most of the bellflowers are blue or lavender, Canterbury bells come in pink and white as well. Common wild species include the southern harebell, with clusters of tiny blue bells, and the tall bellflower, with blooms that are star-shaped rather than bell-like.

Berry See *Fruit.*

Beryl

The radiant emerald and the blue-green aquamarine, two highly prized gems, both are forms of beryl, a mineral found in many parts of North America. Pure beryl crystals are colorless, but most contain impurities, which result in a splendid variety of colors, ranging from red and yellow to blue and green. Not all beryl crystals are of gemstone quality, however; industrial grade beryl is mined for beryllium, an extremely strong, light, versatile metal used by the aerospace industry and in nuclear reactors.

Beryl crystals, which are six-sided and very hard, are usually found in granite pegmatite.

Bigeyes, bright red and glassy eyed, hunt for prey over tropical reefs.

Bellflowers, dainty and colorful, brighten the mossy tundra around Mount McKinley in Denali National Park, Alaska.

This coarse-grained rock cools so slowly within the earth that it often produces crystals of enormous size. One stupendous example, unearthed from the Black Hills of South Dakota, was a beryl crystal that weighed 100 tons.

Biennial See *Annual.*

Bigeye

Small reddish fish with large glassy eyes, bigeyes are found in warmer waters off both the Atlantic and Pacific coasts. Also known as catalufas, they are nocturnal hunters that feed on shrimp, crabs, and other fish. The glasseye snapper—bright red with a covering of rough scales—is found from New Jersey to the Gulf of Mexico. The equally colorful popeye catalufa is a well-known Pacific species. Although bigeyes are relatively common, most members of the family are too small to be of commercial value.

Bighorn See *Mountain sheep.*

Billfish

Marlins, sailfish, spearfish—all the members of the billfish family—are prized by sport fishermen, not only for their large size but also for the spectacular battles they wage when hooked. Surging from the water, they leap and violently twist about as they struggle to break free. All are recognizable by their bills, long, swordlike extensions of their upper jaws. (In contrast to the flattened swords of swordfish, which belong to a

Sailfish, easily recognizable by their large dorsal fins, are vigorous, high-speed swimmers. A favorite with anglers, they wage a fearsome fight on the line.

separate family, billfish bills are rounded in cross section.)

Rapid swimmers, some of the billfish have been clocked at speeds of 60 miles an hour. Knifing through schools of mackerel or herring, they stun their prey by thrashing about with their bills, then swallow their victims before they are able to regain their senses. Although they use their bills mainly to stun rather than stab, billfish have occasionally been known to pierce the sides of sharks, whales, and even wooden boats.

All the billfish have long dorsal fins, but those of the silvery blue sailfish—very high in relation to the diameter of their bodies—are big and dramatic enough to suggest the great sails of clipper ships. Slender, efficient swimmers, they fold their sails against their bodies when racing through the water. Blue marlin are the heaviest billfish, sometimes weighing more than a ton. Spearfish, less common than marlin and sailfish, are smaller and have relatively short bills. Whatever their size or shape, though, billfish make coveted trophies and are often seen decorating the walls of seaside restaurants.

B

Birch bark peels like old paint on a house.

A bittern imitates the reeds around its nest.

Bison, shaggy but dignified, now graze in national parks in Canada and the United States. In the old days, these remarkable beasts roamed the prairies in herds so vast they blackened the landscape as far as the eye could see.

Birch *Betula*

The bark of the birches is their best-known feature, and rightly so, for it is their most striking characteristic. The smooth, chalky white bark of paper birches is the most familiar, but the bark of other species is equally distinctive. It varies from the silvery yellow of yellow birches to the salmon-pink of young river birches and the shiny, deep mahogany of mature sweet birches. It usually has a papery texture, peeling from the trunk in thin, pliable strips.

Twelve species of these handsome trees range far and wide across North America. The cold-tolerant paper birch grows north to the edge of the Arctic tundra, while the river birch flourishes as far south as Louisiana. Widespread in the west is the water birch, named for its fondness for damp soils. Another species, the gray birch, thrives on soils too poor for most other hardwoods; in New England, stands of this so-called "poverty birch" almost always mark the worn-out fields of abandoned farms.

All birches are pioneer trees. Producing tiny, winged seeds so light that they can drift for miles on the wind, the birches are among the first trees to colonize land that has been stripped by fire or logging. In a relatively short time, thick stands of fast-growing, colorful birches hide the scars of man's misuse while protecting the soil against erosion.

Bird See pp.40–41.

B

Bitterroot, the official flower of Montana, also lends its name to a mountain range, valley, and river in that state.

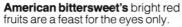
American bittersweet's bright red fruits are a feast for the eyes only.

Bison *Bison bison*

When Europeans first reached North America, bison by the tens of millions roamed the continent. Most lived on the prairies, where several Indian tribes hunted them for meat. Their hides were used for clothing and shelter, and their horn and bone for utensils.

Buffalo, as these magnificent grazers are sometimes called, are unmistakable—with their huge, horned head, massive neck, and high, humped shoulders. A thick, dark, shaggy cape of hair, often matted and mudcaked, hangs from the head, neck, and forelegs. Bulls stand about six feet tall at the shoulder and can weigh more than a ton, while cows average about 900 pounds. During most of the year, cows and calves live in family groups, but bulls join them during the summer to compete for harems that range from 10 to as many as 70 cows.

Slaughtered by the settlers for sport and food, the bison were eventually reduced to near extinction. By 1893 Canada had only 500 bison and fewer than 1,000 had survived in the United States. Now protected in parks and reserves, there are some 15,000 bison in Canada and about 50,000 in the United States.

Bittern

At home amid the reeds and cattails of freshwater and brackish marshes, American bitterns are skilled camouflage artists whose streaky brown plumage helps them blend into their surroundings. Whenever they sense danger, these masters of deception all but disappear by stretching their necks and long bills skyward, mimicking the vegetation. They even waver gently when breezes ripple the reeds.

American bitterns, at two to three feet long, are the larger of the two North American species, which are related to the lankier, longer-necked herons. Thanks to their bellowing springtime calls, they are also known as thunder pumpers and bog bulls. Their smaller cousins, least bitterns, are only about one foot long and utter a more subdued cooing note.

Both species build clumsy nests on the ground near water and lay clutches of three to five eggs. They feed on a wide variety of aquatic animals, including fish, frogs, tadpoles, and insects. Though sometimes seen flying low over marshlands, these secretive birds seldom fly any great distances except during migration.

Bitterroot *Lewisia rediviva*

Though it grows only three inches tall, bitterroot nevertheless makes a bright display on arid western mountain slopes from late April into July, for each plant produces a virtual bouquet of spectacular pink to whitish blooms. Native Americans no doubt admired the show, but they did not pick the flowers. They harvested the thick fleshy roots instead and, after paring away the bitter red bark, roasted them like potatoes or boiled them in soups and stews.

Bittersweet *Celastrus*

Many people cherish bittersweet as a highlight of the autumn landscape, for it is then that the orange husks of its showy fruits burst open to reveal the bright red seeds within. They may look inviting, but despite the plant's name, bittersweet fruits are not edible.

Two species of these twining vines are common across much of the United States. The native American bittersweet thrives in moist, shady spots from Quebec to North Carolina and west to New Mexico. It rambles happily over stone walls and fences, and up shrubs and trees to a height of 60 feet.

The other kind, oriental bittersweet, has escaped from gardens and become naturalized along the eastern seaboard. Its fruits are similar to those of the American species, but the clusters are smaller and hidden among the foliage.

39

Cardinals, a favorite with birders, have stout, seed-crushing bills.

Black-throated blue warblers build neat cup-shaped nests of leaves and grass, lined with cobwebs and hair.

Arctic terns, swift and graceful in flight, have long, tapered wings and deeply forked tails.

Bird

Unique among all animals in having feathers, birds are the most widespread and numerous land-dwelling vertebrates. Of the roughly 9,100 species of birds in the world, about 850 have been found in North America and some 650 of these nest here regularly.

The number of individual birds in North America has been estimated at 5 to 6 billion. Among the most abundant species are the red-winged blackbird, the European starling, and the common grackle, each probably numbering more than 100 million. Runners-up include the American robin, the yellow-rumped warbler, the song sparrow, and the brown-headed cowbird. Among the rarest are the whooping crane and Kirtland's warbler, each with a population of less than 200. The ivory-billed woodpecker and Bachman's warbler, if not already extinct, are even rarer.

Our tallest bird, the whooping crane, stands almost five feet high. The record wingspan, at nine feet seven inches, belongs to the endangered California condor. The heaviest is the male trumpeter swan, which weighs as much as 38 pounds, while the smallest is the Calliope hummingbird, at 2¾ inches long and weighing only a fraction of an ounce.

Built for flight

Except for the extinct great auk, all North American birds known in historic times have been capable of flight. Indeed, flight is one of the characteristic features of birds, and many of their adaptations are related to this ability.

Chief among these are feathers, which, being light and strong, serve the needs of flight very well. The large feathers of the outer wing propel the bird through the air, and the curved flight feathers of the inner wing provide lift. Those of the tail aid in steering by acting as a rudder, while the feathers of the body, known as contour feathers, form a smooth surface that offers little drag, or resistance, to the flow of air. Feathers also provide insulation, important for animals that must maintain high body heat and conserve energy to meet the demands of flying.

Other adaptations for flight include an internal system of air sacs that lower the ratio of weight to volume. The air sacs also allow oxygen-rich air to pass through the lungs during both inhalation and exhalation, another way of meeting the energy demands of flight.

Eggs that develop rapidly and are incubated outside the body also contribute to weight reduction. The reproductive system, moreover, is active and enlarged only during the nesting season; after breeding it shrinks drastically both in size and weight. In addition, birds have a rigid skeleton, which provides a solid base for the powerful breast muscles that drive the wings. Some of the bones are hollow and so help to reduce weight. Finally, birds are equipped with senses—including large, keen eyes—that allow them to operate skillfully in the air.

A variety of lifestyles

Birds have many different flight styles, from the effortless gliding and soaring of vultures, hawks, and eagles to the hovering flight of hummingbirds. Petrels, shearwaters, and albatrosses take advantage of subtle air currents over the ocean, conserving energy by riding on small updrafts over the waves, just as larger birds make use of updrafts over open country or mountainsides. Woodpeckers, starlings, and finches fold their wings during flight, which results in a bounding flight style. Finally, many birds fly with steady, powerful wing beats, often in wedge-shaped formations that allow each bird to ride on the turbulence of the one in front of it.

Flight in many cases is important in obtaining food. Swallows, swifts, and nightjars capture insects in midair, and hummingbirds use their hovering abilities to get at the nectar in flowers. Hawks and eagles soar over vast areas searching for prey, and flycatchers dart out from perches to snap up passing insects.

The bills of birds reflect their methods of foraging and so show many adaptations. Hawks and owls use their hooked bills for tearing flesh. The conical bills of finches, sparrows, grosbeaks, and buntings are ideal for crushing seeds. Hummingbirds and some sandpipers use their long, slender bills for probing, while the bills of flamingos and many kinds of ducks are specially formed for filtering food from water. The fish-catching herons, the anhinga, and the northern gannet, in turn, have spear-shaped bills, and woodpeckers have chisellike bills that are ideal for hacking holes in tree trunks. A number of other birds such as crows and jays, noted for their varied diets, have all-purpose bills.

Habitats are varied, too, for no other group of animals has been so successful in reaching and adapting to so many different environments. From the highest mountain peaks to expanses of ocean thousands of miles from any coastline, birds have found ways of obtaining sufficient food and, in many cases, of nesting. Except for fish, the vertebrate that lives closest to the North Pole in winter is the common raven, which ranges all the way to northern Greenland and the islands of the Canadian Arctic. Many species make their home in North America's harshest deserts, and even the most barren salt flats have their pairs of snowy plovers.

Birds and the environment

Because birds are conspicuous and attractive, concern for their well-being has always been important in conservation movements. They are easy to see and count, and any drop in their populations is easily detected. Birds thus provide an early warning system, often the first indication we have that something is wrong with the environment.

Declines in ospreys, bald eagles, and peregrine falcons provided a clue that DDT and similar chemicals, all of them potentially harmful to humans, were building to dangerous levels in wetlands. As a result of this research with birds, these chemicals are now controlled or banned.

Today, declines in migrant songbirds in North America's woodlands signal the destruction of the tropical rain forests where these species spend the winter. Birds thus are not merely conspicuous and beautiful. They are valuable allies in our efforts to save our planet.

Barbule

Rachis

Feathers must be both strong and flexible. The stiff, central rachis (right) is lined with barbs, which are fringed with hundreds of interlocking barbules (above).

Barb

Shaft

Great blue herons, like all birds, must preen to keep their feathers clean and in good condition.

41

B

Blackberry branches, arching toward the ground, bear berries that turn from bright red to deep black as they ripen.

A red-winged blackbird, while perched on a cattail, keeps on the lookout for rival males.

Yellow-headed blackbirds, when not nesting, tend to gather in dense, colorful flocks.

Black bass *Micropterus*

Several species of freshwater bass, known collectively as black bass, are native to cooler streams in eastern North America. Unrelated to striped bass or the sea bass, they are members of the sunfish family—and most are just as pugnacious as their smaller kin.

Because they are such strong, tenacious fighters, the two best-known species—largemouth bass and smallmouth bass—have been introduced into lakes and rivers all across the continent. They are in fact one of the most popular of the freshwater game fish; armies of anglers try to deceive them with a seemingly endless array of artificial lures.

Largemouth bass may grow to three feet in length and weigh more than 20 pounds—twice the size of smallmouth bass. Even so, the two fish are often mistaken for one another since their coloring—olive above with silvery undersides—is so similar. The best distinguishing feature is the mouth, which on largemouth bass extends back beyond the eye.

During the heat of the day, bass stay in deeper water, swimming among the rocks and preying on crustaceans and small fish. In the evening, they move into the shallows to feed on insects and other creatures near the water's edge.

Black bass breed in spring and early summer. The males build nests near the shore, and after mating, they stand guard, fanning the eggs to keep silt from suffocating them. Since the nesting fish will strike at intruders, they are easy prey for fishing lures. As a result, many states ban bass fishing during the spawning season.

Blackberry *Rubus*

It seems only fair that wild fruits as delectable as those of the blackberries should be well guarded, hidden among thickets of thorny canes. Blackberries, though, are a tangle in more ways than one. Botanists argue endlessly about the number of species there are—one count runs to 122. They probably will never agree, since blackberries cross easily with their close relatives the raspberries and dewberries to produce a continual stream of new hybrids.

The denizens of field and forest do not worry about the scientific status of the fruit; they are too busy eating it. Animals from chipmunks to grizzly bears rely on blackberries as a major part of their summer diet. Some of these foragers even view the thorns as an asset— many small birds rely on them as protection for their nests.

Blackbird

Of the five kinds of blackbirds found in North America, the best known and most widely distributed are red-winged blackbirds (or redwings), named for the males' bright red wing patches, bordered with a band of yellow. Nesting

Black rats, also called ship rats, are crafty stowaways that have traveled the world.

A black widow spider, shiny as patent leather, shows her red identification badge.

in marshes across most of North America, the males stake out their breeding territories with a *con-ka-ree* call familiar to many as one of the earliest signs of spring. In winter, the redwings and other blackbirds gather in such enormous flocks (sometimes numbering in the millions) that they threaten crops and even destroy the trees on which they roost.

Tricolored blackbirds resemble redwings, but the males' wing patches have a white border. They are found only in California and Oregon and live year-round in huge, dense colonies.

Yellow-headed blackbirds, ranging from the Great Lakes to the Pacific, often breed in the same marshes as redwings. But the two do not compete for living space, since yellow-headed blackbirds tend to nest over deeper water.

The other two species, rusty blackbirds and Brewer's blackbirds, lack any patches of red or yellow. Both nest in trees or shrubs near water; the rusty prefers conifers in northern forests and bogs, while the Brewer's often breeds in western towns and parks.

The females of all the blackbirds, drab compared to the males, take charge of nest building and incubation. They fashion sturdy, cup-shaped nests, firmly anchored to reeds, bulrushes, or branches, and lay an average of four to six eggs. In most cases, the males have more than one mate.

Black fly *Simulium*

Only about an eighth of an inch long, hump-backed black flies nevertheless are determined aggressors; attacking man and beast alike, they can inflict painful, sometimes bloody, bites. Their yearly cycle begins in early summer, when adult females lay masses of eggs in fast-flowing streams and rivers. The wormlike larvae attach themselves to rocks by means of sucking disks on the ends of their bodies, and they filter bits of food from the water flowing past. Sometimes the larvae are so numerous that their densely packed bodies look like mossy mats on the

rocks. Eventually encasing themselves in cocoons, the legless wrigglers are transformed into adult flies that go swarming through the north woods—much to the dismay of summer campers. Common examples of these noxious pests are the Adirondack black fly, the buffalo gnat, and the white-stockinged black fly.

Black rat *Rattus rattus*

Along with its cousin the Norway rat, this aggressive, adaptable rodent has been man's uninvited companion for centuries. The two rats, both immigrants from the Old World, are similar in appearance, but black rats have longer tails, larger ears, more-pointed noses, and darker fur. Unlike the more widely distributed Norway rat, black rats in North America are restricted mainly to seaports in the southern United States. Living in or near buildings, they reproduce rapidly and feed by night, usually on human food supplies. Good climbers that like to nest above ground, black rats tend to occupy the upper floors of buildings, while Norway rats prefer ground floors, basements, and sewers. Both species carry diseases, but the black rat is especially notorious for its role in bringing the bubonic plague to medieval Europe.

Black widow spider *Latrodectus mactans*

The most poisonous spider in North America, the female black widow produces a powerful venom that causes severe pain and occasionally even death. Shiny black, she is easily recognized by the red hourglass-shaped mark on the underside of her pea-sized abdomen. (The harmless male is less than half the size of the female.) Although the black widow spider ranges across much of the United States, it is most common in the southern states and is usually found in damp, dark places. It earned its name from the female's habit of eating the male after mating, despite the fact that such cannibalism also is practiced by many other kinds of spiders.

B

Blazing stars, also called gayfeathers, thrive on hot, dry grasslands.

Some blennies are so tiny they can fit inside empty barnacle shells; active little fish, they regularly emerge to feed.

Bleeding hearts are a favorite in old-fashioned flower gardens.

Bloodroots ooze a reddish sap, which Indians used for warpaint.

Bladderwort *Utricularia*

Carnivorous plants with no roots and, in some species, no true leaves, the bladderworts grow in swamps and ponds, where they feed on small animal life. Scattered among the stems and leaves are tiny bladders that function as traps. A watertight door seals the bladder's entrance, and glands pump out any water inside to create a partial vacuum. When an animal touches trigger hairs on the door, the seal breaks and a stream of water rushes in, along with the hapless prey.

Blazing star *Liatris*

The nomadic Indians of the western plains used to wait anxiously each year for the late summer blossoming of the blazing stars. They knew that the appearance of the purplish spikes of thistle-like flower heads, also called gayfeathers, coincided with the ripening of the corn in the fields of neighboring tribes and so marked the beginning of a time of feasting. Though blazing stars of several species grow as far east as the Atlantic Coast, these hardy perennials are uniquely suited to life on the prairie. One kind, for instance, sends its roots a yard or more into the soil during its first season of growth, making the modest above-ground seedling almost invulnerable to drought.

Bleeding heart *Dicentra*

Set amid lacy, finely cut foliage, the pink, heart-shaped blossoms of the eastern and western wild bleeding hearts look for all the world like old-fashioned valentines. Just as descriptively named are their near relatives: Dutchman's breeches, which resembles trousers hung out on a line to dry, and the western steer's head, which looks uncannily like a skull with horns. But beware; despite their charm, several of these plants are also known as staggerweed because of the stupefying effect their toxic foliage has on unwary deer and cattle.

Blenny

Living in tidepools and other shallow waters, blennies are a diverse group of small, slender marine fish. Most are only a few inches long, with a spiny back fin extending from head to tail, and many have branched tentacles and "hairs" on their heads. Some of them, known as the scaled blennies, are predators, while the scaleless combtooth blennies use their teeth to scrape algae from rocks and coral. Some of the blennies use their two front fins as limbs for crawling along the bottom and can even pull themselves out of the water to bask on spray-soaked rocks.

Blizzard

Although any heavy snowstorm is commonly called a blizzard, in its strict sense the term refers to a storm combining freezing temperatures and snowladen winds of 25 miles an hour or more, which reduce visibility to half a mile for three to six hours. Large, dunelike drifts usually form, blocking roads and piling up around buildings, and strong gusts sometimes blow so much snow through the air that visibility is reduced to just a few feet.

Storms of this kind most often occur on the Prairies. Southwestern Saskatchewan is particularly vulnerable. All highways into Regina were blocked for 10 days during a 1947 blizzard. Bitter temperatures and 60-mile-an-hour winds kept Igaluit, N.W.T., residents indoors for 10 days in 1979. Another famous blizzard blasted the northeastern United States for four days in 1888, resulting in the loss of 400 lives.

The Blizzard of '88 was fed by moisture from the Atlantic Ocean, but the Great Lakes spawn blizzards, too. One of the worst in modern times struck Buffalo, New York, on January 28, 1977. Driven by 70-mile-an-hour winds, snow fell for three days and, with nearly 3 feet of snow already on the ground, drifts reached heights of 30 feet. The death toll was 29, including several people who were trapped in stranded cars.

Blowholes (top) shoot geyserlike sprays of seawater from coastal caves. At high tide (above), water rushes into the cave and is forced out through a hole in the roof.

Bloodroot *Sanguinaria canadensis*

Cherished as a harbinger of spring, bloodroot is among the first flowers to appear in eastern woodlands. Its blossoms, pure white or pinkish, are each borne singly at the end of a stem, with the stalk enfolded in a large blue-green leaf. In 1612, British explorer Capt. John Smith commented on bloodroot, noting that it bore a root "the bignesse of a finger and as red as blood." The color was in the sap, which Indians throughout the plant's range, from New Brunswick to Florida and west to Oklahoma, used as a dye to paint their faces, clothes, and weapons. In more recent times, scientists found that an extract of the root helps control dental plaque, and it is the basis of a toothpaste and oral rinse now offered for sale.

Blowhole

When tides are high and seas strong, spectacular fountains of spray can sometimes be seen shooting through vents in the cliffs along rocky shores. The openings, called blowholes, are gaps in the roofs of caves carved by the steady assault of battering waves. At high tide the ocean rushes into the caves, and successive surges force jets of water up through the blowholes.

45

B

The tall bluebell ranges from the north central United States to the Pacific Northwest.

Bluebell *Mertensia*

Of 60 species of bluebells native to North America, some 50 inhabit high meadows and hillsides on the Prairies, and grasslands and slopes in the southern Rocky Mountains. Also known as lungworts, bluebells in eastern Canada are generally found in coastal regions of the Maritime Provinces and in northwestern Quebec. The most common species in the United States is the Virginia bluebell, which flourishes in woodlands and wet fields. Widely cultivated in gardens, this seasonal treat shows its colors only briefly. Bursting from the soil as a tightly wrapped clump of leaves on the first warm days of spring, it unfurls its foliage and sends up stalks topped by clusters of pinkish buds that open to porcelain-blue, bell-shaped flowers.

Blueberry *Vaccinium*

Thriving in poor, acidic soils where few other plants can grow, blueberries are especially common on land that has been ravaged by forest fires. The flames that kill the other trees and shrubs rarely reach the roots of the blueberry bushes, and they soon sprout anew to grow with increased vigor among the fertile ashes. Find a spot that was burned over a few years previously, and there you are likely to find a bumper crop of the luscious fruits that mature from the shrubs' pinkish-white, urn-shaped blossoms.

Humans go to berry patches in pursuit of fruit for pies, muffins, and jams, but they are not alone in relishing blueberries. The fruits sometimes account for half of the summer diet of one of our most reclusive natives, the black bear. Squirrels, foxes, opossums, and raccoons follow in his wake, while colorful bluebirds and scarlet tanagers also have a taste for blueberries.

Despite the name, some blueberry species bear red, purple, or black fruits. All are edible, though some are sweeter than others. The bushes are equally variable. The lowbush blueberry that flourishes through Canada up into the Arctic does not exceed 12 inches in height, whereas the rabbit-eye blueberry found in the southern United States is a vigorous shrub that commonly grows up to 18 feet tall.

Blueberries, on land blackened by forest fires, spring up phoenixlike from the ashes.

Bluebonnets share the stage with crimson phlox in the Texas prairie's annual gala.

Bluebird *Sialia*

With their bright blue feathers and cheerful songs, North America's three species of bluebirds are a welcome presence in fields and gardens across the continent. The most widespread, ranging from the Atlantic Coast to the Rocky Mountains, is the eastern bluebird, which has a rust-colored breast and throat. The western bluebird, similar in appearance but reddish on its back as well, lives only in the Far West. And the all-blue mountain bluebird prefers the higher elevations of western mountains.

Bluebirds feed primarily on insects in summer and berries in fall and winter. Scanning the ground from fence posts or other perches, they

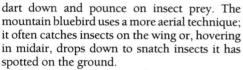
The mountain bluebird (above), an acrobatic hunter, seizes insects on the wing. Birdhouses are welcome homes for the eastern bluebird (right).

dart down and pounce on insect prey. The mountain bluebird uses a more aerial technique; it often catches insects on the wing or, hovering in midair, drops down to snatch insects it has spotted on the ground.

Found mainly in areas with scattered trees, all three bluebirds are hole nesters. They commonly take over abandoned woodpecker nests, but the mountain bluebird sometimes chooses rocky crevices as well. Like most hole nesters, they willingly accept bird houses.

In many areas the bluebirds have declined in numbers. Biologists believe this is due in part to human activities. But the main factor seems to be competition with other hole-nesting birds, especially those two imported aliens, the house sparrow and the starling.

Bluebonnet *Lupinus*

The much-beloved symbol of Texas, these wild lupines are expansive as only Texans can be— their spikes of clear blue blossoms mirror the sky for miles along Texas highways from spring into early summer. (Of the four species of bluebonnets found in Texas, the official state flower is the little *Lupinus subcarnosus*.) A simple device helps these prairie wildflowers succeed in the difficult southwestern climate: their seeds have such a hard coat that they can lie dormant through years of drought and sprout only when rainfall returns. Early settlers called the bluebonnets "buffalo clover," and in fact, they are related to the clovers. Like other legumes, they take nitrogen from the air and fix it in the soil. So this Texas wildflower enriches the land even while cloaking it in beauty.

Blue cohosh *Caulophyllum thalictroides*

Named for the bluish cast of its foliage, blue cohosh is a deceptive plant: what appears to be three separate leaves is actually a single, very complex compound leaf attached to the main stem. And the clusters of blue berries borne by the three- to four-foot-tall wildflowers are not really berries at all, but seeds. Each greenish-yellow flower produces exactly two, which swell to burst free from the enveloping fruit by midsummer. At one time the blue cohosh's root was used by Indian women. Taken as a tea, this "papoose root" helped to hasten childbirth.

Bluefish *Pomatomus saltatrix*

Prized by commercial fishermen as popular tablefare and by anglers as game, bluefish are formidable ocean predators that grow up to four feet long and weigh as much as 20 pounds. The blue-backed, silvery-sided carnivores travel in large schools and swiftly track down and attack other schooling fish such as menhaden, mackerel, herring, and even smaller bluefish.

Bluefish are found off the Atlantic coast, where they travel toward Florida in winter and north again in summer, following the movements of their favorite prey. Slicing easily through flesh with their razor-sharp teeth, these frantic feeders often eat until full and then continue the slaughter, leaving a floating trail of blood and fish parts in their wake. On forays inshore, they have been known to nip bathers caught amid their prey. The young, sometimes called tailors or snappers, begin life in estuaries and bays. Forming schools at an early age, they soon begin to hone their predatory skills on shrimp, anchovies, and other small prey.

Blue moon

A genuine rarity in the night sky, a blue moon occurs only when smoke and dust particles form a layer in the air. The dusty air screens out all colors except blue from sunlight. And since moonlight is actually reflected sunlight, the moon at such times takes on a bluish cast.

B

The rosy boa stays buried by day and comes out to forage for small animals by night.

The bobcat, a well-camouflaged, solitary hunter, is an expert at stalking prey.

Boa

Compared to their awesome tropical relatives, North America's two native boas are small, rather mild-mannered snakes. Like all constrictors, however, they coil tightly around their prey until it suffocates, then swallow the victim whole.

The 18-inch rubber boa, found in the western United States, looks and feels like rubber. It is also called the two-headed snake because its blunt tail looks much like its head; when threatened, it rolls up in a ball and, hiding its head inside, lifts its tail toward its attacker. The three-foot striped rosy boa lives in deserts of the Southwest. Both snakes feed on rodents but also climb small trees in search of nesting birds.

Bobcat *Felis rufus*

The most widespread of our wildcats, bobcats are at home in a broad range of habitats; these versatile hunters are found from western woodlands and deserts to eastern forests and southern swamps. In general appearance they resemble tawny, oversized tabby cats with prominent, tufted ears. The "bob" in their name refers to their short tails, a feature shared with their close relative the lynx.

Masters of the slow stalk, bobcats can also play a waiting game, crouching motionless before pouncing on prey. Scavengers in lean times, they much prefer fresh red meat. Cottontail rabbits are a favorite prey, supplemented by squirrels and mice. At about 20 pounds, bobcats are small compared to mountain lions; even so, they can kill deer many times their size.

Adult bobcats are solitary and seldom meet except to mate, which is done with much loud caterwauling. Reared in dens in rocky crevices, caves, or hollow trees, even as kittens they display the instincts of hunters.

Bobolink *Dolichonyx oryzivorus*

In their flight south for the winter, bobolinks travel from Canada and the northern United States all the way to Argentina, a marathon of some 5,000 miles. Their flight note—a metallic-sounding *pink*—can be heard by night as the migrant flocks pass overhead. In the past, hordes of southbound bobolinks descended on the once abundant rice fields of the Carolinas, where the so-called ricebirds were slaughtered as pests. In the summer, bobolinks settle in open grasslands, where they feed on insects and seeds. The males, black except for a tawny nape and white on the wings and back, court their mates with a delightful bubbling song as they flutter through the air.

Bobwhite See *Quail*.

Bog

Often thought of as bleak and even threatening places, bogs are actually rich and highly specialized environments. In North America, most bogs are relics of the last Ice Age. As the glaciers retreated, they left chunks of ice buried in rocky debris; when the ice melted, steep-sided ponds were formed and later filled by rain and snow.

Too poor in oxygen and nutrients to support most kinds of life, these pockets of moisture offer ideal havens for sphagnum moss. This primitive plant needs no soil, only water, to thrive, and once established, it forms a floating mat that gradually spreads across the surface of the pond. As the mat slowly thickens, it deposits a substantial layer of dead, compressed organic material—peat—on the bottom of the pond.

Because both peat and sphagnum are acidic,

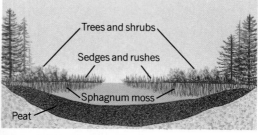

A bog (left) is blanketed by floating mats of sphagnum moss, which over time deposit a thick layer of peat on the bog's bottom, as shown in the cross section (above).

Bonefish inhabit shallow coastal waters.

Borage's hairy stems are used in tonics.

bogs can support only acid-tolerant plants. Larch, black spruce, and white cedar typically take root in the moss around the bog's margin; cranberries, bog rosemary, and labrador tea spring up on the floating sphagnum mat itself; and water lilies hold sway in the open water at the center.

Many plants that cannot compete on dry land find a haven in bogs, which are excellent places to hunt for the rare lady slippers and white fringed orchids. And carnivorous plants, which live on insects, thrive on the sphagnum mat. Few fish can survive in the oxygen-poor waters, but frogs, ducks, moose, wolves, and lynx all take refuge in the remote fastness of bogs.

Bonefish *Albula vulpes*

Up to three feet long with deeply forked tails, slender, silvery bonefish are found along both the Atlantic and Pacific coasts. They can often be seen as they probe shallows near the shore, nudging the sandy bottom with their snouts in search of shellfish, worms, and other food. Bonefish are a great favorite with anglers because of the vigorous fight they wage on the hook. But after losing the tug-of-war, they usually are tossed back alive, since their flesh is filled with so many bones.

Boneset *Eupatorium perfoliatum*

Tall, robust, and crowned with fuzzy, flat-topped flower heads, boneset is found in the St. Lawrence River valley and the eastern United States from late summer into autumn. A white-flowered herb that favors damp meadows, it was sometimes used by pioneers to treat fevers and similar ailments. Ague-weed, feverwort, and sweating plant—all old names for boneset—

testify to its medicinal reputation. Even the name boneset refers not to its virtues in healing broken bones, but in curing "breakbone fever," a type of influenza. As recently as 1900, country people still used the plant as a cough and cold remedy, and every farm had a bunch of boneset hanging up to dry in the attic or woodshed.

Borage *Borago officinalis*

Ever since ancient times, it has been claimed that this sprawling annual herb could drive away sadness and make men merry. And almost certainly it did when taken as traditionally recommended—in a tankard of wine. Though hairy, the young leaves are rich in vitamin C and, with their cucumberlike flavor, make a tasty addition to salads. Bees are attracted to the plant's flowers—five-pointed stars of blue or purple that produce a generous supply of nectar.

B

An eastern box turtle nibbles on clover blossoms; it may also eat berries, mushrooms, insects, snails, and worms.

Brittle stars' flexible arms help them to gather food.

Bowfin *Amia calva*

Often called living fossils, bowfins are the sole survivors of a once widespread family of prehistoric fish. And they demonstrate their survival skills even today: by gulping air at the surface, bowfins thrive in sluggish, oxygen-poor water that few other fish can tolerate. Up to 30 inches long, they are mottled green with a dark spot near the tail and a long fin down the back. Also known as dogfish, grindles, and mudfish, bowfins are found in quiet, plant-choked lakes and streams across most of eastern North America.

Boxfish

A built-in suit of armor—bony plates fused into a protective case—gives boxfish their name. Also called trunkfish, these chunky residents of temperate and tropical seas move about sluggishly, propelled by fins and tail that poke through openings in the rigid case. Boxfish are easily approached by divers as they putter around seagrass beds and coral reefs. Some, such as the smooth trunkfish of the Atlantic coast, use a water-pistol technique to feed: they shoot a stream of water from the mouth, aiming it at the sandy bottom to dislodge small worms and crustaceans that might otherwise remain hidden. Certain species contain a toxin that, if released in an aquarium, can kill every other animal in the tank. Indeed, the boxfish itself sometimes succumbs to its own poison.

Box turtle *Terrapene*

When box turtles sense danger, they not only retract their head, legs, and feet like other turtles, but close up their shells as well. A hinge divides the underside into two halves that can be folded up against the rim of the upper shell, sealing the creature in so snugly that not even a knife blade can be inserted between the shells.

Found only in North America, box turtles are five to eight inches long, with yellow or orange markings on their dark backs. They are more at home on land than in water, with the eastern

This braided stream in Alaska winds and forks its way across glacial debris.

box turtle living in woodlands and meadows and its western cousin preferring the prairies of the south central United States. Active by day, box turtles cool off on hot afternoons by soaking in puddles or resting in mounds of damp leaves. In winter, these expert diggers can hibernate as deep as four feet below the ground.

If removed from their home territories, box turtles can find their way back using the sun as a navigational aid. But if left alone, they spend their entire lives on just a few acres. And their lives are long indeed; box turtles have been known to survive for more than a century.

Brachiopod

Known mainly by their fossil remains, brachiopods flourished hundreds of millions of years ago when much of North America was covered by shallow seas. Some 30,000 fossil species have

Buckeye

Sweet gum

Sassafras

B

The broad-leaved trees
include a remarkable variety
of leaf shapes. The wide
surface area of the leaves
makes them efficient
collectors of solar energy.

Maple

Oak

been found in sedimentary rocks throughout the country, and a few kinds still survive today. Encased in two saucerlike shells, brachiopods are also called lamp shells because of their fancied resemblance to ancient Roman lamps. Most species live attached to the sea floor by an upright fleshy stalk, relying on movement of the water to bring them food.

Braided stream

Networks of interlaced channels that repeatedly divide and then rejoin each other, braided streams create striking patterns of land and water. They tend to form where wide, shallow, slow-moving rivers become choked with sediment, forcing the water to find new paths as constantly shifting sandbars block the channel. Melting glaciers, which release huge amounts of eroded debris, frequently produce intricate braided streams, with rivulets of meltwater weaving across one another. Farther downstream, if the slope becomes steeper, the numerous diverging smaller streams often reunite into a single main channel.

Breccia

Formed of coarse, angular rock fragments that have been naturally cemented together, breccias resemble gravelly, manmade concrete. Although they can be produced by any geologic process that breaks up existing rocks, they most commonly result when rock debris—from a landslide, for instance—is dumped in a valley and buried beneath additional layers of sediment. Eventually the rock fragments are compacted and cemented together as smaller grains fill the gaps between them. The very similar sedimentary rocks called conglomerates are made up of pebbles that have been rounded and worn through long transport by streams, rather than the sharp, angular fragments found in breccias.

Brittle star

With five spiny arms radiating from a small central body, brittle stars resemble their relatives the sea stars, or starfish. Unlike sea stars, however, brittle stars have arms that are long, thin, and flexible, with a snakelike appearance that has prompted their alternate name, serpent stars. The arms are used for moving across the sea floor and for passing food to the mouth, which is located on the underside of the inch-wide central body. If an arm is grasped, the creature escapes by allowing it to snap off; hence the name brittle star. Later a new arm grows in place of the lost one. Congregating by the thousands on the deep ocean floor, brittle stars also live in shallower waters along the Atlantic, Pacific, and Gulf of Mexico coasts. Since they stay hidden under rocks, in seaweed, or buried in sand, these retiring little invertebrates are seldom seen.

Broad-leaved trees

Oak, beech, ash, hickory, and maple, broad-leaved trees common in eastern Canada, dominate temperate forests in the United States. Their success can be attributed to their foliage, for leaves are factories that use energy from the sun to manufacture sugars. And since the typical broad-leaved tree boasts four times the leaf surface of a comparable needle-leaved tree such as a pine, the broad-leaved tree is a much more effective solar collector. In addition, most broad-leaved trees are deciduous—that is, in contrast to the evergreen conifers, they shed their leaves each fall. This not only protects them from winter cold but keeps them from drying out, since moisture is easily lost from the broad leaves. The two classes of trees also differ in their methods of reproduction. Broad-leaved trees are flowering plants that enclose their seeds in fruits, while the needle-leaved trees bear their seeds naked and unprotected in cones.

B

Most bromeliads (above) are epiphytes; they grow perched on the trunks and branches of trees or other supports. Many of them (top) bear colorful flower clusters.

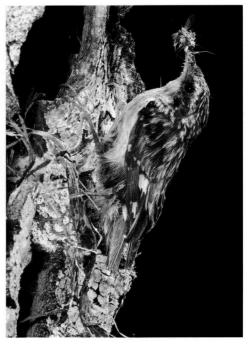

Brown creepers feed on insects picked from crevices in tree bark.

Buckeyes bear spikes of showy flowers that develop into spiny-husked fruits.

Bromeliad

Spanish moss drooping from the branches of a live oak in the Deep South may not seem to have much in common with pineapples on the green-grocer's shelf. Yet both are members of the same strange plant family—the bromeliads. Some 15 species of these tropical and subtropical plants are native to the continental United States, where they range from coastal Virginia south to Florida and west to Texas.

Most of our bromeliads, like Spanish moss, are epiphytes, plants that cling to the branches of trees and shrubs. Their roots never touch the ground, but instead serve mainly to attach the plant to its host. Unlike the dangling threads of Spanish moss, most of our native bromeliads form rosettes of stiff, upright leaves with cuplike bases that collect water. And in contrast to the minute flowers of Spanish moss, most bear conspicuous, brightly colored flower stalks.

Not all bromeliads are tree dwellers. Some make their homes more conventionally on the ground—the pineapple, though originally native to Brazil, grows so well in Hawaii's volcanic soils that it has escaped from plantations and run wild through the Kona region.

Brown creeper *Certhia americana*

Camouflaged by its barklike, streaked, and spotted plumage, the brown creeper is a small and inconspicuous bird that spirals up tree trunks in search of food. Held in place by sharp claws and a stiff, proplike tail, it uses its slender, curved bill to probe for insects and spiders hidden in crevices in the bark. The brown creeper usually begins foraging at the foot of a tree, works its way up the trunk, and then swoops down to the base of the next tree. When alarmed, it spreads its wings and flattens its body against the tree, making itself almost invisible.

Brown creepers depend on bark not only for food and concealment, but for their homes as well. Nests are occasionally built in cavities but most often are hidden behind loose strips of bark. Although their usual call is a single lisping note, in the nesting season brown creepers deliver a melodic song more like that of a warbler.

Bugs molt several times before becoming adults. A green stink bug nymph (above) discards its old skin; a spittle bug (left), completing its final molt, emerges from the froth where the nymph developed.

Bryozoan

Commonly known as moss animals because of the plantlike appearance of many species, bryozoans are tiny invertebrates that live in colonies encrusting rocks, shells, boat bottoms, and other surfaces in both salt and fresh water. Each member is encased in a protective capsule, hard in many species but jellylike in others, and each case has an opening through which the animal extends its tentacles to capture food. The colonies assume a variety of forms. Some resemble seaweed fronds and become dry and brittle when washed up on shore; others grow in bushy tufts on coastal rocks. One freshwater species forms spongelike mats; another lives in colonies that look like strings of snail eggs.

Buckeye *Aesculus*

Ohio claims one species of buckeye as its symbol, but in fact these American relatives of the imported horse chestnut range east to Pennsylvania, south to Florida, and west to Texas, with a California representative as well. One of the great beauties of late spring, buckeyes bear upright clusters of white, yellow, cream, or even pink flowers. The blooms are followed by thick-hulled burs that split in early summer to disgorge large, fleshy seeds with coats like polished mahogany. These may look like chestnuts, but they are bitter to the taste and poisonous. Resourceful Indians, however, still managed to get a meal from the buckeyes by pulverizing the seeds and leaching out the poison.

Buffalo See *Bison*.

Buffalograss *Buchloe dactyloides*

Only two to six inches tall, buffalograss forms a fine, dense, gray-green turf that spreads across portions of the western plains like a natural lawn. Indeed, it once covered such vast expanses from the Canadian Prairies south to Texas and New Mexico that the whole region was known as the short grass prairie.

As the name suggests, buffalograss was a favorite food of our native bison and furnished herds of millions with nourishing winter forage. The grass was nearly as important to the pioneers who went west to tame the plains. They used blocks of the thick, durable turf to build their snug sod houses.

Virtually immune to insects and disease, buffalograss tolerates extremes of temperature and needs little water. For these reasons it is winning new popularity in parts of the United States as a low-maintenance lawn.

Bug

While all insects are commonly referred to as bugs, the term actually applies to just one group—the true bugs. More than 40,000 species of these insects are found worldwide, with some 4,500 of them living in North America. They range from tiny bedbugs to the giant water bugs, aquatic insects that sometimes are more than two inches long.

A few characteristics distinguish the true bugs from other insects. Almost all have two pairs of wings. The forewings are thick and leathery near the base and thin and membranous near the tip; the hind wings, used for flying, are completely membranous. Unlike the many insects that bite and chew, bugs have beaklike mouthparts, which they use to pierce the skin of plants or animals and then suck out the juices. In addition, bugs undergo an incomplete metamorphosis. The young, called nymphs, molt several times and develop into adults without passing through a pupal or resting stage—quite different from the complete metamorphosis of beetles.

B

The bullfrog feeds on worms, fish, insects, and even other frogs.

The bullsnake, despite its bad manners, is a farmer's friend; one snake can rid a barn of rats and mice.

The painted bunting shows off its dazzling colors from lofty perches when trying to attract a mate. When feeding and nesting, however, it keeps out of sight in dense shrubs.

Bullfrog *Rana catesbeiana*

Named for their loud, deep-throated croaks, bullfrogs live in the shallows of permanent bodies of fresh water across most of the continent. Up to eight inches long with smooth, greenish-brown backs, tan bellies, and powerful hind legs, they are our largest frogs.

On spring nights, males shatter the stillness with their booming mating call, a resounding *jug-o-rum*. While the notes may be jarring to human ears, they attract female bullfrogs in large numbers. After mating, the females lay clusters of as many as 20,000 eggs and attach them to underwater vegetation. The eggs hatch into tadpoles, which, depending on the climate, take one to three years to develop into adults.

Hunting mostly by night, bullfrogs prey on insects and other small animals. They can be caught quite easily if dazzled by the beam of a flashlight, and will often "play dead," only to spring back to life and escape at the first opportunity. Many are captured in the wild and raised commercially both for their tasty leg meat and for use as laboratory animals.

Bullhead See *Catfish*.

Bullsnake *Pituophis melanoleucus*

At five to nine feet in length, bullsnakes are among the largest snakes in North America. Their massive bodies are yellow or tannish, marked with dark blotches. Though harmless to man, they can make a tremendous fuss when disturbed, vibrating their tails like rattlesnakes and hissing loudly. Larger specimens even make snorting sounds like those of a bull—hence their name. Powerful constrictors, bullsnakes feed mainly on gophers, rats, and mice. Occasionally seen on the Canadian Prairies, they are known as gopher snakes in the western United States, but called pine snakes in the East.

Bunting

A number of small, plump, finchlike birds with stout, seed-crushing bills are known as buntings. Some, related to cardinals and grosbeaks, are brilliantly colored. The others, more closely akin to sparrows, wear more somber hues.

The brightly tinted buntings are birds of brushy areas. The females, tan or greenish, build their nests well hidden in thickets, while the males flaunt their colors as they sing from conspicuous perches. The male indigo bunting, a rich metallic blue, is one of the few birds that fill the air with song at midday; it performs its recitals well into August. Another, the lazuli bunting, is bright turquoise with orange on the breast. But the most brilliant of all is the painted bunting found in the southern United States. A dazzling patchwork of red, blue, and green, the painted bunting used to be called the nonpareil—French for "unequaled."

The drabber buntings prefer open country and nest on the ground. The well-named snow buntings, mainly white with dramatic black accents, winter in southern Canada and the northern United States and move about in flocks. In spring they head north for the arctic tundra, where males help the females rear their young. Males of the lark buntings, in stark contrast to snow buntings, are almost completely black, except for a large white patch on each wing. They gather in enormous flocks in winter, roaming about in search of seeds.

Burdock *Arctium*

Coarse, invasive weeds up to eight feet tall with large, rhubarblike leaves and clusters of purplish, thistlelike flowers, burdocks thrive in fields and pastures across much of North America. Two factors have guaranteed their spread despite all efforts to eradicate them: the vigor with which they thrust their thick taproots into the earth (even through compacted, uncultivated soil), and their finesse as hitchhikers. Each bur of 10 to 25 seeds is surrounded by a stubble of tiny hooks that cling tenaciously to any passerby. Tangled in the fur of animals, the seed heads may ride for weeks and miles before dropping off to colonize new territory—and so ensure the burdocks' success.

Bur reed *Sparganium*

Well-known to both bird watchers and duck hunters, these freshwater marsh plants are much favored by migratory waterfowl. The long, ribbonlike leaves of the bur reeds, which may rise shoulder high above the water, furnish ducks and other animals with cover in which to hide and nest, while the tough, spiky seed balls serve as an important food source. The plants, in turn, are benefited by the birds; migrating ducks sow the partially digested seeds of bur reeds at stops all along their route.

Burying beetle *Nicrophorus*

The undertakers of the insect world, burying beetles specialize in the interment of dead mice, voles, birds, and other small animals. Usually less than an inch long, these glossy black insects with orange-red markings first locate a dead animal with their sense of smell. A mating pair then teams up to push it to soft ground, where the beetles burrow beneath the carcass until it sinks a few inches below the surface. After the pair has covered the body with soil, the female lays

Burdocks are cultivated by Asians for their vitamin-rich roots and asparaguslike stems.

Bur reeds provide both hiding places and a spiky delicacy for migrating waterfowl.

eggs on the corpse, which becomes both larder and nursery for the offspring. Burying beetles are also called sexton beetles, recalling the fact that in the past the duties of church sextons included the digging of graves.

Bushtit *Psaltriparus minimus*

Tiny, grayish birds with stubby bills and long tails, bushtits spend most of the year in flocks of 20 or more birds, traveling through brushy woodlands mostly in the western United States. Twittering, acrobatic fliers, the birds call constantly to one another with soft lisping notes as they dart among shrubs foraging for insects.

Their nest, built over a period of weeks, is a hanging, baglike structure made of twigs, moss, and lichens and held together with spiderwebs. Both members of a pair build the nest, incubate the eggs, and tend the young. Bushtits often raise more than one brood per year, with the young from the previous clutch remaining to help with the new arrivals.

B

These buteos, a pair of red-tailed hawks, soar and call to each other when courting.

Butter-and-eggs, introduced from Europe, adorns dry fields between July and October.

Buteo

Well-equipped for hours of soaring, buteos are hawks with broad, rounded wings and fan-shaped tails. Their effortless flight lets them scan vast areas of countryside for prey and migrate for long distances by riding on rising currents of warm air. Found throughout North America, many of the buteos—such as the red-tailed, the rough-legged, and Swainson's hawks—prefer open country, while the broad-winged and the red-shouldered hawks frequent wooded areas.

Butte

Flat-topped and steep-sided, the towering red sandstone buttes of Monument Valley on the Utah-Arizona border are familiar to many as the scenery in western films. At sunset, one tall, slender butte known as the Totem Pole casts a shadow that extends for miles across the desert floor. Buttes are also found in western Canada, especially throughout Alberta and in semiarid areas, such as the Big Muddy Badlands, of southwestern Saskatchewan.

The buttes are the lonely remnants of a vanished plateau that once stood high above the present valley floor. Attacked by wind and water for countless centuries, most of the rock has long since been worn away. Only the slender, scattered buttes, protected by erosion-resistant caps, remain standing today.

Butter-and-eggs *Linaria vulgaris*

Also known as toadflax, these charming wildflowers look so much like their cultivated cousins, the snapdragons, that admirers sometimes transplant them into their gardens. Up to three feet tall and topped with jaunty spikes of flowers, butter-and-eggs thrives in fields and on roadsides throughout most of North America. Each pale yellow blossom has an orange lobe on its lower lip that both marks and blocks the entrance to its nectar supply. Since the sweet liquor is hidden at the end of a long spur, only long-tongued insects, such as bumblebees, can get at it. After drinking their fill, they emerge from the blossom thoroughly dusted with pollen, ready to fertilize the next plant they visit.

Buttercup *Ranunculus*

Shiny yellow five-petaled buttercups are a conspicuous sight throughout the country, adding a bright splash of color wherever they spring up. Also called crowfoot because of the shape of their leaves, these wildflowers are fond of moist areas, and a few kinds even grow in water.

One species, the tall buttercup, is a favorite with children, who hold the blossoms under each other's chin in a test that supposedly reveals their fondness for butter. Water crowfoot, which grows underwater, sends up creamy white blossoms that unfold above the surface.

Despite their innocent appearance, some buttercups contain an acrid, toxic juice that can cause dizziness and even death in livestock. Fortunately, most grazers eat buttercups only as a last resort. Once having tasted the weeds, however, farm animals sometimes develop a perverse liking for it and return repeatedly for more, even after suffering from its ill effects. The juice of some kinds, while not as dangerous to humans, can blister the skin.

Butterfish

Silvery, schooling ocean fish with high, thin bodies that from the side seem almost round, butterfish look a bit like shiny, oversized silver dollars. (Some, in fact, are known as dollarfish.) Six to 12 inches long, with tiny mouths and deeply forked tails, they live in temperate to tropical waters along the Atlantic and Pacific coasts. Among the more common species are harvestfish, found in Atlantic waters, and the Pacific pompano; both are valued as food fish.

Showing a marked tendency to seek shelter beneath floating objects, young butterfish often

Butterflyfishes' unique color patterns help them recognize others of their species.

Buttonbush flowers, or honey-balls, are a rich source of nectar late in the season.

B

The common butterwort bears nodding purple blooms, hence this plant's alternate name of bog violet.

take up residence under the bells of jellyfish. One, the man-of-war fish, lives relatively unscathed amid the poisonous stinging tentacles of the notorious Portuguese man-of-war. When grown, however, butterfish abandon the protection of their floating, jellylike umbrellas and travel in schools.

Butterfly See pp.58–59.

Butterflyfish

Like butterflies in a flower garden, these dainty, disc-shaped fish flash with bright colors as they flutter across reefs of rock or coral. Though they prefer shallow tropical seas, a few hardy species venture as far north as New England. Many, like the foureye butterflyfish, have dark bands that mask the eyes and dummy "eyespots" toward the rear of the body; would-be predators mistake tail for head and lunge at the less vulnerable end of the fish.

With tiny, pouting mouths lined with bristly teeth, butterflyfish feed on coral polyps, tubeworms, and algae. The longsnout butterflyfish of Florida can insert its slender nose between the spines of sea urchins to extract prey. Other species are living vacuum cleaners, nibbling parasites from the skins of infested fish.

Butterwort *Pinguicula*

Lying flat on the ground, the butterworts' rosettes of greenish-yellow leaves glisten in the summer sun. Their sheen results from drops of liquid secreted by glands on the upper surfaces. This sticky secretion gives the leaves a greasy feel; hence the name butterwort. It also serves a vital purpose: it transforms the leaves into a kind of natural flypaper designed to trap any small insects that land on them. The leaves then secrete a digestive juice, extracting nitrogen and other vital nutrients from their prey. Found in bogs and other damp places, the carnivorous butterworts make a lovely display from spring into summer as they wave their colorful, spurred blooms atop delicate stems.

Buttonbush *Cephalanthus occidentalis*

Although it is fairly widespread in the United States and found in parts of southeastern Ontario, few people know this handsome shrub, for buttonbush hides in swamps and along the drowned margins of ponds and streams. At summer's end, however, a rich aroma reveals its presence; it is then that the buttonbush bears its creamy, sunburst-shaped, richly fragrant flower heads. The name buttonbush derives from the spherical seed heads, up to an inch across, that follow. Hanging from the barren branches all winter long, they look a bit like buttons dangling from a tattered coat.

Butterfly

A zebra swallowtail, emerging from its chrysalis, hangs upside down and slowly expands its damp, folded wings. Once the wings dry, the exquisite adult is ready for flight.

Among the most beautiful members of the insect world are the butterflies. Together with moths, they make up the order Lepidoptera, from the Greek *lepus,* meaning scale, and *pteron,* meaning wing. The order is well named, for butterflies and moths are distinguished from all other insects by the minute scales that cover their wings.

The differences between butterflies and moths are usually conspicuous. Butterflies ordinarily fly by day and are brightly colored, while moths have dull colors and fly by night. Butterflies tend to rest with the wings folded up over their backs, and moths rest with the wings fanned out. There are, however, notable exceptions to these "rules," and the only sure way to recognize a butterfly is by examining its antennae. Butterfly antennae have a knob at the tip; on moths they are feathery or finely pointed.

Nearly 700 species of butterflies are found in North America, and they vary widely in shape, color, and ornamentation. Some, such as the skippers, are dull, stocky, and mothlike in appearance. The checkerspots and fritillaries, in contrast, have elaborate, boldly colored wing patterns in orange, yellow, and black. The blues, coppers, and metalmarks not only are colorful but have an iridescent glow. The buckeyes, pearly eyes, and satyrs are ornamented with eyespot patterns—prominent black spots or colored concentric circles on the wings. Other butterflies are known for the unusual shapes of their wings. The anglewings have jagged, irregularly shaped wings. Swallowtails and daggerwings have daggerlike extensions on their hind wings, while the hairstreaks have thinner, more hairlike "tails."

Wondrous wings

The particles of "dust" that rub off the wings of a captured butterfly or moth are actually tiny scales. Arranged like shingles on a roof, they account for the variety of colors and patterns on butterfly wings. In some species the scales are colored by pigments. In others, they are grooved in such a way that the play of light on their surfaces produces the effect of color. The iridescence on the wings of blues and coppers is caused in this way, and their metallic glint is accentuated by a thin film of oil on the scales.

Wing scales also play a role in the mating of butterflies, which rely on scent to attract and locate the opposite sex. Glands at the base of some scales produce a distinctive aroma, which is diffused through tufts of very fine hairs at the tips of the scales. As if to confirm his amorous intentions, a male sometimes brushes these hairs over the antennae of the female.

The patterns on butterflies' wings play a significant role in their survival. Many have wings that so closely mimic the leaves, twigs, or bark they rest on that they are nearly invisible to predators. Wings with eyespots and other patterns mislead predators, encouraging them to

Two American coppers mate on a sunlit branch. They sometimes remain together, nearly motionless, for hours on end.

bite in nonvital areas. And bright colors, though conspicuous, often startle would-be predators or deter them in other ways. The brightly colored monarch, for instance, is highly toxic. Once a predator learns this, through trial and error, it will leave the monarch alone. The nontoxic viceroy, nearly identical in appearance to the monarch, survives by capitalizing on mistaken identity.

From egg to butterfly

In the course of its life, a butterfly undergoes a complete metamorphosis, drastically changing in form and appearance. The four stages in its life cycle consist of the egg; the caterpillar, or larva; the chrysalis, or pupa; and finally the adult butterfly, or imago.

The adult female lays a few to several hundred sticky eggs, depositing them on the leaves or stems of plants best suited to the food needs of the caterpillars. Some butterflies lay their eggs singly, others in chains or large clusters. The shapes of the eggs, which are best observed with a magnifying glass, vary with the species; some are simple, smooth spheres, while others have unusual shapes and may be elaborately ornamented, with fluted, ribbed, or pitted surfaces.

Unless the egg is meant to survive the winter, as in some species, the caterpillar normally hatches within a week and begins gorging on food. During the larval stage the caterpillar must eat as much as it can to sustain it through the noneating pupal stage. To avoid being eaten themselves, many caterpillars are well camouflaged, and those that are not are often conspicuously colored, relying on their unpleasant taste or an armor of spines to make them difficult for predators to swallow.

After about a month of eating and several molts to accommodate its increasing size, the caterpillar settles into a suitable spot to pupate. It may hang from a plant by a silken thread, attach itself to a stem with a girdle of silk, or remain on the ground. After a few days the cat-

erpillar's skin shrivels and is cast off, leaving the chrysalis, or pupa. The outside of the chrysalis, though usually blending in with its surroundings, also shows the rudimentary outlines of the developing butterfly's wings, eyes, and legs. Eventually the chrysalis splits open, and the adult insect pulls itself free, climbing onto a twig or leaf to rest while its wings expand and dry. Soon it flies off to begin life as an adult butterfly, a life that will last an average of two weeks but may continue for many months.

The adult butterfly survives on plant nectar, which it drinks through its long, tubelike tongue, or proboscis. The nectar provides the energy needed for flight and for the butterfly's last and most important function: reproduction. Once a male and female of the same species have found each other, they begin an aerial courtship that involves elaborately choreographed movements such as fluttering, diving, and spiraling. Mating itself begins on a branch or other perch and may continue in the air. Finally, some days after mating, the female lays her eggs, and the complex and astonishing life cycle of the butterfly begins all over again.

The ruddy daggerwing is commonly seen in Florida's Everglades National Park.

The zebra longwing is boldly striped.

A silvery blue visits a flower and sips nectar.

Sorting Out the Cacti by Shape and Size

As a group, the cacti are easily distinguished from other plants by their fleshy green stems and sharp spines. Ranging in size from less than an inch to 60 feet tall, their stems assume a wide variety of shapes. Some are round or barrel shaped, while others have cylindrical branches or flattened joints. The shapes and sizes of cactus stems, in fact, provide the best general clues for telling one kind of cactus from another.

Simple, Barrellike

STEMS SMALL (TO 1 FT.) AND KNOBBY

Pincushion cactus

STEMS STOCKY, CYLINDRICAL, AND RIBBED

To 2 feet high, with up to 12 ribs   To 10 feet high, with up to 30 ribs

Hedgehog cactus

Barrel cactus

Cabbage butterfly *Artogeia rapae*

Common in fields and gardens everywhere, cabbage butterflies are serious agricultural pests whose larvae feed on cabbage, mustard, cauliflower, and other crop plants. Accidentally introduced to North America in the 1860's, they have since become the most common butterfly in many areas; they can even be seen fluttering over the scattered patches of greenery in cities. Not the most colorful of their kind, cabbage butterflies have white forewings tipped with black. Dark spots, one on the male and two on the female, dot the wings near the bottom edge. The caterpillars, which hatch from eggs laid on plant leaves, are bright green with yellow stripes.

Cactus

Characterized by fleshy stems and an armament of spines, the cacti are a richly varied plant family. Of the 2,000 species included in the group, all but 1 are native to the New World, and some 1,200 are indigenous to North America alone.

They range from the tiny, buttonlike peyote to the sentinellike saguaro, which grows up to 60 feet tall.

The most notable common characteristics of the cacti are their many adaptations for surviving drought. Their bodies are filled with soft, porous tissue that absorbs water and holds it like a sponge, allowing them to store moisture in wet periods for use through the ensuing dry seasons. Some of the cacti are ribbed with accordionlike pleats that enable them to expand as they fill with water. To minimize the amount of moisture lost by evaporation through the skin, most cacti produce no leaves and have a waxy, waterproof outer covering. Even their shapes—globes, cylinders, and barrels—help guard against dehydration, since they are the forms that allow for the greatest volume with the least surface area. When the rare rain does fall, some of the cacti respond by sending out shallow networks of hairlike roots to tap the moisture, then shed the new growth when the soil dries.

The cacti's spines also play a vital role in survival. More than mere protection against graz-

Complex, Branching

STEMS LONG AND RIBBED

One main stem

Giant saguaro (to 60 ft. high)

Many stems

Organ pipe cactus (to 20 ft. high)

STEMS IN CHAINS OF JOINTS

Treelike

Cane cholla

Low clumps

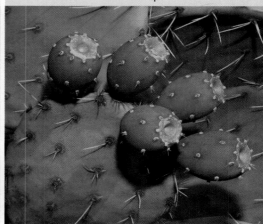

Prickly pear

ers, they cast enough shadow to help shade the plants and keep them cool. (The layer of air trapped under the spines may be 20°F cooler than the outside air temperature.) By slowing the circulation of air, the spines also help minimize the drying effect of wind. In some cases, they even function as water collectors; moisture from fog or light rains condenses on down-curved spines, gradually collecting into drops that fall directly on the roots.

Caddisfly

Found in ponds and streams across southern Canada and most of the United States, caddisfly larvae are freshwater aquanauts. Those of some species tend silken nets that they spin to entrap food, but many others move about in search of their meals, secure in the protection of mobile homes that they build around their own bodies. The cases are usually tubular, with only the larva's head and legs projecting from one end. Building materials, held together by silk or glue, range from sand grains to plant stalks and pieces

of shell. As they approach maturity, the caddis-worms seal up their cases and pupate inside. Eventually they are transformed into delicate, winged, mothlike insects of the night.

Caldera

Far different from the small craters found atop volcanic mountains, calderas are huge circular depressions that result when a volcano completely destroys itself. They usually are formed when an extraordinarily violent eruption spews out so much lava that the magma chamber beneath the volcano becomes empty, causing the top of the mountain to collapse into itself. A well-known relic of such an event is Crater Lake in the Cascade Mountains of Oregon. The six-mile-wide expanse of water fills a caldera left behind by the titanic explosion of Mt. Mazama, an ancient volcano. Almost 2,000 feet deep, Crater Lake is the deepest in North America. Only Wizard Island, a small volcano rising above the water's surface, gives a hint of the fiery mountain that once stood where the lake is now.

61

C

The snowshoe hare is well camouflaged in all seasons by the changing colors of its fur.

A sand grasshopper's mottled form mimics both soil and vegetation.

Killdeer eggs and chicks are virtually invisible on pebbly open ground.

California poppy *Eschscholzia californica*

In late April, when the hillsides of southern California blaze with countless millions of these golden blossoms, it is easy to understand why early explorers sometimes called the area "the land of fire." Borne one to a stem atop mounds of finely cut, blue-gray foliage, the cup-shaped flowers of the California poppy usually have four petals and range in color from brilliant yellow to deep orange. The elongated pods that follow the bloom explode when they mature, scattering seeds for several feet. The official flower of California, this delightful native poppy is at its best there. But it is widely cultivated as a garden flower as well and has established itself in the wild as far afield as Australia.

Camas *Camassia*

Before the arrival of white settlers in the West, these showy members of the lily family were so plentiful that their starchy bulbs were a staple food of several Indian tribes. Five species of camas flourished in damp meadows throughout much of the West, with one, the wild hyacinth, stretching east to Pennsylvania in the United States. Explorers described vast expanses of starry blue, white, and purple blossoms clustered atop wandlike stems that rose two to three feet from tufts of grassy leaves. Nowadays the common camas, or quamash, sometimes colors whole meadows, but the other camases have been wiped out in many areas, the result of cultivation of the land.

Camouflage

Whether hunters or hunted, many animals make use of camouflage to escape enemies or deceive prey. In most cases they rely on color or pattern to blend into their surroundings, but shape and posture can also play a role. The green snakes, for instance, all but disappear as they slither through the grass, and the mottled brown woodcock is nearly invisible on the forest floor. Fawns, brown and spotted, are inconspicuous in sun-dappled woodlands, while on open beaches plover chicks, as well as the eggs from which they hatch, are colored like the sand and pebbles around them.

Another form of deception, called countershading, is practiced by animals with dark backs and light undersides. When seen from above, the dark backs of fish such as bass and mackerel blend in with the dark water; when seen from below, their light bellies are indistinguishable from the sunlit surface. Many birds with dark backs and white breasts wear a similar disguise.

Other animals actually change color to match their surroundings. Flounders and the chameleonlike anoles, for example, change to blend

Ptarmigans in winter (above) wear a coat as snowy as the snowshoe hare's; in summer, the feathers of a nesting female imitate the textures of the surrounding ground (right).

with their backgrounds when they move from one place to another. Ptarmigans, ermines, and snowshoe hares, in contrast, change color with the seasons. During the summer they wear dark, earth-colored feathers or fur. But in winter, their warm-weather colors are replaced by suits as white as snow.

In the insect world, many grasshoppers, katydids, mantids, and others are as green as the plants they rest on, and moths and caterpillars often are patterned like dead leaves, bark, or other vegetation. But the real professionals in the camouflage act are the ones that pose as inedible objects. Walkingstick insects are easily mistaken for twigs, and many of the treehoppers look exactly like thorns.

Campion *Lychnis*

Hardy members of the carnation family, campions are most commonly found in cool northern regions. The white campion, however, ranges as far south as South Carolina. Opening only at night, its inch-wide blossoms are white, making them more visible to the moths on which they depend for pollination. Its day-blooming relatives, such as red campion and ragged-robin, have more-colorful flowers in shades of red and pink. The name campion is also applied to a number of catchflies, similar wildflowers that belong to another genus.

Canine

The domestic dog and its wild, meat-eating relatives, such as wolves, coyotes, and foxes, are all canines. Common characteristics of the wild canines are long, pointed snouts, triangular ears, and bushy tails. Lean, muscular, and long-legged, they are good runners, well suited for the pursuit of prey. They also are intelligent animals, with keen senses of hearing and smell.

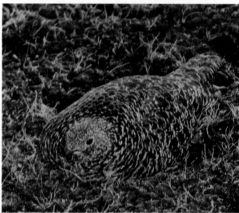

Canyon

A mile deep and 18 miles wide in places, the Grand Canyon in northern Arizona covers a vast area. From the rim, the river that created the awesome abyss can barely be seen. Snaking across the bottom of the gorge, however, the Colorado River continues to slice downward through the rock. Its power to erode is evident in the river's muddy water, which has been carrying away tons of silt, sand, and gravel for some 20 million years.

The river was not the only agent involved in deepening the canyon, however. At the same time that it was cutting downward, upheavals of the earth's crust were raising the Colorado Plateau through which the river had to carve its pathway to the ocean. In the process, layers of rock representing a billion years of geologic time have been exposed. The stepped appearance of the canyon walls results from the fact that the different kinds of rock vary in their ability to withstand erosion.

Canyons generally occur in arid regions where rivers deepen gorges faster than their steep sides can be reduced by weathering. However, Canada's best known example, Ouimet Canyon in Northern Ontario, is a relic of the last ice age.

C

Caracaras are splendid, aggressive birds, easily recognized by their long legs, black crests, and red, unfeathered cheeks.

The box turtle's carapace, a hard, high-domed shell, not only protects the animal but conserves moisture as well.

A male cardinal, unmistakable with its crest and red feathers, stands in bright relief against bare winter branches. During courtship, mates swap song phrases from separate perches.

Caracara *Polyborus plancus*

Large, dark, long-legged, and long-necked, with a distinctive black crown and red, naked face, the crested caracara looks and behaves somewhat like a vulture, although in fact it is related to the falcons. It gets its name from its harsh, cackling cry and makes its home on open scrublands in Florida, coastal Texas, and southern Arizona and New Mexico. In flight this splendid bird can be identified by its long, broad wings with conspicuous white patches. It is more commonly seen on the ground, however, walking in a regal manner or feeding, alongside vultures, on carrion. A brash bully that is not above stealing food from vultures, the caracara also captures frogs, lizards, and other small prey.

Carapace

Protecting the bodies of creatures as diverse as crabs, insects, and turtles, an animal's carapace is a rigid case covering all or part of its back. On turtles, the carapace is the domed upper shell and is composed of a bony layer overlain by hard, horny plates. The carapace of insects and crustaceans, such as crabs and shrimp, is made of a tough, waterproof substance known as chitin. As with turtles, this enveloping armor protects the animals from predators and prevents moisture loss. But it has another function as well: whereas turtles have an internal skeleton of bones, the carapace of insects and crustaceans serves as part of their external skeleton.

Cardinal *Cardinalis cardinalis*

Bright crimson plumage and a regal crest make the northern cardinal unique and unmistakable. Its stout, cone-shaped bill identifies the bird as a seedeater, and indeed the cardinal is a familiar sight at feeders in the midwestern and south-western United States. Originally confined to the southern states, the nonmigratory cardinal is gradually expanding its range northward into Canada.

Aggressively territorial, cardinals sing with a variety of loud, clear whistles. Females, though more subdued in color than the males, have the same distinctive crest and are just as vocal. Nesting in shrubs and thickets, the birds often raise more than one brood a year, with the male caring for the young while the female begins the next brood.

The pyrrhuloxia, a close relative of the northern cardinal, lives in desert scrub in the Southwest. Also known as the Texas cardinal and the parrot-bill, it is mostly gray, with a few prominent patches of red, but nevertheless looks much like its more brightly colored cousin. Both the male and female share in building a tidy, cup-shaped nest in thorny desert scrub, where they raise just one brood each year.

Caribou are crowned with many-branched antlers, which in spring and early summer are covered with a soft, protective skin called velvet. When fall arrives, the males shed their velvet, rubbing against bushes to help the process along.

C

Cardinalfish

Found near coral reefs in warm or tropical seas, most cardinalfish, true to their name, are vivid red. Despite their bright color, however, the tiny fish—most are just one to four inches long—are often difficult to spot. During the day they elude predators by hiding in crevices, caves, burrows, and even in or on other animals. Some species, for instance, dwell among the spines of sea urchins, the tentacles of sea anemones, and between the valves of certain clams. Brownish rather than red, the sponge cardinalfish lives in tube sponges, while the conchfish inhabits the snaillike shell of queen conchs. At night, the cardinalfish emerge from their hiding places and hunt for small prey.

Caribou *Rangifer tarandus*

Like their old-world relatives, the reindeer, caribou are stocky deer of the Far North, with the biggest males weighing as much as 700 pounds. In contrast to most other deer, both sexes have many-branched antlers, though the males' are much larger. Big round hooves ease their passage as they roam across bogs, snow, and soggy tundra. The hollow outer hairs of their coats keep them warm and help make them buoyant (caribou are excellent swimmers), while dense underfur insulates them.

Two races of caribou are found in North America. Woodland caribou live year-round in northern evergreen forests across much of Canada. Barren ground caribou, on the other hand, are migratory and travel in herds that sometimes number in the tens of thousands. They winter in forests just south of the tree line and in spring head north for the Arctic tundra, a journey of up to 800 miles. Following the same routes year after year, they feed along the way on grasses, sedges, and the abundant lichens known as reindeer moss. Calves born on the trek follow their mothers when just hours old.

At summer's end, the herds turn south again. Males battle with each other during the autumn

Mountain lions are solitary carnivores that silently and skillfully stalk prey. When close enough for the kill, the cats pounce and overpower their victims with sharp and savage bites on the neck.

mating season, with the winners establishing and jealously guarding harems. The herds then spend the lean winter months in the forest, browsing on willow and dwarf birch and pawing through the snow with their sharp-edged hooves to reach buried lichens.

Carnivore

To the taxonomist, the term carnivore refers to land-dwelling mammals in the large order that includes such diverse creatures as dogs, cats, weasels, and bears. But in a broader sense the word can be applied to any animal—from birds and fish to reptiles and insects—that feeds on other animals. Herbivores, in contrast, are animals that feed mainly on plants, while omnivores eat both plant and animal matter.

Carnivores have adapted to capturing and eating food in a variety of ways. Hawks and owls, for instance, are equipped with hooked, flesh-tearing beaks, while the specially hinged jaws of snakes enable them to swallow their prey whole. Other animals, such as cats, rely on agility and speed to outmaneuver their victims.

C

The Venus flytrap (left), its hinged leaves open like hungry jaws, is the archetypal carnivorous plant. Once the trap has sprung (above), the insect is locked behind bars.

Carnivorous plants

More than 40 species of carnivorous plants are native to North America, and like their hundreds of relatives around the world, they all thrive on adversity. Although they manufacture most of their food in their leaves just as other plants do, their ability to trap and digest insects and similar prey has enabled them to flourish in habitats where few other flowering plants are able to survive. Most carnivorous plants live in bogs or swamps, where the highly acidic soil lacks vital mineral nutrients and so is too poor to support most vegetation. The carnivores are able to flourish in such places because of the extra nitrogen, phosphorus, and trace elements they derive from their animal prey.

In general, carnivorous plants are of two kinds: those with active traps and those with passive ones. The best known of the active trappers is the Venus flytrap, which has specially adapted leaves that snap shut like bear traps on unwary insects. Passive traps are used by the pitcher plants, which drown their prey in pools of liquid, and by the sundews and butterworts, which secrete sticky fluid on their leaves, turning them into a kind of natural flypaper. The aquatic bladderworts consume any small animals that are sucked into their bladderlike underwater traps.

Because of their unique adaptation to one kind of environment, many carnivorous plants have severely limited ranges. The Venus flytrap, for example, occurs naturally in only one small area of North and South Carolina. On richer soils, few of the carnivores can compete with less specialized but more vigorous plants.

Carp *Cyprinus carpio*

Hardy and adaptable fish, carp thrive in almost any freshwater environment, from weed-infested lakes and rivers to polluted ponds and backwaters. Asian natives, they were introduced to North America from Europe, where they are commonly cultivated for food. Many think the

Catalpa blossoms are followed by long pods that look like leathery string beans.

introduction was a mistake, however, because carp frequently displace more desirable fish. Since they feed by rooting on the muddy bottom for small animals and plants, they often destroy the eggs of other species, as well as the vegetation that the young fish need for cover.

Carp are stout-bodied fish with short, fleshy whiskers near the mouth. Their large, coarse scales are dark on the back and tinged with bronze on the sides. Although they average about 15 inches in the wild, carp raised in captivity may grow to 3 feet and live for 40 years. Some anglers value carp for sport. Ordinarily caught with rod and reel, carp are sometimes shot with bow and arrow. Bow-and-arrow fishing, however, is prohibited in Canada's parks.

Catalpa *Catalpa*

Lush and green, with large, heart-shaped leaves throughout the summer, catalpas have an exotic, almost tropical look. But the trees are at their best when covered with big, upright clusters of showy white flowers in late spring and early summer—a time when few other trees are in bloom. Attractive and fast-growing, they have been valued as shade and ornamental trees in the United States ever since settlers began planting them in parks and gardens there. As a result,

C

The **catbird** sings unique renditions of the songs of other birds, but its best-known call sounds exactly like a cat.

Royal catchfly (upper) is found in woods and prairies from southern Canada to Georgia, while Parry's catchfly (lower) prefers the mountains of Washington and Oregon.

both species native to that country—the northern catalpa, once confined to the Midwest, and the southern catalpa, once found only near the Gulf of Mexico—now are common in all but the coldest states.

The trees also are known as Indian beans because of the long beanlike pods that develop after the flowering season. Turning brown, they hang on the trees all winter long before splitting open and shedding their seeds the following spring. The leaves of the northern species are fed upon by caterpillars of the catalpa sphinx moth. Green and horned, the larvae eventually mature into colorful and convincing mimics of the hummingbird.

Catbird *Dumetella carolinensis*

An uncanny, catlike mewing announces the presence of the gray catbird even before the black-capped, slate-gray bird itself emerges from the underbrush where it usually hides. Like its close relative the mockingbird, the catbird is a talented mimic. Its renderings are not as varied or as accurate as the mockingbird's, but its often melodious, sometimes squeaky phrases clearly suggest the songs of other species.

Breeding across most of North America from southern Canada to the Gulf of Mexico, the catbird is a friendly creature that is welcomed in suburban yards and gardens. Both males and females incubate the four to six shiny, greenish-blue eggs in a cuplike nest of twigs. In spring, the catbird feeds almost exclusively on insects and provides a valuable service by eating the destructive caterpillars of the gypsy moth.

Catchfly *Silene*

Widespread members of the pink or carnation family, the catchflies are so called because crawling insects sometimes get caught in the sticky hairs on their stems. Unlike the carnivo-

rous plants, however, the catchflies do not consume insects as food. The stickiness instead serves as a barrier that prevents crawling insects from pilfering the flowers' sweet nectar, which is reserved for the flying insects that distribute pollen. Known by a variety of names, some of the catchflies are called campions because of their resemblance to their near relatives, the true campions, while still others are called pinks.

C

Some larvae have deceptive eyespots.

Wooly bears have full, furry coats.

Caterpillars come in a range of colors and textures. While many are furry, others have colorful bands or strange spiny growths.

Sphinx moth larvae have showy stripes.

Swallowtail larvae emit a strong odor.

Caterpillar

The wormlike larvae of butterflies and moths, caterpillars got their name from a word meaning "hairy cat"—and many are hairy indeed. The wooly bear, the larva of the Isabella tiger moth, has a thick coat of black hair with an orange band on its midsection that supposedly predicts the length of winter. Such bristly surfaces discourage predators; some caterpillars further protect themselves by secreting irritants from special glands. Smooth-skinned caterpillars include the inchworm, which moves by alternately hunching and stretching its body, and the striped larva of the monarch butterfly.

Catfish

Whiskerlike feelers, or barbels, around their mouths give the catfish their name. Living on the bottoms of lakes, ponds, and slow-moving streams, they use the taste- and touch-sensitive feelers to help locate their food, which includes fish, insect larvae, crustaceans, and a wide variety of other creatures. Catfish have no scales, but some of their fins are armed with sharp spines that can cause painful injuries.

The most abundant of the North American catfish are the bullheads. Popular with anglers, they average 10 inches in length but can grow much bigger. The largest American species, the blue catfish of the Mississippi River system, grows to five feet and weighs as much as 150 pounds. The more slender channel catfish reaches four feet but weighs only 30 pounds. Popular as food fish, catfish are raised on commercial fish farms in the southern United States.

Catkin

Found on a variety of deciduous trees and shrubs, from willows to oaks and birches, catkins are flower clusters pared down to the bare essentials. On pussy willows they are the small silvery tufts that stand erect like furry candle flames, signaling winter's end; on hickories they dangle like long, fuzzy pendants, each one containing dozens of individual flowers along its length. Because most depend on the wind for pollination, these tiny flowers lack petals and sepals—any structures that might impede air circulation. And most catkins appear in early spring, while the branches are still bare. Often the male (pollen-producing) and female (seed-producing) flowers are borne on separate catkins and sometimes on separate plants.

Cattail *Typha*

The tall, sturdy stalks with cigar-shaped tips that give cattails their name are a common sight in marshlands all across the continent. Shooting upward in the spring, they wave the cattail's densely packed flowers aloft where the wind can catch their pollen and carry it far and wide. A single flower head may produce more than 140,000 seeds, each of them equipped with its own parachute of down to help it sail away to new territory. If a seed lands on well-watered soil, it can develop in a single season into a patch of cattails 10 feet across.

Many cave dwellers, such as cave fish (left) and crayfish (right), are colorless and blind.

Cattails have been used in remarkably varied ways. Indians and pioneers wove the leaves into baskets and chair seats, and cattail fluff once served as stuffing for quilts and mattresses. The pollen makes a tasty flour substitute, and the cooked roots are as nutritious as rice.

Cave

Festooned with iciclelike stalactites, rosettes of mineral crystals, and other exotic formations, caves encompass some of North America's most fascinating scenery. Usually found in areas underlain by thick layers of limestone, they are formed when slightly acid water seeps through cracks in the soluble rock and dissolves ever larger openings. Caves sometimes develop into complex systems of rooms and winding passageways, which can be many miles long and extend deep into the earth's interior.

Among the best known of these hidden underground worlds is Carlsbad Caverns in New Mexico. Its "Big Room" covers 14 acres and has a ceiling that, at its highest, could accommodate a 30-story building. Once filled with moving water, the chambers at Carlsbad eventually were raised above the water table and now are relatively dry. Kentucky also is riddled with caves. The largest, Mammoth Cave, has miles of interconnecting rooms linked by twisting passageways. With streams still running through its lowest levels, this remarkable cave system continues to grow. Missouri, too, is pitted with hundreds of caverns. One of them, the labyrinthine Mark Twain Cave near Hannibal, was made famous by Twain's novel *Tom Sawyer*.

Cave animals

Though dark and mysterious, caves nevertheless are home for a rich variety of animal life. Owls roost by day in crevices near the entrances, while phoebes and swallows build mud nests on the walls. Pack rats nest on the floor, venturing outside at night to forage and look for objects to add to their collections of debris.

Deeper inside the cave are the permanent residents, including fish, crayfish, salamanders, spiders, and beetles. In their world of perpetual

Cecropia moths, exquisitely patterned, have large, featherlike antennae.

night, high humidity, and nearly constant cool temperatures, these creatures have developed a number of special adaptations. Many fish have lost all pigmentation and are as white as alabaster. Most cave fish are blind as well, with mere traces of eyes, or none at all; highly developed senses of touch, smell, and hearing compensate for their lack of vision. Many of the crayfish, salamanders, millipedes, and other creatures of the cave also are colorless and blind.

The best known of all cave dwellers are bats, which roost in the caves by day and emerge at night to feed on insects. The roosting bats often are so numerous that they form a dense canopy across the ceiling. And when they leave at dusk, they come out in huge clouds that darken the sky. Carlsbad Caverns in New Mexico were discovered by a cowboy who spotted a cloud of bats. Bracken Cave in Texas, another notable roost, is home to an estimated 20 million bats.

Cecropia moth *Hyalophora cecropia*

Often seen fluttering near bright lights, the cecropia moth is popular with collectors. Its velvety brown wings, with a span of about five inches, are brightly patterned with white and reddish bands and spots. The adults do not eat, but the larvae—green, with spiny red, yellow, and bluish tubercles—feast on the leaves of many trees. Cecropia moths range from southeastern Canada to the southern United States.

69

Celandine was once called wartwort for it was thought to be effective in healing warts.

Centipedes, fast-moving predators with big appetites, help control insect pests.

C

The Octopus and the Squid: Keen-Eyed, Streamlined Cephalopods

Squid average 1 to 2 feet in length, but the giant squid, sometimes seen off Newfoundland, can reach 60 feet.

The octopuses have eight tentacles, equipped with suction disks for grasping and holding fish and other prey.

Common octopus

Atlantic long-finned squid

Cedar

The coniferous evergreen that the ancient Greeks called *kedros* was made famous by King Solomon, who used its timber for the temple at Jerusalem. He chose the cedar for its reddish, aromatic, rot-resistant lumber. While the true cedars are old-world species, some evergreens native to North America have similar wood and were dubbed cedars by the early settlers. This has resulted in a great deal of botanical confusion. The eastern red cedar and southern red cedar, for example, are actually junipers, and the western red cedar, also known as giant arborvitae, is really a thuja. The Atlantic white cedar belongs to yet another genus. Adding to the confusion, a rare tree native to Florida, a relative of the yews, is called stinking cedar because its leaves release a fetid odor when bruised.

This use of the word *cedar* for so many conifers illustrates how misleading common plant names can be. For although all our cedars are evergreens with durable, aromatic wood, none are closely related to Solomon's tree.

Celandine *Chelidonium majus*

One of the earliest spring wildflowers in central Canada and the northeastern United States, celandine unfurls its bright green, deeply cleft foliage before the last snow melts, and opens its small, four-petaled yellow flowers by late April or early May. Farther south the plant is virtually evergreen, especially when it grows in a sheltered spot at the foot of a sun-drenched wall. A member of the poppy family, celandine has orange sap that oozes from any cut stems. And as with many of the poppies, the sap has been used medicinally, in this case to clear the eyes.

Centipede

Unlike some of their tropical relatives, which can be as much as a foot long, our centipedes are rarely more than an inch in length. Even so, they are agile predators that run down insects, spiders, and earthworms. Though their name suggests that centipedes have 100 legs, the actual number varies from fewer than 40 to more than 340. One pair of legs is located on each body segment; they walk by moving the legs in neatly coordinated, rhythmical waves. Centipedes hide in dark, damp places under rocks, logs, and in leaf litter during the day and come out at night to hunt. They use their long, sensitive antennae to locate prey, and then paralyze it with their poison claws. Although most species are harmless to humans, some of the larger southern centipedes can inflict painful bites.

Century plant See *Agave.*

Chamomile grows in dense clumps in dry, sunny spots.

Brook trout are beautifully patterned char. Aggressive fighters, they challenge the most seasoned anglers.

C

Cephalopod

Squid, cuttlefish, octopuses, and the nautiluses all are cephalopods. Their name, from the Greek for "head-feet," refers to the fact that their grasping armlike tentacles grow out from the head. Like clams and snails, cephalopods are mollusks, but only the nautiluses have external shells. Cuttlefish and squid have only rudimentary shells embedded in their bodies, and the octopuses have no shells at all. Among the most extraordinary features of the cephalopods are their "camera" eyes, with lenses that can be focused, like human eyes—an asset in capturing prey. Highly mobile, the cephalopods are jet propelled, moving about by expelling water through a muscular siphon in their bodies.

Chalk

The white, powdery variety of limestone from which blackboard chalk is made, chalk is composed of the remains of microorganisms that once drifted near the surface of the sea. When they died, their calcium carbonate skeletons rained down to the ocean floor and accumulated over the course of millions of years into layers many feet thick. Compacted into rock, the beds eventually were uplifted and exposed on the surface. The most famous chalk formations are the White Cliffs of Dover along the English Channel, but chalk beds were also deposited in shallow seas that once covered parts of North America, and can be seen in Alabama and Kansas.

Chamomile

Two common herbs are called chamomile, and they have much in common. Both have feathery, pale green foliage; pretty, daisylike flowers; and when crushed, a sweet, applelike aroma. Both, moreover, came to our shores in the baggage of European immigrants and have a long history of use among herbalists. Chamomile tea, brewed from the dried flowers of either kind, still is taken as a gentle, pleasant remedy for insomnia and upset stomach. The smaller of the two species, usually called true or Roman chamomile, grows only about nine inches tall and is the more fragrant of the two. The other, wild or German chamomile, at two to three feet in height, towers over its smaller cousin.

Chaparral

Taking its name from a Spanish word for scrub oak, chaparral is a specialized plant community made up of broad-leaved evergreen shrubs. Growing in dense thickets up to 15 feet high, it is found in hot, dry foothills from Arizona and Baja California northward through coastal California to southern Oregon. In addition to scrub oaks, the plants include manzanitas, chamisos, hollyleaf cherries, and dozens of other species. Although seemingly impenetrable, these tangles of vegetation are havens for hosts of animals, from lizards and packrats to wrens and thrashers. As part of the chaparral's natural cycle, thousands of acres fall victim to wildfires every year in the wake of the hot Santa Ana winds.

Char *Salvelinus*

Prized by anglers and gourmets, the beautifully speckled chars are relatives of salmon and trout. In fact, both the brook trout and the lake trout are actually chars; they differ from true trout in having smaller scales and paler spots. Chars thrive in cold, clear waters across North America and spawn every autumn in the gravelly shallows of lakes and streams. The largest char, the lake trout, occasionally reaches 100 pounds, though most are caught before they reach 10 pounds. The brook trout is generally smaller but also puts up a challenging fight when caught. Other chars include the Arctic char, which inhabits northern waters and mountain lakes, and the Dolly Varden trout of the West.

C

The American chestnut, which once thrived in the East, was noted for its rounded crown and graceful, spreading branches.

Black cherry trees bear clusters of creamy blossoms (upper) followed by dark red fruits amid lustrous green leaves (lower).

Cherry

Though modest compared to the splendid show put on by the ornamental cherries grown in parks and gardens, the spring flowering of our several native species nevertheless is a pleasant reminder of the progress of the season. The clusters of delicate, five-petaled, white flowers, like flurries of snow, contrast nicely with the shiny, reddish bark on the twigs. And the fruits that follow, though tarter than the imported cherries we grow in orchards, make tasty jams and jellies, as well as providing food for a wide variety of wildlife.

North America's tallest and most valuable wild species is the black cherry, common in

forests and fields throughout much of the eastern United States. Reaching a height of 100 feet, it is especially prized for its rich, reddish wood, which is second only to black walnut for fine cabinet work, decorative paneling, and musical instruments.

Another species, found from western Canada south to Georgia and Colorado, is the pin cherry. It is also known as fire cherry because of the speed with which it follows in the tracks of forest fires. Its roots halt erosion, and its fallen leaves add humus to the soil, preparing the way for the forest's return.

The most widespread of all the natives, the chokecherry is a common sight in hedgerows across most of the continent. Its dangling clusters of pea-sized fruits are a boon to birds. Like some of the other wild cherry trees, though, its leaves can be a bane to any livestock that eats them; when the leaves wilt, a normally harmless substance contained in them is converted into the deadly poison cyanide.

Chert

A variety of quartz also known as flint and hornstone, chert is a dense, fine-grained sedimentary rock that has been valued for thousands of years. As early as the Stone Age, humans discovered that it can quite easily be chipped into sharp-edged tools and weapons. The first mineral to be deliberately mined, chert was fashioned into spearheads, knives, scrapers, and many other implements. In more recent times the rock again was used for weaponry when another of its properties, the ability to produce sparks, gave it a role as the firing device in flintlock rifles. Most commonly found as round nodules within other sedimentary rocks, chert also occurs in extensive, layered beds.

The black-capped chickadee is common throughout western Canada and the northern United States.

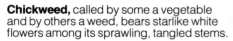

Chickweed, called by some a vegetable and by others a weed, bears starlike white flowers among its sprawling, tangled stems.

C

Chestnut *Castanea dentata*

No tree was more esteemed by early U.S. settlers than the American chestnut. Its soft but durable timber was used for cabins, fences, and furniture. And the sweet, glossy nuts, encased in spiny burrs, were a nutritious food for wild and domestic animals as well as for humans.

Growing rapidly to a height of 100 feet, with a trunk up to 8 feet in diameter, the chestnut was king of the forest from Maine to Florida and westward almost to the Mississippi. Billions of the trees flourished throughout this range; in the Appalachian Mountains alone, their lance-shaped, coarsely toothed leaves shaded untold millions of acres. When the clusters of creamy flowers opened in June and July, the hills had the look of a rolling, foam-capped sea.

Then, in 1904, a fungal blight appeared in New York City on chestnut trees imported from China. Within 50 years its spores had blown west, killing all but a few isolated specimens. Those that survived had been planted in western states, far beyond the tree's natural range. For decades, sprouts kept springing up from stumps of fallen chestnuts, but many of these too succumbed to the tragic blight.

Valiant attempts were made to crossbreed the American chestnut in hopes of developing trees resistant to the fungus. But the experiments took decades and had mixed results. In recent years, however, plant pathologists have detected a weaker strain of the fungus, one that competes with the blight and enables infected trees to heal. By inoculating wild trees with this less virulent parasite, they hope to restore the American chestnut to its original domain.

Chickadee *Parus*

Familiar inhabitants of woodlands and gardens and frequent visitors to feeders, chickadees are among our best-known songbirds. All are active, gregarious, friendly little creatures, with dark caps, black bibs, and gray or brown backs. Named for their cheerful "chickadee-dee-dee" calls, they also make a variety of piping and whistling sounds. While searching in trees for insects and insect eggs, these spirited acrobats often hang upside down from branches as they probe the bark with their bills.

Chickadees nest in cavities in dead wood, in abandoned woodpecker holes, and sometimes in birdhouses. Both male and female share in incubation and all the duties of caring for the young. After the fledglings leave the nest, they gather in small, chattering flocks that roam the woods in winter foraging for food.

The common species across the northern states and Canada is the black-capped chickadee; the nearly identical Carolina chickadee lives in the southeastern states. The mountain chickadee, with a distinctive white eyebrow, makes its home in the western mountains, and the ruddy chestnut-backed chickadee is found in humid forests and parklands along the Pacific coast. The boreal chickadee, also a northern bird, is the most drably colored of the group. During the winter months, if food supplies run short, flocks of these "brown-caps" sometimes stray well to the south in search of seed.

Chickweed *Stellaria media*

Found in lawns and gardens all across the continent, chickweed grows in a sprawling tangle of stems. Commonly regarded as a nuisance, it is a persistent weed that often remains green throughout the winter; its tiny white starlike flowers bloom even when there is snow on the ground, yielding a continual crop of round, reddish-brown seeds. The plant appeals to a variety of animals, however, and the popularity of its seeds with birds both wild and domestic has given chickweed its name. Some people also eat the plant; its tender little leaves and stems, when tossed in salads or served as a hot vegetable, are a tasty substitute for spinach.

C

The chiton's body is covered with flexible plates, enabling it to curl up and protect itself from harm.

A chipmunk, its cheeks already packed, gnaws on food clasped in its forepaws.

Chicory *Cichorium intybus*

By mid-July, chicory's sky-blue, asterlike flowers are a common sight on many roadsides throughout North America. Yet this tall, branching perennial is not a native plant; its first reported appearance on this continent came in 1785, when Governor Bowdoin of Massachusetts imported its seed from Holland. He may have had a taste for the rosettes of tender, dandelionlike leaves the plant produces in its first year of growth; these are still grown for use as a salad green. But it is more likely that he planned to harvest the fleshy taproots, roasting and grinding them to flavor his coffee as the Creoles of Louisiana do today. Unlike many foreign weeds, chicory, which prefers dry soils, has never become a serious pest on farmlands.

Chinook

Mainly a winter phenomenon, the chinook is a warm, dry wind that sometimes rushes down the eastern slopes of the Rocky Mountains. Spilling onto the plains, it can cause temperatures to rise dramatically. In southwestern Alberta, chinooks can raise air temperatures by more than 60°F in one hour. Calgary has some 30 chinook days each winter. Because such winds can rapidly melt any snow cover, chinooks are often called "snow eaters."

Chipmunk *Tamias*

Small, striped, ground-dwelling squirrels, chipmunks are widespread across much of North America. The reddish-brown eastern chipmunk is found nearly everywhere east of the Prairies; the least chipmunk is the most common of more than a dozen smaller, paler western species, which thrive in deserts as well as forests.

Teddy bear chollas have branching stems and a fierce-looking armament of spines.

Active by day, these bold and curious rodents tend to be most conspicuous in the fall, when they dart about in search of food for the coming winter. They stuff their roomy cheek pouches with seeds and nuts, which they then cache in their underground nests. And they live up to their scientific name, *Tamias,* which derives from a Latin word for treasurer: in three days, one eastern chipmunk took in 5 quarts of hickory nuts, 2 quarts of chestnuts, and about 24 quarts of shelled corn; the hoard of one of the western species contained over 67,500 items.

During the winter, chipmunks sleep for long periods, waking regularly to feed. In the spring they emerge to mate, and a litter of two to six young is born about a month later.

Chiton

Often exposed at low tide as they cling to seaside rocks, chitons are primitive, oval-shaped mollusks covered by eight overlapping plates. By day a large muscular foot on the underside holds them firmly in place; at night they creep about feeding on algae scraped from the rocks with a rasping, tonguelike organ. While most are only an inch or two long, one Pacific species grows up to a foot in length.

Chuckwallas, stout-bodied lizards, have loose folds of skin along their sides and neck, giving them plenty of room to expand.

Periodical cicadas can be recognized by their large red eyes and transparent wings.

Cholla *Opuntia*

A large and varied group, the chollas include cacti that sprawl in tangles several yards across but only a foot or so high, as well as others such as the jumping cholla that are branching, tree-like, and grow up to 15 feet tall. All, however, are studded with a fearsome armament of spines, which are often up to 2½ inches long. The spines protect the cactus wrens and thrashers that nest among the cholla's thorny branches. Pack rats also gather fallen joints of the cholla's cylindrical stems and build imposing, intruder-proof nests that are up to two feet high and eight feet across.

For the cacti themselves, the spines function as much for reproduction as for defense. They catch on passing animals, which pull away short sections of the stems and carry them off to new locations; eventually the pieces drop to the ground and take root as new plants.

Chuckwalla *Sauromalus obesus*

A large, dark, stout-bodied lizard that sometimes reaches nearly a foot and a half in length, the chuckwalla lives on dry rocky hills in southwestern deserts. It is active during the day, appearing on rocky ledges early in the morning and basking in the sun until its body temperature rises to about 100°F. Then, climbing about in creosote bushes, a favorite food plant, it forages for buds, fruit, flowers, and leaves. When threatened by predators, the slow-moving chuckwalla escapes by slipping into crevices among the rocks and inhaling large quantities of air; swelling up until it nearly doubles in size, the lizard becomes so securely wedged in place that it is almost impossible to dislodge.

Cicada

One of nature's most intriguing spectacles is provided by periodical cicadas, insects that emerge from the ground at 17-year intervals in southeastern Canada and the northeastern United States and on a 13-year schedule further south. Appearing in huge numbers, the cicadas first shed their nymphal skins, which can often be seen clinging to trees and other supports like ghostly duplicates of the insects themselves. Then the cicadas move higher into the trees, where they mate, lay eggs, and—most notably—sing.

Males serenade females by vibrating membranes on the sides of the abdomen. Their loud trills and soft buzzes, produced by throngs of insects, make up a deafening chorus. After mating, females insert their eggs in twigs, and the hatched nymphs later drop to the ground, burrow into the soil, and begin sucking juice from the tree's roots. After years of feeding in the dark, the nymphs tunnel to the surface, emerge as adults, and repeat the cycle.

Often erroneously called locusts, cicadas are not related to true locusts, which are a kind of grasshopper. The periodical cicadas look like giant, broad-headed flies with bright red, bulging eyes and four transparent wings. Like their relatives the aphids and leafhoppers, they have mouthparts adapted for sucking plant juices.

Similar to the periodical cicada are the dog-day cicadas of the Northeast and the grand western cicadas of the Southwest. Both differ from the periodical cicadas in their greenish color and their much shorter life cycles, which span just one or two years.

Cinquefoil *Potentilla*

The name *cinquefoil* means "five-leaf," and many of these perennial wildflowers and shrubs do indeed bear leaflets in groups of five, spread out like the fingers of a hand. Sometimes, however, the number varies; the shrubby cinquefoil, a dense, four-foot plant that ranges from Alaska to New Jersey, may bear leaflets in groups of 3 or 7, while other species have as many as 15 leaflets per leaf. The flowers, however, are more consistent in their arithmetic. The petals, usually yellow but occasionally white or crimson, always number five, and the many stamens invariably occur in multiples of five. The plants' generic name means "little potent one" and refers to the supposed medicinal properties of silverweed, one of the commoner species.

C

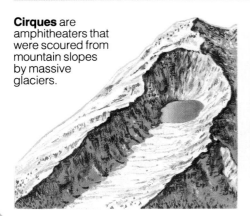

Cirques are amphitheaters that were scoured from mountain slopes by massive glaciers.

The gaper, a giant clam of the Pacific coast, digs into the mud with its extended foot.

The multihued clay cliffs on Martha's Vineyard in Massachusetts are unique in the East.

Cirque

Common features on glaciated mountains, cirques are steep-walled, basin-shaped hollows carved into the slopes. They were formed at the heads of glacier-filled valleys; plucking away blocks of underlying rock, the moving tongues of ice gradually excavated the hollows. With the glaciers now gone, the bottoms of the basins are often filled with the picturesque little mountain lakes known as tarns.

Clam

Living on the bottom of oceans, rivers, and lakes, clams spend most of their time buried in mud or sand. Their soft bodies are protected by hinged, two-part shells of various shapes, depending on the species. The shell can be opened and closed, allowing a muscular foot to protrude. The foot propels the animal across the bottom by expanding and contracting in such a way that the clam alternately anchors the tip in the sand and then pulls itself forward.

Clams eat and breathe by drawing water into the shell through a fleshy tube called the siphon, then passing it across their gills and expelling it through another tube. They feed on microscopic bits of food that become trapped in mucus on the gills. Since clams have no need to move

about in search of prey, they can remain buried indefinitely on the bottom.

Many of the clams are popular as seafood. One of the commonest kinds along the Atlantic coast is the quahog, or hard-shelled clam, which is often served in chowder and on the half shell. Another, the eastern surf clam, grows up to nine inches across. Soft-shelled clams, with shells that are more fragile than those of other species, are known familiarly as steamers.

On the Pacific coast, the eight-inch Washington clam, or gaper, can squirt a three-foot stream of water when disturbed. Another, the pismo clam, may live for 25 years. And the geoduck (pronounced "gooey duck"), sought as a delicacy, can weigh as much as 12 pounds.

Freshwater clams, called river mussels, are less well known and less palatable than their marine cousins. Darker on the outside than sea clams, they are often harvested for their pearly inner shells, which are used for making buttons.

Clamworm

Well known to fishermen who often use them as bait, clamworms once were thought to prey on clams because they were sometimes found in empty clam shells. In fact, most of these marine worms live in burrows or under rocks and snatch small animals that pass within their

White clematis brightens moist valleys in the Pacific Northwest.

The eyed click beetle, nearly two inches long, has spots that mimic a perpetual stare.

C

reach. During the mating season, some species swarm to the surface and perform a kind of nuptial dance as they spawn. The larvae drift for a time with the plankton, then settle to the bottom for the rest of their lives.

Clarkia *Clarkia*

Some three dozen species of these charming annuals ornament British Columbia and the western United States. Growing up to three feet tall, the clarkias tend to prefer dry open areas such as the slopes and foothills of the Coast Ranges and the Sierra Nevada. An outstanding attraction of these four-petaled wildflowers is suggested by one of their colloquial names, farewell-to-spring. Blooming at the onset of hot weather, the clarkias open their pink, lavender, or white blossoms after most other wildflowers have faded and the turf has begun to brown with drought.

Clay

An extremely fine-grained earthy material that can be molded when moist but hardens when dried or fired, clay is an important component of soil. It also is a valuable resource that has been used for centuries in architecture and industry. Its numerous applications range from the manufacture of bricks, fine china, and high-technology ceramics to the coatings that give book papers their whiteness and glossy shine.

Clematis *Clematis*

Most of the wild clematises, like their cultivated cousins, are vines. Their leafstalks coil around the twigs of neighboring shrubs and so help hoist the plants up into sunlight. The most common species in the East is virgin's bower, a vine that scrambles over streamside brush. Its other common name, old-man's beard, was inspired by the clustered fruits, each one tipped with a long silky plume.

A few of the clematises are not vines at all, but upright, earthbound wildflowers. Typical of the nonclimbing sorts is the pine-hyacinth of Florida. Its knee-high stems bear as many as three blue or lavender bells in late winter.

Click beetle

Noisy little acrobats, click beetles are also known as skipjacks and snapping bugs—and with good reason. When threatened, the inch-long insects drop to the ground and play dead. If they happen to land upside down, they arch their backs, then snap them straight—an action that launches their bodies into the air with an audible click and, with luck, lands them on their feet again. One of the largest, commonest, and most conspicuous North American species, the eyed click beetle is easily recognized by the pair of large eyelike spots on its back. The larvae of click beetles—hard and wiry—are called wireworms. Burrowing through the soil and feeding on seeds and roots, many of them are serious agricultural pests.

Climate

The difference between weather and climate is, in effect, the difference between days and decades. Weather, which changes daily, includes such things as the temperature, wind, rain, snow, and cloudiness at a particular time and place. An area's climate, in contrast, is the average pattern of weather that occurs there over tens or even hundreds of years.

Among the factors influencing a region's climate are its latitude, its distance from the sea, and the existence of mountain barriers. Widely varying conditions in North America result in such extremes as the frigid climate of Canada's High Arctic, the humid, subtropical climate of southern Florida and the hot, dry climate of deserts in the southwestern United States.

Although in the course of a human lifetime climate appears to be fixed, it can in fact change. Some 20,000 years ago, for example, much of North America was covered by glacial ice—and many scientists believe that such ice ages recur in cycles. In more recent times, the amount of carbon dioxide in the atmosphere has been increasing as a result of the burning of fossil fuels. Preventing the escape of heat from the earth—the so-called greenhouse effect—this build-up of carbon dioxide could cause a gradual warming of climates all around the world.

Clouds offer good indications of coming weather. Fleecy cumulus clouds (left) signal the continuation of fair weather; altocumulus clouds (right) with thick, billowy layers often bring rain.

C

Climax community

Ecologists have long recognized that any plant community—the association of species growing on a given site—tends to change over time in the process of natural succession. Eventually, however, a state of equilibrium is reached; the species are so finely attuned to each other and to the overall environment that changes cease. This stable, self-perpetuating mix of vegetation is called the area's climax community. Only a change in climate, a catastrophic event such as a forest fire, or more often, man's interference will alter the vegetation.

The nature of the climax community is determined by climate, soil, and other environmental factors. The abundant precipitation and mild winters of central North Carolina, for instance, foster an oak/hickory climax—a hardwood forest dominated by those trees. And Oklahoma's hotter summers, colder winters, and periodic drought result in a tallgrass prairie.

Clingfish

Shaped more or less like tadpoles, these scaleless, broad-headed bottom dwellers are made for the sedentary life: on their undersides, the pelvic fins are fused into suction discs that enable clingfish to get a grip on rocks, oysters, and other hard surfaces, and so steady themselves against the ebb and flow of the tide. Even when plucked from the water, they sometimes hold fast to their moorings.

Clingfish are most common in tropical seas, but the hardy skilletfish—named for its frying-pan shape—is often seen in oyster beds as far north as New Jersey. In the West, the northern clingfish, large at six inches, ranges all the way to Alaska and lives in kelp beds.

Clintonia *Clintonia*

Bride's bonnet is the common name of the western clintonia, and the one or sometimes two dainty white blossoms that top its 18-inch stems in early summer would indeed be suitable adornment for a bride. Also called queen cup, this graceful perennial produces bright blue ber-

An acre of clover can add as much as 150 pounds of nitrogen to soil annually.

ries, a characteristic it shares with a clintonia found in northern California and Oregon. The bluebead, or dogberry, of northeastern forests and bogs also bears blue fruits. The only nonconformist is the speckled wood lily of eastern mountains; its berries are pitch black.

Cloud

Everyone, no doubt, has marveled at the sight of billowing, cottonlike clouds drifting slowly overhead and changing constantly in size and shape. Substantial as they may seem, however, these fantastic sky sculptures are nothing more than water vapor made visible. They form when warm air rises and cools, causing the water vapor in it to condense into tiny droplets or ice crystals. And these droplets and crystals are what we see as clouds.

Based on their appearance, clouds are classified into three basic types: cumulus, or heaped; stratus, or layered; and cirrus, or wispy. The shapes of clouds are significant because they can help us predict coming changes in the weather. Fleets of mile-high, puffy, cumulus clouds, for instance, indicate fair weather. If very large cumulus clouds develop and their domes rise five miles or more into the sky, their tops often spread out into the shape of an anvil. Such ominous-looking clouds are described as cumulonimbus (*nimbus* means rain) and usually foretell impending thunderstorms and heavy rain.

Stratus clouds form when there is little wind and a warm front flows across a wedge of colder air. Uniform in appearance, these layered clouds

Tree clubmosses (left) and ground pines (right) produce highly flammable spores. Called vegetable sulfur, the dust has been used in the manufacture of fireworks.

C

often lie close to the ground and may produce drizzle or light rain. In contrast, wispy cirrus clouds, also known as mares' tails, form at very high altitudes and are composed of ice crystals; advancing ahead of a front, they usually indicate the approach of rain or snow.

Clover *Trifolium*

Distinguished by their three-part leaves and dense, fragrant flower heads, clovers are a familiar element in many North American landscapes; they thrive in lawns, fields, vacant lots, roadsides—virtually everywhere. Although we have several native species, almost all the common cultivated clovers are imports that have long since spread across the continent. White clover and crimson clover, from Europe, were introduced as forage crops; both are also valued as honey plants. Red clover, another immigrant and the state flower of Vermont, is one of the more important species grown for hay.

In lawns, however, the clovers are sometimes regarded as pests. But turf purists who try to eradicate them do so at their own expense, since clovers, like other members of the pea family, have nodules on their roots that host nitrogen-fixing bacteria. These valuable microorganisms enrich the soil by converting atmospheric nitrogen into a form usable by plants—and nitrogen is the major active ingredient in most lawn foods. Appreciating their value as natural fertilizers, farmers often sow clovers in their fields to be plowed under as "green manure."

Clubmoss

Despite their name and sometimes mossy appearance, clubmosses are not mosses at all. Growing in woodlands, bogs, and meadows, many of these low-growing evergreens, such as ground pine and running cedar, have narrow, scalelike leaves and are topped by erect, clublike cones. Looking much like miniature conifers,

they are, in fact, related to ferns and horsetails. They are the descendants of huge prehistoric trees that flourished hundreds of millions of years ago—in the forests that later were transformed into tremendous coal deposits.

Clubmosses spread mainly by means of long, wiry stems that creep across or just under the ground and send up new shoots every few inches, but they also reproduce by means of spores. The clublike structures atop the plants—or in some species, the tiny sacs at the base of the leaves—produce the fine, yellow, dustlike spore granules that are dispersed by the wind. When the spores settle to the earth, they develop into tiny plants that live hidden underground for years before emerging as adults.

Coal

An important and abundant mineral resource, especially in the United States, coal had its beginnings hundreds of millions of years ago in vast prehistoric swamps. Forests of gigantic, fernlike trees up to 100 feet tall and 6 feet in diameter flourished in these wetlands, along with amphibians 8 feet long and dragonflies with 2-foot wingspans. When the plants died, their remains accumulated into layers many feet thick and gradually decomposed into peat.

Layers of sediment eventually were deposited over the peat, and heat and pressure transformed it into coal. Fern fronds and other fossils from the prehistoric forests are often found preserved in coal seams—compelling evidence of their origin as living plants.

Variations in conditions produced different kinds of coal in different areas. Lignite, the type most like peat, is soft, crumbly, and brown. Bituminous, or soft, coal—by far the most abundant sort—is dull black and harder than lignite. Anthracite, produced by tremendous pressures generated by folding of the earth's crust, is extremely hard, black, and shiny; almost pure carbon, it burns the most efficiently of any coal.

C

Coatis walk with their tails held high like banners. Active most of the day, they retreat to shady spots when the sun grows too intense.

American cockroaches, long-lived and prolific, are obnoxious, persistent pests.

Coati *Nasua narica*

A lively relative of the raccoon, the coati ranges just north of the Mexican border into southern Arizona, New Mexico, and Texas. Foraging by day with its long, striped tail held high, this 15- to 25-pound mammal eats almost anything, from prickly pears to tarantulas. It probes the earth with its nimble snout in search of grubs and roots but also takes small prey such as scorpions and lizards. Leaping into trees like troops of monkeys, coatis feast as well on eggs, nuts, and especially, fruit. An agile climber, it uses its tail as a balancing pole on the way up and as a holdfast on the way down.

Females and young males feed, nap, groom, and play in boisterous bands of a dozen or more. Adult males, however, are loners and join the groups only during the breeding season. Some seven weeks after mating, the females retire to tree nests or rock dens and give birth to four to six kits. There they remain until, about five weeks later, the noisy young are brought forth and introduced to high-spirited coati society.

Cobia *Rachycentron canadum*

With no close kin among any fish in the sea, the cobia is one of a kind. Sleek and fast-moving, it has a long, dark body, a pointed snout, and a line of short spines in front of the dorsal fin. While they are usually one to four feet long and weigh 30 to 50 pounds, specimens more than five feet long and weighing as much as 100 pounds have been hooked.

Traveling alone or in small schools, cobias rove warm inshore waters and are often seen hovering beneath larger fish, boats, buoys, and other floating objects. Most prefer the balmy Gulf of Mexico, but during the summer some cobias travel north to brave the cooler waters off New England. Voracious predators, their keen appetite for crustaceans has earned them the nickname crabeaters.

Cockroach

With a lineage of some 350 million years, cockroaches are obviously born survivors. Voracious eaters, they feed on almost anything, including paper, soap, and glue. Usually dark brown or black, with a flattened oval body, cockroaches are creatures of the night that, with few exceptions, scuttle frantically away from light. Body hairs that are sensitive to air currents and sound vibrations warn them of approaching danger; long legs and lightning reflexes help them dash to safety. While many species have wings, most household varieties do not fly.

Fifty-five species of cockroaches are found in North America. Luckily, only five of them are household pests; the majority live outdoors in plant litter, woodpiles, and crevices. The giant palmetto bug of Florida, at more than two inches in length, is North America's largest cockroach. More common and much smaller is the Croton bug, or German cockroach, which is found in urban dwellings all around the world.

Codfish

Abundant and valuable food fish—annual catches amount to tens of thousands of tons—several members of the codfish family are prized for their tasty flesh. The premier member of the family, the Atlantic cod, has been a vital part of Atlantic Canada's economy for generations. The species' bounty off Newfoundland's Grand Banks has drawn fishermen to that area since the 1500s.

Coltsfoot, with its bright yellow flower heads, looks very much like a dandelion.

Red columbine is a hummingbird favorite.

C

Dark-spotted, with three back fins and a single chin whisker, Atlantic cod live in cold waters and probe the ocean bottom for a variety of foods. Active predators, they eagerly devour other fish, squid, and shellfish, often swallowing the shells along with the flesh inside. The average cod hauled in by fishermen weighs less than 25 pounds, but they can grow to great size; the record holder was a hefty 200-pounder.

Other important members of the codfish family include the Pacific cod, found in waters off the northwest coast; haddock, which live in the north Atlantic and are among the most valuable of all food fish; tomcod and pollock, found off both coasts; and the burbot, a freshwater codfish found in northern lakes.

Coltsfoot *Tussilago farfara*

One of the earliest of spring flowers, coltsfoot seems intent on getting a head start on the season: its yellow, dandelionlike blooms open atop scaly 4- to 18-inch stems, then wither and set seed before any leaves appear. Because of this two-stage growth pattern, herbalists called the plant son before the father. When the large, roundish leaves do unfurl, they explain coltsfoot's common name; toothed along the edge, they are shaped more or less like a hoofprint.

Columbine *Aquilegia*

Their delicate blue-green leaves and dainty flowers may have an appearance of great fragility, but columbines are tough. Blue columbine, for instance, the state flower of Colorado, climbs well above the timberline on mountain peaks, while the yellow-blossomed Chapline's columbine sprouts from desert cliffs in New Mexico. Even the red and yellow wild columbine of eastern North America ventures out of its preferred moist woodlands to colonize rocky crevices and ravines. Although the color varies from species to species, the form of the flowers remains the same: each of the five petals extends backward in a long, pointed tube, or spur. Our ancestors likened the blooms to five birds perched around the edge of a fountain, and the plant's name derives from the Latin for "like a dove."

Comb jelly

Sometimes seen dotting sandy beaches after storms or drifting at the surface in quiet lagoons, comb jellies look like small, transparent blobs of gelatin. No relation to the true jellyfish, they are named for the eight rows of comblike projections that circle their body like lines of longitude on a globe. Moved in unison, the combs propel the creatures weakly through the water.

By day, sunlight reflects off the moving combs, producing an iridescent glint; at night the animals sometimes glow in the dark with a lovely greenish or bluish light. Most comb jellies feed by sweeping tiny planktonic organisms into their mouth with their long, sticky tentacles. Common species include the sea gooseberry, less than an inch in diameter, and the pinkish, two-inch sea walnut.

Comfrey *Symphytum officinale*

An immigrant from Europe that now grows wild on roadsides and in waste places, comfrey is abuzz with activity when it blooms, for bees find its dangling clusters of pink, blue, or yellowish bell-shaped flowers irresistible. The plant's large, hairy leaves supplied generations of countryfolk with salad greens and pot herbs, and they were traditionally used in a variety of herbal remedies. Unfortunately, however, while the foliage is rich in protein, vitamins, and minerals, the plant has also been found to contain a cancer-causing alkaloid, particularly in its long, black-skinned root. No longer recommended for internal use, the leaves nevertheless can be crushed and safely applied to wounds as a soothing poultice.

The California condor's remarkable eyes can locate dead animals from miles away.

Coneflowers proliferate in grassy fields.

Conch

Found in warm, shallow tropical seas, especially off the coasts of Texas and southern Florida, conchs (pronounced "conks") are large, spiral-shelled marine snails. Docile plant eaters, conchs move quickly across the sandy bottom by means of a horny, clawlike plate attached to the end of the muscular foot. By digging the claw into the sand and quickly contracting a muscle, conchs can actually leap or somersault. Queen conchs, prized by collectors for their beautiful pink shells, are up to a foot long and weigh as much as five pounds. Florida fighting conchs, about four inches long, are particularly agile leapers, hence their name. Conch flesh is used in fritters and chowders, and the shells are occasionally fashioned into horns for signaling.

Condor *Gymnogyps californianus*

With a nine-foot wingspan—the greatest of any North American land bird—the California condor used to be a master of the sky. Now rare and seriously endangered, this extraordinary vulture once soared high above the land, gliding 10 miles at a time without flapping its wings. Thousands of years ago the birds ranged east as far as Florida, feeding on the carcasses of once-plentiful large mammals, but by the middle of this century, the huge, cliff-nesting birds were confined to the mountains of southern California. Raising only one young every other year and beset by habitat loss, food shortages, and contamination of their food with pesticides and poisons, their numbers dropped to fewer than 40 by 1975. In the mid-1980's the remaining wild birds were captured and placed in zoos, where only a few young have so far been successfully hatched. Researchers are trying to build up a population of captive-bred condors and hope eventually to return them to the wild.

Coneflower

The cheerful, golden yellow rays encircling a dark, domed center have fixed the name black-eyed Susan in the minds of flower lovers all across the continent. But the black-eyed Susan is just one of many coneflowers, members of the sunflower family with petallike ray flowers that surround a thimblelike cone of disc flowers. The prairie coneflowers, found on the Great Plains and eastward, have drooping yellow ray flowers, and their cones give off a licoricelike aroma when crushed. The purple coneflowers, also native to the plains, have more bristly cones. Their lovely, magenta flowers are prized by gardeners.

Conglomerate

Naturally cemented jumbles of rounded stones, conglomerates are a type of sedimentary rock. The pebbles they contain usually were worn smooth as they were rolled and bounced along by fast-flowing water in ancient streams. When the stones eventually came to rest, the spaces between them filled with smaller grains and the mass was gradually cemented together to form the potpourri referred to as a conglomerate.

Conifer

The scaled cones that protect the seeds of conifers come in a variety of shapes and sizes and are one of the main distinguishing characteristics of these trees and shrubs. Their needlelike leaves are another feature common to conifers, although cedars and junipers, for example, have flat, scalelike leaves instead. Most also are ever-

Getting to Know the Needle-Leaved Conifers

A walk in the woods can be more of an adventure when you know how to tell a pine from a larch or a fir from a spruce. Some important clues, such as the grouping of the needles and the positions of the cones, are outlined in the chart. Note also that the larches and bald cypresses, unlike most conifers, shed their needles in the fall. Not included here are the yews, which have needles but do not bear cones.

Needles bound in clusters

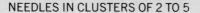

NEEDLES IN CLUSTERS OF 2 TO 5

PINES

Eastern white pine (East)   **Ponderosa pine (West)**

NEEDLES IN TUFTS OF 20 OR MORE

LARCHES

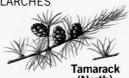

Tamarack (North)

Needles not in clusters (evenly distributed on branch)

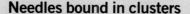

CONES STAND UPRIGHT ON BRANCHES

FIRS

Balsam fir (North)   **White fir (West)**   **Subalpine fir (West)**

CONES HANG FROM BRANCHES

Cones at tips of branches	Cones not at tips of branches
Cone scales flat	Bracts between cone scales

HEMLOCKS

Eastern hemlock (Northeast)

DOUGLAS FIRS

Douglas fir (West)

Cone scales wrinkled

BALD CYPRESSES   REDWOOD

No bracts between cone scales

SPRUCES

Bald cypress (Southeast)   **Redwood (Far West)**   **White spruce (North)**

green: the exceptions are the larches and bald cypresses, which lose their needles in winter.

An ancient order of plants, the conifers developed millions of years ago, long before the first broad-leaved trees. Their stately descendants include our oldest trees (the 4,600-year-old bristlecone pines), our biggest (the giant sequoias), and our tallest (the California redwoods).

Broad-leaved trees are better adapted to temperate climates, however. The conifers are dominant in northern regions where the evergreens' ability to make and store food year-round is a major advantage. Because needles are better at retaining water than broad, flat leaves, conifers also thrive in hot, dry areas and often on poor, rocky soils.

American coots, also known as mud hens, are jet-black, but the chicks sport bright reddish heads and shoulders.

Female copepods carry fertilized eggs in tiny sacs.

Continental Divide

Gentle rivulets, rushing streams, and mighty rivers—all are affected by a line of high ridges in the Rocky Mountains that we call the Continental Divide. To the west of the line water flows toward the Pacific Ocean; to the east it flows into the Atlantic or the Gulf of Mexico. Marking the boundary between two drainage systems, the Continental Divide, sometimes called the Great Divide, continues north through Canada and south into Mexico.

Lesser divides can also be traced. One, near Duluth, Minnesota, runs from east to west, separating the water flowing north into the Great Lakes and the St. Lawrence River from the water that flows south into the Mississippi.

Coot *Fulica americana*

Noisier and more quarrelsome than their relatives the rails, American coots are known for their unmelodic medleys of cackles, grunts, and croaks. Ducklike water birds, they are slaty gray with a white bill, red eyes, and lobed toes that facilitate both swimming and walking on muddy shores. The birds take flight awkwardly, spattering water as they run across the surface trying to lift off. Feeding on aquatic plants, insects, worms, and snails, coots often gather in dense flocks on open water. The young have a remarkable means of escaping danger: at the first warning from an adult, chicks dive underwater and grasp a plant stem in their bill, anchoring themselves to the bottom until the danger has passed.

Copepod

Tiny (the largest are no bigger than a grain of rice) but incredibly abundant, copepods play a vital role in oceanic food chains. These small, shrimplike crustaceans feed on microscopic plants and are in turn consumed in vast quantities by other invertebrates, as well as by fish and even whales. The copepod's body, enclosed in a protective shell like that of a shrimp, is equipped with two pairs of antennae and several pairs of flattened limbs. The limbs, in fact, give the copepod its name, which is derived from Greek words meaning "oar foot." In addition to the marine copepods, freshwater species live in ponds and quiet streams. Easily captured with a fine net, they can be observed with a hand lens.

Copper

A shiny, pliable, orange-red metal that is easily shaped and immune to rust, copper has been pounded into tools and implements since ancient times. The Coppermine River of the Northwest Territories and Lake Superior's southern shores were prime sources of native copper for Canada's aboriginal peoples. The metal still is widely used for utensils, coins, and roofing. An excellent conductor of heat and electricity, copper also is used for pots, pans, wire, and tubing, and it can be combined with other metals to form brass and bronze. Copper is sometimes found in its pure form (called native copper). More often, copper is mined as an ore, from which the metal is extracted.

Copperhead *Agkistrodon contortrix*

Up to 4½ feet long, the copperhead is a poisonous snake named for the coppery color of its head. It lives in rocky, wooded areas from Massachusetts to Texas, where the chestnut-brown hourglass pattern on its back keeps it well camouflaged among fallen leaves. Copperheads are related to cottonmouths and rattlesnakes and, like those other pit vipers, have heat-sensitive organs on their faces that are used to locate warm-blooded prey. In addition to small mammals, they feed on lizards and frogs, which are killed by venom delivered through sharp, hollow fangs. Fortunately, their bite, though painful, is seldom fatal to humans.

Copperheads hibernate in large groups during the winter. In late summer, these snug dens serve as nesting sites for the females, who return to bear litters of live young.

C

Elkhorn corals are so named because of the antlerlike shape of their branches.

Coral polyps sting prey with the whiplike tentacles that surround their mouths.

Coquina *Donax variabilis*

Less than one inch long, the glossy-shelled Florida coquina is a pretty wedge-shaped clam found in the surf zone of sandy beaches from New York to Texas. Coming in a variety of pastel hues, these dainty little mollusks burrow into the sand with each receding wave, then resurface to feed on the next incoming wave. Despite their small size, coquinas make an excellent chowder, and their shells, compacted into rock, are used as a building material in parts of Florida.

Coral

Relatives of sea anemones and jellyfish, the stony corals are tiny invertebrates found in warm, shallow tropical and subtropical seas. Some live as solitary individuals, but most form large colonies. Each animal, called a polyp, is usually only a fraction of an inch long, and its tube-shaped body is fixed at one end to a limestone cup formed of its own secretions. At the other end is a mouth leading to a gullet, and around the mouth are tentacles used to sting small prey. Less common than the stony corals, soft corals have horny or leathery skeletons.

Colonies of the stony corals grow in size by building on the skeletons of their ancestors. Different species develop characteristic and sometimes wonderfully exotic forms, as suggested by such common names as brain coral, lace coral, star coral, and elkhorn coral. Individual polyps reproduce by forming buds, each of which matures into a new polyp alongside the old one. The same corals also reproduce sexually; the fertilized eggs hatch into free-swimming larvae that, unlike the buds, can swim off on their own to begin new colonies.

Coralbean *Erythrina*

Covered with showy spikes of tubular, brilliant scarlet blossoms, these handsome shrubs and small trees stage a dramatic show each year from late spring through early summer. The flowers are followed by pods of attractive, but poisonous, shiny red beans. The most familiar species are the eastern coralbean, which ranges from North Carolina to Texas, and the southwestern coralbean, native to the dry, rocky soils of Arizona and New Mexico. The buoyant, light wood of a Hawaiian coralbean is used for the manufacture of surfboards, floats, and similar items.

Eastern coral snakes feed on reptiles.

C

Coral reef

Individual coral polyps, the marine animals that spend their lives anchored in self-made limestone cups, are relatively small. Colonies of these little creatures, however, have created the largest structures ever produced by any living thing; generation after generation builds upon the limestone remains of their ancestors, forming underwater reefs that can continue to expand indefinitely.

Found in warm, shallow seas off the coast of Florida and farther south, coral reefs support an incredible variety of life. Snails, crabs, and spiny lobsters creep through crevices in the coral rock. Starfish, worms, and parrot fish "graze" on the living polyps. And everywhere there are sea fans, sponges, and other exotic creatures.

Divers have long been enchanted by coral reefs, where they marvel at the intricate formations of the corals themselves and the astonishing array of brightly colored fish that flit through these incredible underwater seascapes. Among the most fascinating reef dwellers are the small, low-profile cleaner fish, at whose "stations" the larger fish patiently wait in line to be nibbled free of parasites.

Coral snake

To recognize the difference between the colorfully banded, poisonous coral snakes and harmless look-alikes such as the scarlet kingsnake, generations of children in the southern United States have been taught a helpful ditty:

Red next to black, a friend of Jack;
Red next to yellow can kill a fellow.

For only on coral snakes do the red and yellow bands touch each other.

In fact, the snakes are seldom even seen; both native species are mainly nocturnal and spend most of their time hiding under logs or in burrows. When people do encounter the smallish, handsomely banded reptiles, the snakes tend to be docile and bite only if handled.

Sometimes called harlequin or candystick snakes, coral snakes live in a variety of locations and habitats, from dry, rocky slopes and canyons in the Southwest to pine woods and wet hammocks in the Southeast.

Double-crested cormorants lay two to four eggs, which hatch in about a month.

Cormorant *Phalacrocorax*

Long-necked, duck-sized, and glossy black, cormorants are fast and efficient water birds. Diving underwater, they paddle furiously with their webbed feet and seize fish in their long, sharply hooked bill. Unlike most aquatic birds, they do not have water-repellent feathers and so can often be seen perched on rocks or pilings with their wings spread out to dry.

Found along seacoasts and on inland lakes and rivers, cormorants are highly social; they sometimes form communal fishing groups that include hundreds or even thousands of birds. Assembling into long lines, they herd a school of fish toward the shallows and snatch those feeding near the surface. Cormorants also breed in colonies, building crude, bulky nests on rocky cliffs or in treetops.

The most widespread of the six North American species and the only one likely to be seen far inland is the double-crested cormorant, named for the pair of curly plumes it wears on the sides of its head during the breeding season. Others include the Brandt's and pelagic cormorants of the Pacific coast and the great cormorant, found along the Atlantic coast.

C

Cotton grasses' hairy white tufts inspired their botanical name, too; it derives from the Greek for "wool bearing."

The cottonmouth does its most serious hunting at night.

Cornetfish *Fistularia*

Long, slender fish that sometimes reach a length of six feet, cornetfish have an elongated, tubular snout and a whiplike filament trailing from their tail fins. These near relatives of trumpetfish occur mostly in the West Indies, but in summer are found further north. Camouflaged by their vertical stripes and dark color, they swim just below the surface and stalk prey near corals and grassy seabed flats. They drift slowly toward unsuspecting small fish and feed by quickly sucking prey into their tiny mouth. The blue-spotted cornetfish ranges from Nova Scotia to Florida and the Gulf of Mexico. The less common red cornetfish travels only as far north as Virginia.

Cotton grass *Eriophorum*

Despite their name, the cotton grasses are not grasses at all but members of the sedge family. In bloom from summer into fall, they bear tiny flowers amid tufts of long, cottony white hairs atop their triangular stems. Found in bogs and moist meadows all the way north to the Arctic Circle, the cotton grasses often grow in dense stands, their tufted white flower heads looking like unseasonable snow covering the land.

Cottonmouth *Agkistrodon piscivorus*

Often spotted on branches overhanging water, cottonmouths are highly venomous snakes whose bite can be quite dangerous. When threatened, the snake rears its chunky head and gapes to display the cottony white interior of its mouth—hence the name. Also called water moccasins, they are closely related to the copperhead and infest swamps, rivers, lakes, and rice fields in the southern United States. From two to six feet long, the cottonmouth has a broad flat head and stout body, either unpatterned or

Cotton rats look cute but are major pests.

marked with dark, ragged blotches. Like other pit vipers, cottonmouths have deep, heat-sensitive facial pits that detect warm-blooded prey. They also feed on frogs and insects.

Cotton rat *Sigmodon hispidus*

One of three rats native to the United States, the hispid cotton rat is an agricultural pest noted for its destruction of cotton crops. It also devours sugarcane, alfalfa, and sweet potatoes and eats insects, birds' eggs, and carrion as well. With grizzled fur and a short, scaly tail, the cotton rat occurs mainly on farmlands of the Southeast. Although primarily nocturnal, it is sometimes seen along roads during the day, where it quickly disappears into weeds, ditches, or its own well-made runways. One of the world's most prolific mammals, the cotton rat begins to breed at six weeks of age and produces several litters each year. Predators such as cats, hawks, and snakes, however, help control its population.

87

Fruit

Cottonwoods grace the banks of Wyoming's Snake River. Their shiny, saw-toothed leaves (above) have a balsamic aroma.

C

Cottontail See *Rabbit.*

Cottonwood *Populus*

Found in almost every region of North America, cottonwoods are named for the parachute of cottony down attached to each of their seeds. When the tiny fruits burst open in late spring, the seeds drift away by the millions and collect in fluffy white windrows.

Favoring damp soils in low-lying areas, these fast-growing members of the willow family may add four to five feet to their height annually. They peak at an early age, however: cottonwoods begin to decline when about 75 years old, and very few live more than a century.

During its relatively short lifespan, the eastern cottonwood may reach a height of 150 feet. Though settlers in the East paid little attention to it, on the prairie, where it was often the only tree around, the eastern cottonwood was treasured by pioneers. In the Pacific Northwest the black cottonwood is the largest broad-leaved tree; old accounts describe specimens 225 feet tall, with trunks 8 feet in diameter.

Cougar See *Mountain lion.*

Cowbird *Molothrus*

Named for their habit of feeding among grazing cattle, cowbirds are best known as opportunists that raid the nests of other birds—not to take eggs, but to leave them. Both the bronzed cowbird of the Southwest and the more widespread brown-headed cowbird lay their eggs in the nests of other songbirds, such as warblers, vireos, and flycatchers, and then abandon them to be raised by foster parents.

While such behavior may seem easier than incubating eggs and feeding nestlings, brood parasitism is costly for both the cowbird and its victims. Many species thwart the cowbirds by removing their eggs, burying them beneath a new nest lining, or abandoning the nest alto-

Cowbirds are about eight inches long.

gether. As a result, female cowbirds must lay many more eggs than other birds do. And the cowbirds that do hatch crowd out and starve some of the rightful nestlings. Most experts believe that the cowbirds' nest parasitism accounts for the decline of such songbirds as the endangered Kirtland's warbler in Michigan and Bell's vireo in California.

Cowrie *Cypraea*

Noted for their glossy shells, brilliant colors, and intriguing patterns, these handsome snails have long been prized by collectors. On Pacific islands, royalty once wore golden cowries as symbols of rank. Although the cowries live mainly in tropical seas, a few species are found off the southern United States. The chestnut cowrie, about two inches long, inhabits rocky coasts in California, and the four-inch measled cowrie lives in bays in southern Florida.

Coyote *Canis latrans*

"Life span, if lucky, about 13 years," one text says of the wide-ranging coyote, and certainly few animals have needed more luck to reach old age in the face of human persecution. For centuries coyotes have had an exaggerated reputation

Coyotes, alert and animated canines, have spread from coast to coast.

Ghost crabs, camouflaged by their sand-colored shells, are elusive crustaceans.

C

as ruthless predators of domestic livestock, especially sheep and poultry. Although studies show that these midsize wild dogs feed mainly on rabbits, ground squirrels, small rodents, and carrion, the truth is that they eat almost anything. They have even been known to feed on watermelons and persimmons.

Despite man's poisons, traps, and guns, coyotes have not merely survived; they have actually expanded their range as well. Their distinctive nocturnal yaps and howls now are heard from the suburbs of Los Angeles to river deltas in the Northwest Territories.

Coyotes mate in winter, and in spring the females give birth to litters of 4 to 10 tiny, helpless pups that grow with astonishing speed. Beginning at three weeks to take food provided by their fathers, they reach independence in the fall, when most disperse in search of home territories—and mates—of their own.

Crab

Among the most familiar seashore creatures, crabs are easily identified by their broad backs, formidable pincers, and their habit of scuttling sideways on four pairs of walking legs. Adapted to a variety of habitats, they can be seen racing across the sand, burrowing into muddy salt marshes, and crawling across the sea floor.

A few kinds live mainly on land, but all crabs must return to the water to reproduce. The eggs, which the females carry on their undersides, hatch into tiny free-swimming larvae that go

through several molts before settling to the ocean bottom and developing into adults. Most crabs are scavengers and eat a variety of foods, which they seize in their pincers.

Lady crabs and other swimming crabs have oarlike tips on their last pair of legs, enabling them to move swiftly through the water. The nocturnal ghost crabs run across beaches with astonishing speed, then burrow into sand above the high-tide line. Fiddler crabs are well known for the males' one enormously oversized pincer, which they brandish to court females and to fend off competing males. Blue crabs, one of the most important commercial species, are found in bays and estuaries all along the Atlantic coast. The soft-shelled crabs listed on seafood menus are usually blues; their shells are edible because the crabs have just molted.

Crab Spider

Masters of camouflage, some of the crab spiders can change their color to match the flowers on which they wait for passing prey. Once settled in, they grab any insect that comes close, poison it with their bite, and enjoy a meal. Like their namesakes, crab spiders can easily and nimbly scuttle sideways. Although they do not spin webs, the females produce silken sacs to protect their eggs. They usually die, however, before the young emerge.

Cranberry *Vaccinium*

Low, creeping vines with tough, wiry stems, cranberries flourish in bogs and other moist, acidic soils from Labrador to Alaska and south to North Carolina. Though Indians of the northeast relished the fruit, there is no proof that cranberries were served at the first American Thanksgiving in 1621. In 1663, a recipe for cranberry sauce appeared in a Pilgrim cookbook, and colonists later sent 10 barrels of the crimson berries to King Charles II. Valued mainly for their fruits, cranberries nevertheless provide a colorful display over the seasons. In summer the vines are dotted with pretty pink flowers, which are followed in the fall by plump red berries; and in winter the leathery, oval leaves turn from dark green to blazing scarlet.

Crane *Grus*

The two North American members of the ancient crane family are birds of open wetlands, plains, and prairies. The whooping crane, standing more than four feet tall, is the giant of our waders. It is also one of the most endangered of birds. In the 1940's the entire population of whoopers totaled fewer than two dozen. Now, however, with strict protection and careful management, the majestic white cranes are slowly increasing in number. Each spring the growing flock migrates from its winter home in Texas to its nesting ground in northern Canada.

Sandhill cranes—regal, gray, and three to four feet tall—are more numerous than whoopers but also depend on shallow wetlands and open prairies for survival. In an experiment begun in 1975, sandhill cranes that nest in Idaho have served as foster parents to eggs and young of captive-bred whooping cranes.

Cranes mate for life and may live for 30 years. Their remarkable calls can be heard a mile away, but even more compelling are the musical duets sung by mated pairs. The most striking aspect of crane courtship, though, is their dancing. Male and female bow low to each other and then bound high in the air, like bouncing balls, in the annual mating rite. Some Indian tribes copied the dance as part of their ceremonies. And one biologist, caring for a captive female whooper, induced her to lay an egg by repeatedly joining her in this courtship dance.

A sandhill crane stalks a western grassland for frogs, snakes, insects, and tender roots.

Crane fly *Tipula*

Long-winged and long-legged, crane flies are often mistaken for huge mosquitoes. They are harmless, however; the adults feed only on nectar or, in some species, nothing at all. Walking and flying slowly and rather awkwardly, crane flies are usually found in dense vegetation or near water. They also are attracted to buildings, where, after dusk, clouds of them are frequently seen swarming about lights. The tough-skinned larvae, called leatherjackets, live in damp soil or shallow ponds and are often used as bait.

Crater

Formed at the summit of volcanoes or by the impact of meteors crashing into the earth from outer space, craters are steep-walled, circular depressions. Meteor Crater in Arizona, nearly a mile wide and 600 feet deep, is one of the best known of its type. The gaping hole was formed in prehistoric times when a meteor some 80 feet in diameter, traveling at more than 30,000 miles per hour, collided with the earth.

Much more common are volcanic craters. Almost all volcanoes have small craters around their vents, caused by the slumping of molten lava at the end of an eruption. Later eruptions, such as the one that rocked Washington's Mount St. Helens in 1980, can destroy the summit and greatly enlarge the crater. Calderas, in contrast, are deep, broad basins often several miles in diameter, usually formed by the collapse of a volcanic cone into its empty magma chamber after an especially violent eruption.

Crayfish

Also called crawfish and, sometimes, crawdads, crayfish are freshwater crustaceans that look very much like miniature lobsters. Common in streams and quiet ponds, they grow to three or four inches in length. Four pairs of walking legs allow them to move in any direction. When danger threatens, however, they flex powerful abdominal muscles and dart abruptly backward, out of harm's way.

Feeding on vegetation and a variety of small animals, crayfish in turn are prey for birds, turtles, raccoons, and otters. Some species live in deep burrows with a water-filled chamber at the end that serves as a refuge in times of drought. A few inhabit damp meadows and have earned a reputation as crop-eating pests.

Crayfish are popular menu items, particularly in the Mississippi River basin. In Louisiana, residents and visitors alike savor such local favorites as crayfish bisque.

Creosote bush *Larrea tridentata*

The most common shrub of the southwestern deserts, the creosote bush is superbly adapted for survival. It sends out roots in two directions: a taproot reaches down to find deep hidden re-

Crayfish prefer to stay hidden under rocks and logs by day, but at night they feed actively on worms, snails, insect larvae, and tadpoles.

The crater at Mount St. Helens, with walls 2,000 feet high, was created by a volcanic blast whose force was the equivalent of 500 Hiroshima-type atomic bombs.

Creosote bush (left) keeps its distance from neighbors, thereby conserving moisture; its flowers (above) appear after spring rains.

serves of water, while a network of shallow roots quickly absorbs any rainfall at the surface. It also secretes an herbicide into the surrounding soil, killing any seedlings that might compete for moisture. A waxy coating on the leaves helps protect the creosote bush against dehydration, but in periods of extreme heat or drought it simply sheds its normally evergreen foliage, then sprouts new leaves when the weather becomes more moderate. And while some desert animals, such as the chuckwalla, thrive on the creosote bush's leaves and twigs, most mammals are warned off by an acrid odor that inspired the plant's nickname, stinkweed.

Crevasse

An ever-present peril on glaciers, crevasses are gigantic vertical cracks that form in the slowly moving rivers of ice. Sometimes dozens of feet wide and more than 150 feet deep, they usually are caused by stresses that develop as the ice passes over obstructions or begins to descend steep slopes. Crossing a crevasse field on a glacier can be extremely hazardous, especially when a cover of snow hides the narrower gaps. Sometimes, however, the wider gaps can be crossed safely where wind-blown snow has formed bridges over the chasms.

C

Male field crickets make various chirps and trills, and often even dance, to attract females.

Red crossbills are quite conspicuous as they clamber like parakeets among pine branches.

Crinoids, more abundant in the distant past, are often found preserved as fossils.

Cricket

The subject of a great deal of superstition, crickets have been regarded as signaling both good fortune and bad. Having a cricket in the house brought good luck, while harming one was believed to cause all manner of woes.

The most common of these familiar chirping, hopping insects are the black field cricket and the similar brown house cricket. The latter, an old-world import, thrives in North American homes on food crumbs and even on bits of fabric.

Smaller and pale green, the snowy tree cricket is known mostly by its sounds. Rubbing their wings together, the males sing in unison on summer nights and unwittingly tell us how warm it is: adding 40 to the number of times they chirp in 15 seconds yields the approximate temperature in degrees Fahrenheit.

Crinoid

Although they look like showy flowers of the sea, crinoids actually are invertebrate animals related to sand dollars and starfish. The two types of crinoids—sea lilies and feather stars—trace their ancestry back to fossil forms that

lived hundreds of millions of years ago. Sea lilies, the more flowerlike of the two, live atop long slender stalks that are permanently attached to the ocean floor, and use their feathery arms to strain food from the surrounding water. Feather stars, on the other hand, break free of their anchoring stalks as they mature, and use their arms to swim about in shallow water.

Crocodilian

The closest living relatives of the long-extinct dinosaurs, crocodilians include alligators, caimans, crocodiles, and a single species of gavial. While the American alligator is quite plentiful in southeastern swamps and bayous, the American crocodile is an endangered species found only in southern Florida. In appearance, crocodiles differ from alligators in having narrower, more pointed snouts and bigger teeth that show more prominently even when the mouth is closed.

Crossbill *Loxia*

Crossed at the tips, the distinctively twisted beaks of crossbills look at first glance like a handicap. In fact, they are delicate tools that serve very well for removing seeds from the cones of pines and other conifers. The birds use the crossed tips to pry the cone scales apart, then deftly extract the seeds with their tongue.

Our two species of crossbills—white-winged and red—are primarily birds of northern forests. In years when cone crops fail, however, large flocks of crossbills often wander far beyond their normal range.

Red crossbill males are brick-red, with dark wings and tail, and tend to favor pine seeds. Snowy wing bars highlight the rosier white-winged crossbills, which prefer the seeds of spruces and hemlocks and often fly to the ground to open fallen cones.

A solitary crow looks relatively docile, but groups of crows frequently turn into noisy, mischievous mobs that gang up on larger birds such as hawks and owls.

Lobsters, among the larger crustaceans, can grow to a length of two feet and weigh over 40 pounds; such giants are estimated to be more than 50 years old.

C

Crow *Corvus*

Bold, brash, mischievous, and black from beak to toe, crows are big, imposing birds with a three-foot wingspan. Adapting to a variety of habitats and resourceful in securing food, they also are extremely intelligent. Crows raiding cornfields, for example, have an uncanny ability to tell the difference between a farmer's gun and such harmless articles as brooms or sticks. Crows adopted as pets have actually learned to count and utter coherent phrases. And they solve the problem of cracking mollusks such as clams by carrying them into the air, then dropping them on rocks to smash the shells. Omnivorous in their eating habits, crows also devour eggs, worms, berries, insects, fish, grain, and animals killed on roadways.

The familiar caw of the common crow is heard throughout the country in parks, farmlands, woods, and suburbs. Our other two crows, both slightly smaller than the common crow, are the fish crow of the Atlantic and Gulf coasts and the northwestern crow, which lives along the north Pacific coast from Washington to Alaska. More sociable than the common crow, they forage year-round in groups. Like all crows, they nest in pairs, but in winter they often gather by the thousands to roost.

Crustacean

Hard-shelled crabs scurrying along seashores, sowbugs living under logs, fairy shrimp swimming in temporary ponds—all are crustaceans. Like their relatives the insects, spiders, and scorpions, they have jointed legs and external skeletons, which they shed periodically as they grow.

The continent's largest crustacean is the Alaskan king crab. A record specimen measured six feet two inches from claw tip to claw tip.

Although crustaceans are found in oceans from polar regions to tropical climes, they are not limited to the sea. Tiny brine shrimp, for instance, thrive in the ultrasalty waters of the Great Salt Lake, while others, such as crayfish, inhabit fresh water. A few specialized types live in the outflow of natural hot springs, and some, such as the land crabs of southern Florida, are terrestrial air-breathers.

Some of the crustaceans are pests. Crayfish riddle dikes and levees with their burrows; land crabs devour crop plants; and barnacles on the hull of a ship can cut its speed in half. But others, including lobsters, crabs, and shrimp, are valued human foods. And as a link in marine food chains, copepods and other tiny members of the class are swallowed up by a vast array of sea creatures, from arrow worms to whales.

Bald cypress trees, draped with vines and Spanish moss, may grow to a height of 150 feet.

CYPRESS SWAMP

The rich and wondrous world of the cypress swamp is peculiar to the Southeast, where wetlands and warm temperatures combine to create a unique habitat for luxuriant vegetation and a wealth of animal life. The towering bald cypress trees are festooned with masses of Spanish moss. Colorful orchids and delicate ferns grow here as well, and the water's surface is often blanketed with water lilies, duckweed, and water hyacinths. In southernmost swamps such as Big Cypress and Okefenokee, alligators bask on the banks, and venomous cottonmouth snakes dangle from branches. At dusk the swamp becomes a concert hall resounding with animal voices, from the baritone bellowing of alligators to the soprano chirping of tree frogs. And in the dimming skies, elegant egrets and wood storks fly home to roost for the night in the giant trees.

The anhinga, about to dine on a sunfish, is the only bird that actually spears its prey.

The great egret, over three feet long, flies gracefully and speaks with a hoarse croak.

Green tree frogs make a melodious chorus that fills the swamp at night.

A female alligator guards her nesting mound, where dozens of eggs are slowly incubating.

Water hyacinths form vast carpets across the swamp.

Carnivorous bladderworts feed on tiny animals captured in underwater traps.

A white-tailed deer is dwarfed by the massive trunks of a stand of bald cypresses.

95

Citrine crystals, a type of quartz, are often mistaken for their more precious look-alike, the gemstone called yellow topaz.

Yellow-billed cuckoos, up to a foot in length, slip quietly from branch to branch, occasionally uttering their telltale calls.

Crystal

Disparate as they may seem, salt, snowflakes, gemstones, metals, and sugar all have one thing in common: they are made up of crystals, as are most nonliving substances. Crystals are characterized by symmetrical atomic structures whose orderly patterns are repeated again and again, often yielding beautiful shapes. Some crystals, such as quartz, are large and conspicuous, but in most substances they are much too small to be seen with the naked eye.

Cuckoo *Coccyzus*

Unlike the brash character that leaps out of clocks to announce the hour, the cuckoos of North America are shy birds. Both the black-billed cuckoo and the yellow-billed cuckoo prefer to hide in thickets at the edges of forests and orchards and are more likely to be heard than seen. (A third species, the mangrove cuckoo, lives only along the Florida coast.)

Nest building is not one of the strong points of these slim, long-tailed birds; they raise their young on crudely assembled platforms of sticks and twigs. From the moment of hatching, the chicks are studded with stout quills that finally open into feathers just before the birds are ready to begin flying.

The cuckoos' voracious appetite for insects, especially hairy caterpillars, makes them welcome allies in the fight against such pests as the gypsy moth. Tent caterpillars, which veil trees with their big cobweblike nests, are also a favored food. Yellow-billed cuckoos, in fact, have been known to consume more than 300 of these destructive larvae in a single meal.

Currant *Ribes*

Valued for their tart, juicy berries, which are used in jams, jellies, and pies, currants are low to midsize shrubs that prefer cool, moist climates. Their arching branches, with lobed, maplelike leaves, bear clusters of tiny, bell-shaped yellow-green flowers that mature into shiny red, black, or amber fruits. Unfortunately, however, currants are host to a fungus called blister rust that attacks the eastern white pine and a number of other pines prized for their timber. Thus, while many species of wild currants are native to North America, they have been systematically eradicated from many areas.

Cusk-eel

Long, slender, and snaky, cusk-eels resemble true eels but have a pair of feelers (actually modified fins) under the chin. Although they are not common, cusk-eels are found in temperate and tropical seas around the world. The spotted cusk-eel, a dweller in deep water off the west coast, ranges from one to two feet in length; the striped cusk-eel of the east coast averages just six inches. To hide from predators, these shy and secretive fish back into rock crevices or burrow tail-first into sandy bottoms.

Cyclone See *Hurricane.*

Cypress *Cupressus*

Perched on rocky cliffs above the Pacific, their crowns flattened and their trunks contorted by driving winds, Monterey cypresses seem the perfect symbol of persistence. But their romantic beauty is rare indeed, for the trees' entire wild population is restricted to two groves in Carmel, California. In fact, all our continent's native cypresses—evergreens with scalelike foliage, woody cones, and fragrant wood—prefer dry, austere western habitats. The Modoc cypress, for example, flourishes in lava fields of the Siskiyou Mountains in California and Oregon, while the Arizona cypress is found only in arid canyons of the southwestern United States.

Cypress swamp See pp.94–95.

Daddy longlegs, when fleeing enemies, sometimes shed one or more of their stiltlike legs.

Oxeye daisies, the state flower of North Carolina, often fill whole meadows with their charming blossoms.

Daddy longlegs

Familiar to almost everyone, the daddy longlegs has a plump, oval body supported by eight long, threadlike legs. (The biggest of North America's 200 species boasts a three-inch leg span.) Although they are related to spiders, daddy longlegs lack silk glands and so spin no webs. They are not poisonous but can defend themselves by emitting a foul odor. Usually found in damp places, they feed on small insects, spiders, carrion, plant juices, and even each other. In the North most daddy longlegs hatch in the spring and die after the females lay their eggs in the fall. In the South they often hibernate. Because they mature in late summer and are often seen at harvest time, they are also known as harvestmen.

Daisy *Leucanthemum vulgare*

Relatives of the florist's chrysanthemums, oxeye daisies are among the first wildflowers that most children learn to recognize. Their cheerful flower heads—bright yellow central disks encircled by haloes of white, petallike ray flowers—embellish fields and roadsides from coast to coast. Growing up to three feet tall, daisies have narrow, jagged leaves that when young are tender enough to be eaten in salads. When older, however, they become so pungent that even grazing cattle shun them.

Damselfish

Brilliantly colored and adorned with stripes, spots, and bars, damselfish are among the most striking of the small reef fish. Characterized by a single nostril in front of each eye (most fish have

Damselfish, pugnacious reef dwellers, are known for launching aggressive attacks against much larger foes.

two), they are found in tropical and some temperate seas. Despite their name, these colorful fish are anything but delicate damsels. Daring warriors instead, they aggressively defend their home ground—a patch of kelp or coral or a crevice in the rocks—from other reef fish, spiny sea urchins, inquisitive barracudas, and even snorkelers and scuba divers. The sergeant-major, named for its stripes, often travels in small platoons as far north as New England. Pacific coastal waters from southern California southward are the domain of the ferocious garibaldi. Not only does the bright orange male zealously defend its nest, but the nest site is often passed from one generation to the next.

97

Dandelions are considered by many to be pernicious weeds, but the tender young leaves are delicious in salads, and wine can be made from the flower heads.

D

Damselflies are sharp-eyed insects that rest on waterside plants when not on aerial forays for mosquitoes and other insect prey.

Dayflower blossoms have two showy blue petals, far larger than the third, tiny white petal.

Damselfly

Flashing with brilliant metallic hues of green, blue, violet, and other colors as they dart through the summer air, damselflies are beautiful, slender-bodied insects. They often are mistaken for dragonflies, but while at rest, most damselflies fold their wings parallel to their body, while dragonflies hold them straight out. Like dragonflies, damselflies are found around water; they prey on mosquitoes and other small insects, which they trap in a cage formed by their legs. Damselfly nymphs are aquatic predators that usually creep along the bottom, but they can also scull through the water, using their three feathery gills as oars.

Dandelion *Taraxacum officinale*

Though gardeners might find it difficult to believe, North America used to be almost entirely free of dandelions. Once it had been imported by early colonists, however, the familiar yellow-flowered weed proceeded to do some colonizing on its own, its downy seeds floating off and eventually taking root across the continent. Fecundity is one reason for the dandelion's success. Its flower heads contain as many as 200 individual florets, each of which sets seed without need for pollination. The blossoms, moreover, release ethylene gas in the late afternoon, which poisons competing plants. And the dandelion's hollow stem contains a bitter white sap that effectively discourages grazing animals.

Darter

Little minnowlike fish that range from one to nine inches in length, darters are named for their habit of darting swiftly from one resting place to the next. More than 100 species live in streams and lakes east of the Rockies, where they feed on a variety of small aquatic animals. Many of the darters are brightly colored, with the males' hues becoming particularly intense during the breeding season. Common species

Daylily plants are long-lived, but the handsome flowers last only a day.

Decomposition, whether by bark beetles (top right) or fungi (right), recycles nutrients.

D

include the widespread Johnny darter; the sand darter, which burrows into sandy stream bottoms and leaves only its eyes and snout exposed to detect prey; and the celebrated snail darter, which made news in the 1970's when concern over destruction of its habitat delayed completion of a U.S. dam.

Dayflower *Commelina*

Thriving in shady dooryards, roadsides, and woodland clearings, dayflowers furnish a pretty show of three-petaled blue flowers from May to October. When the blooms open, the two larger, upper petals arch back to expose the nectar and invite visits from pollinating bees. After a few hours, the petals wilt, wrapping a moist blanket around the flower's pistil and stamens. This allows for self-pollination, so that even without the help of bees, fertile seed is assured.

Daylily *Hemerocallis*

Roadside wildflowers of beauty and elegance, daylilies are hardy perennials that long ago escaped from cultivation. Both the orange and the yellow daylily, the latter lemon-scented, bloom in loose clusters atop four-foot stalks. Though each trumpet-shaped flower lives only a day, as the name suggests, the plants produce a succession of blossoms over several weeks. Resistant to insects and disease, daylilies also are extremely resilient: their fleshy, fibrous roots easily survived the long ocean voyages of the settlers who introduced them, and they have since become established in the wild.

Death camas *Zigadenus*

Aptly named, the death camases are poisonous in every part. They can easily be distinguished from their edible relatives, the true camases, when in bloom. On death camases, the spikes of small, six-pointed flowers are greenish yellow, white, or bronze, while most of the true camases have blue flowers. In early spring, however, the differences are not so apparent, since all are simply tufts of grasslike leaves. Indians, who used to gather camas bulbs for food, occasionally made fatal mistakes in identification. Even today, the death camases sometimes poison sheep and cattle on the western mountains and plains.

Deciduous forest See pp.100–101.

Decomposer

When a plant or animal dies, hosts of other organisms feed on its remains. The most numerous of these decomposers are bacteria and fungi, indispensible recyclers that break down organic compounds into simpler components and so return vital nutrients to the environment. A host of small animals, from earthworms to insects, also feed on the remains. The wood-gnawing larvae of bark beetles, for instance, tunnel beneath the bark of rotting logs, where they in turn become hosts to the parasitic larvae of tiny wasps. Termites, too, may consume the wood but must rely on microscopic protozoans in their bodies to actually digest the fibers. Thus a single rotting log on the forest floor can be a thriving metropolis of interrelated life.

Eastern redbud, whose luminous pink flowers appear before the heart-shaped leaves, is a hardy tree that thrives in the rich, loamy soils of eastern forests.

Trilliums often carpet acres of moist woodland with dainty spring blooms. The plant's name comes from the Latin for "three."

DECIDUOUS FOREST

Dominated by lofty and elegant broad-leaved trees that shed their foliage in autumn, deciduous (as opposed to evergreen) forests flourish in moist, rich soils over much of eastern North America. Oaks, maples, beeches, birches, and other tall trees, their crowns merging into a continuous canopy, spread their leaves in the sunlight to manufacture food. Squirrels, hawks, and owls nest in the treetops, insects feed on the leaves, and birds in turn feed on the insects. Below the canopy is an understory of shade-tolerant trees. Deer wander among the low-growing ferns and scattered shrubs on the sun-dappled forest floor, woodcocks probe the soil for worms, and bears search for wild berries. The forest floor is also a place where decaying logs and leaves are broken down by insects, worms, fungi, and bacteria, renewing the soil by releasing vital nutrients.

With the cool of autumn, the green leaves turn to yellow, orange, and red, and for a short time, especially in New England, the forests are ablaze with colors that rival those of the most dazzling flowers. By winter, most of the leaves have fallen to the forest floor, leaving bare branches silhouetted against the sky. In spring, before the canopy of leaves has had a chance to fill in again, the sun-drenched forest floor is carpeted with a tapestry of wildflowers.

Mushrooms assist the process of decay and help enrich the soil.

Male ruffed grouse fan their tails and raise their neck feathers as part of their springtime courtship ritual.

A stand of maples puts on a fiery show in autumn. The colors are produced when green chlorophyll fades with the onset of cold weather. Other pigments, previously masked by the green, are then revealed.

Male scarlet tanagers flit like embers through the treetops, devouring beetles and caterpillars that harm oaks and other trees.

Hepatica is one of the first woodland wildflowers to greet the spring.

Raccoons are voracious omnivores for whom the forest provides a smorgasbord of nuts, berries, birds' eggs, insects, and crayfish.

Spotted salamanders, in spring, migrate to shallow woodland ponds, where they mate and lay their jelly-coated eggs.

Deer, such as the dappled mule deer fawns (above) and the majestic white-tailed buck (right), often stand motionless while waiting for danger to pass. But the adults run so swiftly that they can easily outpace most predators.

D

Deer *Odocoileus*

Our only animals with antlers, North America's deer include three giants—moose, caribou, and wapiti, or elk. The most widespread and abundant members of the family, however, are the alert, elegant bucks, graceful does, and dappled fawns of the white-tailed and the mule deer.

Especially common throughout the East, the delicate white-tailed, or Virginia, deer prefers woodland edges but can also be found in many suburban areas. Up to 3½ feet tall and weighing as much as 250 pounds, it is a fleet, elusive creature that, when frightened, flashes the white underside of its tail like a banner. The stockier, long-eared mule deer lives in the West on forested mountain slopes as well as in deserts and chaparral. The black-tailed deer of the Northwest is a subspecies of the mule deer.

Both white-tails and mule deer browse by day and on moonlit nights on the buds and twigs of trees, feeding on tender grass, berries, and acorns when they are available. During hard winters they barely subsist on the meager food that is available, and starvation is common.

In fall, the antlered males battle other bucks for mates. Some seven months later, first-time mothers generally give birth to a single fawn, while older does commonly bear twins. The young have spotted coats that provide camouflage when they crouch motionless on the forest floor or in tall grass. And they are scentless, which further protects them from predators.

Deer mouse *See White-footed mouse.*

Delta

Formed at the mouths of rivers or streams, where the water slows and drops its burden of sand, silt, and clay, deltas are often triangular in shape and take their name from their resem-

blance to the Greek letter delta. Not all are wedge shaped, however: some are rounded, and some, like the Mississippi River's, are pronged like bird feet. The size and shape depend on the size of the river, the amount of sediment it carries, and the currents where it empties. The Mississippi River, with a delta that covers hundreds of square miles, dumps more than 5 million tons of sediment each year into the Gulf of Mexico, extending the delta another 200 feet into the Gulf annually. Other notable examples include the Red River delta, formed where the river flows into Lake Winnipeg, and the Mackenzie River delta on the shores of the Beaufort Sea.

Desert *See pp.104–105.*

Desert pavement

Long before humans were paving roads, wind and water were at work paving parts of deserts with mosaiclike expanses of closely packed rock fragments known as desert pavement. These barren, windswept areas result where finer particles of sand and soil have been carried away by erosion, leaving the surface covered with a solid armor of rocks. Though we usually think of deserts as sandy places, rocky areas sheathed with desert pavement, such as those found in parts of California's Death Valley, are actually far more common than sand.

Desert poppy *Kallstroemia grandiflora*

In late summer the desert poppy spreads brilliant coverlets of bloom over dry, sandy flats and slopes from western Texas to southern California. Bright orange and bowl-shaped, the five-petaled blossoms are two inches across and grow on sprawling hairy stems. Later in the season the handsome flowers are followed by seed-filled fruits with long beaks and spiny, swollen

The devil's walking stick, despite its fearsome armament of spines, is sometimes eaten by hungry white-tailed deer. The small, five-seeded black berries, however, are ignored by all but a few mammals and birds.

Desert pavement forms a tough armor in arid areas, yet seedlings manage to push through.

D

As sand and soil on the desert floor...

are worn away, buried stones are exposed...

and eventually form an interlocking pavement.

Dew collects in tiny, glistening beads on a copper butterfly poised for the night on a leaf.

bodies that look like miniature replicas of medieval maces. Though not poppies at all, these tough annual wildflowers are also known as Arizona poppies and summer poppies.

Devil's walking stick *Aralia spinosa*

Sometimes growing as a 40-foot tree, the devil's walking stick more often has just a single stem some 15 feet tall, topped by a parasol of huge, twice-divided leaves. Up to three feet long, they are the biggest leaves borne by any native shrub or tree. Also known as Hercules' club, the devil's walking stick is armed with a fearsome array of thorns, which even bristle from the leaf stalks. In summer the plant's forbidding aspect is softened by huge clusters of little greenish flowers that, by autumn, turn into small black berries. Ranging from New York to east Texas, the devil's walking stick often forms dense thickets along streambanks and other low-lying areas.

Dew

When the sun goes down at the end of the day, objects near the ground begin to cool off and chill the warmer air that surrounds them. As the air cools, it becomes more saturated with the water vapor it contains, because cool air cannot hold as much moisture as warm air can. When the air reaches the temperature at which it is completely saturated with water vapor—its dew point—some of the vapor condenses as dew, glistening drops of water that appear on grasses, flower petals, spiderwebs, and other outdoor surfaces. (If the dew point is below freezing, the excess moisture freezes directly onto surfaces and is called frost.) Most likely to form on calm, clear nights, dew is an important source of moisture for many desert plants.

Dewberry See *Blackberry*.

California poppies explode into bloom after rare rainfalls that soak the desert soil.

The cactus wren, seen here perched on a prickly pear, nests in the arms of cacti.

DESERT

Though the word suggests blistering heat and vast stretches of sand, a desert is more aptly defined by its lack of moisture and its sparse vegetation. The Great Basin Desert of Nevada, Utah, and Oregon, where sagebrush dominates, is actually relatively cold. Hotter and more famous are the Mojave, Sonoran, and Chihuahuan deserts of the Southwest, where mesquite, creosote bush, and cactus are uniquely adapted to perennial drought. Here the daytime heat is so intense that most animals stay hidden in the shade. With the cool of evening, however, coyotes get up from their siestas to chase black-tailed jackrabbits, sidewinders stalk kangaroo rats, and bats catch insects on the wing. In the morning, when the scorching heat returns, only a few birds and an occasional butterfly animate the torrid but starkly beautiful desert landscape.

Desert lilies' tangy bulbs were consumed by Indians.

Kangaroo rats, able to live on the tiny amounts of water produced by the digestion of seeds, never need to drink.

The Joshua tree, found in the Mojave Desert, is a yucca that sometimes grows to a height of 40 feet.

Gilded flickers are woodpeckers that nest in the saguaro cactus.

Century plants, pollinated by long-tongued bats, are agaves that live for many decades.

The black-tailed jackrabbit's big ears not only sense predators but also help dissipate body heat.

The yellow-headed collared lizard often scampers across rocky slopes on its hind legs.

D

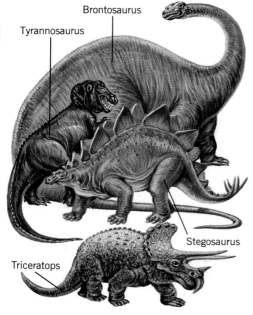

Diatom shells, two halves that fit together like a pillbox, are etched with intricate markings.

Dippers are fearless birds; they dive for prey even in rushing water that is icy cold.

Dinosaurs were not all giants like these; in fact, some were no bigger than chickens.

Tyrannosaurus
Brontosaurus
Stegosaurus
Triceratops

Diamond

The hardest of all natural substances, diamonds are formed from carbon that was dissolved in molten rock and cooled under enormous pressure. Looking like glassy, irregular pebbles, they can be cut and polished to produce gems. Most, however, are not of gem quality and are used instead as industrial abrasives. The only significant diamond field in North America is in Arkansas, but diamonds scattered by glaciers and streams have been found near the Great Lakes, in the Appalachians, and in California.

Diatom

Among the most abundant of all living things, diatoms are so tiny that as many as 20 million of these one-celled plants can live in a single quart of seawater. Unlike other algae, they have shell-like cell walls made of silica and come in a be-

wildering variety of shapes—round, square, needlelike, triangular, starlike, and more.

Golden brown in color, diatoms live in both salt and fresh water. They sometimes form slimy films or jellylike lumps on underwater stones and sticks, but most float free in the plankton. Key links in aquatic and marine food chains, they are eaten in countless numbers by planktonic animals that are in turn the food of larger creatures of the sea. After death the empty shells of diatoms accumulate in deposits of diatomaceous earth, valued as an ingredient in scouring powder and other abrasives; as a filter; and as a filler in paints, plastics, and other products.

Dinosaur

Dominating the earth for 140 million years, dinosaurs were the largest land animals that ever lived. The earliest of these giant reptiles appeared more than 200 million years ago, and the last of them mysteriously disappeared some 65 million years ago. In North America, dinosaurs lived mainly on the plains and badlands just east of the present-day Rocky Mountains—Alberta's Dinosaur Provincial Park is one of the world's richest sources of dinosaur fossils—in the U.S. southwest, and on the coastal plain between the Appalachian Mountains and the sea. Among the hundreds of species were the fearsome three-horned triceratops; the stegosaur, with a deadly spiked tail used in self-defense; and the 75-foot, 30-ton brontosaur ("thunder lizard"). The largest dinosaur, the seismosaur ("earthquake lizard"), was up to 120 feet long and weighed perhaps 100 tons. Preying on these herbivores were a variety of awesome carnivores, notably the *Tyrannosaurus rex* ("tyrant lizard king"), which was 40 feet long, 18 feet high at the hip, and had a huge head and a mouth filled with 6-inch-long daggerlike teeth.

D

A female dobsonfly's jaws, smaller than the male's, are still formidable.

Curly dock's leaves have been cooked as greens, its seeds ground into flour, and its roots used in tonics.

Dipper *Cinclus mexicanus*

Stocky, gray, short-tailed songbirds that favor waterfalls and cold rushing mountain streams of the Far West, American dippers earn their living in an extraordinary way. Undaunted even by water too turbulent for humans to stand in, they fearlessly plunge in and pump their wings to reach the bottom, where they stride along the streambed in search of food. Small fish and insect larvae are their main prey.

Also known as water ouzels, dippers have big feet and thick plumage that is waterproofed by oil from large preen glands. Flaps over the nostrils, and transparent membranes that close over the eyes complete their diving outfits.

The dippers' fluid song, often delivered from streamside boulders, can be heard even over the roar of rushing water. The birds always build their domed nests near waterways. Some even raise their families behind the curtains of waterfalls—one reason why the young must be accomplished swimmers when they leave the nest.

Dobsonfly

Long, fearsome-looking insects with a five-inch wingspan, male dobsonflies have a daunting pair of jaws: an inch long on some species and gracefully curved, they look like crossed sabers. (The females' jaws are much smaller.) During their brief two-week existence as adults, these fluttery fliers sometimes are seen congregating around outdoor lights. After mating, they lay waxy clusters of eggs on leaves or branches above rapid streams. When the larvae hatch, they drop into the water and spend two years or

so as ravenous aquatic predators, lurking under stones and gobbling up small prey. Known as hellgrammites, dobsonfly larvae can inflict painful bites on swimmers. They are, however, relished by bass and prized by anglers as bait.

Dock *Rumex*

Found on roadsides and in fields and gardens from coast to coast, docks are ubiquitous members of the buckwheat family. Thanks to long, penetrating taproots, they also are among the most persistent. Leaves vary with the species, but most docks look alike in flower and seed. In June they send up tall stems topped with spikes of small greenish flowers, which by September yield an abundant crop of reddish-brown, three-sided fruits. All parts of the plants are avidly consumed by wildlife.

Dodder *Cuscuta*

A threadlike parasite that twines around other plants, dodder is a nuisance that sucks the juices from ornamentals and valuable crop plants. Each seed sends up a thin stem that attaches itself to a nearby plant, penetrating the host's tissue and drinking in its sap. Dodder's own roots then wither, leaving the parasite with no attachment to the soil. Its leafless stems are light orange, lacking the chlorophyll that enables other plants to make their own food. Dodder does bloom like a normal plant, however, bearing dense clusters of tiny, bell-shaped, white or yellow flowers. Its seeds can lie dormant for five years, but once they sprout, each can produce a half mile of coiling stems in just four months.

D

Spreading dogbane has fragrant, bell-shaped flowers that spring from curved stems.

Dogtooth violets, like the trout lily (above) and the glacier lily (below), are named for the shape of the small white underground bulb from which the leaves and flowers sprout.

Dogwood is useful and lovely—the bark was substituted for quinine in the U.S. Civil War.

Dogbane *Apocynum*

Despite their sinister name, our several species of dogbanes are of little threat to dogs. Nor, despite their poisonous milky sap, are they any threat to grazers: the juice is so bitter that animals generally avoid the plants. From June to September, all the dogbanes are arrayed with clusters of pink or whitish flowers. The tallest species, a five-foot plant sometimes called Indian hemp, has especially stringy bark that Indians used for making rope and fishnets.

Dogtooth violet *Erythronium*

The dozen or more wildflowers known as dogtooth violets all are members of the lily family and are among the first to bloom in spring. In the East the common species is the trout lily, named for its mottled green leaves. Often growing in large patches, each plant bears a single yellow bloom atop a four- to eight-inch stem. Of the several western dogtooth violets, one of the best known is the glacier lily, a white-flowered species found near snow fields.

Dogwood *Cornus*

British Columbia, Virginia and North Carolina all claim the dogwood as their official flower, but in fact the much-loved, white spring blooms are not flowers at all. Their four notched "petals" are actually bracts, modified leaves that surround the real flowers—the cluster of tiny greenish-yellow blossoms at their center.

Seldom exceeding 30 feet in height, the flowering dogwood of the East is overshadowed by the Pacific dogwood of the West, which grows up to 60 feet tall. Four to six white bracts encircle its flower clusters, and it sometimes blooms twice a year. Both trees, unfortunately, are sus-

D

Common dolphins follow ships for miles, often leaping in the air as if to announce their presence.

ceptible to a fungus disease that in recent years has caused an epidemic of deaths among these beautiful ornamentals.

Well known—and easily recognized—among the smaller species is the red osier dogwood, a shrub with blood-red bark that adds a welcome note of color to winter landscapes. Another, silky dogwood, is a spreading species with purplish twigs that favors streambanks and similar moist places. Notable berry producers, the dogwoods rank high among trees and shrubs as a source of food for wildlife.

Dolomite

Composed of calcium carbonate, dolomite is nearly identical to limestone—with one crucial difference. It contains magnesium, which makes it harder and less soluble than limestone and therefore more resistant to weathering. Most dolomite was formed when magnesium-rich water seeped into preexisting limestone and replaced some of the rock's calcium with magnesium. Dolomite is used as a building stone, a lining for furnaces, and in smelting.

Dolphin

Often seen cavorting off the bows of moving ships, schools of dolphins move in graceful arcs as they leap above the waves. These playful, intelligent mammals are actually small, toothed whales, whose beaklike snouts distinguish them from their blunt-nosed relatives, the porpoises. With a highly varied repertoire of whistles, clicks, and chirps, dolphins can signal to each other and even carry on conversations. They also produce ultrasonic sounds, which they use for navigation and locating prey. Using their teeth to capture and hold prey rather than to chew it, dolphins feed on fish and squid, swal-

Dolphinfish, known for their vivid colors, fade within minutes of being pulled from the water.

lowing them whole. Like other whales, dolphins breathe through a blowhole on the back and sleep while floating near the surface.

Found off both the Atlantic and Pacific coasts, the eight-foot common dolphin has a black back, white belly, and yellowish stripes on its sides. The larger bottle-nosed dolphin is 9 to 12 feet long and mostly gray in color. Famous for its ability as a performer, the bottle-nosed dolphin thrives in captivity, is easily trained, and has made innumerable appearances in films and aquarium shows.

Dolphinfish *Coryphaena hippurus*

Though no relation to the acrobatic marine mammals known as dolphins, dolphinfish also are well known for their agile antics: lightning speed, dramatic leaps, and ferocious fighting ability make them a favorite with deep-sea fishermen. Unmistakable in appearance, dolphinfish are up to 6½ feet long, with a dorsal fin that tapers all the way from their blunt head to their forked tail. The fish also are brilliantly colored, with deep blue and green on the back and bright golden flanks (which no doubt inspired their other name, dorado). Roaming in schools, dolphinfish feed on squid, crustaceans, and especially, flying fish, which they often pursue by leaping above the waves.

D

Douglas firs, somber in winter, are decorated in spring with cheerful, red-orange buds.

The white-winged dove's monotonous cooing carries over considerable distances.

Dragonflies are harmless, despite such names as snake doctor and devil's darning needle.

Douglas fir *Pseudotsuga*

Towering, majestic trees that sometimes reach heights of more than 300 feet, Douglas firs are exceeded in size only by the redwoods and giant sequoias. The largest specimen on record stood 385 feet tall and had a trunk 15 feet thick. On the tallest trees, the trunks soar straight up for 100 feet or more and are crowned by a compact pyramid of branches covered with flattened needles and pendulous cones. In 1825, botanist David Douglas, for whom the tree is named, failed in his first attempt to collect seeds because his shotgun would not shoot high enough to dislodge a cone. Unmistakable in appearance, the cones have three-pointed, ribbonlike bracts projecting from between their scales. Though the biggest trees are found in coastal forests from British Columbia to northern California, Douglas firs range through much of the West. Prized as ornamentals and for Christmas trees, they also are one of our most valuable timber trees.

Dove

Known for their gentle, cooing calls, doves have been symbols of peace and love since ancient times. Stocky, small-headed, and usually brown or gray, they scuttle along on short legs with their heads bobbing back and forth. Although there is no technical distinction between doves and pigeons, doves tend to be smaller, more graceful birds with pointed tails, while pigeons are larger and have fan-shaped tails.

Doves nest on flimsy platforms of twigs and usually lay two pale, unmarked eggs. The newly hatched young are fed pigeon milk, a substance that looks like cottage cheese and is produced in the parents' crops. Mature doves feed mainly on seeds and fruit and are among the few birds that can drink without lifting their heads to let the water run down their throats.

The most widespread species is the mourning dove, whose repeated coos add a poignant, mournful note to forests, deserts, suburbs, and even cities from coast to coast. Because of its

Drought can devastate crops and turn productive soil into a powdery dust that blows away on the wind.

abundance and fast flight, the mourning dove is a popular game bird in parts of the United States. So is the white-winged dove of the U.S. southwest. The sparrow-sized common ground-dove is found in southern grasslands, and the similar Inca dove prefers to nest in deserts.

Dragonfly

Quick and agile fliers, dragonflies are long, slender insects equipped with two pairs of gauzelike wings that shimmer in the sunlight. Although our largest species has a wingspan of nearly six inches, fossils reveal that some of their ancient ancestors were five times that size. Dragonflies are usually seen hovering over ponds and quiet streams, where they hunt for mosquitoes and other insects. Gathering their legs together to form a sort of basket, they scoop up their victims as they dart through the air. Even as aquatic nymphs, immature dragonflies are accomplished predators. Their hinged lower jaws, armed with sharp hooks at the end, can shoot out with lightning speed to snatch tadpoles, small fish, and insects. After one or more years, the homely nymphs emerge from the water and begin their lives as graceful, winged adults.

Drizzle

Associated with gloomy days and low-lying clouds, the form of precipitation we call drizzle is neither mist nor rain but something in between. It is made up of water droplets that are just large enough to drift slowly downward. They are not so small that they float in the air as do the tiny particles of mist or fog. Nor are they so large and heavy that they fall rapidly like rain. And unlike rain, which is associated with high, turbulent clouds that tend to pass quickly overhead, drizzle usually continues to fall over longer periods of time.

Drought

When the amount of precipitation in a region drops far below its normal level over an extended period of time, the resultant shortage of moisture is called a drought. In their severest form, droughts can cause a succession of calamities and take an enormous toll on life, land, and the economy. Streams and reservoirs dry up; crops wither and perish; animals starve or die of thirst; the soil turns to dust and is carried away by the wind; and grass and forest fires rage out of control.

In the 1930's, for example, the Prairies were devastated by one of the worst droughts in history. Crops failed, much of the land was ruined, and families were forced to abandon their homes forever.

Drum

Also known as croakers, drums are named for the low-pitched sounds they make by contracting muscles next to the swim bladder. The family includes about 160 species of mostly oceanic fish, though not all of them croak, because not all are equipped with the swim bladder that serves to amplify the sound. The various species range from 1 to 100 pounds in weight, but all have in common a conspicuous notch dividing the dorsal fin into two parts.

Found mostly in shallow coastal waters, the drums are popular commercial and sport fish. Millions of red drums, or channel bass, are caught off Florida every year, and black drums and spotted seatrout are sought from New England to the Gulf of Mexico. Off the west coast, the white seabass, up to four feet long, also is prized by fishermen. Other drums include the weakfish and kingfish, found in the Atlantic, and the freshwater drum of the central United States.

Drumlin

Ice Age relics, drumlins are long, low, oval-shaped hills composed of glacially deposited debris. Molded into their characteristic streamlined form by moving ice sheets, they lie with their long axis in line with the direction of the ice's movement. Up to 150 feet high and half a mile long, drumlins often occur in groups on flat plains, where they look like schools of leaping porpoises. Among the most famous drumlins is Bunker Hill in Boston, Massachusetts. Thousands of drumlins are found in southern Ontario, in Nova Scotia and in the Northwest Territories. Smaller groups occur in other provinces.

D

Mallards, like other dabbling ducks, leap out of the water directly into flight; diving ducks, in contrast, need a running start along the surface before they become airborne.

Duckweed, littering ponds like green confetti, is a favorite and nutritious food for waterfowl.

Duck

Web-footed waterfowl with waterproof feathers, ducks are birds of oceans, lakes, rivers, and ponds. In contrast to their larger cousins, geese and swans, they generally have shorter legs and necks and broader, flatter bills; and instead of trumpeting or honking, they quack or whistle.

Male ducks are more brightly colored than females, but after mating they molt into drab browns similar to the females' plumage. Most species build down-lined nests on the ground near the water's edge, but a few kinds nest in cavities in trees. Unlike geese and swans, ducks do not mate for life; once the eggs have been laid, the males abandon the females and troop off to molt and congregate with other males.

Our many kinds of ducks fall into several groups based on appearance and feeding habits. Most familiar are the freshwater dabbling ducks such as mallards, black ducks, teals, and wigeons. Dabblers feed by filtering small plants and animals from the surface or by tipping tail-up to pull underwater plants from the bottom.

Diving ducks are found on both fresh and salt water. Some, such as canvasbacks and redheads, are mainly vegetarians, while scaups, eiders, scoters, goldeneyes, and buffleheads dive for shellfish and crustaceans. Mergansers are streamlined divers that seize fish with their long, sawtooth-edged bills. Oldsquaws, the deepest divers, can descend to depths of 200 feet.

Other ducks include ruddy ducks, which are chunky, broad billed, and stiff tailed, and the whistling ducks of southern marshes, long-legged, long-necked birds with shrill calls.

Duckweed

Of the more than 300,000 known species of flowering plants, the duckweeds are the smallest; one kind is so tiny that a dozen individuals could fit on the head of a pin. Found in still, warm waters, duckweeds are simple, free-floating fronds that have no stems or leaves, and in a few species lack roots as well. Their tiny flowers rarely produce seeds. Duckweeds propagate instead by developing buds that break off and grow into mature plants. Extremely prolific, duckweeds sometimes multiply so rapidly that they completely cover a pond's surface.

Getting Acquainted with the Dabbling Ducks

As a group, these closely related freshwater ducks all have the same way of feeding. Dabbling ducks, unlike divers, probe for food by "upending"—tipping their tails in the air while dunking their heads under water. The females, with mottled brown plumage, all look pretty much alike. But the males have distinctive colors that enable both female ducks and human bird-watchers to tell one species from another. When you see a male dabbling duck, notice first whether the head is a solid color or patterned, then use the guidelines in the chart below to give the duck a name.

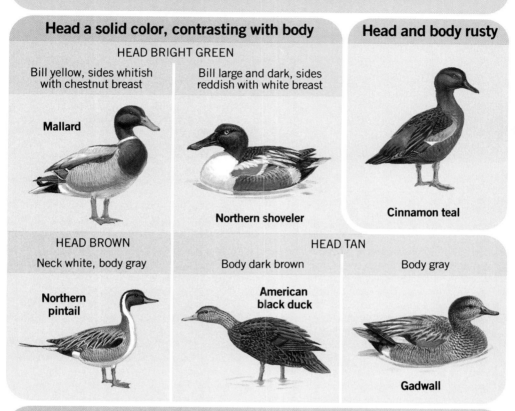

Head a solid color, contrasting with body

HEAD BRIGHT GREEN

Bill yellow, sides whitish with chestnut breast

Mallard

Bill large and dark, sides reddish with white breast

Northern shoveler

Head and body rusty

Cinnamon teal

HEAD BROWN

Neck white, body gray

Northern pintail

HEAD TAN

Body dark brown

American black duck

Body gray

Gadwall

Head patterned, contrasting with body

GREEN EAR PATCH

Forehead white, body brownish

American wigeon

Head rusty, body gray

Green-winged teal

WHITE CRESCENT NEAR EYE

Head gray, body brownish

Blue-winged teal

Dudleya *Dudleya*

Plants of harsh places where little else can survive, dudleyas of various species cling to seaside cliffs in California, hide under the scrub on coastal mountain ranges, and poke up from desert slopes in the Southwest. The plants lie withered and dormant through the summer's heat, but winter rains revive their tidy rosettes of succulent leaves, and in spring they send up stalks of pretty yellow, red, or white flowers. One of the better-known species is the powdery dudleya, a yellow-flowered plant of coastal cliffs that is named for the mealy white coating on its leaves. Another widespread species, canyon dudleya, produces red to yellow flowers; it brightens rocky outcrops in California's Sierra Nevada and the coastal mountain ranges.

D

Great Sand Dunes National Monument in Colorado boasts crests as high as 700 feet.

Dune

Unstable monuments to the combined action of wind and time, dunes are hills of sand found in deserts and along shorelines. Formed in much the same way as snowdrifts, they build up when wind, slowed by an obstacle such as a rock or plant, drops its load of sand on the leeward side. The resultant mound gradually increases in size, in some cases reaching hundreds of feet in height. Some dunes are anchored by vegetation; others migrate many feet each year.

Among Canada's best known dunes are those on Prince Edward Island's north shore and in Manitoba's Spruce Woods Provincial Park. In the United States, notable seashore dunes are found on Cape Cod in Massachusetts, and along the Oregon coast. On the shores of Lake Michigan, many dunes are piled 500 feet high and extend for miles.

Dust devil

On hot, still days when the midday sun blazes down in arid regions, air near the ground heats up and begins to rise. As air rushes in to replace it, the rising air starts to spin. Dust, sand, leaves, and debris also are pulled up into what then becomes visible as a slender, wavering dust devil. Looking like tiny tornadoes, dust devils may rise hundreds of feet. But because they are small and easily disturbed by surface winds, they seldom last more than a few minutes.

Dust storm

Sweeping across the land—often for hundreds of miles—dust storms are strong, dust-laden winds that smother animals and plants, bury crops, and reduce visibility to nighttime darkness. Destructive and awesome, they occur in arid regions with little protective vegetation and

Dust storm warnings recall the devastating Dust Bowl destruction of the 1930's.

in areas where drought has reduced the soil to powdery dust. As winds sweep across the ground, particles are stirred up and held aloft, forming great dark walls that can reach heights of 10,000 feet or more. Although dust storms have always been part of the Prairie scene, the most devastating occurred in the 1930's. During those Dust Bowl years, the land dried to dust and millions of acres of farmland were destroyed.

Dusty miller *Artemisia stelleriana*

A common plant on eastern seashores, dusty miller sports little yellowish flower heads in summer. But its outstanding feature is its felty gray-green foliage, which does indeed have a dusty look, as if it had been sprinkled with flour. The covering protects the leaves from drying out in sun and wind, so that it flourishes even at the ocean's edge. An import from Asia, the plant is cultivated for its attractive foliage. But since escaping from the garden, this perennial has proven an important stabilizer of beaches. As sprawling stems take root across the dunes, they cast a silvery net that slows the shifting sands.

The bald eagle, seen here in an ancient tree in Alaska's scenic Tongass National Forest, was named for the striking white feathers on its head, which give it an appearance of baldness. In 1782 the stately bird became the official national emblem of the United States.

E

Earwigs are identified by a characteristic pair of pincers at the rear of their bodies. These appendages are straight on females but curved on males. When handled, the tiny insects may give a sharp pinch, but they are otherwise harmless.

Eagle

Bold and proud in appearance, eagles have symbolized power since ancient times. Like other hawks, they have keen eyesight, hooked beaks, and long, curved talons for seizing prey. The two North American species, the bald eagle and golden eagle, are similar in size, with eight-foot wingspans, but otherwise differ in several ways.

Despite its fierce appearance, the bald eagle is a rather timid hunter. Usually found near water, it feeds mainly on fish, which it often steals from ospreys. Its nest, or aerie, generally built in tall trees, is enlarged year after year and may be as much as 9½ feet wide and 20 feet high. In the 1960's bald eagles were reduced in numbers by DDT but have made a comeback since the pesticide was banned.

The golden eagle, which nests on cliffs in western mountains and across Canada, is a bolder hunter than the bald eagle. It captures prey in long swoops and sometimes attacks animals larger than itself—even some as big as deer. Golden eagles build large stick nests in trees or on rocky ledges. They have been known to defend breeding areas up to 75 miles square.

Earthquake See pp.116–117.

Earthworm

Cylindrical, segmented, legless animals, earthworms move with the help of tiny bristles, called setae, on each body segment. They feed on decaying organic matter in the soil and deposit the residue on the surface as granular castings. Charles Darwin considered earthworms to be among the most important creatures on earth because they encourage plant growth by mixing and aerating the soil as they burrow through it. He estimated that the worms on a single acre of land bring as much as 18 tons of soil to the surface each year. Although they often appear after storms, earthworms do not rain down from the heavens as was once thought: they simply are forced to flee from their water-filled burrows.

Earwig

Inch-long insects with fierce-looking pincers at the rear of their bodies, earwigs trace their name to the superstition that they crawl into the ears of sleeping people. They are, in fact, nocturnal but are harmless to humans. Earwigs do, however, hide in cracks and crevices by day and, because they sometimes cause an unpleasant odor, can be household pests. Those in the West and South sometimes damage cultivated plants.

Alaska's 1964 earthquake turned soil to mud, causing houses to slide downslope.

Earthquake

Among the most dreaded of natural phenomena, severe earthquakes are terrifying events. Their awesome force can topple buildings, buckle bridges, rupture highways, and cause catastrophic loss of life and property. Fortunately, the most powerful quakes are rare. Of the million or so earthquakes that occur around the world every year, the vast majority are too small to be detected except by sensitive instruments. In North America, about 700 a year are strong enough to be felt, but most cause no more rumbling than a passing truck.

The causes of quakes

The earth's crust consists of about 20 gigantic, slowly moving plates. As these collide, grind past, or sink below one another, stress builds up along their edges. Finally, the crust suddenly gives way, sending shock waves in all directions. The slippage temporarily relieves the stress, but it also causes the earth to tremble and crack. The largest, most destructive quakes tend to originate near so-called subduction zones, regions where one plate is being pushed beneath the edge of the adjoining plate. When earthquakes occur on the ocean floor, the shock waves can produce swift and devastating tidal waves known as tsunamis. Twenty-seven people were drowned in 1929 when one such tsunami swamped Newfoundland's Burin Peninsula.

Earthquakes can also be triggered by volcanic eruptions and even by human activities. In a few instances, liquids pumped into oil fields to force petroleum to the surface lubricated fissures in the bedrock, causing slippage.

The magnitude of earthquakes is usually measured on the Richter scale, devised by a California geologist. Each successive whole number on the scale represents a tenfold increase in the force of the shock waves. For example, a magnitude of 7 is 10 times greater than a magnitude of 6, and 100 times greater than a magnitude of 5. The most powerful, recent earthquake to strike North America, the Alaskan quake of 1964,

San Francisco's 1906 earthquake reduced much of the city to rubble. Many newer steel-framed buildings withstood the force of the tremors, only to be destroyed when fires, ignited by live wires and broken gas mains, engulfed the crippled metropolis.

During an earthquake, improperly constructed buildings can collapse into heaps of rubble.

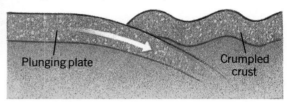

Plunging plate

Crumpled crust

In subduction zones one crustal plate dives beneath the edge of another, crumpling its surface.

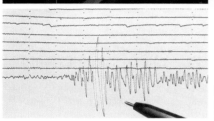

Seismographs (left, above) record all earthquake tremors. Major jolts produce the longest strokes (left).

registered 8.4 on the Richter scale. Canada's largest, which registered 8.1, occurred in 1949 off the Queen Charlotte Islands.

Quakes in the past

Although the majority of earthquakes in Canada occur along the British Columbia coast, several of the earliest quakes recorded took place in Quebec. One rocked the Charlevoix/Kamouraska region in 1663, causing vast landslides. Dishes were shattered, buildings shook and some 300 houses were damaged in Montreal in a 1732 quake. In 1755, another quake that struck New England was felt from Nova Scotia to South Carolina.

A more devastating earthquake centered on the frontier town of New Madrid, Missouri, in 1811. Its terrified settlers watched helplessly as the ground heaved and split, the Mississippi River churned violently, overflowing its banks, and riverside bluffs collapsed into the water.

In the next few months, two more major earthquakes struck, leveling New Madrid. The second was so powerful it caused church bells to toll in Washington, D.C., and stopped clocks in Charleston, South Carolina. This time, the Mississippi reversed its course and then rushed into a newly created depression in the ground, forming gigantic Reelfoot Lake. The shocks continued almost daily for two years.

In 1886 a violent earthquake hit Charleston, South Carolina, killing 60 people and destroying much of the city in just 70 excruciating seconds. As in the Missouri quakes, the ground split open, casting silt and water 20 feet into the air, a phenomenon that occurs when powerful shock waves suddenly rip through loose, watery

soil. Tremors from the devastating earthquake were felt as far away as Canada.

The trembling West Coast

The Pacific Coast, where two of the earth's giant shifting plates meet, is the continent's leading earthquake zone. More than half the U.S. quakes occur in California because of its extensive, branching system of faults. The largest of these is the San Andreas fault, where the Pacific Plate slides northwestward against the North American Plate at about two inches per year. Visible on the surface, the fault stretches nearly 700 miles.

San Francisco, built astride the San Andreas fault, has a long history of earthquakes. The most violent, estimated at 8.25 on the Richter scale, struck in 1906 with a roar that survivors compared to a thousand runaway trains. Streets rippled and heaved, water and gas mains ruptured, houses collapsed, and whole sections of the city went up in flames.

On Canada's west coast, earthquake risk from the shifting Pacific and North American plates is compounded by the interaction of the Juan de Fuca crustal plates. Vancouver Island suffered some damage in a powerful 1946 quake, but the region has never experienced the destruction suffered by California and Alaska.

The devastating Good Friday earthquake in Anchorage, Alaska, struck on the afternoon of March 27, 1964. At 8.4 on the Richter scale, the quake released energy equivalent to 12,000 Hiroshima-type atomic bombs. Fissures sliced through the city, and entire neighborhoods sank 30 feet below the surface. Nearly 2,000 miles away, a tsunami hit Crescent City, California, drowning 12 people and demolishing the town.

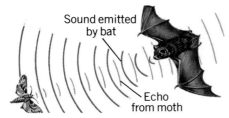

Echolation enables bats to home in on mosquitoes and even tiny midges.

King eider drakes have strikingly patterned plumage and colorful bills.

Echolocation

Bats, porpoises, and a few birds are among the animals that use echolocation to navigate and locate prey. For bats, cave dwellers that live in a world of darkness, this system of sonar provides a means of capturing flying insects even on the inkiest of nights. As they flutter through the air, bats emit short bursts of high-pitched sounds that bounce off objects around them and are reflected back to their large ears. These echoes enable the bats, in effect, to "see" pictures in sound. Porpoises emit clicking sounds whose echoes tell them about the location, size, and shape of prey, and some cave-dwelling birds navigate by means of high-pitched calls.

Eel *Anguilla rostrata*

Long, slender, snakelike fish, American eels have a ribbonlike look as they undulate through the water. They are found in lakes, ponds, rivers, and streams all along the eastern seaboard, but they migrate to the Sargasso Sea in the Atlantic Ocean to spawn. There each female lays as many as 20 million eggs, which the males cover with milt. This prodigious effort is the final act of the adults, for they die before the eggs hatch. The young drift with the currents toward the coast and gradually metamorphose from flat, transparent, leaf-shaped larvae into elvers, miniature, light-colored versions of the adults. The journey to the shore takes about a year; once there, the males remain near the river mouths while the females continue upstream, sometimes slithering across mud flats and wet grass on their way to inland lakes and ponds. When fully grown, from 8 to 20 years later, the eels begin their long swim back to the Sargasso Sea.

Elms are prized for their graceful symmetry.

Eelgrass *Zostera marina*

One of the few flowering plants found in the sea, eelgrass is named for its long, ribbonlike leaves that sway gently with the currents. Growing in dense stands in shallow waters along the Atlantic and Pacific coasts, it was long regarded by fishermen as little more than a propeller-fouling pest. Then in 1931 a mysterious blight virtually wiped out the eelgrass beds. When the thriving bay scallop fishery also collapsed, ecologists realized that the beds are in fact vital nurseries, not only for scallops but for a host of other creatures, too. The subsequent starvation of thousands of brants demonstrated the importance of eelgrass to these geese as well. Fortunately, the eelgrass eventually recovered and once again fulfills its vital role in coastal ecology.

Egret *See Heron.*

Eider

Stocky ducks of northern climes, the eiders are best known for their down. Famed for its softness and superb insulating qualities, it has for centuries been harvested from their nests to make eiderdown bedding and parkas.

Common eiders, at 27 inches and nearly five pounds, are the largest North American ducks. They winter along the north Atlantic and Pacific coasts and migrate farther north each spring. Feeding on mollusks and crustaceans, these expert divers routinely plunge to depths of 60 feet. The other three species—king, spectacled, and Steller's eiders—all dwell somewhat farther north year-round. Or so it is assumed, for the wintering grounds of the spectacled eider remain largely unknown to this day.

Elder *Sambucus*

Famous for its fruits, which are made into elderberry jam, pie, and wine, the common elder of the East is a shrub up to eight feet tall. In contrast, the treelike blueberry elder of the West often grows 20 feet tall with a trunk 2 feet wide.

Endangered species: can we help?

Whooping cranes

Florida panther

Black-footed ferret

Some endangered species are managing to make a slow comeback thanks to programs aimed at protecting them. A 30,000-acre refuge has been created in southern Florida to help preserve and extend the range of the panther; a Canadian-American program has increased the whooping crane population from 15 to about 100; and the black-footed ferret is now part of a captive breeding program.

E

In summer the elders bear broad clusters of creamy flowers, which are followed by red or purple fruits. A favorite with wildlife, the fruits often are so abundant that the plants' stems break under their weight. All elders, in fact, have brittle wood and pithy twigs that are easily hollowed out to make whistles and drinking straws.

Elk See *Wapiti*.

Elm *Ulmus*

Countless North American towns have an Elm Street, a reminder that earlier residents found elms to be ideal shade trees. Fast-growing and up to 100 feet tall, the graceful vase-shaped trees formed cathedrallike gothic arches over hot roadways; they prospered even in the compacted streetside soil; and they tolerated both drought and periodic flooding.

Since the 1930's, however, the trees have been decimated by the deadly Dutch elm disease. Caused by a fungus that is spread from tree to tree by elm bark beetles, the fatal ailment arrived on these shores with a shipment of logs infested with fungus-carrying beetles. One estimate puts the death toll of the last half century at 100 million trees.

Of 25 species of elm worldwide, only the white, or American, elm, the hard-wooded rock, or cork, elm and the slippery elm are native

to Canada. All produce small, winged fruits and have elongated, oval leaves with typically lopsided bases and, unfortunately, all are susceptible to Dutch elm disease.

Endangered species

Plants and animals whose populations have dwindled to such low levels that they are threatened with extinction are known as endangered species. In some cases species have become so specialized in their requirements that even the slightest change in the environment imperils their existence. In modern times, however, the threats more often result from human interference. In the last century, bison were so ruthlessly slaughtered that they were nearly wiped out before efforts were undertaken to save them from extinction. Even more sinister than hunting and trapping is the destruction of habitat. The elimination of forests and wetlands to build suburbs and shopping malls, and the fouling of whole ecosystems with pollutants and pesticides have taken a devastating toll on wildlife. Before it was banned, for instance, DDT threatened such birds as bald eagles and peregrine falcons by causing them to produce eggs with abnormally thin shells. From the Florida golden aster and the Santa Cruz cypress to the wood stork, the red wolf, and the magnificent blue whale, the list of endangered species is a long one.

E

The ermine's remarkable agility and dogged hunting style give it the advantage over squirrels, chipmunks, and other rodent prey.

Epiphytes, such as these bromeliads clinging to cypress trunks in the steamy Florida Everglades, rarely harm their hosts; unlike parasites, they do not extract vital juices.

English sparrow See *House sparrow.*

Epiphyte

Perched on trees, utility wires, and even buildings, the so-called air plants use their roots only to anchor themselves in place; having no contact with the soil, epiphytes get all their nourishment from wind-blown dust and from minerals in rainwater. Epiphytic ferns, orchids, and bromeliads are plentiful in subtropical Florida, while Spanish moss drapes trees throughout the South. In other areas, mosses, liverworts, and lichens are common epiphytes.

Ermine *Mustela erminea*

Small and agile, with a lithe and sinuous body, the ermine is a ferocious nocturnal hunter that can slip through even the tightest spaces in pursuit of mice and other small mammals. Sometimes known as the short-tailed weasel, it is 12 to 14 inches long, including its 2- to 4-inch black-tipped tail.

Twice a year, ermines molt and undergo a complete color change. Chocolate-brown with white underparts in summer, in winter they turn snow-white except for their black tail tips. The beautiful winter pelts are valued as luxury furs and have traditionally been a symbol of European royalty.

Found as far north as the Arctic and south to New Jersey in the East and New Mexico in the West, ermines live alone in forests and brushy areas—anyplace with an abundance of prey and water. Almost perpetually hungry, they help keep rodent populations in check.

Erosion

Bit by bit, the face of the earth is constantly changed by the never-ending process of erosion. Its agents—water, wind, waves, and ice—all have amazing power to move, sculpt, and scar the land. Falling rain, each drop like a little hammer, pounds away at the soil. Streams and rivers strip off sediment and carry it toward the sea. Waves gnaw at sandy shores and pummel seaside cliffs. Mighty glaciers gouge out valleys and, over time, reshape entire mountain ranges. And in the desert, intermittent downpours deepen gullies, while wind-blown sand scours away the surfaces of solid rock.

Erosion does not work alone. Weathering first breaks down the rocks by dissolving them with acidic groundwater, by alternate freezing and thawing, and by other means. The smaller pieces can then be moved from place to place.

The results of this slow but steady change can be harmful. Millions of tons of topsoil are lost from farmlands every year. But erosion has also created some of our most spectacular scenery—from the Grand Canyon and Niagara Escarpment to the sheer cliffs along parts of the Pacific and Atlantic coasts.

Erratic

When the massive ice sheets of the last Ice Age moved slowly across the land, they carried along pieces of bedrock and deposited them far south of their places of origin. Such rocks, called erratics, often differ dramatically from the surface on which they rest in their new surroundings. As a result, they have provided geologists with im-

Erosion has sculpted some beautiful landscapes, from the curves of Arches National Park, Utah (above left), to the spires of Bryce Canyon, also in Utah (above right).

E

Erratics, the boulders resting on this rock surface, testify to the power of the mammoth sheets of ice that carried them from the North.

portant clues as to the routes taken by the long-vanished ice sheets. These well-traveled relics of the Ice Age range in size from mere pebbles to building-size boulders that weigh tens of tons.

Esker

Steep-sided winding ridges made up of sand and gravel, eskers are remnants of the last Ice Age. The ridges of debris were deposited by streams of water that snaked through passages in and under glaciers, and were exposed when the ice melted. To modern eyes some of the narrower eskers look like railroad embankments. Eskers can be seen in many areas of Canada and in parts of the northeastern United States that were covered by the great ice sheets. Many of them, however, have long since disappeared, mined for the sand and gravel they contained.

Estivation

The hot-weather equivalent of hibernation, estivation is a state of dormancy that allows animals, particularly those that dwell in the desert, to survive in times of excessive heat and drought. During such periods, the animals become torpid, their breathing and heart rates are reduced, and the need for oxygen and water are greatly diminished. Many insects and snails estivate, as do spadefoot toads and fish that live in ponds subject to drying out. Estivators sometimes wrap themselves in moisture-retaining cocoons; others burrow into the ground while waiting for rain. A few mammals, such as ground squirrels, also become dormant in the hot summer months, but scientists disagree as to whether their metabolic slowdown can be described as true estivation.

121

Evening primroses produce an oil that recent medical research has shown to be of promise in the treatment of a variety of ills.

An estuary's brackish water, often reaching far inland, is a rich breeding area for fish, crustaceans, and shellfish, especially in the fringing salt marshes that are alternately drained and flooded by the tides.

Estuary

When coastal land subsides or melting glaciers cause sea levels to rise, the mouths of rivers are drowned, producing bodies of mixed salt and fresh water called estuaries. They may be broad and shallow like Chesapeake Bay, the largest inlet on the eastern United States, broad and deep like the St. Lawrence estuary, or narrow and deep like Quebec's Saguenay River or an Alaskan fjord. Many great port cities—Quebec, Baltimore, New York—were built on estuaries.

While an estuary may look placid on the surface, it is in fact a battleground: the sediment-laden river current drives seaward, only to be rebuffed by the relentless tides. A battleground might seem an unlikely setting for a nursery, but the estuary's brackish waters are just that—a rich reproductive habitat for marine life.

Eucalyptus *Eucalyptus*

Native to Australia, where they are called gum trees, eucalypti are famous for being the sole food source of koala bears. In the 1850's these attractive evergreens were first introduced to California, where, because of their amazing vigor and tolerance for dry soils, they were widely planted both as ornamentals and in reforestation projects. The blue gum is the tallest and most vigorous species, attaining heights of 50 feet in five years and 180 feet at maturity. On some eucalypti the bark is shed in flakes, giving the trees a mottled appearance, while on others it peels off in shaggy strips. The leathery, lance-shaped leaves contain aromatic oils used in medicines, deodorants, and perfumes, and the wood is used for lumber and fuel.

Eutrophication

As a lake evolves over time, it becomes enriched with nutrients in a natural aging process called eutrophication. The nutrients, released by the decay of plants and animals, stimulate even more growth and decay, causing silt and organic remains to accumulate on the bottom. Over thousands of years, the lake is transformed into a marsh and finally into dry land. Man-made pollutants, however, speed up the process, causing lakes to age prematurely. The nutrients in sewage and fertilizers foster the rapid growth of algae, which, when they die and decay, use up so much oxygen that fish and other animals literally suffocate. And so, ironically, the lake chokes to death from its own excessive fertility.

Evening primrose *Oenothera*

Though the evening primroses favor sunny sites such as roadsides and vacant lots all across North America, most of them bloom only in the evening hours. The four-petaled flowers open

Extinction was the sad plight of the passenger pigeon, seen here mounted in a museum. Once so plentiful that great flocks darkened the sky, they were exterminated by merciless hunting and other factors. The last survivor died in a zoo in 1914.

In the Everglades, herons and egrets gather near a stand of cabbage palmettos.

at sunset and wilt the next morning, a schedule that suits the night-flying moths they depend on for pollination. The blossoms' light colors—yellows, pinks, and whites—show up in the dark, and a sweet lemon fragrance adds to their allure. The most abundant species, the common evening primrose, has six-foot stems that help its inch-wide flowers stand out against the night sky. The Missouri evening primrose, less than one foot tall, compensates for its modest stature with bolder flowers—bright yellow saucers three inches across.

Everglades

Called Pa-Hay-Okee—the grassy river—by the Seminole Indians, Florida's Everglades are a 4,000-square-mile wetland extending from Lake Okeechobee south to Florida Bay. Most of the Everglades is a vast, nearly flat expanse of sawgrass, a sharp-edged sedge that grows 10 to 15 feet tall. Ponds and channels of open water lace the sawgrass prairie, and here and there the monotony is interrupted by small stands of trees—bald cypresses in low places, and virtual jungles of mahoganies, gumbo-limbos, and other tropical species on the hammocks, low islands that rise only a foot or two above the water level. Where the marsh meets the ocean, it is fringed with a broad belt of mangroves, salt-tolerant trees that protect the land from the ravages of wind and waves. And everywhere there is wild-

life. Teeming with a staggering variety of species, the Everglades serve as a sanctuary for many rare plants and animals. Ibises, egrets, and other long-legged waders fish in the shallows, while bald eagles roost in the cypress trees. Alligators, deer, marsh rabbits, bobcats, and even the endangered Florida panther all find a haven in this unique waterlogged wilderness.

Evergreen forest See pp. 124–125.

Extinction

The disappearance of plants and animals from the face of the earth is an ongoing process in the life of the planet. Scientists, in fact, estimate that perhaps 90 percent of all the species that have ever lived are now extinct. Mammoths and mastodons, saber-toothed tigers, and countless other creatures have long since died out and are known to us only as fossils. Gone too are all the dinosaurs, victims of a mysterious mass extinction that took place some 65 million years ago.

In modern times, however, the pace of extinctions has increased alarmingly. All too often human activity has been to blame, both directly through wanton slaughter and indirectly through destruction or degradation of habitat. Unless vigorous steps are taken to protect and replenish them, more and more endangered plants and animals are doomed to slip into the eternal oblivion of extinction.

A **bull moose's** antlers, here covered with the fuzzy skin called velvet, are used to battle other males.

Red-breasted nuthatches often creep headfirst down tree trunks.

EVERGREEN FOREST

Twinflowers hang in nodding pairs.

Stretching from coast to coast across North America, just south of the arctic tundra, is a broad band of northern evergreen forest. Sometimes called boreal forest, taiga, or simply the great north woods, the expanse is dominated by firs, spruces, and other coniferous trees. Unlike the broad-leaved trees that dominate farther south, the conifers are well adapted to the cold temperatures and poor, shallow soils of the north. The trees provide a cornucopia of seeds that sustain a variety of wildlife from crossbills and nutcrackers to chipmunks and red squirrels. Warblers and other insect-eating birds populate the forest in summer, feeding on hordes of flies, mosquitoes, and caterpillars. Even in winter, woodpeckers and nuthatches probe under bark for dormant insects and their eggs. The frigid, snowy winters provide a challenge to mammals. Some, such as beavers and squirrels, rely on stored food. Moose, porcupines, lynxes, and wolves forage or prowl all winter long, while woodchucks, ground squirrels, and black bears prefer to sleep through the harsh months until spring.

Snowshoe hares become brown in summer and white in winter; this one is in the midst of change.

The lynx, an expert at stalking and pouncing, is adept at catching agile, elusive snowshoe hares.

Tranquil ponds, remnants of ancient glaciers, punctuate the northern evergreen forest.

The spruce grouse, well camouflaged, feeds on the needles and buds of conifers.

Magnolia warblers nest in evergreens and feed on insects that inhabit the treetops.

Bunchberry's blooms (left) and berries (right) resemble those of flowering dogwood, a relative.

The gyrfalcon (right) is the world's largest falcon. A bird of the far north, it breeds on the Arctic tundra, from Alaska to Labrador, and frequently builds its crude nest on rocky ledges (below). The hatchlings are often cared for in the nest for a month.

F

Falcon *Falco*

With pointed wings and streamlined bodies, falcons are fast-flying, open-country birds of prey that specialize in catching other birds in flight. Most seize their prey in steep power dives, or stoops, but some also drop to the ground to catch small mammals, insects, and lizards. Unlike hawks, which use their talons to kill their prey, falcons do in their victims with a quick bite on the back of the neck.

Falcon nests are simple affairs with little or no lining, usually placed on ledges or in the old nests of other birds. The females lay three to five eggs, which, like the hatchlings, are tended by both parents.

The peregrine falcon, clocked at speeds of 175 miles an hour, is the fastest of the falcons. Once found across most of North America, it has declined drastically in numbers because of pesticide residues in the ducks, pigeons, and shorebirds that it feeds on. The prairie falcon lives in dry regions of the West, where it often skims low and flushes birds from the ground. Merlins, small falcons of savannas and open woodlands, prey on songbirds, which they often overtake in swift horizontal attacks rather than downward stoops. The American kestrel takes more insects and mammals than birds, and hovers as it scans the ground for prey. While most falcons raise only one brood each year, kestrels produce a second in years when mice and voles are abundant.

False hellebore *Veratrum*

Stately summer-blooming perennials, the false hellebores bear plumes of green, yellow, white, or purplish star-shaped flowers atop stems three to seven feet tall. The delicacy of the blooms provides a pleasing contrast with the plants' broad, boldly pleated leaves, which clasp the stem at their bases. Members of the lily family, the false hellebores are unrelated to the true hellebores, which are old-world relatives of buttercups. And although one western species is known as skunk cabbage, the false hellebores are in no way related to the malodorous wetland plants of that name. All the false hellebores are believed to be poisonous and are occasionally fatal to grazing livestock. Yet the same toxic alkaloids also have the power to heal; they are used in medications for treating hypertension.

Fang

Operating something like hypodermic needles, fangs are the specialized teeth that poisonous snakes use to inject venom into prey. Modified salivary glands produce the poisons, which kill the snakes' victims and assist in digesting them. When a snake is ready to strike, toxins secreted by the glands pass into the hollow fangs, where they are injected into the victim. Some snakes, such as copperheads, have fangs in the front of the mouth that fold back when not in use. On other snakes the fangs remain erect. A third group delivers venom with grooved fangs at the rear of the mouth.

Fault

Caused by tremendous pressures deep within the earth, faults are fractures in bedrock where the rocks on one side have slipped past those on the other. Faults range in length from a few feet to many miles, and the movement along them may occur a bit at a time or—at high levels of stress—in dramatic, devastating leaps. North America's most famous fault is the San Andreas

False hellebores, like the Indian poke (above) and the corn lily (right), contain powerful chemicals, which have been used effectively in insecticides.

F

Block-faulting created the steep, rugged peaks of the Teton Range in Wyoming. The eastern face of the range is the edge of a crustal block that was lifted and tilted along a fault.

On some faults blocks of crust move horizontally past each other.

On other faults rocks slide up or down on opposite sides of the fracture.

fault, which slashes across California. It marks the boundary between two of the giant plates that make up the earth's crust, and sudden slips along its length have caused major earthquakes. Other faults are found far from plate boundaries. But no matter where they lie, most are created as the moving plates jostle one other, straining the rigid bedrock until it snaps and thrusts blocks of rock up or down, right or left, along the fracture. So-called fault-block mountains, such as the Sierra Nevada in California, formed when a crustal block was heaved up and tilted along a fault.

Feldspar

The most common group of minerals in the earth's crust, feldspars are the main components of many types of rocks and occur in a range of colors. One kind provides the fleshy pink tone that characterizes some of the granites. Another variety, labradorite, displays a rainbow of colors and can be polished into gemstones, as can milky white moonstone and the green variety called Amazon stone. When decomposed by weathering, feldspars form clay, which can be used in the manufacture of glass and ceramics.

127

A male fiddler crab brandishes a single large claw in an elaborate display of courtship or bravado.

Young fern fronds, called fiddleheads, are gathered in the spring and eaten as vegetables.

F

The filefish (right) is a strange-looking creature with small, high-set eyes, a tiny mouth, and a single, jagged spine that projects from the top of its head. The pancake thinness of its body is revealed in the head-on view (far right).

Fern

An ancient class of plants that dominated the earth hundreds of millions of years ago, ferns are indeed rather primitive looking. Most have delicate, feathery leaves, or fronds; grow close to the ground; and prefer damp, shady areas. When the young leaves, aptly called fiddleheads, first appear, their tips are tightly coiled, and they gradually unfurl into mature fronds. The small dark spots on the undersides of the fronds are clusters of spore sacs that eventually burst open and scatter dustlike spores to the wind. When the spores land, they develop into tiny intermediate plants that reproduce sexually, and it is their offspring that grow into the familiar spore-producing fern plants.

Of our 300 species of ferns, two of the more common and typical examples are the elegant ostrich fern and the ubiquitous bracken. Some of the others are nonconformists. The walking fern, for example, sprouts new plantlets at the tips of its long, narrow leaves and reroots itself as it "walks" across the soil. The shoestring fern, an epiphyte that never touches the ground, has yard-long strap-shaped fronds, which dangle like ribbons from rough-barked trees in Florida and Georgia. Other mavericks include ferns that float and a few climbing vines.

Ferret *Mustela nigripes*

A secretive but inquisitive member of the weasel family, the endangered black-footed ferret is one of our rarest mammals. In Canada, it is found only in Alberta and Saskatchewan. This slim-bodied, short-legged Prairie native is an appealing creature with a black mask across its eyes and with dark feet and a dark tail tip accenting its yellowish coat. The ferret feeds on ground squirrels, mice, and ground-nesting birds, but its favorite prey is the prairie dog, whose underground burrows it takes over as its home. Active at dusk and by night, the ferret makes chattering sounds and hisses when alarmed.

With the decline of prairie dogs—considered pests by farmers, who have waged constant war against them—the black-footed ferret's very existence has been threatened. An intensive captive breeding program aimed at saving the ferrets and returning them to the wild has been underway in the United States for some time.

Fiddler crab *Uca*

Low tide on sandy or muddy seashores and in salt marshes brings out fiddler crabs in droves. Emerging from their burrows, where they find protection from fish and other predators, the lit-

Purple finches are enjoyed for their melodious mating songs.

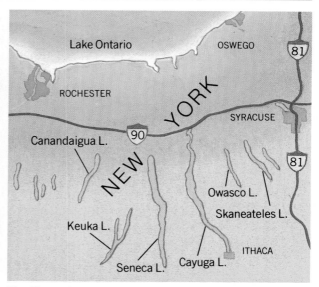

The Finger Lakes of western New York are classic examples of long, narrow glacially carved basins.

tle crustaceans scuttle sideways across the surface, feeding on algae and other plant material. Then, when the tide comes in, the fiddlers head back for the safety of their burrows and carefully plug the entrances.

Male fiddlers are easily recognized by their one greatly enlarged pincer, or claw, which they wave about in self-defense and as part of their courtship rituals. The crabs are named for the males' habit of moving the oversized claw back and forth with a sawing motion that looks much like a fiddler fiddling.

Filefish

With bodies flattened from side to side and a single spine projecting, unicorn-style, from the top of their heads, filefish are strange-looking creatures that were named for the sandpaperlike texture of their scales. Usually found near wharves and reefs along the Atlantic coast, filefish swim along slowly, stopping now and then to munch on sea fans, algae, sponges, and even stinging corals. They often hover head down as they forage, and can change color to blend with their surroundings.

Finch

In addition to finches and goldfinches, the finch family includes the pine siskin, the redpolls, the crossbills, and the evening and pine grosbeaks. Seedeaters all, most of the finches have stout conical bills that are ideal for crushing such fare. Many finches even feed seeds to their nestlings. (Most other seed-eating birds raise their young on a diet of insects.) And one, the American goldfinch, delays nesting until late summer when seeds are most plentiful.

Most of the finches are birds of open woodlands or fields. Rosy finches, however, nest on alpine and arctic tundra, and house finches,

once exclusively southwestern birds, now thrive in eastern cities. The eastern birds are descendants of caged finches that were released in 1940. In winters when northern seed crops fail, finches sometimes fly south in exceptionally large numbers. Pine siskins, for instance, may roam from Canada and the northernmost states all the way to the Gulf Coast in search of food.

Finger lake

During the last ice age, tongues of glacial ice sometimes advanced along north-south river valleys, gouging them out and greatly deepening them. When the ice later retreated, it sometimes left small moraines that dammed the ice-gouged hollows and created long, narrow lakes. Such lakes are called finger lakes after the most famous examples of their kind, the Finger Lakes of western New York.

Fir *Abies*

Though a few other evergreens are called firs, our nine species of true firs are unmistakable. Their cones, unlike those of other conifers, stand upright on the branches; the axis of each cone, moreover, remains attached to the tree after its seeds and scales are shed, leaving an erect pencillike spike. The firs also are known for the blisters of aromatic resin that collect under their bark. It is this sticky substance that gives the popular Christmas tree, the balsam fir, its pleasant holiday fragrance. While the balsam fir ranges across much of Canada and the northeastern United States and the white fir grows from California to the Rockies and south into Mexico, some of the other firs have more limited ranges. The Fraser fir, for example, survives only on the highest peaks of the Appalachians, and the bristlecone fir is confined to canyons in California's Santa Lucia Mountains.

The firefly's heatless, neonlike glow is produced by a chemical reaction in the insect's abdomen.

Fireweed's purple spires illuminate a northern landscape. Yukon's floral emblem and a member of the evening primrose family, the plant is also known as rosebay, purple rocket, and great willow herb.

F

Firefly

Also called lightning bugs, fireflies are actually small, slow-flying beetles that brighten the sky with their blinking lights on summer evenings. Each species has its own characteristic pattern of flashes, which the insects use for finding mates. The males fly about flashing a signal from a light organ on the abdomen, and females hiding on vegetation respond with flashes that announce their readiness to mate. Some females can also mimic the signals of other species: males fooled by this apparent invitation fly down, only to be eaten by the deceptive temptress. After mating, the females lay eggs on moist ground. The larvae, sometimes seen glowing on damp lawns, prey on snails and small insects.

Fireweed *Epilobium angustifolium*

Often the first plant to grow in fire-scorched areas, fireweed adds a striking note of color as it springs to life from charred soils. Useful as well as beautiful, it produces seeds by the thousands, each one equipped with a tuft of silken hairs that allows the seeds to drift for long distances on the wind. After settling to the ground, the seeds lay dormant, sometimes for years, until fire strips away the shade and sunlight warms the soil, enabling them to germinate at last. Taking nutrients from the ashes, fireweed spreads a mat of roots through the soil, protecting it from erosion until shrubs and trees reestablish themselves.

Yukon's floral emblem, also found from Labrador to Alaska and south to California and the Midwest, fireweed stages a spectacular show when it comes into bloom. From July to September, spires of showy four-petaled magenta-

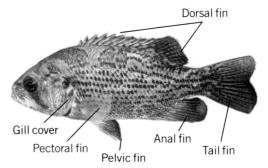

Dorsal fin

Gill cover

Pectoral fin

Pelvic fin

Anal fin

Tail fin

Fish are as various as eels, rays, and seahorses, but this rock bass is fairly typical.

pink blossoms top its six-foot stalks, which are lined with willowlike leaves. The flowers are followed by slender pods, which soon burst open to launch their downy seeds.

Fish

By far the most numerous of all our animals with backbones, fish are cold-blooded, water-dwelling creatures that breathe through gills. Beyond that basic definition, however, it is difficult to generalize. Almost anyone would recognize a carp or a tuna as a fish: like most of their kind, they have paired gills, fins for swimming, and scale-covered bodies that are tapered at both ends. But fish come in an enormous array of shapes and sizes, ranging from less than half an inch to more than 40 feet and weighing from less than an ounce to thousands of pounds.

Fish also display vastly different characteristics. They are as varied as the pancake-flat flounder, with its oddly placed eyes; the batfish, which uses its fins for walking across the ocean

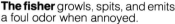

The fisher growls, spits, and emits a foul odor when annoyed.

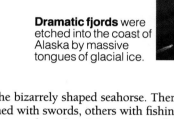

Dramatic fjords were etched into the coast of Alaska by massive tongues of glacial ice.

F

floor; and the bizarrely shaped seahorse. There are fish armed with swords, others with fishing lures, fish that produce electricity, and even fish that can crawl about on land. And fish live in nearly every imaginable watery habitat, from mountain lakes to murky ocean depths and from steaming hot springs to frigid polar seas.

The vast majority of the 2,000 or so North American species are bony fish, meaning their skeletons are made primarily of bone. These most advanced of all fish are usually equipped with gas-filled swim bladders, used for controlling buoyancy. Other fish, such as sharks, rays, and skates, have skeletons of cartilage rather than bone. Lacking swim bladders, they must remain constantly on the move to keep from sinking. The most primitive fish—the eellike lampreys and hagfish—lack jaws and instead have sucking mouths lined with teeth. The bony and the jawless fish usually reproduce by spawning, with the males fertilizing the eggs after the females have released them into the water. On the other hand, sharks and rays mate, and in most cases the females bear live young.

Fisher *Martes pennanti*

A brownish-black, bushy-tailed member of the weasel family, about the size of a small fox, the fisher is a stong, aggressive, agile hunter active by night. It lives in dense forests across Canada, where it roams widely over a home territory of up to 10 square miles. Although the fisher occasionally eats fish, its diet consists primarily of rodents, porcupines, and snowshoe hares.

Running, swimming, and climbing trees in pursuit of prey, it can track with the persistence of a wolverine, fend off dogs, and kill animals as large as deer and lynx.

Solitary for most of the year, fishers pair off with mates from January through April. Well before giving birth to one to four blind, helpless young, the females make dens in hollow trees, logs, or under rocky ledges. Overtrapped in the past for its handsome pelt, the fisher is now protected and is valued for its role in controlling porcupine numbers.

Fjord

As Ice Age glaciers moved slowly down existing river valleys on their journey to the sea, they carved deep into the bedrock and excavated the spectacular inlets that we know today as fjords. Although fjords are relatively shallow at their entrances, farther inland they may reach depths of 4,000 feet. Distinguished by dramatically soaring walls, these unique waterways often have waterfalls cascading down their sides, which further enhance their beauty.

Although fjords are most often associated with Norway (the word itself is Norwegian), many spectacular examples can be seen in North America, among them several on Alaska's southern coast and others at Albeni Inlet on Vancouver Island, on the Saguenay River in Quebec, and at Bonne Bay in Newfoundland. But Somes Sound, on the picturesque coast of Mount Desert Island in Maine, is the only fjord in the United States mainland.

F

Flamingo *Phoenicopterus ruber*

A bird that has come to symbolize not only Florida but all things tropical, the greater flamingo is unmistakable with its exotic pink plumage, stiltlike legs, and graceful, swanlike neck. Standing three to five feet tall, it feeds by dipping its curved bill upside down in brackish water, then using its thick, fleshy tongue to force mud and water through sievelike structures on the bill that strain out algae, tiny shellfish, and other small animals. Gregarious birds, flamingos live in large colonies on isolated lagoons, where they build moundlike nests of mud and where each pair raises a single chick. The few truly wild flamingos that turn up in Florida come from colonies in the Bahamas. The ones most often seen there are not wild at all, but the semidomesticated denizens of parks and gardens.

Flatfish

In contrast to other fish, the bottom-dwelling flatfish—flounder, sole, halibut, and the like—swim on their sides. They begin life swimming upright like "normal" fish, but then something peculiar happens: one eye begins to migrate across the head toward the other eye, and in some species the mouth becomes twisted as well. The body also develops the typical flattened, oval form of adult flatfish and becomes colored on the eyed upper side and pale on the eyeless underside. Once the transformation is complete, flatfish sink to the bottom of the sea, where they often lie partially buried in mud or sand. Frequently covered with spots and blotches, they are perfectly camouflaged. Some flatfish can even change their color to match almost any background. Active predators, they dart quickly upward to snatch unwary crustaceans, squid, and smaller fish.

While flatfish average a foot or two in length, some kinds are much larger. The Atlantic halibut can be more than eight feet long and weigh some 700 pounds, and the Pacific halibut is nearly as big. The most beautiful flatfish, the peacock flounder of warm Florida waters, is named for the brilliant blue markings on its body. Another, known as the windowpane, is a remarkably thin-bodied flatfish that ranges from Canada to South Carolina. Unlike its relatives, most of which are featured on seafood menus, the windowpane is simply too flat and meatless to be valued as a food fish.

Flamingos, often seen posing in shallow water, even sleep standing up, although balanced on just one leg.

Some flounders, marine flatfish, can change color to blend with the bottom.

Flatworm

Simple, soft-bodied invertebrates, flatworms fall into three main classes: the mostly free-living turbellarians and the parasitic tapeworms and flukes. The best-known turbellarians are the freshwater planarians. Less than an inch long, these worms have been much studied because of their remarkable regenerative abilities; if cut in two, the rear end of a planarian grows a new head, while the head end grows a new rear. The parasitic tapeworms, which absorb food through their body walls, live inside other animals. Beef tapeworms, which mature in the human intestine, can be as much as 30 feet long. They may weaken their hosts by competing for food but usually cause no damage. Many of the parasitic flukes, in contrast, cause serious diseases. The sheep liver fluke, for instance, inhabits the bile ducts of sheep and cattle and is responsible for the disease known as liver rot.

Flax, a graceful plant with slender stems, grows wild on western hillsides, covering them with a sea of sky-blue blossoms.

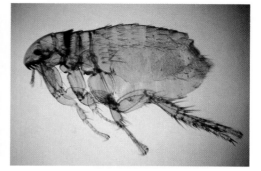

Dog fleas, translucent, wingless, and almost microscopic, are nonetheless a bane to animals and humans alike.

Daisy fleabane, while lovely, often invades hay fields and ruins the taste of the crops.

Flax *Linum*

Once grown on pioneer farms to produce the yarn from which settlers wove linen cloth, flax cultivation is now limited to California and western Canada, mostly Manitoba. However, it is no longer grown for fiber, but as an industrial oil seed crop: flaxseeds yield the linseed oil used in linoleum, oilcloth, paints, and varnishes. Most of Canada's crop is exported to the United States, Europe and Japan.

Originally imported from Europe, where it had been used for making rope, fishnets, and fabric since ancient times, flax has long since escaped from cultivation. It now survives in fields and waste places of western Canada and the United States as a graceful annual wildflower up to three feet tall. Clusters of small five-petaled sky-blue flowers open from February to May and blossom until September, adding cheerful splashes of color to the sandy, well-drained sites the plant favors. Several native flaxes also grow throughout the United States, including a yellow-flowered species found in Eastern woodlands and a copper-colored variety that thrives from Texas to Canada.

Flea

Tiny blood-sucking insects that live on dogs, cats, rodents, birds, and humans, these wingless pests can move easily through hair and feathers. Equipped with powerful leg muscles, fleas also can leap indiscriminately from one host to another. The dog flea, one-tenth of an inch long, can jump seven inches high and more than one foot horizontally. As they move from animal to animal, fleas help spread a number of ailments. The dog flea, for example, is involved in the transmission of the dog tapeworm. Another, the oriental rat flea, is notorious for its role in spreading the dreaded bubonic plague.

Fleabane *Erigeron*

Whether low and sprawling or growing up to three feet tall, the fleabanes all bear daisylike flowers in shades of white, pink, purple, blue, or more rarely, yellow or orange. Found from coast to coast in habitats that range from moist meadows to dry rocky slopes, the plants might easily be confused with asters, except that most of the fleabanes bloom earlier, in summer rather than the fall. Their name recalls a time when pungent fleabanes were hung in homes to drive away fleas. Today some of them serve a similar purpose, with oil of fleabane being used as an ingredient in insect repellants.

Flicker See *Woodpecker*.

Flint See *Chert*.

A flood can turn a relatively placid river into a raging torrent that cuts a swath of destruction across the land, undermining roads and buildings, ripping out buried pipes and wiring, and etching gullies into formerly flat terrain.

F

Flood

Among nature's most destructive phenomena, floods occur when heavy rains or rapidly melting snow cause streams or rivers to overflow. A river flood of this sort may produce a mild soaking of the surrounding land, or it may result in a major disaster in which people, homes, and bridges are swept away. In mountainous areas, torrential downpours sometimes result in flash floods, which often strike without warning. In 1972 a flash flood in Rapid City, South Dakota, killed more than 200 unwary people.

Floods also occur in coastal areas, when hurricanes batter the shore and swamp low-lying areas with storm-driven walls of water. Such was the case when Hurricane Hazel swept southern Ontario in October 1954 causing 81 deaths. Coastal regions may also be submerged by tsunamis, mountainous tidal waves generated by earthquakes on the ocean floor. Twenty-seven people drowned when a tsunami pummeled Newfoundland in 1929.

One of North America's worst floods, in 1889, was caused not by nature but by human neglect. A dam burst near Johnstown, Pennsylvania, and sent a raging torrent into the valley below, sweeping away homes, locomotives, and everything else in its way. More than 2,000 people lost their lives in the disaster.

Flood plain

The flatlands bordering a river and composed of sediments deposited by the river are called its flood plain. When a river is moving swiftly, particles of sand and silt are carried along in suspension, but when the river overflows its banks in flood, the water immediately slows down and drops its load of sediment, forming the plain. The flood plains of young streams may be only a few feet wide, while those of older, meandering rivers like the Mississippi can stretch for miles.

Flounder See *Flatfish*.

Flower

Whether large and showy or small and inconspicuous, all flowers serve the same purpose: they produce the seeds that enable flowering plants to perpetuate their kind. While their structure varies from species to species, the basic design includes one or more female organs, called pistils, at the center; these are surrounded by male organs, called stamens, and then by rings of petals and sepals. The sepals, usually green, enclose the bud before the flower opens. The petals, often colorful, serve to attract pollinators such as bees and butterflies.

Each stamen consists of a pollen-bearing structure (the anther) atop a slender stalk (the filament). The pistil has a sticky or fuzzy top, called the stigma, which traps pollen. Once a grain of pollen has landed on the stigma, a tube grows down the necklike style into the ovary, where the plant's egg cells, or ovules, are fertilized and develop into seeds.

There are countless variations on this basic plan. Besides differences in the number, size, shape, and arrangement of the various parts, for example, some species have separate male and female flowers or even male and female plants.

Flowering plant

From grasses and wildflowers to towering trees, flowering plants far outnumber such nonflowering types as conifers, ferns, and mosses and truly dominate the earth today. Despite differences in size, shape, and habitat, all flowering plants are similar in the way they reproduce. In contrast to the seeds of conifers, which are borne unprotected on the scales of cones, the seeds of flowering plants are enclosed within ovaries that, sometimes along with other floral parts, develop into fruits.

Rockrose

Common blue violet

Blossoms come in an astonishing variety of colors, scents, sizes, and shapes, from the simple rockrose and the elegant lady's slipper to the complex sunflower, a composite made up of hundreds of tiny individual flowers.

Yellow lady's slipper

Sunflower

F

Ohio spiderwort

Style   Stigma

Petal

Ovary

Anther
Filament

Stamen

Ovule

Sepal

Receptacle

Flower stalk

The anatomy of a flower reveals an array of structures whose combined purpose is reproduction. Ovules, or eggs, within the ovary must first be fertilized by pollen before yielding the seeds that produce new plants.

135

The American hover fly is a gardener's friend; its larvae prey on destructive insects.

The male vermilion flycatcher has a Spanish name that means "little coal of fire."

Fly

Distinguished by having just one pair of wings (most insects have two pairs), the true flies nevertheless are able fliers. The adults of some species drink nectar and other liquids, some kinds suck blood, and others eat nothing at all. The larvae of many flies are known as maggots and feed on dead and decaying organic matter.

Perhaps the best-known member of the group is the house fly, a pest that breeds in filth and transmits such diseases as typhoid fever and cholera. Mosquitoes also are true flies. The females are the ones that bite, with various kinds transmitting malaria, yellow fever, and other illnesses. The black fly, another pest, has a vicious bite that is all too familiar in wooded areas of the Northeast in early summer.

Flies can, however, be useful as well. Some kinds parasitize insect pests and help keep them under control. Many are eaten by larger animals. Because of their impressive reproductive potential, flies have found their way into the research laboratory: geneticists are quick to point out that significant advances have been made in the field of heredity by studying the characteristics of succeeding generations of fruit flies.

Flycatcher

Nearly three dozen species of flycatchers, including the kingbirds, the phoebes, and the wood pewees, are found in North America. They earned their name from their habit of darting from perches to snatch passing insects in flight. Alert and upright in posture, the birds flit swiftly out to snap up prey, often with an audible click of their broad, flattened bills.

Ranging up to 16 inches in length, most flycatchers are rather drab and nondescript, clad in olive, brown, or dull gray. One exception is the male vermilion flycatcher, which is bright red and black. Another, the scissor-tailed flycatcher, is pale gray with pinkish sides and very long outer tail feathers. Besides being beautiful, the scissortail is notable for its courtship ritual. The male flutters downward in an intricate flight pattern, concluding his descent with several neatly executed somersaults. The scissortail and most other flycatchers build cup-shaped nests, generally in the open but sometimes in tree cavities or crevices in rocks. All species are territorial, with the kingbirds even attacking crows and hawks that trespass on their turf.

Flying fish

Often taking to the air in swarms, silvery, bullet-shaped flying fish can sail above the sea at 35 miles per hour. By spreading their enlarged pectoral (forward) fins like wings and sculling with their tails, they become airborne and glide above the waves, sometimes for hundreds of feet. They fly not to amuse themselves but to escape predators such as tuna and dolphinfish. Each species is dubbed either monoplane or biplane, depending on whether its members use just the pectoral fins alone or both the pectoral and pelvic (rear) fins to glide. Among the more common biplanes are the Atlantic and the California flying fish. The latter, at 18 inches, is one of the largest members of the family and is considered excellent eating.

Flying squirrel

Big-eyed and covered with soft velvety fur, these charming creatures of the treetops do not actually fly, as their name implies, but glide from tree to tree. Launching themselves from limbs, flying squirrels spread out the folds of skin that extend along each side between front and hind legs, and sail through the air. Using their broad tails as rudders, they can glide for 150 feet.

Strictly nocturnal, flying squirrels love old, rotten trees with plenty of cavities and snags. Some build nests of leaves and lichens, but most prefer to use old woodpecker holes as dens and nurseries. Sociable creatures, they frequently share their dens with other squirrels.

About 10 inches long, including the tail, the

F

Along the Atlantic Flyway, the Chesapeake Bay area is a vital rest stop for migrating waterfowl.

F

The thick fogs for which San Francisco is famous are formed when warm, moist air from the Pacific passes over the chilly waters offshore. As the air cools, its water vapor condenses into soupy fog that is carried inland and obscures the city.

southern flying squirrel inhabits broad-leaved and mixed forests throughout the eastern United States. Its larger relative, the northern flying squirrel, is found in evergreen forests in Canada and the northern United States, as well as farther south in the mountains.

Flyway

On their seasonal flights to and from their breeding grounds, many migratory birds travel along well-defined north-south routes known as flyways. Broad in some places and narrow in others, these paths provide links between feeding areas, where the birds can stop to rest and refuel. The four main flyways in North America are the Atlantic Flyway, along the Atlantic Coast; the Mississippi Flyway, which follows the Mississippi Valley; the Central Flyway, more or less parallel to the Rocky Mountains; and the Pacific Flyway, along the Pacific Coast.

Ducks, geese, and swans are the birds that most commonly use these migratory corridors. For these waterfowl, the flyways connect impor-

tant marshes, lakes, and wildlife refuges. Other birds, such as shorebirds, also rely on feeding areas along the routes—stopovers that are essential for their survival. The loss of even one feeding site (to development, for instance, or to pollution) could interfere with migration, because the next stop on the route might be too far away for the hungry, tired birds to reach.

Fog

The dense, ground-hugging clouds of suspended water droplets known as fog can cover the land like clammy shrouds. They often occur on calm, clear nights when the ground cools, chilling the air above it enough for water vapor in the air to condense into visible droplets. Fog may also result when cold air passes over warm water, causing a steamy cloud to form. Conversely, it can form when warm, moist winds blow over chilly land—along a seacoast, for example—or a cool ocean current. In many areas, dense fogs pose a hazard to motorists and sometimes cause delays at airports.

Fossil footprints preserved in solid rock are exciting reminders of long-extinct dinosaurs. The fossil tracks of mammals, birds, and many other creatures have been found.

F

Dramatic folds contort the limestone layers exposed in this rugged California outcrop.

Most forget-me-nots have sky-blue blooms. One species is the state flower of Alaska.

Fold

Caused by movements in the earth's crust, folds are bends in rock layers. Although rocks are rigid, if enough pressure is applied they become plastic and can be bent or warped without breaking. The resultant rumples vary greatly in size. Some folds are mountainous in scale and extend for miles. Others are gentle ripples only a few inches long. Folds that sag downward are called synclines; those that arch up are known as anticlines.

Fool's gold See *Pyrite*.

Foraminiferan

Single-celled, mostly marine animals found in all oceans, foraminiferans are best known for their beautiful, elaborately structured shells, which in most species are composed of calcium

carbonate. Threadlike extensions of the body protrude through tiny holes in the shells, enabling the animals to move and feed. When the creatures die, their shells sink to the bottom. So numerous are they that their remains form an ooze covering about 30 percent of the ocean floor. And so abundant have they been over the past 420 million years that in many areas foraminiferan fossils are the major component of massive deposits of limestone and chalk.

Forget-me-not *Myosotis*

Flourishing along stream banks and in other moist locations across the continent are several kinds of forget-me-nots, among them the familiar five-petaled sky-blue flower with the bright yellow eye at its center. Erect or sprawling plants no more than two feet tall, these delightful wildlings bear their dainty nosegays of blue, white, or occasionally pink blooms from late spring until early fall.

Fossil

Each one a bit of evidence in the mystery of life's past, fossils are remnants of plants and animals that have been preserved from prehistoric times. Most were formed when dead plants or animals were quickly buried, protecting them from scavengers. Since flesh and other soft parts usually decayed before they could be preserved, the most common fossils are teeth, bones, shells, and other hard parts.

The majority of fossils are petrified, or turned to stone. In some cases dissolved minerals simply filled the tiny air spaces in bones or shells,

Four-o'clocks, with blooms that open late in the day and fade the following morning, are usually pollinated by night-flying moths.

Red fox pups, playful and inquisitive, can often be seen near the entrance to their den, which is usually the abandoned burrow of some other animal.

F

strengthening the original object. In other cases all of the original animal or plant gradually dissolved and was replaced bit by bit by minerals. Natural molds were formed when entire organisms disappeared after sediments hardened around them. If minerals later filled the mold, the result was a natural cast—an exact replica of the organism. Flat objects such as leaves or feathers often left thin molds called prints.

Fossils of insects are often found in amber, or fossilized resin, where they were trapped in ancient times. The footprints of dinosaurs and other extinct animals were sometimes preserved in hardened mud and clay. In rare instances, the entire bodies of mastodons and other large animals were preserved in ice or tar.

Fossils are found only in sedimentary rocks, such as limestone, sandstone, and shale. While erosion sometimes exposes them on the surface of the earth, most collectors know that manmade quarries and road cuts are among the best places to hunt for these clues to life long ago.

Four-o'clock *Mirabilis*

Named for their habit of blooming as the day wanes, the four-o'clocks are handsome, brightly colored wildflowers. The Southwest claims the greatest variety, including the sweet four-o'clock, which flaunts six-inch tubular blossoms of white or pink atop sticky three-foot stems. Another one—the Colorado, or desert, four-o'clock—is a sprawling annual that yields spectacular displays of two-inch purplish trumpets.

Fox

Traditional symbols of cunning and craftiness, foxes are, in fact, agile, intelligent, and above all, adaptable creatures. Bushy-tailed, long-snouted members of the dog family, they are quick and skillful hunters that eat a broad range of wild fare, including insects, rabbits, berries, and all sorts of rodents.

The most common and widespread of the North American foxes are red foxes. Surprisingly small under their luxurious, usually flame-red coats—on the average, about 10 pounds—they hunt in fields and along woodland edges with catlike stealth. Gray foxes, also widespread but most common in the South, are unusual in their ability to climb trees—a rarity in the dog family. The Prairies and arid parts of the southwestern United States are home to the tiny kit foxes, nocturnal hunters with oversized ears. The Arctic foxes live in the Far North. Brown or gray during the summer months, they spend their time hunting on the tundra; in winter they turn white and move out onto the pack ice, scavenging in the wake of polar bears.

F

The foxgloves' name is of uncertain origin, but its tubular blooms have inspired a number of equally fanciful nicknames, including witches' thimble and bluidy (bloody) man's fingers.

Foxglove *Digitalis*

Pretty but poisonous, the foxgloves are powerful medicinal plants. An extract of their leaves, digitalis, is one of the most effective medicines for certain heart diseases.

During their first year of growth, these robust biennials form lush rosettes of ground-hugging, wrinkled, tongue-shaped leaves. Then, in their second season, they send up tall stalks lined with lovely bell-shaped flowers. The common foxglove, native to Europe, was introduced by physicians in the 1700's; its spires of purple-flecked rose or white blossoms now brighten moist clearings, stream banks, and shady spots across most of North America.

Fritillary

Boldly patterned with dark spots on the upper sides of their wings and, in many cases, with silvery spots on the undersides, the tawny to orange fritillaries include some of North America's most striking butterflies. The larger kinds, known as the greater fritillaries, are so named for their broader wingspans; they flit over meadows and bogs, visiting thistles and other flowers. One of the more common species, the great spangled fritillary, is found from Canada south to Georgia, New Mexico, and central California. The lesser fritillaries are small, swift fliers that range as far north as the Arctic.

Frog

Smooth-skinned, tailless creatures with bulging eyes and powerful hind legs adapted for leaping and swimming, frogs are the most familiar of our amphibians. They are found from the Arctic to the tropics, and range in size from tiny cricket frogs, sometimes a mere half inch long, to bass-voiced, eight-inch bullfrogs. Most have thin, moist skin and must live in or near water; others live on land but return to the water to breed.

In spring the males raucously summon the females with a variety of mating calls, each species sounding its own particular notes. After joining them in the water, the females lay eggs by the hundreds or even the thousands. Covered with a protective, jellylike coating, the fertilized eggs hatch into tadpoles a week to a month later. The tadpoles undergo an amazing transformation as they develop from long-tailed, round-bellied, gill-breathing larvae into tailless, strong-limbed, lung-breathing adults. Bullfrog tadpoles take up to three years to develop into frogs, but most species take just a few months.

Although frogs begin life as vegetarians, they are voracious carnivores as adults. Skilled hunters, they devour huge quantities of insects, as well as spiders, earthworms, and other small creatures, which they catch with their long sticky tongues. Cold-blooded animals, many of the frogs hibernate in winter by burying themselves in mud at the bottom of ponds.

Great spangled fritillaries range from Canada to the southern states.

Gray treefrogs climb with the aid of suction pads on the tips of their toes.

Frost, as on these highbush blueberries, forms when moisture in the air freezes directly onto a cold surface.

F

Frogfish

Plump, round-bodied inhabitants of warm-water seas, frogfish are intricately camouflaged anglers. They entice their prey—usually small fish—within range of their wide mouths by waving a wormlike lure from the end of their "fishing rod," actually a modified spine on the dorsal fin.

Most frogfish rest quietly in place on the ocean floor or crawl about with the help of arm-like pectoral fins. The sargassumfish, one of the best-known species, in contrast, lives not at the bottom of the sea but instead drifts near the surface amid floating forests of sargassum weed. Looking very much like the algae in which it dwells, it creeps among the plants, stalking other inhabitants of the sargassum weed. Sargassumfish have the ability to inflate their bodies by swallowing water or air, most likely as a means of preventing predators from extricating them from their seaweed world.

Froghopper See *Spittlebug*.

Front

Associated with changing weather, a front is the moving boundary between two air masses of different properties. If the advancing air mass is colder than the one it is replacing, the leading edge of colder air is called a cold front; if the advancing air is warmer, the leading edge is called a warm front.

Cold fronts move rapidly, as the denser, heavier cold air drives a wedge under the warm air. Most cold fronts cause brief showers and gusty winds, followed by clear skies and cool, dry conditions. Warm fronts move more slowly, with the advancing warm air gradually sliding up over the heavier, low-lying cold air. They bring layered clouds and longer, steadier rains, which are usually followed by clearing skies and warm, humid air.

When a fast-moving cold front catches up with a slowly advancing warm front, the result is an occluded front. The warm air, now surrounded by colder air, is forced aloft. Trapped over a trough of cool air, the warm air produces rain that lasts for hours.

Frost

The delicate ice crystals that turn grass to silvery white, create feathery patterns on window-panes, and lend a magical quality to other surfaces are known as frost. It is formed—usually on cold, cloudless nights—when air saturated with moisture comes in contact with below-freezing surfaces near the ground. Unlike frozen dew, which occurs when dewdrops freeze after a fall in temperature, frost is formed from water vapor that has crystallized directly into ice without passing through the liquid stage.

141

Not All Fruits Are Sweet and Juicy

Fruits fall into a number of botanical categories. Simple fruits, which may be fleshy, hard, or papery, are formed from a single ovary, while complex fruits develop from more than one ovary.

Simple fruits

DRUPE

BERRY

LEGUME

Locust pod

Peach

Tomato

SAMARA

NUT

Maple

Acorn

Complex fruits

AGGREGATE FRUIT

Achene

Strawberry

MULTIPLE FRUIT

Mulberry

Fruit

Botanically speaking, acorns, cucumbers, bean pods, and even grains of wheat all are fruits. The mature seed-bearing structures of flowering plants, fruits develop from the flowers' ovaries and, sometimes, associated floral parts. They can be sweet and fleshy, like apples and cherries, or dry and papery, like milkweed pods. Fruits are classified according to their structure. Simple fruits, for example, develop from a single ovary, while complex fruits derive from more than one. Those with stony pits, such as peaches and plums, are called drupes; pods, like those of peas and beans, are legumes; and the winged fruits of maples and elms are known as samaras. Apples and pears are called pomes; their edible flesh is actually swollen stem tissue. So is the ripe flesh of a strawberry; the seeds on its surface are in fact tiny individual fruits called achenes.

Fruit fly

Tiny insects that lay their eggs on fruit or decaying vegetation, fruit flies of various kinds are found all over the country. The Mediterranean fruit fly, for example, is a serious pest that periodically infests citrus crops. The well-known vinegar fly, *Drosophila melanogaster,* in contrast, has benefited humanity, for it has proved to be an ideal subject for the study of heredity.

Fulmar *Fulmarus glacialis*

Stocky seabirds that look like thick-necked gulls, fulmars spend most of their life gliding over far northern seas. They feed mainly on fish and squid but also trail fishing boats to scavenge for cast-off wastes. Like their relatives the petrels, fulmars have tubelike nostrils atop their beaks. When disturbed, they regurgitate a thick, smelly oil and spit it at enemies. The name fulmar, in fact, means foul gull.

Fumarole

Often hissing with steam, fumaroles are vents in the earth that emit water vapor, carbon dioxide, and other volcanic gases. They are found in volcanic areas such as Yellowstone National Park, where molten magma lies relatively close to the surface. The discharge from some fumaroles is mainly steam; in others the water vapor carries along a mixture of volatile, sometimes noxious, gases escaping from the lava.

Fungus

Molds, mildews, yeasts, and the familiar mushrooms all are fungi. Although they have traditionally been considered plants, fungi differ in so many ways that some scientists now place them in a separate kingdom. Unlike green plants, for example, fungi have no chlorophyll to make their own food and so must absorb nutrients from other organisms, living or dead.

Most fungi are microscopic, but even those that yield mushrooms or other visible structures consist mainly of underground masses of fine cottony threads. A mushroom is the fungus's fruiting body and exists solely to make spores that, scattered by wind and water, develop into new fungi.

Many of the fungi form partnerships with plants. Lichens, for instance, consist of algae and fungi that live in close association. Other fungi are attached to the roots of living plants, providing them with mineral nutrients and receiving food in return. Many plants, such as orchids, cannot survive without the help of fungi.

Fungi also cause diseases, including ringworm, athlete's foot, and the rusts and smuts that afflict many crop plants. But mostly they are beneficial. Fungi enrich the soil by assisting in decay; they cause the fermentation that results in alcohol; they produce antibiotics and other life-saving drugs. And of course many mushrooms are good to eat.

The Fanciful Forms of Fungi

Fungi can assume a variety of fascinating shapes. Although some detective work is needed to pinpoint a particular species, the broad groups are easy to identify. Most familiar are the mushrooms, which have distinct stalks and caps. Others may grow in the form of cups, crusts, shelves, coral-like stalks, or irregular masses of jelly.

Fungi without distinct caps and stalks

SHELF-SHAPED
Bracket fungi

JELLYLIKE MASS
Jelly fungi

LEATHERY CRUST
Parchment fungi

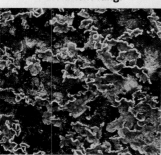

UPRIGHT STALKS
Coral fungi

Fungi with distinct stalks and caps

CAP DOMED OR UMBRELLA-SHAPED

Gills under cap	Smooth under cap
Gilled mushrooms	**Boletes and others**

CAP ROUNDED AND PITTED | CAP FUNNEL-SHAPED

Morels	**Chanterelles and others**

SPHERICAL MASS

Ball only	Ball with starlike "husk"
Puffballs	**Earthstars**

SMALL BOWL-SHAPED STRUCTURE

Bowl empty	Bowl containing "eggs"
Cup fungi	**Bird's nest fungi**

F

Crystals of galena glimmer with a grayish sheen. This principal ore of lead is sometimes called "lead glance," a reference to its distinctive luster.

The gallinule is a strong swimmer despite the fact that its feet are not webbed.

Galls on plants such as maple trees (upper) and goldenrod (lower) are often opened by birds that want to get at the larvae inside.

G

Gabbro

A dark, coarse-grained igneous rock, gabbro forms by slow cooling and crystallization of magma deep within the earth. Common in the Adirondack Mountains of New York, it often contains the green mineral olivine, as well as feldspar and large amounts of iron-rich minerals such as pyroxene. Sometimes sold under the name black granite, gabbro is widely used as a building stone, and it is especially popular for decorative facings.

Galena

The shiny blue-gray mineral known as galena is the principal ore of lead. It forms impressive cubic or eight-sided crystals, and fine specimens have been uncovered in Oklahoma, Kansas, Missouri, and Illinois. (Galena, Illinois, was named for the extensive deposits of ore that gained it prominence as a 19th-century lead mining center.) Often found in limestone, many galena deposits also contain silver and are frequently mined for that metal as well. Extracting lead from galena is a simple process; pioneers, in fact, simply tossed lumps of the ore into hot fires to obtain lead for bullets. Galena was important in the early years of radio, when its crystals were used in crystal radio sets.

Gall

The warty or tumorlike growths often seen on the leaves, stems, and other parts of plants are known as galls. Most of them are caused by small insects that lay their eggs in the plant tissue. When the larva hatches from the egg, its

The northern gannet, with its majestic six-foot wingspan, alternately flaps its wings and glides as it soars above the sea. When its spots a school of fish, it plunges headfirst into the water.

presence stimulates the abnormal growth of the tissue surrounding it. The larva is not only protected inside the gall but also feeds on the swollen plant tissue. Chief among the gall-forming insects are gall flies, tiny wasps, midges, and aphids. Bacteria, fungi, and minute worms called nematodes can also stimulate the production of galls, often on the roots of plants. Each gall maker has its own particular host plant and forms galls of characteristic shapes and sizes. Although galls are usually small, crown galls on tree trunks, caused by bacteria, can be as much as two feet across. Most galls cause little damage to their host plants, but others, such as those produced by Hessian flies, can result in serious crop damage.

Gallinule *Porphyrula martinica*

At home in freshwater wetlands in the South, the purple gallinule, or marsh hen, is shaped like a chicken. Its brilliant colors, however, make it stand out like a jewel. In addition to its handsome green and purple plumage, the gallinule sports a striking yellow-tipped red bill and a powder-blue shield on the forehead. Ill-equipped for swift flight, it prefers to wade through reeds and pickerelweed and occasionally climbs into low bushes. Its long yellow toes also enable the gallinule to tread with quiet grace across the tops of lily pads.

Living on the bounty of the marsh, gallinules eat frogs, snails, aquatic insects, eggs, and seeds. They build nests one to five feet above the water in shrubs or other vegetation and raise broods of six to eight young. Their similar-looking cousin, the common moorhen, used to be known as the common gallinule.

Gannet *Morus bassanus*

Goose-sized seabirds with stout, pointed bills, northern gannets are renowned plunge divers. Sighting a school of fish—usually herring or mackerel—they hurtle seaward from heights of 50 feet or more and hit the water with a tremendous splash. A reinforced skull and air cells in the neck and breast help absorb the impact.

In winter northern gannets range from Massachusetts to Florida and the Gulf of Mexico; in summer they gather in the North Atlantic to breed in huge, noisy colonies on seaside cliffs. Gannets mate for life and return to the same nesting spot each year. When one bird arrives at the nest of dried seaweed and debris to relieve its mate on their single egg, it is welcomed with rituals that include the tossing of seaweed. Both birds may bow, point their bills skyward, and strike them like swords against each other. When their young finally takes wing, it spends the next three or four years at sea before returning to shore for the first time to breed.

Gap

Rivers sometimes slice straight across mountain ridges in deep valleys known as water gaps. The valleys usually began forming long ago when the river flowed across a level plain. As the surrounding land was worn away, exposing a layer of more resistant rock, the river etched its course downward through the ridge, forming the defile. The Delaware Water Gap is one of many found in the Appalachians. The Oldman River Gap is well known in southern Alberta. If the stream is later diverted, leaving the gap dry, it is called a wind gap.

G

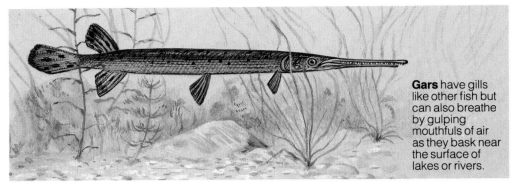

Gars have gills like other fish but can also breathe by gulping mouthfuls of air as they bask near the surface of lakes or rivers.

G

A garter snake, enjoying a moment in the sun, remains on the alert for passing prey.

Gar *Lepisosteus*

Bullet-shaped fish with pointed snouts and rows of needle-sharp teeth, gars have skins covered with thick, diamond-shaped scales so tough that they can deflect spears and arrows. Several species inhabit lakes and rivers of the eastern and central United States, and they sometimes venture into brackish coastal waters. They often float in the water with an eerie stillness, springing to life only when prey fish blunder near.

Gars can grow up to 10 feet in length. The largest species, the alligator gar, weighs up to 200 pounds and is one of the most formidable freshwater fish. They are not, however, much sought as sport fish; their flesh, though edible, is not very tasty, and their roe is poisonous.

Garnet

Glassy, hard, and richly colored, garnets have been prized as gemstones since antiquity. The intensely red variety called pyrope (Greek for "fire-eyed") has even been sold as imitation ruby. Though the garnets valued as gems usually are red or purplish, the crystals also come in shades of orange, yellow, green, and black. Composed of silica and a variety of metallic elements, they get their colors from their differing metallic contents. The crystals, found embedded in various, usually metamorphic rocks, are generally less than an inch across, though a mine at Gore Mountain, New York, has yielded specimens some three feet in diameter. Most of the garnet mined commercially today is used in industrial abrasives for grinding and polishing.

Garter snake *Thamnophis*

Marked with three light stripes along the length of their bodies, garter snakes were named for their supposed resemblance to the fancy garters men once wore to support their hose. Garden snake might, however, be a more appropriate name, for these familiar, harmless reptiles thrive in parks and gardens as well as in pastures, meadows, and marshes. With a dozen or so species found from coast to coast, garter snakes are most often seen in early spring, their mating season. Bearing live young instead of laying eggs, they are among the most prolific North American snakes: though litters average fewer than 20, the common garter snake sometimes produces nearly 100 offspring at a time.

Gayfeather See *Blazing star*.

Gecko

Named for the *geck-o* cry of an Oriental species, the geckos are unusual among reptiles for their ability to produce sounds at all. While some bark and others chirp, the commonest species, the banded gecko, simply squeaks in protest when alarmed. A harmless little lizard up to six inches long, it lives in canyons and among the dunes and rocky hillsides of the arid Southwest. Hiding in crevices by day, it comes out at night to feed on insects and spiders, which it captures with lightning-quick flicks of its long, sticky-tipped tongue.

Gemstone

Minerals prized for their beauty, durability, and rarity are known as gemstones. Used since ancient times for jewelry and ornament, they also have been kept as talismans and credited with curing ills as diverse as snakebites and dysentery. Of the 2,500 or so rock-forming minerals, less than 100 are considered gemstones, and only about 20 are of extreme value.

The banded gecko, a little ground-dwelling lizard, is the most widely distributed species of its kind in the United States.

Western fringed gentians provide a summery ribbon of color along the Rocky Mountains from Canada as far south as Arizona.

When removed from the earth, most gemstones look like dull lumps of rock. Their beauty is brought out by cutting, shaping, and polishing. Stones such as amethyst are faceted to reveal their brilliance, or "fire"; others with interesting colors or patterns—opal or cat's-eye, for instance—are polished, not cut. Among the several gemstones found in North America are nephrite jade in British Columbia, agates and opals in Manitoba, amethysts in Ontario and Nova Scotia, sapphires in Montana, and tourmalines in California and Maine.

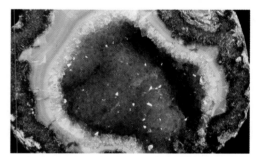

A geode, cut open to reveal its inner beauty, is lined with a dazzling array of jewellike, perfectly formed crystals of amethyst.

Gentian *Gentiana*

Lovely, brightly colored wildflowers, gentians are relatively rare in the East but are a chief ornament of the western mountains. The Rockies alone host some 20 species, most notably the western fringed gentian. Adopted as the official symbol of Yellowstone National Park, this hardy annual paints moist meadows throughout the summer with a palette of purple-blue blossoms. The four petals on each vase-shaped flower are edged with a fringe that fences out plundering insects, reserving the sweet nectar for pollinating bees. The very similar eastern fringed gentian, a three-foot biennial of sunny meadows, bears up to 100 cerulean blooms in early fall. Another—the closed, or bottle, gentian—has deep blue flask-shaped flowers that never open; bumblebees can shoulder their way in, but if lesser insects follow, they risk entombment.

Geode

Hollow nodules of stone with inner cavities that are lined with crystals or layers of minerals, geodes are among nature's surprises, for their beauty is not revealed until they are cut open. They form over long periods of time when cavities in rocks are filled with water containing dissolved quartz or other minerals; the minerals in the water gradually come out of solution and are deposited on the walls of the cavity. If the quartz has few impurities and is deposited relatively quickly, colored layers of fine-grained quartz called agate are formed. Slower deposition results in a lining of beautiful inward-pointing crystals. In North America these delightful oddities are most common in the limestones of the Mississippi and Ohio valleys.

Wild geraniums have been a mainstay in herbal medicine for hundreds of years.

Beehive geyser, one of Yellowstone's wonders, sends a dramatic plume 150 feet into the air at unpredictable intervals.

Geranium *Geranium*

Whether white, pink, or purple, the flowers of the many kinds of wild geraniums found in North America always have five petals, five sepals, and stamens in multiples of five. The leaves are usually lobed or deeply divided. The most distinctive features of the plants, however, are their fruits—long beaklike capsules that have earned some species the name cranesbill. Other well-known species include the pink-flowered herb Robert, widespread in the East, and the dove's-foot geranium, a common weed on lawns in the West.

Geyser

Periodically erupting with explosive bursts of steam and hot water, geysers are one of the great spectacles of nature. Some are notable for the regularity of their eruptions; the world's most famous geyser, Old Faithful in Yellowstone National Park, emits its scalding plume more or less on schedule. With a total of some 3,000 geysers and hot springs, Yellowstone ranks as the world's largest geyser field. Geysers are also found in California.

These fascinating natural fountains occur only in areas where pockets of magma, or molten rock, lie close to the earth's surface and heat the overlying rock. Groundwater seeping into a geyser's tube is heated by contact with the rock. The water does not readily come to a boil, however, since an increase in pressure (caused in this case by the weight of the water above it) raises the boiling point of a liquid. Eventually, however, some of the water does reach this elevated boiling point and flashes into steam, forc-

ing water to spill from the top of the tube. With this sudden drop in pressure, superheated water farther down is vaporized, causing the entire column of steam and superheated water to erupt in one explosive jet. As soon as the eruption ends, more water begins to seep into the geyser's tube, setting the stage for the next show.

Giant sequoia *Sequoiadendron giganteum*

Among the most massive of living things, the giant sequoias, while not the tallest trees, often weigh more than 1,000 tons. Yet these stately evergreen behemoths sprout from seeds so tiny that 5,500 of them weigh barely an ounce. Remarkably hardy and long-lived, the trees grow only at altitudes of 5,000 to 7,000 feet in a few dozen groves that lie scattered along a 280-mile stretch of the Sierra Nevada's western slope. Sheathed in rich reddish-brown bark that is resistant to both fires and insects, many have lived for 3,000 years or more. Pyramidal in outline when young, the giant sequoias, which have scalelike needles, become craggy and rounded as they age.

Gila monster *Heloderma suspectum*

Easily identified by its bold colors and patterns, the Gila monster is a stocky lizard up to two feet long. It has a thickened tail in which it stores fat for use when food is in short supply, and it is covered with small scales that give its skin a

The bird's-eye gilia, native to the foothills of California, is distinctly tricolored and has become a well-known rock garden plant.

Giant sequoias filter sunlight through their sky-scraping branches. The 275-foot General Sherman tree, its trunk almost 103 feet around at the base, holds the current record for size.

G

mainly on small mammals, which are killed by its venom. It also eats the eggs of other reptiles and of birds.

The Gila monster is a sluggish creature that usually avoids human beings. But it can, if disturbed, twist its body with surprising speed and deliver a powerful, bulldog-stubborn bite that permits its poisonous saliva to seep slowly from its lower jaw into the victim's wound. Although the Gila monster is widely feared, its bite, though painful, is rarely fatal to humans.

Gilia *Gilia*

Found mainly in the western states, the gilias are a group of some two dozen rather modest wildflowers. Most have delicate, finely cut foliage and trumpet-shaped flowers that flare out with five lobes at the top. The blooms of the bird's-eye gilia, a common wildflower on grasslands throughout most of California, are attractively tricolored in shades of pale blue, dark blue, and yellow. The densely clustered flower heads of blue-headed, or globe, gilia each contain up to 100 individual flowers; with stamens protruding from the trumpets, the rounded clusters look a bit like pastel pincushions. California gilia, found mainly in the Coast Ranges, is quite similar, but its clusters contain fewer flowers and are sometimes fan shaped.

The Gila monster gets its name from the Gila River, which flows through the southwestern United States. The river, in turn, takes its name from an Indian tribe.

beaded look. Native to the deserts of Arizona and New Mexico, the Gila monster and a close relative, the Mexican beaded lizard, are the only venomous lizards in the world.

Shy and largely nocturnal, the Gila monster remains hidden by day in rocky crevices or burrows. But by dusk it starts to prowl, preying

149

Gills Come in Many Forms

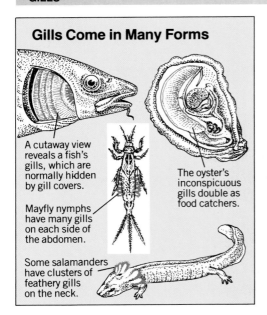

A cutaway view reveals a fish's gills, which are normally hidden by gill covers.

The oyster's inconspicuous gills double as food catchers.

Mayfly nymphs have many gills on each side of the abdomen.

Some salamanders have clusters of feathery gills on the neck.

The ginkgo is easily identified by its distinctive fan-shaped leaves.

American ginseng flowers are later replaced by red berries.

Gills

Many freshwater and marine animals are equipped with gills, specialized breathing organs that take up dissolved oxygen from the water and release carbon dioxide. Gills have thin, membranous walls through which these gases can pass easily, and they are usually filled with blood or body fluids.

The gills of fish, tadpoles, and permanently aquatic salamanders are located in the neck region. On fish they are usually protected by hard plates (the gill covers), but they are exposed and feathery on tadpoles and salamanders.

On clams, oysters, and other bivalve mollusks, the gills are thin flaps of flesh. Straining food particles from the water that passes across them, they are used for feeding as well as breathing. Other mollusks, including many snails, have feathery gills.

The aquatic larvae of many insects, such as mayflies, damselflies, and stoneflies, also are equipped with gills—usually feathery or leaflike structures on the tip or sides of the abdomen. No insects have gills as adults, however. Nor do a host of very small aquatic animals that absorb oxygen directly through the skin and so do not need gills.

Ginkgo *Ginkgo biloba*

The sole survivor of an ancient family of trees, the ginkgo is notable for its unusual leaves. Quite different from those of any other tree, they are fan shaped, with the veins fanning out from the narrow end. Bright green in spring, they turn yellow before dropping in the fall.

This native of the Far East, also known as the maidenhair tree, probably was saved from extinction by monks who centuries ago began cultivating it in temple gardens in China and Japan. Highly valued as an ornamental, the ginkgo is especially popular in cities because it can tolerate air pollution. Female trees are often destroyed, however, because of the foul odor of their plumlike fruits.

Ginseng *Panax*

The celebrated, supposedly man-shaped roots of these low-growing woodland herbs have long been treasured as a cure-all by Orientals, who claim them effective for treating everything from impotence to diabetes. American ginseng, a close relative of the Chinese species, once carpeted the eastern hardwood forests. But centuries of harvesting for export to China, where the root is in great demand, has severely depleted the native stock. A plant of rich, well-drained soils, American ginseng bears three compound leaves that resemble those of the horse chestnut.

Glacier

The gentle, rolling hills and fertile soils of the Prairies, the cobbled fields and kettle ponds of New England, and the rugged peaks of the West all are evidence of the actions of one of nature's most potent forces: glaciers. Far from being a thing of the past, these great masses of ice still cover 10 percent of the world's land surface. Some, called valley glaciers, form in hollows on high mountain slopes and flow downhill as nar-

The glasswort, when it turns bright red, adds its own touch of color to autumn's palette.

Alaskan glaciers (top) are in the process of creating characteristic U-shaped valleys like this one in the state of Washington (left), carved out long ago during the Ice Age.

G

row rivers of ice. In Canada they are found mainly in the Rocky Mountains and the high-lands of the High Arctic. Others, known as con-tinental glaciers, are giant ice sheets such as those found today in Greenland and Antarctica.

Glaciers form in areas where annual snowfall exceeds melting. As the snow accumulates year after year, it is gradually transformed into ice. Buried under more and more snow, the ice be-comes denser still and, when it reaches a critical thickness and weight, begins to move.

Most glaciers creep along at only a few inches to a few feet per day, plucking, grinding, and tearing at the land on their relentless journey. Alberta's Athabasca Glacier in Jasper National Park glides along at about 23 feet a year, but Yukon's Steele Glacier in Kluane National Park has sometimes surged as many as 75 feet in a day. Whatever their speed, glaciers scour the earth and deposit rocks, sand, and debris in a distinctive fashion. Valley glaciers transport huge blocks of rock, sharpen peaks, and widen and deepen valleys, while the great continental ice sheets override hills, incise grooves into bed-rock, and leave behind deep lakes and gently sloping mounds of debris.

Glasswort *Salicornia*

Stripped down to bare essentials, the glassworts consist of little more than fleshy, jointed stems. The leaves have been reduced to clinging scales, and the tiny flowers are practically hidden in

Globeflowers are increasingly rare in the East and should not be disturbed or picked.

hollows on the upper joints. Plants of salt marshes and other saline areas, the glassworts have a pleasantly salty flavor and so are often picked as salad ingredients. Because they can also be pickled, the glassworts are sometimes known as pickle weeds.

Globeflower *Trollius*

Attractive members of the buttercup family, globeflowers are widespread across much of North America. The Eastern species, found in swamps and marshes, bears yellow springtime blooms. As the snows melt on mountain slopes, the western globeflowers dot high meadows with flowers that are creamy or greenish white. While abundant in the Rockies, globeflowers are endangered in other regions.

The blue-gray gnatcatcher is a lively, alert bird always on the lookout for its next meal.

Goatfish, sporting typical reds and yellows, are a colorful sight, whether in schools (upper) or individually (lower).

The goatsbeard (upper) gets its name from the long hairs on its fruits (lower), which are scattered, parachute-style, by the wind.

Glowworm See *Firefly*.

Gnat

Troublesome pests in many areas, gnats are any of several kinds of tiny, mosquitolike flies. Some are especially irritating because they form large, marauding swarms that attack humans and animals with annoying bites. The eye gnats, which are attracted to human and animal secretions, are thought to transmit pinkeye and other diseases. The larvae of most species live on plants, and some, such as Hessian flies, pose a serious threat to crops.

Gnatcatcher *Polioptila*

Small, active birds, gnatcatchers, as their name implies, feed primarily on tiny insects. Flicking their long tails, they are quite conspicuous as they flit from perch to perch in search of prey. The blue-gray gnatcatcher, the most widespread species, lives in woods and thickets throughout much of the United States. It builds a dainty cuplike nest lined with flower petals, feathers, spiderwebs, and hair and often decorates the outside with bits of lichen.

Gneiss

Coarse-grained and usually marked with alternating light and dark bands, gneiss (pronounced "nice") is a common metamorphic rock. It forms when sedimentary or igneous rocks, such as sandstone or granite, are altered by heat and pressure rearranging and often recrystallizing their minerals. Gneisses are abundant in the Appalachian Mountains in the East and in the Rockies, Cascades, and Sierra Nevada in the West.

The nighthawk, a goatsucker, nests on bare gravelly soil, rocks, or graveled urban roofs.

G

Goatfish

Some 50 species of goatfish, or red mullet, are found around the world in tropical and warm temperate seas. Usually traveling in small schools, they are distinguished by the pair of whiskerlike barbels that hang from their chins. Supposedly resembling a goat's beard, the barbels are sensory probes that the fish use to find the bottom-dwelling invertebrates on which they feed. When not in use, the barbels are folded back in special grooves along the lower jaw.

Goatsbeard *Tragopogon pratensis*

Bearing flowers that resemble dandelions, the yellow goatsbeard is named for its large, white-plumed seed heads. Like the purple-flowered oyster plant, a close relative, it was brought to America by colonists who found the flavor of its taproots reminiscent of oysters. Both species have escaped to the wild and become common weeds in many areas. The goatsbeard's alternate names, noonflower and Jack-go-to-bed-at-noon, allude to the fact that its flowers close at midday.

Goatsucker

Named for the ancient belief that their gaping mouths enable these birds to steal milk from goats, the goatsuckers also are called nightjars, an allusion to the jarring calls of these nocturnal fliers. The goatsuckers' very large mouths in fact are ideally suited for their diet—insects caught in flight. Typically camouflaged in mottled shades of brown and gray, the birds spend most of the day resting on the ground or perched lengthwise along tree limbs.

Perhaps the best-known member of the family is the whip-poor-will, whose name echoes its loud, persistent call. The foot-long chuck-will's-

The bluebanded goby dwells in waters off the coast of southern California.

widow, the largest of our goatsuckers, has a similar call but delivers it at a somewhat slower tempo. Another species, the common nighthawk, is more often seen in flight and is notable for its voracious appetite: one hungry bird was shown to have eaten more than 2,000 insects in a single night.

Goby

Members of an enormous family of fish found mainly in tropical and temperate seas, the gobies are a remarkably varied group. A few kinds are transparent, many are brilliantly colored, and most are less than six inches long. Some burrow in the mud, some live on coral reefs, and others cling to slippery rocks, using suction cups formed from their partially fused pelvic fins. Still other species move into the burrows of shrimp and crabs; live in or near tube sponges and feed on parasitic worms; or even hover, unscathed, among the stinging tentacles of sea anemones. Still others spend their time at "cleaning stations," dining on the parasites that they pick from larger fish.

The American goldfinch, an appealing songster, is sometimes called the thistlebird because it prefers thistle seeds for eating and thistledown for nest building.

Goldenrod, dappling a field with graceful yellow plumes, marks the end of summer. Kentucky and Nebraska both claim goldenrod as their state flower.

G

Gold

Perhaps the most versatile and beautiful of all metals, gold has been treasured by mankind since prehistoric times. Its popularity is not a mystery: gold combines rarity with strength, durability, and shimmering beauty. It can be hammered into paper-thin sheets, stretched into wire, and pounded, cut, or molded into shape. Because it is also soft, however, gold is usually mixed with other metals, such as platinum or nickel, when used for jewelry.

Gold is found in veins, or lodes, and in placer deposits. Glittering in streambeds, placer deposits consist of flakes and nuggets eroded by water from veins or rocks elsewhere. It was the glint of gold in a stream in Georgia that touched off North America's first gold rush in 1828. But the real frenzy began in California in 1849 and continued in 1898 in Yukon, where the Klondike River and its tributaries eventually yielded more than $100 million in gold.

Goldenrod *Solidago*

Flourishing in fields and clearings all across North America, nearly 100 species of goldenrod gild late-summer and autumn landscapes with plumes and spires of mellow gold. Though long condemned as the cause of hay fever, the goldenrods in fact are innocent of the charges. The real culprits are ragweed and other plants that bloom at the same time and produce huge amounts of wind-blown pollen. The Indians valued goldenrod as a cure for numerous ailments. (In

fact, the plant's Latin name means "to make whole.") Early settlers also gathered leaves of the sweet goldenrod to brew a soothing, anise-flavored tea and used the flowers to produce a rich yellow dye.

Goldenseal *Hydrastis canadensis*

The fat yellow roots of goldenseal are marked with leaf scars that do indeed resemble seals stamped into bars of bullion. But those same roots also account for the scarcity of the plant: they were so heavily collected in the past as herbal remedies that goldenseal, once common in eastern woodlands, is now endangered in many areas. A foot or so tall and topped by a pair of maplelike leaves, each stalk bears a single greenish-white flower in spring, which gives way to bright red berries in the fall.

Goldfinch *Carduelis*

Noted for their bright colors and cheerful songs, the goldfinches are sometimes called wild canaries. They are small, gregarious birds that prefer open country and, like other finches, feed primarily on seeds. Even the young are fed a diet of regurgitated seeds.

The most widespread species by far is the American goldfinch. Common across southern Canada and most of the United States, it tends to nest late in the season, when thistledown is available for lining its tightly woven, cup-shaped nest. Breeding males are bright yellow, with a black cap and black wings and tail. The

Majestic snow geese take wing amid a splash of lakewater. Although they are most often white, some snow geese have dark plumage and are known as blue geese.

A boat-tailed grackle, its black feathers shining in the sun, uses its long keellike tail to steer while in flight.

lesser goldfinch, a western species, also has a yellow breast and black cap, but its back varies from greenish to black in different parts of its range. Lawrence's goldfinch, yellow breasted with a distinctive black face patch, is found in California and in areas just north of the Mexican border.

Goose

Honking from on high, clamorous V-shaped flocks of migrating wild geese always are stirring reminders of the changing seasons. Generally larger than ducks, with longer necks and sturdier legs for walking, these widespread waterfowl differ from their smaller cousins in other ways as well. The sexes look alike, making it difficult to tell males from females. Geese are more sociable, migrating and wintering in huge flocks and often nesting in large colonies. While ducks form pairs that last for only a few months, geese usually mate for life, with both parents caring for the young. Geese, moreover, tend to be vegetarians, with short, stout bills that are well suited for grazing on fields, croplands, and even lawns and golf courses.

In North America the most familiar species is the Canada goose, with its long black neck and white chin patch. The snow goose is most common in the western states. The greater white-fronted goose, which often flies with snow geese,

can be recognized by its white face and brown plumage. Another common species is the brant, a small, dark, chunky maritime goose that winters along both the Atlantic and Pacific coasts.

Goosefoot *Chenopodium*

Found along roadsides and in gardens all across North America, the goosefoots are wild relatives of beets and spinach. Our several species range from one to six feet in height, with the lower leaves on some looking a bit like a goose's foot. Plain but prolific, they bear tiny greenish flowers and produce huge crops of seeds—as many as 50,000 per plant. Indians made flour from the seeds, and the leaves of one kind, lamb's quarters, are still used as a substitute for spinach.

Gopher See *Pocket gopher.*

Gopher snake See *Bullsnake.*

Gopher tortoise See *Tortoise.*

Grackle *Quiscalus*

Our three species of grackles are big, glossy members of the blackbird family, with exceptionally long tails. Equipped with stout, all-purpose bills, they are opportunists that eat a wide variety of foods, from grain and grubs to small birds and even minnows. Sociable creatures, they travel in flocks, roost together in winter, and nest in loose colonies.

The common grackle, the smallest, most familiar species, is found almost everywhere east of the Rockies. Both sexes are black and richly iridescent. The boat-tailed grackle, a large bird of coastal marshes in the East, is named for its very long, keeled tail. Males are black, but females are a warm brown. The very similar great-tailed grackle lives from Louisiana to southern California and ranges northward to the southern Great Plains.

G

Stark domes of granite dominate the breathtaking vistas at Yosemite National Park in California, which boasts the world's largest collection of granite domes.

Grass, a large and varied plant family, includes foxtail grass (top) and big bluestem grass (bottom).

Granite

A mosaic of colorful, interlocking crystals, including quartz, feldspar, and mica, granite is one of the principal rocks forming the continents. Its name comes from an Italian word meaning "grainy" and refers to the rock's coarse texture. Granite formed as molten magma slowly cooled deep within the earth's crust. Hard, strong, weather-resistant, and taking a fine polish, it is widely quarried for use as tombstones and in construction.

Grape *Vitis*

Vinland was what the ancient Vikings called North America, and the name still fits, for wild grapes continue to flourish in thickets and woodlands from Canada to Mexico. Fox grapes, frost grapes, and scuppernongs are among the more familiar, widespread species. Climbing by means of twining tendrils, the pliant vines can clamber up to 100 feet into the treetops. Shading their hosts with their own canopies of leaves, grapevines sometimes kill the trees on which they grow. Catbirds, cardinals, and other birds strip shreds of bark from the vines and weave them into their nests. And in the fall, just as in Aesop's fable, foxes are among the many kinds of wildlife that come to feast on the clusters of tart, juicy fruits.

Graphite

Shiny, black, and greasy to the touch, graphite is one of nature's softest minerals. It is composed of carbon atoms arranged in thin layers that slide easily past one another, and so is an excellent lubricant. When mixed with clay for hardness, it makes up the "lead" in pencils. (Its name is derived from the Greek for "to write.") Graphite is also used for battery electrodes, the cores of nuclear reactors, and a number of other industrial purposes.

The lubber grasshopper, which cannot fly, has "ears" located on its abdomen.

Grass

From lawns and pastures to meadows, prairies, and croplands, about half of North America is covered by grasses of various kinds. The cereals that we rely upon for much of our food—corn, rice, wheat, oats, rye, and barley—all are grasses, as is sugar cane. Even more widespread than the cultivated kinds are the wild grasses—some 1,500 species in all—which grow in almost every conceivable habitat, from coastal dunes topped by swaying stands of sea oats to the high mountains of the West, where alpine timothy grows on lofty meadows. Prairie grasses such as buffalo grass and little bluestem once blanketed the Great Plains, thriving in a climate that is too dry to support trees and shrubs.

Most grasses have long, bladelike leaves and hollow stems that are reinforced by solid nodes. They spread both by means of seeds produced by their tiny, inconspicuous flowers, and by creeping stems that take root at intervals and send up new plants. The grasses' fibrous roots protect the soil from erosion, and as the plants decay, they help enrich the topsoil.

G

Grebes are fine swimmers, divers—and parents. A horned grebe (left), with golden "horns" glistening, guards its nest. A graceful western grebe (right) gives its downy chick a ride.

Grasshopper

Well-known for their extraordinary leaps, grasshoppers are also noted for their summer songs. Depending on the species, they produce the sounds by rubbing rough-edged legs against their wings or by rubbing two wings against each other.

The long-horned grasshoppers such as katydids are named for their long antennae. Among short-horned grasshoppers are the lubber grasshoppers, notorious for the havoc that they sometimes produce in the Prairies: occasionally erupting in enormous numbers, the insects become the voracious plagues of locusts that swarm in clouds over cropland, devouring every plant in sight.

Grasshopper mouse *Onychomys*

Unlike most small rodents, which feed on seeds or other plant foods, North America's two species of grasshopper mice are feisty carnivores. Inhabitants of western plains and deserts, the stocky, relatively short-tailed creatures move into the burrows of prairie dogs and other animals and come out at night to hunt. They are sometimes called scorpion mice, an allusion to one of their favorite foods. But they also capture insects, lizards, and small mammals.

Grasslands See pp.158–159.

Grayling *Thymallus arcticus*

Deep, cold lakes and chilly, rushing northern streams are home to the American, or arctic, grayling, esteemed as a sport fish and admired for its beauty. Varying from silvery to brownish in color, these handsome relatives of trout are adorned with high, colorful saillike back fins. Although graylings once ranged south to Utah and Wyoming, they are now scarce in the western states. But they remain plentiful in Canada and Alaska, where prized five-pounders are regularly caught. Game fighters, they rise readily to artificial flies.

Grebe

Among the most skillful of all diving birds, grebes not only plunge headfirst underwater; they also can sink slowly out of sight by compressing their feathers and driving out trapped air, thus making themselves less buoyant. Grebes, in fact, are so well adapted to life in the water that they seldom fly, and many birders have never seen one on the wing.

Most of the grebes are noted for their elaborate courtship dances. Mated pairs build floating, raft-like nests anchored to marsh plants, where both parents tend the clutch of two to eight chalky, plant-stained eggs. Feeding on a wide variety of aquatic life, grebes also eat large quantities of their own feathers. Besides lining the stomach and protecting it from damage by fish bones and shell fragments, the feathers apparently slow down the bones' passage through the digestive system, giving them more time to dissolve.

The long-necked western and Clark's grebes are the largest of the seven North American species. Others include the somewhat smaller red-necked grebe, the wide-ranging pied-billed grebe, and the handsomely plumed horned and eared grebes of western prairie marshes.

Greenbrier *Smilax*

Woody vines that inch their way upward by clinging with twining tendrils to any available supports, the dozen or so greenbriers—most of them armed with thorns—create impenetrable tangles along eastern streams, roadsides, and woodland edges. They bear rounded clusters of tiny greenish-white flowers, which mature into hard, red to black berries. One species, the carrion flower, is thornless but armed instead with a repugnant odor.

Pronghorns are built to run; when threatened, they can sprint off at 60 miles per hour.

GRASSLAND

From the Rocky Mountains to Indiana and from Canada's prairie provinces to Texas, the heart of North America at one time was dominated by grasslands that stretched as far as the eye could see. Though much of the region now is cropland, pockets of the original prairie still exist. Also known as the Great Plains, this is an area that has always been too dry to support trees, but not so dry as the deserts of the Southwest. The grasslands range from the moist tallgrass prairies of the Midwest to the drier shortgrass prairies farther west, where bison and pronghorns graze. Other wildlife includes small rodents and reptiles, preyed upon by hawks, owls, coyotes, and badgers, and numerous ground-nesting birds. Among the hordes of insects, crickets and grasshoppers sing from the grasses, while bees and butterflies flit from place to place sipping nectar and pollinating an endless array of wildflowers.

Prairie dogs are sociable rodents; they greet each other with kisses and warn each other with shrill barks.

Burrowing owls often move into deserted prairie dog dens.

Coneflowers explode with color on tallgrass prairies at summer's end.

The bison is the grasslands' most majestic beast. During the mating season a bull's thunderous bellowing can be heard for miles.

Spring wildflowers of many kinds paint the Texas grasslands with a bold array of reds, whites, and blues.

The rough blazing star turns the prairie into a sea of purple in late summer.

The greater prairie chicken lures females with fancy dances and booming calls.

Shortgrass prairie stretches for unspoiled miles across the plains of South Dakota.

159

The rose-breasted grosbeak (left) gets its name from its showy plumage, while the evening grosbeak (right) was named in the mistaken belief that it starts to sing at sunset.

Greenhouse effect

Like the glass on a greenhouse, the small amounts of carbon dioxide and water vapor in the atmosphere allow solar rays to warm the earth but prevent heat from radiating back into space. This so-called greenhouse effect has helped maintain life-sustaining temperatures on earth since the atmosphere formed. In recent years, however, a dramatic increase in the burning of fossil fuels has raised the amount of carbon dioxide in the air, intensifying the greenhouse effect. As a result, some experts fear that temperatures around the globe will rise, disrupting climates everywhere.

Greenling

Found in cool coastal waters from California to Alaska, greenlings are popular game fish with colorful markings. The brownish kelp greenlings, for instance, are daubed with blue spots on the males and reddish-brown spots on the females. Fishermen seek greenlings for their flesh, which, though greenish, is very tasty. While most are less than two feet long, the five-foot, 100-pound lingcod is big enough to be harvested commercially.

Grosbeak

Named for their stout, conical bills, grosbeaks are attractively colored, finchlike songbirds. The rose-breasted grosbeak of the East has been dubbed the potato-bug bird by farmers, who appreciate its voracious appetite for harmful beetles. The closely related black-headed grosbeak lives west of the Rockies, while the South is home to the blue grosbeak, which incorporates into its nest such varied materials as corn husks and strips of plastic. The two remaining grosbeaks nest in northern coniferous forests, where seeds are plentiful. The evening grosbeak, famous for raiding bird feeders, actually finds most of its food in the wild. And flocks of pine grosbeaks, which are fond of evergreen seeds, have been known to strip trees of their cones.

As ground cherries mature, papery husks like those of their relatives, the ornamental Chinese lanterns, form around them.

Ground beetle

Emerging at night from under logs and litter, ground beetles dash about frantically as they search for insects, slugs, and other small prey. Many of our 3,000 or so species are patent-leather black, but others shine with color. Some climb trees to devour gypsy moth caterpillars, and others can extract snails from their shells. When annoyed, those known as bombardier beetles make an audible pop as they expel a foul fluid that instantly vaporizes into a noxious gas.

Ground cherry *Physalis*

Their name to the contrary, these wild fruits of fields, waste places, and open woodlands are kin not of cherries but of tomatoes. Low, branching annuals, the ground cherries are adorned in summer with bell-shaped white or yellow flowers, which mature into plump, usually golden berries, each one enclosed in an inflated, papery husk. Though the cherry-sized fruits are prized by country people for use in jams and pies, the leaves and unripe fruits are poisonous.

160

This ground beetle is a caterpillar hunter.

The groundsel's cheery yellow flowers belie the fact that most species are weeds.

The thirteen-lined ground squirrel's "stars-and-stripes" pattern has caused it to be known in the United States as "the federation squirrel."

Groundsel *Senecio*

Preferring moist, rich soils, many of the groundsels have become troublesome weeds of barnyards, fields, and gardens. Their name, in fact, is thought to be derived from an Old English word meaning "ground swallower." Members of the sunflower family, most groundsels have small yellow daisylike flowers, and their tiny airborne fruits, equipped with tufts of silken down, are distributed far and wide at the whim of the wind. A number of species, such as common groundsel, have a history of use in herbal medicine. Another, threadleaf groundsel, is notorious in the West as one of the most poisonous of all range plants.

Ground squirrel *Spermophilus*

Sprightly cousins of the tree squirrels, ground squirrels are true groundlings; most of them dwell in subterranean burrows that are complete with sleeping chambers and grass-lined dens to accommodate large litters of fast-growing young. The labyrinths also provide snug quarters in which the squirrels can hibernate,

particularly at times when food is scarce. A hibernating squirrel typically curls up into a ball, a position that is ideal for conserving heat; as its body temperature and heart rate plummet, the squirrel slips into a deep torpor. Ground squirrels in the Arctic hibernate for up to eight months of the year, while other species that dwell in arid regions become dormant during the hot months of summer.

More than a dozen species of ground squirrels live in the western and midwestern states. Inhabiting meadows, rocky hillsides, prairies, and deserts, they feed by day on greenery, seeds, and insects. Ever alert as they forage, the jaunty little rodents regularly rise up on their haunches to survey their surroundings. When threatened by enemies—including eagles, hawks, coyotes, and badgers—they signal their fellows with a sharp, distinctive warning whistle and then run for cover themselves.

Ground water

Beneath the surface of most of the world's land area lies an unseen reservoir of water. Renewed constantly by rain and melting snow, this so-called ground water fills the spaces between particles of soil, sand, and gravel, as well as pores and cracks in the bedrock. The top of the water-saturated area, which may be near the surface or far underground, is called the water table. Ground water sometimes flows onto the surface in springs and riverbeds.

In many areas, from New Jersey in the East to the deserts of the Southwest, ground water tapped by wells is the main source of water for drinking, irrigation, and household and industrial use. Although it is less easily contaminated than surface water, ground water is nevertheless subject to pollution. Chemical fertilizers, sewage, and gasoline that leaks from underground storage tanks are but a few of the contaminants that can foul this precious resource.

Grunions, attuned to the tides, come ashore to spawn during full and new moons.

Herring gulls often engage in raucous disputes.

G

Guillemots are deep divers that plunge underwater to nab fish from the ocean bottom.

French grunts add to the beauty of a coral reef.

Grouse

Chunky and chickenlike, grouse are ground-dwelling birds that normally take to the air only to escape enemies. Relying instead on their remarkable camouflage, they usually sit tight until predators come dangerously close, then take off with an explosive whirring of wings.

The family, which includes ptarmigan and prairie chickens, is renowned for the spectacular shows the birds put on during the spring mating season. The forest-dwelling ruffed grouse stands on a log and drums the air with his cupped wings, producing a deep booming sound that can be heard more than a mile away. Even more elaborate are the rituals of the western sharp-tailed grouse, sage grouse, and prairie chickens. Males gather at special dance grounds, called leks, where they strut, bow, stamp their feet, and spread their tails like fans, all the while making booming sounds that are amplified by brightly colored air sacs on either side of the neck.

Favorite game birds, grouse are admired by hunters for their crafty last-minute escapes. But some kinds, such as the spruce grouse, present less of a challenge: they tend to simply stand in place staring at the hunters.

Grunion *Leuresthes tenuis*

Small silvery fish found off the coast of southern California, grunions are best known for their remarkable spawning behavior. Every two weeks from March through June, when the full or new moon brings the tides to their highest, millions of grunions ride the night waves onto sandy shores. Boring into the damp sand with their tails, the females lay their eggs while the males, curled around the females, quickly fertilize them. The next wave carries the grunions back out to the ocean. So predictable is their spawning that fishermen take advantage of grunion runs and scoop up the tasty fish by the bucketful. Two weeks later, during the next peak tide, the eggs hatch and the fry are washed out to sea. Members of the silversides family, grunions can grow up to eight inches long and have a blue-bordered silvery stripe along each side.

Grunt

A large family of colorful warm-water ocean fish, grunts are named for the piglike noises they make, not only while underwater but also after they are caught. The sounds, amplified by their

Gypsum forms dazzling white dunes in New Mexico.

Female gypsy moths, unable to fly, spend their short lives laying felty, amber-colored egg masses on tree bark.

swim bladders, are produced by grinding together powerful teeth in their throats.

Ranging in length from six inches to two feet, grunts live in large schools around reefs and weeds and feed on a variety of creatures, from crabs to sea urchins. Several species, including the yellow-striped French grunt, engage in a curious kissing behavior: two fish, with mouths wide open, swim together, touch lips, and then part. Other varieties include the white grunt, an Atlantic food fish, and the California sargo.

Guillemot *Cepphus*

Penguinlike birds of the auk family, guillemots nest in rocky crevices along northern coasts. About one foot long, both the black guillemot of the North Atlantic and the pigeon guillemot of Pacific waters are jet black with conspicuous white wing patches and bright red legs. They dive underwater in search of fish, mussels, and other prey and use their wings to paddle. Like other auks, the birds forgo nest building and lay their eggs directly on rocks.

Gull

Whether perched on piers, soaring over surf, or filling the air with raucous, scolding cries, gulls seem virtually synonymous with seashores. Yet the birds, typically white or gray with black markings, are just as likely to be seen inland, where many of them nest and scout for food in fields, marshes, lakes, and garbage dumps.

By far the most common species, found on every coastline and on inland lakes and rivers, is the herring gull. An important scavenger, it is also known for its habit of cracking clams open by dropping them on rocks. The largest gull, with a wingspan of more than five feet, is the great black-backed gull of the Atlantic Coast. In mixed gatherings of gulls, this imposing bird always occupies the highest perch and often robs smaller gulls of their food.

The California gull, which winters on the West Coast and breeds inland, is the state bird of Utah, an honor it earned by saving the crops of early Mormon settlers from a plague of grasshoppers. Breeding even farther inland, on the Prairies, is the Franklin's gull; sometimes called the "prairie dove," it builds floating nests in marshes. Another common inland species, the ring-billed gull, is often seen in flocks, gleaning in plowed fields for insects and rodents.

Bonaparte's gull (named not for the emperor but for his ornithologist nephew) breeds in forested wetlands and, unlike most other gulls, nests in trees. The laughing gull, found mostly on the Atlantic and Gulf coasts, often follows fishing boats for handouts. The bird is named for its robust *ha-ha-ha,* which sounds much like human laughter.

G

Gypsum

A soft whitish mineral best known for its use in plaster of paris, gypsum is found in many areas in North America. It was usually formed by the evaporation of mineral-laden water in shallow seas and occurs in thick, extensive beds. Other varieties include crystals, lovely reddish rosettes, and a waxy type, called alabaster, that is carved into vases and statuary. Gypsum is also used in the manufacture of such varied products as plasterboard, tile, cement, paper, and paint.

Gypsy moth *Lymantria dispar*

Since their introduction from Europe in 1869, gypsy moths have spread throughout the Northeast and turned up as far west as Oregon. While the adults do not eat, the caterpillars, marked with red and blue spots, are voracious feeders. Hatching in May, they can strip entire trees of their leaves by the time they spin their cocoons in July. Some 10 days later the dusky brown or whitish moths emerge, and in late summer the females lay their eggs, starting the cycle anew.

Hail creates danger and havoc along highways. Sometimes falling at speeds of up to 100 miles per hour, hailstones can do serious damage to vehicles, buildings, and crops. Hailstorms are most common in Alberta and Saskatchewan and in the central United States between Texas and the Dakotas.

H

The halfbeak is no doubt well suited to scooping up food as it skims the surface of the water. Its remarkable lower jaw is equal in length to its entire head.

The hairstreaks, along with their relatives the blues and coppers, are sometimes called gossamer-winged butterflies.

Habitat

Frequently compared with an address, a habitat is the specific place where a plant or animal lives. A dog's furry back, for instance, is the habitat of fleas, while the moist, shaded forest floor is the place where we would expect to find ferns. A habitat is also a community, like a neighborhood, and includes all the living and nonliving things that make up an area—the plants, the animals, the soil, and everything else that shapes a particular environment.

Haddock See Codfish.

Hagfish

Among the most primitive—and homely—of all fish are the hagfish. Like their relatives the lampreys, they lack scales and paired fins; their skeletons are formed of cartilage, not bone. Seldom

exceeding two feet, the slimy, eellike creatures have poorly developed eyes, jawless mouths, and fleshy tentacles. Most species burrow into the muddy bottom beneath deep, cold ocean water. Hagfish eat dead or injured fish, using rasplike tongues to bore a hole into the fish's body, then devouring everything but its skin and bones.

Hail

Dramatic but dangerous, hail consists of rocklike lumps of ice that hurtle down from the sky. Hailstones can be as small as peas or as big as grapefruits and are capable of causing tremendous damage. They can break windows, dent cars, ruin crops, and occasionally even kill people. Hail begins as ice pellets that are tossed about in thunderclouds. Kept aloft by powerful updrafts, they accumulate layer after layer of ice on their surfaces until, too heavy to be supported by the updrafts, they fall to earth.

Hairstreak

Named for the fine lines on the undersides of their wings, hairstreaks are brownish, fast-flying butterflies that dart through meadows and forests all across the country. Most hairstreaks also have streamerlike "tails" on their hindwings—a further clue to their identity. Depending on the species, the short, sluglike larvae may feed on leaves, fruits, or small insects. A few kinds have glands that secrete a substance called honeydew, a sweet liquid much craved by ants. The ants, in fact, sometimes tend the caterpillars in their nests, where they "milk" them with gentle strokes on the abdomen.

164

Halite, everyday salt, forms in an evaporating pond (left). A close-up (above) reveals the geometry of its crystals.

Each hammock in the Florida Everglades is a treasure trove of colorful butterflies and other fascinating wildlife. A mere sampling of the rich mix that grows on hammocks includes live oak, pigeon plum, strangler fig, nakedwood, and mulberry trees.

H

Halfbeak

Though they are close cousins of the flying fish, halfbeaks never quite become airborne: instead, they skitter along the surface of warm coastal seas, where they feed on small fish and algae. Named for their long, protruding lower jaw, halfbeaks are slender, streamlined fish, with dorsal and anal fins set far back near the tail. A common East Coast species, the foot-long bally-hoo, is often used as bait by anglers trolling for sailfish, marlins, and other game fish.

Halite

Commonly called rock salt, halite is the naturally occurring mineral (sodium chloride) used to flavor food. It is formed by the evaporation of salt water and occurs as clear or colored crystals. Huge deposits are located in Michigan, Ohio, and western New York. Since halite is light and plastic, deep deposits are sometimes squeezed upward by underground forces, causing the rocks above them to arch up into domes. Common in Texas and Louisiana, salt domes are often associated with oil deposits. Though most familiar on dinner tables and on icy roads, halite also has an astonishing range of industrial uses.

Halo

When the sun or moon shines through high, wispy clouds, ice crystals in the clouds can play strange tricks with the light. The most common effect, called a halo, is a bright ring of light that sometimes completely encircles the sun or moon. Variations on the light show, created as the light is refracted and reflected by the ice crystals, include colored halos, double halos, vertical "pillars" of light, and even bright spots of light on either side of the sun, known as sun dogs or mock suns.

Hammock

In southern parlance, a hammock is an elevated area with fertile soil that supports a hardwood forest. In Georgia the term usually refers to islands in salt marshes, while in Florida the best-known—and best-preserved—examples are the densely forested islands that rise only a foot or two above the marshes in Everglades National Park. Havens for dozens of plant and animal species, the hammocks are thick with mahoganies and royal palms, festooned with orchids, and alive with a daunting array of tree snails, indigo snakes, and other exotic creatures.

165

Antelope jackrabbits, like all hares, leap away from enemies; true rabbits, in contrast, prefer to hide.

Hanging valleys, such as the one at California's Bridalveil Fall, can produce astounding natural beauty; the stream here plunges 600 feet into the deep valley below.

H

Hanging valley

Tributary valleys that enter a main valley at levels far above that valley's floor are called hanging valleys. Typically, as streams or rivers in hanging valleys flow into the main valley, they tumble down rapids or waterfalls. Takakkaw Falls in Yoho National Park in British Columbia, Cameron Falls in Waterton Lakes National Park in Alberta, and Bridalveil Fall and Ribbon Fall in Yosemite Valley in California, for instance, all flow from hanging valleys.

Products of glaciation, they were formed by tributary glaciers that flowed into a major valley glacier. Because they were smaller, the tributary glaciers did not cut such deep trenches as the one in the main valley. Thus, when the ice melted, the hanging valleys remained perched above the main valley's floor.

Hare *Lepus*

Large, long-eared mammals with powerful hind legs, hares are related to rabbits but differ in a number of ways. Unlike the blind and helpless young of rabbits, for example, hares are born fully furred with their eyes open and are soon able to hop about.

The most familiar hares are the long-legged jackrabbits, which are often seen bounding across western grasslands and deserts. Their long ears act as antennae, picking up faint sounds, and also help to radiate body heat. Like other hares, they bolt away at the approach of danger, and for short bursts can reach speeds of 35 miles per hour.

The snowshoe, or varying, hare of northern and alpine forests and brushlands is brown in summer but turns white in winter. In the fall it also develops dense fur pads on its feet that enable it to leap more easily through the snow. Active by night, it is, like all the hares, a vegetarian, feeding on green plants in summer and on twigs and bark in winter.

Harvestman See *Daddy longlegs.*

Harvest mouse *Reithrodontomys*

Though they look very much like house mice, American harvest mice are more at home in fields and grasslands. There they forage by night for seeds, often bending stems to the ground to "harvest" the seeds. The mice weave blades of grass into six-inch spherical nests that they build on supports just above the ground. Harvest mice are found in most parts of the United States. One species, now endangered, lives only in salt marshes around San Francisco Bay.

Salt-marsh harvest mice, unlike their dry-ground kin, prefer to be near water.

The Swainson's hawk (above) feeds on crickets and grasshoppers; red-tailed hawks (below) perform a midair courtship ritual.

Orange hawkweed, or devil's paintbrush, is admired in the wild but despised in lawns and gardens.

H

Hawk

Keen-eyed birds of prey that hunt by day, hawks are most often seen soaring gracefully overhead. But when one of these imposing hunters spots a prospective meal, it swoops down with lightning speed, seizes the animal in its viselike talons, and tears it into bite-sized pieces with its powerful hooked beak.

The hawk family includes the accipiters (such as the northern goshawk) and the buteos (such as the red-tailed hawk) as well as eagles, ospreys, marsh-dwelling northern harriers, and the graceful kites. (Falcons, which are often called hawks, differ in several ways and belong to a separate family.) Our largest species is the bald eagle, with a seven-foot wingspan; the smallest, with a wingspan of just under two feet, is the sharp-shinned hawk.

Following a courtship that often includes spectacular displays of aerial acrobatics, most hawks build nests of sticks high in trees. A few, such as the golden eagle, nest on rugged cliffs, while the northern harrier nests on the ground in or near marshes.

Hawks eat almost any kind of small animal, from birds to beetles and from rodents to reptiles. Some, however, are more specialized: the snail kite dines only on large snails, and the osprey feeds almost exclusively on fish.

Hawkweed *Hieracium*

Though its orange-red flowers add sprightly dashes of color to fields and roadsides in summer, orange hawkweed well deserves its nickname, devil's paintbrush. To gardeners, it and other hawkweeds, such as mouse ear and king devil, are indeed works of the devil, for they are tenacious weeds. Their creeping stems form dense mats of hairy, oblong leaves, and their dandelionlike flowers produce downy seeds that sail on the wind to lawns far and wide.

Hawthorn *Crataegus*

The long, needlelike thorns and zigzagging branches of the hawthorns form dense, tangled silhouettes against the winter sky. Then, in spring, the small, prickly trees are covered with coarsely toothed leaves and showy white to pink flowers that resemble apple blossoms. The similarity to apple trees continues in the fall, when the blossoms give way to clusters of small, usually red fruits, called haws, which are eagerly sought by grouse, pheasants, and deer. Many kinds of hawthorns, also known as thorn apples, are found across North America, often forming dense stands in abandoned fields and pastures. Because of their attractive blossoms and bright fruits, the trees make charming ornamentals.

Western hemlocks sometimes take root on "nurse logs"—the decaying trunks of fallen trees.

H

Hazel *Corylus*

Common shrubs or small trees of fencerows and woodland borders, hazels often form dense, twiggy thickets. Their branches, tough and flexible, are sometimes woven into baskets, but the plants are valued mainly for their abundant crops of tasty nuts. Also known as filberts, the fruits are enclosed in distinctive, leafy husks. Those of the American hazel have tattered, ragged edges, while the husks of the beaked hazel are joined in long, tubular snouts.

Hellbender *Cryptobranchus alleganiensis*

So named, no doubt, because of its grotesque appearance, the hellbender is a flat-headed, wrinkled, dull-colored salamander that grows up to 30 inches long. It is so homely, in fact, that although entirely harmless, it is widely presumed to be poisonous. An ungainly resident of rivers and streams in the eastern and midwestern United States, it usually hides under rocks by day and emerges only at night to hunt for crayfish, shellfish, worms, and insect larvae.

Hemlock *Tsuga*

Slow-growing but long-lived, the hemlocks are softwood conifers that may endure for centuries and reach heights of 100 feet or more. The trees are conical in form, and their drooping branches are covered with short, flattened needles that are dark green above and whitish below. The trees take up to 300 years to reach maturity and, when full grown, cast a dense shade that prevents all but hemlock seedlings from taking root beneath them. Once threatened by overcutting,

the eastern hemlock, which flourishes from the Atlantic Coast to Minnesota, was prized by the leather industry for the high tannin content of its bark. The western hemlock is the most common tree of the Pacific Coast rain forests.

Hemlock, poison *Conium maculatum*

An imported weed of roadsides, pastures, and waste places, poison hemlock is akin to and closely resembles Queen Anne's lace, or wild carrot. Up to five feet tall, with branching stems and lacy, parsleylike foliage, it bears flat-topped clusters of tiny, dull white flowers from June through August. Unlike Queen Anne's lace, however, the hairless stems of poison hemlock are marked with purple spots and its leaves emit a foul odor when crushed. Well-known as the source of the deadly potion used to execute the Greek philosopher Socrates in 399 B.C., poison hemlock contains in all its parts the powerful, often deadly alkaloid coniine. Today this ingredient is extracted for use in sedatives and other medications. Water hemlock, a related weed that flourishes on wet soils, is even more deadly. A single bite of its white, parsniplike taproot has been known to fell a full-grown adult.

Hepatica *Hepatica*

Despite their delicate appearance, the hepaticas are in fact quite sturdy: their dainty lavender, pink, or white blooms are among the earliest performers in the annual parade of wildflowers that grace eastern woodlands in the spring. Their broad, three-lobed leaves play a role in the hepaticas' early flowering. Lying flat on the ground throughout the winter, they catch the

Poison hemlock, while lovely and lacy, contains a powerful toxin in all of its parts.

Pocket gophers, herbivorous rodents, feed on roots, tubers, and other plant matter.

first rays of spring sunlight and so help melt the snow around the plants. Only after blooming ends do the old leaves wither and die, to be replaced by fresh new growth.

Herbivore

Animals that feed primarily on plants are called herbivores and include creatures as diverse as leaf-chewing insects, fruit-eating birds, and wood-boring beetles. Most are specially adapted for their particular diets. Beavers, for example, have chisellike incisors that are perfectly suited for felling trees and gnawing on bark; cattle have flattened molars for grinding food; and seed-eating finches have stout, conical bills that are ideal for cracking seeds. A vital link in all food chains, herbivores convert the energy provided by plants into animal tissue and are in turn consumed by carnivores, or flesh eaters.

Herb Robert See *Geranium.*

Hercules club *Zanthoxylum clava-herculis*

Stout thorns sprout from the trunk, branches, and leaf stalks of Hercules club, a shrub or small tree of southeastern coastal plains. On older specimens, warty growths on the trunk give it the look of an ancient weapon, which accounts for the plant's name. Another common name, toothache tree, was inspired by the pungent bark and foliage, which have a long history of use in folk medicine. When chewed, they numb the mouth, temporarily relieving toothache pain. The featherlike compound leaves are nearly evergreen, with the old foliage often persisting until early spring. The tiny greenish flowers appear before the new leaves open, and later give rise to clusters of small reddish pods. As they mature, the pods split open, and a solitary black seed dangles from each one on a thread.

Hermit crabs are denizens of tidal pools and sandy ocean bottoms.

Hermit crab

Many a beachcomber has picked up a snail shell, only to find its entrance blocked by the head and claws of a hermit crab. Unlike other crabs, this squatter has a soft, unarmored abdomen and so must use an empty shell for protection. Twisting its body, the hermit crab fits itself into the snail shell; leaving its strong pincers hanging out, it uses its hindmost pair of legs to hold itself firmly in place. When the crab outgrows its borrowed home, it moves into a larger shell, often evicting another hermit crab in the process. Hermits have also been seen pulling live snails from their shells and then eating the former occupants before moving in. Found on both coasts, most species are about an inch long, but the large hermit crab of the Atlantic coast sometimes grows to a length of five inches.

How to Recognize the Herons and Egrets

Herons and egrets differ from other long-legged waders. Their spear-shaped bills, for example, are unlike the curved bills of ibises, and their S-shaped necks contrast with the straight necks of wood storks and cranes. To tell one species from another, check the colors of the plumage, bill, and legs and the bird's overall size and shape.

Plumage white

BILL YELLOW

LARGE AND SLENDER

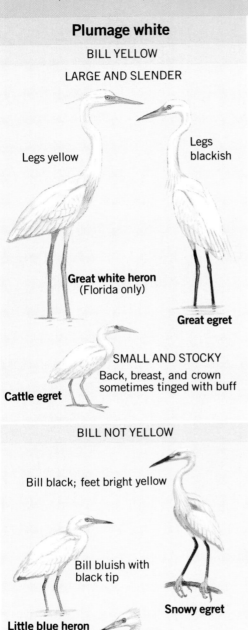

Legs yellow

Legs blackish

Great white heron
(Florida only)

Great egret

SMALL AND STOCKY

Back, breast, and crown sometimes tinged with buff

Cattle egret

BILL NOT YELLOW

Bill black; feet bright yellow

Bill bluish with black tip

Snowy egret

Little blue heron
(immature)

Bill pinkish with dark tip

Reddish egret
(white phase)

Plumage colored

BREAST OR BELLY WHITE

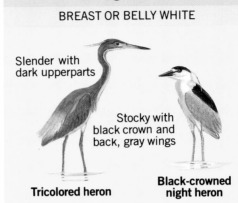

Slender with dark upperparts

Stocky with black crown and back, gray wings

Tricolored heron

Black-crowned night heron

NECK AND BODY PALE GRAY

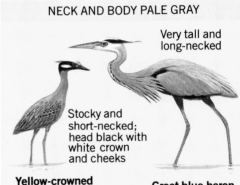

Very tall and long-necked

Stocky and short-necked; head black with white crown and cheeks

Yellow-crowned night heron

Great blue heron

BODY DARK GRAY OR BLUE-GRAY

Slender and long-necked; head and neck dark purple

Little blue heron
(adult)

Slender and long-necked; head and neck rusty

Reddish egret
(dark phase)

Small and stocky; neck deep chestnut

Green-backed heron

H

170

Heron

Elegant, long-legged wading birds with graceful, sinuous necks, herons are widespread across much of North America. The family also includes the egrets, which are simply herons with white plumage, and the closely related bitterns.

All herons have long, pointed bills that are used for snapping up fish, frogs, crustaceans, insects, and an occasional bird or mouse. Although they generally nest in colonies, most species hunt alone by day and fly back to their roosts at dusk. The night herons, however, rest by day and work the night shift. Sometimes walking slowly through the water in search of prey, herons may also stand perfectly still and wait for victims to come within reach, then snatch them with quick thrusts of the beak.

The great blue heron (which also occurs in Florida in a white form known as the great white heron) has a six-foot wingspan and is our continent's largest species. Equally beautiful are the great and snowy egrets, whose elegant breeding plumes, once sought for hats, nearly caused the birds' extinction. A smaller species, the cattle egret, has expanded its range northward since its first nesting in Florida in 1952. It lives in grasslands, where it feeds on insects stirred up by tractors and livestock.

Herring *Clupea harengus*

Silvery throngs made up of tens of thousands of herring are found off both the Atlantic and Pacific coasts. Feeding on plankton filtered from the seawater, the foot-long fish are in turn preyed upon by salmon, tuna, seals, and gulls. Because they travel near the surface in such enormous schools, herring are easily accessible to commercial fishermen and are netted by the ton. Among the most valuable of all food fish, herring are marketed fresh, smoked, and pickled, and young fish are canned as sardines. They are also used as bait for catching cod and halibut and are processed for oil and fish meal.

Hibernation

As winter closes in, woodchucks, ground squirrels, and some other animals go into a deep sleeplike state called hibernation. Their temperature, pulse rate, and breathing rate all plummet, and they survive on the energy in body fat. When the weather warms, they slowly reawaken. Other animals, such as raccoons, are inactive in cold weather but are not true hibernators. Their temperature and respiration rate are not greatly reduced, and they can easily be roused.

Hickory *Carya*

Synonymous with toughness, the hickories are well known for producing the strongest, most resilient wood of any North American trees. Their wood, in fact, is the timber of choice for tool handles but also makes excellent firewood

When hibernating, the golden-mantled ground squirrel is beyond sleep; the animal can even be picked up without waking.

The eastern hognose snake, despite its bluster, is a danger primarily to toads.

and is especially esteemed as a smokehouse fuel. Common throughout eastern and central North America, all the hickories have long-stalked, featherlike compound leaves. Rough, scaly bark is another common trait, though the shagbark hickory is identified by the long, peeling strips of skin. And all bear oily, hard-shelled nuts enclosed in fibrous green husks. The nuts of one kind, the pecan, are an important commercial crop; those of other species provide a feast for chipmunks, squirrels, and other wild creatures.

Hognose snake *Heterodon*

Renowned as a bluff, the nonpoisonous, totally harmless eastern hognose snake puts on quite an act when threatened or surprised. Swelling its body and spreading its neck like a cobra, it hisses fiercely as it lunges and thrashes to frighten the intruder. Then, if the interloper is not deterred, the snake tries another tactic. It writhes convulsively, rolls over on its back, and goes completely limp, playing dead. The ruse usually works, and as soon as the coast is clear, the snake slips away to safety. The western hognose relies on similar but more subdued displays. Both snakes, up to three feet long, are named for their upturned, armored snouts, which they use for digging in the soil.

Worker honeybees gather pollen for food. They carry the dusty substance on their legs, where special hairs keep it together in a "pollen basket." Later, back at the hive, the pollen is kicked off and deposited in special storage cells.

H

Swarms of honeybees (above) are usually made up of a queen and a throng of workers looking for a new hive. At the right is a nest of wild bees. The insects must consume eight pounds of honey to produce one pound of wax for the combs.

Hog potato *Hoffmanseggia densiflora*

The tubers produced by the hog potato's roots furnish welcome fodder for creatures inhabiting southwestern U.S. deserts. In addition to nourishing many kinds of wild animals—the plant's name in Spanish means "mouse's sweet potato"— the tubers were gathered by Indians when other food was in short supply. Though edible, nutritious, and useful in emergencies, hog potatoes do not provide a very tasty meal.

Bearing dainty compound leaves, the plants in summer produce 16-inch spikes of yellow-orange flowers, which give way to beanlike seed pods. While hog potatoes make a pretty show along roads and railways, they can be troublesome pests on farmlands.

Holly *Ilex*

Venturing as far north as Cape Cod, the American holly is a sturdy tree that may reach a height of 100 feet. Like the imported English holly, its spiny evergreen leaves and bright red berries are instantly recognized by almost everyone, thanks to their widespread use as Christmas decorations. Many other hollies are less familiar, however, for their leaves are neither leathery nor evergreen, and they lack spines. One such example is possumhaw, a native of the southern United States, which, at 30 feet, is the tallest of the deciduous species. Winterberry, a large shrub that thrives in moist areas, also sheds its foliage in autumn. It is sometimes called black alder because its leaves turn black before they fall.

The trumpet honeysuckle, a vine of eastern woods and thickets, is a high climber that is often cultivated in gardens and trained to coil through trellises. The long, fingerlike blooms, which inspired the plant's other name, coral honeysuckle, are followed by bright red, egg-shaped berries.

Honeybee *Apis mellifera*

Living together in colonies that number in the thousands, honeybees form complex and efficient societies, with each individual insect performing its preordained role. Preeminent in the colony is the queen, a large, long-lived female bee whose sole mission is to lay eggs. The relatively few males, called drones, exist only to fertilize future queens on special mating flights. The thousands of remaining bees, called workers, are sterile females that perform the colony's day-to-day chores. Toiling industriously, they gather pollen and nectar from flowers, tend the developing larvae, care for the queen, and maintain the nest, or hive.

The hive is filled with honeycomb, which is made up of thousands of six-sided cells built with wax secreted by the workers. Honey and pollen are stored in most of the cells; in others the queen lays the eggs, which develop from larvae to pupae to adult bees.

Humming from flower to flower, honeybees perform an invaluable service in the natural world. Even as they ensure their own survival by gathering food, they ensure the survival of plants by pollinating their blooms.

Honeydew

A sweet, sticky liquid excreted by treehoppers, aphids, and other sap-sucking insects, honeydew sometimes coats the leaves of plants attacked by these pests. The accumulation can harm the plants by encouraging the growth of mold. While gardeners may disapprove of honeydew, however, ants, wasps, and other insects regard it as an elixir. Ants sometimes approach aphids, tap them with their antennae, then drink the drops of liquid that the aphids excrete in response. Some species even protect the aphids, like herds of cattle, and return regularly to "milk" their charges.

Honeylocust *Gleditsia triacanthos*

Even adventurous squirrels avoid climbing the honeylocust, for the tree has clusters of nasty branching thorns on both its trunk and branches. But this fast-growing tree, a native of the midwestern and southern United States, has a less menacing aspect as well, provided by its delicate, compound leaves and dangling clusters of greenish-yellow flowers. The fruits are long, leathery pods that contain the tree's "honey," a sweet pulp that surrounds the beanlike seeds.

H

Honeysuckle *Lonicera*

Attractive shrubs and vines with smooth, oval leaves, honeysuckles are admired for their lovely trumpetlike flowers and sweet nectar. By far the most common is Japanese honeysuckle, a climbing vine with fragrant, white to yellow flowers. Introduced as an ornamental, it has become so pervasive that many regard it as a weed. Trumpet honeysuckle, one of the showiest species, is a woodland vine with beautiful blossoms that are red on the outside and golden within. The tubular blooms are so deep that the plant depends entirely on hummingbirds for pollination. In contrast, mountain fly honeysuckle, a low woodland shrub, bears shallow yellow flowers that are more accessible to insects.

Hoof

Sheep, goats, pigs, cattle, deer, and horses all have hooves, which are essentially large, thick toenails that encase and protect the bottoms of the feet—natural shoes. Made of the same material as claws and fingernails, hooves are derived from the outer layer of an animal's skin. On single-toed mammals such as horses, the hoof is one continuous sheath. On others, such as sheep and cattle, it is divided into two halves and is called a cleft hoof.

Fruit

Male catkins

The hop-hornbeam's oval leaves have hairy stems, and its nutlets are encased in scaly, bladderlike sacs.

Mountain sheep, also known as bighorns, have been overhunted for their remarkable horns. Rams sport massive spiraling horns, while those of the females are smaller and only slightly curved. Horn size helps establish rank among male herd members.

H

Hop-hornbeam *Ostrya virginiana*

Although the dangling papery fruits of the hop-hornbeam resemble the hops used to flavor beer, its seeds serve instead as forage for ruffed grouse and other wildlife. Ranging across eastern North America, this slow-growing, long-lived tree rarely exceeds 30 feet. It is adapted to a wide range of soils and flourishes in shady spots. The hop-hornbeam's bark is rough and shaggy, its leaves toothed, and its timber so hard and tough that the tree is nicknamed ironwood.

Horn

The sturdy headgear of cattle, bison, goats, sheep, and some other mammals, horns serve as more than ornaments. The formidable, paired structures are also weapons used to fend off predators and to joust with males of the same species during the mating season. Horns consist of a core of bone surrounded by a layer of hard fingernail-like material. In contrast to antlers, which are branched and are shed every year, horns are unbranched, permanent fixtures.

Hornbeam *Carpinus caroliniana*

Rounded ridges spiral up the trunk and limbs of the American hornbean, giving the tree a muscular look that accounts for one of its alternate names—musclewood. Though in fact it is more closely related to the birches, it is also called blue beech because its smooth bluish-gray bark

is similar to the beeches'. Thanks to its remarkably hard wood, this small tree of eastern streamsides and bottomlands, like its close relative the hop-hornbeam, is also called ironwood.

Horned lark *Eremophila alpestris*

Among the first birds to nest each year, horned larks sometimes begin raising families as early as February. Birds of wide open spaces, they favor fields, prairies, and beaches, where they are often seen in enormous flocks. Although they feed and nest on the ground, horned larks sometimes circle high in the sky, singing a twittering flight song, then plummet earthward once again. Two small feather tufts on their heads, not always conspicuous, give horned larks their name.

Horned lizard *Phrynosoma*

Looking a bit like tiny dinosaurs, horned lizards have squat, oval bodies, sharp spines projecting from the back of the head, and rows of pointed scales along their sides. Also known as horned toads, they live in arid and semiarid areas west of the Mississippi River. Protective coloration helps them to blend with their surroundings. When threatened, horned lizards hiss, bite, lower their heads to brandish their spines, and inflate their three- to seven-inch bodies to look larger than they actually are. They can even spurt thin jets of blood from the corners of their eyes. Despite this arsenal of defenses, horned lizards are prey to roadrunners, coyotes, and the

174

Horned larks build shallow nests on bare ground and produce up to three broods each year.

Horned lizards were at one time called "sacred toads" because they seemed to weep tears of blood.

Bald-faced hornets build large nests, with room for thousands.

occasional snake that risks swallowing the well-armored body. Able to tolerate higher temperatures than most reptiles, horned lizards forage by day for ants and other insects. At night and when the daytime heat becomes too intense, they burrow into the sand, leaving only their heads exposed.

Horned toad See *Horned lizard.*

Hornet

Familiar across North America, hornets are social wasps that build large hanging nests. (The similar yellow jackets build underground nests.) Stout-bodied insects, most are black with yellow or white markings and inflict very painful stings. Hornets chew rotten wood and other plant fibers to form the gray pulp (much like papier-mâché) used for nest building. Consist-

ing of tiers of cells, the nests are enclosed in the same papery material. While colonies last just one season, queens overwinter and in spring begin constructing new nests. Adhering to a rigid caste system, female workers, produced in the first broods, assume most of the duties of the nest, with drones appearing in later generations.

Horntail

Though related to wasps and bees, horntails lack the narrow waists and nasty stings of their kin. A projection resembling a horn, at the tip of their elongated bodies, gives them their name. Females also have a sharp ovipositor for drilling into dead trees to lay their eggs. The larvae pupate after tunneling through the wood for up to two years, and emerge as winged adults. The pigeon horntail is the most common species in the East; smoky horntails predominate in the West.

Wild horses, their number greatly diminished, still enjoy western scrub country. In Canada, small herds may be seen roaming Rocky Mountains Forest Reserve in Alberta.

H

Flower cluster

Compound leaf

Nut

Spiny fruit

The stately horse chestnut, admired for its striking, upright flower clusters, is popular as a shade or ornamental tree.

Horse, wild *Equus caballus*

Swift, smart, feisty, and free, the wild horses that roam the West today are descendants of the horses brought here centuries ago by Spanish settlers. Also called mustangs (from a Spanish word for "stray"), the horses travel in small bands over plains and grasslands. Stallions battle each other in fierce competition for harems of mares, while the younger males usually congregate in bachelor bands. Tough and hardy, the horses live for about 20 years. Though generally smaller than the average domestic horse, mustangs nevertheless belong to the same species.

Wild horses once numbered in the millions. But over the years, so many were hunted or rounded up, to make way for farms and cattle ranches, that their numbers have been drastically reduced. Protective legislation has been in force in Canada since 1974.

Horse chestnut *Aesculus hippocastanum*

According to tradition horse chestnuts long ago were used as a medicine for horses. Hence the name of this old-world tree, which was brought here in pioneer times. While the glossy, dark brown nuts do resemble true chestnuts, their meat is bitter and inedible. The two trees are not even closely related. The horse chestnut is instead a close kin of the native American buckeye, known as Ohio buckeye.

Most common in the Northeast and Midwest, horse chestnuts have large, attractive leaves,

The horsefly, a stealthy pest, lands quietly on victims before delivering a sharp bite.

The horseshoe crab has a shell shaped somewhat like the foot of a horse.

The horsetail's ancestors covered most of the earth some 300 million years ago.

H

with seven leaflets radiating from the end of a single stalk. But the horse chestnuts' chief beauty is the array of upright clusters of showy white flowers that in June transform the trees into giant candelabras. In September the spiny green fruits fall from the branches and split open to reveal the nuts, which look like polished mahogany.

Horsefly *Tabanus*

Known for the painful bites they inflict on animals and humans alike, horseflies are robust, fast-flying insect pests. They are found from coast to coast in fields, forests, and pastures near the ponds and streams where they live as larvae. The males, which feed on pollen and nectar, are harmless. The females, however, have piercing, cutting mouthparts that can penetrate even the toughest hides in order to suck blood. Repeated attacks by horseflies can seriously weaken animals, and their bites can transmit diseases from host to host.

Horseshoe crab *Limulus polyphemus*

Little has changed with the horseshoe crabs since they first appeared on earth millions of years ago: every spring these seafaring relatives of spiders and scorpions still head for beaches by the thousands in an ancient spawning ritual, with the males riding ashore atop the larger females. Dome-shelled and dull brown, horseshoe crabs grow to about three feet in length, including their slender, pointed tails. They live in shallow waters all along the Atlantic and Gulf coasts, where they root on the bottom for worms and mollusks. Once ground up by the thousands for fertilizer and still used to bait fish traps, horseshoe crabs are valued for nobler purposes today. Their blood is used in pharmacological research, and scientists study them to learn about the electrical link between eye and brain.

Horsetail *Equisetum*

Fossils preserved in coal reveal that the ancient ancestors of present-day horsetails grew to the size of trees. Surviving today as weeds of moist places, the modern horsetails are much more modest, rarely exceeding two or three feet in height. Some are virtually all stem, growing in clumps of hollow green stalks with their leaves reduced to mere sheaves encircling the stems; others bear whorls of branches on the stalks. Producing neither flowers nor seeds, horsetails reproduce instead by releasing spores from special conelike structures. Permeated with silicon crystals, the abrasive stems once were used for cleaning pots and pans and so earned the horsetails their alternate name, scouring rushes.

177

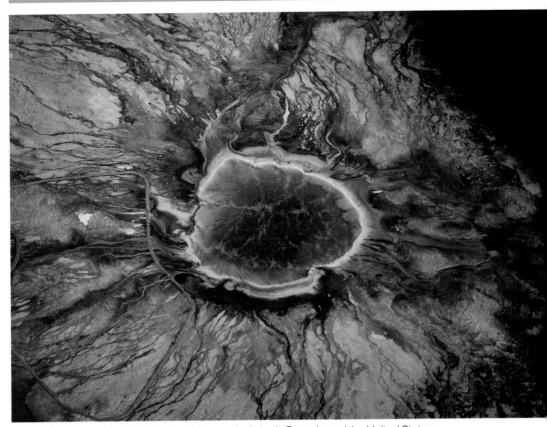

Hot springs are major attractions of some parks in both Canada and the United States.

Hot spring

Ever since antiquity, people have drunk and bathed in the mineral-rich water of hot springs in search of relief from all sorts of ailments. Such springs are usually found in areas where molten rock, or magma, lies fairly close to the surface and heats groundwater that seeps down through cracks and crevices in the overlying rock. Rising back to the surface through natural vents, the steaming water forms calm pools or steadily flowing streams.

Housefly *Musca domestica*

Zigzagging through the air in search of food to light upon, houseflies have been the annoying companions of humans for thousands of years. Suspected of carrying diseases, the insects are attracted to manure and rotting plant and animal matter, where they feed and lay their eggs. Most prolific in warm weather, the housefly develops from egg to maggot to adult in only 10 days, and a single female can theoretically produce millions of offspring in a single summer.

House mouse *Mus musculus*

For thousands of years house mice have been uninvited guests in human homes. Choosing warm, dark places to set up housekeeping, the little rodents tear strips of cloth or paper to build their nests, which are often lined with pilfered feathers. Though they usually eat whatever scraps of human food they can find, in lean times they may resort to such fare as glue and soap. House mice also live outdoors, where they feed on plants and are preyed upon by owls, snakes, and other animals. Since the mice can begin to breed at only a few weeks of age, tremendous populations can build up in a short time. On rare occasions, croplands have been known to host more than 80,000 mice per acre.

House sparrow *Passer domesticus*

Also known as the English sparrow, the hardy, adaptable house sparrow was imported from Europe in the 1850's and is now abundant in cities, suburbs, and farmlands from coast to coast. Like many other introduced species, it turned out to be a pest—a noisy, aggressive bird that steals the nesting sites of bluebirds, wrens, and other native hole-nesters. Building crude, untidy nests of straw, feathers, and trash, the interlopers raise as many as three broods of young each year.

Hover fly

The nonstinging look-alikes of bees and wasps, hover flies are named for their habit of hovering and darting among flowers in their relentless search for nectar and pollen. Most are brightly

House mice, natives of the Old World, were stowaways on the first ships from Europe.

House sparrows look harmless, but they can tear up the nests and destroy the eggs of other birds.

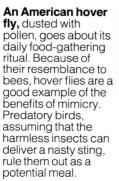

An American hover fly, dusted with pollen, goes about its daily food-gathering ritual. Because of their resemblance to bees, hover flies are a good example of the benefits of mimicry. Predatory birds, assuming that the harmless insects can deliver a nasty sting, rule them out as a potential meal.

patterned with yellow and black; some are slender and narrow-waisted like wasps, while others are plump and fuzzy like bumblebees. Depending on the species, the larvae may live in water, tunnel through flower bulbs, or lodge in the nests of ants or bees. And the larvae of some kinds are gardeners' allies, preying on aphids and other plant pests.

Humidity

On some days the air is dry and pleasant, while on others it seems sticky and uncomfortable. The difference is due to humidity—the moisture content of the air. Because the amount of water vapor the air can hold before it becomes saturated varies with temperature, the moisture content is expressed in terms of relative humidity—a ratio comparing the amount of water vapor actually present in the air with the amount that would saturate it at the same temperature.

Thus a relative humidity of 50 percent means the air is only halfway to its saturation point; a relative humidity of 100 percent means the air can hold no more moisture.

Hummingbird See pp. 180–181.

Hummingbird moth *Hemaris thysbe*

Commonly seen hovering at flowers as it sips nectar through its long tongue, the stout-bodied hummingbird moth does indeed look remarkably like a hummingbird. Also known as the common clearwing because of the large transparent areas on its wings, it has a hairy, dull green body with reddish bands across the abdomen and a fuzzy tuft at the rear. Flitting from flower to flower, the moth feeds during the day in meadows and gardens all across southern Canada, the northern United States, and south to the Gulf of Mexico in the East.

An Anna's hummingbird prepares to take a midair sip of nectar with its needlelike bill. Brilliant red coloring on its head and throat marks the four-inch male of this West Coast species, which was named for an Italian duchess.

Hummingbird

When European settlers first glimpsed North America's hummingbirds, they were dazzled by their glowing iridescence, incredible speed, and ability to hover before flowers, poised on almost invisible wings. One 18th-century writer called them "the miracle of all our winged animals," and few of us are so blasé, even now, that we can ignore such amazing little creatures.

Twenty-one species of these exclusively new-world birds have been sighted in the United States. Only one, the ruby-throated humming-bird, lives east of the Mississippi River, and most of the western species venture just a short distance north of the Mexican border. But four, including the diminutive calliope hummingbird, range northward into Canada, and one, the rufous hummingbird, even reaches southern Alaska. As autumn nears, hummers head for warmer climates, with some migrating thousands of miles—an incredible feat for such tiny birds.

Fast-flying nectar feeders

Most of our hummingbirds are a rich iridescent green above and whitish or buff below. Males usually have a throat patch, or gorget, of bright red, violet, or blue, and in some the color extends to the crown. Exceptions include the magnificent hummingbird, which is black below with a green gorget and a purple crown, and the violet-crowned hummingbird, which has pure white underparts. Females are similar but lack the bright gorgets and crowns.

Beating their wings with powerful muscles, hummingbirds are noted for their ability to hover in midair as they feed. But these aerial acrobats can play other tricks as well. They also are able to fly up and down, shift sideways, and even fly backward.

When hummingbirds feed, their wings beat more than 50 times a second as they hover before flowers to probe for nectar and tiny insects with their long, slender bills. As they reach deep into the blooms, their tubular tongues function like drinking straws. Because of their exceptionally high metabolic rate, hummers feed almost continuously throughout the day. At night they sustain themselves on food stored in their tiny crops, and in cool weather they conserve energy by becoming temporarily dormant.

Territorial imperatives

Fiercely territorial, hummingbirds boldly defend the flowerbeds they have staked out as their own. The males also make spectacular display flights that further proclaim their flowers off limits to others. The ideal territory is a large patch of plants in bloom, but where these are scarce, the birds make the rounds of flowers that are scattered here and there—a so-called "trapline," which is defended as vigorously as a typical territory.

A patch of flowers bright with blooms is more than just a source of food, however; for males it is also a means of attracting mates. After building their nests elsewhere, females visit males in their territories. Darting, swooping, and plummeting, the males indulge in the stunning court-

Calliope hummingbirds—at three inches and one-tenth of an ounce, the continent's tiniest birds—build well-camouflaged nests.

Shimmering broad-tailed hummingbirds spend summers in the Rockies, where wildflowers depend on them for pollination.

Beautiful blue-throated hummingbirds live near the Mexican border, preferring territories close to water.

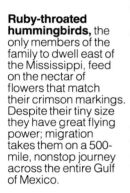

Ruby-throated hummingbirds, the only members of the family to dwell east of the Mississippi, feed on the nectar of flowers that match their crimson markings. Despite their tiny size they have great flying power; migration takes them on a 500-mile, nonstop journey across the entire Gulf of Mexico.

ship flights that are a vital part of their breeding ritual. Once a pair has mated, the female leaves to carry out the duties of parenthood alone.

All our hummingbirds build tiny cup-shaped nests of plant down, spider silk, and moss, often covering them with bud scales or bits of lichen. The female usually lays two pure white eggs, which hatch after 12 to 18 days, a surprisingly long time for such small birds. Fed on a diet of nectar and insects, the young leave the nest at about three weeks, often spending the last few days perched on the rim. There they exercise their wings, preparing themselves for their lives as fast-flying adults.

Of birds and flowers

Just as hummingbirds have adapted to flowers, many flowering plants have come to rely on hummingbirds for pollination. Mostly red or orange, hummingbird blossoms are usually tubular and open during the day. They have little or no scent, since perfume is not needed to attract these little birds. The stamens or pistils extend beyond the petals, where they can touch hovering hummers and transfer the pollen. Lacking the "landing platforms" of plants visited by bees or butterflies, these blooms make their nectar accessible only to hummingbirds.

Among the hummingbird favorites in the East are cardinal-flower, trumpet vine, bee balm, and columbine. In the West, Arizona honeysuckle, Indian pink, scarlet larkspur, many paintbrushes, and the bush monkeyflower are adapted to visits by hummers.

Since hummingbirds require flowers for survival, it is quite easy to attract these feathered gems to gardens. Even some of the more elusive species can be lured with feeders, glass or plastic containers filled with sweetened water and decorated with the bright red that the birds seem to find irresistible. With the feeder filled, it is easy to enjoy, closeup and firsthand, these delightful sprites that John James Audubon called "glittering fragments of the rainbow."

A hurricane, viewed from a spacecraft, is seen as a massive, rotating storm system.

Hummingbird trumpet *Zauschneria*

A small shrubby plant of the Far West and Southwest, the hummingbird trumpet enlivens dry slopes and mountain ridges with dazzling displays of bright red tubular blossoms. The nectar-filled flowers open late in the season, providing hummingbirds with energy-rich food as they begin their fall migration. Also known as California fuchsia, the desert plant bears small woolly leaves, while the plants that grow on mountain slopes have less hairy foliage.

Humus

When leaves, branches, dead insects—almost any kind of plant or animal material—fall on warm, moist soil, microorganisms immediately begin breaking them down to their constituent elements. The roots of nearby plants absorb nutrients released by the decay, and carbon dioxide escapes into the air. What remains to enrich the soil is humus. This fine-textured black or brown material promotes healthy plant growth, both by helping the soil retain moisture and by keeping it loose and crumbly so that air can penetrate to roots. As it gradually decomposes, humus continues to benefit surrounding plants with a small but steady supply of nutrients.

Hurricane

Monstrous in both their size and ferocity, Atlantic hurricanes are severe tropical storms that develop over warm oceans. Called typhoons in the Pacific, the giant circular storm systems are also known as tropical cyclones. Their violent winds, which may blow at speeds of more than 150 miles per hour, are accompanied by huge churning waves and torrential rainfall.

Seen from a satellite, the swirling clouds of a hurricane resemble a giant pinwheel. At the center is the eye, a low-pressure area about 30 miles in diameter where the weather is eerily calm. The eye is surrounded by a wall of clouds and winds that may spread over an area measuring from 300 to more than 1,000 miles in diameter.

Hurricanes usually form over the Caribbean Sea and western Atlantic Ocean in August or September, when the surface of the ocean is warmest. Fueled by heat energy, their power increases as long as they remain over warm water. Those that head for land are prescriptions for disaster, with winds that can smash windows, tear the roofs off buildings, and snap large trees like toothpicks. Ninety percent of the deaths caused by hurricanes, however, result from drowning. The storms' low pressure elevates the level of the sea, and this, combined with huge waves and heavy, pounding rain, causes catastrophic flooding when a hurricane reaches shore. The effects are even worse if a storm hits at high tide. Fortunately, because they are no longer fueled by warm ocean water, hurricanes gradually die out as they move over land.

Hydra

Tiny freshwater relatives of sea anemones, hydras are carnivorous animals with built-in weapons systems. Consisting of hollow central stalks with crowns of tentacles radiating from the top, hydras anchor themselves to stones or plants and wait for passing prey. When tiny insects or crustaceans swim by, stinging cells on the tentacles shoot out poisonous threads, like miniature harpoons, paralyzing the victims, which the hydras then digest.

Icebergs, here shimmering under the bright arctic sun, possess an awesome beauty. Sun, wind, and seawater melt the tops of the bergs, sculpting them into magnificent forms.

Ibis

Denizens of shallow marshes, ponds, and coastal lagoons, where they stalk a variety of prey, ibises are easily distinguished from other long-legged, long-necked wading birds by their downward-curving bills. At dusk the gregarious creatures form large V-shaped flocks and fly to groves of tall trees, where they roost together for the night. They also nest in colonies. Each pair builds a loose cup of sticks or aquatic plants and tends a clutch of two to four pale blue, green, or buff-colored eggs.

Of the three species found in North America, the white ibis—snow-white except for its black wing tips and red bill, face, and legs—inhabits southern marshes and mangroves. The glossy ibis, a medium-size bird with bronzy plumage, is found on the U.S. East Coast, occasionally venturing as far north as Canada. Similar except for the band of white circling its face, the white-faced ibis lives on fresh water in the West.

Iceberg

Massive and menacing, icebergs are floating mountains of ice, sometimes with awesome facades and spires like those of castles and cathedrals. They are formed when huge chunks break off, with a thunderous rumbling, from the ends of glaciers or ice sheets and tumble into the sea. Icebergs present a serious hazard to shipping in such places as the North Atlantic, where most originate in Greenland. Although the largest bergs may tower hundreds of feet into the air, more than 85 percent of their bulk remains hidden below the surface, giving rise to the expression "That's just the tip of the iceberg."

White ibises are seldom caught standing alone. In summer, they gather into giant roosts of tens of thousands of birds. When they take to the air, the V-shaped flocks stretch a mile or so across the sky.

Glittering ice plants carpet the ground with their succulent stems, fleshy leaves, and spiky flowers.

A giant ichneumon bores into a log to lay its lethal egg.

The brittle beauty of an ice storm belies the terrible havoc that it can cause.

Ice plant *Cryophytum crystallinum*

Covered with tiny, water-filled beads, the stems and leaves of ice plants sparkle like hoarfrost on hot, dry slopes of the southern California coast. They put on a splendid show from March to October, bearing a profusion of pink or white flowers that open only on bright, sunny days. Originally imported from Africa to help control erosion, ice plants also are abundant on dunes, roadsides, salt marshes, and sea cliffs.

Ice storm

Among the most destructive forms of winter weather, ice storms occur when rain falls from warm air into a layer of colder air. As it nears the ground, the water freezes, coating wires, trees, and almost any other object it hits. Also known as silver thaws, the storms result in glittering layers of ice that can be breathtakingly beautiful. But they are also extremely dangerous. Less than half an inch of ice can snap power lines, break branches, and create havoc on roads and highways. If strong winds accompany the storm, the effects on forests can be devastating. And even a thin coating can freeze over the food supply, causing animals to starve. Fortunately, ice storms are usually short-lived. In most cases, the warm air mass that brought the storm slowly displaces the colder air and melts the ice.

Ichneumon

While they rarely sting humans, these relatives of wasps are deadly enemies of the insects that damage trees and crops. The female giant ichneumon, for instance, walks along tree trunks,

A massive igneous monolith—Stone Mountain—emerges from the earth in Georgia. On one of its granite walls is a memorial carving 190 feet wide and 90 feet high.

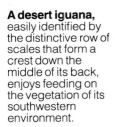

A desert iguana, easily identified by the distinctive row of scales that form a crest down the middle of its back, enjoys feeding on the vegetation of its southwestern environment.

listening for larvae of the pigeon horntail, a wood-boring insect. When she finds one, she pierces the bark and lays an egg in the horntail's tunnel. The ichneumon larva that hatches from her egg then slowly devours the horntail larva, pupates, and emerges as a winged adult. Other ichneumons parasitize harmful caterpillars, such as the tobacco hornworm, eating them from the inside out.

Igneous rock

Deriving their name from the Latin word for fire, igneous rocks are formed when molten magma cools and crystallizes. Some, such as granites, harden slowly deep within the earth and have a coarse-grained texture. Others, such as basalt, cool rapidly and are finer grained. They form from magma that explodes from volcanoes or oozes out through fissures on the earth's surface. Although often covered by sedimentary rocks or soil, igneous rocks form the bulk of the earth's crust.

Iguana

Some of the hottest, driest areas of the Southwest are home to the large and varied iguana family. The collared and horned lizards, for example, are iguanas, as is the chuckwalla. But the only species that bears the family name is the desert iguana. Unlike most other lizards that return to their burrows when the sun is high in the sky, this iguana is active at midday, often sunning or foraging even when temperatures soar above 100°F. For relief from the searing heat of the desert floor, it clambers into low shrubs, but at the first hint of danger it scurries into underbrush or into the burrow where it spends the night. Although it resembles a miniature dragon, the foot-long desert iguana prefers eating flowers to breathing fire. The yellow blooms of the creosote bush are its favorite meal, but it also relishes the buds, leaves, and flowers of cacti and other plants, as well as occasional carrion and insects.

The imperial moth can be sighted east of the Rockies from Canada to Mexico.

During incubation the diminutive chestnut-sided warbler sits on its eggs for 12 to 13 days.

Imperial moth *Eacles imperialis*

With a wingspan of four to six inches, the imperial moth is one of the largest in North America. The short-lived, nonfeeding adults have bright yellow wings that are streaked and spotted with purplish brown. Strongly attracted to artificial lights, they sometimes linger near them after daybreak and are eaten by birds. The larvae, four inches long, are horned and hairy caterpillars that feed on the foliage of both broad-leaved and coniferous trees.

Incubation

Left alone, a bird's eggs would not hatch, for the embryos must be kept warm if they are to develop. Incubation is the process by which the eggs are maintained at a fairly constant temperature. Usually birds accomplish this by sitting on the eggs and warming them with body heat. Since feathers block the flow of heat from a bird's body, females (which do most of the sitting) molt the feathers on part of the belly to form a brood patch. This bare area, which is well supplied with blood vessels, transfers more heat to the eggs. Ducks and geese pluck feathers from the brood patch, but on most other birds they fall out naturally.

During incubation, birds turn their eggs several times a day, both to ensure even heating and to keep the embryos from settling to one side of the eggs. After the eggs hatch, the parents often continue to brood the chicks until they are able to maintain a steady body temperature—anywhere from a few days to a few weeks, depending upon the species. Incubation periods range from 12 days for some of the songbirds to as long as 55 days for shearwaters.

Most birds lay one egg a day and do not begin

Colorful Indian paintbrush plumes brighten the meadows, forest clearings, fields, and prairies of the West.

The Indian pipe bears its blooms atop stems that are 6 to 10 inches tall.

incubating until the clutch is complete. Others—owls, hawks, and herons, for instance—start sitting as soon as the first egg is laid. As a result, their chicks do not hatch in unison, and in lean times the youngest nestlings sometimes starve to death.

Indian paintbrush *Castilleja*

The bright orange, red, yellow, pink, or lavender plumelike flower heads of the Indian paintbrushes look as if they have been freshly dipped into pots of paint. The colorful display, however, is provided not by flowers but by bracts, modified leaves that nearly hide the actual, pale, tubular, two-lipped blooms. Most at home in the West, though a few species do wander to the East, the paintbrushes range from a few inches to five feet in height. Besides the food they manufacture with their own green leaves, these semiparasitic wildflowers also derive nourishment by tapping into their neighbors' roots, a trait that makes them unsuitable for gardens.

Indian pipe *Monotropa uniflora*

Rising in ghostly white or pinkish clusters from the shadowed forest floor, the Indian pipe, also known as the corpse plant, is sometimes mistaken for a fungus. It is, however, a true flowering plant, although its leaves, lacking chlorophyll and reduced to mere scales along the stem, are unable to manufacture food. Instead, the Indian pipe's tangled mass of rootlets lives in intimate association with subterranean fungi that take sustenance for both of them from decaying organic matter and the roots of living trees. Each of the Indian pipe's pale, waxy stems is topped in summer by a single nodding cup-shaped flower that does indeed give it the look of a small clay pipe. The closely related pinesap is similar in appearance but is reddish or yellow in color, and each stalk bears not one but several nodding flowers. Often found growing beneath pines and oaks, it too lives in partnership with a fungus.

Indigo *Baptisia*

In pioneer times settlers cultivated the native wild indigo as a substitute for the traditional old-world dye plant. But they also used it to brush flies off their horses and so called it shoofly and horsefly weed. A bushy plant found on sandy soils throughout the East, wild indigo has gray-green compound leaves resembling clover and is covered with pretty yellow flowers from May to September. A pair of taller Midwestern species bear similar blooms. The prairie false indigo produces creamy white flowers. The blue false indigo has flowers of a true indigo-blue, and its sap turns purple upon exposure to the air.

Insect See pp. 188–189.

Insect

Astonishing in their number and diversity, the insects of the world outnumber all other animal species by about four to one. North America alone has more than 100,000 kinds, and on average, a square mile of land is home to more insects than there are people in the world. And this may be only the tip of the iceberg, for scientists discover thousands of new insect species every year.

Yet despite their diversity—from beautiful butterflies to chirping crickets to lowly lice—all insects have certain features in common. For one thing, an insect's body always has three parts: the head, thorax, and abdomen. Most insects also have a pair of antennae on the head and three pairs of jointed legs on the thorax.

Though a few primitive, soil-dwelling types are wingless, most insects have wings. Usually there are two pairs, attached to the thorax. Flies, however, have only one pair. And on beetles the outer pair of wings are hardened cases that protect the membranous inner pair.

Spiders, centipedes, and ticks are often mistaken for insects, but there are basic differences. Spiders, for example, may look like insects, but they have eight legs rather than six, and their bodies are in two parts rather than three.

Growing and changing

The life cycle of certain insects—among them butterflies, moths, bees, ants, beetles, and flies— involves a remarkable transformation, or metamorphosis, that takes place in four stages: egg, larva, pupa, and adult. Most larvae, such as caterpillars (butterfly larvae) and maggots (fly larvae), are eating machines. As they grow in size, the wormlike larvae shed their skin several times and then pass into the pupal, or resting, stage, in which they are sealed inside a protective covering, such as a cocoon. The pupae of some butterflies are beautifully marked with gold spots and have been given the name chrysalis, which derives from the Greek word for gold. Once the changes of the pupal stage are complete, the insect emerges from its cocoon as a fully formed, winged adult.

Many other insects, such as grasshoppers, dragonflies, cockroaches, cicadas, and lice, develop differently, with a life cycle of just three stages: egg, nymph, and adult. In a process called incomplete metamorphosis, the nymphs, which have traces of wing buds, undergo several molts as they increase in size and gradually assume the adult form. Some nymphs—for instance, those of grasshoppers—bear an obvious resemblance to their parents. Others, such as dragonfly nymphs, are homely, voracious predators that live underwater and breathe with gills—a far cry from the beautifully colored, gossamer-winged adults they become.

Insects are survivors

Insects are among the most successful forms of life on earth. For one thing, they are enormously adaptable. Some live in ice-cold water, others in hot springs, salt lakes, or pools of crude oil. They thrive from the frozen polar regions to the tropics, and from deserts to streams. Their small size is helpful too. Insects can hide, build

Treehoppers are odd-looking insects that resemble thorns and suck sap from plants.

Large milkweed bugs, half an inch long, are seen here with developing nymphs.

Cicada-killer wasps use their formidable stings to paralyze cicadas, then haul their quarry to underground nests.

Paper wasps construct hanging nests made of finely chewed wood pulp. They feed on nectar and the juices of fruits.

homes, and find food in tiny places that are inaccessible to other animals. And individual insects not only need very little to eat, but they can make a meal of almost anything, from cloth and paper to plaster and glue.

Defense against predators is another facet of survival. Insects, for instance, have external skeletons—in effect, hard coats of armor that protect them from injury. When confronted with an enemy, however, most insects escape by flying, jumping, or running away. Others rely on camouflage: walkingsticks, treehoppers, and many moths and caterpillars look exactly like the vegetation on which they rest.

Some kinds of insects use weapons to defend themselves. Caterpillars are often armed with poisonous barbs; ants and beetles have sharp, pincerlike jaws; and bees and wasps can deliver powerful stings. Other insects, such as stinkbugs and carrion beetles, emit offensive odors, while earwigs and bombardier beetles can release noxious sprays. Still others survive simply because they are unappetizing. The monarch butterfly, for example, is avoided by birds because of its unpleasant taste.

Our constant companions

Humans have often wished that insects were not such expert survivors. For thousands of years people have suffered bites and stings, diseases,

damaged property, and devastated crops—all thanks to these tiny but ubiquitous creatures.

By far the most costly and destructive insects are the agricultural pests. Every year such important crops as cotton, potatoes, and many fruits are seriously harmed by insects. The damage they do, combined with the cost of controlling them, amounts to many billions of dollars.

Without insects, however, the world as we know it would be seriously impoverished. Many thousands of plants would disappear without insects to pollinate them; we would have no silk or honey; and countless kinds of birds, fish, reptiles, and other insect-eaters might simply vanish from the earth.

Tiger swallowtails are boldly colored as adults, but the young larvae look like bird droppings, and the overwintering pupae resemble sticks.

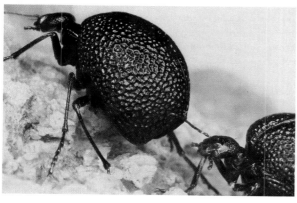

Desert blister beetles are found in the arid Southwest. Like other blister beetles, their bodies contain chemicals that, when released on human skin, cause blisters."

189

The invertebrates, which include more than a million different species, have very little in common except that they all lack backbones. Some, however, are more closely related than others. The sea star (left) is grouped with sea urchins and sand dollars; the scorpion (below) is the cousin of insects and crabs; and the sea anemone (bottom) is a relative of jellyfish and corals.

Invertebrate

Any animal without an internal backbone, or spine, is called an invertebrate. A vast and varied assemblage, such creatures constitute about 95 percent of all animal species, and they range in size and complexity from microscopic protozoans to the 50-foot giant squid. The largest group, the arthropods, includes insects, crustaceans, spiders, and other creatures distinguished by the possession of jointed legs and hard outer coverings. The mollusks, found in almost every habitat, form another large and adaptable group; it includes animals with shells, such as clams and snails, as well as others whose shells are buried in their bodies (squid) or missing altogether (octopuses). Worms, sponges, corals, brachiopods—these and many more creatures are numbered among the invertebrates. Their activities, from pollinating flowers to aerating the soil, are vitally important in the food chain and in every kind of ecosystem.

Iris *Iris*

Anyone who has ever bought a spring bouquet will recognize these striking flowers and their dramatic swordlike leaves, for the wild irises that adorn our countryside bear an unmistakable resemblance to the cultivated species. Like the florist's blooms, the wildlings—many of them known as flags—flaunt three upright petals and three drooping petallike sepals, which on some kinds sport a fuzzy ridge, or "beard."

In spring and early summer the irises put on a spectacular show across much of the continent. Violet-colored blue flags dot moist meadows and woodlands in the East, while the similar-looking Rocky Mountain iris is well known throughout the West. In the Southeast, marshes, streambanks, and bayous are -enlivened by tall and tawny red flags, and the yellow flag is a familiar ornamental from coast to coast.

Iron

The fourth most abundant element in the earth's crust, iron lacks the shimmering beauty of silver and the lustrous yellow sheen of gold but is nevertheless of inestimable value, for it is the most widely used of all metals. All plants and animals contain small amounts of iron. Humans especially need it for healthy red blood cells, where it plays a crucial role in the transport of oxygen. But iron is also the basis for the manufacture of steel and countless other products. The silver-gray shiny metal is extremely malleable; it can be magnetized and is a good conductor of heat and electricity. Iron seldom occurs in its pure state in nature but combines with other elements to form many minerals. When oxidized, it rusts, thus adding magnificent color to rocks.

Irises, all beautifully colored, get their name from the Greek goddess of the rainbow.

Jack-in-the-pulpit, hooded in spring (top), produces bright fruits in autumn (bottom).

Crevalle jacks, up to two feet long, form dense schools that travel as far north as Cape Cod.

J

Jack

Popular as both game and food fish, the jacks are a large family that can challenge even the most experienced angler. Fast swimmers that are apt to head for deep water and shoot straight downward, these fish of tropical and temperate seas display fight and strength far out of proportion to their size. And they are able predators, sometimes herding anchovies and other small fish into dense schools before striking. Ranging in length from six inches to five feet, the jacks have deeply forked tails and, often, an iridescent silvery sheen. Well-known members of the family include the amberjacks, tenacious game fish named for their golden hue; the pompanos, delectable food fish; and the California yellowtails, so prized that their numbers have dwindled. Another, the pilotfish, which travels alongside sharks and ships to pick up scraps, was once thought to lead sharks and whales to food and guide lost ships to land.

Jack-in-the-pulpit *Arisaema triphyllum*

A familiar sight in eastern woodlands, the Jack-in-the-pulpit is a member of the arum family, which includes such related plants as skunk cabbage and calla lilies. Up to three feet tall, it blooms in early spring, producing distinctive hooded flower spikes. The purple-striped or green "pulpit," called the spathe, arches over "Jack," a fleshy clublike spike—known as the spadix—with many tiny flowers hidden at its base. By fall, after the flowers have passed, the spathe withers to expose a cluster of bright red berries. Also known as Indian turnip, Jack-in-the-pulpit has corms, or bulblike roots, that long ago were cooked and eaten as vegetables by the aboriginal peoples. Inedible when raw, the corms were also ground for poultices and dried for a variety of medicinal uses.

Jackrabbit See *Hare.*

The jaegers, which get their name from the German word for hunter, are fiercely protective of their nests and nestlings. Powerful, fast flyers as well as bold thieves, they have been known to swoop down on colonies of seabirds and feed on their eggs.

The blue jay (left) and the Steller's jay (right) are brazen, noisy members of a large family of birds that also includes the well-known ravens, crows, and magpies.

J

Jaeger *Stercorarius*

Hawklike relatives of gulls, jaegers are pirates of the high seas. Swift and streamlined, with long central tail feathers, they shamelessly bully terns and gulls, grabbing fish from their bills, making them drop hard-won prey, and even forcing them to disgorge fish already eaten. They are also formidable hunters in their own right, equipped with hooked beaks and sharp talons. On their nesting grounds on the Arctic tundra, all three species of jaegers feed regularly on such prey as lemmings and small birds.

Jay

Far more colorful than their larger, somber-hued cousins, the crows, jays are adaptable, aggressive birds that usually live in woodlands and often nest in gardens and backyards. Just as inquisitive as the crows, they are often the first birds to spot predators and sound the alarm. They feed on insects and the eggs and young of other songbirds, as well as seeds and nuts, including acorns, which they thriftily bury for winter use.

The handsomely crested blue jay is a familiar bird at backyard feeders in the East, where its nest-robbing habits and raucous cries have given it a reputation as a pest. A western relative, the Steller's jay, inhabits coniferous forests in the mountains. The scrub jay lives in chaparral, pine-oak woodlands, and juniper thickets in the West; an isolated population in Florida is separated from its relatives by more than 1,000 miles. The stocky, crow-shaped pinyon jay likes to travel in large flocks and feeds on the seeds of pinyon pines. Another type, the fluffy gray jay, is a bird of northern spruce and fir forests. It often flies into camps to steal food—a habit that has earned it the epithet camp robber.

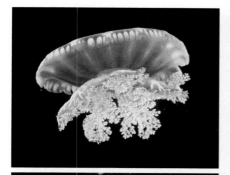

Jellyfish occur in a fascinating variety of shapes and sizes.

The toxic jimsonweed has a large, fragrant flower.

Jellyfish

These primitive marine animals without backbones or brains are not fish at all but are related to corals, sea anemones, and hydras. Jellyfish have broad, bell-shaped bodies made of translucent gelatinous material. The mouth and four trailing lobes hang from the underside of the bell, and many long, threadlike tentacles dangle from its edge. The tentacles are armed with poisonous stinging cells, which jellyfish use to capture small fish, planktonic animals, and other prey. Since they can also sting humans, they are unwelcome at bathing beaches.

Jellyfish can swim feebly by contracting and relaxing their bells, but for the most part they drift with the currents and winds. Occasionally they swim upside down, their tentacles floating above them. The moon jelly, a species that is common off the Atlantic, Pacific, and Gulf of Mexico coasts, is 8 to 10 inches in diameter. Another, the by-the-wind sailor, is less than four inches across and has a triangular "sail" projecting from its body. The lion's mane, the giant of the clan, is a venomous resident of northern waters. Over 6 feet in diameter, it has tentacles more than 100 feet long.

Jet stream

Giant rivers of air that flow at high velocity about seven miles above the surface of the earth, the jet streams circle the globe from west to east. They blow in narrow bands at an average of 60 miles an hour, though speeds of 300 miles an hour and more have been recorded. Associated with turbulence in the lower parts of the atmosphere, jet streams have a definite effect on weather patterns.

These ribbons of wind were first discovered by airplane pilots during World War II. Flying eastward, they found that they could arrive at their destinations well ahead of schedule if they were able to catch a jet stream.

Jimsonweed *Datura stramonium*

With derivatives whose effects range from medicinal to downright poisonous, jimsonweed has a long history of use by cults and witches. Its name derives from Jamestown, Virginia, where early settlers ate the leaves and became crazed for days. Others used jimsonweed to make a paste that, absorbed through the skin, produced wild hallucinations.

Growing up to five feet tall in parts of central and western Canada and coast to coast in the United States, jimsonweed has coarsely toothed, foul-smelling leaves but its huge trumpetlike white or lavender flowers are pleasantly fragrant. They open at night and attract swarms of moths that, apparently developing an addiction for the narcotic nectar, often return again and again for more.

Alternate names for the plant include devil's apple, mad apple, fireweed, stinkweed, and devil's trumpet. Jimsonweed's fruits, bristling with sharp spines and about the size of golf balls, inspired yet another nickname: thorn apple.

J

Joshua trees assume remarkably varied shapes. Perhaps flowering for the first time, the specimen on the left has not yet developed the many-branched form of the mature tree (right).

Joe-pye weed's many other common names include king of the meadow, marsh milkweed, and purple boneset.

J

Joe-pye weed *Eupatorium*

The curious name of the joe-pye weed honors an Indian healer who, according to legend, used the plants to cure an epidemic of typhus in the Massachusetts Bay Colony. In moist meadows and woodland clearings, they are among the most conspicuous wildflowers of late summer, when their broad, fuzzy clusters of pinkish-purple blooms appear atop stout stems three to seven feet tall. When bruised, the lance-shaped leaves of one species, sweet joe-pye weed, give off an aroma very much like vanilla. The similar-looking spotted joe-pye weed has purple or purple-spotted stems.

Jojoba *Simmondsia chinensis*

A hardy survivor that can live for a century, jojoba is a shrub that thrives in the dry, salty soils of southwestern deserts, where rain is scarce and temperatures often soar. The plant grows up to 8 feet tall and gets much of its moisture by sending a taproot 35 feet into the ground. This attractive evergreen has stiff, branching stems and oval, leathery leaves. Its pale greenish flowers are unremarkable, but the acornlike fruits are unique and valuable. Their peanut-size kernels yield a liquid wax that is much in demand for cosmetics and as an industrial lubricant. Very similar to the oil of sperm whales, the substance has been valued as a substitute for whale oil since the great mammals became endangered. Because it resembles boxwood, jojoba is gaining favor in parts of the Southwest as an ornamental shrub. In other arid regions of the world, it has been transplanted to help stabilize soils and stop the spread of deserts.

Joshua tree *Yucca brevifolia*

A plant unlike any other, the Joshua tree ornaments the Mojave Desert with picturesque, grotesquely branching silhouettes. It was named by early Mormons, who likened the tree to the biblical Joshua beckoning them to the Promised Land. Starting life as a dense rosette of blue-green, daggerlike leaves, this oversized member of the agave family sends a single stem 8 to 10 feet into the air. Then, after its first flowering, it begins to spread its branches in characteristically striking patterns. At maturity the Joshua tree may reach a height of 30 to 50 feet, with a trunk 3½ feet in diameter. From late February to early April, it produces clusters of six-petaled yellow-green blossoms, fertilized by the night-flying yucca moth. The blooms produce abundant crops of seeds, which Indians used to grind into meal. The tree's wood has been used for everything from paper pulp to surgeon's splints.

Woodland jumping mice, which live near ponds and streams, are able swimmers as well as nimble leapers.

Dark-eyed juncos, familiar visitors at bird feeders, are sometimes called snowbirds. The active creatures are unfazed by winter storms.

Common junipers produce dark bluish berrylike cones, whose fragrant, resinous flesh is relished by many birds.

Jumping mouse

Named for their habit of moving across the ground with bounding leaps, jumping mice inhabit woodlands and meadows. The small yellowish rodents have long hind legs that enable them to jump up to six feet, and exceptionally long tails that help them maintain balance when leaping. Jumping mice are elusive creatures that hide by day and forage at night for grass seeds, fruit, and insects. Unlike most mice, they do not store food but put on a thick layer of fat in the fall in preparation for six to eight months of hibernation. After emerging in spring, they mate and give birth to a litter of young several weeks

later. The woodland jumping mouse of the Northeast prefers brushy areas near water; the meadow jumping mouse is found across Canada and in the northern United States.

Junco *Junco*

Small, gregarious birds that resemble sparrows, juncos are found in coniferous and mixed forests and at the edges of woodlands throughout North America. Hopping about on the ground, they forage for seeds in winter and include insects, spiders, and wild fruits in their diet in summer. They also nest on the ground, building well-hidden cups of rootlets, grass, and moss. After nesting, juncos gather in flocks that migrate south or into lowland areas. Tame and trusting, they are welcome visitors at bird feeders.

Several races of juncos formerly regarded as separate species are now known as dark-eyed juncos. All have pink conical bills and white outer tail feathers but are otherwise quite variable. The yellow-eyed junco, a second species, lives in the mountain forests of the Southwest.

Juniper *Juniperus*

These aromatic evergreens flourish on dry, rocky soils throughout most of North America. Though all junipers have durable, close-grained, soft wood, and pungent, semifleshy cones resembling berries, these trees are a diverse group that varies in form and height. The alligator juniper of the Southwest, for instance, is a spreading tree that reaches heights of 65 feet and has scalelike foliage that overlaps like the shingles on a roof. The widespread common juniper, in contrast, is a sprawling shrub with pointed needles. Cedar chests are made from the wood of another common species, known as eastern red cedar, and the berries of the common juniper are used for flavoring gin.

J

195

A kangaroo rat's long hind legs enable it to bound great distances, just like its namesake. It also uses its strong legs to strike opponents in fights. When not out foraging, the little rodent lives in an underground burrow, where it sometimes stores a supply of dried food.

A katydid, its folded wings resembling a tent, blends in with its surroundings.

The Kentucky coffeetree has compound leaves up to three feet long. Its pods often grow to a length of 10 inches.

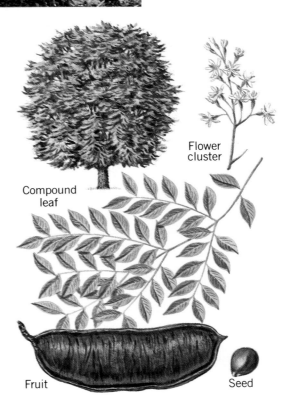

Flower cluster

Compound leaf

Fruit

Seed

K

Kame

Domelike hills of glacial debris, kames were deposited by streams of meltwater flowing into crevasses or pouring off the leading edges of stagnating glaciers and ice sheets. They range in height from just a few feet to 100 feet or more and are generally composed of a mixture of sand and gravel. Especially common in Wisconsin, Michigan, Indiana, and other areas near the southernmost limits of the vast continental ice sheets of the Ice Age, kames are a good source of sand and gravel for road construction as well as for other purposes.

Kangaroo mouse *Microdipodops*

At six inches long, including the tail, kangaroo mice are about half the size of their more familiar cousins, the kangaroo rats. Like their kin, though, they have powerful hind legs that enable them to leap across the deserts and sagebrush flats of the Great Basin in Nevada and neighboring states. Relatively rare, by day the little rodents retreat into burrows among the roots of desert plants and seal the entrances with sand to keep out the heat. They come out at night to feed on seeds and insects but have no need for drinking water, obtaining it instead from their food as it is metabolized.

196

A kettle hole filled with water forms a quiet pond beside dunes on Cape Cod in Massachusetts.

Kangaroo rat *Dipodomys*

Like their Australian namesakes, kangaroo rats have sturdy hind legs and long tails. Agile creatures of the night, they leap gracefully across deserts and dry plains in the West, using their tufted tails for balance. They are gentle, attractive animals, with large heads, large eyes, and tawny, silklike fur.

Kangaroo rats stay in their burrows during the heat of day, emerging after dark to forage for seeds, grass, and roots, which they carry back to the nest in fur-lined pouches on their cheeks. Well-adapted to life in the desert, they do not need to drink water. The little moisture that they require is obtained as a by-product of digestion of their food.

Kaolinite

A soft, whitish clay mineral, kaolinite is produced by the decomposition of feldspar and similar materials. As water seeps into soil or rock that is rich in feldspar, the feldspar gradually weathers to form kaolinite. Sometimes called china clay, it is widely used in pottery and ceramics and as a coating and filler in paper products. Important deposits of kaolinite are found in Georgia, North and South Carolina, Florida, and Pennsylvania.

Katydid

More often heard than seen, katydids fill summer nights with shrill, monotonous music. Best known is the so-called true katydid of the East, which seems to recite its own name over and over again. Their chirping sounds, produced by rubbing one wing against the other, are courtship calls that enable the sexes to find each other and mate. The males' loud serenades are usually answered by the shorter chirps of the female.

Closely related to the grasshoppers, katydids have long, threadlike antennae. Most are green, matching the vegetation on which they rest, and their wings are often ridged and veined to resemble leaves. The insects feed on the leaves and tender twigs of trees and shrubs.

Kentucky coffeetree *Gymnocladus dioicus*

Native to the Midwest, where it prefers deep, rich, moist soils, the Kentucky coffeetree is, throughout its range, one of the last trees to leaf out in spring and one of the first to shed its enormous, twice-compound leaves in the fall. In late spring it is covered with large upright clusters of greenish-white flowers, with those on female trees producing broad, leathery, reddish-brown pods. They contain large seeds that pioneers used to brew a coffee substitute.

K

Kettle

Bowl-shaped depressions, often filled by ponds, are a common sight on the outwash plains of long-vanished Ice Age glaciers. Known as kettles, they usually are quite deep and can be up to a mile in diameter. They formed where blocks of ice were buried in the sand and gravel left behind by retreating glaciers. As the ice slowly melted, the covering debris collapsed, leaving a gently sloping depression on the surface of the land. Many kettle ponds are found in Manitoba, Ontario, Michigan, Minnesota, and on other dumping grounds of the great Ice Age glaciers.

197

Adult killdeer have two black bands across the breast, while the chicks have only one.

Striped killifish, found from Cape Cod to Florida, reach eight inches in length.

Killdeer *Charadrius vociferus*

Perhaps the best-known shorebird in North America, this member of the plover family nests in much of Canada and throughout the U.S. mainland. A bird of open places—from pastures and meadows to airports and golf courses—the killdeer is named for its piercing *kil-dee* call, which it often rings out while in flight.

The killdeer lays its buff-colored, dark-blotched eggs in a nest that is nothing more than a shallow depression in the ground lined with pebbles or a few bits of vegetation. Choosing any open stony area, it even nests on driveways and little-used gravel roads.

The killdeer is famous for its "broken wing" display. When intruders appear in the nesting area, they are confronted by a creeping, wing-dragging, piteously crying adult. Its splayed tail reveals the bright orange rump, a beacon that further distracts potential predators and helps draw them away from the nest full of eggs or tiny chicks.

Eastern kingbirds are brash and bellicose inhabitants of forest edges, woodland clearings, and open areas.

Killifish

Only a few inches long, the killifish are often confused with minnows. Some of them, in fact, are called topminnows because of their habit of feeding at the water's surface. Equipped with upturned mouths adapted for that purpose, killifish consume large quantities of mosquito larvae and are valued for their role in keeping the insects under control.

Of the several dozen species of killifish in North America, most live in the South. They thrive in fresh, salt, or brackish water, and some of the desert dwellers—called pupfish—can

The belted kingfisher will often perch on a branch, then plunge down to nab its prey. It swallows fish whole, headfirst.

Golden-crowned kinglet males have conspicuous orange crowns, while those worn by the females are yellow.

survive temperatures of up to 100°F. A few killifish, such as mummichogs, are used for bait, while many of the brightly colored kinds, such as pygmy killifish, are popular aquarium fish.

Kingbird *Tyrannus*

Bold and belligerent, the kingbirds are indeed lords of their domain, as their name *Tyrannus* implies. When a larger bird, such as a hawk or crow, flies through a kingbird's territory, the fearless little defender immediately takes chase. Scolding the larger bird with staccato squeaks, the kingbird even goes so far as to land on the interloper in flight, pecking at its back until feathers fly and the trespasser is driven away. The kingbirds' aggressive instincts are so strong, in fact, that the birds have even been sighted attacking low-flying airplanes.

Found mostly in the United States, the two most widely distributed species are the black-and-white eastern kingbird and the pale gray and lemon-yellow western kingbird. Like other flycatchers, they feed by swooping out from exposed perches to snatch up flying insects, often with an audible snap of the bill. Especially fond of honeybees, the birds have earned the nickname bee martins. Kingbirds also feed on berries in summer and fall: hovering near shrub dogwoods and elderberry bushes, they dart in repeatedly to nip off the ripening fruits.

Kingfisher

Spirited and able anglers, kingfishers regularly station themselves on branches over lakes or streams and intently eye the water below. When a fish flashes by, the bird plunges into the water and snaps it up with its stout, daggerlike bill. Flying to a nearby perch, it often beats the wriggling fish against a branch, tosses it into the air,

and swallows it headfirst. Kingfishers sometimes vary their hunting technique, hovering in midair as they scan the water for fish. Whether perched or on the wing, they frequently fill the air with loud, rattling calls.

In summer, male and female kingfishers take turns excavating a nesting burrow up to 15 feet long in a steep sand or gravel bank, usually near a stream or river. They loosen the dirt with their beaks and kick it out with their feet. Then, in a chamber at the end of the tunnel, the female lays her glossy white eggs on a bed of fish bones and scales. The young, fed on small fish, leave the nest when they are some three weeks old.

The species seen throughout North America is the belted kingfisher, a chunky, blue-gray bird with a big head and a ragged crest. Two others, the ringed kingfisher and the green kingfisher, are found only in southern Texas in the United States.

Kinglet *Regulus*

Tiny, plump, grayish-olive birds, the kinglets are most often seen in trees, flitting restlessly from branch to branch as they pluck insects and their eggs and larvae from the foliage and crevices in the bark. They summer in northern coniferous forests, where they build elaborate, globular nests of moss and spiderwebs, lined with feathers, fur, and plant fibers. Their eggs, up to nine to the clutch, are creamy white with dainty speckles. In winter they range south as far as Mexico and often roam the woodlands in mixed flocks, keeping company with chickadees, brown creepers, and other small birds. The ruby-crowned kinglet is named for the males' red crown patch, though it is visible only when they are excited. About four inches long, these birds produce a surprisingly loud, melodic song. Golden-crowned kinglets are named for the crowns worn by both sexes.

K

199

Kingsnakes, up to six feet in length, come in a wide range of distinctive colors and patterns.

Kudzu grows rapidly, draping trees, fences, and buildings with lush tangles of vines. This rampant, uncontrollable weed, formerly confined to the southern United States, is eradicated wherever possible. But despite the efforts, it has been spotted as far north as New England.

Kingsnake *Lampropeltis*

Formidable enemies of both rats and mice, kingsnakes are valued by farmers for keeping down populations of the rodent pests. Since they are immune to the venom of rattlers and copperheads, kingsnakes sometimes feed on these poisonous reptiles as well. They kill by constriction, coiling around their victims and suffocating them, as do their close relatives the milk snakes (so named for their supposed ability to suck milk from cattle).

Knapweed *Centaurea*

Adorning fields and roadsides throughout the summer and into fall, the knapweeds are best recognized by their thistlelike flower heads—tufts of tubular blue, purple, pink, or white florets that emerge from a sheath of prickly bracts. Many species are found across the continent, including a garden favorite, the bachelor's button. The knapweeds range from one to four feet in height, with lance-shaped or divided leaves.

Knotweed *Polygonum*

Among the most aggressive, widespread weeds of roadsides, lawns, and cultivated ground, the knotweeds are named for their swollen stem joints. Some, because of their leaves' biting flavor, are also known as smartweeds. Blooming through summer and fall, the knotweeds bear small pink or greenish-white flowers which usually grow in dense spikes. The water smartweed has large pink flower clusters and thrives in ponds and muddy places. Japanese knotweed forms thickets of bamboolike 10-foot-tall shoots and is almost impossible to eradicate. Others—such as lady's thumb, with a dark 'thumbprint' near the center of each leaf, and pinkweed, named for its pink flower spikes—flourish in yards virtually everywhere.

Kudzu *Pueraria lobata*

In 1911, the fast-growing kudzu was imported from Japan to the United States and hailed as the Savior of the South. With roots that penetrate deep into the soil, the vine promised a solution to the problem of erosion. Its ability to take nitrogen directly from the air and fix it in the soil seemed to make it ideal for restoring fields exhausted by generations of tobacco and cotton culture. And its broad, bright green, three-part leaves were even more nutritious than alfalfa.

But kudzu turned out to be too successful, adding a foot of growth each day and sending vines to the tops of tall trees in a single season. While insects, diseases, and colder weather kept kudzu in check in the Orient, the pest flourished in the warm, moist South, smothering 11,000 square miles by the 1980's.

Ladybird beetles gather in large numbers in the fall, just before their winter hibernation. Savvy farmers, aware that the insects congregate in the same places every year, often collect the hordes for use in control of aphids and other pests.

Lacewings emit a foul odor when disturbed and so are also known as stinkflies.

The showy lady's slipper is the emblem of Prince Edward Island and Minnesota.

Lacewing

Delicate insects with diaphanous, conspicuously veined wings, lacewings are found throughout North America. Their abdomens are long and slender, and their folded wings resemble tiny tents. Green lacewings live in meadows and gardens, while the less common brown lacewings are more often seen in wooded areas. The larvae of both kinds, like the adults, feed so ravenously on aphids and other soft-bodied insects that they are often known as aphid lions.

Ladybird beetle

Small, round, and colorful, ladybird beetles, or ladybugs, are among our most beneficial and popular insects. Red or yellow with black spots, or black with red or yellow spots, they look like brightly enameled half-peas. They were named after Our Lady, the Virgin Mary, in the Middle Ages. Over the centuries since then, legends about these attractive insects have abounded.

Their usefulness, however, is not a matter of folklore: formidable predators, both adults and larvae devour huge numbers of aphids and other harmful insects. Over 150 species of ladybird beetles are found in North America, and almost all are helpful to farmers and gardeners. In the late 1800's an Australian species was imported to combat an insect pest that was plaguing California citrus orchards. The venture proved to be so successful that ladybird beetles are now raised commercially as natural pest controls.

Lady's slipper *Cypripedium*

Among the most elegantly beautiful of all wildflowers, lady's slippers are easily recognized by the distinctive slipper-shaped pouch formed by one of their petals. The structure is more than decorative, however. Insects lured into the pouch can escape only through an exit where they are well dusted with pollen, ensuring cross-pollination of the plants.

These hardy members of the orchid family flourish in bogs and moist woodlands all across the continent. Their lovely pink, yellow, or white blossoms often tempt would-be transplanters. But because the plants cannot survive without the aid of microorganisms in their native soil, they must be admired only in the wild.

L

LAKE

Scattered like jewels across the North American landscape, lakes are rich in both beauty and wildlife. Most of these sizable inland bodies of water were formed by glaciers. The icy bulldozers either scarred the bedrock with depressions that later filled with water, or dumped tons of debris in the paths of rivers, creating natural dams. Some lakes occupy volcanic craters, some are man-made, and others were created by the erosion of limestone or movements of the earth's crust.

Whether fed by runoff from rain and melting snow or by underground springs, lakes often seem as eternal as the earth itself, but in fact they are short-lived on the scale of geologic time. Some are destined to dry up after a change in climate, and others will be filled with stream-fed sediment. Most shallow lakes, however, expire from eutrification, the process by which the accumulation of organic debris turns lakes into swamps and eventually dry land.

Some glacial lakes were formed when deposited debris dammed the glacier's own meltwater.

Western grebes build floating nests that are tethered to reeds. Here an adult feeds a chick.

Largemouth bass (above right) are a favorite of fishermen. They feed on insects, crayfish, frogs, and other fish.

Mallard ducklings, still downy, sun themselves on a log. The adults are agile fliers that can leap from the water directly into flight.

202

Moose have a particular fondness for aquatic plants. Despite their enormous bulk, they are surprisingly adept swimmers.

Whirligig beetles carry air bubbles underwater.

Dragonflies, before becoming winged adults, are nymphs that live and feed underwater.

Waterlilies, their roots anchored to the lake bottom, float like miniature islands.

Longnosed gars, unlike most fish, can use their swim bladder to absorb oxygen from the air.

This mountain lake, located in the Bighorn Mountains in Wyoming, will be several inches deeper in spring, when it is filled by the runoff from tons of melting snow on the surrounding slopes.

A **lamprey has** seven gill openings on either side of its body. Its round mouth is used to suck the blood of the host fish.

Larkspur blossoms yield a blue dye, which early settlers used to make ink.

Landslides can collapse entire mountainsides, reshaping the terrain with astonishing speed.

Lamprey

Primitive, scaleless fish that resemble eels, lampreys grow up to three feet long. They lack the jaws, bony skeletons, and paired fins of their more advanced relatives. Most, armed with a circular mouth and horny teeth, live as parasites, attaching themselves to other fish and sucking their blood.

Some lampreys live entirely in lakes and rivers, while others venture into the sea. In spring they swim up freshwater streams to scoop out nests and spawn. The wormlike larvae, called ammocoetes, burrow into the mud of riverbeds, where they feed on tiny particles of organic matter. After several years they mature into adults and make their way back to the lake or ocean from which their parents came.

Lampreys have at times been used as food; in some cultures, they are a delicacy. But generally they are regarded more as pests, especially in the Great Lakes, where parasitic lampreys killed vast numbers of trout and other fish before measures were devised to keep their numbers in check.

Landslide

Terrifying and destructive, landslides occur when soil and rock on steep hillsides come loose and hurtle downward, sweeping everything in their path. Sometimes landslides are triggered by earthquakes, but more often they are caused by heavy rain that soaks the ground and acts as a lubricant. One of North America's worst landslides occurred in Alberta in 1903, when 90 million tons of limestone plummeted off Turtle Mountain onto the sleeping town of Frank, damming the Crowsnest River, and burying a mine plant and sections of CPR tracks under 100 feet of debris. At least 70 people died in the slide.

Larch *Larix*

Two traits distinguish the larches from all other coniferous trees: their soft, flat needles grow along the twigs in tufts that resemble brushes, and the needles are shed in autumn, leaving the trees naked except for their little upright cones. The eastern larch, or tamarack, can be found

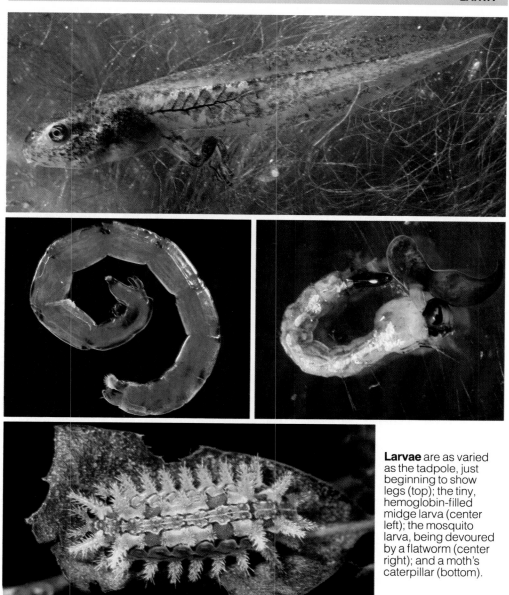

Larvae are as varied as the tadpole, just beginning to show legs (top); the tiny, hemoglobin-filled midge larva (center left); the mosquito larva, being devoured by a flatworm (center right); and a moth's caterpillar (bottom).

throughout eastern and central Canada and in the northeastern United States. The western larch, twice as tall at 150 feet or more, is an important timber tree in the Pacific Northwest.

Larkspur *Delphinium*

Arranged on slender stalks up to seven feet tall, the showy blue, white, or purple blossoms of the larkspurs each have a long, pointed "spur." Actually a narrow tube, the structure serves as a repository for the nectar that tempts the plant's pollinators, which include bumblebees, moths, and butterflies. Flourishing in a wide range of habitats, larkspurs are found from moist, northeastern woodlands to the dry prairies and the slopes of western mountains. Because all parts of the plants are poisonous to livestock as well as humans, the larkspurs have earned a sinister reputation in cattle country.

Larva

At birth or hatching, many animals look like miniature versions of the adults, while others begin their lives as larvae completely different from the adults. The latter must undergo a dramatic transformation, or metamorphosis, before they become fully mature. Larval stages are most common among invertebrates, especially insects and creatures that live in water. Beetle grubs and the caterpillars of butterflies are examples of air-breathing insect larvae. The larvae of other insects, such as dragonflies and alderflies, may spend up to two years in the water, eating voraciously, before they develop into winged, short-lived adults. Marine animals such as sponges, oysters, crabs, and jellyfish also have larval stages. Among vertebrates, some fish produce larvae, but the most familiar examples are the tadpoles of frogs and toads.

L

205

Fiery lava erupted to create the desolate landscape at Craters of the Moon in Idaho.

Lava

Molten rock that erupts onto the surface of the earth through volcanos or fissures in the crust is called lava. It can be thick and viscous or fluid and fast flowing. It also is fiery hot, with temperatures as high as 2200°F. As lava cools, it forms many kinds of igneous rocks. Some are very dense in composition but harden too rapidly to produce visible crystals. Others, like pumice, have a spongy texture and are almost weightless because gases are quickly trapped as the lava becomes solid. Rapid chilling of lava results in obsidian, a black glassy rock. When extruded underwater, lava sometimes solidifies into blobs known as pillow lava. So-called basaltic lavas tend to be more fluid and often pour out of fissures in the earth, burying hundreds of square miles (such as the eastern two-thirds of Oregon and Washington) under thick sheets of rock.

Lead See *Galena*.

Leaf

Fundamentally, a leaf is a factory that, by the process of photosynthesis, uses the energy from sunlight to manufacture the sugars and starches that nourish the growth of an entire plant. The flat part of a leaf, its "blade," is actually a highly efficient solar collector, while the veins serve not only as reinforcing ribs but also as a circulatory system.

The interior of the leaf, where most of the photosynthesis occurs, is protected on both top and bottom by an epidermis, a tough, wax-coated skin that protects the leaf against dehydration. Pores, or stomata—many thousands per square inch—perforate the epidermis. They can be opened and closed to control the movement of carbon dioxide and oxygen in and out of the leaf. The pores also regulate the escape of excess water, for a leaf serves, too, as an evaporative cooler that keeps the plant from overheating when the temperature rises.

The shapes of leaves vary widely from species to species and are among the most reliable clues in plant identification. Needles and scales identify the many different types of conifers, while among broad-leaved plants leaves may be simple (undivided, like those of elms or birches) or compound (composed of numerous leaflets, like the leaves of locusts and ash trees).

Leafhopper

Tiny, wedge-shaped jumping insects that often are colorfully patterned, leafhoppers feed by sucking juice from the stems and leaves of plants. In the process the host plants, deprived of sap, are stunted and eventually wither. Widespread pests that also cause havoc by transmitting plant diseases, leafhoppers are harmful to a wide range of shrubs, trees, and grasses; apple, bean, potato, beet, and grape crops are particularly susceptible to infestation. The bane of many a gardener, leafhoppers also attack a rainbow of flowers, among them roses, asters, and forsythia. As they sip plant fluids, the insects expel a sweet liquid, called honeydew, that attracts ants, wasps, and flies.

Leaf miner

Pale lines winding just beneath the upper surfaces of leaves usually mark the tunnels of leaf miners, the tiny larvae of several kinds of insects, including flies, sawflies, moths, and bee-

Leafhoppers number some 2,500 species in North America alone.

Baby leatherbacks head for the sea immediately after emerging from their nests.

Leaf miners mar foliage with unsightly lines as they tunnel through the tissue.

tles. When an adult female lands on a leaf, she cuts a hole in its epidermis and deposits an egg in the soft tissue inside. The colorless, wormlike larva that hatches from the egg then gnaws an erratic path through the tissue until, about a week later, it pupates and is transformed into an adult. Though unsightly, the damage done by leaf miners seldom results in serious harm to the host plants.

Leatherback *Dermochelys coriacea*

Weighing up to 1,200 pounds, the leatherback is the world's largest turtle. This seafaring giant, named for its dark, ridged, rubbery carapace, navigates vast distances across the Atlantic and Pacific oceans, swimming strongly with its huge, oarlike forelimbs. While it generally prefers tropical waters, the reptile has been spotted off Canada's shores.

Leatherbacks usually mate every other year, with the females then swimming thousands of miles to warm nesting grounds. There they haul themselves ashore at night, dig a hole with their hind flippers, lay 80 to 100 round white eggs, and then return to the sea. The turtles, however, are in dire danger of extinction. Their nests are often plundered, and many adults are killed by accident. They also drown while entrapped in fishnets or die after eating floating plastic, which they mistake for jellyfish, their primary food.

Leech

Relatives of the earthworm, leeches are generally found in fresh water (though some inhabit moist soil) and live as bloodsucking parasites. Using a sucker at the hind end of the body, they attach themselves to passing animals or humans. Then they pierce the skin and feast on blood with a front sucker. An anticoagulent keeps the victim's blood flowing freely until the sated worm drops off. One such meal can last a leech for months. Used by medical practitioners in the past, leeches are making a comeback, having proved useful for taking up unwanted blood during microsurgery.

L

207

Acacias, tree-size legumes, flourish in the Southwest.

Sage grouse conduct energetic courtship rituals on their leks, which are also called dancing, or booming, grounds.

Legume

A huge family of flowering plants, the legumes include some 15,000 species of trees, shrubs, herbs, and vines. Although they exhibit a great deal of variability, all species are distinguished by their pealike fruits—pods that, as they dry, split along both sides to scatter the seeds.

Legumes are found almost everywhere, and much of their success is due to their ability to enrich the soil in which they grow. Most species have nodes on their roots inhabited by bacteria that can transform atmospheric nitrogen into nitrates that are usable by plants. As a result, legumes are among the first colonizers of poor or disturbed soils.

Second only to the grasses in economic importance, the legumes yield a wide variety of useful products. Because their seeds contain an abundance of protein—two to three times as much as wheat or corn—many legumes, such as soybeans and peanuts, are valuable food crops. Others, including clover and alfalfa, provide nutritious forage for livestock. Some, such as the desert shrub mesquite, are harvested for firewood, and some are used for cabinetmaking and fine furniture. Still others—wisteria and sweet peas, for example—are enjoyed simply for their lovely, sweet-scented flowers.

Lek

Probably derived from a Swedish word meaning "to play," the term *lek* refers to an area where birds gather communally to enact their courtship rituals. Male prairie chickens and several other grouse, for example, compete for females on the lek by strutting, bowing, and displaying their plumage. At the same time, they inflate colorful air sacs on their necks or breasts to produce loud booming sounds that can be heard for miles. The hens, meanwhile, stroll among the performers and choose a mate, then go off to nest and rear their young alone.

Lemming

Plump rodents that look like overgrown voles, lemmings are about six inches long with stubby tails and thick, silky fur. Most species are creatures of the Far North, where they live in colonies on damp meadows and open tundra and feed on tender grasses and roots. They nest in burrows, with each female producing as many as 30 young per year.

Though tales of lemmings committing mass suicide are false, it is easy to see how the truth has been misinterpreted. Every few years, for unknown reasons, lemmings experience population explosions that trigger mass migrations. On occasion the processions become so frantic that great numbers of lemmings drown while trying to swim across lakes and rivers, and this has given rise to the myth of the suicide march.

Lichen

Find a crust of lichen clinging to a rock or tree trunk and you have discovered not one plant but two, for lichens are actually algae and fungi living together in intimate partnership. The alga, through photosynthesis, produces food to nourish both, while the fungus absorbs water, which keeps the alga moist, and shades its light-sensitive partner. In addition, some lichens serve the environment by secreting acids that help break rocks down into soil.

Despite their amazing diversity of form, lichens can be grouped into three broad categories. The leafy types that cling to trees and rocks are foliose lichens; the granular kinds that form crusty patches on rocks are crustose lichens; and the branching tufts that are attached at the bottom or hang from trees are fruticose lichens.

Though commonly green, lichens are also found in bright colors and are a source of natural dyes. One kind, called reindeer moss, is the major food of caribou and other foragers in the Far North.

L

Forked lightning leaps from a cloud, sending jagged, high-voltage branches toward the ground. Zigzagging downward, lightning creates brilliant pyrotechnic displays, which are best observed from an enclosed place.

Fruticose lichens include the pyxie cups (top left), British soldiers (bottom left), and the ladder lichen (bottom right). Crustose lichens (top right) encrust rocks, enlivening bare surfaces with vivid colors.

Lightning

Beautiful but terrifying, the natural fireworks called lightning are the result of electrical discharges from clouds. As a storm cloud churns in the sky, it builds up a positive charge at the top and a negative charge at the bottom. When the voltage within the cloud becomes great enough, a powerful current of electricity passes between the negatively charged base of the cloud and the positively charged earth, creating the bright flash we see as lightning. The tremendous heat of a lightning bolt, greater than that on the surface of the sun, causes the air to expand explosively, and the resultant shock waves produce the sound we hear as thunder. Extremely dangerous, lightning causes the deaths of more than 100 North Americans every year. The worst places to be during thunderstorms are under isolated trees or on high ground; the safest places are in cars or buildings.

Lignite

Brown and crumbly, lignite can be thought of as coal in the making. Like the harder coals that are most often used for fuel, it is formed from dead plant material, or peat, that originated in ancient swampy forests. But it has not been subjected to the intense heat and pressure required to produce the harder coals. Lignite is burned for fuel in some places. Because it deteriorates during transport, however, it is used mainly by consumers located close to the mines.

L

Wood lily　　　Turk's cap lily　　　Sierra wild onion

Clintonia　　　Chocolate lily　　　Madonna lily

The lily family is remarkably diverse and includes agricultural crops as well as colorful flowers.

Lily

In its broadest sense the term *lily* refers to a plant family that includes thousands of species, from onions and asparagus to tulips and trilliums. Most are perennial herbs that grow from bulbs, but some are woody, and a few, such as the greenbriars, are evergreens. On all, however, the floral parts—sepals, stamens, and so on—occur in multiples of three.

In the lily family, members of the genus *Lilium* are the so-called true lilies. These include a number of wild species, such as the wood lily and Canada lily, which brighten moist meadows and roadsides with showy trumpet-shaped blooms, and the chaparral lily, a plant of dry slopes in the West. Lilies are the floral emblems of Quebec—the Madonna, or garden, lily—and of Saskatchewan—the wood, or prairie, lily.

Limestone

A common, widely distributed sedimentary rock, limestone is composed of the mineral calcium carbonate. It is usually grayish white, but iron and other impurities can stain it yellow, brown, and occasionally red. Often rich in fossils, most limestones are formed from the re-

mains of ancient marine animals and plants. When the organisms died, their shells and skeletons rained down onto the ocean floor and were eventually compacted into thick beds of rock. Limestone can also form from the precipitation of calcium carbonate that is dissolved in seawater and hot springs.

Limpet

Small snails with flattened, conical shells, limpets are found along both coasts. They cling to rocks by means of a muscular, suckerlike foot and can survive the battering of even the most powerful waves. At high tide limpets creep about and scrape algae from the rocks with their rasping tongues. When the water recedes, each one returns to its home base—a slight depression hollowed into the rock—where it anchors itself until the return of high water.

Limpkin *Aramus guarauna*

A denizen of freshwater wetlands in Florida and southern Georgia, the limpkin looks like a heron, flies like a crane, and acts like a rail. Named for its peculiar, halting gait, the chocolate-brown, white-streaked bird wades the shallows

Limestone, etched by rainwater, erodes to form fascinating natural sculptures.

Earless lizards are desert dwellers and, unlike other lizards, lack ear openings.

Limpkins teach their young to forage for shellfish at water's edge. Almost wiped out by aggressive hunters, limpkins are now protected.

and mud flats, capturing snails and other prey with its long, heavy, slightly down-turned bill. The bird's shrill wail, which can sound almost human as it echoes in the night, has earned the limpkin such nicknames as crying bird and mourning widow. In early spring mated pairs build shallow nests of sticks near the water, where they raise four to eight young.

Liverwort

Primitive, prostrate relatives of mosses, liverworts are plants of moist, shady places, where they often spread in dense mats across soil, rocks, and rotting logs. Some are mere leathery, leaflike fronds; others are branched and lined with tiny rounded, overlapping leaves. Lacking true roots, they are anchored in place by threadlike rhizoids. Liverworts produce spores but also reproduce by means of tiny buds, called gemmae, that dot their surfaces.

Lizard

Closely related to snakes, lizards are reptiles and, like their legless cousins, have dry, scaly skins that protect them from dehydration. They are especially common in warm regions and can thrive in deserts and other places where moisture is scarce. Unable to regulate their internal body temperature, lizards warm up by basking in the sun and cool off by scuttling into the shade. Some species are vegetarians, but most feed on insects, rodents, and other small prey.

Lizards may hiss, bite, inflate their bodies, or lash their tails in self-defense, but some have developed more unusual strategies. Horned lizards can squirt blood from the corners of their eyes. Others, including the glass lizard, rely on an even odder trick: when seized, the glass lizard's tail breaks off, and the amputated section, which continues to wriggle, distracts the enemy while the lizard escapes.

L

Cardinal flowers (left) are pollinated by hummingbirds; bay lobelias (right) rely on bumblebees.

Lobsters, when taken from the ocean, are a dark greenish red. On the sea floor they rove about waving their antennae and swiveling their eye stalks as they search for food and watch for enemies. If lucky, they may live 50 years, but most caught in pots are far younger.

L

Lobelia *Lobelia*

Filled with an acrid, milky juice, the upright stems of the lobelias are topped by lovely tubular flowers. Each has two lips, the upper divided into two lobes and the lower into three. Of our several native lobelias, the most spectacular by far is the cardinal flower, admired for its brilliant crimson blooms. Another, Indian tobacco, was once used medicinally and so earned such colorful nicknames as gagroot and asthma-weed.

Lobster

Well-known for their intimidating claws, protective shells, and tasty flesh, American lobsters are found off the Atlantic Coast from Labrador to the Carolinas. Hiding by day in burrows or under rocks, they roam the ocean floor at night to scavenge and prey on crabs, snails, fish, and others of their own kind. Their two foreclaws are specialized: the larger one is used to crush hard-shelled prey, and the smaller one, equipped with sharp teeth, is used for tearing food apart. When confronted by enemies, lobsters flip their powerful abdomens to swim backward out of harm's way.

Female lobsters produce thousands of eggs, which are carried under the abdomen until they hatch. The free-swimming larvae drift near the surface for a time, then sink to the bottom, shedding their hard shells periodically as they increase in size. Barring mishaps, lobsters may reach a length of two feet, weigh more than 20 pounds, and live for many decades.

Spiny lobsters, found off the coasts of Florida

Loess blankets much of the Midwest, providing excellent topsoil for corn and other crops.

The black locust's clustered flowers fill the spring air with their sweet fragrance.

and California, are named for the spines on their shells. Though they lack the large, meaty claws of the American lobster, they are often caught for the flesh in their muscular abdomens.

Locoweed *Oxytropis*

Loco is Spanish for "crazy," and loco is indeed the way livestock behave after eating these low-growing prairie plants. Horses, cattle, and sheep become disoriented, unable to walk or see normally, and prone to violent frenzies. With no known antidote, the slow-acting poison in the plants often leads to death. Ironically, the loco-weeds are an acquired taste, for animals avoid them when other food is available. Once they begin eating the plants, however, they keep coming back for more. Many species are native to dry soils in the West. Members of the pea family, all bear clusters of purple, red, or white flowers. The milk vetches also are called loco-weeds and have the same deadly effects.

Locust

First appearing as huge gray clouds on the horizon, dense swarms of voracious locusts descend on western farmlands from time to time, devouring crops and grasslands, denuding shrubs and trees, and generally ravaging the countryside. The insects are actually various species of short-horned grasshoppers, whose populations explode in years when spring rains are particularly heavy. Abandoning their normally solitary ways, the locusts then gather into ravenous swarms that can number in the billions. A particularly notorious plague of locusts invaded the Prairies in the 1870's and caused many millions of dollars' worth of damage.

Locust *Robinia*

Trees of the pea family, the locusts can be recognized by their compound leaves, gracefully drooping flower clusters, and the armament of thorns on their branches. In spring the black locust, an attractive shade tree up to 80 feet tall, fills the air with the sweet perfume of its creamy flowers. In fall the blooms are followed by long, leathery pods containing hard, glossy seeds, which are eaten by squirrels and other animals. Its hard, durable wood is used for fence posts and railway ties. The clammy locust, named for the sticky hairs on its twigs and pods, bears showy clusters of rose-colored, scentless blossoms and is also planted as an ornamental.

Loess

A sediment composed of fine rock particles created by the grinding action of Ice Age glaciers, loess was carried south by meltwater streams and later was blown eastward in what must have been enormous dust storms. Subsequent weathering of this blanket of sediment has created some of the richest soil on earth. It is thickest near the rivers, such as the high bluffs of the Mississippi not far from St. Louis.

L

213

Loggerhead females dig a deep hole in the beach, where they lay more than 100 leathery eggs the size of Ping-Pong balls. Afterward, they cover the eggs with sand and crawl back to the sea. When the eggs hatch eight weeks later, the tiny turtles immediately scramble down the beach into their ocean home.

Loggerhead *Caretta caretta*

Large, lumbering sea turtles, loggerheads swim along at an average speed of one mile per hour, pausing now and then to bask at the ocean's surface. They are imposing animals that often weigh 500 pounds or more and are topped by domed shells up to four feet long. Their big heads are equipped with powerful jaws well suited for crushing the hard-shelled crabs and mollusks they sometimes eat; they also feed on sponges, fish, jellyfish, and plants.

Every other year the females crawl out of the sea to lay their eggs on warm, sandy beaches, including a few sites on the South Atlantic coast. Despite the large numbers of eggs that they deposit, coastal development and overcollecting have caused their population to decline.

Longshore current

Flowing parallel to seashores and driven by prevailing winds, longshore currents occur where waves strike the shore at an angle. As they flow along the coast, longshore currents pick up sand and redeposit it farther downcurrent. Together with tides and rip currents, they are constantly reshaping the contours of sandy beaches, sandbars, and barrier islands.

Trouble occurs when man interferes with this natural, dynamic process by building seawalls, jetties, and other devices meant to halt erosion. These structures trap sand on their windward side but prevent sand from being redeposited on the leeward side—thus saving one beach at the expense of others.

Longspur *Calcarius*

Named for their elongated hind claws, longspurs are chunky, gregarious, sparrowlike birds. They are dull colored much of the year and can be hard to spot as they travel with flocks of horned larks and snow buntings, foraging for seeds on windswept plains. In the summer, however, the males wear brightly patterned breeding plumage.

Lapland longspurs start nest building within days of returning to their breeding grounds.

Even so, few people ever see them, for the chestnut-collared and McCown's longspurs nest only on northern plains, and the Lapland and Smith's longspurs on Arctic tundra.

Loon *Gavia*

A characteristic and haunting sound of northern lakes is the loud, yodeling call of the common loon; echoing through the night air, it shatters the silence with what seems to be hysterical human laughter. Like all the loons, the common loon is a sturdy, goose-size diving bird with a stout, spear-shaped bill and webbed feet placed far back on the body for propulsion under water. During dives for fish, loons can remain submerged for five minutes or more and reach depths of 200 feet.

Although the birds have difficulty walking, during the breeding season they venture ashore to incubate one to three speckled eggs in loose nests at the water's edge. Both parents share in the feeding and care of the downy chicks, which sometimes hitch rides on the backs of the adults. The four species found in North America nest on Arctic tundra or northern inland lakes but winter as far south as Florida on the Atlantic Coast, and southern California in the West.

L

The common loon builds a nest of dry grass on a secluded lakeshore.

Prolific purple loosestrife paints meadows and marshes with bright blooms.

The American lotus's remarkable seeds are able to germinate after a century or more.

Loosestrife *Lythrum*

Tall, attractive wildflowers, several native loosestrifes grace moist soils from the salt marshes of New Jersey to damp meadows in southern California. Up to six feet tall, the plants have pairs of narrow lance-shaped leaves and six-petaled tubular flowers of varying hues. None of the native North American species, however, are as aggressive or conspicuous as the imported purple loosestrife, a showy immigrant from Europe that bears spectacular spikes of magenta blooms from June through September. It is so prolific that in many areas its impenetrable tangles of stalks and roots have crowded out native wetland plants. Providing little in the way of food or cover, the vast stands of purple loosestrife have also displaced much native wildlife.

Lotus *Nelumbo lutea*

Rooted in the muck of shallow lakes and streams, the American lotus flaunts its fragrant, creamy yellow flowers on stems that rise three feet above the water. The leaves are picturesque as well: olive-green discs up to two feet wide that are set like parasols atop stout stalks. The waxy blossoms, each six to eight inches across, last about five days before their petals fall, leaving behind the seedpods, which resemble the spouts of watering cans. Pitted with holes, they are embedded with shiny black seeds, which Indians once gathered for roasting and grinding into meal. The starchy, tuberous roots were also harvested and eaten like sweet potatoes. Today the pods are sought for use in dried flower arrangements. Though lotuses are found throughout the eastern United States, they are becoming increasingly rare.

L

215

Luna moths have exotic, gemlike eyespots. The one shown here is approximately life-size.

Elephant heads have "trunks" that serve as perches for pollen-gathering bumblebees.

Louse

Tiny, flat, wingless insects that feed on humans and other animals, lice fall into two broad categories. Chewing lice attack birds and mammals, subsisting on feathers or hair. Sucking lice cling to the bodies of mammals, including humans, and feed on their blood. Associated with unsanitary living conditions, sucking lice are tenacious pests that cement their eggs, called nits, to hair and clothing. They are also unhealthy, with some kinds transmitting serious diseases.

Lousewort *Pedicularis*

With finely divided, fernlike foliage and spikes of tubular two-lipped flowers, the louseworts are pretty plants whose name derives from a mistaken belief that they transmit lice to any animals grazing on them. Wood betony, with red to yellow blossoms, is a widespread example. Another, elephant heads, is a rose-red wildflower of mountain meadows and swamps; its blooms do indeed look like elephant heads, complete with ears and trunks.

The Canada lynx, about three feet long and weighing up to 45 pounds, is an expert stalker. When snowshoe hares are scarce, lynxes turn to birds, rodents, and deer. They pose no danger to man, and only when particularly desperate do they prey on domestic animals.

Luna moth *Actias luna*

Named for the ancient Romans' goddess of the moon, the green-winged luna moth is one of the loveliest creatures of the night. It is found only in eastern North America, where, in its spiny caterpillar stage, it feeds avidly on the leaves of trees. Then it spins a silken cocoon, sometimes incorporating a fallen leaf, and metamorphoses into a mature moth.

The adults never eat but spend their brief lives searching for mates. The males are ever on the alert for the enticing scent given off by courting females. At one time the fluttering dance of dozens of males on the trail of female lunas was a common sight around street lights on summer evenings. Exposure to pesticides and pollutants has, however, reduced the population of these beautiful, now endangered, insects.

Lupine *Lupinus*

In early summer the flower spikes of wild lupines brighten fields and roadsides throughout the East. But it is in the West that these legumes really flourish, with more than 70 species tinting mountains and plains with blues, pinks, yellows, and whites. Eastern or western, all lupines bear bonnet-shaped flowers and compound leaves with the leaflets radiating from their stems like the spokes on a wheel. As do all legumes, lupines have nitrogen-fixing nodules on their roots and so do well in poor, dry soils. Texas bluebonnet may be the best-loved lupine, but California claims the biggest: three times taller than its relatives, the yellow-blossomed tree lupine grows to an astonishing nine feet.

Lynx *Felis lynx*

Solitary and seldom seen, lynxes are cats of the cold coniferous forests of Canada and the western mountains. They sleep by day in caves or hollow trees but at night are very active, some-

Lupines got their name from the Latin for wolf. Once thought to "wolf" nutrients from the soil, the plants actually enrich it.

L

times traveling for miles in search of prey. Expert stalkers, they can creep to within a few feet of a prospective meal before bounding out for the capture. They also hunt by lying in ambush, waiting quietly for hours on a limb over a trail.

Similar in appearance to bobcats, which live farther south, lynxes are about three feet in length, with tufted ears, long legs, and a stubby tail. Their long, silky fur is grayish with darker spots, and their large, furry feet serve as snowshoes in winter—an adaptation that allows lynxes to pursue their favorite quarry, the similarly equipped snowshoe hare, even in deep snow. Since lynxes depend on hares for most of their food, their population rises and falls in 10-year cycles that match those of the hares.

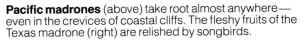

Pacific madrones (above) take root almost anywhere—even in the crevices of coastal cliffs. The fleshy fruits of the Texas madrone (right) are relished by songbirds.

Magnolias bear large, showy blossoms in early spring.

Mallards are naturally gregarious waterfowl that frequently flock together by the thousands.

Mackerel

Close relatives of the tunas, the oceangoing mackerels share their larger cousins' stream-lined torpedo shape, silvery blue iridescence, and forked tails. Up to two feet in length, they are valuable food fish and are regularly netted in large quantities. Mackerels fight fiercely when hooked—sometimes leaping high into the air—and are highly regarded game fish as well.

Roving the seas in huge schools, mackerels prey on smaller fish and squid. They in turn are eaten by porpoises, whales, seabirds, and other fish. In the Pacific, mackerels range from Alaska to California, while in the Atlantic they are found from the cold northern waters off Labrador south to the Carolinas.

Madrone *Arbutus*

The Texas madrone, native to central Texas, is a little tree with a crooked trunk and rarely exceeds 20 feet in height. In contrast, the Arizona madrone, found in the mountains of the South-west, reaches 50 feet, while the Pacific madrone of coastal forests sometimes soars to 125 feet.

Despite these differences in stature, however, the family resemblance is strong. All three species of madrones have a smooth, red, paper-thin bark that peels away to expose the bright new growth beneath, and their oval evergreen leaves are a dark, glossy green. They bear clusters of fragrant, white or pinkish urn-shaped flowers, and all produce mealy, red or orange fruits that are relished by band-tailed pigeons and other birds.

Magma

The molten rock found deep beneath the earth's crust is known as magma. It contains a complex mix of chemicals and gases, which eventually crystallizes into igneous rocks. Magma that wells up and flows onto the surface through volcanoes or fissures is called lava.

Magnolia *Magnolia*

On spring evenings in the South, when the creamy white blossoms of the southern, or ever-green, magnolia are on display, filling the air with lemony perfume, it is easy to understand why many people consider it to be the most beautiful

M

Yellow-billed magpies, normally found only in parts of California, have become city birds as their preferred wild habitats have been lost to agriculture.

Mountain globemallow's lovely pink blossoms color the wet meadows of Glacier National Park from June through August.

of all flowering trees. While the southern magnolia may reach a height of 100 feet or more, most others are small to medium-size trees, 30 to 50 feet tall. Magnolia leaves—deciduous on some species, evergreen on others—are oval and large. Those of the bigleaf magnolia, so glossy that they look polished, may be 32 inches long, perhaps the largest of any North American tree. The gray or brown bark is smooth and thin, releasing a spicy aroma when bruised or cut. All species bear magnificent cup-shaped white or greenish blossoms in spring, but not all have the compelling sweetness of the southern magnolia. Borne in conelike clusters, the seeds dangle for a time on threads before falling to the earth.

Magpie *Pica*

Long-tailed and boldly patterned in black and white, magpies are conspicuous, noisy birds of the West. Like their relatives the crows and jays, they travel in small flocks and feed on everything from insects and fruit to carrion and birds' eggs. They often breed in loose colonies, building their domed nests of sticks in tall shrubs or thorny trees. The black-billed magpie is a widespread species, while the yellow-billed magpie is found only in parts of California.

Mallard *Anas platyrhynchos*

The most widespread and numerous of all our ducks, the mallard is found in wetlands throughout the Northern Hemisphere. The males are distinguished by their glossy green heads and single white neck ring, while the females are a mottled brown. Mallards are often

seen foraging in shallow water, with their tail ends sticking straight up as they dabble for food on the bottom. They also filter seeds at the surface and graze on land. Their varied diet consists of seeds, shoots, and grain, as well as insects and small aquatic animals.

Mallards nest across most of the continent and can be found even in city parks. The nest, a shallow bowl of grasses and marsh plants, is usually concealed near the water. As the eggs are laid, the female lines it with down plucked from her breast. Soon after hatching, the 7 to 10 downy yellow young waddle after their mother, who leads her brood to the water.

Mallow

In times past, the sweets known as marshmallows were made from the roots of a wetland wildflower of that name. Though today's confection contains not a trace of the plant, the mallow family supplies a number of important food, fiber, and floral crops. Cotton, which covers millions of acres in the South, is a mallow. So is okra, the plant whose mucilaginous fruits thicken Creole gumbos. Ornamental mallows include hollyhocks and hibiscus.

Mallows are characterized by five-petaled symmetrical flowers with the stamens united in a cylindrical column that encloses the pistil. The leaves, covered with fine, fuzzy-tipped hairs, alternate along the stem, and the fruits are dry five-parted capsules that split lengthwise to release their seeds. Most of the mallows are herbs or shrubs, though two tree-size tropicals, the upland cotton and the sea hibiscus, have become naturalized along the Florida coast.

M

Mountain lions usually prefer solitude, but a mother will stay with her kittens for up to two years.

Mammal

At first glance, a mouse and a whale do not seem even remotely alike, but as different as they appear, both the tiny land dweller and the giant sea dweller are mammals. The two, in fact, have a number of traits in common, not all of which are unique to mammals. Both are air-breathing vertebrates, but so are lizards and toads. Both are warm-blooded, but so are birds. And both bear live young, but so do a number of snakes, frogs, and insects.

What makes mammals special?

What the mouse and the whale share with no other class of animals are two deceptively simple characteristics: hair and mammary glands. Like the mouse, most mammals are completely covered with fur. Others, however, have only small patches of hair or very little at all. Whales and walruses, for instance, have just a few bristles, and armadillos have mere tufts of hair between their armor plates.

The main function of fur is to insulate; it keeps the body warm. This is especially important because, unlike fish, reptiles, and other cold-blooded creatures, whose body temperature fluctuates with their environment, mammals must maintain a constant temperature. For some animals, hair serves other purposes as well. The mottled brown fur of fawns and the snowy white fur of snowshoe hares provide excellent camouflage. Structures such as porcupine quills (used for defense) and cat whiskers (used as sensory devices) are specially modified hairs.

Another trait unique to mammals—mammary glands—is the one that gives them their name. While the young of other animal groups often are dependent on uncertain food supplies, baby mammals always have milk, for the mother's body continues to produce it even when solid food is scarce. The richest milk of all is produced by sea dwellers such as whales and seals.

Containing enormous quantities of fat, it allows the young to put on weight very quickly (baby whales can gain 200 pounds a day). The fat content also results in a layer of blubber that insulates the body from the frigid sea.

Mammals live just about anywhere

North America supports some 400 species of mammals—about one-tenth of the world's total. Extremely adaptable, mammals are found in almost every conceivable habitat, from scorching deserts to the arctic tundra and from mountaintops to the watery deep. Some fly or glide through the air, while others spend their entire lives in the darker realms underground. Though several mammals are active in daylight, a surprising number prefer to sleep by day and hunt for food at night.

Many mammals that live in forests are specially adapted for life in trees. Opossums, for instance, have a prehensile tail for grasping branches, and squirrels have sharp claws that enable them to scurry up and down tree trunks. Flying squirrels have folds of skin which they stretch out to glide through the air, while bats, the only true fliers among mammals, have wings made of thin membranes that extend between their elongated "fingers."

Gophers, moles, and other burrowers spend much of their time underground. Equipped with strong claws and enlarged forelimbs, they move with ease through the soil. Many have short fur and lack external ears, and some that rarely come up to the surface have poor vision or are completely blind.

Mammals that live on the ground have their own special adaptations. Deer and horses, for example, with their long legs and sturdy hooves, are built for running, and their teeth are shaped for cutting and grinding vegetation. Wolves and bobcats, on the other hand, live on animal prey and have highly developed canine teeth for piercing and tearing flesh.

Spotted skunks give warning with a handstand, then release a foul spray.

Sure-footed mountain goats can take refuge from enemies on the steepest cliffs.

Walruses use their imposing tusks to break up ice and fend off polar bears.

Aquatic mammals, such as whales, porpoises, seals, and manatees, are uniquely adapted for life in the water—so much so, in fact, that some of them resemble fish. On many, the forelimbs are enlarged into paddlelike structures, the tail or combined hindlimbs look like a fish's tail, and the entire body is streamlined.

The smart and the sociable

Mammals, equipped with superior brains, have relatively sophisticated social organizations and forms of communication. Wolves, which spend their lives in hierarchical groups called packs, exchange information about dominance and territory through scent, sound, and body language. Beavers and prairie dogs cooperate with others of their kind in building and excavating and by warning each other of danger. Among the most intelligent of mammals, whales and porpoises communicate with their species through a complex system of squeaks, trills, and bellows.

In respect to communication, however, one mammal surpasses all others. Humans not only can communicate detailed information, but they can also store that information for the benefit of succeeding generations.

White-footed mice, like all mammals, nurse their young with milk from their mammary glands. Since females can conceive less than six weeks after birth and each may have several litters a year, the population can increase dramatically. Though moderately destructive, white-footed mice have the redeeming virtue of eating huge numbers of harmful insects.

The mammoths' gigantic tusks were probably not used as weapons, but for scraping snow and ice from edible plants.

Mantids, unlike most insects, can swivel their heads.

Manatees are gentle, slow-moving creatures of Florida's brackish inlets and estuaries. Group members greet one another by touching muzzles, and they sometimes warn each other of danger with high-pitched chirps. Though the resemblance is far from obvious, manatees supposedly inspired the folklore about mermaids.

Mammoth *Mammuthus*

Majestic beasts that lived during the last ice age, mammoths have been extinct for thousands of years. These relatives of modern elephants were massive creatures with domed heads, huge curved tusks, and ridged molars for grinding coarse grasses. Of the several kinds that roamed North America, the imperial mammoths, standing 13 feet high, were the largest. The slightly smaller Columbian mammoths were sometimes hunted by tribesmen on the western plains, while woolly mammoths, with tusks up to 16 feet long, were masters of the Far North. A shaggy outer coat of hair over dense underfur, plus a thick layer of fat, protected them from frigid weather. The frozen carcasses of woolly mammoths are occasionally unearthed in the Arctic. Often perfectly preserved, they are vivid relics that make the Ice Age seem like only yesterday.

Manatee *Trichechus manatus*

Plump, placid mammals that live in warm coastal waters and river mouths in Florida, manatees have blimplike bodies up to 15 feet long and weigh as much as 1,500 pounds. Sometimes called sea cows, they move about slowly, propelled by two front flippers and a broad, flattened tail. Manatees surface every few minutes to take in air but spend most of their time underwater, grazing on aquatic plants. Their prodigious consumption—up to 100 pounds of plants per animal each day—plays a useful role in keeping channels clear of water hyacinths and other weeds. Since they often linger near the surface, many of these gentle giants have been killed or maimed by the propellers of motorboats. In winter, manatees, unhappy in chilly water, seek out warm springs and even the heated outflow from factories and power plants.

Mangrove

The shores of south Florida are lined for miles with dense stands of red mangroves, North America's only trees able to live in salt water. Topped with a canopy of leathery green leaves, the trees have roots that arch out like buttresses from the main trunks and serve as props. Columbus, when he first encountered tangled thickets of mangroves, described them in his log as being "so thick a cat couldn't get ashore."

Seeming to march out across the shallows,

M

Trees That Make New Land

Red mangroves' tangled roots trap silt and debris that would otherwise be at the mercy of erosion by wind and water (below). On a massive scale, the plants play a role in the formation of islands by extending their domain into the sea (right).

White mangrove

The three mangroves are not close relatives, as reflected by the differences in their fruits and flowers. The black mangrove's pencillike, aerial rootlets take oxygen to larger roots below.

Black mangrove

Red mangrove

the roots of the trees not only protect the shoreline from erosion by wind and wave but also help build land. By trapping sediment and debris, the roots create new islands and extend old shorelines seaward. Nurseries for a teeming community of marine life, they also serve as barriers that keep predators from the throngs of water birds that nest among their branches.

While red mangroves prefer the seashore and the edges of brackish estuaries, two other species live in salt marshes farther inland. Black mangroves thrive in mucky areas between salt water and dry land and are surrounded by little forests of pencillike pneumatophores. Projecting from the mud, these odd structures serve as snorkels, allowing the buried roots to breathe. White mangroves are found on still-drier soils farther inland.

Manta

The giants of the skates and rays, mantas live in warm waters of both the Atlantic and Pacific oceans. Their name comes from a Spanish word for "blanket"—a reference to their wide, winglike pectoral fins. A pair of fleshy "horns" on their heads accounts for the nickname devil ray; a whiplike tail adds to their evil appearance.

Some mantas are enormous, with a span of more than 20 feet from fin tip to fin tip and a weight of well over a ton. Despite their bulk, they "fly" gracefully through the water by rhythmically undulating their fins, and sometimes make spectacular leaps into the air.

Mantid

Long, slender insects with prominent eyes, mantids are formidable predators. They hold their front legs folded forward, as if in prayer, and so are commonly called praying mantises. But this pose is less pious than it appears, for mantids so positioned are in fact waiting in ambush for prey. Their grasping forelegs, which can lash out in an instant, are lined with needle-sharp spines from which no victim can escape. In fall, the females, notorious for eating their mates, produce foamy masses containing up to 200 eggs, which hatch the following spring. Several species are native to North America, but the largest and best known are the introduced European and Chinese mantises.

M

The Magnificent Maples

Two main characteristics help distinguish most maples from other trees: their lobed leaves grow in opposite pairs, and their winged fruits, called keys or samaras, also come in pairs. Telling one species from another, however, is a little trickier. Helpful clues include the shape of the leaf, the number of lobes it has, and whether the margins are toothed or smooth. Note also the shape of the paired keys. The wings are widely spread on some species and nearly parallel on others. A tree's flowers or even its sap can provide clues for identifying some of the common maples.

Leaves with 3 or 5 broad lobes

LOBES POINTED, WITH TOOTHED MARGINS; STALKS RED

Flowers greenish, in short clusters

Rocky Mountain maple (West)

Flowers red to yellow, in short tufts

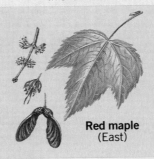

Red maple (East)

Flowers yellow, in long, upright clusters

Mountain maple (Northeast)

LOBES POINTED, WITH SMOOTH MARGINS; STALKS GREEN

Sap in stalks milky

Norway maple (introduced)

Sap in stalks clear

Sugar maple (East)

LOBES WITH ROUNDED TIPS

Florida maple (Southeast)

Leaves with 3 pointed lobes

Striped maple, or moosewood (Northeast)

Leaves with 5 deeply cut lobes

LEAVES 6" WITH TOOTHED MARGINS

Silver maple (East)

Leaves with 7 or 9 pointed lobes

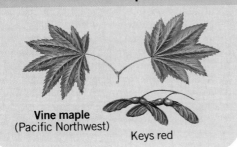

Vine maple (Pacific Northwest) Keys red

LEAVES 12" WITH SMOOTH MARGINS

Bigleaf maple (West Coast)

M

Mariposa lilies, which come in a variety of shapes and hues, get their name from the Spanish word for "butterfly." The bulbs, when eaten raw, have a nutty taste; cooked, they have a flavor similar to potatoes.

Manzanita *Arctostaphylos*

Although the manzanitas range in size from creeping mats of foliage to trees some 30 feet tall, most are vigorous evergreen shrubs. Easily recognized by their tough, twisting branches and smooth, shiny reddish bark, they often form dense, virtually impenetrable thickets on arid slopes in the West. The clusters of pink or white urn-shaped flowers that droop from the twig tips in spring are later replaced by berrylike fruits that yield a tasty jelly.

Maple *Acer*

Handsome and hardy, maple trees come in all shapes and sizes. Perhaps the best known are the sugar maples, which explode with brilliant color in autumn, a brilliance now enshrined in the Canadian flag. The trees are famous both for the sugary sap that yields maple syrup and for the durable wood used for fine furniture.

Silver maples, common in the East, are named for the silvery undersides of their leaves. Turning easily on slender stalks, the leaves seem to shimmer with the slightest breeze. The bigleaf maple of the West Coast, though shorter in stature at 40 to 60 feet, has leaves up to a foot wide. Smaller and more shrublike, the Rocky Mountain maple manages to survive in the poor, gravelly soils of cliffs and canyons.

All the maples have leaves that grow in opposite pairs. The flowers, though small, are often in conspicuous clusters; red maples, for instance, cast a scarlet haze over moist woods in early spring, flowering well before the leaves appear. Maple seeds come in paired keys, or samaras. Once they dry, the winged fruits whirl earthward like tiny toy helicopters.

Marble

Prized for its beauty, strength, and durability, marble is limestone that has been recrystallized by heat and pressure within the earth's crust. Pure marble is snow-white, but impurities give a range of colors, including gray, red, pink, green, yellow, and black. Marble has been used for building and sculpture since ancient times. The Alberta Legislature in Edmonton has Quebec, Pennsylvania, and Italian marble. The Lincoln Memorial in Washington, D.C., is built of Alabama, Colorado, and Georgia marble. Marble is also found in Vermont and Tennessee.

Mariposa lily *Calochortus*

Flourishing on the dry slopes of western mountains and foothills, in hard-packed desert soils, and in the shade of coniferous forests, mariposa lilies offer a charming contrast to the austerity of their environment. Although the flowers of some kinds are globe shaped and others dangle like bells, most are open, upright, and as cheerful looking as tulips. The blooms range in color from white to yellow, orange, scarlet, and purplish, with each of the three petals commonly marked at its base with a darker spot. The tasty bulbs of some of the mariposas were valued as food by Indians and early settlers. One kind, the sego lily, is credited with saving Mormon pioneers from starvation and is now honored as the state flower of Utah.

Marlin

Aristocrats among sport fish, the speedy, streamlined marlins are known for their fighting ability and their spectacular leaps when hooked. Related to sailfish, they have a prominent back fin that folds down into a groove when they are swimming at full speed. (Marlins can attain bursts of 60 miles per hour.) They use their spearlike bills to stun prey as they swim through schools of smaller fish, then turn back and swallow their victims whole. Marlins are found in warm water off both coasts. Striped marlins live in the Pacific, and white marlins swim in Atlantic waters. But the most highly prized of all is the wide-ranging blue marlin; at 15 feet or more, and weighing up to 1,000 pounds, it can challenge the most dedicated fisherman.

M

Yellow-bellied marmots, unlike their cousins the woodchucks, live together in colonies.

A marsupial, this baby opossum takes in the view from its mother's pouch.

Marmot *Marmota*

These largest members of the squirrel family are stocky, ground-dwelling rodents about two feet long, with short legs and bushy tails. They live in burrows in rocky slopes and open fields. Hibernating throughout the winter, marmots emerge in spring to feed on grasses and other plants. The most widely distributed species is the feisty woodchuck, or groundhog, of Canada and the eastern United States. Others include the yellow-bellied marmot, or rockchuck, of the Rockies and Sierras, and the hoary marmot of the Pacific Northwest. Often sitting up alertly as if on guard duty, marmots respond to danger with sharp, piercing whistles—sounds that account for their nickname, whistlers.

Marsh See pp. 228–229.

Marsh marigold *Caltha*

Two species of marsh marigolds—both of them perennial wildflowers of wet soils—share the continent. The easterner makes its home in swamps and moist lowlands, while the western marsh marigold thrives on soggy alpine meadows and beside icy mountain streams. Both kinds are often called cowslips, though the plants are actually related to buttercups. Eastern marsh marigolds, in fact, look much like large buttercups, greeting April with a splendid show of bright yellow flowers up to two inches across. The western species, also known as elkslip, blooms later—from June until September—and has white flowers with knots of golden stamens at their centers.

Marsupial

A maternal pouch distinguishes most marsupials from all other mammals. Born at a very early stage of development—hardly more than embryos—marsupial young make their way into the pouch on the mother's belly, immediately begin nursing, and remain there until they are able to get about on their own. The most familiar examples are the kangaroos and koalas of Australia, and the hardy, adaptable opossum, the only marsupial native to North America.

Marten *Martes americana*

A solitary, bushy-tailed member of the weasel family, the marten lives in the cool coniferous forests of the Far North and western mountains. It is a fast and agile climber, well equipped for pursuit of the red squirrels that are its favorite prey. (Indeed, as it bounds from limb to limb, it might easily be mistaken for a large, dark squirrel itself.) On the ground the marten is equally quick and curious, nosing into nooks and crannies in search of insects, small animals, nuts, and fruit. It dens in hollow trees and meets others of its kind only during the summer mating season. Trapped extensively for its soft, lustrous fur, the marten has disappeared from parts of its former range.

Martin *Progne subis*

Purple martins, our largest swallows, used to nest primarily in abandoned woodpecker holes in dead trees. Some also took up residence in hollow gourds hung up for them by Indians,

M

Marsh marigolds' foliage, though mildly toxic when raw, can be boiled and eaten as a potherb.

Mastodons were shorter and more heavily built than modern elephants. Hunting by humans may have played a role in their extinction.

who enjoyed their company. Today, however, most martin colonies live in special man-made multiunit birdhouses to which they return year after year. In some regions starlings and house sparrows have crowded them out, but where competition is light, colonies sometimes number more than 200 pairs. Like other swallows, martins feed mainly on insects caught in flight. They not only help control these pests but also delight humans with their musical chirping.

Mastodon *Mammut americanum*

Distant relatives of elephants and mammoths, American mastodons died out about 8,000 years ago. The imposing beasts stood 10 feet tall and wielded impressive, curved tusks up to 8 feet long. Shaggy, reddish-brown fur protected them from the cold, and their grooved teeth—the size of large bricks—were used for grinding up huge quantities of plant food. Fossils of these ancient behemoths—found from Alaska to Florida, but mostly in the East—are proof that mastodons were once a familiar presence on the North American landscape. Huge tusks have even been unearthed in New York City, evidence that the hairy giants once trudged through spruce forests where skyscrapers now stand.

Mayapple *Podophyllum peltatum*

Maylemon might be a more fitting name for the mayapple, since its fruit resembles the lemon in color, shape, and flavor. Found on rich soils in the East, the plant sends up stems one to two feet tall, topped with deeply lobed, umbrellalike leaves. A creamy cup-shaped flower emerges from a fork in the stem, followed by a yellow oblong berry one to two inches in length.

The fruit is sometimes used to make jams and beverages, and the roots have a long history of use in folk medicine. Known as mandrake to early herbalists, the mayapple contributed potent treatments for everything from warts to jaundice. Even today, extracts have proved valuable in treating several kinds of cancer.

M

MARSH

A red-winged blackbird perched on a cattail, rudely scolding anyone who comes near, or a lazy turtle basking on a log amid a patch of fragrant waterlilies—such scenes are commonplace in freshwater marshes. In contrast to swamps, which are dominated by trees, these shallow, richly productive wetlands support a vast array of nonwoody plants. In addition to the familiar cattails and waterlilies, they are home to pickerelweed, sedges, sawgrasses, and even such unusual plants as sundews and bladderworts, which capture and consume insects. Mosquitoes and dragonflies hum and hover in the air, while fish and frogs lurk in the water below. Marsh-loving mammals include muskrats, mink, and masked raccoons. But the most elegant denizens of all are the birds: herons, egrets, ibises, coots, rails, and especially the huge numbers of ducks and geese that depend on marshes both as permanent homes and as resting places on their long annual migrations.

Male red-winged blackbirds claim their nesting territories with a loud *con-ka-ree*. They build a cup-shaped nest in marsh grass.

American bitterns, usually quite shy and secretive, make bold, bellowing calls in spring.

Painted turtles spend many warm, daylight hours basking on logs, often piled on top of each other.

Muskrats feed on marsh plants as well as snails, frogs, and fish. They live in burrows or, like beavers, in lodges constructed in open water.

The male ruddy duck puts on quite a show when courting. With his stiff tail feathers cocked upward, he puffs out his breast, bows his head, and drums on his throat and chest with his bright blue bill. The agitation forces air from his feathers, making the water in front of him bubble like seltzer.

Pickerelweed is so named because those prized fish are likely to be found nearby.

Cattails' flower heads produce thousands of seeds, each with its own downy parachute.

A white-faced ibis, standing over its nest, shows off its bronzy plumage. The long curved bill is used to probe in the mud for crayfish, as well as to snap up fish, frogs, and insects.

A western meadowlark feeds her eager young at a partially domed nest built on the ground.

Mayflies are the only insects that molt after they have developed wings.

Mayfly

In late spring and early summer, huge clouds of fragile mayflies swarm over lakes, ponds, and streams to mate, lay their eggs, and die within a day or two. Prior to this grand finale, these gauzy-winged insects live as aquatic nymphs complete with six legs, seven pairs of gills, and three feathery "tails." After as long as two years in the water, where they molt many times, they crawl out and molt twice more, the second time developing from winged subadults into fully mature adults. Mature mayflies eat nothing; their digestive systems simply fill with air for added buoyancy. Fish eagerly devour both the nymphs and adults, and many anglers' fishing flies are designed to imitate them.

Maypop See *Passionflower*.

Meadowlark *Sturnella*

Stocky, short-tailed birds that are well camouflaged on the back with streaks of brown, meadowlarks can easily be recognized by the black V on their bright yellow breasts. Two species, whose ranges overlap, look so much alike, however, that they are readily distinguished from each other only by their different singing styles: the eastern meadowlark's loud, clear whistles contrast dramatically with the melodious, flutelike song of the western meadowlark. Ground dwellers, the birds build dome-shaped nests in grassy fields and feed on insects and seeds. Despite their name, meadowlarks are related not to larks but to blackbirds.

Meadow rue *Thalictrum*

Rarely wandering far from streamsides or moist woodlands, meadow rues are moisture-loving plants that flourish all across North America. They are erect, branching perennials that range in height from a foot or less on western mountains to almost 10 feet in eastern ditches, and are much admired for their delicate blue-green foliage. The blooms are pretty, too: from late spring to late summer the meadow rues are covered with airy clusters of dainty white, yellow, or purple petalless flowers.

Meadowsweet *Filipendula*

Tall, fragrant wildflowers, the meadowsweets were named not for any preference for meadows and prairies, but because their sweet-scented blooms once were used for flavoring that old English beverage, mead. The best-known spe-

Meanders are the wide loops formed by erosion as a river snakes its way across silty terrain.

cies, called queen of the prairie, is an eight-foot-tall perennial with huge compound leaves and branching clusters of deep pink flowers that last all summer. In the East the closely related wild spireas also are known as meadowsweets.

Mealybug

Named for the waxy white powder that covers their bodies, mealybugs are notorious insect pests that live by sucking juice from the leaves and stems of plants. The females—soft, oval, and wingless—are often found feeding in clusters on the underside of leaves, while the slender, winged males fly from plant to plant in search of mates. Left unchecked, mealybugs can weaken or kill the plants they infest, but in most cases they are easily controlled.

Meander

As a river flows across its floodplain, it often forms the broad, looping curves known as meanders. (The word is derived from a winding Turkish river so named by the ancient Greeks.) On the outside edge of a curve, where the current is fastest, the riverbank erodes, while sediment is deposited on its inner edge, gradually changing a small twist into a large, looping curve. Ever-changing, meanders sometimes are transformed into crescent-shaped oxbow lakes.

Measuring worm

The larvae of a widespread family of delicate moths, measuring worms are named for their peculiar looping gait. By arching up the middle of its body, a measuring worm pulls the rear part

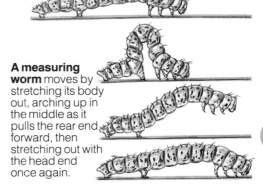

A measuring worm moves by stretching its body out, arching up in the middle as it pulls the rear end forward, then stretching out with the head end once again.

M

forward, then stretches out its head end to repeat the process. Giving the impression that they are measuring the surface as they move across it, measuring worms are also called inchworms. North America alone harbors some 1,200 species of these tiny foliage-eating acrobats, some of which damage shade trees.

Male red-breasted mergansers make catlike sounds when courting females. Sometimes a flock of these birds will form a long moving chain across the water's surface, driving fish into shallower areas where they can easily be plucked from the water.

Mesas are majestic testaments both to the power of erosion and to its limitations, since these huge flat-topped hills are capped with harder layers that could not be worn away. Aptly enough, *mesa* is Spanish for "table."

Menhaden *Brevoortia tyrannus*

One of the most abundant and important fish of the Atlantic coastal waters, menhaden are named for an Indian word meaning "that which enriches the soil." Their flesh is so oily that these large-headed, silvery members of the herring family are seldom eaten by humans. Indians of the U.S. east coast, however, used menhaden as fertilizer, burying one fish in each hill of corn. Today the oil is an ingredient in soaps, paints, and other products, and the fish meal and scraps are used in livestock feed and fertilizer. Up to 18 inches long, menhaden travel in enormous schools: their general range is from Nova Scotia to Brazil. Bluefish, striped bass, and many others eat huge numbers of menhaden, which are also used for bait.

Merganser

Slim and swift on the wing, mergansers are unique among ducks in having slender, saw-toothed bills that they use for seizing fish and other prey in underwater dives. All three North American species nest in forested regions and migrate south to open lakes, rivers, or coastal waters for the winter.

The smallest and most elegant species is the hooded merganser, which has a fan-shaped white crest bordered with black. Unlike the other mergansers, "hoodies" rarely gather in flocks

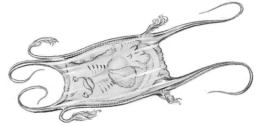

Mermaid's purses, the leathery egg cases of skates and certain sharks, protect the young as they develop.

and usually winter on ponds and quiet estuaries. The common merganser is large and sleek; the male has a glossy green head without a crest, while the somewhat smaller red-breasted merganser has a distinctive spiky crest. Common mergansers nest in holes in trees and winter on fresh water, whereas red-breasted mergansers nest on the ground and prefer to spend the cold months on salt water.

Mermaid's purse

Often seen littering the seashore or attached to clumps of seaweed at low tide, mermaid's purses are the egg cases of skates and certain sharks, such as dogfish. Those of the skates are black, leathery, and pillow-shaped, with a hornlike projection at each corner. The purses of dogfish are similar in shape but are translucent and have long tendrils, which are used for anchorage.

M

Honey mesquite's delicate flowers are replaced by long, sweet-tasting seedpods, a favorite of many grazing animals.

Metamorphic rocks often have a banded texture, with layers of light and dark minerals. This one is ornamented with a vein of quartz.

Skates lay their eggs in the sand well offshore, so the cases found on the beach are generally empty. But dogfish and other egg-laying sharks deposit their purses in seaweed beds near shore, and intact cases can frequently be found when the tide recedes. The embryos within take several months to hatch.

Mesa

Often ochre or deep red in color, mesas are steep-sided, flat-topped tablelands that rise in stark splendor from the deserts of the southwestern United States. They range in size from a few acres to hundreds of square miles and are isolated remnants of much larger plateaus that once stood high above the present desert floor. Mesas are capped by a hard layer of rock that withstood the assault of wind and water while the softer layers below were worn away, forming steep slopes. One of North America's most famous table mountains, Mesa Verde, looms above its surroundings in southwestern Colorado. Twenty miles long and 15 miles wide, this mesa is incised with caves that were home to the cliff-dwelling ancestors of the Pueblo Indians.

Mesquite *Prosopis*

The hardy and tenacious mesquites are thorny shrubs and trees that thrive in the hot, dry climate and poor soils of the southwestern United States. Their remarkable taproots probe downward more than 60 feet in search of groundwater, while extensive lateral roots fan out from the trunk to soak up newly fallen rain. In very dry areas mesquites may be only a few feet tall, but with adequate moisture they can grow to some 50 feet in height, with a girth of up to 3 feet. The twisted trunks are covered with thick, craggy bark, and the twigs bear sharp spines up to two inches long. Mesquite leaves, in contrast, are delicate and feathery. The dainty spikes of greenish-white flowers that appear in spring and summer give rise later to long pods filled with pulpy seeds. Sweet and rich in protein, the seeds were once a staple in the diet of native peoples. They also are relished by deer, rabbits, peccaries, and domestic livestock. Mesquite wood makes good lumber, and it also yields an aromatic smoke used to flavor grilled meats.

Metamorphic rock

Rocks that have been altered by intense heat or pressure within the earth's crust are known as metamorphic rocks. They originate as sedimentary or igneous rocks, such as sandstone or granite, but are transformed into new types of rocks when their minerals recrystallize or are realigned. Metamorphism can occur when buried rocks come in contact with magma pushing its way to the surface. It can also result from major regional geologic events, such as movements of the earth's crust, which produce tremendous heat and pressure and so alter all the rocks in the area. Many metamorphic rocks, such as gneisses, are characterized by alternating light and dark bands; others, such as slate, occur in plates. The skyscrapers in New York City rest on a solid foundation of metamorphic rocks, mainly schist, gneiss, and marble.

M

233

Spotted salamanders deposit clusters of gelatinous eggs (top) in water, and the tiny, developing larvae are easily seen inside the translucent eggs. After a month or so the eggs hatch, and the slender, legless larvae (below left) remain in the water as they metamorphose into land-dwelling adults. Spotted salamanders (below right), common in the eastern United States, are up to nine inches in length.

Metamorphosis

Many kinds of animals undergo astonishing transformations as they mature. These changes, called metamorphosis, are so dramatic that creatures at various stages in their life histories sometimes appear to belong to completely different species. Wormlike beetle larvae, for example, become winged adult insects; legless, fishlike tadpoles turn into tailless frogs with powerful hind legs; and microscopic, free-swimming oyster larvae are transformed into hard-shelled, stationary adults.

In the course of metamorphosis, some organs are lost while others are gained. An earthbound caterpillar develops wings, and its chewing jaws are replaced by a long, sucking snout. The tadpole trades its gills for lungs, and its tail shortens to nothing as its legs grow longer. A tiny, translucent, floating lobster larva becomes an armored giant with legs and claws.

Some insects, such as beetles, bees, and butterflies, undergo what is called complete metamorphosis. That is, they pass through four separate stages of development: egg, larva, pupa, and adult. During the inactive, nonfeeding pupal stage, their bodies are completely reorganized into winged adults. Other insects, such as grasshoppers and dragonflies, in contrast, undergo incomplete metamorphosis, a three-stage process. They do not pupate but gradually assume the adult form during a series of molts.

Red milkweed beetles are found in the eastern United States and Canada.

Meteorite

Stony or metallic objects that drop to earth from outer space are called meteorites. While most are quite small, the largest measure several feet in diameter and weigh thousands of pounds. Meteorites offer scientists clues about the composition of the planets and other extraterrestrial bodies. Relatively rare (most burn up as they hurtle through our atmosphere, where they are visible as "shooting stars"), some 500 meteorites are estimated to hit the earth each year, though very few are ever recovered. In 1982, however, a six-pound meteorite crashed through the roof of a house in Connecticut—just a mile from another home that had been hit 11 years earlier.

M

Milkweed blossoms (left) are sweetly fragrant; the silk-tufted seeds (right) scatter far and wide.

Mica

Occurring in thin, flexible, shiny sheets, layers of the familiar mineral known as mica can sometimes be peeled apart with the fingernail, almost like the pages of a book. Composed mainly of aluminum, oxygen, and silicon, mica has a crystal structure with perfect cleavage, the property that allows it to be split into sheets. Depending on the type, it may be black, brown, violet, or transparent, and in fragmented form it appears as the shiny flecks in blocks of granite. The most common kind, called muscovite, was so named because the Russians once used large sheets of mica as window glass. Mica still is used in the manufacture of electronic components, ceramics, plastics, and paints.

Midge

At dusk, midges often swarm in such dense clouds near bodies of water that they produce an audible hum. Tiny but prolific, these fragile-looking flies closely resemble mosquitoes, but they do not bite. The females lay their eggs in ponds or streams, where the wormlike larvae scavenge for bits of food in the bottom sediments. The larvae of some, called bloodworms, are used as bait by anglers. Eaten by trout and many larger animals, the larvae are important links in freshwater food webs.

Migration See pp. 236–237.

Milksnake See *Kingsnake.*

Milkvetch See *Locoweed.*

Milkweed *Asclepias*

The fragrant blossoms and spindle-shaped seedpods of the milkweeds are familiar sights along roadsides and in meadows and forest clearings across North America. Sturdy plants with stout stems and large oval leaves, most are filled with poisonous, milky sap. In summer the milkweeds bear clusters of colorful five-petaled flowers that are ingeniously constructed to aid cross pollination. The nectar-filled blossoms contain wishbone-shaped structures with a waxy mass of pollen hanging from each end. Catching on the legs of foraging insects, the pollen masses are carried away like saddlebags and dislodged on the next milkweed the insect visits. The blooms are followed by warty pods that burst open to scatter their seeds on the wind.

Milkweed beetle *Tetraopes*

For their entire lives milkweed beetles are irrevocably linked to milkweeds. They lay their eggs on the plants, the larvae feast on milkweed tissue as they tunnel through roots and stems, and the adults feed on the leaves. The acrid, milky sap of the milkweeds makes the beetles themselves distasteful to predators—and their bold red and black coloring advertises this fact. Finicky feeders, each of the several species found in North America relies on just one or two kinds of milkweed. One of the most common, the red milkweed beetle, produces squeaking sounds by rubbing together rough areas on its body.

M

235

Migration

Twice every year, as the spring thaw begins and again as summer wanes, many birds, mammals, and other animals migrate between their seasonal homes. In the course of these periodic, round-trip movements between summer and winter habitats, the migrants often battle tremendous obstacles and cover vast distances. Arctic terns, for instance, fly thousands of miles, trading one polar locale for another; eels undertake arduous journeys from inland lakes and rivers to spawning grounds in the Atlantic Ocean; and salmon hurl themselves against the current as they swim from the sea back to the freshwater streams where they were hatched.

These large-scale movements, involving thousands of individuals or even entire populations, enable animals to find food during times of scarcity or to congregate for mating. Most migrations are triggered by changes in day length, the onset of cold weather, or the phases of the moon. But migration is a complex phenomenon, with animals responding to both environmental and physiological cues.

Aerial navigators

Birds are the most familiar and spectacular migrants, with about 90 percent of our North American species moving south in the fall and north again in spring. Some, such as the lesser golden-plover, fly thousands of miles from the Arctic tundra to winter in the southern hemisphere. Others, such as robins and goldfinches, travel a few hundred miles to their wintering grounds, while the mountain quail of the West migrates just a few miles, walking from alpine nesting areas to valleys below the snow line.

Many birds travel along well-defined routes called flyways. Songbirds and some waterfowl often fly by night, using the stars and moon as a guide, and pause to rest and refuel during the day. Raptors, cranes, and others migrate by day, relying on the sun for orientation. Still others seem to depend on such clues as the earth's

magnetic field and even barometric pressure to guide their flight.

Migrating birds generally fly at altitudes of 5,000 feet or less, but in clear weather they may soar to more than 20,000 feet. Their speed varies with the weather, and birds tend to travel faster in spring than in the fall. The current speed record is held by a lesser yellowlegs. Banded on Cape Cod, it was found six days later in the West Indies, some 1,888 miles away, and so averaged more than 300 miles a day.

Mammals on the move

Mammals also are accomplished migrants. Each year as winter approaches, caribou trek more than 600 miles south from the arctic tundra to the shelter of the far northern forest, where food is easier to find. Come spring, the massive herds once again head north toward their breeding grounds. Not all treks are so extensive, however. Wapiti, mountain goats, and mountain sheep move downslope at summer's end to feed in sheltered valleys, journeys that seldom amount to more than 10 miles.

Wintering monarchs gather in huge numbers on evergreen trees.

American robins, harbingers of spring, migrate in large flocks as they head north at winter's end.

Caribou travel in vast herds as they trek toward their breeding grounds on the Arctic tundra.

Brown bears (left) are attuned to the migrating habits of salmon and pluck the fish from the water as they swim upstream. Some species of salmon (right) turn bright red before spawning.

Many bats, especially the red and hoary bats, summer in the northern United States and winter in the southern states. Those that hibernate may well travel hundreds of miles to reach the caves where they spend the winter.

Among the migrating marine mammals, northern fur seals shuttle between Alaska and California, a trip of up to 1,700 miles. Some of the whales also make astonishing seasonal journeys, leaving frigid polar regions to bear their young in tropical seas thousands of miles away.

Reptiles, fish, and insects

Several snakes, including rattlers, travel many miles to gather in winter dens. But of all the reptiles, the sea turtles are the ones that undertake the most extensive migrations; they often swim hundreds or even thousands of miles between feeding grounds in the open ocean and the beaches where they lay their eggs.

The most celebrated migratory fish are the salmon, which leave the rivers where they were hatched, and swim to sea; then after a journey of as much as 3,000 miles and four years, they return to the same river to mate and die. Migrant marine fish include striped bass and bluefin tuna.

Even insects migrate. Each fall, millions of monarch butterflies travel as much as 1,800 miles from their northern summer range to a few wintering sites in central Mexico and California. The return trip is made in stages, as females stop to lay eggs and die. Their offspring complete the flight back to where their forebears lived the previous summer.

The mysteries of navigation

The routes of most migratory animals are well known, but the question of how they navigate on their journeys is still debated. Birds use topographic features, the sun and stars, wind direction, and even the earth's magnetic field to find their way. Whales, caribou, and wapiti follow ancient routes that older individuals remember. And salmon recognize the distinctive "odors" of the rivers where they were spawned.

No one is sure what triggers the urge to migrate, but as the time approaches, birds, for instance, fatten up, often increasing their body weight by as much as 50 percent. The study of these age-old journeys is far from complete, with many mysteries remaining about navigation and the mechanisms that compel migration.

Fringed polygala, also known as gaywings, is a milkwort that grows in rich, moist woods; the blossoms have showy winglike sepals.

This millipede, sensing danger, has curled itself into a spiral to protect the vulnerable underside that bears its many legs.

River chubs, like most other minnows, play an important role in the freshwater food chain. Feeding on aquatic insects, insect larvae, and crustaceans, minnows in turn are consumed by the larger game fish. A number of species of minnows, in fact, are used by anglers as bait.

Milkwort *Polygala*

Named for an old belief that nursing mothers gave more milk after eating these wildflowers, milkworts of many species thrive all across the continent and are found everywhere from dry, open fields to moist meadows and swamps. Most are low, branching plants crowned with clusters of tiny flowers in a rainbow of hues. Variously shaped, the flower heads of some, such as orange milkwort and the purplish field milkwort, resemble the flower clusters of clover. In contrast, Seneca snakeroot, so named because Indians used its leaves to treat snakebite, bears its pale flowers in long spikes; and fringed polygala, or gaywings, has much larger flowers that look like fanciful magenta birds in flight.

Millipede

Slinking along on dozens of tiny legs, a millipede looks like a cross between an earthworm and a caterpillar. (While some species have fewer than 30 legs and others have several hundred, none have anywhere near the thousand suggested by their name.) Denizens of dark, damp places, millipedes wriggle through soil and un-

der stones and logs, where they feed on rootlets and decaying vegetation. Unlike their relatives the centipedes, which are equipped with poison fangs, millipedes do not bite. When provoked by would-be predators, they coil up tightly to protect their tender undersides, and as a last resort, they can release a foul-smelling toxin.

Mimicry

Plants and animals sometimes bear a striking resemblance to entirely different plants, animals, or nonliving things. Use of these built-in disguises, called mimicry, plays an important role in survival. A bird in search of insects, for example, is likely to avoid what appears to be an inedible leaf, unaware that it is passing up an entirely edible katydid. The boldly colored viceroy butterfly, though perfectly palatable to birds, likewise is avoided because it looks almost exactly like the foul-tasting monarch. Similarly, the harmless scarlet kingsnake mimics the bright colors of the venomous coral snake.

In aggressive mimicry it is the predator who wears a disguise—much like the proverbial wolf in sheep's clothing. Alligator snapping turtles, for instance, lure fish by wiggling their

M

Minks are most often found near water; excellent swimmers, they dive for frogs and small fish.

wormlike tongues, while trumpet fish imitate the colors of harmless species in order to sneak up on their prey.

Plants also practice mimicry. Certain kinds of trilliums, for example, smell like carrion and so attract the flies and beetles that pollinate their blooms. The aptly named stinking Benjamin is the rankest of these floral mimics.

Mineral

The building blocks of rocks, ores, and gems, minerals are as ordinary as table salt or as rare as rubies. Geologists define a mineral as any naturally occurring solid that was never part of a living organism, has a fixed chemical composition, and has its atoms arranged in a regular crystal pattern. Some 3,000 minerals have been identified, but only about 100 are common.

With their varied colors, textures, and wide range of uses, minerals have long intrigued mankind. Some, such as sulfur and fluorite, have important industrial uses; others, such as amethysts, have been imbued with mystical properties; and still others—sapphires, for example—are prized as gems.

Mink *Mustela vison*

Valued for their glossy, luxurious fur, minks are bushy-tailed weasels that live in marshes and in thickets near lakes and streams. Though found in nearly every area except the southwestern United States, minks are rarely seen because they spend the day hidden in burrows or abandoned beaver lodges. At night they hunt for frogs, fish, crayfish, and other aquatic creatures, as well as larger fare, such as muskrats and rabbits.

When threatened by foxes, owls, or other en-

emies, minks put up a terrific fuss, spitting, hissing, and emitting a foul, skunklike odor. They even fight with each other and prefer to spend their lives alone except during the mating season. The young can feed themselves in a few months and mate when one year old.

Once widely sought for their fur, wild minks are rarely trapped nowadays. Instead, the animals are raised in captivity. Brown-furred in the wild, ranch-reared minks have been bred to yield coats of various colors, including blond and black.

Minnow

Though the word *minnow* is commonly used to mean any small fish, it actually refers to members of the largest family of freshwater fish—a family that in North America alone embraces some 280 species. Some of them are indeed small; shiners, goldfish, dace, and chubs, seldom more than a few inches long, all belong to the minnow family and serve as food for larger fish. Others, such as carp and western squawfish, in contrast, grow up to four feet in length and are themselves sought as game fish.

In spring and summer many spawning minnows take on showy colors and sprout warty tubercles on their heads—the trappings of courtship. Fallfish protect their fertilized eggs with a layer of stones that they carry to the nest in their mouths. The most unusual breeding behavior, however, belongs to the bitterlings: the female develops a tubelike ovipositor and uses it to inject her eggs into the gill cavity of a freshwater mussel. After being showered with the male's sperm, the eggs develop and hatch within the protective mantle of the mussel, which is unharmed by its nursery duty.

M

239

Mistletoe, often used to steal a kiss, steals its own nourishment from host trees.

Field mint, like many of its relatives, has flowers that grow in dense clusters at intervals along the stem.

Velvet mites, in bright crimson, are found in moist woods and prey on insect eggs.

In mixed forests in autumn, the green conifers contrast with the red and gold deciduous trees.

M

Mint

Peppermint and spearmint are the celebrities of the mint family, lending their freshness to candies, liqueurs, toothpastes, and of course juleps. But botanically, a host of other plants also qualify as mints. These include rosemary, oregano, thyme, sage, and basil—in fact, the mints account for 25 percent of our culinary spices. Bee balm, wild bergamot, and catnip are among the many wild species found in fields and along roadsides all across North America. Whatever the species, all the mints are characterized by square stems; oval, tooth-edged leaves borne in opposite pairs; and two-lipped tubular flowers of pale purple, pink, or white. The tiny blossoms are massed in whorls or spikes, usually reaching their peak display in midsummer. Volatile oils stored in resinous dots on the stems and leaves give mints their fragrance. In some species, such as peppermint and thyme, the oils are reported to have medicinal properties as well.

Mockingbirds are renowned for reciting the songs of other birds, from the melancholy coos of mourning doves to the fatuous clucking of chickens. They will typically repeat a phrase over and over again before going on to another.

Mirage

Often appearing in the distance as shimmering ponds in the middle of roads on hot summer days, mirages result from the bending of light rays by layers of air of different temperatures. The "ponds," in fact, are simply images of the sky, produced when light rays are bent by the hot air just above the pavement. Under certain conditions objects such as trees or even ships at sea may appear magnified, upside down, or high above their actual locations.

Mistletoe *Phoradendron flavescens*

Though today it is an enduring symbol of the holiday season, in the past mistletoe represented supernatural powers. Awed by the way this parasite sprouts from tree limbs and prospers without sustenance from the soil, primitive man hung it over his doorways to ward off witches.

Mistletoe is found in western Canada and it flourishes in most parts of the United States. Clinging to tree branches, its ball of fleshy green leaves and stems may measure several feet across. The flowers are inconspicuous, but the shiny white winter berries attract flocks of birds. The seeds, which are sticky, adhere to the birds' beaks and so are carried from tree to tree to sprout into new clusters of mistletoe.

Mite

Tiny cousins of spiders and scorpions, mites are eight-legged animals that live in soil or water as well as on plants and animals. Of the thousands of species found in North America, some are large enough to be seen, while others are microscopic. Many feed on important crops as well as on stored grain and other products, causing enormous damage.

Best known, however, are the parasitic mites, which burrow into the skin of humans and domestic animals. The minuscule larvae of harvest mites, called chiggers, often torment campers in the woods. These pests virtually strip-mine the skin, releasing irritating chemicals that make for endless itching. Various mites also live in nasal passages and other body cavities.

Mixed forest

Between the deciduous forest of the eastern United States and the northern coniferous forest of Canada lies an intermediate zone of mixed forest. Stretching from the Great Lakes to Nova Scotia, this broad belt of mixed woodland is characterized by warm summers, cold winters, moderate rainfall, and rich soil. Its trees include a mingling of southerly broad-leaved species, such as maple, beech, basswood, ash, and oak, and northerly conifers, such as white pine, hemlock, balsam fir, and tamarack. Local conditions determine which trees grow where. The cool, shaded north side of a hill in New England, for example, might be all "north woods," with hemlock and fir. But its sunny south slope might support sugar maple, oak, and hickory.

Moccasin See *Cottonmouth.*

Mockingbird *Mimus polyglottos*

Though mockingbirds have a sweet, melodious song of their own, they are best known for their imitations of the songs of dozens of other birds. So versatile are these mimics, in fact, that their repertoire also includes the sounds of crickets, frogs, and even dogs. Tireless balladeers, they sing for hours at a time, both day and night.

Neatly attired in gray and white, mockingbirds are often seen in U.S. gardens, thickets, and low trees, where they aggressively defend their nests against all intruders. In spring and summer they consume huge quantities of insects. In fall and winter, however, their diet turns to fruit, and they sometimes damage orchard crops. Popular nonetheless, these cheerful mimics are the state bird of Arkansas, Texas, Mississippi, Florida, and Tennessee.

M

241

Eastern moles are more help than harm, since they aerate the soil and destroy insect pests.

Mojarra

Silvery, heavily scaled fish with forked tails, mojarras commonly cruise the bottoms of warm, shallow coastal seas in extensive schools. Equipped with mouths that can be stretched out to form long, downward-pointing tubes, they root through the bottom sediments, sucking in small shrimps, crabs, and worms.

Mojarras often enter the brackish water of bays and estuaries. Some species, such as the spotfin mojarra and the silver jenny, even venture into fresh water.

Mole

Built for burrowing, moles have pointed noses, tapered heads, and thick, glossy fur. Shovellike forelegs push soil aside, while powerful hindlegs propel the creatures forward. Though moles are blind or nearly so, their hearing is acute.

The eastern mole tunnels near the surface when searching for worms and insects, often leaving unsightly ridges on lawns throughout the eastern United States. Deeper burrows are used for raising young and escaping winter's cold. The star-nosed mole, found in many parts of eastern Canada, lives near water, diving for snails and aquatic insects. It is named for the fleshy sensory projections on its nose. Our largest species, the seven-inch Townsend's mole, and our smallest, the three-inch shrew mole, both live in the West.

Mollusk

Clams, oysters, snails, slugs, squids, and octopuses—all are mollusks, members of the group of animals second only to insects in number and di-

Limpets are marine snails that creep on coastal rocks. Forming the largest group of mollusks, snails are called univalves because they have only a single shell.

versity. Mollusks are characterized by contrasts. Some, such as certain clams and oysters, live deep in the ocean, while others, including some kinds of snails, live high on mountain slopes. Though the vast majority have hard shells, others, such as slugs and octopuses, have no shells at all. And while most are smaller than a human hand, the giant squid may grow to a length of 60 feet.

All share several bodily traits, however, though they take different forms in different species. All mollusks are soft-bodied invertebrates with a layer of tissue, called the mantle, that surrounds the gills, intestines, and other organs and secretes the substance that hardens into shell. Many feed by means of a rasplike structure called the radula, covered with tiny teeth. Most also have a muscular foot, used both for locomotion and for digging.

A few mollusks are destructive. Shipworms, for example, bore into wood pilings and boats,

M

Monarch caterpillars (upper) are as boldly hued as the adult butterfly (lower). The colors warn of the insect's unpleasant taste.

Molting in spring, mountain goats look rather scraggly. The molting process is regulated by hormones.

causing enormous damage. For the most part, however, mollusks are beneficial. Their shells and pearls provide beautiful jewelry, and the flesh of oysters, clams, scallops, mussels, snails, and even squids is a valuable source of food.

Molt

The process of shedding old feathers, hair, or skin is known as molting. In amphibians and reptiles this is a dramatic event, with the whole outer layer of skin being sloughed off at once. When it is time to molt, a snake rubs its snout against a rock or tree until the skin tears, then wriggles out, leaving the old covering behind.

Temperate-zone mammals typically molt twice a year. The fall molt produces a heavy winter coat, which is shed the following spring.

The situation is more complicated among birds. Most species, including the familiar songbirds, lose their feathers gradually—a few at a time—over the course of one to three months, and the birds can fly throughout. Ducks and some of the other water birds, in contrast, molt all their flight feathers at once and remain grounded until the new growth is complete.

Monadnock

When erosion wears away a broad plateau, leaving an isolated peak surrounded by lowlands, the resulting landform is called a monadnock. The archetype for these geological features is Mount Monadnock in southwestern New Hampshire; composed of sturdy metamorphic rock, it rises to a height of 3,165 feet. Another famous example, Stone Mountain in Georgia, is a great granite monolith that towers some 825 feet above the surrounding plains. Monadnocks generally survive because they are formed of rock that is highly resistant to erosion.

Monarch *Danaus plexippus*

Boldly patterned orange and black butterflies, monarchs are among the greatest migrators of the insect world. At summer's end monarchs from eastern and central North America head south, flying thousands of miles to congregate by the millions in winter havens in the mountains of Mexico. In one colony 20 acres of trees were found to be carpeted by the resting butterflies. Western monarchs gather at wintering sites along the California coast, roosting in groves of Monterey pines and eucalyptus trees. In spring they leave their refuge and start the long trip north; stopping en route, they lay eggs and die. Once mature, the offspring continue the journey northward.

Monarchs are milkweed butterflies; the caterpillars feed on the plant's leaves, ingesting its poisonous sap with impunity. The noxious juice protects the fat caterpillars, and later the mature butterflies, from being eaten by birds and other predators: after one taste, they learn not to meddle with monarchs.

M

Pink monkey flowers bloom along streams and other moist, mountainous areas from the Canadian Rockies south to the Sierra Nevadas of California.

Western monkshood contains a powerful toxin, which has been used for poison arrows.

Monkey flower *Mimulus*

Few wildflowers put on as colorful a display as the monkey flowers. Related to snapdragons, they bear a profusion of tubular two-lipped blossoms that, to many observers, look very much like grinning monkey faces. The charming blooms—in yellow, orange, red, purple, blue, or white—brighten streamsides and other damp locations in the East. In the West, where the monkey flowers are most numerous, some kinds also thrive in dry, gravelly soils and on high mountain slopes.

Monkshood *Aconitum*

Named for their hood-shaped blossoms, which resemble monks' cowls, these wildflowers prefer the rich soils of mountain meadows and ravines. The blooms—purple, blue, or white—are borne in spiky clusters. A powerful poison called aconitine is contained in the roots of all monkshoods. Used in ancient times to execute criminals, it was once thought to cause the death of wolves as they foraged for roots in winter—hence its alternate name, wolfsbane.

Mooneye *Hiodon*

Mooneyes and their smaller cousins, the goldeyes, are aptly named fish that live in lakes and rivers throughout central North America. Equipped with teeth on the tongue and on the roof of the mouth, they catch and devour minnows, aquatic insects, and small shellfish. The

mooneyes' resemblance to other, better-known fish has earned them the alternate name "toothed herring." Up to 18 inches long, they are sometimes sold as smoked fish.

Moon snail

Housed in the whorls of large, rounded shells, moon snails are able predators that plow across the sandy sea floor, leaving a telltale trail. When the snail encounters a clam, it uses its finely toothed tongue, or radula, to drill a hole through the victim's shell, then feasts on the soft flesh within. Females glue their eggs to sand grains, forming curious ring-shaped structures, called sand collars, that are sometimes found washed up on sandy shores.

Moorhen *Gallinula chloropus*

Chickenlike birds formerly known as common gallinules, common moorhens live in marshes and weedy ponds, where they feed on insects, snails, and seeds. These waterbirds are agile swimmers, but they also have long toes that enable them to run about on lily pads and other floating plants. Though they sometimes fly to safety when they sense danger, they are weak and clumsy on the wing and are more likely to dash into the vegetation for cover. Moorhens build cuplike nests on platforms of reeds or in shrubs at the water's edge, raising two, and occasionally three, broods a year. The downy chicks follow their parents, catching insects on their own as they roam through the dense vegetation.

M

A common moorhen leads her brood of downy, bald-headed chicks toward the marsh grass, where they will feed on insects. At times the chicks ride upon the back of one of the parents. The adults have distinctive red face shields, yellow-tipped bills, and white patches on their glossy black wings.

Moose often give birth to twins. Weak and gangling at birth, within two weeks the calves are able to roam with their mother in search of food. The next spring, before giving birth again, the mother chases off the yearlings, forcing them to fend for themselves at last.

Moose *Alces alces*

Inhabiting dense forests throughout Canada, Maine and Alaska, moose are the giants of the deer family. They may lack the grace of other deer, but they are nevertheless among North America's most magnificent mammals. A bull moose crashing through the underbrush in a northern bog is a sight not soon forgotten.

Alaska boasts the largest males: they weigh some 1,800 pounds, stand more than seven feet tall at the shoulder, and have antlers with a spread of over six feet. In addition to a massive body and a big, overhanging muzzle, the moose is characterized by a fold of skin on the throat called the bell. Though long and spindly-looking, its legs are well suited for moving swiftly across snow, wading in water, and swimming.

During the fall rutting season, when their low, mooing calls echo through the forest, bulls battle over cows in savage antler-to-antler confrontations. By December the contests end and the bulls shed their hefty headgear.

In summer, moose wade into ponds and streams to eat aquatic plants, and in winter they browse on twigs and bark. Once exterminated in parts of their range—they were used as food by native peoples and early settlers, and their antlers have always been prized as trophies—moose have lately made a comeback.

Moraine

The accumulations of boulders, rocks, sand, and other material carried along by glaciers and deposited when the ice melts are called moraines. Lateral moraines form along the sides of valley glaciers and consist of debris that falls down from adjoining slopes. Medial moraines result when two glaciers merge and two lateral moraines unite as a stripe of rubble down the center of the compound glacier. Terminal moraines form along the leading edges of glaciers, where the melting ice drops its cargo of rocks and sediment in a line across the valley. A ground moraine is a layer of debris deposited beneath a glacier. Many moraines in northern regions were left by the great continental ice sheets.

M

Moray eels spend the day lurking in rock crevices, their heads often protruding to catch a glimpse or a whiff of a prospective meal. Unwary fish or squid that happen to pass by are quickly engulfed by the moray's sharp teeth and powerful jaws. Divers may take some consolation from the fact that the moray's bite, though vicious, is never poisonous.

Moray

Thick-bodied eels that swim with serpentine undulations, morays are among the meanest-looking characters in the sea. Though intimidating and large—some are more than six feet long—these denizens of rock and coral reefs are basically shy. Their unnerving habit of keeping their toothy jaws agape is simply the morays' means of breathing.

By day, morays seek the solitude and shelter of caves in rock and coral formations, but aided by an extraordinary sense of smell, they can strike out fiercely when a smaller fish swims by—or when a foolhardy diver's hand intrudes on their privacy. After dark, morays leave their lairs to stalk fish and other creatures of the reef.

Morning glory *Ipomoea*

Truly a glory of the early hours, morning glories unfurl their colorful trumpet-shaped flowers shortly after dawn, then close them again just a few hours later. The twining vines, which may climb to 10 or 20 feet, are widely planted to decorate fences and trellises. Wild morning glories, however, can also be serious pests, causing damage to crops such as corn and cotton. Yet one species—the familiar sweet potato—is an important crop in its own right. Less well known is the wild potato vine, or man of the earth; its giant edible root, growing several feet long and weighing up to 30 pounds, served as an important source of food for both native peoples and early settlers.

Mosquito

Found all across North America, mosquitoes are notorious insect pests. Females lay clutches of 150 to 300 eggs almost anywhere that they can find water, whether in marshes or in discarded tin cans. After hatching, the hyperactive larvae, called wrigglers, eat prodigiously, using bristly brushes on either side of the head to sweep food particles into their mouths. The larvae pupate within a week, and a few days later the long-legged, fragile-looking adults emerge.

Males live on a diet of plant juices, but the females of most species need a meal of blood to nourish their developing eggs. They pierce their victims' skin with stilettolike mouthparts, then sip their bloody feast. This strategy is not merely annoying; it can result in the transmission of such serious diseases as malaria and yellow fever. Fortunately, in North America these ailments have been largely eliminated through stringent control efforts.

Mosquito fish *Gambusia affinis*

Only 2½ inches long, the stout-bodied little mosquito fish earned its name from its voracious appetite for mosquito larvae. A native of the southeastern United States, where it thrives in ponds, ditches, streams, and even brackish water, it has been transplanted to other areas of the world to help control the insect pests.

Mosquito fish are live bearers, with the females annually giving birth to three or four broods of some 200 or more fully formed miniature fish. Though inconspicuous themselves, mosquito fish have a number of colorful relatives, including guppies and mollies, that are popular with aquarium hobbyists.

Moss

Among the most primitive of land plants, mosses lack true roots, stems, leaves, or even an internal system of tubes for transporting water and nutrients. In addition, they are incapable of flowering or setting seed and reproduce instead by means of tiny, single-celled spores produced

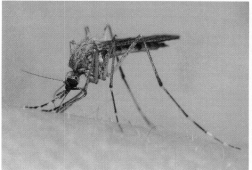

A female house mosquito on human skin positions her needlelike proboscis (left). After inserting it (right), she sucks in blood—like soda through a straw—until her abdomen is full.

Cecropia moths, found from the Atlantic coast to the Rockies, may have a wingspan of more than five inches. Males locate females with their large feathery antennae, which can sense the odor of a prospective mate more than a mile away.

in special capsules. Seldom more than a few inches tall, mosses grow in dense mats.

Primitive though they are, mosses are hardy, thriving even on Arctic tundra. Their ability to live on bare and burned-over areas gives them an important role in soil formation. By colonizing bare rock, mats of moss prepare a toehold for higher plants. By absorbing large amounts of water, they help prevent erosion.

The most extraordinary of our North American species is luminous moss. Glittering like gold, this cave-dweller produces its own tiny lenses that concentrate the feeble light of its gloomy environment and so allow it to carry on photosynthesis. The most valuable mosses are the sphagnums, the mosses that form peat. Gradually filling bogs, they convert wet land to dry. The decomposed peat is also mined and used to improve poor soils.

Moth

Generally thought of as lackluster cousins of the beautiful butterflies, moths are indeed usually the stouter and less colorful of the two. Like butterflies, they have patterned wings covered with scales, and most have hollow, coiled tongues for sipping nectar. Moths are best distinguished from their showier relatives by their antennae, which may be feathery or threadlike but never have the clubby tips found on butter-

fly antennae. Most moths, moreover, are nocturnal, while butterflies are active by day; on many summer evenings the dusky forms of moths are seen fluttering about porch lights.

Of the more than 11,000 species of moths and butterflies in North America, the vast majority are moths. Their life cycle, like that of butterflies, includes four stages—egg, larva (caterpillar), pupa (usually a silken cocoon), and adult. Moths generally deposit their eggs on the plants that their larvae eat, although some kinds feed on such fare as fungi, fabrics, and even beeswax. The caterpillars, some of which are quite colorful, feed almost constantly; many, in fact, are destructive agricultural pests. Hawk moths, tiger moths, and tussock moths are some common North American varieties.

M

Moth mullein Verbascum blattaria

Found in fields and roadsides throughout North America, the moth mullein sends up three-foot spikes of pretty five-petaled flowers from June through October. Some say the plant was named for the fancied resemblance of its fuzzy stamens to a moth's antennae. Others claim it received its name because its white or yellow blooms attract those night-flying insects. Whatever the origin, country folk used to pack its leaves among their woolens in the belief that they would ward off clothes moths.

Mount Shuksan, in the Cascades, in the state of Washington, is a monument to volcanic forces.

MOUNTAIN

Ascend any mountain, whether along the rugged trails of the Rockies or the gentler slopes of the ancient Appalachians, and you will witness astonishing changes. From their forested foothills to their craggy, snowcapped summits, mountains are layered with a series of life zones, each characterized by its own distinct community of plants and wildlife.

The towering peaks of the West best dramatize the broad range of conditions encountered from foothills to mountaintop. Douglas firs form dense, fragrant stands on the lower slopes;

elk and mule deer graze in flower-filled mountain meadows; farther up, at the timberline, gnarled bristlecone pines and other stunted conifers weather the fierce winds, and delicate forget-me-nots, moss campions, and gentians carpet the alpine tundra with a vivid patchwork of color. Beyond are the perpetually snowcapped summits, virtually devoid of life.

Running from Alabama to Newfoundland, the lush, rounded ridges of the East, remnants of peaks once as lofty as those in the West, also exhibit a range of habitats on their slopes.

Parry's primroses are hardy wildflowers found in crevices on soggy tundra slopes.

Mountain bluebirds often nest in abandoned woodpecker holes.

Golden eagles are magnificent mountain predators that soar for hours on end looking for prey.

Mountain lions, graceful and solitary, are becoming increasingly rare.

Mountain goats climb to dizzying heights, well beyond the reach of most predators.

Blue columbine, the state flower of Colorado, thrives in moist woodlands.

Moss campion brightens rocky summits during the spring and summer.

Pikas store hay throughout the summer in preparation for the long mountain winter.

Mountain beavers, though not true beavers, often live near water and dig tunnels that divert the flow of streams.

Mountain laurel leaves were once used to cure skin rashes.

Mountain ashes, elegant trees with showy blossoms and shiny fruits, are popular ornamentals.

Mountain ash *Sorbus*

The slow-growing, relatively short-lived mountain ashes are pretty little trees that tolerate cold, marginal conditions. As their name suggests, they are most common at higher elevations, on rocky hillsides or along stream banks. Though the European mountain ash, widely planted as an ornamental, grows to heights of 60 feet or more, the native American species seldom exceed 30 feet. With straight trunks and rounded crowns of feathery foliage, the trees wear broad, showy clusters of white flowers in late spring and shiny red fruits in the fall. The fruits persist long after the leaves have fallen, providing a winter feast for many birds. In northern regions moose browse extensively on the twigs.

Mountain beaver *Aplodontia rufa*

Neither mountain dwellers nor beavers, these stocky, burrowing rodents live in damp, forested regions of California and the northwestern United States. Also called sewellels, mountain beavers are about a foot long, with coarse, grayish-brown fur, rounded ears, and a tiny stub of a tail. Mainly nocturnal, they emerge after dark to forage for small plants. Their burrows, which are often dug into stream banks, usually include special chambers for storing food.

Mountain goat *Oreamnos americanus*

Surefooted despite a weight of up to 300 pounds, mountain goats are native to the Canadian Rockies and spend most of their time high above the timberline. Sharp-edged, skid-resistant hooves enable them to maneuver along narrow ledges and clamber up steep, icy slopes as they search for grasses, lichens, and other food. A dense coat of thick white fur keeps them well insulated in this cold and windy world. Both males and females have backward-curving black horns and bearded chins. Mountain goats migrate up and down the slopes with the seasons, descending from the tundra to the tree line when winter snows threaten their food supply. The kids are born in early spring—usually in single births, but sometimes as twins. They can stand up and walk within minutes of birth, and in just a few days they are able to follow their mothers across incredibly rugged terrain.

M

Mountain lions kill with a bite to the neck. They prefer deer and elk but, in lean times, have been known to pursue hares and even an occasional skunk or porcupine.

Mountain sheep, by negotiating sheer cliffs, can avoid such enemies as wolves and coyotes. The ram (left) has bulkier headgear than the ewe.

Mountain laurel *Kalmia latifolia*

In Appalachian woodlands the spring flowering of mountain laurel provides one of nature's loveliest displays. Often growing in dense thickets, this shrub or small tree, which may reach 30 feet in height, is covered with glossy evergreen leaves, two to four inches long—a handsome foil for the large, showy flower clusters. Each pale pink, cup-shaped bloom resembles a tiny, colorful skirt, giving mountain laurel the alternative name calico bush.

Favoring acid soils, mountain laurel is native to open woods and abandoned pastures from Maine to Florida and west as far as central Tennessee. No relation to the old-world laurel used by the ancients for victory wreaths, mountain laurel is poisonous to livestock, though white-tailed deer browse on its foliage with no ill effect.

Mountain lion *Felis concolor*

As elusive as they are powerful, mountain lions are large cats that live in more areas than one might imagine—from the swamps of Florida to the deserts and mountains of the West. Known by different names in different places, mountain lions are variously called cougars, pumas, panthers, painters, and catamounts.

Up to five feet long, with gray to tawny fur and a black-tipped tail, mountain lions are solitary creatures that hunt by night, primarily for deer and elk. These furtive predators generally stalk their prey, then rush in for the kill, but they sometimes pounce from overhanging trees or cliffs. Despite the fears of ranchers and campers, mountain lions rarely attack livestock and tend to avoid humans completely.

Their bloodcurdling mating call—a scream that sounds like a terrified woman—is sometimes heard in remote areas. Litters of as many as five playful, spotted cubs are usually born in summer, and the young cats remain with their mother for a year or more before setting out on their own.

Mountain sheep *Ovis canadensis*

Thanks to their massive, spiraling headgear, mountain sheep are also known as bighorns. Though heavily built, these mountain dwellers are amazingly nimble. Equipped with an excellent sense of balance and cushioned hooves that provide good traction, they are extraordinary climbers and jumpers—well adapted to the rugged, rocky terrain of western mountains from Canada to Mexico. During the rutting season in late fall, the rams compete for females in impressive jousting matches. Charging each other head on, they butt their enormous horns with explosive crashes as the smaller-horned ewes look on. Though the strongest rams usually win these contests, they use up so much energy that they seldom live as long as the losers.

M

251

Mudpuppies are salamanders with powerful flat tails that are used for balance and propulsion.

A mourning cloak butterfly spreads its wings and displays its striking blue spots— a marked contrast to its drab underside.

Mourning cloak *Nymphalis antiopa*

Flashy in flight, the mourning cloak butterfly displays a row of electric blue spots along its shiny gold wing margins. Common from coast to coast, the insect shows its colors not just in summer but in the winter months as well. Hibernating as an adult, it sometimes emerges from the crevices where it winters, and can be seen fluttering about on warm days, even while snow is still on the ground. The caterpillars— black and bristly with a row of red spots—feed on the leaves of willows, poplars, and elms.

Mouse

Originally used for the old-world house mouse, which was introduced to North America as early as the 1500's, the word *mouse* now refers to a number of small rodents with soft gray or brown fur, large rounded ears, and a long thin tail. Among the many native North American mice are the tiny harvest mice, which prefer open grassy areas; pocket mice, with pouches on their cheeks for carrying food; jumping and kangaroo mice, noted for their remarkable hopping ability; and the ubiquitous white-footed mice.

Since most mice are easy prey for hawks and other birds, as well as four-footed predators, they tend to be nocturnal and remain in hiding during the daylight hours. Abundant throughout North America, mice generally feed on seeds or vegetation, but one, the grasshopper mouse, is itself an aggressive predator.

Mudminnow

Though not minnows at all (they are more closely related to pikes), the mudminnows are in fact very much associated with mud. They live in weed-choked ponds, sloughs, and slow-moving streams, where they frequently bury themselves tail-first in the bottom mud. Remarkably hardy little fish, they can thrive in water with a very low oxygen content. North America's biggest mudminnow, the Alaska blackfish, grows up to eight inches in length. It used to be caught in large numbers in the fall, then frozen for use as winter food for sled dogs.

Mudpuppy *Necturus*

Oversized salamanders up to 17 inches long, mudpuppies live in lakes and streams. They are slimy and dull colored with darker spots, and have three pairs of bushy red gills on each side of the neck. Hiding on the bottom by day, mudpuppies go on the prowl at dusk, hunting for fish eggs, crayfish, insects, and other small aquatic prey. In spring, after mating, the females lay several dozen eggs, depositing them one by one beneath sticks, stones, and other underwater objects. The larvae hatch several weeks later and are mature when about eight years old.

M

The red mulberry tree bears juicy, purplish-red fruits. Eaten mainly by wildlife, they can be used to make jelly. In earlier times the tree's light, durable wood was sometimes used for fenceposts and farm tools, and the Choctaw Indians wove cloth from the dried bark of young mulberry shoots.

Some mule ears produce large, hairy leaves, but desert species bear narrow, water-conserving foliage. Aboriginal peoples sometimes ate the taproot and young shoots of the plant.

Mulberry *Morus*

Only two species of mulberries are native to North America: the red mulberry, a good-sized tree up to 70 feet tall, which grows widely in the eastern United States, and the smaller Texas mulberry, which occurs in the U.S. Southwest. Others have been introduced to the United States from Eurasia, including the black mulberry, which was brought over by early settlers. Another, the white mulberry, has long been cultivated in the Orient, since its foliage is the main food of the silkworm. Widely planted in the southeastern states in an attempt at domestic silkworm culture, it escaped to the wild and now grows throughout the eastern United States. A cold-tolerant variety of white mulberry, called Russian mulberry, has been widely planted in windbreaks in the U.S. West. The sweet, knobby multiple fruits of all the mulberries are shaped like blackberries but range in color from white to red to black. Though all are edible, most are consumed by songbirds and other wildlife.

Mule ears *Wyethia*

Natives of our western mountain slopes, mule ears paint hillsides, meadows, stream banks, and open woods with their cheerful yellow blossoms from spring until midsummer. Reaching a height of two feet, they do not come anywhere near the stature of their stately relatives the sunflowers. Mule ears owe their common name to the shape of the large, hairy leaves that grow in clusters at the plant's base. The botanical designation for mule ears reflects the name of the 19th-century fur trader and explorer Capt. Nathaniel J. Wyeth.

M

253

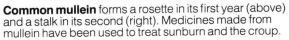

Common mullein forms a rosette in its first year (above) and a stalk in its second (right). Medicines made from mullein have been used to treat sunburn and the croup.

Musk oxen are as heavy as they are hairy: males, five feet high at the shoulder, weigh up to 800 pounds.

Murres return year after year to the same narrow ledges on steep coastal cliffs.

Mullein *Verbascum*

The common mullein is easily identified by its spirelike form and woolly gray-green leaves, which have inspired such names as velvet plant and old man's flannel. (People used to line their shoes with the leaves for warmth.) A biennial found in pastures and waste places across North America, this Eurasian native produces a broad, ground-hugging rosette of large, felty leaves in its first year. In its second season it sends up a ramrod-straight stalk six to eight feet tall, covered with cheerful yellow flowers.

Mullet

Several species of these fish are found in North America's coastal seas and estuaries. The most abundant are the striped mullet, which sometimes reaches a length of three feet and a weight of 15 pounds, and the very similar but unstriped white mullet. Preferring warm and temperate waters, mullets range from Cape Cod to the Gulf of Mexico; the striped mullet is also found in the Pacific from California south.

Mullets feed on algae and small animals that they filter from the bottom mud, grinding them in their gizzardlike stomachs and digesting them in exceptionally long intestines. They travel in large schools and are often seen leaping into the air with a silvery flash, then flopping back into the water with a splash. Although they are mainly saltwater fish, mullets sometimes swim for long distances up coastal rivers.

Murre *Uria*

Among the most numerous of all seabirds, murres are handsome members of the auk family. Both the common murre and the slightly larger thick-billed murre can be recognized by their prim black-and-white plumage, their long, pointed beaks, and their upright, penguinesque stance. Although their wings are stubby, murres are rapid fliers. They also use their wings to "fly" under the water, diving more than 200 feet in pursuit of small fish and other prey. Murres winter at sea but in summer gather in huge nesting colonies on coastal cliffs, mostly in Newfoundland. Each pair tends a single egg,

Fly agaric Bleeding mycena Painted bolete

Scarlet waxy cap Chanterelle

Mushrooms, enormously varied in appearance, are the fruiting bodies of underground fungi.

laid directly on the bare rock. Strongly tapered at one end, the egg tends to roll in a circle when disturbed, rather than falling off the cliff. At three weeks old, the chicks jump into the sea and are fed there by the adults until they can fly.

Mushroom

Intriguing and diverse, mushrooms come in a wide variety of sizes, shapes, and colors. Most of these fascinating fungi have the familiar umbrella form, with stalk and cap, but on some the tops are conical, and a few even flare out like trumpets. From red and purple to yellow and white, mushrooms are adorned with a rainbow of hues. And while some are deadly poisonous, others are prized by gourmets.

Often seeming to spring from the ground overnight, mushrooms sometimes grow in circles, called fairy rings, which were once believed to be footprints left by dancing sprites. The parts we see, however, are only the spore-producing reproductive bodies of the fungus, most of which is hidden underground in the form of a mass of cottony threads called the mycelium.

On the underside of their caps, many mushrooms have thin gills radiating like the spokes of a wheel; the undersides of others are perforated with minute pores. These structures produce spores by the millions, to be scattered by the winds. If the spores land on moist soil or rotting wood, new mycelia develop and can live underground for years before sending up mushrooms.

Muskeg

Dotting the vast northern coniferous forests of Canada and Alaska are countless sphagnum bogs known as muskegs. Drainage is poor in these lands of low relief, and glacier-carved depressions are numerous. The result is a patchwork of bogs where ponds have gradually filled in with soggy sphagnum. Slow to decay in these cold climes, the moss eventually accumulated into thick deposits of peat, permitting black spruces and other conifers to take root where there once was open water.

Musk ox *Ovibos moschatus*

Beyond the tree line on the wind-whipped tundra of the Far North and on nearby Arctic islands lives the stocky, long-haired musk ox. Both sexes wear broad horns that are plastered against the skull like helmets and curve up at the tips. Feeding on grasses, willows, and other tundra vegetation, musk oxen live in small herds consisting of a single bull and several cows. During the fall mating season, bulls engage in savage battles to establish dominance; in early spring each cow gives birth to a single calf. When threatened, musk oxen form a circle around their calves and face outward, presenting their foes with a daunting array of horns. This defensive ploy works well against wolves but not against humans, who have exterminated the musk ox in much of its former range.

M

Muskrats swim by sculling their tails and paddling with their hind feet. Extremely prolific, they sometimes produce several litters a year, with an average of six young in each litter.

Common musk turtles, also known as stinkpots, have two conspicuous light stripes on either side of their dark heads and necks. Usually spotted in ponds or swamps, they sometimes climb on tree branches that overhang the water.

Muskrat *Ondatra zibethicus*

Well adapted for life in ponds, marshes, and slow-moving rivers, muskrats are stocky rodents that can swim for long distances underwater and remain submerged for minutes at a time. They reach a length of two feet and have partially webbed hind feet, a long scaly tail that is flattened from side to side, and lustrous fur that ranges in color from pale brown to almost black.

Muskrats build two kinds of shelter: burrows in the banks of streams, and dome-shaped lodges of grasses and reeds in the shallows of marshes; both have underwater entrances. During the summer muskrats can often be seen carrying mouthfuls of cattails or bulrushes to their dens; they also feed on crayfish, clams, and fish.

Musk turtle *Sternotherus*

Close relatives of mud turtles, musk turtles live in bayous, ponds, and other quiet waters, which they seldom leave except to nest and bask in the sun. They forage on the bottom for insects, carrion, and other morsels—including the bait on fishhooks. They are not at all appreciated by the anglers who catch them, however: these pugnacious little reptiles not only bite when handled, but also emit a foul-smelling musky fluid. Of our several species of musk turtles, only the aptly named stinkpot extends its range beyond the Deep South.

Mussel

Found both in fresh water and in the sea, mussels are bivalve mollusks that resemble clams. The saltwater kinds live mostly in shallow waters and in the intertidal zone, where they are found partially buried in the bottom or attached to rocks, pilings, and other supports. Often living in clusters or even huge colonies, mussels anchor themselves in place with tough threads secreted by a special gland. The widespread blue mussel is edible and highly esteemed as food.

North American Indians also ate large quantities of freshwater mussels, whose shells were at one time used for making mother-of-pearl buttons as well. Unlike saltwater mussels, whose larvae float with the plankton, the larvae of many freshwater species are parasitic. Looking much like miniature clams, the larvae are expelled by the adult mussels and clamp shut on the fins and gills of fish. There they are enclosed in fleshy cysts and feed on fish tissue until they mature and drop off into the water.

M

Many mustards, such as Pallas's wallflower (above), toothwort (above right), and western wallflower (below right), have colorful blossoms that brighten open meadows and roadsides.

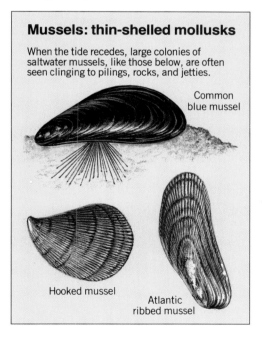

Mussels: thin-shelled mollusks

When the tide recedes, large colonies of saltwater mussels, like those below, are often seen clinging to pilings, rocks, and jetties.

Common blue mussel

Hooked mussel

Atlantic ribbed mussel

Mustard

Of all the members of this large plant family, black mustard is the most familiar. Its yellow flowers turn whole fields golden in spring; its young leaves are cooked and eaten as greens; and its dark brown seeds flavor the popular condiment that bears its name. Food plants such as cabbage, kale, broccoli, turnips, and radishes, as well as many garden flowers, also are family members. Wild mustards, many of them back-yard weeds, include the desert candle, prince's plume, winter cress, and shepherd's purse. All have four-petaled yellow, purple-red, pink, or white flowers. The petals form a cross that gives the family its scientific name, Cruciferae, or crossbearers.

Mutualism

The close association of individuals of two different species for the benefit of both is called mutualism. A cow, for example, provides both living space and food for the bacteria that live in its digestive tract; the bacteria, in turn, help break down cellulose in the cow's food, rendering it digestible. The yucca plant and the yucca moth likewise have a mutually beneficial relationship. The plant relies on the moth for pollination, while the moth's larva depends on the plant for seeds, its sole source of food. In the case of lichens—plants composed of an alga and a fungus living together—the alga manufactures food for both, while the fungus absorbs water and helps shade the alga.

M

257

N

Some natural bridges, such as Hickman's Bridge in Capitol Reef National Park, Utah, were formed when meandering streams gradually eroded their way through a wall of sandstone.

Natural bridge

Arches formed of solid rock, natural bridges are elegant erosional remnants. Some are created when most of the roof of a limestone cave collapses, leaving a small section as a natural span. A famous example of this type is Natural Bridge in Virginia. Ninety feet long and rising almost 200 feet above Cedar Creek, it was once owned by Thomas Jefferson and now has a highway running across its top. Other natural bridges occur when meandering streams or percolating groundwater undercut walls of rock, gradually enlarging an opening to form a graceful arch. The world's largest natural bridge is Rainbow Bridge in Utah. Spanning 275 feet and towering to a height of almost 300 feet, it is, according to Indian legend, a rainbow turned into stone.

Natural gas

An important energy resource, natural gas is a mixture of methane and other flammable gases. Like coal and oil, it was formed from long-buried organic matter and is usually found with or near petroleum deposits. (Natural gas provides the pressure for oil gushers.) Nonpolluting and easy to transport, it is used for cooking, heating, and many industrial purposes. The major natural gas fields in North America are found in Alberta, Louisiana, Oklahoma, and Texas.

Needlefish

Sleek and flashy speedsters of coastal seas, needlefish are streamlined creatures with elongated bodies that taper to long, pointed beaks. Armed with sharp teeth, they prey by night on smaller

Stinging nettles bear tiny greenish flowers in long, feathery clusters throughout the summer. The plant's scientific name comes from the Latin *uro,* meaning "I burn."

fish, overtaking their quarry with bulletlike runs and spectacular out-of-the-water leaps that are worthy of their relatives the flying fish.

Edible despite the unappetizing greenish hue of their flesh, needlefish have a strange history of turning the table on fishermen. Dazzled by nighttime lights on boats and propelled by vibrating tails, they sometimes hurl themselves headlong out of the spray and smash into unsuspecting boatmen. The five-foot houndfish, the

The eastern newt goes through two adult stages. After hatching and developing in water, the red eft (below) lives on land for two to three years. When mature, it turns a dull olive-brown (left) and returns to the water to breed.

largest of the needlefish, can become a truly lethal weapon: hurtling through the air, it can strike with enough force to seriously injure anyone who happens to be in its path.

Nematode

Ranging in size from microscopic to many feet in length, nematodes are incredibly abundant roundworms that live virtually everywhere. The many free-living species abound in soil and water—and even in such hostile environments as hot springs and cider vinegar. Others live as parasites on plants and animals. Numerous kinds are food or crop pests, and some nematodes—such as hookworms, lungworms, and trichinae—cause serious illnesses in humans as well as in dogs, sheep, horses, and other animals.

Nest See pp. 260–261.

Nettle *Urtica*

Best-known for the itchy, burning rash they cause on contact with the skin, nettles are natural practitioners of chemical warfare. The bristly hairs that cover the leaves and stems are actually hollow tubes filled with an irritating fluid. When a person brushes against the plant, the hairs inject their noxious contents, causing a rash that can last for hours.

Thriving in rich, moist soil, nettles grow as weeds across much of North America. Though universally cursed by gardeners with ungloved hands and by walkers with bare legs, the plants were once regarded as valuable. Rich in vitamin C, the young shoots, boiled to remove the irritants, make a tasty soup or vegetable. Nettles also yield a strong fiber and have been cultivated for textiles, paper, and rope.

Newt

Like other salamanders, some of our newts are strongly aquatic, others primarily terrestrial. But still others, including the wide-ranging eastern newt, manage to be both by turns. The newt's gilled aquatic larva hatches in the spring and spends its first summer in the natal pond. The gills then disappear, and the larva transforms into a brightly colored land-dwelling creature known as a red eft. Foraging for insects and worms, the diminutive predator roams the forest floor for the next two or three years. Then, at sexual maturity, the eft returns to water and changes once again—this time into a larger, dull greenish adult newt—and spends the rest of its life as an aquatic hunter.

Pileated woodpeckers, giants of their kind at 18 inches in length, excavate roomy nest holes in dead trees. So large are these cavities, in fact, that when abandoned, they often become the homes of wood ducks.

Nest

While some creatures spend their lives in the open, exposed to the elements and to enemies, others build nests—safe havens that serve as warm beds, cozy homes, protected nurseries, hibernation chambers, or even, in some cases, small cities. Nests may be used year-round or only during the breeding season, and they may be built of found materials or of substances produced by the nest builder itself.

Feathered and furry nest builders

Since birds and mammals are warm-blooded animals whose bodies must be kept at a constant high temperature, most of them build nests to help keep their offspring warm. Though they sometimes serve to shelter the adults as well, their primary purpose is to provide a safe, warm place for the developing young.

Birds' nests, which are usually cup shaped, saucer shaped, or domed, are placed in bushes, trees, buildings, or even on the ground. Most are one-family structures built of grass, sticks, mud, or other material. Woodpeckers, in contrast, dig holes in trees, while kingfishers and some seabirds and swallows nest in burrows. Others, including cormorants, herons, gulls, and terns, seek safety in numbers and take advantage of limited space by nesting in colonies.

Though birds are the best-known nest builders, some kinds don't make nests at all. A number of seabirds and a few land birds simply lay their eggs on ledges or on the ground; goatsuckers, for example, incubate their eggs on bare soil or forest litter.

Nor do all mammals build nests. Bats retreat to caves, tree holes, or buildings, while large, fast-moving animals such as deer, bison, and whales give birth to well-developed young and so have no need for nests.

Red foxes use ground burrows not only to rear their young but to make quick escapes. Males provide the family's food until the young can forage for themselves.

Prothonotary warblers, birds of moist woods and swamps, often choose unusual nesting sites.

American alligator

Yellow jacket

American robin

Barn swallow

Black-tailed prairie dog

American dipper

An assortment of nests, fashioned in different styles, is as varied as the builders.

A great many mammals do build nests, however, often in the form of burrows lined with grass or fur. A few carnivores, such as foxes and weasels, use burrows to protect their young, and many rodents—pocket mice and chipmunks, for instance—use them not only as nurseries but for food storage and as permanent homes.

The nests of other mammals come in a variety of forms. Jumping mice construct domes of grass, while squirrels build both leafy platforms and domed nests high in trees. Wood rats assemble large piles of sticks, bones, and other debris, which they place in trees, shrubs, or among rocks. Beavers, perhaps the most ingenious engineers of all, build sizable lodges complete with underwater entrances.

Of alligators and ants

Amphibians, rather than building nests, lay eggs that are protected in jellylike strings or masses. Few reptiles build nests, either, preferring to bury their eggs in the ground and leave them to hatch unattended. Alligators and crocodiles, however, lay their eggs in large mounds of vegetation, and the female stands guard until the hatchlings can fend for themselves.

Among the few fish that build nests are the sunfish, which lay their eggs in sandy depressions that are swept clean of debris. Much more complex are the nests of male sticklebacks; constructed of grass and other plant material, they are used to attract females and shelter the eggs.

While most nests are thought of as beds, nurseries, or single-family dwellings, the nests of social insects such as ants, bees, and wasps are more like small cities. They include nurseries, food storage areas, the queen's chambers, and other specialized zones, all connected by intricate networks of passageways. Hundreds of sterile workers are constantly busy collecting food, defending and cleaning the nest, making repairs, and tending the young.

A few other invertebrates build nests. Tarantulas, for instance, live in burrows, while trapdoor spiders reside in web-lined tunnels fitted with hinged doors at the top. And webworms and tent caterpillars spin webs that shelter large numbers of larvae.

A nest has many lives

A nest that has been built and abandoned by one animal is likely to be used again by others. Woodpecker holes, for example, are commonly taken over by other cavity-nesting birds and even by bats and squirrels. When a catbird leaves its nest, a cup-shaped structure placed in a low shrub, a white-footed mouse may roof it over and use it to raise its own young; and once the mouse has left, a bumblebee queen might move in and start a colony. The chambers and tunnels excavated by prairie dogs likewise may later be adopted by burrowing owls.

In some cases nests are occupied by intruders long before their builders move out. Ants' nests almost always contain a variety of other insects; some prey on the ant larvae, while others are simply harmless freeloaders. And a few species of wasps, bees, and ants never build nests of their own but take over those of other insects, often by force.

The nests of birds and mammals are not immune to intruders, either. They often contain fleas, mites, and other irritating parasites. But perhaps the most flagrant interlopers of all are cowbirds; they regularly shirk their parental responsibilities by laying eggs in the nests of other birds, leaving their offspring to be raised by unwitting foster parents.

261

N

Common nighthawks do not build nests; instead, the females lay one to three mottled eggs directly on bare ground or, in cities, on gravel rooftops. When threatened, roosting females try to distract predators from their broods with noisy displays.

Night herons, the yellow-crowned (left) and black-crowned (right), are crested in spring.

Niche

The role a species or individual plays in relation to all the other kinds of plants and animals in its habitat is known as its ecological niche. In a coniferous forest, for example, some of the animals are insect eaters, others are large carnivores, and still others feed on seeds; each kind occupies a separate niche. The hawks and owls that live there, in turn, are both large birds of prey that eat smaller birds and mammals. But since the hawks operate by day and the owls by night, they occupy different niches.

Nighthawk *Chordeiles*

Not hawks at all, the nighthawks are close relatives of the whippoorwill. And like their cousin, they are active by night, especially at dawn and dusk, snatching up insects in flight in their large gaping mouths. Birds of open places rather than the forests preferred by whippoorwills, nighthawks nest on burned-over areas, fields, and deserts. The common nighthawk has also taken to nesting on the flat gravel roofs of buildings in cities. The display flight of the male is a familiar sight at dusk: hovering high above the building where its mate is guarding her two eggs, the bird dives suddenly downward, with its wings making a loud booming sound. In early fall the nighthawks begin drifting south toward their wintering grounds in the tropics, traveling by day in large, silent flocks.

Night heron

Stocky birds with shorter necks and legs than other herons and egrets, the night herons are nonconformists in their habits as well. Whereas most of their kin feed by day and gather to roost

Norway rats originated in Asia before making their way to Europe and finally to North America. Voracious, indiscriminate eaters, they thrive from coast to coast.

Bittersweet nightshade, a mildly poisonous plant, is so named because when chewed, its fruits first taste bitter, then sweet.

at night, the night herons set out at dusk to begin their search for food. While it is true that they occasionally hunt during the day, especially when skies are overcast, for the most part they spend the daylight hours hidden in trees and wait until dark to prowl in shallow streams, marshes, and lagoons.

The wide-ranging black-crowned night heron, which breeds on every continent except Australia and Antarctica, is found across parts of Canada and most of the United States. It feeds primarily on fish but also takes frogs, mice, and even the young of other birds. The yellow-crowned night heron, found in the U.S. Southeast, has a stouter bill than its cousin and preys mainly on hard-shelled crayfish and crabs.

Although night herons usually nest in colonies in trees, shrubs, or dense cattails, returning year after year to the same nests, the less gregarious yellow-crown sometimes nests alone. Both parents incubate their clutch of three to five blue-green eggs and share in feeding the young. Immature birds are streaked and spotted with brown and do not acquire full adult plumage until they are three years old.

Nightshade

A large and varied group of plants, the nightshade family is notorious for its many poisonous species. Yet it also includes some of our most important crop plants, among them tomatoes, potatoes, sweet and hot peppers, eggplants, and tobacco. Like other, more dangerous species, however, even potatoes and tomatoes have slightly toxic leaves and stems, and some of the hot peppers contain compounds so irritating that they can easily cause blisters.

Among the wild species are bittersweet nightshade, a rampant weed, and black nightshade, named for its dark fruit. Though poisonous as it develops, the fruit makes delicious jams and pies when ripe. Buffalo bur and horse nettle also contain poisons but are so thorny that they are avoided by both humans and livestock. The edible ground cherries and toxic thornapples are nightshades, too—members of a family so diverse that it also includes the innocent petunia.

Nocturnal animal See pp. 264–265.

Norway rat *Rattus norvegicus*

Native of the Old World, the Norway rat did not reach our shores until the late 18th century. Before long, however, it became the dominant rat of both city and countryside. Slightly larger than its cousin the black rat, another old-world immigrant, this gray-brown rodent grows up to 10 inches long, excluding its scaly tail, and often weighs over a pound.

Omnivorous and extremely destructive, Norway rats eat almost anything from garbage to grain, often gnawing their way into stored supplies and contaminating the food. They live practically everywhere—burrowing into trash heaps, invading the spaces between walls, digging tunnels in fields—and form well-organized colonies. Extremely prolific, females can breed at three months, and produce an average of five litters a year. Norway rats have been known to attack humans, and like the black rat, they carry a number of serious diseases.

Nut See *Fruit*.

Nocturnal Animal

During the night, when daytime creatures such as human beings are fast asleep, a host of nocturnal animals are wide awake and on the move —whether searching for food, escaping from enemies, or courting the opposite sex. Well-suited to darkness, these creatures depend less on eyesight than on smell and hearing—senses that are quickened by the cool, calm, damp night air, through which sounds and odors carry especially well.

In the night woods

Unlike their human cousins, most mammals are nocturnal. The timid, wide-eyed woodland rodents, which nibble on plants and seeds under cover of darkness, are in turn consumed by such predators as foxes, bobcats, and weasels. Three familiar omnivores—raccoons, skunks, and opossums—take advantage of the smorgasbord available in loose-lidded garbage cans. And high overhead, flying squirrels emerge from their dens to chatter among themselves and glide from tree to tree, while sonar-guided bats flutter through the air in pursuit of insects.

Among the birds that work the night shift, the best known are the owls, which, guided by moonlight as well as by sound, swoop down on unwary mice and voles. Night herons also set out at dusk to search in shallow water for fish and crayfish. Whippoorwills and nighthawks are up and flying as well, sweeping the air for moths and other night-flying insects.

In spring and fall hordes of migrants add to the action. While many of the larger birds migrate by day, the smaller, more vulnerable songbirds travel under the stars. This enables them both to avoid diurnal birds of prey and to spend the hotter daylight hours resting and feeding.

At ground level, nightcrawlers inch from their tunnels in the earth, while centipedes scurry among fallen leaves in search of food. All kinds of beetles and moths collect on our window screens, while garden spiders busily spin their webs and throngs of crickets and katydids fill the night air with their serenades.

Desert nightlife

In the deserts of the Southwest, the majority of animals are active by night, since few can survive the searing heat of day. During the sunlit hours only a few birds and butterflies make themselves known, while the cool of evening brings out a parade of sidewinders, scorpions, kangaroo rats, owls, and coyotes. Even some of the plants are more "active" by night. Yuccas and cereus cacti, for example, bloom after dark and so accommodate the night-flying moths that are their pollinators.

By the moonlit surf

Nighttime seashores are less noisy but no less populated than during the day. Beach fleas and sandhoppers by the thousands emerge from their burrows and are joined by multitudes of sideways-scuttling ghost crabs—all gleaning tiny morsels of plant and animal matter that

Little brown bats zigzag through the night air, consuming insects. By day they roost in caves or hollow trees.

Opossums, equipped with sharp claws and a prehensile tail, are expert climbers. Their eclectic diet includes insects, birds' eggs, small animals, fruit, grain, carrion, and a variety of edible items discarded by humans.

Raccoons will eat almost anything. Clever, adaptable, and unfazed by man, they are found in suburban and rural areas from coast to coast. These masked bandits, having spent the night raiding garbage cans, pass the daylight hours snoozing in hollow trees or caves.

The hog sphinx moth of eastern woodlands feeds on fermenting tree sap and decaying fruit.

Eastern screech owls often punctuate the night's stillness with ghostly hoots and wails.

have been left by the beach's day visitors or dumped by the tide.

Loggerheads and other sea turtles lumber from the surf to scoop out sandy nests and deposit caches of leathery eggs that resemble Ping-Pong balls and hatch some eight weeks later. The California grunion also lays its eggs at night. Hosts of these silvery fish flop ashore on the highest tides in spring. There the females work their tails into the wet sand to deposit their eggs, while the squirming males fertilize them. Their task accomplished, the grunions then ride the next wave back into the sea.

Within the oceans themselves, darkness moves vertically, retreating far below the surface under the penetrating light of day, then returning to the surface after sunset. Following this daily fall and rise of darkness are millions of copepods and other tiny crustaceans that sink as the light advances, then slowly make their way upward at dusk to feed on microscopic plants. These animals attract night-feeding fish, shrimp, and squids, which are in turn consumed by larger fish, such as sharks, whose voracious feeding frenzies often roil the silvery moonlit surface.

Life carries on even in the darkest ocean depths. Sponges, clams, sea cucumbers, fish, and other animals live far below the blue-green twilight zone, where they survive by preying on each other and by scavenging the table scraps that filter down from meals consumed by their neighbors above. These creatures of the murky deep are remarkably adapted—like the blind and colorless salamanders of deep caves—to a life of eternal night.

Clark's nutcrackers, like their close relatives the crows, are smart, aggressive, and gregarious.

White-breasted nuthatches are also called upside-down birds.

Nutcracker *Nucifraga columbiana*

Bold and lively members of the crow family, Clark's nutcrackers live in the chilly coniferous forests of the Rocky Mountains and the Sierra Nevada, where they specialize in prying the seeds from pinecones. They are particularly fond of the large, nutritious nuts of pinyon pines. In late summer and fall the birds eat some of the seeds on the spot, but they also begin storing them for a winter food supply. Tucking them into a pouch under the tongue, they fly to less-snowy lower slopes, where they poke holes in the ground with their pointed bills and bury several seeds in each. A single nutcracker making many such trips can cache over 30,000 seeds in a year. Remarkably, by remembering the positions of nearby landmarks, nutcrackers find and retrieve their hordes months later—even when the ground is covered with snow.

Nuthatch *Sitta*

Unique in their ability to climb headfirst down tree trunks, nuthatches busily probe the bark for insects and spiders; they also eat acorns and nuts, which they wedge into crevices. Their name derives from the term *nut-hack,* referring to the way in which they use their beaks to hack open these wedged bits of food.

Common winter visitors to suet- and seed-filled bird feeders, nuthatches range from Canada south into Mexico. Our best-known species is the white-breasted nuthatch, nattily patterned in blue-gray, black, and white. Others include the red-breasted, brown-headed, and pygmy nuthatches. Forest dwellers that nest in tree cavities, they are especially partial to abandoned woodpecker holes. These appealing little creatures, quite fearless around humans, have endeared themselves to bird lovers far and wide.

Nutrias are larger than muskrats and smaller than beavers. At dusk, when they begin their foraging, these rodents sometimes fill the air with a chorus of bleats and piglike grunts.

Nutria *Myocastor coypus*

An immigrant from South America, the nutria, also known as the coypu, is a whiskered, muskratlike aquatic rodent some two feet long, excluding its long naked tail. Introduced years ago in the southern United States to stock fur farms, some escaped and their descendants have since made themselves at home in scattered locations all across the continent.

Nutrias excavate snug burrows in muddy waterside banks and feed by night on the varied water plants growing at their doorsteps. Like raccoons, they grasp their food with their dexterous paws and deftly feed themselves by hand. Able swimmers, even baby nutrias can paddle about in swamps and ponds within a day of their birth. The unusually high position of the mother's mammaries along her sides enables the precocious young to cling to her back and suckle even as she swims.

266

The ocean is ever restless, from the pounding surf to the currents that sweep around continents.

Live oaks are renowned for their huge, spreading branches.

Oak *Quercus*

Of all North America's broad-leaved trees, oaks comprise the most species, 68 in all, and occupy the greatest variety of habitats. Oaks are, in the main, slow-growing woodland monarchs favoring well-drained soil. But some prefer swamps, others grow on prairies, and shrubby evergreen oaks thrive in the arid U.S. Southwest.

The toughness of their wood has made oaks symbols of stout endurance. Some species yield the densest of all North American timbers—wood so hard and resistant to decay that in the days before steel, it was the material of choice for shipbuilding. Oaks also supplied barn timbers, axles, and mine props.

As an aid to identification, the oaks are divided into two broad groups: red oaks and white oaks. The leaves of the whites have rounded lobes, and their sweet acorns take six months to mature. The red oaks, in contrast, have tiny bristles at the tips of their leaves or pointed lobes, and bitter acorns that take two years to mature.

Ocean

One great, continuous body of salt water that encircles the globe, the ocean covers some 70 percent of the earth's surface. This vast circulatory system provides moisture for the rain that sustains life on land; it buffers our climate; and it teems with an astonishing variety of life, from microscopic plankton to gargantuan whales. The water is rich with dissolved minerals that were washed in from the land, especially sodium chloride—ordinary table salt—which accounts for its characteristic taste and smell.

Winds keep the seas in constant motion and help produce the currents that circulate in well-defined patterns. One of the best-known currents is the Gulf Stream. Flowing northward in the Atlantic Ocean, its relatively balmy waters warm coastal regions all along the eastern seaboard. In the Pacific Ocean the California Current chills the coastal strip in summer but makes its winters mild. Meanwhile, the sea level rises and falls with the tides, which roll in and out on a regular schedule in response to the gravitational pull of the moon and sun.

The relentless movement of the sea, driven by winds, currents, and tides, generates waves that batter the coast, constantly altering the profile of the land. The continents themselves do not end at the shoreline; instead, they slope off gently into the ocean, creating underwater plains known as continental shelves. Along the east coast the shelf is quite wide, in some areas extending dozens of miles out to sea before plunging steeply to the ocean floor. On the Pacific coast the shelf is much narrower—barely present at all off parts of California. Penetrated by sunlight and loaded with nutrients, the continental shelves host a wealth of marine life and, in places, hold huge reservoirs of petroleum.

267

0

The ocotillo, after a good rain, bears clusters of flame-shaped blossoms at the tips of its whips.

Ocotillo *Fouquieria splendens*

One of the strangest, most colorful shrubs of the southwestern deserts, the ocotillo through most of the year resembles nothing so much as a loose bundle of long, spiny coachwhips. The arrival of winter rains, however, prompts the shrub to sprout small, rounded leaves along the length of each branch; though the ocotillo sheds this foliage as soon as the soil dries again, the leaf stalks persist and harden into spines. The rains also bring an explosion of color as the ocotillo bursts into bloom, with 6- to 10-inch clusters of scarlet flowers at the ends of the whips. Because of these displays, the ocotillo has been adopted as an ornamental in its native range. Desert-dwelling Indians also planted it in hedgerows to make coyote-proof chicken runs, and cut its branches to weave walls for their huts.

Octopus *Octopus*

Bizarre creatures of the deep, octopuses are named for the eight sucker-lined tentacles that radiate from their sac-shaped bodies. The several species that live in North American waters range in size from the giant Pacific octopus, with a diameter (including tentacles) of up to 30 feet, to a tiny 2- to 3-inch species found in deep water north of Cape Cod. Living on the sea floor, octopuses use their tentacles to crawl about and to ensnare their prey. Tough, parrotlike beaks enable these soft-bodied creatures to crush and eat such hard-shelled fare as lobsters, crabs, and snails. When threatened by morays or other enemies, octopuses eject a murky cloud of ink and then, by forcing water from their bodies, jet off to the nearest crevice for cover.

Octopuses change color when they are agitated, becoming blue, red, brown, purple, white, or even striped.

Omnivore

Unlike herbivores, which eat only plants, and carnivores, which eat only animals, omnivores are creatures that feed on the full range of available food. Snapping turtles, for example, consume everything from aquatic plants to fish, frogs, and even small mammals. Opossums and raccoons also enjoy a whole smorgasboard of

Baby opossums, after nursing in their mother's pouch for several weeks, crawl out and ride about on her back, clutching her fur with their tiny, dexterous paws. Like human hands, the opossum's hind feet are equipped with opposable thumbs.

O

plant and animal matter, from berries and mushrooms to bird's eggs and insects. Rats and other rodent pests have eclectic tastes as well, which often lead them to food discarded by humans, the most omnivorous omnivores of all.

Onion *Allium*

Odor is the identifying characteristic of the wild onions—when bruised, their leaves and bulbs are just as pungent as their cultivated relatives. The wild sorts are edible, too, and were eagerly gathered by aboriginal peoples. They are found on the Canadian prairies and throughout the United States, especially in the West. Growing from underground bulbs, the leaves of the wild onions are flat green straps or hollow quills, depending upon the species, and the sunbursts of blossoms that appear by midsummer range from white or greenish to purple and pink.

Opossum *Didelphis virginiana*

A marsupial about the size of a cat, the Virginia opossum is the only North American mammal that carries its offspring kangaroo-style, in a pouch. A dozen or so larvalike babies are born at a time, each one so tiny—smaller than a honeybee—that an entire litter can fit in the palm of a hand. Blind and hairless, they make their way through their mother's coarse fur to the warm pouch, where they immediately begin to nurse. After two months the young, recognizable at last as miniature opossums, go topside to ride on their mother's back until they are old enough to fend for themselves.

Roaming by night, these adaptable omnivores are well known as raiders of garbage cans. By day they hole up in second-hand burrows, tree cavities, or abandoned squirrel nests. At home in treetops, opossums use their long, naked tails as extra hands as they clamber through the branches. When threatened by predators, they occasionally feign death by lapsing into a comatose state—the classic and sometimes life-saving ruse called playing possum.

Orb-weaving spiders make quick work of spinning their webs, often completing the elaborate trap within just one hour.

Orb-weaving spider

The classic spider web, with a silken spiral spun over radiating threads, is the handiwork of orb weavers. Marvels of geometric design, the delicate orb webs are also death traps for flying insects; once ensnared on the sticky threads, they rarely escape. Alerted by the slightest movement in the web's network, the resident spider quickly pounces on its flailing victim, devouring it on the spot or wrapping it in silk for later consumption. Orb weavers often eat their web at the end of the day and, working in darkness, construct a new one in about an hour. Baby spiders spin miniature versions of the orb web.

The showy lady's slipper, floral emblem of Prince Edward Island, boasts a pouchlike lip and a scent that attracts pollinating insects.

Night-smelling orchids, epiphytes that grow on trees in southern Florida, derive their name from their scent, which is particularly strong after sundown.

Striped coral root orchids sprout only once in several years from a subterranean network of stems and associated fungi.

Orchid

Often called the royal family of flowering plants, the orchids, with some 35,000 species worldwide, outnumber every other family of flowers. And to those who think of them only as exotic hothouse blooms, it often comes as a surprise to learn that some 200 species of native wild orchids grow—often literally—in North America's backyards.

Supremely adaptable, orchids have wandered north beyond the Arctic circle to thrive in climates too harsh for any tree. In less frigid climes, they have colonized habitats ranging from the hammocks of subtropical Florida to the dry woodlands of the West and wet northern bogs. Florida boasts the most native orchids—over 100 species. The Northeast also has a rich assortment, with more than 60 kinds flourishing in meadows, bogs, and woodlands, while in the Southwest they are found mainly in canyons and high valleys, where mountain streams supply a constant source of water.

Fascinating flowers

Many of our native orchids, with lilting names like rose pogonia and twayblade, calypso and grass pink, have smaller blooms than their tropical relatives, but they are every bit as fascinating. Like their hothouse kin, their blossoms flaunt three petals and three petallike sepals, with the pollen-producing stamens and pollen-receptive stigmas fused into a central structure called the column. One of the petals, "the lip," is generally distended and serves as a landing platform for pollinators, which include moths, bees, flies, bats, birds, butterflies, and even mosquitoes.

Specific orchids often depend on a single type of pollinator, and many have developed ingenious strategies for attracting that one visitor. Vivid colors, scents, and nectar draw bees and butterflies to some orchids, while those that rely on flies smell like rotting meat. Still others attract male insects by posing as potential mates; the flowers not only mimic female insects in appearance but also release similar perfumes. When the males try to mate, they cover themselves with pollen and then carry it to the next flower they visit. Some orchids appeal to insects' aggressive instincts. The tropical, multibranched oncidiums, found as far north as the Florida Everglades, mimic swarms of bees and so provoke attacks from nearby hives.

Orchid seeds are tiny travelers

As remarkable as the flowers are, the orchids' dustlike seeds—so tiny that a single pod may contain millions—also are one of nature's wonders. Light enough to blow for hundreds of miles on the wind, they have economized on their weight by eliminating the stores of food customary in other seeds. As a result, they can germinate only with the aid of special fungi that provide nutriments. Often this partnership continues throughout the life of the plant—the orchid deriving its nourishment from the fungus, which lives in association with the plant's roots.

Depending on the species, orchids are either epiphytic or terrestrial. Living without contact with the soil, epiphytes attach themselves to tree branches. They draw nutrients from airborne dust and decayed matter that washes in among their roots, and absorb moisture from rain showers. Typical of tropical habitats, North American epiphytic orchids are limited to the extreme Southeast. A notable example is the vinelike vanilla orchid of Florida, whose seedpods are the source of natural vanilla flavoring.

More-northern regions are home to the terrestrial orchids, which take root in the soil. Because they live as perennials, dying back to the ground in autumn and sprouting anew from the roots in spring, they are far less vulnerable to winter frosts. Some survive for years in this fashion. Lady's slippers, for example, may be 15 years old before bearing their first flowers; those dainty, moccasin-shaped pink, white, or yellow blossoms are unforgettable, however, and have made lady's slippers among the most beloved of woodland flowers.

Magic, medicine, and more

The downy rattlesnake plantain, in contrast, bears only tiny blossoms; its appeal lies instead in its rosette of green and white checkered leaves. Pioneers thought the leaves resembled snakeskins, and so believed them to be an antidote for snakebite. Indeed, given the many unusual features of our native orchids, it is not surprising that they have inspired a vast array of superstitions.

Besides their supposed value as antitoxins, orchids were once taken as remedies for ills ranging from gout to insomnia, while lady's slippers, when boiled in milk, were held to be an aphrodisiac. In addition to rousing passion, these innocent blooms were said to mark the sites of crimes and tragedies.

Though no longer much sought for herbal medicines, orchids are, unfortunately, victims of their own surpassing beauty. Everywhere they are increasingly rare, for wildflower enthusiasts, ignorant of the plants' dependence on soil fungi, yearly transplant thousands to gardens, where the orchids almost invariably starve and die.

The fringe-lipped rose pogonia flowers atop single-leaved stems up to 24 inches tall.

The delicate butterfly orchid blossoms year-round across southern Florida.

271

0

Oregon grapes produce bright, fragrant yellow flowers (above), followed by edible blue berries (right). These features, combined with their shiny, hollylike leaves, make them popular ornamentals.

Altamira orioles, formerly known as Lichtenstein's orioles, are found at the southern tip of Texas, where their nests hang from the branches of tall trees.

The osage orange's fruits are not at all like true oranges; they contain a bitter, milky sap and are inedible.

Oregon grape *Mahonia*

Evergreen members of the barberry family, the Oregon grapes are also known as holly grapes. Like the hollies, they sport shiny, spiny leaves, and like grapes, in autumn they are arrayed with clusters of dark blue berries that can be made into jams, jellies, and even wines. They are valued also for the clusters of fragrant, small, cupped yellow blossoms borne at the tips of the twigs in spring, and one of the showier species has been adopted as the state flower of Oregon. This 3- to 10-foot shrub is a native of the Pacific Northwest, where it forms thickets in open woodlands. Enthusiastic gardeners, however, have transplanted it to temperate regions across the continent. Another common species, the creeping holly grape, thrives in shady canyons and on rocky slopes from the foothills of the Coastal Ranges of California to the Rockies.

Oriole *Icterus*

Their striking colors—orange and black or yellow and black—make orioles the most flamboyant members of the blackbird family. Shy birds whose musical whistles resound from the treetops, they weave distinctive, pouch-shaped hanging nests of grass, string, hair, and various plant fibers. The more modestly colored females build the nests, while the males provide insects and fruit to feed the family.

Most orioles, such as Scott's oriole of the Southwest and the spot-breasted oriole of Florida, prefer warm climates. Two species, however, manage to thrive in more northerly regions. The orchard oriole, a rust-breasted bird, nests in eastern fruit trees. The other, the northern oriole, includes two races: the famed Baltimore oriole of the East and the very similar Bullock's oriole of the West.

Ospreys, which feed on fish that swim near the surface, have special dense, oily feathers that permit them to splash into the water without getting soaked. After a meal ospreys sometimes fly close to the water, dragging their feet as if to clean them.

0

Orpine See *Stonecrop.*

Osage orange *Maclura pomifera*

A tree native to the south-central United States, the osage orange is distinguished by the odd round fruits it bears. Up to five inches across and sometimes weighing several pounds, they look like unripe oranges and exude a milky sap when bruised. The tree's common name also refers to the Osage Indians, who used the hard, resilient wood for bows and clubs. Up to 30 feet tall with zigzagging, thorny branches, osage oranges grow rapidly and are resistant to heat and drought. Pruned to form hedges, they were, until the introduction of wire fencing, the standard enclosures for prairie farms, serving both as animal-proof barriers and as sturdy windbreaks.

Osprey *Pandion haliaetus*

Brown and white, with wingspans of nearly six feet, ospreys are formidable birds of prey that feed exclusively on fish. Also known as fish hawks, they hover over rivers, lakes, and seacoasts as they search for prey. Once they spot a tantalizing flash, ospreys plunge feet-first into the water, often with a great splash, and seize their slippery catch in sharp talons. On the flight home they usually hold the fish facing forward and so reduce wind resistance.

Osprey nests, made of sticks, driftwood, and odd debris that has washed up on shore, are usually built in places that command panoramic views, including treetops, telephone poles, chimneys, and man-made nesting platforms. When the chicks hatch, the father delivers about six pounds of fish per day to the nest, where the mother feeds shredded morsels to the young.

A few decades ago, osprey populations were severely reduced because the birds ate fish from water polluted with DDT. The poison, which affected reproduction, caused the birds to lay eggs with thin, easily broken shells. Thanks to conservation efforts, however, the noble fish hawks in recent years have made a dramatic and welcome comeback.

Otter See *River otter, Sea otter.*

Outcrop

Ranging in size from the small patches of bare rock found in fields to rugged, towering cliffs on mountainsides, outcrops are sections of bedrock that are not covered by soil or loose boulders. Bedrock can be exposed in a number of ways. Soil may slump down a hillside, for example; glaciers may bulldoze the land; or erosion by wind and water may scour away all the surface debris. Outcrops are "windows" to the crust below, often giving evidence of valuable ores.

Saw-whet owls are named for their rasping calls. Tiny, nocturnal creatures about eight inches long, they have large yellow eyes that make them look less stern than other owls. Saw-whets, found from Alaska to Nova Scotia and south to Mexico, are so tame that they can be captured by hand.

Owl

Well-known for their solemn, studious appearance and their haunting nighttime calls, owls are birds of prey that are most active at dusk and after dark. While some also hunt by day, many are entirely nocturnal. In addition to rodents and other mammals, their prey includes insects, frogs, toads, and small birds.

Owls are characterized by short, stout bodies, strong, hooked beaks, and sharp talons for seizing prey. Many also have feathery tufts, called ears or horns, on their heads. The birds range in size from the tiny elf owl, no bigger than a sparrow, to the great gray owl, which reaches nearly three feet from head to tail.

Hunting in the dark

In his play *Love's Labour's Lost,* William Shakespeare wrote "then nightly sings the staring owl"—words that certainly apply to any of these big-eyed, big-headed birds, for owls do indeed stare. And in that staring face we can see some of the owl's adaptations for life in the dark. Unlike the eyes of other birds, an owl's eyes face straight ahead, like our own, giving the bird binocular vision. Unlike human eyes, however, they do not move in their sockets, so the bird must swivel its head to follow moving objects.

Although owls see well in dim light, most depend on superkeen hearing when searching for prey. Many, in fact, can locate prey in total darkness, relying on sound alone. The owl's large ear openings are hidden under the ruff of feathers framing the face—its facial disk—an arrangement that helps funnel sound into the ears. On some species, moreover, the ears are placed asymmetrically, resulting in a stereo effect that allows the bird to home in on the source of a sound with amazing accuracy.

Once an owl hears an animal rustling in leaves or grass, it drops from its perch and swoops silently toward the noise. At the last instant, the bird swings its feet forward and, with its sharp talons outspread, strikes the ground at exactly the right spot to seize its victim.

Swift on the wing, owls are also noiseless in flight. Their soft, fluffy feathers muffle the sound of their broad wings, enabling them to swoop toward prey in absolute silence.

Many kinds of owls

Owls are divided into two families: the barn owl, whose single species is distinguished by its heart-shaped face, and typical owls, of which there are 18 species in North America. Most of the latter are forest dwellers that spend the day roosting in trees or in other sheltered places. Their colors, mainly browns and grays, and their patterns of streaks and bars help them blend into their surroundings, making them difficult to spot even in broad daylight. The snowy owl, which hunts by day on the arctic tundra, is also camouflaged. Its plumage—white with a few black bars—blends almost perfectly with a background of snow or ice.

Our largest species, the great gray owl, lives in the vast coniferous forests of Canada and preys mainly on rodents. Its hearing is so acute that it can plunge into snow and capture voles as they scurry about hidden in their tunnels. Nearly as large is the great horned owl, an aggressive predator with large ear tufts. Found in forests, deserts, swamps, and even city parks, it is big enough to attack skunks, porcupines, and other large prey. Its deep five-noted hooting is one of the most familiar of all owl calls.

At the other extreme is the diminutive elf owl, a resident of deserts and dry woodlands along streams near the Mexican border. It feeds on insects and, at times, lizards. Other small species include the screech owls—plump, robin-size birds with short ear tufts, best known for their whistled calls—and the northern saw-whet owl. Slightly smaller than a screech owl and lacking ear tufts, the saw-whet nests in a variety of wooded habitats but is usually found roosting by day in small, dense conifers.

Most owls nest in cavities in trees or giant saguaro cacti, or in the abandoned nests of crows or hawks. Snowy and short-eared owls, however, build crude nests on the ground, while burrowing owls lay their eggs in prairie dog dens or in burrows they dig themselves. Incubation begins with the first egg, so that the young hatch consecutively. Both parents tend to the nest and defend it vigorously. In years of food scarcity, some species, among them the snowy owl, do not breed at all.

Owls in folklore and legend

In view of their humanlike faces, nocturnal habits, and loud, often ominous-sounding calls, it is not surprising that owls figure prominently in tradition and folklore. Symbols of the Greek goddess Athena, the deity of wisdom, owls have long been considered the epitome of wise old birds. Their calls are said to portend significant events. Three hoots, for example, indicate a marriage, while five hoots foretell a journey.

Oddly enough, however, owls are considered harbingers of ill as well. In parts of the South, an owl perching on the roof of a house is said to be a sure sign of death. But this misfortune can be averted by turning shoes upside down.

The long-eared owl, a medium-size bird, is rarely seen during the day.

Great horned owls, powerful, aggressive birds, often take over abandoned hawk or crow nests.

Young screech owls are covered with thick, fluffy down. These owls come in two color phases: reddish and grayish.

Snowy owls nest on the tundra, but they fly south in winter and are often seen on sandy beaches.

As oxbow lakes age, they become more and more isolated from the meandering rivers that formed them. The one at the top, entirely separated from the river, is clearly much older than the still-muddy backwater in the center of the photo.

O

Owl clovers sometimes grow in large patches, carpeting the deserts and dry plains of the West with radiant color.

Owl clover *Orthocarpus*

Despite their name, the owl clovers are not clovers at all. Common wildflowers of western plains and open woods, they are more closely related to Indian paintbrushes. Their clustered blooms are set, like the paintbrushes' flowers, among showy bracts that in some cases are more colorful than the flowers themselves; on some species the bracts completely hide the blossoms. The plants, up to 16 inches tall, have narrow threadlike leaves. Spots on the flowers of some species make them look a bit like peering owls.

Oxbow lake

Named for the U-shaped bows on old-time ox yokes, oxbow lakes are formed from the loops of meandering rivers. Eroding their banks, the rivers eventually cut across the necks of the curves, leaving the old channels as backwaters. Sediment then fills in the ends of the loops until they become isolated lakes. As more sediment accumulates, the lakes turn into marshes and then into dry land. Though best-known in the lower Mississippi Valley, oxbow lakes are found on floodplains all across North America.

Oyster

Like mussels and clams, oysters are bivalve mollusks; their soft bodies are protected in hinged pairs of shells. They live in shallow coastal seas, where, cemented to rocks or pilings, they feed on tiny organisms filtered from the water.

Beginning their lives as microscopic eggs, oysters soon hatch into free-swimming larvae. Most are gulped down by fish, but those that survive sink to the bottom after two weeks or so and attach themselves to rocks and other hard surfaces. Oysters grow about an inch a year, starting out as males and later developing into females that lay eggs by the millions.

Oysters are preyed upon by all sorts of creatures. Oyster-drill snails bore holes into the shells, starfish pull them open, and birds called oystercatchers pry the shells apart to get at their flesh. Humans relish oysters too, of course, and most of those sold commercially are raised on undersea "farms."

Oystercatcher *Haematopus*

Large, chunky shorebirds with long orange-red bills and pinkish legs, oystercatchers feed on small marine animals found by the seaside. They use their flattened, bladelike bills to pry open

Oysters are harvested from shallow coastal waters (left). Oystermen sometimes use giant tongs (above) to pluck their catch from the bottom. North American oysters are used for food; the ones that produce pearls occur in tropical seas.

Oystercatchers wander along beaches or wade through shallow water at low tide, looking for oysters and clams, which they pry open with their chisellike bills.

the shells of oysters, mussels, and clams; to probe in the sand for worms and crustaceans; and to dislodge barnacles from rocks.

Oystercatchers nest in shallow depressions in the sand or in rock crevices. The two or three spotted eggs yield precocious, downy gray young that, shortly after hatching, are able to follow their parents on foraging expeditions.

Our eastern species, the American oystercatcher, has black-and-white plumage and lives on beaches from Virginia to the Gulf of Mexico. The black oystercatcher, outfitted in brownish black, prefers rocky western shores from California north all the way to Alaska.

Oyster plant See *Goatsbeard*.

Ozone

A form of oxygen with three oxygen atoms per molecule instead of two, ozone is a gas present in very small amounts in the atmosphere. At low altitudes it is considered an air pollutant and is an irritating component of smog. High in the atmosphere, in contrast, ozone plays a role vital to the survival of life on earth. Ultraviolet sunlight colliding with oxygen in the upper atmosphere produces an ozone layer that shields the earth from radiation harmful to many forms of life—including humans, in whom it can cause skin cancer. Recently, gases called fluorocarbons have been shown to deplete the ozone layer, and so efforts are being made to reduce the levels of these pollutants in our atmosphere.

P

The cabbage palmetto is honored as the state tree of Florida.

Paddlefish, up to six feet in length and weighing over 150 pounds, are valued food fish.

Pack rat See *Wood rat.*

Paddlefish *Polyodon spathula*

A long, broad, flattened snout distinguishes paddlefish from all other fish. Fully one-third of the length of their bodies, the spoon-shaped structures may be sensory organs used for locating the plankton and other small animals on which the fish feed. Hatchlings are born with no sign of the snout but start to grow one when they are just two to three weeks old.

Also known as spoonbills and shovelnose cats, paddlefish, which grow up to six feet long, inhabit lakes and rivers in the Mississippi River basin. Primitive, scaleless creatures with skeletons made of cartilage, they have only one close relative, a large, similarly snouted species that lives in the Yangtze River in China.

Painted turtle *Chrysemys picta*

North America's most wide-ranging turtle, the painted turtle is aptly named: its smooth olive-to-black shell is edged with red; its underside is yellow; and its head, neck, and legs are marked with red and yellow. Found in weedy freshwater marshes, quiet ponds, and slow streams, it feeds on almost anything it can find, whether plant or animal. In fair weather, groups of painted turtles bask on rocks or logs. In winter those that live in cold climates hibernate.

Palm

Elegant and graceful, most palms are trees with a single, slender, unbranched trunk topped by a featherduster crown of fan- or feather-shaped leaves. Although they are most common in the tropics, several kinds are native to warmer parts of North America, including the stately royal palms of southern Florida, the palmettos that grow from the Carolinas to the Gulf of Mexico, and the Washington palms of the Southwest.

Both native and exotic palms are commonly planted as ornamentals in the Sun Belt. In the past, however, aboriginal peoples built huts with palm trunks and used the leaves to thatch them. Leaves were sometimes woven into hats, mats, and baskets. Indians also relished the trees' edible fruits and the honey that bees harvested from the huge, drooping clusters of fragrant white or yellow flowers. Today imported coconut palms are grown in Florida, and date palms from overseas are an important crop in California and the Southwest.

Getting to Know the Common Palms

Whether trees or shrubs, North American palms are topped with fan-shaped or feather-shaped leaves. To pin down the species, note the height and examine the leaves, trunks, and fruits. Of the palms shown here, all are native to the Southeast except the Washington palm of the West and the introduced date and coconut palms.

Leaves feather-shaped

Trunk gray, upper part bright green. Fruits bluish purple.

To 100 ft.   **Florida royal palm**

Trunk gray-green, ringed. Fruits orange-red.

To 25 ft.   **Florida cherry palm**

Trunk smooth, usually leaning. Fruits massive.

To 100 ft.   **Coconut palm**

Trunk rough, covered with leaf stubs. Fruits in large clusters.

To 100 ft.   **Date palm**

Leaves fan-shaped

LEAF STALKS ARMED WITH SPINES

Trunk with skirt of dead leaves. Fruits black.

To 75 ft.   **Washington palm**

Trunks in many-stemmed clumps. Fruits black.

To 25 ft.   **Everglades or paurotis palm**

Shrublike with creeping stems. Fruits blue-black.

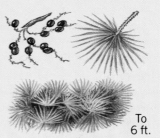

To 6 ft.   **Saw palmetto**

LEAF STALKS WITHOUT SPINES

Leaves 5–8 ft. wide with prominent midrib. Fruits black.

To 80 ft.   **Cabbage palmetto**

Leaves 2–3 ft. wide, nearly circular. Fruits whitish.

To 30 ft.   **Florida thatch palm**

Leaves 1½–2 ft. wide, silvery below. Fruits purplish.

Top

Bottom

To 25 ft.   **Florida silver palm**

P

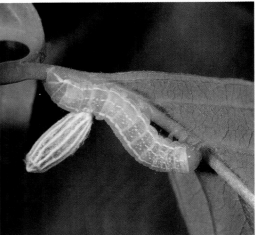

Some parasitic wasps lay their eggs in the bodies of living caterpillars (above). Dodder, a plant parasite, twines around and draws juices from the stems of host plants (left).

Paloverde *Cercidium*

Through most of the year these small trees of the southwestern deserts remain leafless, smooth-branched skeletons. But with the first warm rains of spring, the paloverdes burst into leaf and bloom, covering their branches with a mantle of tiny, featherlike leaves and clusters of yellow blossoms. Bees eagerly seek the nectar-rich flowers. The pods that appear later on contain seeds that Indian tribes traditionally collected to cook as vegetables and to grind into meal. Some 20 or 30 feet in height, the paloverdes are an important food for jackrabbits, mountain sheep, and deer. Domestic livestock, on the other hand, are deterred by the short, sharply pointed spines on the twigs and seek the thorny paloverdes only as a last resort.

Parasite

Ticks and fleas, as well as many kinds of worms, fungi, protozoans, and even certain plants, are all considered parasites—organisms that sustain themselves at the expense of other living things, called hosts. In some cases the parasites have parasites of their own. The fleas that pester our pets, for instance, are themselves hosts to much tinier mites.

In ordinary concentrations most parasites do little or no harm to their hosts. A few flatworms in the digestive tract do not cause their animal host much of a problem; nor is a beech tree bothered by a scattering of beechdrops, modest plants of the forest floor that, lacking chlorophyll, tap into the tree's roots for nourishment.

Other parasites, however, cause serious damage. The protozoans that cause malaria and amoebic dysentery, for example, can drastically weaken their hosts, and parasitic fungi are responsible for many plant diseases, such as wheat rust and potato blight.

Paloverdes lose their leaves early but can produce food in their green bark.

Parrotfish

With dazzling colors and imposing size—some species are four feet long—parrotfish are among the favorites of snorkelers and scuba divers who visit tropical reefs. The fish are named not for their rainbow of hues but for the birdlike beaks, formed of fused teeth, with which they scrape algae and bits of coral from the reef. Parrotfish also have large grinding teeth in the throat, used for crushing their food.

Active by day, some parrotfish retire to crevices at night. Others, however, rest in the open on the ocean floor and protect themselves in a remarkable way. They secrete a jellylike cocoon—a kind of self-made sleeping bag—that apparently serves as a defense against nocturnal predators while they sleep.

Parsley

From parsnips to pennyworts, the parsley, or carrot, family is made up of thousands of species of plants. What all have in common are umbels—flat-topped or umbrella-shaped clusters

Stoplight parrotfish, up to 20 inches long, add dashes of brilliant color to reefs, which they patrol in search of food. They use their toothy beaks to scrape morsels of algae or other plant food from the coral.

Partridgeberry's fuzzy white flowers are followed by two tasteless red berries.

Passionflowers were named by Spanish priests who visited colonial South America.

of tiny flowers. But various members of the family have their differences as well. Some, such as Queen Anne's lace, yellow pimpernel, and golden alexanders, are dismissed as lowly weeds, while others, including sea holly and blue lace flower, are esteemed as ornamentals. Culinary parsleys include carrots, celery, and parsnips, as well as such herbs as anise, dill, fennel, cumin, coriander, and caraway. Fool's parsley and water hemlock, in contrast, both are highly toxic and can kill if consumed.

The family's namesake—the small biennial herb known simply as parsley—is a Mediterranean plant that has been cultivated since ancient times both as a garnish for food and for its reputed medicinal properties.

Partridgeberry

Though it thrives in woodlands throughout the eastern United States, the partridgeberry is easily overlooked through most of the year. In winter, however, its scarlet berries (edible but flavorless) show up against the plant's ground-hugging mat of lustrous evergreen leaves. It is

worth searching out in early summer, too, when pairs of tiny, fragrant flowers adorn the tips of its trailing stems. Pink in bud, they open into fuzzy, white to purplish tubular blooms.

Passionflower *Passiflora*

Seventeenth-century Spanish priests named the passionflower, seeing in its intricate blooms symbols of the crucifixion of Christ. The three stigmas at the center, they said, represented the nails that held Him on the cross; the five stamens, His wounds; and the petals and sepals, the 10 disciples who remained faithful throughout His suffering. The halo of threads encircling the flower they likened to the crown of thorns.

Attractive perennial vines, passionflowers are most common in the southern United States. The yellow passionflower, however, clambers through moist thickets as far north as Pennsylvania and west to Kansas. Reaching a height of 10 feet, it bears small blossoms that are followed by purple berries. The maypop, a lavender species, ranges north to Maryland and Oklahoma and yields tasty yellow fruits the size of hen's eggs.

P

Pawpaws can be identified by their large, pungent leaves and six-petaled flowers.

Pearly everlasting is quick to grow on burned-over soils or other disturbed areas.

Pawpaw *Asimina triloba*

Thriving in rich, moist soil from the lower Mississippi Valley to southern Michigan, these small trees with large leaves and purplish flowers are relatives of the mostly tropical custard apples. The stubby, cylindrical fruits that appear on the pawpaw's branches in late summer account for its alternate name, false banana. Yellowish-green at first, the fruits begin to darken in the fall and finally turn nearly black—a sign that the sweet, custardy flesh is ready for eating.

Collared peccaries are also called javelinas, a reference to their sharp upper canines.

Early settlers made jelly from pawpaws and extracted a yellow dye from the pulp. Ripe fruits can be hard to find, however, since many animals seek them as eagerly as do humans.

Pea See *Legume.*

Pearly everlasting *Anaphalis margaritacea*

A favorite wildflower for dried bouquets, the well-named pearly everlasting keeps its shape and color indefinitely. Its woolly stems, one to three feet tall, are topped with wide clusters of pearly white flowers with yellow centers. The leaves, narrow and straplike, are sage green on top and whitened underneath with woolly hairs. North America's only native everlasting, this cheerful wildflower is found in fields and along roadsides from coast to coast.

Pecan See *Hickory.*

Peccary *Tayassu tajacu*

Bristly, piglike mammals up to three feet long, collared peccaries trot through the cactus and mesquite country of the Southwest in bands of five to a dozen or more. They use their long, sensitive snouts to sniff out roots and herbs, as well as other morsels such as worms, insect larvae, birds' eggs, and lizards.

Long-legged compared to true pigs, peccaries flee nimbly from coyotes and other predators. If cornered, however, they can put up a ferocious fuss, attacking enemies with their formidable tusks. Secretions from musk glands help define a herd's territory, and individuals occasionally sound an alarm by chattering their teeth or making barking sounds.

White pelicans (above) fly in tight formations. They often form a line on the water and beat their wings as they herd schools of fish toward the shallows. Brown pelicans (right), the smaller of our two species, fish on their own and perform impressive headlong dives from as high as 50 feet. Gregarious birds, both white and brown pelicans nest in large colonies.

Peeper See *Spring peeper.*

Pelican *Pelecanus*

Known to readers of light verse as the bird whose bill holds "more than his belican," a pelican—with a roomy pouch suspended from its long, broad beak—cannot be mistaken for any other bird. Stocky and short-legged, pelicans may be clumsy on land, but they are amazingly graceful in the air.

The brown pelican, one of the two species found in North America, is a seabird that lives along the south Atlantic, Gulf of Mexico, and Pacific coasts. Flying above the water until it spots the silvery flash of a fish near the surface, it plunges into a headlong dive—often from as high as 50 feet—that culminates in a great splash. Returning to the surface with a fish, the pelican then pauses for a moment to let the water drain from its pouch before swallowing its prey.

The American white pelican, a larger bird that nests on inland lakes in the West, is less acrobat-ic. Rather than diving, it fishes from the surface, dipping head and bill underwater to seize its prey. White pelicans often fish in teams, swimming abreast in a line or semicircle to herd fish into shallow water. The birds coordinate their movements in the sky as well. With the precision of a chorus line, the members of a flock sometimes flap their wings in unison as they fly.

Peppertree *Schinus molle*

Producing neither the familiar table spice nor the garden peppers used in salads and cooking, the peppertree is named instead for the pungent flavor of its ruddy, berrylike fruits. Native to Peru and a member of the cashew family, this handsome ornamental has become such a common sight along streets on the West Coast that it is often called California peppertree. It grows up to 40 feet tall and has branches that droop like a weeping willow's, with evergreen compound leaves filled with milky, aromatic sap. Many songbirds relish the tree's red fruits.

P

Brown thrasher

Yellow-rumped warbler

Northern cardinal

Blue jay

Perching birds all have four-toed feet made for grasping branches. The birds, mostly small to medium in size, are solitary nesters and eat huge quantities of fruit, grains, and insects.

Perch

Fish of clear lakes and streams, perches range in size from the hefty walleye to the diminutive darters. The walleye—sometimes called the pike perch—weighs up to 25 pounds and is named for its large, glossy eyes, which, in the beam of a flashlight, shine with an eerie orange glow. The walleye is a favorite with anglers, as is its smaller relative, the yellow perch, easily recognized by its yellowish color and dark vertical stripes. Both the yellow perch and our other medium-size perch, the sauger, weigh up to three or four pounds. The smallest members of the family are the dozens of species of brilliantly colored darters, named for their abrupt movements on the bottoms of streams. Among them are the widespread Johnny darter and the endangered snail darter.

Perching bird

Also known as passerines, perching birds are so named because of the form of their feet: all have four flexible toes—three facing forward and one facing backward—an arrangement that enables them to grasp twigs, wires, and other perches. Approximately 60 percent of all the world's bird species are perching birds, including such common and widespread groups as wrens, thrushes, titmice, finches, warblers, and jays. They range in size from tiny kinglets and sparrows to the common raven, a bird that is two feet long and has a four-foot wingspan. While all can perch, a few ground-based passerines, such as larks and pipits, have feet that are slightly modified for walking and running. Often brightly colored, many of the perching birds are well known for their ability as songbirds.

Perennial See *Annual.*

Periwinkle

Dainty little snails with spiral shells, periwinkles live where land meets sea—on rocky shores, on wharf pilings, in salt marshes, and in mangrove swamps. Like other snails, they leave trails of mucus as they creep along, using their rasping tongues to scrape algae and other edibles from rocks and similar surfaces. The common European periwinkle, introduced to Nova Scotia in the mid-1800's, now ranges south as far as Maryland. Growing up to 1½ inches long, it is one of the largest species and is considered a delicacy by some. A smaller relative, the northern rough periwinkle, lives high on rocks along both the north Atlantic and Pacific coasts and, like other periwinkles, is relished by ducks.

Permafrost

On the frigid tundra—the treeless expanses of the Far North—and on some very high mountains above the timberline, the land is underlain by permafrost, a nearly impenetrable layer of permanently frozen soil and rock. In some places the permafrost extends downward for thousands of feet, but in the Canadian arctic it averages about 1,000 feet in thickness.

Covering and insulating the permafrost is a thin mantle of soil, known as the active zone, that thaws in summer, then freezes again in winter. Because drainage is so poor, the land in summer is dotted with countless ponds and marshes, and the surface soil becomes so spongy and waterlogged that it is difficult to walk upon.

In places, seasonal freezing and thawing of the active zone sorts rocks into neat circles and polygons, creating so-called patterned ground. Pingos, another characteristic landform, are hills with cores of solid ice. And on slopes in summertime, great lobes of thawed surface soil at times ooze slowly downhill in this strange, otherworldly landscape.

Persimmon *Diospyros*

Country folk call persimmons "possum apples" because of the animal's enthusiasm for the plumlike orange fruits that persimmon trees bear in autumn. Though soft and sweet when fully mature, the unripe fruits are so full of tannic acid that they will pucker a person's lips.

Persimmon trees are normally only 30 to 50 feet tall but grow to heights of 70 feet on Mississippi bottomlands. They are most common in the Southeast, where farmers use the fruit to fatten hogs, but range north to Connecticut and west to Texas. Sheathed in scaly grayish-brown bark that resembles alligator hide, persimmons have glossy green oval leaves and are covered with bell-shaped white flowers in May and June. The only North American members of the ebony family, persimmons produce a hard, heavy wood sometimes used for golf clubs.

Marsh periwinkles, about one inch long, are found in estuaries and salt marshes from the middle Atlantic states to Florida. Clinging to reeds and tall grasses, they use their long rasping tongues to feed on tiny scraps of plant food. Like other periwinkles, they are a favorite food of ducks, gulls, and various shorebirds.

P

Persimmons figured strongly in the diet of southeastern Indians, who baked bread with a meal made from the dried fruits.

Petrel *Pterodroma*

Gull-size seabirds of the shearwater family, the petrels include several species that, collectively, are known as gadfly petrels. They nest on tropical islands and, during the nonbreeding season, roam the open sea, feeding on small squid and fish snatched from the water's surface. Most frequently seen are the black-capped petrel of the Atlantic and the mottled petrel, a rare winter visitor off the Pacific coast. The smaller birds called storm petrels belong to a different family.

Petrified wood often displays colorful inclusions of agate, chalcedony, and other minerals.

Petrified wood

Petrified wood is the fossil remains of ancient trees whose tissues were replaced by the mineral silica. Examples have been found in many parts of North America, including the world's largest collection of multicolored logs, which is contained in Petrified Forest National Park in Arizona. Once the trunks of coniferous trees, the logs were buried in sediments and transformed to rock when mineral-saturated groundwater seeped into them, replacing the original wood cell by cell. Petrified trees often are so well preserved that the annual growth rings and other internal structures are visible. Such details provide fascinating insights into the kinds of trees found in North America millions of years ago.

Petroleum

A vital natural resource, petroleum is used for fuel and lubricants, and in the manufacture of plastics and a host of other synthetic products. Crude oil, as it is also called, is a mixture of various hydrocarbons (compounds of hydrogen and carbon), along with traces of sulfur and other impurities. The exact composition of petroleum varies from site to site; so the oil pumped from one field may be thick, black, and tarlike, while that from another field is as light and fluid as motor oil.

Petroleum is thought to be derived from the remains of tiny plants and animals that flourished in ancient seas. When these organisms died, they drifted to the ocean floor, where they mixed with and were buried under thick layers of sand and mud. Over millions of years, the layers compacted into sedimentary rock, such as

Oil wells are often drilled offshore from platforms standing on the sea floor.

sandstone and shale. The heat of compaction combined with decomposition of the organic debris, converted the ancient plants and animals into enormous deposits of crude oil and natural gas. North America has vast reservoirs in Alberta, Yukon, the Northwest Territories, Louisiana, Texas, Oklahoma, and Alaska.

Peyote *Lophophora williamsii*

Also known as mescal button, peyote is a small, knobby, bluish-green cactus found in limestone soils in southern Texas and northern Mexico. Stubby and spineless, it contains a number of alkaloids, including mescaline, and is best known for the hallucinogenic effects it can induce. Southwestern Indians have long used it as

Phacelia blossoms are frequently borne in crowded clusters and have protruding stamens, giving the flowers a furry look.

Phainopeplas oftentimes build their nests in the forks of mesquites or other small trees.

Red phalaropes breed on the tundra and winter on the rough seas of the North Atlantic, often following herds of whales.

part of their religious rituals, chewing pieces cut from the cactus. Tapering from a mushroomlike top to a thick taproot, the mature plant averages only two inches high and some three inches across. In summer a white to pinkish flower opens on the peyote's upper surface and later gives rise to a stubby red fruit that ripens the following year.

Phacelia

Ranging in height from a few inches to four feet, phacelias bear clusters of colorful flowers on stalks that are coiled like scorpions' tails but straighten out as the blossoms open. Most U.S. species inhabit dry areas in the West. One of the best-known, the California bluebell, is a two-foot-tall annual that flourishes in dry soils of southern California. The eastern United States has several phacelias, including Miami mist, with delicately fringed blue blossoms.

Phainopepla *Phainopepla nitens*

With a prominent crest, blue-black plumage, and gemlike red eyes, the phainopepla has an air of jaunty elegance. Its name, derived from the Greek for "shining robe," was inspired by the male's bright, glossy feathers.

Phainopeplas live in the arid Southwest, where they zigzag through the air and, flycatcher-style, nab insects on the wing. But their main foods are berries, especially those of the parasitic mistletoe. Growing on the mesquites in which the birds nest, the plants are valiantly defended against incursions of other fruit-eating birds.

In some areas phainopeplas have developed the unusual habit of breeding in two different places in the same year. After raising a brood in southern California deserts in early spring, the birds sometimes travel to moister chaparral country, where they breed again in summer.

Phalarope *Phalaropus*

Sandpiperlike shorebirds with longish legs, necks, and bills, phalaropes are nonconformists when it comes to courtship. Practicing a most unusual role reversal, the females—larger and more brightly colored than the males—aggressively seek out mates and fend off competitors. And it is the drably plumaged males that build the nests, incubate the eggs, and care for the young. Phalaropes are unconventional in their feeding habits as well; they spin around like tops on the water's surface, dabbling with their bills for crustaceans and tiny fish.

Two of the phalaropes—the red and the red-necked—nest on the tundra of the Far North and spend their winters at sea in the southern hemisphere. Before setting off for the south, the birds gather offshore by the thousands in such well-known meeting places as the Bay of Fundy. The only other species, the Wilson's phalarope (named for American ornithologist Alexander Wilson) prefers freshwater habitats; it nests on ponds and marshes on the western plains and winters in South America.

The ring-necked pheasant was introduced so successfully in the western plains that it was designated South Dakota's state bird.

Pheasant *Phasianus colchicus*

Brought to North America from Asia in the 1800's, the ring-necked pheasant now thrives across southern Canada and the northern United States, where it is at home on croplands, pastures, fields, and brushy areas; it even nests on the outskirts of cities. The male is especially dramatic looking, with his long, tapering tail, and his colorfully iridescent head set off by a distinctive white collar. While this flashy plumage helps the cock attract mates, the delicate brown feathers of the hen serve as camouflage when she sits on her ground nest. If disturbed, she often feigns injury to lure intruders away from her brood of as many as 15 chicks. A startled male, on the other hand, heads almost straight up in a burst of flight, or he may dash away on foot to seek cover in a nearby patch of underbrush.

Phlox *Phlox*

Numbering some 60 species, the phloxes all are North American natives, though one species is also found in Siberia. Because their flowers blaze with a rich variety of hues, especially reds, whites, pinks, purples, and blues, the plants were named for the Greek word for "flame." Early settlers, however, often called them sawpit flowers, an allusion to the fondness of the tall eastern summer phlox and blue phlox for the moist, organic soil of lumberyards.

Actually, the plants flourish in a wide range of soils and habitats, especially in the West. In California, for example, the two-foot-tall showy phlox, with lancelike leaves and bright pink flowers, thrives both in forests and on sagebrush flats, while the Rocky Mountain phlox prefers dry mountain ridges, dotting them from May to August with symmetrical, ground-hugging cushions

Blue phlox—also called wild sweet William—was used by aboriginal peoples as an herbal remedy for digestive problems, and its roots were cooked to make eyewash.

of snowy white blooms. Another low-growing species, the creeping moss pink, is an easterner found on sandy soils and rocky ledges from Maine to North Carolina.

Phoebe *Sayornis*

Medium-size flycatchers, phoebes build moss and mud nests beneath bridges or under the eaves of buildings. The best known of the three North American species, the eastern phoebe, ranges from the Gulf of Mexico to southern Canada and west to the Rockies. It is among the earliest spring migrants, and perching males are often seen busily pumping their tails as they repeat their characteristic *feebee* call. The eastern phoebe is less colorful than its cousins, the Say's phoebe of the West and the black phoebe of the U.S. Southwest. All three hunt actively for insects, often snatching them in midflight.

Phoebes, including eastern (left) and black (right), prefer waterside habitats.

Pickerelweed tints a shallow freshwater pond (above) with spikes of violet blooms (above, right).

Photosynthesis

One of the miracles of the natural world is photosynthesis, the process by which green plants manufacture their own food. The two basic ingredients are water and carbon dioxide, which plants—with the aid of sunlight—are able to transform into sugar and oxygen. Water is taken up through the roots of higher plants, and carbon dioxide enters the leaves through special pores called stomates. Meanwhile, chlorophyll, the green pigment in plants, absorbs energy from sunlight and serves as a catalyst in the chemical reactions that break down the water and carbon dioxide. The water is split into oxygen, which is released into the atmosphere, and hydrogen, which combines with the carbon dioxide to produce simple sugars. These sugars are crucial building blocks that can be converted into more complex sugars and into starches, fats, and proteins.

Plants are not the only benefactors of photo-synthesis, for all animal life depends, directly or indirectly, upon the process. The grains and vegetables we eat, as well as the meats and other animal products, could not exist without it. Equally essential to life is the oxygen released by photosynthesis, for without it we could not breathe. Our breathing, in turn, plays a reciprocal role, for the carbon dioxide we exhale is one of the essential ingredients of photosynthesis.

Pickerelweed *Pontederia cordata*

Growing in profusion across eastern North America, pickerelweed is a perennial aquatic plant that flourishes in freshwater marshes, ponds, and streams. It takes root in shallow water (the same habitat preferred by the fish known as pickerels) and sends up large shiny long-stemmed leaves and attractive spikes of purplish-blue flowers. Bees visit the blossoms for nectar, muskrats relish the foliage, and ducks feed on the nutritious nutlike seeds.

Pikas harvest green plants and dry them in the summer sun for use during the winter.

Chain pickerels, a favorite of fishermen, are pikes named for their chainlike markings.

Pigeon

The stout, small-headed birds known as pigeons could just as easily be considered large doves since, except for their names, no clear-cut distinctions separate the two kinds of birds. Pigeons and doves are much alike in behavior as well. When courting, for example, the male makes gentle cooing sounds, bows to the female, and feeds her seeds. The young hatch in flimsy nests of twigs, where they are fed a cheesy white substance, called pigeon's milk, that is produced in the throats of the adults.

The pigeons in our cities are well adapted for urban life. Also known as rock doves, they are attracted by the ledges of high buildings, which resemble the cliffs their old-world ancestors used as nest sites. The only other common species, the band-tailed pigeon, lives in western forests and feeds on seeds, nuts, and berries. The passenger pigeon, now extinct, was once this continent's most abundant bird. Traveling in huge flocks, it probably died out as a result of overhunting and the destruction of forests.

Pika *Ochotona*

Related to rabbits and hares, pikas do look a bit like short-eared rabbits as they scamper among mountain rocks. Nicknames such as rock rabbit, whistling hare, and little chief hare are further testimony to the family resemblance. Found year-round above the timberline on high mountains in the West, pikas live in colonies among loose boulders. When danger threatens, usually in the form of eagles or other predators, pikas warn each other with loud, squeaky barks. Cautious about their food supply as well, the provident little creatures harvest leaves and grasses, stack them in the sun to dry, then store them in their rocky dens for the long cold winter.

Pike *Esox*

From the 10-inch, 1-pound grass pickerel to the 7-foot, 75-pound muskellunge, all five North American species of pikes are such aggressive predators that they have earned the nickname

Pileated woodpeckers cling to trees with the help of their sharply clawed feet.

waterwolves. All are freshwater fish with long, slim, muscular bodies and powerful, jutting jaws armed with sharp teeth. The pikes satisfy their voracious appetites by lurking in weedy shallows and darting out to seize their victims. Although they feed mainly on other fish and frogs, even waterfowl and young muskrats do not escape the larger species. Strong fighters, the pikes are popular game fish and, once caught, make a tasty meal.

Pileated woodpecker *Dryocopus pileatus*

Striking black-and-white birds with rakish red crests, pileated woodpeckers are—except for the probably extinct ivory-billed—our largest woodpeckers. Though nearly as big as crows, they are rarely seen. The best signs of their presence in the mature woodlands they prefer are the large rectangular holes they hack into tree trunks in search of carpenter ants, their favorite food. Listen, too, for their loud, ringing calls and the rhythmic hammering as they bore new

Limber pine

Lodgepole pine

Bristlecone pine

White pine

Pines are often classified into two groups, white (soft) and yellow (hard), according to the strength of their heartwood. Except for the lodgepole, all species pictured here are white pines.

holes. In spring the males also drum on dead stubs to attract mates and proclaim territory. Mated pairs chisel tidy nest holes in tree trunks, where they raise broods of three to five young.

Pillow lava

Formed when lava solidifies underwater, pillow lava consists of heaps of rocks that look like piles of sandbags. When molten lava erupts under the sea, its surface quickly chills and develops a brittle skin. Tongues of hot liquid then break through the surface and harden into the characteristic pillow shapes. Examples can be seen in California, New Jersey, and other places where ancient sea floors are exposed on land.

Pine *Pinus*

The pines are trees that invite superlatives: oldest, tallest, most useful, and more. Bristlecone pines, for example, claim the prize for longevity among trees, with some of them reaching ages of

5,000 years or more. The giants of the group are sugar pines, which can top out at 200 feet and produce cones to match—up to 2 feet long. Still other species, valued as timber, supply countless board feet of lumber for myriad uses, among them home construction, railway ties, and even matchsticks.

All the pines have evergreen, needle-shaped leaves that are usually borne in clusters of two to five. And they all produce seeds in cones formed of overlapping woody scales. While young trees are usually conical in form, with whorls of horizontal branches radiating from the trunks, older trees sometimes assume more spreading, irregular shapes.

Except for parts of the Midwest and Far North, pines range throughout North America. Though some grow on soggy soils, most species prefer dry, sunny uplands. Since they can prosper on soils too thin and rocky for agriculture, pines are extensively planted in the reforestation projects that are so vital to the enhancement of the environment.

Deptford pinks have old-world origins and trace their name to Deptford, England, now part of London.

Tiny pipsissewa flowers, less than an inch across, cluster atop stems that are not quite one foot tall.

Pink *Dianthus*

Named not for their colors, which include hues from red to white, these wildflowers are called pinks because of the fringed edges of their petals, which look as if they were "pinked" with shears. Pinks came to North America as garden flowers (carnations and sweet Williams are pinks) but have long since escaped to sandy fields and roadsides. Our commonest species are the maiden pink, with trailing stems, and the Deptford pink, which grows up to three feet tall.

Pinyon *Pinus*

Picturesque pines of arid regions in the western United States, pinyons produce nutty white seeds relished by all sorts of wildlife, from black bears to wild turkeys. Also avidly consumed by humans, the so-called pine nuts or Indian nuts are gathered by American Indians and shipped to urban markets. The thin-shelled, cylindrical, half-inch-long seeds are not only tasty; they are nutritious as well, containing more protein than lentils or chick peas. The trees, which range from California to Texas and from Idaho to Mexico, are generally small and spreading. Averaging 20 to 30 feet in height, they prefer the dry, rocky soils of foothills and canyons.

Pioneer plant

When a farmer's field is left unplanted, such hardy plants as ragweed and thistles soon spring up. And after a forest fire the charred ground is often taken over by legions of fireweed, topped with plumes of pink flowers. These pioneer plants, so named because they are the first to arrive on the scene, are able to withstand such harsh conditions as intense sunlight and poor soil. Once established, they protect the soil from erosion, enrich it by their own decay, and shelter the seedlings of other plants such as vines, shrubs, and trees, which eventually take over.

Pipefish

Odd little relatives of seahorses, pipefish are long, slender creatures with bony scales that form rings of armor around their bodies. They range from 1 to 16 inches and have flexible tails and tubelike snouts that end in small, sucking mouths. Stranger than their appearance, however, is their mating behavior. Females deposit eggs in brood pouches on the males, where they remain until hatching several weeks later. Usually found in warm, shallow seas, pipefish move through the water by rippling their back fins, and often live in eelgrass or seaweed beds.

P

Carnivorous pitcher plants—such as cobra plants (above), northern pitcher plants (top, right), floral emblem of Newfoundland, and trumpets (right)—all entrap insects. When prey falls into the tube-shaped leaves, it drowns and then is digested by the plant.

Pipit *Anthus*

Small, slender birds with streaked or mottled brown plumage and white outer tail feathers, pipits characteristically bob their tails as they walk along catching insects on the ground. Though generally inconspicuous, courting males are noted for their impressive displays: they fly straight up, then flutter back down, their songs descending in pitch as the birds float down from the sky. The American pipit, our commonest species, nests on arctic and alpine tundra and winters in open country in the South. The less common Sprague's pipit is a bird of short-grass prairies.

Pipsissewa *Chimaphila umbellata*

Producing clusters of fragrant, pinkish-white star-shaped flowers above whorls of evergreen leaves, pipsissewa brightens dry midsummer woodlands all across temperate North America. Its name, from a Cree Indian word meaning "it breaks into small pieces," refers to the Crees' belief that an extract from the leaves could break up kidney stones. Pipsissewa remained a popular home remedy until the early 1900's, and it is still used for flavoring candy and soft drinks.

Pitcher plant

Among the carnivores of the plant world, pitcher plants are distinguished by their urn-shaped leaves. Within the leaves' rims, the plants serve up drops of nectar to lure insects. An unwary explor-

ing insect will occasionally fall into the urn, or pitcher, where a band of downward-pointing hairs prevents the victim from crawling back up. Below the bristles, the interior wall of the leaf is sleek and waxy—a further impediment to climbing out. Trapped, the insect drowns in the rainwater accumulated in the pitcher. Enzymes secreted by the plant hasten the digestion of the insect's body, which is absorbed for nourishment.

While the best-known pitcher plants are colorful bog-loving curiosities of the East and Midwest, other species prosper in various habitats in the South and West. Thriving primarily in places where little nitrogen is available to their roots, pitcher plants compensate for the shortage by extracting this important nutrient from the insects they trap.

P

The **copperhead,** a widespread pit viper, delivers a venomous bite, but it is rarely fatal to humans.

Broadleaf plantain is a well-known and persistent lawn and garden weed.

Pit viper

The cottonmouth and copperhead, as well as our various rattlesnakes, are all pit vipers—a group of poisonous snakes named for the distinctive sensory organs they have in common. Located on either side of the head between the eye and nostril, these sensory pits are extremely responsive to heat and are used to determine the whereabouts of warm-blooded prey. Pit vipers are nocturnal, and by moving their heads from side to side, they are able —with these special sensors—to gauge the exact location of birds and mammals in the dark. Once they have homed in on their targets, they strike rapidly and accurately, injecting venom with their long, hollow fangs.

Plankton

Derived from a Greek word meaning "wander," the term *plankton* refers to the huge numbers of plants and animals that drift with currents in the ocean and other bodies of water. The plants, known as phytoplankton, live in the well-lit surface waters, where they carry on photosynthesis. Consisting mainly of microscopic algae, they are the basic source of food in the ocean.

Zooplankton, the floating animals, range from minute protozoans to tentacled jellyfish several feet in diameter. The larvae of many kinds of fish and shellfish also drift as plankton before maturing into adults. Many of these animals graze on the phytoplankton. They are in turn eaten by larger drifters, which are themselves food for other creatures, including the massive blue whale, which subsists on plankton strained from seawater.

Plantain *Plantago*

Unrelated to the tropical bananalike plants of the same name, the various plantains are all too familiar to gardeners and lawn keepers, who despise them as persistent, troublesome weeds. The leaves, ribbed and broadly oval on many species, are arranged in ground-hugging basal rosettes from which rise tall, slender stalks topped with spikes of inconspicuous greenish flowers. Both wild and caged birds, as well as a number of rodents, are fond of the tiny seeds, and rabbits nibble on the foliage. Richer than spinach in several vitamins, the tender young leaves used to be served as a potherb at family dinner tables. The two most widespread species, the oval-leaved common plantain and the aptly named narrow-leaved plantain, are both old-world natives that thrive from coast to coast.

Plateau

Broad, flat expanses of terrain that rise high above their surroundings are called plateaus. They range in height from a few hundred to many thousands of feet and may encompass vast areas. The Colorado Plateau, for instance, covers about 150,000 square miles and in most places stands about one mile above sea level.

Deeply incised with canyons, including the Grand Canyon, the Colorado Plateau was uplifted by titanic movements within the earth's crust. Other plateaus were built up as successive lava flows buried preexisting landscapes under thick layers of basalt. Measuring about 75,000 square miles, the Columbia Plateau in the Pacific Northwest is made up of basaltic lava that poured from enormous fissures in the earth.

Lesser golden plover

Piping plover

Black-bellied plover

Semipalmated plover

Plovers, plumpish wading birds with big eyes and bold markings, are a common sight on mudflats and beaches, though a few species prefer fields and grasslands.

Playa

Named for the Spanish word for "beach" or "shore," a playa is a flat, dry lakebed on a sunparched desert floor. The lake may be filled after heavy downpours, but it dries out again within a few days or weeks. After the water evaporates, the playa is often left encrusted with a layer of salts, and continued flooding and drying can produce thick accumulations of halite, gypsum, and other economically important minerals. Playas are common in Death Valley, California, where they were at one time mined for borax. The Bonneville Salt Flats in Utah are another large—and spectacular—example of a playa.

Plover

Stocky, large-headed shorebirds with big eyes and short bills, plovers are generally found on beaches and mudflats. Unlike their relatives the sandpipers, they rarely probe under the mud for food. Instead, they stand still for several minutes to scan the ground in front of them and snatch up small prey, then run a few paces and pause to watch again.

Our best-known plover, the raucous killdeer, is a bird not of beaches but of open fields. It is named for its persistent ringing *kill-dee* call. Another widespread species is the semipalmated

plover, whose name refers to its half-webbed toes. Despite its bold markings, this handsome little bird in fact blends perfectly with the mudflats where it forages. Far less common are the snowy and piping plovers. Both are denizens of sandy beaches, where their pale plumage provides camouflage as they scurry along the shore.

The strikingly patterned lesser golden plover is famous as a champion migrant, sometimes making round-trip journeys of 16,000 miles. After nesting on the Arctic tundra, flocks of these birds fly to Labrador, then set off on a nonstop trip over the Atlantic to the plains of southern South America.

Poacher

Bottom dwellers that inhabit cold ocean waters, poachers are slim-bodied fish that range from 2 to 10 inches in length. Clad in bony plates and bristling with spikes and spines, they include such aptly named characters as the spinycheek starsnout, the northern spearnose, the pricklebreast, the sawback, and the warty poacher. One species, the kelp poacher, uses its fins to scale craggy rocks and is often festooned with camouflaging seaweed and sponges that make it look like a bit of red and brown jetsam. Though often abundant, especially in the North Pacific, poachers are of no commercial value.

P

Clouds of pollen, carried by the wind from pine trees to a lake (above), form spectacular swirls on the water. Male pussy willow catkins (right), loaded with pollen, await a strong breeze.

Pocket gophers lead solitary lives, burrowing in loose soil. The roots and grasses they feed on are carried in pouches in their cheeks.

Pocket gopher

Pouches on the outside of their cheeks—noticeable only when they are bulging with roots, tubers, and other vegetation—are the pockets that give pocket gophers their name. Stocky little rodents, they have strong feet and sharp teeth that are used for digging their extensive burrows. Though rarely seen above ground, they are easily located by the fan-shaped mounds of earth that they push out of their tunnels.

Most of the 15 or so species in the United States are found in western mountains. Their burrows aerate the soil, but the animals at times destroy root crops and pull forage plants into their tunnels—destructive habits that have led to efforts at extermination. Since pocket gophers reproduce at a prodigious rate, however, such campaigns have had limited success.

Pocket mouse

Some 20 species of pocket mice inhabit deserts and dry prairies west of the Mississippi River. Expert burrowers, they use their tunnels for nesting, food storage, and as daytime retreats. At night the tiny rodents emerge from their burrows to forage for seeds on the surface. Like their distant cousins the pocket gophers, they have fur-lined, external cheek pouches, which they stuff with seeds that they carry back to their underground larders.

Poisonous plant See pp. 298–299.

Poisonous snake

Though widely feared, poisonous snakes pose relatively little danger to humans. The fact is that in North America, only a dozen or so deaths per year are attributed to snakebites. And most of the victims are people who regularly handle venomous snakes.

North America's poisonous snakes fall into one of two categories. The more numerous pit vipers—including the copperhead, cottonmouth, and all the rattlesnakes—have a deep,

Pollination is inadvertently accomplished by bees, which fly from flower to flower in their search for food.

heat-sensitive pit, used to detect warm-blooded prey, in front of each eye. Pit vipers strike quickly; the venom, which they inject through long, hollow fangs, attacks the victim's blood vessels and red blood cells.

Coral snakes, brightly banded with yellow, red, and black, live only in warm areas. Instead of striking quickly, they gnaw on their victims, releasing a venom that impairs the nervous system and can sometimes paralyze such vital organs as the lungs and heart.

Pokeweed *Phytolacca americana*

Up to 10 feet tall with branching stems and foot-long leaves, pokeweed flourishes in fields and along roadsides throughout the East. Its spikes of tiny greenish-white flowers are followed by purple berries borne on scarlet stems.

Its root, which resembles that of a horseradish, is known for its medicinal uses. And in spring, especially in the South, the plant's young shoots are boiled and consumed as a vegetable.

Despite its array of benefits, however, pokeweed must be approached with caution. It is so poisonous that if it is not properly prepared, the food and medicines it offers can be lethal—hence the pokeweed's other epithet: the Jekyll and Hyde of the plant world.

Pollen

Consisting of tiny grains that play a vital role in the reproduction of seed-bearing plants, pollen looks to the naked eye like a yellowish dust. Under an electron microscope, however, the grains are revealed in their astonishing variety. With surfaces that are smooth, grooved, spiked, pitted, or ridged, pollen grains are shaped like everything from flying saucers to cantaloupes.

Pollen is produced by the stamens, or male structures, of flowering plants and by the male cones of conifers. In the process of pollination, pollen is transferred to the plant's female structures, where fertilization takes place and seeds then develop. Typically, much more pollen is produced than is ever used. And the pollen of some plants, such as ragweed, is, of course, a major nemesis of hay fever sufferers.

Pokeweed's purple berries contain a dark juice that was once used for ink, inspiring one of the plant's nicknames, inkweed.

Pollination

Wind and water, as well as bees, butterflies, birds, bats, and other animals, all play a part in pollination—the process by which pollen is transferred from the male parts of plants to the female parts. Plants that depend on wind or water produce huge amounts of pollen to ensure that at least some of it arrives at its destination. Others have showy petals or enticing odors that attract pollinators such as honey bees, hummingbirds, or other creatures. The pollinators, searching for nectar or pollen to use as food, are dusted with pollen as they alight on a flower, and then unwittingly transport it to others.

Once the pollen has reached its female counterpart, fertilization takes place. In conifers, whose ovules are exposed on cones, the process is simple. In flowering plants, however, a pollen grain that lands on top of the female pistil must first germinate, sending a pollen tube down into the pistil until it reaches an ovule. There it releases a sperm nucleus that unites with an egg cell to develop into a seed.

Poison ivy, often found growing as a vine, can be recognized by its glossy three-part leaves.

Foxgloves, source of the heart drug digitalis, are popular garden plants, prized for their showy flowers.

Poisonous Plant

Some 700 species of plants native to North America are classed as poisonous. The toxins they contain present an array of complicated compounds, including alkaloids, glycosides, and resins, each of which affects victims in different ways. Some attack the nervous system, producing weakness or paralysis; others interfere with the heart and circulatory system; and many irritate the skin and the digestive tract.

Some poisons are fast acting, producing symptoms almost immediately. The acrid juice of buttercups, for instance, inflames the mouth and stomach within seconds. The toxins of the deadly amanita mushrooms, in contrast, may take up to 24 hours to show their full effect.

One man's poison

A number of poisonous plants can heal as well as harm, for a plant that is toxic in large quantities may have medicinal value in smaller amounts. Indeed, many medicines are essentially extracts of poisonous plants administered in controlled doses. The common foxglove, for example, is the source of digitalis, a drug used to strengthen the heartbeats of cardiac patients. In large doses, however, digitalis can cause heart failure.

Further complicating this situation is the fact that a plant may be poisonous at one stage of its life cycle and not at another. Pokeweed, for instance, is relatively harmless when young, and in many areas country people gather the shoots in spring to boil as a potherb. But as the plant matures, it accumulates such high concentrations of toxins in all its tissues, that consumption of any of its parts can be lethal.

Skin irritants

While many poisonous plants are toxic when ingested, others inflict their misery simply by being touched, producing a skin rash called contact dermatitis. The rash is commonly caused by close encounters with a notorious plant: poison ivy (also known as poison oak). It contains an oil, urushiol, that blisters the skin of allergic individuals. The poisonwood, a small tree with purple leaves that is found in the Southeast, also causes severe dermatitis, while in the West snow-on-the-mountain, prized for its showy white blossoms, yields a milky sap so caustic it has been used to brand cattle.

Mistaken identities

In recent years the incidence of plant poisonings has been increased by the renewed popularity of foraging for wild foods. Many toxic plants resemble common food plants and so fool inexperienced harvesters. Someone seeking the edible roots of the wild carrot, for instance, might accidentally pick those of its similar-looking relative, poison hemlock; and the fleshy tubers of the water hemlock are frequently mistaken for wild parsnips—with fatal effect, since one or two bites can deliver a lethal dose.

Mushrooms suffer from the most sinister rep-

Jimsonweed, a member of the nightshade family, produces potent—and toxic—hallucinogens.

Baneberry's fruits cause severe stomach upset when eaten.

utation of all the wild edibles. This is somewhat unfair, for of the 5,000 or more kinds found in North America, only about 100 are poisonous. But positive identification can be tricky, and some of the deadliest kinds closely resemble benign species.

Innocent victims

Despite the great number and variety of poisonous plants, human deaths remain relatively rare. Young children are most at risk, since their natural curiosity prompts them to taste every new thing they discover. Because of their low body weight, moreover, children are susceptible to far smaller doses of toxins.

Parents often unwittingly compound the problem by putting poisonous plants about the house and yard, right in harm's way. Dumbcane and philodendron, both popular house plants, contain needlelike crystals of calcium oxalate in their stems and leaves. When eaten, the crystals embed in the tissues of the mouth and tongue and cause an intense burning sensation. Far more dangerous are the juicy red fruits of the yew. Though their flesh is edible, the seeds (and

needles) contain taxine, a poison that can cause respiratory failure in as little as one half hour.

Mountain laurel, a common wild shrub and a popular ornamental, is poisonous in all its parts, including the honey made from its nectar. Another dangerous domestic is the oleander, a common landscaping shrub in the Southeast. Every part is toxic: people have even died after using oleander twigs as barbecue skewers.

Perilous pastures

Poisonous plants also take a toll on livestock, particularly in the arid West, where hungry animals may have difficulty finding other fodder. The white snakeroot, an upright weed with candelabras of fuzzy white blossoms, is often eaten by cattle, causing nausea and trembling, as well as poisoning their milk.

Among the most dangerous plants of western prairies are the locoweeds. They contain a slow-acting toxin that causes disorientation, frenzied behavior, and sometimes death. Fortunately, locoweeds and most other poisonous species are so foul-tasting that one bite is usually enough to convince livestock to graze elsewhere.

False hellebores, up to six feet tall at maturity, are among the many poisonous plants whose toxins have been used for medicinal purposes. They contain powerful alkaloids that help lower blood pressure and slow the heartbeat.

P

Junkyards choked with debris, belching smokestacks, and smoggy skies are grim reminders of our pollution problems.

Liquid wastes threaten North America's rivers.

Illegal dumping—from household trash to toxic chemicals—is more than an eyesore.

Oil spills have sullied pristine shores, even in such remote areas as Alaska, killing animals and crippling the fishing industry.

An oil spill in Alaska in 1989 killed thousands of birds, despite desperate rescue efforts.

Pollution

An unpleasant by-product of human activities such as industry, mining, and even agriculture, pollution is the contamination of our air, water, and land. Sludge-clogged rivers, soup-thick smog, and roadways littered with bottles and other debris—these are just a few of the pollution problems facing all of North America. Detergents, fertilizers, pesticides, and industrial pollutants have sullied streams and contaminated water supplies, while heaps of nonbiodegradable trash choke our waste disposal sites.

Other less visible enemies also imperil our planet. Acid rain, caused by industrial and auto emissions, has killed fish, corroded buildings, and devastated forests. The burning of fossil fuels adds carbon dioxide to the air, which could produce the greenhouse effect: a warming of the atmosphere that would disrupt climates around the world. And burgeoning stores of nuclear wastes pose an ominous threat.

Human health is directly endangered by some pollutants. Many industrial chemicals are known carcinogens; smog can cause severe respiratory problems; and in some communities, tainted water supplies have resulted in an increased incidence of leukemia and other illnesses.

The first step toward healing a sick environment is to eliminate as many pollutants as possible. The use of certain aerosol propellants, for instance, has been prohibited in an effort to save the ozone layer. Strict compliance with pollution regulations, waste treatment, recycling, and the use of biodegradable products are ways in which communities and corporations can take active roles in cleaning up the planet.

Polyphemus moth *Antheraea polyphemus*

One of North America's native silkworm moths, the polyphemus moth, was named for the one-eyed giant of Greek mythology, an allusion to the eyespot on each of its brownish wings. As a fat, leaf-green caterpillar, the polyphemus feeds on the foliage of hardwood trees, then overwinters in a cocoon. When the adults emerge, ready to mate, the males' antennae are especially feathery—the better to detect pheromones, the alluring female scents that waft on the breeze.

Pond See pp. 302–303.

Pond lily *Nuphar*

Though pretty, the sunny yellow flowers of pond lilies, or spatterdocks, are not so large and lovely as those of the lotuses and water lilies. The plants, in fact, are sometimes scorned as weeds because they grow so vigorously that they crowd out other plants. They do, however, provide a feast for wildlife. Ducks eat the seeds, moose graze on the floating leaves, and muskrats and beavers store the sweet roots, which were also eaten by Indians and early settlers.

Pondweed *Potamogeton*

Bottom-rooted aquatics, pondweeds flourish in lakes, ponds, and streams. Some species are entirely submerged, while others have narrow underwater leaves and larger leaves that float on the surface. Their tiny green flowers are borne on spikes that project from the water. Though far from showy, pondweeds are of vital importance to wildlife. Fish and other animals find cover in thickets of pondweed, and waterfowl eat the nutlets as well as the plants themselves.

Poppy

A large and attractive family of flowers, the poppies are prized for their colorful but short-lived blossoms. Most have milky or colored sap and many have deeply cut foliage. Each flower stalk ends in a single bud that opens to reveal four to six broad petals surrounding a knot of stamens. The blooms are followed by fruit capsules that open to release their seeds through pores. One of the best known is the California poppy, whose golden blossoms blanket grassy hills and arid slopes from California to Utah. Up to eight feet tall, the shrublike Matilija poppy has giant white flowers with yellow centers.

California poppies cover a western field with a sea of golden blossoms.

Porcupine *Erethizon dorsatum*

Easily recognized by the long, sharp quills that cover its stocky, short-legged body and stubby tail, the porcupine is the only rodent of its kind in North America. The quills—approximately 30,000 on each animal—are modified hairs that come loose when they are touched. Any predator that attacks a porcupine retreats with its face and paws covered with the barbed spines, which work their way deep into the flesh, causing infection and, sometimes, death.

A forest dweller in Canada and the western and northeastern United States, the porcupine spends its days sleeping. At night it forages in trees, feeding on bark, twigs, and buds and often causing extensive damage. In spring the female leaves the trees and moves into a den to give birth to a single young. The newborn's quills are soft but harden within minutes. And within hours the youngster can climb trees with its mother.

Porcupinefish

When pursued or perturbed, porcupinefish balloon from bite-size to basketball-size by gulping air or water. The sharp spines that give the fish their name bristle from the taut skin and act as a further deterrent to would-be predators. Unlike those of their cousins the burrfish (whose spines are always erect) the "quills" of the porcupinefish lie flat against their bodies when they deflate. Their beaklike teeth—one big tooth in the upper jaw, and another in the lower jaw—enable them to crush mollusks and other hard-shelled prey. Found off the Atlantic and Pacific coasts, the whimsical-looking creatures are sometimes inflated, dried, and sold as souvenirs.

P

301

Beavers' expertly built dams actually create ponds, in the midst of which these busy engineers construct the lodges where they rest by day and raise their young.

Green-backed herons remain perfectly still until they spot a fish, then dart forward and snatch it from the water.

Pond lilies' sweet rootstocks were cooked and eaten by Indians.

The alligator snapping turtle is a natural angler. By wiggling a wormlike projection on its tongue, this predator lures fish within range of its powerful, viselike jaws.

POND

A placid, mirrorlike surface dotted with lily pads, where dragonflies shimmer in the sunlight and chorusing bullfrogs can be heard at dusk—such is the scene that comes to mind when we think of a typical pond. Though hard to define precisely, a pond is generally considered to be a small body of standing fresh water—often of uniform temperature—that is shallow enough for sunlight to penetrate to the bottom, allowing rooted plants to grow even in the deepest parts. Here pondweed and other plants live completely submerged, while duckweed floats on the sur-

face, its tiny roots dangling below. Water lilies require shallower water, and even closer to shore are cattails, arrowheads, and arums.

For its rich variety of animal life—from microscopic plankton to visiting moose—the pond serves as food factory, nursery, and battleground. Here all manner of insects, fish, amphibians, birds, and mammals compete for food, shelter, and breeding space. As a pond ages, however, its cast of characters changes, for built-up sediment and encroaching vegetation eventually turn it into a marsh and then dry land.

Water smartweed, named for the sharp taste of its leaves, has long, sprawling, underwater stems. Its seedlike fruits provide meals for a variety of ducks.

This woodland pond, though still beautiful, is showing its age. Much of its surface is covered by water lilies and cattails are gradually advancing toward the center of the pond.

Longear sunfish are named for the large black flap extending from the gill cover. By fanning with their fins, the males clear away debris from a small area on the bottom to form a circular nest.

Lesser giant water bug males carry their mate's eggs piggy-back-style until they hatch.

Minks prefer to live close to water, where they pursue fish, snakes, and other prey.

American toads spend most of their mature lives on land but breed in shallow ponds.

P

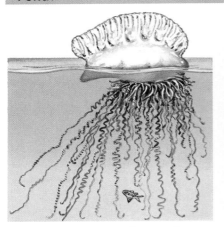

The Portuguese man-of-war trails its stinging tentacles underwater.

Greater prairie chickens show off to females during their age-old sunrise courtship ritual.

Porgy

Abundant in U.S. waters on the Atlantic and Gulf of Mexico coasts in habitats ranging from rocks and reefs to pilings and seagrass beds, porgies are popular food and game fish. Most species eat shellfish and weigh less than one pound. Exceptions include the 30-pound sheepshead and the 10-pound jolthead porgy, which is named for its habit of dislodging mollusks with its head. One of the most familiar species, found from Cape Cod to the Carolinas, is called the scup in New England, the northern porgy in New York, and the fair maid in the South.

Porpoise

Small relatives of whales, porpoises resemble their cousins the dolphins but are chunkier, with snouts that are short and blunt rather than beaked. Streamlined sea mammals with a torpedo shape designed for efficient swimming, they travel in pairs or in larger groups, moving through the water at speeds of up to 14 miles per hour. Like whales and dolphins, they breathe through a blowhole on the top of the head and must surface regularly for air. When swimming rapidly, they sometimes leap out of the water to take a breath.

Porpoises are intelligent creatures that communicate by means of high-pitched whistles and squeals. They also emit ultrasonic clicks in order to find their prey—primarily fish and squid—by means of echolocation. They breed in summer, and each female gives birth to a single calf about one year later. Like dolphins, porpoises are sometimes inadvertently caught and drowned in the nets of commercial fishing vessels.

Harbor porpoises, which live off both the Atlantic and Pacific coasts, often venture into bays and the mouths of large rivers, where groups sometimes cooperate in rounding up schools of fish. More playful and gregarious are Dall's porpoises. Patterned in black and white like miniature killer whales, they live in the North Pacific, where they are frequently seen swimming near the bows of moving ships.

Portuguese man-of-war *Physalia physalis*

Looking like a large jellyfish as it drifts on the surface of warm seas, the Portuguese man-of-war is actually a colony of organisms, called polyps, that work in concert to capture and devour prey. Buoyed by a balloonlike float, the beautiful but dangerous man-of-war hides its arsenal underwater: dangling from the float are long, trailing tentacles armed with deadly stinging cells. When touched by fish or other prey, the tentacles paralyze the victim and pull it toward specialized polyps that digest the food for the entire colony.

Although encounters with this notorious creature can be painful, some animals fear it not at all. Certain fish live unharmed among its tentacles, and loggerhead turtles eat the man-of-war with impunity.

Pothole

Deep circular depressions in the bedrock floor of rivers, potholes are a testament to the erosive power of running water. As turbulent water forms eddies in the stream, stones and pebbles often get caught in the swirl. Churning around and around in the same spot, the stones gradually scour deep holes in the underlying rock of the riverbed. The abrasive tools—pebbles, stones, and even grains of sand—can often be found at the bottom of the hole.

Prairie See *Grassland.*

Prairie chicken *Tympanuchus*

Grouse of the grasslands, prairie chickens are best known for their remarkable springtime courtship displays. Gathering at dawn on traditional mating grounds, groups of males begin to leap, stomp, and strut about, their tails fanned and their neck feathers erect. At the same time, inflated pouches on their throats resonate with booming calls that can be heard two miles away. Females view the entertainment, then mate and go off to nest and raise their young alone.

A watchful prairie dog (left) and some pups (right) survey their "town" from burrow entrances. For ventilation, and to provide an escape route, most of the burrows have two entries.

The prairie pothole region is a vital waterfowl nesting area; it includes only about 10 percent of North America's wetlands, yet produces some 50 percent of its ducks.

The greater prairie chicken, now extinct in Canada, is still found in the United States from Michigan westward, while the lesser prairie chicken lives farther south. Because farmland has gradually usurped their habitat, all prairie chickens have declined in number over the years. One subspecies, the Attwater's prairie chicken, found along the Texas coast, is seriously endangered; and another, the heath hen of the eastern United States, is extinct.

Prairie dog *Cynomys*

The playful and sociable prairie dogs are squirrel-like, burrowing rodents that live in colonies, or towns, on the Prairies. They are named for their high-pitched staccato barks, signals that warn each other to hide from badgers, hawks, or coyotes. Prairie dogs also communicate by nuzzling, kissing, and grooming, which reinforce the bonds within each coterie, or extended family, in the larger colony. Each coterie may have up to 100 burrows, elaborately interconnected and sometimes a dozen feet deep.

Until early in this century, vast numbers of prairie dogs were found on the western plains. A single colony in Texas, for example, covered thousands of square miles and was populated by some 400 million prairie dogs. Today the

great towns have disappeared. Poisoned and shot by ranchers because they were thought to compete with livestock for food, prairie dogs now survive only in small, isolated towns in parks and wildlife refuges. The last prairie dog towns in Canada are in southern Saskatchewan. One colony near Val Marie is protected by the Saskatchewan Natural History Society.

Prairie pothole

Across the southern parts of the prairie provinces, western Minnesota, and the Dakotas, the plains are dotted with glacial "thumbprints" created over 10,000 years ago. Water-filled depressions called prairie potholes, they cover some 300,000 square miles and are the breeding grounds for more than half of the continent's ducks. These miniature marshes range in size from more than 100 acres to fewer than 10 and are home to an array of plants and animals, including the ubiquitous cattails and muskrats. Despite the fact that many of our prairie wetlands have been lost to drainage and development, the potholes still provide nesting places and rest stops along North America's waterfowl flyways.

Praying mantis See *Mantid.*

P

Predators, such as the eagle swooping toward a fish (top left), the toad dining on an earthworm (top right), or the brown bears feasting on salmon (left), are equipped for catching prey. Eagles rely on sharp vision and talons, bears on a keen sense of smell and strong claws, and toads on their hairtrigger reflexes.

Precipitation

Rain and snow, as well as drizzle, sleet, and hail, are all forms of precipitation—moisture that falls from clouds to the earth. Clouds are formed when water vapor rises in the air, becomes chilled, and condenses into droplets or flakes. If the clouds become dense enough, droplets adhere to each other, increasing in size until they become heavy enough to fall as rain. When the clouds are low and the air is relatively still, moisture often descends as a fine mist, called drizzle.

Freezing temperatures produce precipitation in the form of sleet, hail, and snow. Sleet, which consists of moisture that has frozen into small pellets of ice, falls only in winter. In warmer weather the pellets, though frozen in the upper atmosphere, melt before they reach the ground, and fall as rain. Hail is formed when frozen pellets are tossed around in the air by updrafts, adding numerous layers of ice until they become so large and heavy that they fall to earth. (Hailstones can be dangerous; they have been known to injure livestock and break the windshields of cars.) Unlike sleet and hail, which begin as frozen rain, snow is made up of delicate crystals formed directly from supercooled water vapor. Though every snowflake has a six-sided shape, the design of each one is unique.

Whatever form it takes, precipitation provides the water that feeds rivers, lakes, and streams. Eventually it flows off the land into the sea, where it evaporates, beginning the cycle of precipitation all over again.

Predator

When we think of predators, we tend to think of animals with fangs and claws, or hooked beaks and talons. Indeed, wolves, bobcats, owls, and hawks are all predators, but strictly speaking, so is any animal that kills and feeds on other animals. A robin pulling a worm out of the ground, for example, has much in common with an eagle swooping down on a prairie dog, and an insect-eating dragonfly is a predator, too.

In fact, few animals are exclusively predatory or vegetarian. Foxes, for example, occasionally feed on berries and grapes, while other creatures that we think of as vegetarians sometimes prey on other animals. Chipmunks, for instance, feed mainly on seeds and nuts, but when the opportunity arises, they also capture and consume insects and young birds.

Prickly ash *Zanthoxylum americanum*

A shrub or small tree of rocky woodlands and riverbanks, the common prickly ash is one of the few nontropical members of the citrus family. It bears clusters of small greenish-yellow flowers in early spring before the feathery leaves emerge. Like its relative Hercules' club, the ash's branches are armed with stout thorns—a superfluous defense, since the whole plant is infused with a bitter, lemony oil that wildlife avoids. Early settlers, however, chewed the aromatic bark to numb toothache pain, dubbing prickly ash the toothache tree.

Prickly pears attract insect pollinators with their colorful, waxy-petaled blossoms.

Prince's plumes, lovely though they are, present a threat to grazing animals.

P

Prickly pear *Opuntia*

Close relatives of the cholla cacti, prickly pears can be recognized by their jointed stems, which are formed of broad, flattened pads that resemble spiny green beaver tails. Found in many places throughout the prairie provinces and the southwestern United States, prickly pears of various species may grow as tall as 15 feet or spread in thickets 30 feet across. New pads sprout small, fleshy leaves, but they soon drop off, leaving behind needle-sharp spines and clusters of tiny, irritating barbed bristles. In spring prickly pears produce flowers up to four inches across in brilliant shades of yellow, orange, and red; these are followed by juicy, reddish-purple, figlike fruits. In the Southwest the fruits are made into syrup and jelly, while the pads are peeled and eaten as a vegetable.

Primrose *Primula*

Partial to cool moist places, our many species of primroses grow along stream banks, in meadows, and on damp mountain slopes. Since their name derives from the Latin word for "first," it is not surprising that many of them bloom in early spring. A single stalk shoots up from a rosette of leaves and is topped by a cluster of five-petaled flowers. Though the blooms come in a rainbow of colors, they usually have yellow centers that lead pollinating insects to the flowers' hidden troves of nectar. The bird's-eye primrose, for instance, is pink with a yellow center, and the rosy mountain primrose also has a yellow "eye."

Prince's plume *Stanleya*

These royally named plants, which flourish on deserts and plains throughout much of the West, are members of the mustard family. Conspicuous in bloom, they produce tall showy plumes of four-petaled flowers that on most species are bright lemon-yellow. Desert plume, the commonest species, flaunts its flowers on stalks up to five feet tall. But because, like all the other prince's plumes, it thrives on soils rich in the poisonous element selenium, desert plume is toxic and poses a threat to grazing animals.

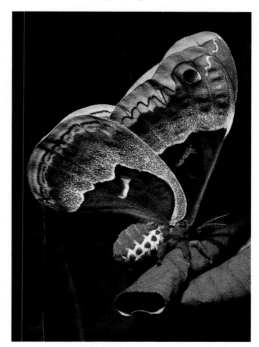

Female promethea moths are more brightly patterned than their mates, and unlike the males, they fly only at night.

Promethea moth *Callosamia promethea*

Attractively patterned members of the silkworm moth family, these insects are found in southern Ontario and parts of Quebec, and throughout the eastern and central United States. In the larval stage promethea moths are easy to identify: the caterpillars are green with five conspicuous tubercles on the back—four bright red ones at the head end and a yellow one at the rear. They feed on the foliage of the spicebush and on sassafras, cherry, and other trees. Overwintering as pupae, they hang from the twigs of their food trees in two-inch-long, leaf-wrapped silk cocoons and emerge as adults in the spring.

P

The pronghorn is the only animal that sheds the sheaths of its horns annually.

When puffballs mature, they release powderlike spores by the millions.

Pronghorn *Antilocapra americana*

North America's swiftest mammal—the graceful and agile pronghorn—can leap 20 feet in a bound and is able to sprint over prairies and sagebrush flats at speeds of 60 miles per hour. Sometimes called the American antelope, the pronghorn is unique; it has no close relatives and is virtually unchanged from ancestors that roamed the earth some 2 million years ago.

Mainly brown, with two white stripes across the chest, a large white rump patch with hairs that are raised in warning when danger looms, and two-pronged horns, the creature is easily recognized. Males are strongly territorial and compete with each other for harems during the autumn rut. The fawns, often twins, are born the following spring. True to their heritage, they can run faster than humans within days of their birth. Pronghorns feed in the morning and evening, grazing on grasses and weeds and occasionally browsing on shrubs.

Protozoan

Amoebas, paramecia, and thousands of other kinds of protozoans flourish worldwide in fresh and salt water and in damp soil. Though they consist of but a single cell and most are microscopic in size, protozoans lead remarkably complex and varied lives. Many can reproduce sexually, but others simply divide in two or sprout buds that develop into new individuals. Some move about, propelled by whiplike flagella or tiny, hairlike cilia. While many kinds require oxygen, others survive in such airless environments as septic tanks and the intestines of larger animals. Some are parasitic, including those that cause malaria and dysentery. And a few protozoans, like plants, can manufacture food through photosynthesis.

Ptarmigan *Lagopus*

Small, stocky grouse that live on chilly Arctic tundra and on treeless mountaintops in the West, ptarmigans are masters of camouflage. In summer their mottled black and brown plumage blends with the scrubby tundra vegetation, and in winter their feathers are as white as the surrounding snow. Like all grouse, they have feathered legs, but in winter their feet and toes are also feathered, conserving heat and acting in effect as snowshoes.

Ptarmigans feed on insects, berries, and tender leaves during the warm months and turn to buds, twigs, and seeds in winter. During the spring mating season the males are adorned with prominent red combs over their eyes and display by strutting, cackling, and making short, fluttering flights. The females build the nests and incubate the eggs alone, but the males stand guard and sometimes help to tend the young.

Of the two species that live in the Arctic, the willow ptarmigan inhabits birch and willow thickets, while the rock ptarmigan prefers higher, more barren ground. The white-tailed ptarmigan is found on alpine meadows high in the Rocky Mountains from Alaska to New Mexico.

Puffball

Like mushrooms, puffballs are the spore-producing fruiting bodies of underground fungi. Forsaking the umbrella shape of their mushroom kin, most are spherical, but others are shaped like clubs, pears, or toy tops. Their surfaces may be warty, spiny, pitted, or smooth. When they are young, the flesh of most is white and spongy; but as they age, it darkens, and if poked or kicked, the mature fungus emits a dusty cloud of tiny spores. While most puffballs are just an inch or two across, some grow as big as basketballs. Many species are edible when young and fleshy, but since a few are poisonous, puffballs should be sampled only with expert guidance.

The white-tailed ptarmigan has snowy feathers that provide protective coloring during the Rocky Mountain winter; in the summer its feathers become mottled brown.

The Atlantic puffin (left) and the tufted puffin (right) both boast distinctive, brightly colored beaks, which accounts for the fact that the birds are sometimes referred to as sea parrots.

Puffer

Aptly named, the puffers—also known as blowfish or swellfish—discourage predators by gulping air or water until they are inflated to twice their normal size. Turning belly up, they bob at the surface of the sea until the danger passes, then deflate with a great belch and go on their merry way, searching for crabs and clams, which they crush with their tough beaks.

Puffin *Fratercula*

These squat little seabirds may look comically awkward on land and rather heavy in the air, but once in their element, the water, they become able predators. "Flying" through the sea on stubby wings, they dive-bomb shoals of herring, sand eels, sardines, and other small fish, as well as squid. Though they dispatch their victims one by one, they can carry as many as 20 small fish crosswise in their brightly colored beaks.

Atlantic puffins ply the cold waters off Canada and New England. Their western cousins, the horned and the tufted puffins—named for their eye ornaments and head plumes—are at home in the North Pacific. All remain at sea in winter, returning to land only during the breeding season.

Puffins often nest in well-populated colonies usually on remote, rugged islands free from egg- and chick-eating land predators. They deposit a single egg deep within a burrow excavated in soft earth, or in a feather- or grass-lined lair in a rocky cleft. After fattening up their hatchling on fish, the parents return to the sea. The young puffins, still unable to fly, eventually scramble to the shore by night and plunge into the water.

Pyrite

Known as fool's gold, pyrite is a shiny yellow metal that has tricked many a prospector. In fact, its striated crystals do sometimes occur in gold-laden veins. Pyrite is found in Yukon, the Northwest Territories, Ontario, Newfoundland and many other North American locations.

Q

Mountain quail

Gambel's quail

Scaled quail

California quail

Quails are monogamous upland game birds that live on open farmlands, deserts, and plains, as well as in forests. Ranging from small to medium in size, most species are less than 12 inches long.

Quack grass *Agropyron repens*

A native of Europe, quack grass—also known as quick grass and couch grass—is an immigrant that thrives in fields and waste places all across the continent. Three to four feet tall with narrow leaves and erect flower spikes, it spreads rapidly by means of underground stems. Since quack grass is difficult to eradicate, most farmers consider it an aggressive weed. It can, however, be harvested as hay, and it helps anchor the soil against erosion.

Quahog *Mercenaria mercenaria*

Hard-shelled clams, or quahogs, are among the most popular shellfish with seafood fanciers along the East Coast. Small ones are savored as littlenecks, slightly bigger ones are called cher-

rystones, and the largest are diced for clam chowder. Their strong, hinged shells—gray and conspicuously ridged on the outside, but smooth and white or purplish within—were fashioned into wampum and used as currency by aboriginal peoples.

These bivalves live buried in the sand or mud, with a pair of tubelike siphons exposed. They feed by drawing water into one siphon, filtering out edible morsels, then expelling the water.

Quail

Small chickenlike creatures less than 12 inches long, these relatives of grouse and pheasants are among North America's most beautiful birds. The males wear bold, attractive patterns, while the females, though more subdued, look enough like their mates to be easily recognized.

Clear, colorless quartz crystals not only make lovely gemstones, but the mineral is also the basic ingredient of the sand on our beaches.

Queen Anne's lace, found from coast to coast across North America, blooms in the summer. As the flat flower heads age, they form cups that look like tiny bird's nests, with the seeds ripening inside.

Quails form pairs in spring, when the male's loud calls advertise his territory. In some species only the female builds the nest and incubates the clutch of 10 or more eggs, but the male always assists in rearing the chicks. The family remains together, often joining other families to form large coveys in winter.

The only eastern quail is the northern bobwhite, named for its whistled call. The bird is not migratory and, since severe winters can destroy whole bobtail populations, it is seldom seen in Canada. The most familiar western species, the California quail, sports a jaunty black head plume. Gambel's quail, at home on southwestern deserts, has a similar topknot. Another southwesterner, the secretive Montezuma quail, hugs the ground and slips away when danger threatens. Sometimes, however, it just freezes on the spot, a habit that has earned it the nickname fool quail.

Quartz

Hard and durable, quartz is one of the most common rock-forming minerals. Composed of silica, it is also the basic component of beach sand. Pure quartz is clear and colorless, but impurities yield a whole range of colors. Among the many kinds of quartz are prized gem-quality crystals such as amethyst and citrine; agate, which has wavy bands of color; and chalcedony, a translucent, waxy variety. Of great economic importance, quartz sand is used in glassmaking; sandstone and other rocks formed of quartz are valuable building stones; and quartz crystals are used in watches and electronic equipment.

Queen Anne's lace *Daucus carota*

Recognized by its familiar flowers that brighten fields and roadsides with splashes of white, Queen Anne's lace is also called wild carrot. In fact, this biennial, a member of the parsley family, is the ancestor of the garden carrot. The flower head that appears atop each stem is actually composed of many tiny blooms—one three-inch flower head may contain thousands of florets. A single red-purple bloom often appears at the center of the white florets. According to legend, it symbolizes the blood of Queen Anne of Great Britain, who pricked her finger while making lace. It is a tale that not only gives the summertime bloom its name but at the same time recalls the plant's old-world origins.

Quicksand

Folklore, films, and fiction are filled with tales of hapless travelers who step into quicksand and are slowly sucked down into a soupy grave. But while quicksand is quite real and can cause death, the stories about its dangers are somewhat exaggerated.

Simply a mixture of sand and water, quicksand is found in places where groundwater flows up through loose sand. Objects heavier than water sink in it, but it does not suck them down. It is possible to escape quicksand either by being pulled to safety or by discarding heavy objects such as backpacks, lying on the back with arms and legs spread out to distribute body weight, and slowly rolling to solid ground.

311

Eastern cottontails' enemies include hawks, owls, cats, and human hunters.

The rabbitbrushes' aromatic wood and bark are chewed like gum by the Paiute Indians.

R

Rabbit *Sylvilagus*

Furry mammals with long ears, short, fluffy tails, and long hind legs for hopping, rabbits flourish all across the continent. In contrast to the larger, longer-eared hares, rabbits bear young that are naked and blind, while those of jackrabbits and other hares are fully furred and have their eyes wide open at birth.

Rabbits live in a broad range of habitats, from forests and swamps to dry brush country and suburban areas. The most widespread species, the eastern cottontail, is found virtually everywhere east of the Rockies. Like other rabbits, it is active from dusk to dawn, feeding on green plants in summer and on bark and twigs in winter. The 10-inch pygmy rabbit, which lives among the sagebrush in the Great Basin, is the only species with gray instead of white on the underside of its tail.

The pygmy rabbit digs tunnels for nesting, but most others nest in shallow, fur-lined depressions among grass, shrubs, or leaves. Females give birth to as many as four litters a year, with up to seven young in each. Able to leave the nest within two weeks, the young can reproduce when they are less than six months old.

Rabbitbrush *Chrysothamnus*

Abundant in the western United States, the rabbitbrushes are hardy shrubs found on deserts, plains, and mountain slopes. Though some species grow 12 feet tall, most are compact bushes 1 to 3 feet in height. In late summer the plants are covered with dense clusters of small flowers that tint the land with a golden haze. The narrow, pointed leaves, though often pungently aromatic, are nevertheless eaten by rabbits, deer, and other wildlife. Because of their tolerance for salty and disturbed soil, rabbitbrushes are useful for erosion control, and one species shows promise as a source of rubber.

Raccoon *Procyon lotor*

Easily recognized by their bushy, ringed tails and the black masks across the eyes, raccoons are familiar mammals across most of southern Canada and the United States. Stocky yet agile, they are good climbers and swimmers that den in hollow trees and spend the night foraging.

Raccoons are adept at catching fish, frogs, and crayfish by groping in the shallows of swamps and streams with their remarkably dexterous forepaws. (The tendency of captive individuals to wash their food is probably not an act of cleanliness but a reflection of the fact that wild raccoons find so much of their food in water.) Adaptable omnivores, raccoons also relish birds, mice, insects, earthworms, fruits, nuts, and just about anything else that is edible.

Because of their eclectic appetites, raccoons sometimes earn a reputation as pests. Gardeners and farmers regret their taste for corn, and conservationists deplore their fondness for loon eggs. And when the masked marauders move from the wilds into the suburbs, they soon become skilled at raiding garbage cans.

Though not true hibernators, raccoons sleep through much of the winter. By February, however, the mating urge sends the males out regardless of the weather. Nine weeks later each female bears three to six kits. Educated by their mothers in the warm months, they enter their first winter well trained for life on their own.

Racer *Coluber constrictor*

A swift, slender snake up to six feet long, the racer glides through its grassy or wooded haunts with its head held high off the ground. If chased, it often climbs into bushes or small trees, and when cornered, it strikes repeatedly while vibrating its tail. If it is in dried vegetation, the resulting sound is easily mistaken for a rattlesnake's rattle. Nonpoisonous, the racer seizes

Racers can move as fast as an adult human walking at a brisk pace.

Some raccoons are no bigger than stocky cats, but large males can grow over three feet long and weigh more than 40 pounds.

The reclusive sora, our commonest rail, is known for its plaintive, whinnying call; it is more likely to be heard than seen.

mice and other small prey, which it swallows whole. Although only one species is found in North America, its color and markings differ dramatically from region to region.

Radon

Colorless, odorless, tasteless—and radioactive—radon is a gas produced by the gradual decay of uranium, which is present in small quantities in rocks and soil. Outdoors it occurs in low, harmless concentrations. But the gas sometimes seeps into housing, where it can reach levels hazardous to human health. While some areas, such as eastern Pennsylvania, are radon hot spots, contamination zones are found throughout Canada and the United States.

Ragweed *Ambrosia*

Though numbingly ordinary in appearance, the ragweeds are an extraordinary menace to hay fever sufferers. Their spikes of inconspicuous greenish-yellow flowers produce billions of pollen grains, which in late summer are carried by the wind not only to other ragweeds, where they enable the plants to set seed, but to the noses and throats of millions of allergic humans. Viewed through an electron microscope, the pollen, covered with nasty hooks and spines, looks just as troublesome as it actually is.

Of several native ragweeds, which flourish in vacant lots and neglected fields all across the continent, two are most abundant. Common ragweed, with finely cut, fernlike leaves, reaches a modest height of one to four feet. Giant ragweed, with leaves divided into three to five broad lobes, grows up to 15 feet tall.

Rail

More often heard than seen, rails are secretive marsh birds that prefer to stay hidden among reeds and grasses. When pursued, they are more likely to run than fly, taking advantage of their slender shape, long legs, and large feet to slip away through dense vegetation.

Rails build bulky nests on the ground or among reeds over water, usually concealing them under a canopy of surrounding plants. The downy black chicks follow their parents through the marsh in search of insects, worms, snails, and seeds.

The Virginia rail and the sora—both robin-size birds of freshwater marshes—are the most common and widespread in North America. The Virginia rail has a long, thin bill and a grating call, while the sora's bill is stubby and yellow and its calls include a medley of whinnying and piping notes. The king rail of freshwater marshes and the clapper rail of salt marshes resemble the Virginia rail but are twice its size.

A rainbow arching above the horizon adds a note of exquisite drama to a brooding Arctic sky.

Rainbow

Whether seen nearby in the spray of a garden hose or miles away on the clouds of a distant rainstorm, the multicolored arcs we call rainbows are produced in the same way. Myriads of water droplets act as tiny prisms that bend sunlight into its spectrum of colors. The backs of the droplets then reflect the colored light back to our eyes. Since the light is bent at a slightly different angle for each color, we see bands of red, orange, yellow, green, blue, and violet.

Rain forest

Although the term rain forest usually conjures up images of lush tropical jungles, North America also boasts a unique temperate rain forest—a ribbon of incredibly luxuriant vegetation along the coast from northern California to the Alaska panhandle. Where moist winds from the Pacific Ocean meet the coast ranges, rain and snow fall in abundance. A continual dousing of up to 200 inches of precipitation each year results in a phenomenal growth of trees and shrubs. Conifers such as Sitka spruces, western hemlocks, and western red cedars tower to heights of 200 feet or more and often have trunks over 10 feet in diameter. Beneath this canopy flourishes a rich mix of bigleaf maples, alders, and other hardwood trees; shrubs such as blueberries and elderberries; and in places, a lush carpet of ferns, mosses, and club mosses. A wealth of wildlife, from bald eagles to deer and elk, also finds a haven in this magnificent forest.

Rain shadow

Just as mountains cast shadows by blocking sunlight, they can also create so-called rain shadows by preventing moisture in the air from reaching their leeward side. When moist air blows against a

In the temperate rain forest bigleaf maples and other trees, draped with thick mantles of moss, filter the light of the sun, creating a soft greenish glow throughout the forest.

mountain range, it is forced upward. The air cools as it rises, and the moisture condenses and falls as rain or snow on the windward slopes. Once the air has crossed the mountains, it descends and warms up. By now it not only is too dry to produce rainfall, it also evaporates moisture from the leeward land, creating very arid conditions. In Vancouver Island, in British Columbia's lower mainland, and in Washington State, for example, the coastal fringe receives over 100 inches of rain per year, while the area east of the lofty Cascade Mountains gets barely 10 inches. Since rain shadows create such dry conditions, they play a major role in the formation of deserts.

Rapids on the Gallatin River in Montana present a turbulent challenge for rafting enthusiasts. But the massive boulders and hidden rocks that produce the roiling "white water" are a major hazard.

Wood rats, which feed on fruit, seeds, and nuts, live alone in rocky crevices. They often clutter their nests with found objects.

Rapids

Rapids—areas where water flows quickly over a rocky, uneven streambed—can be formed where large chunks of debris block a watercourse or where rivers flow down steep slopes or across ledges of erosion-resistant rock. Because they are navigational hazards, these stretches of shallow, turbulent water often must be circumvented by man-made waterways; the "Soo" (Sault Ste. Marie) Canals, for instance, bypass the rapids between Lake Superior and Lake Huron. Whether the rapids occur in mighty rivers or modest streams, their well-aerated water is home to a surprising variety of life, from microscopic plants to insect larvae, equipped with all manner of hooks and suckers for clinging to the rocks. Rapids provide sheer beauty, too, a fact confirmed by just one view of the rushing Colorado River in the Grand Canyon.

Raspberry *Rubus*

From woodlands and waste places in the East to canyons and moist slopes in the West, the delectable, thimble-shaped fruits of wild raspberries provide welcome snacks for hikers and are also harvested for jams and other treats. Many kinds of wildlife relish the fruits as well and find cover among the thickets of prickly, arching canes. The plants' five-petaled blossoms are similar to wild roses, which is hardly surprising, since the raspberries, like their kin the dewberries and blackberries, are members of the rose family.

Rat

Looking much like overgrown mice, rats are furry rodents with pointed snouts and long tails. The most familiar are the Norway rat and the black rat, introduced from the Old World. Aggressive, adaptable, and prolific, these rats have plagued mankind for centuries, infesting barns and dwellings and causing substantial damage.

A number of North America's native rodents are also called rats. More closely related to mice and voles than to the old-world rats, they include cotton rats, rice rats, and wood rats. They thrive in all sorts of habitats, from sun-parched deserts to temperate rain forests, feeding on everything from grain to bird eggs. They also vary dramatically in their habits. The kangaroo rat, for instance, hops about kangaroo-style on its hind legs, while the muskrat is a large, aquatic member of the vole family.

Rat snake *Elaphe*

Agile, powerful predators that kill by constriction, rat snakes have an appetite for rats that has earned them the gratitude of farmers from southern Canada to Mexico. The various species also eat mice, frogs, and lizards and are at home in woodlands, swamps, and farmlands. While rat snakes usually forage on the ground, they are experts at climbing trees in search of birds and their eggs. When threatened, they rear up, vibrate their tails, and hiss menacingly. Up to eight feet long, some species are quite colorful.

315

Sidewinders, desert rattlesnakes, leave telltale J-shaped tracks.

Ravens, intelligent birds, have occasionally been tamed and taught to mimic human speech.

R

A spotted eagle ray dives gracefully toward the ocean bottom to search for shellfish.

Rattlesnake

Rattlesnakes are venomous pit vipers well known for their trademark warning device: hollow, horny segments at the tip of the tail that are loosely connected and produce a buzzing sound when vibrated. A new rattle is added each time the snake sheds its skin, but they are easily broken off and so, contrary to folklore, offer no clue to the snake's age. Rattlesnakes range in length from a mere 18 inches (the diminutive pygmy rattlesnake) to a record 8 feet (the eastern diamondback).

Most rattlesnakes live in arid areas of the U.S. West and feed on small mammals, birds, and lizards. Timber rattlers, one of the few species found in the eastern United States, often hibernate in large groups in caves and rocky crevices. Like other rattlesnakes, they bear live young in broods of a dozen or more. Other common species include the large and colorful western diamondback and the sidewinder, noted for its unusual looping locomotion.

Raven *Corvus*

Large, glossy black birds with thick bills, ravens make deep croaking sounds rather than the familiar caws of their smaller cousins the crows. Ravens also prefer wilder places than crows and are most likely to be seen near rocky hills, seaside cliffs, and remote areas of the Far North. Ravens are primarily scavengers but also feed on insects, clams, worms, and even young birds. Like crows, they are extremely intelligent.

The more widespread of two species, the common raven, is found all across Canada and much of the western United States. (Some isolated populations also manage to thrive in the Appalachians.) The smaller Chihuahuan raven, formerly known as the white-necked raven, lives in the arid U.S. Southwest.

Ray

Like sharks, rays are primitive fish with skeletons of cartilage rather than bone. They are distinguished by their broad, flattened bodies, which are extended by enlarged, winglike pectoral fins. The biggest ray, the manta, has "wings" that are more than 20 feet across. Occurring in both the Atlantic and Pacific oceans, rays live for the most part on the seafloor, where they feed on shellfish and crustaceans. Although most species are harmless, the electric ray produces powerful shocks both to stun prey and to defend itself, while the stingray can deliver painful blows with its venomous tail spine. Most rays give birth to live young, but skates lay eggs in horny capsules known as mermaid's purses.

Razor clam

Mollusks found in shallows along the seashores of both coasts, razor clams, also known as jackknife clams, are easily recognized by their distinctive shells. Long, narrow, and blunt on both ends, they look much like old-fashioned straight razors. Most species dig into the sand and mud

Redbuds, prized for their display of delicate pink blossoms, enliven woodlands in early spring.

Redwoods, the titans of coastal forests, thrive in cool, moist regions near the Pacific Ocean. Their trunks are sheathed in thick, fire-resistant bark.

on the ocean floor and, like other clams, feed by filtering protozoans and organic particles from the water. Members of the family vary considerably in size; the West Coast's rosy razor clam is 1 to 3 inches in length, while the common razor clam of the Atlantic grows up to 10 inches long.

Redbud *Cercis*

Small, elegant, and valued as ornamentals, redbuds are among the first flowering trees to bloom in spring, when they are covered with purplish pink blossoms even before their leaves unfurl. The flowers—delicate and reminiscent of sweetpeas—grow in clusters all along the older branches and even sprout from the trunk. The fruits that follow are flat, beanlike pods containing shiny brown seeds.

Two species are native to North America. The eastern redbud, found in moist soils and along stream banks in the eastern half of the United States, has large heart-shaped leaves and seldom exceeds 25 feet in height. The smaller, shrubbier California redbud, which grows on dry hillsides and along mountain streams in the U.S. West, has leaves that are more rounded.

Redpoll *Carduelis*

These robust little finches with red caps and black chins breed in the Far North, but in winter twittering flocks of redpolls venture south as far as Missouri and Virginia. They feed on seeds, especially those of birches and alders, knocking them from the catkins and picking them off the ground. When dusk approaches or severe weather threatens, redpolls store seeds in tiny throat pouches, an adaptation that allows them to take cover and eat at their leisure. During incubation, the females, which lay five to seven eggs, are fed by their rosy-breasted mates.

Redwood *Sequoia sempervirens*

Redwoods are nature's skyscrapers, the tallest trees of all. Splendid 275-foot giants are not uncommon, and the loftiest living specimen, at 368 feet, is the tallest known tree in the world. Redwoods take four or five centuries to mature, and survive easily twice that long. As they age, the lower branches fall away, leaving stately trunks that are 15 feet or more in diameter and sheathed in bark up to 1 foot thick. The foliage of these titans is surprisingly delicate; the flattened needles lying in two rows along the twigs are only half an inch long. The seed-laden cones are also small—about one inch long.

Redwoods thrive only along the Pacific Coast from central California to southern Oregon, flourishing in the areas where summer fog rolls in regularly from the ocean. The reddish, straight-grained wood is light, splits and cuts easily, and resists insects and decay better than almost any other timber, making redwoods highly desirable for home building, outdoor furniture, water tanks, and railway ties.

Reed grass has stiff stems that have been used to thatch roofs and weave mats.

Reptiles can be as different as a sluggish box turtle and a nimble fringe-toed lizard, but all are cold-blooded, breathe with lungs, and have dry, scaly skins.

Regeneration is most astonishing among invertebrates such as this starfish, which has begun to grow back a missing arm.

Reed grass *Phragmites communis*

Growing in dense patches and attaining heights of up to 15 feet, reed grass is a common sight in marshes, in brackish estuaries, and along damp roadsides. The upright stems of the giant grass, topped with brown to purplish plumes of tiny flowers and long, silky hairs, are a pretty sight swaying in the breeze. But the flowers rarely produce seed; instead, reed grass spreads by means of creeping underground stems that are sometimes more than 30 feet long.

Regeneration

A crayfish that loses a claw and grows a new one is demonstrating regeneration—the ability to replace lost body parts. Commonest among invertebrates, regeneration can be quite dramatic

in certain worms and sponges: when they are cut into pieces, each one grows into a new individual. While salamanders can grow new limbs and lizards new tails, regeneration is limited in vertebrates. Humans, for example, can replace skin, hair, nails, and liver tissue, but little else.

Remora

These oceangoing hitchhikers, also known as sharksuckers, get their nickname from the suction disks on the tops of their flat heads. The fish use the disks to cling to sharks, barracudas, turtles, whales, and other hosts and so travel effortlessly through tropical and temperate seas. Some species prefer specific hosts, while others are less choosy about their transportation. Up to three feet long, remoras eat scraps dropped by their hosts but can also forage on their own: detaching themselves with a sliding motion, the fish join other remoras in pursuit of prey.

Reptile

Snakes, lizards, turtles, and crocodilians all belong to the class of animals known as reptiles. Of the 275 or so species found in North America, there are about 115 kinds each of snakes and lizards, nearly 50 turtles, and just 2 crocodilians (the American alligator and the American crocodile).

No single trait distinguishes reptiles from all other creatures, as do the feathers of birds or the

Rhododendrons, elegant shrubs used in landscaping, form dense thickets on moist mountains slopes.

Rhyolite, spewed from ancient volcanoes, has been sculpted into spectacular shapes at Chiricahua National Monument, Arizona. Identical in composition to granite, it is less resistant to weathering.

hair of mammals. But all are cold-blooded vertebrates that breathe with lungs rather than gills and have dry, scaly skins. Lizards and snakes are covered with scales that overlap like the shingles on a roof, while turtles and crocodilians wear a covering of larger adjoining plates. Both scales and plates conserve moisture and serve as suits of armor that protect against predators.

Unlike birds and mammals, which have their own built-in thermostats, reptiles cannot regulate their body temperature internally. Since excessive cold makes them sluggish, many must bask in the morning sun before they begin moving about. Those that live in deserts, however, often have to take refuge in the shade or in burrows to escape the scorching midday sun.

In contrast to amphibians, which depend on water to reproduce, all reptiles breed on land. Though most species lay eggs, some give birth to live young. Unlike salamanders and frogs, which go through a larval stage, young reptiles look like miniature versions of the adults.

Rhododendron *Rhododendron*

Natives of cool, moist regions, rhododendrons form dense thickets on rocky hillsides and along stream banks in the Northeast and Pacific Northwest. On high mountain slopes they also range south into Georgia and Alabama. Some of the 20 or so wild rhododendron species are in bloom from April into July, bearing showy clusters of five-lobed, bell-shaped blossoms of white, pink, or purple touched with spots of green, yellow, or brown. The shrubs range in size from the 16-inch-tall Lapland rosebay, found in Alaska, to the treelike rosebay rhododendron of the Appalachians, which can grow to a height of 40 feet. Rhododendrons typically have oval leathery leaves that are dark green and

glossy on the upper surface. Up to 10 inches long, the leaves persist through the winter, curling into cylinders in cold weather to prevent loss of moisture.

Rhyolite

An igneous rock with the same composition as granite, rhyolite is formed from viscous lavas that erupted from volcanoes or squeezed through fissures in older rock. Light-colored and fine-grained, rhyolite contains quartz and feldspar, with flecks of mica and other minerals. Frothy, gas-filled flows of rhyolite form the spongy rock known as pumice. The shiny black volcanic glass called obsidian results when lava of the same chemical composition cools too rapidly for individual crystals to form.

Rice, wild *Zizania aquatica*

Though both wild rice and true rice, like most cultivated grains, are members of the grass family, the two are only distantly related. The wild species is a tall, reedlike aquatic plant that once flourished in still, shallow waters from the Great Lakes south to Texas but now is confined mainly to parts of Ontario and Manitoba and northern Minnesota and Wisconsin. The plants, up to 10 feet tall, are anchored in the bottom mud in water up to 6 feet deep. Long, narrow leaves are scattered along the stems, which in summer are topped with foot-long plumes of tiny green or purplish flowers. The seeds—thin, black, protein-rich kernels that ripen in the fall—have for generations been a mainstay of Indian tribes, such as the Ojibwa and Chippewa. Indians still harvest the crop each year by shaking the ripe grains into their canoes. Today, however, most wild rice comes from cultivated paddies.

319

River otters are gregarious, fun-loving animals that seem to spend as much time romping and playing as they do hunting and fishing. Not even a deep covering of snow will deter them from sliding down riverbanks and plunging into the icy water.

Ringtails, smaller and more agile than raccoons, are usually found in wooded, rocky parts of the U.S. Southwest. During the day, a long, bushy tail dangling from a high branch may betray the presence of a dozing ringtail.

Rice rat *Oryzomys palustris*

Small rodents of wet places in the U.S. Southeast, marsh rice rats got their name from their fondness for the shoots and seeds of rice. Able swimmers and divers, they also feed on crayfish, clams, and other aquatic vegetation. Several litters are born each year, with the young leaving the nest in seven weeks. Since females are by then able to breed, their numbers increase quickly where food is plentiful and predators, such as hawks, are scarce.

Ringtail *Bassariscus astutus*

A long, bushy tail banded in black and white and a sharply pointed snout make this shy relative of the raccoon easy to identify—if you manage to spot one. Active mainly at night, the ringtail is an agile climber that often sleeps the day away in trees. It also likes rough, rocky places, where it moves easily along the most pre-

cipitous ledges. Wherever it settles down, preferably near water, the ringtail feeds on small mammals, birds, insects, and fruits. Born in late spring, the young are tended by both parents.

The ringtail's alternate name, cacomistle, is derived from Indian words for "half" and "mountain lion." Its nickname, miner's cat, can be traced to the fact that it was once kept in mines to control rodent populations.

Rip current

A real danger to swimmers and surfers, rip currents are fast-moving, narrow streams of water that flow to sea from land. They form along seacoasts where waves strike the shore at an angle; there water from successive waves builds up until it escapes by rushing seaward in a sudden surge. Since rip currents are narrow, experts recommend that swimmers not fight them but swim parallel to the shore until safely beyond their pull.

Roadrunners— running swiftly on long, sturdy legs, with necks outstretched— chase lizards and other prey. Desert dwellers, they build cup-shaped nests of sticks in low trees or among clumps of cacti. The four to six eggs are incubated mainly by the males.

R

Robber flies seize damselflies and other insects in their spiny legs, then stab the victims with their sharp mouthparts.

River See pp. 322–323.

River otter *Lutra canadensis*

With dense, sleek fur, webbed feet, and a layer of insulating fat under the skin, these playful, appealing members of the weasel family are well suited for aquatic life. Streamlined swimmers with powerful tails that help propel them through the water, otters can travel as far as a quarter of a mile before surfacing to breathe. They live in lakes, rivers, and marshes, where they eat fish, frogs, crayfish, and other prey.

Born in burrows or in abandoned muskrat or beaver lodges, otter pups are helpless and blind at first; but when they are several months old, their mothers teach them how to swim, dive, and hunt. The fathers begin to assist in the pups' schooling in about the sixth month. The sociable family group is often joined by others to to-boggan in the snow, slide down muddy riverbanks, or frolic in the water, occasionally "talking" to each other with a varied repertoire of growls, chirps, and squeals.

Roadrunner *Geococcyx californianus*

Comical in both appearance and behavior, the greater roadrunner, North America's only species, is an entertaining bird to watch. An inhabitant of dry country in the Southwest, the two-foot-long ground-dwelling cuckoo is a bit disheveled looking, with a shaggy crest, wings that seem too short, and a bill and tail that seem too long. The bird can coo like a dove or crow like a cock, and it would rather run than fly. It moves along furtively, pausing to peer about, until it spots a lizard. Then the roadrunner gives chase, sprinting forward at up to 15 miles an hour until it nabs its prey. Holding the lizard in its bill, the bird whacks it against a rock and then swallows it whole. Other meals consist of snakes, scorpions, crickets, mice, and even small birds snatched from the air as they fly by. Honored as the state bird of New Mexico, the roadrunner is also known by such names as snake killer and chaparral cock.

Robber fly

Also known as assassin flies, robber flies are formidable predators that ambush other insects on the wing. They perch watchfully until a prospective meal flies by, then give chase. Capturing their prey with their long, spiny legs, they suck the bodies dry. Big-eyed and bristle-faced, some robber flies are long and slender, while others are as stout as bumblebees. Each species has a characteristic hunting ground—some, for example, the grass; others, the beach.

RIVER

With stretches of roaring white water as well as placid, slow-moving sections that meander across plains to terminate in brackish estuaries, rivers change in character as they make their way from their upland sources to the sea. Their inhabitants change too, for the plants and animals that thrive in swift currents are quite different from those that prefer to live in lazier waters.

The clear, fast-moving rivers that rush down hills and mountains are home to creatures adapted for survival in strong currents. Crayfish hide under rocks; salamanders attach their sticky eggs to fallen logs; insect larvae anchor themselves with hooks, claws, suckers, or cement; and trout and salmon, their bodies streamlined, manage to hold their own against the current and even swim upstream.

In quieter waters the wildlife is more like that of marshes, lakes, and ponds. Water lilies, pondweeds, and numerous other plants thrive in the relatively warm, slow-moving water, and a variety of birds and mammals come to feed on the river's abundant supply of insects, reptiles, fish, amphibians, and crustaceans.

Mountain rivers become torrential in spring, when they are swollen by melting ice and snow.

Male wood ducks have superb breeding plumage. The birds nest in tree cavities.

Great blue herons are stealthy waders, snapping up fish and frogs with their scissorlike bills.

Manatees, gentle plant-eating mammals that live in the brackish estuaries of Florida, are now endangered.

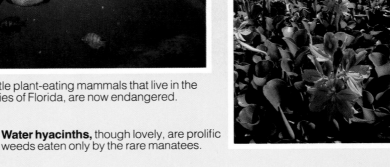

Water hyacinths, though lovely, are prolific weeds eaten only by the rare manatees.

Fast-flowing rivers often harbor trout, salmon, crayfish, and aquatic insects, but except for algae and mosses, few plants can survive the strong currents.

River otters, among the most playful of mammals, are active throughout the year and feed on fish and frogs.

Bald eagles, which gather in large numbers on Alaska's Chilkat River, are never far from water. Feeding on fish, carrion, and even other birds, bald eagles are also known for stealing meals from their cousins the ospreys.

Sandhill cranes perform spectacular dances both in and out of the mating season. Bowing, skipping, and leaping high into the air, hundreds of birds at a time may join in the ballet.

Rodents, the world's most abundant mammals, are well adapted for a variety of tasks and habitats. Some, such as least chipmunks (right), have dexterous, handlike forepaws; marmots (below left) post sentries at their grazing grounds to stand guard while the others feed. Porcupines (below right) fend off aggressors with a bristling armor of barbed quills.

R

Robins, often seen pulling worms from the ground, also feed on fruits and insects.

Robin *Turdus migratorius*

Easily recognized by its reddish-orange breast, the American robin has adapted handily to life in suburban gardens and city parks and is now more abundant in settled areas than in its ancestral woodland habitat. Each spring it builds a grass-lined, cup-shaped nest cemented together with mud. Although trees are the favored site for nests, they also appear on windowsills and other ledges on buildings. When the robin's delicate blue eggs hatch, both parents tend the nestlings. As the chicks grow older, the female begins laying a second clutch of eggs, and the male takes over nursery duty, feeding the young a diet of earthworms, insects, and fruit.

To winter-weary Canadians, robins are often the harbingers of spring. In the United States, many do migrate early in the season, but others remain in the northern states throughout the winter, living on berries in sheltered places.

Rock

Rocks, composed of one or more minerals, are the solid materials that make up the earth's crust. They are an ingredient of soil and provide us with building materials, valuable ores, and a great deal more. They also hold important clues to the history of the planet.

Rocks are divided into three major groups—igneous, sedimentary, and metamorphic—depending on the way in which they were formed. Igneous rocks solidified from molten magma. Coarse-grained varieties, such as granite, cooled slowly deep within the crust. Denser types, such

Wild roses, the floral emblem of Alberta, often form dense thickets in fields and fencerows, providing cover for a variety of wildlife. Long the symbols of luxury and love, roses also have practical value: their nutritious hips, rich in vitamin C, are widely used in dietary supplements.

as basalt, are volcanic and cooled quickly at or near the earth's surface.

Sedimentary rocks consist of material deposited by natural processes, such as windblown sand, decaying plant or animal matter, and chemicals precipitated from water. Over long periods of time, the material accumulated in layers and was compacted into rock. Examples include sandstone, composed of eroded sediments cemented into dense beds; and limestone, layers of calcium carbonate, often containing fossils.

Metamorphic rocks form when sedimentary or igneous rocks are altered by heat or pressure. Marble, a popular building stone, forms from limestone; and slate, a roofing tile, from shale.

Rocky shore See pp. 326–327.

Rodent

Rodents are the most numerous mammals in the world. In North America they comprise some 200 species—about half of all our mammals—and range in size from the pygmy mouse, which is four inches long, including its tail, to the beaver, which reaches a length of four feet and can weigh 60 pounds. Among the most familiar rodents are chipmunks, squirrels, mice, voles, rats, lemmings, gophers, and porcupines.

Some rodent populations are huge. (As many as 400 voles, for example, may inhabit a single acre.) In part this is because many rodents breed year-round. Moreover, seeds, their principal food, are plentiful in most habitats. Another secret of their success is their distinctive, chisel-like incisors. These teeth, one pair on each jaw, keep growing throughout the rodent's life. As the animal gnaws, its incisors are constantly renewed and sharpened, making them ideally suited for opening nuts and tough seed coats.

The success of rodents is a mixed blessing. Some carry diseases, and many cause considerable damage to crops and property. But rodents are also the mainstay in the diets of a host of other animals.

Rose *Rosa*

Though virtually all of our garden roses are descended from European or Asian ancestors, North America is richly endowed with native wild roses—some 170 species by one count. They include the arctic rose, a three-foot-tall prickly shrub of the Far North with deep pink flowers; the widespread pasture rose, with delicate, rosy-red blooms; and the prairie rose, a four- to six-foot shrub with arching canes and pale to dark pink blossoms. Wild roses typically have hooked thorns or needlelike prickles; compound leaves with 3 to 11 toothed leaflets; and fragrant, five-petaled flowers. After their season of bloom, usually in late spring, roses produce hips, fleshy orange fruits filled with seeds. Rich in vitamin C, wild rose hips are harvested for making jam and tea.

Rosinweed *Silphium*

Resembling sunflowers in appearance, the rosinweeds are coarse, vigorous wildflowers that grow up to 10 feet tall and are most common on the Prairies. Their yellow flower heads, two to five inches across, are borne atop stems filled with the resinous sap for which the plants were named. The paired leaves of one species, the cup plant, join at the stem to form cups, while those at the base of the aptly named compass plant almost always point north and south.

Rush *Juncus*

Found in marshes and wet meadows, rushes are grasslike plants that have long cylindrical stems with clusters of tiny flowers near the top. People used to fashion the stems into rope, baskets, mats, and chair seats. When stripped of their skin and dipped in fat, the stems' pithy cores also served as wicks for crude candles called rushlights. Though a few other plants, such as bulrushes, scouring rushes, and spikerushes, borrowed the name, they are not true rushes.

The rocky coast of Big Sur, California, a popular tourist attraction, features dramatic headlands, pounding surf, deep coves, and sheltered beaches.

ROCKY SHORE

Dramatic, jagged cliffs rising straight out of the sea; colorful, kelp-draped rocks; and clouds of salty mist sprayed from seething surf—these are all features of the rocky shore. Here seabirds nest among rugged crags; sea otters dive and frolic in the waves; and tufts of seaweed soften the contours of wave-cut rocks.

As the tide recedes, a series of life zones is revealed. Blue-green algae and lichens grow in the uppermost zone, where snails called periwinkles cling to cliffs that are moistened only by the splashing of the waves. Rubbery strands of branching, ribbonlike rockweeds cushion the barnacle-encrusted rocks of the intertidal zone,

which is alternately washed by the waves and exposed to the air. In the lowest zone, laid bare only by the lowest tides, sea urchins and starfish live in jungles of leathery kelp and other seaweeds. When the waves recede, tide pools are left behind among the rocks. They are often filled with a surprising array of life, from sea anemones to sponges.

On the Pacific Coast, sculpted cliffs shelter nesting seabirds, while sea lions bask on the rocks below. The rocky coast of the Northeast, shaped by glaciers as well as the steady assault of the sea, is dotted by islands and incised with deep bays and quiet coves.

Sea lion pups bask atop rocks on the Pacific Coast. Noisy and playful, they are well-loved circus performers.

Sea anemones and acorn barnacles ornament tide pools.

326

Kelp and other seaweeds hold fast to wave-splashed rocks.

Sea otters sleep and eat among kelp beds, tethering themselves with the weeds to keep from drifting.

Chitons, common on rocky coasts, creep about at night to feed on algae.

Murres return to the same nesting sites year after year and lay their eggs on bare rock.

Rough limpets cling so tightly that they can survive a battering by the strongest waves.

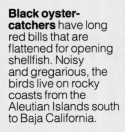

Black oyster-catchers have long red bills that are flattened for opening shellfish. Noisy and gregarious, the birds live on rocky coasts from the Aleutian Islands south to Baja California.

Sages, such as the scarlet sage (left) and thistle sage (right), prefer dry, sandy soils.

S

Saber-toothed cats roamed North America thousands of years ago hunting large plant-eating animals, especially mastodons. But just as those elephantlike creatures became extinct, so too did the saber-tooths, perhaps falling victim to a profound climatic change.

Saber-toothed cat *Smilodon*

Also known as saber-toothed tigers, these long-extinct carnivores were giant members of the cat family. Larger than lions, with powerful neck and shoulder muscles and two enormous fangs, saber-toothed cats must have been terrifying creatures to behold. They probably used their eight-inch-long, daggerlike teeth to rip open the bellies or slash the throats of mammoths, giant ground sloths, and other prey.

Once widespread in North America, the saber-tooths died out over 10,000 years ago. The remains of hundreds have been discovered in the La Brea tar pits in California; the beasts most likely were lured there by struggling animals that were about to perish in the tar.

Sage *Salvia*

Relatives of the familiar culinary herb, the wild sages range from low-growing annuals to substantial shrubs. They all bear two-lipped tubular flowers, usually in clusters along the stems, which, like the stems of others in the mint family, are square in cross-section. Various wild sages bloom throughout the summer, tinting fields and roadsides with shades of violet, blue, red, and pink. Chia, a blue-flowered western species, yields small, nutritious seeds that aboriginal peoples ground into flour. Other kinds have been used medicinally for everything from flesh wounds to digestive problems.

Sagebrush *Artemisia*

Plants of contrasts, the sagebrushes have a spicy odor that belies their bitter taste. Cattle shun the shrubs, and so they spread over western plains and foothills wherever overgrazing has damaged the land. Big sagebrush, the most common species, ranges from 3 to over 12 feet in height, depending on growing conditions. It has small, wedge-shaped leaves that end in three rounded teeth, and bears clusters of tiny yellow flowers on the twig tips. Sagebrush withstands drought by sending roots deep into the soil and by shielding its leaves with a down of silvery, reflective hairs. Though despised by ranchers, sagebrush was used as fuel by pioneers, and Indians wove moccasins from the strips of gray bark that peel naturally from older branches. Deer and antelope depend upon sagebrush for fall and winter forage, and sage grouse feed on its buds and leaves.

Sagebrush, found in arid parts of the West, is easily ignited, and in earlier times settlers and native peoples used the plant for fuel. Today the fragrant wood finds favor in backyard barbecues.

season, absorbing up to a ton of water through a vast network of shallow roots. The cacti, which live for up to 200 years, are the ultimate late bloomers, passing an entire human lifetime before developing their first buds. White-winged doves visit the creamy white blooms by day, and bats seek them out at night, pollinating the flowers in their search for nectar. The juicy red fruits, eagerly consumed by desert wildlife, are also gathered by Papago Indians, who eat them raw or use them to make cakes and syrup.

S

St. Elmo's fire

An eerie glow that was first observed on the masts of ships during stormy weather, St. Elmo's fire is caused by electrical discharges between turbulent air and high, pointed objects. The phenomenon, which also occurs on the propellers and wingtips of airplanes and at the tops of steeples, can be thought of as a gentle, harmless form of static electricity. Seen by such voyagers as Columbus and Magellan, St. Elmo's fire was named for the patron saint of sailors.

St. Johnswort *Hypericum*

Herbs and small shrubs that are most common in dry, rocky waste places, the St. Johnsworts typically have five-petaled yellow flowers with a tuft of yellow stamens at the center. The oblong opposite leaves of most species are dotted with tiny, translucent glands. The plants, named for St. John the Baptist, were once thought to ward off evil spirits. Recently, a substance from one species has shown promise in fighting viruses.

Saguaros are in decline in much of their range, partly due to poachers, who steal the magnificent cacti for sale to landscapers.

Saguaro *Carnegiea giganteus*

King of the cacti, the majestic saguaros of southern Arizona and nearby California tower to heights of 50 feet. Their tall columnar trunks and upright branches consist mainly of spongy, water-storing tissue wrapped in a pleated, accordionlike skin. Living storage tanks, saguaros can swell to twice their normal size during the rainy

Salal *Gaultheria shallon*

Flourishing on the Pacific Coast from California to Alaska, this handsome shrub reaches a height of eight feet in redwood forests, though it generally is much shorter. Like its close relative, wintergreen, salal is adorned with waxy white or pink urn-shaped flowers in spring and early summer. Its blue-black berries are used for jam and are eaten by wildlife, and its aromatic, evergreen foliage is a popular holiday decoration.

Some salamanders, such as the marbled salamander (left), lay their eggs in holes on the ground, while others, like the long-tailed salamander (right), deposit their eggs in water.

Sockeye salmon live in the Pacific Ocean for four to six years before entering rivers for the long swim toward their breeding grounds, which may be over a thousand miles inland. As they head upstream, the males turn bright red, their backs become humped, and their snouts hooked.

S

Salamander

Long-tailed and short-legged, salamanders look like lizards but have skin that is thin and moist instead of scaled. In North America, which has more of these amphibians than any other continent, they are found primarily in the East (especially in the Appalachians) and along the West Coast. These harmless creatures prefer wet habitats, but most salamanders live in damp burrows or under logs or rocks, visiting ponds and streams only to lay their eggs. Except for the feathery gills on their necks, the tadpoles resemble those of frogs and toads. Some species lay their eggs on land, producing hatchlings that bypass the tadpole stage and look like the adults. Many salamanders breathe with lungs, but others absorb oxygen directly through the skin. A few species spend their entire lives in water and breathe with gills even as adults. Among these aquatic salamanders are the pale, blind species that live in caves or underground streams.

Salmon

Although these cold-water fish are prized for their commercial and sport value, their astonishing migrations are the salmon's most famous characteristic. Born in clear lakes and streams,

the young fish swim out to sea, and then, years later, they return. Driven by a remarkable instinct, they undertake a grueling odyssey back up the swift rivers, battling currents and leaping waterfalls, to the very same lakes and streams where they hatched. On the way their silvery scales take on new hues, and the snouts of males become beaklike. Pacific salmon arrive with just enough energy left to spawn before they die. One kind, the chinook, routinely swims hundreds of miles at sea, then travels 2,000 miles more up the Yukon River to spawn. Atlantic salmon also make arduous spawning trips—but survive to return another year.

Salt See *Halite.*

Salt lake

Unlike other lakes, salt lakes have inlets but no outlets: the water they contain is trapped in enclosed drainage basins. Seasonal rains keep them supplied with water, but since it escapes only by evaporation, mineral salts are left behind and become more concentrated year after year. Often much saltier than the sea, salt lakes occur mainly in deserts. Many, for instance, are located in the Great Basin, where the renowned Great Salt Lake is found.

A southern salt marsh offers a haven to a host of wildlife, including an elegant egret.

Salt marsh

Flat expanses of coastal land that are washed by tidewater and that support salt-tolerant grasses and other plants, salt marshes are among the world's most productive habitats. They serve as vital nurseries for commercially important fish and shellfish. As dead plant matter decays, it forms the basis of a rich and complex food web. When the tide is out, sandpipers probe the mud for worms and crustaceans, and fiddler crabs scuttle about in search of edible debris left by the receding water. Legions of migrating ducks and geese find food and shelter in the marshes. Rails slip secretively through the grass; herons and egrets wade in the shallows; and airborne ospreys, gulls, and terns scout for meals. Mammals such as minks and raccoons also hunt for prey here. But perhaps those most at home in salt marshes are muskrats. They build domed lodges with underwater entrances, where they can hide from predators and raise their young.

Saltwort *Salsola kali*

Also known as Russian thistle, saltwort is a prickly herb that flourishes on beaches. Its tolerance for dry, sandy soils has enabled this old-world immigrant to spread across the western plains as well, where it is one of many ubiquitous tumbleweeds. Bushy and up to three feet tall, saltwort has spine-tipped leaves and tiny green flowers. Once the fruits have matured, the plant dries out, breaks free from its roots, and tumbles across the windswept land.

Sand

Most abundant on beaches and in deserts, sand consists of rock particles that are larger than silt and smaller than gravel. The tiny grains are formed by the decomposition of solid rock by

Sand, composed of quartz and colorful mineral grains, provides camouflage and cover for insects and other creatures.

such agents as wind, rain, frost, and glacial ice. Made up mostly of quartz, sand may also contain feldspar, gypsum, basalt, and other substances, and the sand on beaches often includes fragments of shell and coral. Huge amounts of sand are carried by rivers to the sea, whose currents sculpt it into sandbars and barrier islands. It is easily blown by the wind as well, forming the graceful dunes found on beaches and in deserts. A valuable resource, sand is used to make abrasives, glass, and other materials.

Sandbur *Cenchrus*

Wherever the soil is sandy—on beaches, along roadsides, and in abandoned fields—sandburs are likely to make an appearance. In spring they look like just another coarse, sprawling grass. But in summer the sandburs produce tiny flowers enclosed in annoying burs, whose barbed spines are sharp enough to pierce the skin. Once the seeds inside mature, the burs break easily from the plant, clinging to passing humans and grazing animals.

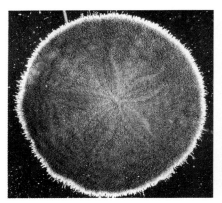

Sand dollars are covered with tiny, fuzzy spines that, in motion, resemble a windblown field of grass. They are used to crawl and burrow into the sand.

Spotted sandpipers, nicknamed teeter-tails, bob forward and then back as they walk along.

S

A sandstone butte in the Southwest has sweeping layers that hint at its complex origins.

Sand dollar

Marked with a five-petaled motif on the upper surface, sand dollars are flat, round marine animals related to sea urchins and sea stars. They grow to about three inches in diameter and are covered with minute, movable spines that give them a fuzzy feel. Burrowing in the sand, they feed on bits of organic material that they find among the grains. Empty skeletons, bleached white, are often found washed up on beaches on both the Atlantic and Pacific coasts.

Sandpiper

The most diverse family of shorebirds, our sandpipers include some 40 small to medium-size wading birds found mainly near fresh water and along seashores. In addition to those known as sandpipers, other waders such as sanderlings, dowitchers, snipe, and godwits also belong to the family. Sandpipers range in size from the sparrow-size least sandpiper to the chicken-size long-billed curlew, and most are inconspicuously patterned in browns, grays, and white. The varied shapes of their bills enable different species to specialize in different prey, including mollusks, insects, and crustaceans. Sanderlings, for instance, are a familiar sight on beaches, where they scurry after the receding waves, seeking food by pecking in the sand with their short, pointed bills. Woodcocks, in contrast, use their long, slender bills to probe deep in the mud for earthworms. Gregarious birds, sandpipers are often seen in large flocks as they migrate between their northern breeding grounds, usually in the Arctic, to wintering areas that may be as far away as South America.

332

Rock sandwort has many wiry stems that are covered with small, needlelike leaves.

Desert sand verbena stands in sharp contrast to the white flowers of the dune primrose, adding a splash of color to an arid Arizona landscape.

S

Sandstone

A common sedimentary rock that is sometimes beautifully tinted by iron and other minerals, sandstone is the basis of such awesome scenery as the towering cliffs of Mesa Verde in Colorado, the wind-sculpted spans that astonish visitors at Arches National Park, Utah, and the startling towers and monoliths of the Southwest's Monument Valley. Sandstone forms when grains of sand, deposited in thick beds by wind and water, are subjected to immense pressure and cemented together by lime, silica, iron oxide, or other minerals. A rich repository of fossils, sandstone can also reveal the ripple marks of long-vanished seas and the bedding of dunes in bygone deserts.

Sand verbena *Abronia*

Charming wildflowers that sprawl over dry, sun-drenched ground, sand verbenas thrive on beaches, deserts, and other dry areas in the West. The stems of many species are sticky, and the leaves of most are thick and juicy. Although the sand verbenas' rounded heads of trumpet-shaped flowers resemble those of true verbenas, the two plants are not related. Fragrant and colorful, sand verbenas are frequently planted in rock gardens and seaside gardens.

Sandwort *Arenaria*

Growing in low creeping mats or tall open tufts, sandworts are attractive wildflowers of rocky ledges and sandy soils. The pointed, needlelike leaves are arranged in pairs or clusters along the plants' wiry stems, which are topped with five-petaled white flowers that glisten like tiny stars. Among the many species that thrive in rocky crags on high alpine slopes are mountain sandwort of the Appalachians and Fendler's sandwort, a Rocky Mountain species. The lovers of dry, sandy soils include Nuttall's sandwort found along the Pacific Coast and the pine-barren sandwort, found on the East Coast.

Sandy shore See pp. 334–335.

Santa Ana wind

During the winter in southern California, the wind blows westward across the Santa Ana Mountains. As it ascends the windward slopes, the air loses most of its moisture in the form of rain or snow. Then as it rolls down the leeward slopes, it is compressed and warmed, producing a strong, hot, dry wind known as the Santa Ana. Sucking moisture out of the chaparral as it blows toward the coast, the wind greatly increases the risk of raging brushfires.

Saprophyte

Organisms that get nourishment from dead and decaying plants and animals are called saprophytes. Chief among them are many bacteria, as well as fungi such as mushrooms, molds, and even the mildew on an old leather shoe. All these saprophytes secrete enzymes into the nonliving host and break it down into substances that can be digested. While some cause food spoilage and other damage, saprophytes perform an essential service in recycling vital nutrients.

Bayberry fruits are a favorite food of myrtle warblers.

Marbled godwits probe the moist sand with their long, slender bills in search of food.

SANDY SHORE

Gulls—their scolding cries resounding above the swash of foaming surf—are often the most obvious signs of life on sandy seashores. But many other, less conspicuous creatures also inhabit the ribbons of beach where land meets sea. Countless clams, mole crabs, lugworms, and other animals lie hidden in the sand, filtering plankton and bits of organic debris from the water of each breaking wave. Also feasting at the water's edge are throngs of shorebirds, such as sanderlings, sandpipers, and plovers. Higher on the beach, ghost crabs and sand fleas stay safely buried in the sand by day but emerge in droves after dark to feed on plants and animals that have washed ashore. A variety of visitors, among them horseshoe crabs and sea turtles, use beaches as breeding grounds, gathering each year at customary places to perpetuate their kind.

Farther back from the shore, beyond the reach of the relentless surf, is the domain of plants that not only thrive in sand but can tolerate the salty air and blazing sun as well. Sea oats, wild roses, silverweed, and other sturdy survivors serve both to anchor the otherwise shifting dunes and to provide shelter for colonies of nesting gulls and terns.

Least terns, which nest on the ground, have chicks that are the color of sand.

A sand dollar skeleton, bleached white by the sun, lies nestled among scallop and coquina shells.

Horseshoe crabs come ashore in early spring to lay their eggs on beaches along the Atlantic Coast.

Dunes, which build up beyond the reach of the waves, are often held in place by sea oats and other plants that anchor the sand against the onslaught of the winds.

Black skimmers fly just above the water, snapping up fish with their lower bills.

Ghost crabs remain in their burrows by day, except for brief forays to the surf to moisten their gills.

Wild roses, which produce bright red hips, are common on seashores in the Northeast.

Sand collars, structures made of sand and mucus, contain the moon snail's eggs.

Yellow-bellied sapsuckers nest in Canada and winter as far south as Central America.

Sassafras leaves have different shapes, all on the same tree.

Sapsucker *Sphyrapicus*

The appropriately named sapsuckers are highly specialized woodpeckers that use their sharp beaks to drill neat rows of small holes in the bark of trees. Then, with brush-tipped tongues, they lap up the sap that oozes out and also eat the insects it attracts. They sometimes snatch insects in midair, as well, and occasionally feed on wild fruit. In typical woodpecker fashion, sapsuckers excavate nest holes in trees, often dead ones. Females incubate the eggs during the day, and males take over at night. Both parents share in feeding the young. Unlike other woodpeckers, the sapsuckers are strongly migratory. Yellow-bellied sapsuckers, for instance, travel thousands of miles when the seasons change.

Sassafras *Sassafras albidum*

An eastern tree that sometimes reaches a height of 65 feet, the sassafras is instantly recognized by its foliage, for its leaves come in three distinct shapes—oval, mittenlike, and trilobed. The tree is particulary lovely in autumn, when its foliage takes on fiery hues that contrast dramatically with red-stemmed, dark blue fruits.

Indians used sassafras to treat complaints ranging from rheumatism to malaria, and colonists prized sassafras tea as a tonic. For many years oil from the root bark flavored root beer, chewing gum, and toothpaste and was even used as a dental antiseptic. The oil has now been declared unsafe, however, because its chief ingredient, safrole, may be carcinogenic.

Sawfish *Pristis*

Large rays that look and swim much like sharks, sawfish are named for their long, flat snouts, which are edged on both sides with razor-sharp teeth. When they spot a school of fish, sawfish

Sawfly larvae not only look like caterpillars but are just as destructive, attacking oaks and elms as well as conifers and fruit trees.

slash through the shoal with this double-edged tool, then eat the dead and injured prey. They also use their snouts to probe the bottom for shellfish and other morsels. Sawfish live in warm, shallow waters off the Atlantic and Gulf of Mexico coasts but also enter the lower reaches of rivers, where they give birth to live young.

Sawfly

A saw-toothed egg-laying apparatus gives the sawflies their name. Using this organ, the female sawfly cuts slits into stems or leaves and inserts her eggs, which hatch into caterpillarlike larvae. The voracious larvae feed on the young leaves of

Saw palmettos are small, low-growing palms, unlike their treelike cousins the cabbage palmettos, which sometimes tower nearby.

Purple saxifrage, found on rocky ledges as far north as Newfoundland, produces dainty, half-inch-wide flowers from May to August.

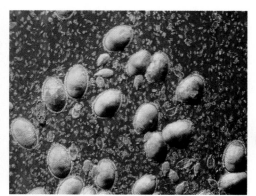

Scale insects, camouflaged in their waxy shells, scarcely look like insects at all.

roses, currant bushes, and other plants, sometimes burrowing into the tissue to form galls. Other highly destructive species attack conifers and can quickly denude a tree. Sawflies are closely related to ants and wasps but lack the narrow "waists" typical of their kin.

Saw palmetto *Serenoa repens*

Unlike most other palms, the saw palmetto is a low, sprawling shrub that often forms dense thickets extending for miles. Common on dunes and in sandy pine barrens, the saw palmetto ranges from South Carolina to the Florida Keys and west to the Mississippi Delta. Its fan-shaped leaves, up to three feet in diameter, vary in color from yellowish green to silvery white, and the leafstalks are armed with small, curved spines that resemble the teeth of a saw. The tiny, creamy white flowers that bloom among the saw palmetto's graceful leaves are followed by black, olivelike fruits. Fleshy and juicy when ripe, the fruits are an important winter food for Florida's white-tailed deer.

Saxifrage *Saxifraga*

Often springing up in crevices on cliffs—as if their roots had split the rock—saxifrages are hardy wildflowers whose name means "rock breaker." The name also may be traced to the plants' early use in a remedy for breaking up kidney stones. Saxifrages produce stems up to three feet tall and bear clusters of five-petaled, usually white blooms. A species common in the East is early saxifrage, which has a rosette of hairy leaves at its base and bears clusters of white flowers atop a hairy stem in early spring. Another, the low-growing purple saxifrage, found on mountain ledges from Newfoundland to Washington and Oregon, is notable for its rich reddish-lavender flowers. A number of other saxifrages are cultivated in rock gardens.

Scale insect

A bane of gardeners and fruit growers, scale insects are named for the waxy, usually oval shells that cover their bodies. Huge numbers of these pests sometimes infest fruit trees and other plants, which they weaken or even kill by sucking sap. The males do not eat, living only long enough to mate with the legless, wingless females. Among the more destructive species are the San Jose scale, the oyster shell scale, and the cottony cushion scale.

S

Some scavengers are opportunists, feasting on remains wherever they happen to find them. Crows, for instance, are always quick to home in on any road-killed animals they encounter along the sides of highways.

S

A scallop, its shell agape, displays its tiny, bright blue eyes and fringe of tentacles. Barnacles often encrust their shells.

Scorpions assume a dramatic pose when ready to strike. Fortunately, most would much prefer to flee than fight.

Scallop

Fan-shaped mollusks with earlike projections at the hinges of their fluted shells, scallops are found off all our coasts. While some species live permanently attached to rocks or pilings, most propel themselves through the water by vigorously clapping their shells together. (The large muscle that closes the shells is the part we eat.) The shells are lined with a fleshy mantle fringed with sensory tentacles and a row of tiny blue eyes. Although the eyes can distinguish only light and dark, they enable scallops to detect approaching predators in time to jet away. Two common species are the three-inch bay scallop, found in shallow water along the East Coast, and the deep-sea scallop, which can grow to eight inches.

Scavenger

Animals that feed primarily on carrion are known as scavengers. By eating these unwanted remains, they serve as nature's cleanup crew, ridding the landscape of decaying carcasses. Vultures, which soar in sweeping circles as they search for carrion, are among the few animals that live primarily as scavengers. Others scavenge only when the opportunity arises. Arctic foxes, for instance, often tag along after polar bears, picking up their scraps.

Schist

The coarse-grained metamorphic rock called schist is composed of wavy bands of minerals that tend to split into layers. Mica schist, named for the thin, flaky sheets of mica that run through the rock, is the most prevalent type. Common from Quebec and New England through the Appalachian Mountains to Georgia, it is often silvery and is strongly banded. Talc schist, named for its dominant mineral and found in the Appalachians, is grayish green and has a greasy feel.

Scorpion

Four pairs of legs mark the scorpions as arachnids, relatives of spiders, ticks, and mites. Solitary nocturnal predators found in the South and West, the creatures emerge from crevices and other hiding places at dusk and use their pincerlike foreclaws to grasp and tear apart prey. In addition to insects, they feed on spiders and various small animals.

The scorpion's most notorious characteristic, curved ominously over its back, is its segmented tail, tipped with a venomous stinger. Used to subdue larger prey and for self-defense, the scorpion's sting usually causes only local pain and swelling in humans, though the neurotoxic venom of a few species is potentially fatal.

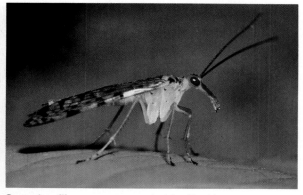

Scorpion flies, common east of the Rockies, are easily recognized by their prominent beaks.

Many scorpionfish, ornamented with flaps and spines, are well camouflaged for life on reefs.

White-winged scoter

Surf scoter

Black scoter

Scoters are underwater feeders that can plunge to great depths in search of shellfish.

Scorpionfish

Carnivorous bottom dwellers with a tendency to lurk among reefs and other rocky places, scorpionfish are also known as rockfish. They live in temperate or tropical seas, with some species favoring shallow water and others living at depths as great as 1,000 feet. Up to three feet long, many scorpionfish are brightly colored (deepwater species are usually bright red), and their heads are frequently ornamented with fleshy flaps and spines. Scorpionfish also have strong, sharp spines on their back fins. In a few species the spines are venomous, but even without the poison they can deliver painful wounds— hence the name scorpionfish. Among the commercially important species are the redfish, or ocean perch, of the Atlantic, and the bocaccio, common off the Pacific Coast.

Scorpion fly

Slender insects with long, thin, many-veined wings, threadlike antennae, and elongated, downturned "snouts," scorpion flies are harmless scavengers. They are named for the males' upturned, bulb-tipped abdomens, which resemble scorpion tails. The many species found across North America live mainly in moist deciduous woods and other cool, damp places. They feed primarily on dead insects but also eat some plant material. Females lay their eggs in the soil; and the larvae, which resemble caterpillars, emerge a week or so later and immediately begin scavenging on their own.

Scoter *Melanitta*

Excellent swimmers and deep-sea divers, our three species of these sea ducks nest in the Far North—the surf scoter in boggy woodlands, the black scoter and the white-winged scoter on open tundra. Females lay six to eight eggs, which they incubate for about a month. Almost as soon as the downy ducklings hatch, they are able to walk, swim, and find their own food.

On their breeding grounds the scoters' varied diet includes freshwater mollusks, fish, and vegetation. But when at sea (they winter along both coasts), the dark, stocky ducks become specialists. Gathering in huge flocks over mussel beds, they dive to depths of up to 40 feet and use their powerful bills to wrench mussels and other mollusks from underwater rocks.

Groupers, the largest sea bass, hide in reefs and wrecks on the ocean floor waiting to ambush prey.

Sea anemones feed by using their tentacles to sweep food particles into the mouth.

Puffins, like other members of the auk family such as murres and guillemots, are true seabirds. Excellent swimmers and divers, they spend most of their lives at sea, where they feed on fish and other animals; the birds return to land only to nest.

Sculpin

Homely creatures with broad heads and short tapering bodies, sculpins are scaleless fish that live on the bottom in both fresh and salt water. Though most are more bone than flesh, the 30-inch cabezon of the Pacific is sometimes eaten. The slightly smaller sea raven of the North Atlantic, bizarrely ornamented with prickles and spines, can inflate its body when annoyed. Their freshwater cousin—the four-inch muddler, or miller's thumb—lives in lakes and streams.

Sea anemone

Looking very much like flowers, sea anemones are brightly colored marine animals that add a patchwork of hues to tide pools, rocky coastal areas, and the sea floor. Their bodies are cylindrical, attached at the bottom to rocks or other objects and topped by waving, petallike tentacles that surround a central mouth. Some species feed on plankton, but others have stinging cells on the tentacles that paralyze fish and other small prey, which is then swept into the mouth to be digested. When alarmed and when tides are particularly low, sea anemones retract their tentacles and cover their mouth openings, protecting themselves from injury and dessication. They reproduce both by sprouting new individuals at the bases of their bodies and by shedding eggs and sperm into the water.

Sea bass

This varied family of nearly 400 species encompasses many commercial and sport fish, some of which are delectable while others are deadly. Among the sea basses are kelp bass, sand bass, coneys, hinds, and groupers. All have full bodies and big, broad mouths, and most live on the bottom in warm seas. In size, however, variety prevails, with lengths ranging from two inches to six feet or more. The giant of the family is a grouper, the jewfish, which can exceed 600 pounds. The sex life of sea bass is also varied.

A sea fan, though plantlike in appearance, is actually a kind of coral—a colony of tiny animals.

Most are hermaphrodites, with both male and female reproductive organs. Groupers, on the other hand, begin life as one sex and, as they mature, are transformed into the opposite sex.

Seabird

The term *seabird* is often loosely applied to any bird that spends time on the ocean, including sea ducks, gulls, loons, and many others. Strictly speaking, however, a seabird is one that obtains its food entirely at sea and comes ashore only to nest. Under this narrower definition the true seabirds are albatrosses, shearwaters, and storm-petrels (collectively known as tubenoses), as well as auks, gannets, kittiwakes, some of the cormorants, and a few terns.

Sea chub

Because of their habit of following ships in large schools, the sea chubs have earned the nickname rudderfish. Typically dark in color, these ocean dwellers have deep, oval bodies and small heads and mouths. They feed on seaweeds and other underwater plants, as well as the small animals that live on the vegetation. In the Atlantic Ocean, the Bermuda chub ranges from Cape Cod to the Caribbean. The halfmoon, a Pacific relative, is most often found in shallow water near rocky coasts.

Sea cow See *Manatee.*

Sea cucumber

Like their namesakes, sea cucumbers are long, cylindrical, and warty. But they are animals, not plants, and are related to sea urchins and sea stars. Seldom more than a foot long, sea cucum-

Sea cucumbers, when irritated, can expel a mass of sticky filaments—and sometimes all of their internal organs, which then grow back.

bers have a circular mouth ringed by branched tentacles at one end of the body. They are creatures of the ocean floor, where they find food in the mud. When threatened, some species eject a tangle of sticky filaments into the face of the enemy, creating enough confusion to deter the would-be attacker.

Sea fan *Gorgonia*

Despite the fact that they look much like lacy trees swaying with the current, the gracefully branched sea fans are really a type of coral. They consist of colonies of individual animals, called polyps, that grow together in the fanlike patterns for which these underwater beauties are named. Anchored at the base to rocks, sea fans have flexible internal skeletons covered by a thin layer of brightly colored living tissue. The polyps extend their tentacles through this tissue to gather the plankton on which they feed. Growing to a height of two feet or so, these exotic-looking creatures are especially abundant in the reefs and shallow waters off the coast of Florida and in the Caribbean.

341

Seahorses, when not tethered to weeds, navigate by fluttering their dorsal fins.

Fur seal pups gain weight very quickly because their mothers' milk is rich in fat.

S

Sea hare

Mollusks with much-reduced shells or no shells at all, sea hares are so named because of their prominent tentacles, which resemble rabbit ears. Grazing on seaweed along both coasts of North America, the creatures creep about on a large, muscular foot, much as snails do, but they can also swim by flapping fleshy lobes on both sides of their bodies. Though harmless, sea hares can startle anyone who disturbs them by emitting a cloud of inky purple-red fluid.

Seahorse *Hippocampus*

With horselike head and bony armor, a seahorse seems an unlikely fish. But the several species, from 2 to 12 inches long, that live in warm, shallow seas along our coasts are, in fact, true fish. Weak swimmers, seahorses resist strong currents by grasping seaweed with their prehensile tails. Securely tethered, they use their tubular snouts to suck in animals that pass by.

Seahorses reproduce in a most unusual way: In mating, the pair produces musical sounds as the female deposits eggs in a pouch on the male's belly. There they are fertilized, and several weeks later the male contorts his body and expels as many as 200 tiny young, one at a time.

Seal

Marine mammals that seem half dog and half dolphin, the seals and sea lions are well adapted to life in the sea. Descended from land-dwelling carnivores, they have the canine muzzles and teeth—and in some cases, even the voices—of their terrestrial ancestors. But their streamlined bodies and flippers allow them to swim as gracefully as fish. Equipped with ears and nostrils that close up tightly when they dive, seals can descend hundreds of feet below the surface and can hold their breath for more than half an hour. Because they are protected by dense fur and a thick layer of blubber under the skin, seals are comfortable even in the iciest water. Most feed mainly on fish, but some also eat squid, octopus, crabs, and clams.

Seals are divided into two families: the earless, or true, seals, which lack external ears and have small hind flippers that cannot be turned forward; and the eared seals, also known as sea lions and fur seals, which have visible external ears and large hind flippers that do turn forward. Some sea lions have a leonine mane on the neck. California sea lions, which are very playful, are the "trained seals" seen in circuses.

While most earless seals are monogamous, others have multiple mates. Fur seals and sea lions, for example, assemble each year at traditional breeding grounds called rookeries—stretches of beach where the males compete for territories and for harems of 3 to 30 or more females. The females almost always give birth to a single pup, born on land or on an ice floe.

Aside from sharks, killer whales, and polar bears, the seals' worst enemies are human hunters, who in the past have decimated a number of species for their fur. Thanks to enlightened legislation, however, seal numbers have rebounded in recent years.

Sea lion See *Seal.*

Sorting the Sundry Seals

Seals are of two families: earless seals, with small, inconspicuous ear openings; and eared seals, with visible external ears. But more noticeable is the fact that earless seals have small hind flippers which cannot turn forward, so that on land the animals must drag themselves along. The eared seals, in contrast, have large hind flippers that can turn forward, enabling them to walk on land. Within the two groups, a species can be recognized by such clues as size, color, and where it lives.

Earless seals
Hind flippers small, do not turn forward

4 TO 6 FEET LONG

Harbor seal
(Atlantic and Pacific)

Body gray or brown, spotted.

Harp seal
(North Atlantic)

Body pale gray with black band on back. Head black.

7 TO 11 FEET LONG

Snout long and doglike. Body gray, spotted.

Gray seal
(North Atlantic)

Males with inflatable sac (or hood) on snout. Body gray, spotted.

Hooded seal
(North Atlantic)

Eared seals
Hind flippers large, turn forward

4 TO 8 FEET LONG

Northern fur seal
(Pacific)

Body brown, belly reddish, shoulders gray.

California sea lion
(Pacific)

Body brown all over. Barks constantly.

TO 10 FEET LONG

Northern sea lion
(Pacific)

Body tan. Males with mane on neck.

TO 20 FEET LONG

Northern elephant seal
(Pacific)

Males with large, overhanging snout. Body nearly hairless.

S

Sea oats, with tenacious roots that hold the dunes in place, are often deliberately planted.

Sea oats *Uniola paniculata*

Growing up to six feet tall, the grass called sea oats is found on sandy seashores from Virginia and southern California southward. Long, narrow leaves grow along the stems, which by the end of summer are topped with graceful, plumelike clusters of golden yellow fruits.

Unlike most plants, sea oats easily tolerate the strong winds, salt spray, and blowing sands of the seashore. Their fast-growing roots, which penetrate deep into the sand in search of moisture, enable them to survive drought, one of the principal hazards of life on the exposed, sunny dunes. And their networks of shoots that spread just beneath the surface make them very effective for anchoring the dunes against erosion.

Sea otter *Enhydra lutris*

A resident of the great offshore kelp forests along the Pacific coast, our smallest marine mammal, the sea otter, is best known for its tool-using talents. Diving to depths of as much as 180 feet and able to stay underwater for four minutes at a time, it snatches sea urchins, abalones, mussels, and clams from the bottom, then returns to the surface, often bringing along a flat stone. Floating on its back with the stone on its belly, the sea otter hammers its prey on this improvised anvil until the shell cracks open, and so gets at the flesh inside.

Sea otters not only eat on their backs but also rest—and even sleep—floating along belly-up. When a pup is born—just one to a litter—the mother carries it, too, on her stomach until the youngster starts diving on its own, at about two months. Inveterate mariners, sea otters spend virtually their entire lives at sea, heading for shore only during severe storms.

Once hunted nearly to extinction for their glossy pelts, sea otters are now protected and have made a dramatic comeback. Today they flourish along the West Coast from central California to Alaska, with as many as 100,000 cavorting in the kelp offshore.

Sea robin

Bottom-dwelling fish that are found mainly in shallow coastal waters, sea robins typically have big, broad heads covered with bony plates; slender, tapered bodies; and enormous winglike pectoral fins. The first few rays of the pectoral fins are separate, resembling fingers, and are used for walking across the sea floor and feeling for crabs and other food. Notable for their noisy repertoires, especially during the spawning season, sea robins make a variety of grunts, groans, and drumming sounds by vibrating their oversized swim bladders.

Sea shell *See Mollusk.*

Sea slug

These mollusks without shells are among the sea's most spectacular inhabitants. Some are as smooth as ribbons, others bristle with elaborate fingerlike projections, and nearly all are painted with dazzling hues. Predators should not be deceived by their beauty, however, for many sea slugs defend themselves by exuding acids and poisons. While some are content to graze on algae and plankton, most are carnivores. Those that feed on creatures such as sea anemones and

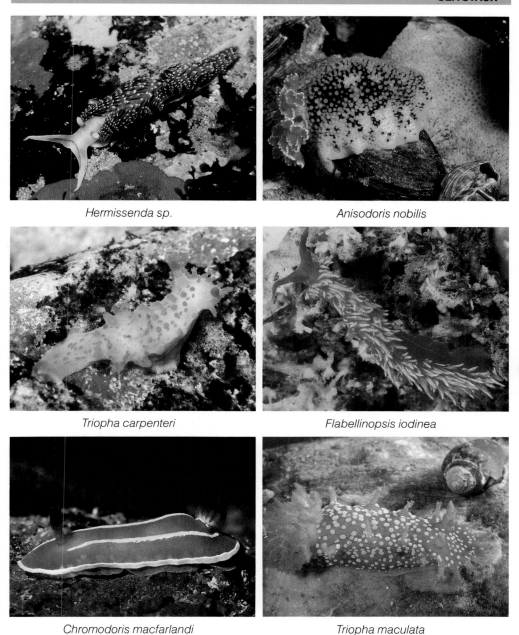

Hermissenda sp.

Anisodoris nobilis

Triopha carpenteri

Flabellinopsis iodinea

Chromodoris macfarlandi

Triopha maculata

Sea slugs, marine mollusks without shells, exhibit an astonishing variety of shapes and colors.

S

jellyfish are immune to those animals' stings; swallowed whole, the stinging cells are shunted to projections on the sea slug's back, ready to be fired if the slug is harassed.

Sea squirt

Touch the saclike body of a sea squirt, and it will live up to its name by squirting out a jet of water. These leathery, bottle-shaped creatures live attached to rocks and other objects (either singly or in colonies) and filter food from water pumped through the body. They begin life as free-swimming, tadpolelike larvae with primitive, flexible backbones, but they soon settle to the bottom and mature into sedentary adults.

Sea stack

Shaped by the steady hammering of waves, sea stacks are isolated, often picturesque columns of rock that rise from the sea off rocky shores. They form as waves attack coastal cliffs, wearing away the weaker rocks and leaving headlands composed of the more resistant. Over time, these promontories are narrowed as water cuts through the rock, producing natural arches. Eventually these, too, give way to the assault of the sea: the tops of the arches collapse, leaving behind the pillarlike sea stacks. Because the stacks provide a safe haven from shoreside predators, they are often colonized by seabirds for use as rookeries.

S

Sea stars drape themselves over shellfish and pull the valves open with their sucker-lined tentacles.

Sea urchins, armed with purple spines, decorate a bed of kelp.

Seaweed: suited for ocean living

Diverse plants, seaweeds are equipped to withstand the rigors of ocean living. Hold-fasts anchor them in place, and flexible fronds, whose air bladders keep them afloat, sway in the surf without tearing.

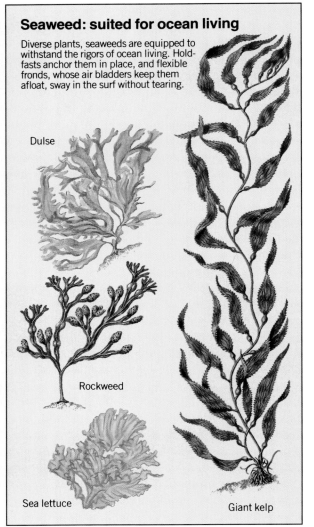

Dulse

Rockweed

Sea lettuce

Giant kelp

Sea star

Also known as starfish, sea stars are spiny-skinned marine animals that usually have 5 arms but can have as many as 40, arranged symmetrically around a central disc. If they lose an arm to a predator or an accident, a new one grows in its place.

The undersides of the arms are lined with hundreds of tiny, rubbery tube feet, each one tipped with a suction cup. Operated by a combination of muscular contraction and hydraulic pressure, the tube feet enable sea stars to crawl across the sea floor. The animals also use them to slowly but steadily open the shells of clams and mussels, their principal prey. Once the valves have been pulled apart, the sea star slips its stomach, turned inside out, between the shells and digests the soft parts.

Sea stars are commonly seen along rocky coasts, especially at low tide when they are often stranded in tide pools. Most reproduce by releasing sperm and eggs into the water, where the fertilized eggs develop into free-swimming larvae, which later settle to the bottom to mature.

Sea turtle

Rovers in the open ocean, sea turtles are so completely adapted to marine life that they rarely come ashore except to lay their eggs. Their streamlined shells are thinner and lighter in weight than those of land turtles, and their paddlelike limbs, though clumsy on shore, enable the huge reptiles to swim through the water at speeds of up to 20 miles per hour.

Every two or three years, sea turtles migrate hundreds or even thousands of miles to nest on sandy beaches. After mating in shallow water, the female heaves herself up on the shore at night, digs a deep hole with her hind flippers, and lays dozens of eggs in it. Then she covers the clutch with sand and returns to sea. About eight weeks later, the young turtles hatch and rush toward the water, dodging gulls and other hungry predators. When they mature, the turtles return to nest on the very same beaches where they were born.

The sea turtles include leatherbacks (at up to 1,200 pounds, the giants of the clan), loggerheads, green turtles, ridleys, and hawksbills.

Sedges, such as the Arctic cotton grass, cover large tracts of the boggy tundra. Tall, dense stands of various sedges offer protective cover to nesting birds and other small animals.

Once abundant in North American waters, all the sea turtles have been drastically reduced in numbers as a result of coastal development, nest plundering, and overhunting.

Sea urchin

Common both in rocky tide pools and in offshore waters, sea urchins are globular relatives of sea stars and sand dollars. Their hard outer skeletons bristle with green or purple movable spines, which, in a few species, are poisonous. They are also equipped with tiny, sucker-tipped tube feet arranged in long rows; working in concert with the spines, the feet allow them to creep over rocks and through beds of kelp. Sea urchins feed mainly on algae, though some are also scavengers. They rasp the food off rocks and other surfaces using five sharp teeth that are located on the underside of the body. When sea urchins die, their spines break off, and the empty limestone skeletons, called tests, frequently wash up on shore, where they are collected by beachcombers. Sea urchins are a favorite food of sea otters, and many gourmets consider the eggs of some species a delicacy.

Seaweed

Such names as sea palm, sea staghorn, and feather boa attest to the varied forms of the marine algae commonly called seaweeds. Most are anchored to rocks and other surfaces by rootlike structures called holdfasts, and some, such as the rockweeds, are studded with little air bladders that serve as flotation devices. Although the branching fronds of many species resemble stems and leaves, seaweeds lack the internal plumbing systems of higher plants and instead take in nutrients directly from the water.

Seaweeds are classified into three groups on the basis of color. The brown algae, including gulfweeds and kelps, are the largest, with the giant kelp of the Pacific growing to lengths of more than 200 feet. Red algae, such as laver, dulse, and Irish moss, tend to be smaller and more delicate and are associated with relatively warm waters. Sea lettuce and other green algae are less common than the red and brown kinds.

Sometimes used for food, seaweeds have many other commercial uses. Some supply thickeners for ice creams and pharmaceuticals, as well as the agar used in laboratories. Others, such as kelp, are harvested for use in the production of everything from paint to beer.

Sedge

Though often mistaken for grasses, the various sedges—usually found in marshes and other moist places—belong to an entirely separate plant family. A glance at the stems, however, is enough to tell them apart: grasses have round, hollow stems, while those of most sedges are triangular and solid. Even so, the confusion persists and is reflected in the names of many species. The saw-toothed sedge that covers much of the Florida Everglades, for example, is called sawgrass. Another widespread sedge is called yellow nutgrass; regarded as a weed by some farmers, it is cultivated in parts of the U.S. South for its edible tubers, known as earth almonds.

Sedimentary rock, easily recognized by its layers, is sometimes thrust skyward by powerful forces deep within the earth.

Seeds, like those of common milkweed, sometimes come equipped with parachutes.

S

Sedimentary rock

The terra-cotta walls of the Grand Canyon and the colorful pinnacles looming over Bryce Canyon are both made up of sedimentary rock. They formed from natural debris that built up, layer upon layer, over millions of years and was finally compacted into rock. Some sedimentary rocks, such as sandstone and shale, formed from particles eroded from preexisting rocks. Others, like limestone and dolomite, are composed of the skeletons of ancient sea creatures or of minerals that were dissolved in water. Still others—gypsum and halite, for instance—are products of evaporation. Many sedimentary rocks have a bedded structure, and some are loaded with fossils that provide clues about ancient life.

Seed

Serving as links between generations, seeds are the self-contained reproductive structures produced by flowering plants, conifers, and a few others. Each seed contains a miniature plant, or embryo, and a supply of food, both of which are enclosed in a protective coat. This durable package can remain viable for a long time—the record is held by arctic lupine seeds that were able to germinate after more than 10,000 years.

Self-heal *Prunella vulgaris*

Also known as heal-all and hookheal, self-heal has a long history of medicinal uses. The plant was used to cure ailments of the mouth and throat, and the bruised leaves, when applied to

Self-heal, because of the yawning shape of its blooms, was once believed to cure ailments of the mouth and throat.

cuts and scrapes, were supposed to promote healing. The plant does in fact make a most convenient bandage, since it flourishes throughout the continent. Sometimes erect and sometimes forming dense, ground-hugging mats, this ubiquitous member of the mint family has square stems and spikes of two-lipped, usually purple flowers.

Senna *Cassia*

Esteemed for centuries for their medicinal properties, senna leaves still serve as the basis for a number of modern laxatives. Our several native species thrive in a variety of habitats, from dry

348

Sennas are sun-loving, often shrubby plants, many of which thrive in deserts.

Shad are caught by anglers, as well as netted en masse, as they head upstream to spawn.

S

Serviceberries are also called shadbushes, servicetrees, Juneberries, and sugarplums.

grasslands to moist woods. Perennial members of the pea family, with feathery compound leaves, they bear clusters of bright yellow, five-petaled flowers, which are followed in autumn by flattened, beanlike seed pods.

Sequoia See *Giant sequoia.*

Serpentinite

A greenish-black metamorphic rock with a greasy feel, serpentinite forms when rocks rich in olivine and other magnesium minerals are altered by moderate amounts of heat and pressure. It frequently contains veins of the fibrous mineral chrysotile, which is the chief source of asbestos. Because of its color and its resemblance to marble, serpentinite is often used as a decorative stone. It is common in mountainous regions of California, Montana, and Maine.

Serviceberry *Amelanchier*

One of the first trees to bloom in spring, service-berries are covered with clouds of dainty white five-petaled flowers just as the shad are running upriver to spawn. It was for this reason that colonists called them shadbushes—just one of many common names. Extremely hardy, several species grow across North America; some are small trees, but many are shrubs no more than 15 feet tall. Their purple fruits, which resemble blueberries, ripen in June and are quickly devoured by birds and other woodland creatures. Settlers used the fruits for jams and pies, and aboriginal peoples mixed them with venison or buffalo meat to make pemmican.

Shad *Alosa*

Members of the herring family, shad live in the ocean but, like salmon, swim up coastal rivers to spawn. The commonest species, the American shad, is about two feet long and weighs from two to five pounds. An important food and game fish in the East, it has been introduced in Pacific waters as well.

Signaled by the warming of coastal rivers in spring, shad swim upstream to lay their eggs. The young hatch within a week or two and grow about five inches long over the summer, then head for the sea, where they mature in three to five years on a diet of plankton.

In the past, shad were heavily netted during spring spawning runs. But overfishing, dam building, and pollution have depleted the numbers of these once-plentiful fish, which are prized for both their flesh and their roe.

349

S

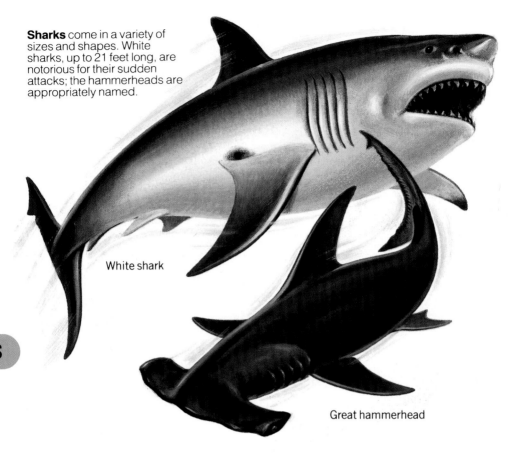

Sharks come in a variety of sizes and shapes. White sharks, up to 21 feet long, are notorious for their sudden attacks; the hammerheads are appropriately named.

White shark

Great hammerhead

Shadbush See *Serviceberry.*

Shaggymane *Coprinus comatus*

Like other inky-cap mushrooms, the shaggymane goes through a strange transformation as it ages: its white, shaggy, torpedo-shaped cap and gills gradually turn black and disintegrate into an inky liquid. Once used as a substitute for ink, the fluid contains the spores that propagate the fungus. The shaggymane, which grows in grassy places from coast to coast, is delightfully edible when young, but once it begins to change color, it should be left alone.

Shale

Shale, the most common sedimentary rock, is formed of thinly bedded layers of clay, mud, or silt that were deposited in ancient lakes or shallow seas. As the debris accumulated, it was gradually compacted into relatively soft rock that can easily be split into thin layers. Some shales, called oil shales—often found sandwiched between beds of sandstone or limestone—are rich in organic matter. In the process of compaction, the trapped organic debris was converted to hydrocarbons that can be distilled to produce oil. While extraction is expensive and difficult, the oil is usable as fuel. Alberta, Colorado, Wyoming, and Utah have large deposits of oil shale.

Shark

Though universally feared, the speedy, torpedo-shaped fish known as sharks are also widely misunderstood. Of the more than 250 species, for example, only a few behave aggressively toward humans, and shark attacks in fact are extremely rare. Ironically, the largest sharks—the whale sharks, which grow up to 45 feet long and are the biggest of all fish—are among the most harmless, feeding only on microscopic plankton. Others have been known to swallow such inedible objects as cans, bottles, and rubber tires, but more typical fare consists of everything from fish and crabs to dolphins and seals, as well as other sharks.

Equipped with unusually keen senses, sharks detect prey not only by sight, sound, and smell but also by sensing faint electrical fields in the water. They are on the move continuously, though not because they are always hunting, as is commonly believed (some go for days without eating); lacking the air-filled swim bladders that make other fish buoyant, sharks would sink if they remained still. They also differ from most other fish in having skeletons composed of cartilage rather than bone and in possessing several rows of teeth, which are constantly replaced as they wear out. The sharp scales that cover the skin are toothlike as well; tough and abrasive, dried shark skin was once used as sandpaper.

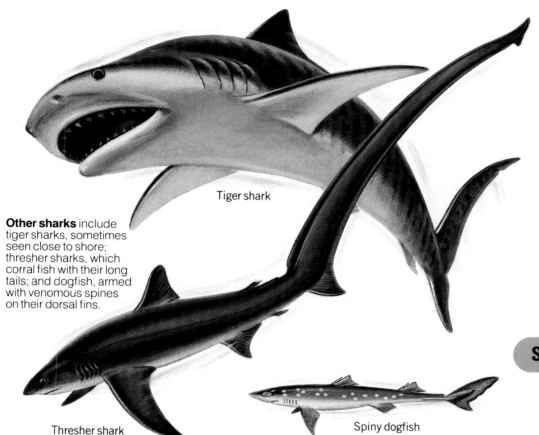

Tiger shark

Other sharks include tiger sharks, sometimes seen close to shore; thresher sharks, which corral fish with their long tails; and dogfish, armed with venomous spines on their dorsal fins.

Thresher shark

Spiny dogfish

S

Shearwater

Gliding between ocean waves with their narrow wings outstretched, shearwaters adeptly snatch fish, squid, and other food from just beneath the water's surface. The birds—one to two feet long, with tubed nostrils atop their hooked beaks—are related to fulmars and petrels. They spend most of their lives at sea, coming ashore only to nest in island burrows. Tireless travelers, most shearwaters seen off our coasts could easily have nested on islands of such distant lands as Chile or New Zealand.

Shell See *Mollusk.*

Shepherd's purse *Capsella bursa-pastoris*

Heart-shaped capsules filled with tiny reddish seeds give the shepherd's purse its name, for they resemble the leather pouches that shepherds used to wear on their belts. An old-world weed that has become established in croplands, gardens, lawns, and waste places practically everywhere, shepherd's purse first produces a low rosette of sharply toothed leaves that look much like dandelions, then later sends up a branching stem as much as 20 inches tall. The plant flowers practically year-round, its stem tips bearing clusters of tiny white blossoms, which mature into the "purses." Herbalists have traditionally

recommended this member of the mustard family as a remedy for internal bleeding. Today its tender young leaves are sometimes gathered and eaten as salad greens.

Shiner *Notropis*

The midgets of the minnow family, shiners are little freshwater fish that live in streams, ponds, and lakes all across North America. Averaging two to four inches in length, they feed mainly on tiny insects but also eat algae—and are in turn eaten by larger fish. In fact, anglers commonly use shiners as live bait. Though generally silvery, the males of some species, such as the common shiner and the bleeding shiner, take on brilliant colors during the spawning season.

Shipworm *Teredo*

Despite their name, shipworms are not worms but marine mollusks—relatives of clams—that bore into wood and often do serious damage to piers and other structures. Unlike the shells of most mollusks, those of shipworms have developed into filelike drilling instruments. Located at one end of the creature's long, worm-shaped body, the shells are used to tunnel deep into wood, some of which is eaten. The other end of the animal remains attached to the burrow's entrance, taking in food and oxygen from the sea.

351

Shooting stars are self-pollinating and so are able to survive when insects are scarce.

Many shorebirds, such as the lesser yellowlegs, are long legged and graceful.

Shooting star *Dodecatheon*

With stamens joined in a downward-pointing cone and petals swept back like trailing flames, these charming wildflowers do indeed resemble shooting stars. According to legend, they spring up wherever a real star has fallen to earth. In fact, shooting stars are versatile plants that are found in many places; they grow both in sun-drenched grasslands and in shaded woods, especially in mountains in the West. In early spring a ground-hugging rosette of oval or spatula-shaped leaves appears. Then at blossom time a single leafless stalk up to 20 inches tall arises from its center, with a constellation of as many as 25 fragrant red, purple, pink, or white flowers dangling gracefully from the top.

Shrew families frequently form chains, with the mother leading the frenetic litter.

Shorebird

The birds known collectively as shorebirds are a varied assemblage that includes a number of closely related families—the plovers, the oyster-catchers, the stilts and avocets, and the many sandpipers. Most are long legged and use their bills to probe for food along the shores of fresh and salt water. Many are familiar sights on ocean beaches, often pausing on their migrations. But a few, such as the killdeer (a plover) and the common snipe (a sandpiper), live far from the sea.

Shrew

Found all across North America, shrews live in habitats as diverse as deserts (the desert shrew), moist forests (the smoky shrew), tundra (the arctic shrew), and mountain streams (the water shrew). They also vary in size; the pygmy shrew is our smallest mammal, but even the largest, the short-tailed shrew, is only four inches long.

Shrews are bundles of nervous energy, active at any hour (though mostly at night) searching out invertebrates and carrion to support their geared-up metabolism. The short-tailed shrew, our only poisonous mammal, even tackles frogs and mice much larger than itself. The shrews' frenetic lives burn out quickly, however, with few of them ever reaching a second birthday.

Shrike *Lanius*

Equipped with strong, slightly hooked beaks, shrikes are songbirds that hunt for a living. They survey their surroundings from exposed perch-es, then chase down insects and small birds, ro-dents, and reptiles. Since they often hang their prey on thorns or barbed wire fences, shrikes have been nicknamed butcherbirds.

Two species are native to North America: the northern shrike of boreal Canada and Alaska, which wanders south in winters when food is scarce, and the more southerly loggerhead shrike, a widespread but increasingly scarce bird of fields and fencerows. Both build bulky cup-shaped nests in trees or shrubs and raise families of four to six young.

Loggerhead shrikes build bulky cup-shaped nests, where both parents incubate up to six eggs. A month after hatching, the young are able to snag and impale prey. Shrikes have remarkable eyesight, as keen as that of hawks and eagles.

S

Cleaner shrimp provide an important service by removing parasites from the gills, mouths, and scales of fish. Many of these shrimp are characteristically colored, which helps their clients find them.

Shrimp

Semitransparent, delicate-bodied relatives of lobsters and crabs, shrimp are common marine and freshwater crustaceans. Many are commercially harvested and represent the shellfish industry's most valuable catch.

Ranging in size from less than half an inch to about eight inches long (the larger ones are often called prawns), shrimp have flexible bodies, long antennae, and numerous pairs of jointed appendages. Those nearest the head are used for handling food. Behind them are five pairs of walking legs and, along the abdomen, five pairs of appendages known as swimmerets, which are used for sculling through the water. By sweeping their fanlike tails downward, shrimp can also move rapidly in reverse.

Many shrimp live on ocean bottoms, where they scavenge for plant and animal matter; others prey on krill and shellfish larvae; and still others, known as cleaner shrimp, eat parasites off the bodies of fish. Some shrimp simply lay their eggs and abandon them. But the females of most species carry them attached to the swimmerets until the eggs hatch into larvae, which gradually metamorphose into adults.

Shrub

The term *shrub* applies to any woody plant less than 10 feet tall with several stems branching from the ground. Unlike trees, shrubs have no single stem that dominates as a trunk. Branching in various patterns, shrubs can be low and spreading, broad and round, or tall and narrow. Under favorable conditions, shrubs such as honeysuckles sometimes form small trees, while certain trees—willows and sumacs, for instance—grow as shrubs in harsh environments.

Sidewinder See *Rattlesnake.*

Silver

Treasured since ancient times, silver is among the most lustrous and malleable of the precious metals. Though it is sometimes mined in pure form, most silver is obtained as a by-product in the refining of other metals. In the 1800's, prospectors were lured by discoveries of silver in the Rocky Mountains, and much of our silver is still mined there. Most familiar as jewelry, flatware, and coins, silver also has important uses in photography, electronics, and dentistry.

The greater siren, which can grow about three feet long, lives in swamps and weedy ponds from Maryland to Florida and west to Alabama.

Sinkholes can open up quite suddenly, resulting in the kind of devastation shown here. Occurring in central Florida, an area that is well known for its sinkholes, this collapse created a chasm 400 feet across.

S

Silverfish

A bane of tidy housekeepers, silverfish are small, primitive, wingless insects with long antennae and three spearlike tail filaments. They lurk in warm, dark cupboards and behind partitions but venture out at night to feed on such starchy delicacies as wallpaper, book-binding glues, and even starched fabrics. Silverfish lay their eggs in household nooks and crannies; the young, which look like miniature adults, require two years or more to mature.

Sinkhole

Sinkholes are deep round holes, sometimes filled with water, that form in areas where the bedrock is limestone and rainfall is moderate to heavy. Some are produced when the roof of an underground cavern collapses. Others are created as acidic rainwater percolates through limestone, gradually dissolving the rock until the overlying soil suddenly subsides. Sinkholes vary in size and depth, but some are large enough to cause considerable damage, swallowing up cars, trucks, and even houses. Parts of Kentucky, Alabama, Indiana, and Missouri are dotted with sinkholes, and they formed many of Florida's lakes.

Siren

Odd, eellike salamanders with bushy external gills and no hind legs, sirens never mature into land-dwelling adults. Instead, they remain in water throughout their lives, which may be as long as 25 years. They hide by day in weedy ponds and on the muddy bottoms of swamps and lakes, foraging at night for worms, snails, insects, and small fish. The three species found mainly in the U.S. Southeast range in size from the six-inch-long dwarf siren to the greater siren, which reaches nearly three feet.

Skate

Flat-bodied relatives of sharks, with broad, winglike pectoral fins, skates belong to a family of rays that lay eggs in leathery cases instead of giving birth to live young. The cases, called mermaids' purses, often wash up on beaches.

Skates are harmless, unobtrusive creatures that spend the day half-buried in sand on the ocean floor, moving about at night to hunt for shellfish, which they crush with their powerful flat teeth. Like big exotic birds, they propel themselves along the sea bottom by gracefully undulating their huge fins.

The largest North American species is the eight-foot-long big skate of the Pacific Ocean. Smaller kinds, including the little skate and the barndoor skate, are found in the Atlantic.

Skimmer *Rynchops niger*

Black skimmers, also known as cutwaters and scissorbills, fly low over the sea, slicing the surface with their knifelike bills. When the lower mandible—up to an inch longer than the upper one—strikes a small fish or shrimp, the bill instantly snaps shut. The bird then angles its head back, swallows its prey, and continues its inflight fishing without missing a beat.

Black skimmers fish by skimming the water with the lower bill (left) or by jabbing at prey while wading in the shallows. They nest in colonies of up to 200 pairs, laying their eggs in simple depressions in the sand (above).

The broad-headed skink, found in the eastern United States, is at home among fallen leaves and rotting logs.

Cobweb skippers sip nectar from blossoms or take nutrients from damp organic matter. Their caterpillars feed on grasses and sedges that grow in open fields.

About the size of crows, but with a slender build, skimmers are black above and white below, with red feet and black-tipped red bills. Their eyes have vertical pupils, like those of cats, that can be narrowed to thin slits to reduce the glare from sand and sea. Nesting on beaches and islands along the Atlantic and Gulf of Mexico coasts, skimmers lay their speckled eggs in depressions in the sand. The chicks sometimes hide by scooping out shallow holes and then kicking sand into the air; falling onto their tawny backs, the sand serves as camouflage.

Skink

So shiny that their scales seem polished, skinks are small, secretive lizards that feed by day on insects, spiders, and worms. When seized by a predator, a skink's tail breaks off, distracting the would-be attacker. Fleeing to safety, the skink later grows a new tail. North America's largest species, at 13 inches long, is the Great Plains skink of the central and southwestern United States. An aggressive creature, it will bite if handled. The five-lined skink—about eight inches long, with five pale stripes down its dark back—lives in parts of Ontario and in eastern U.S. woodlands. The young, with yellow stripes and bright blue tails, look very different from the adults. The two other skinks found in Canada are the western skink, in British Columbia, and the northern prairie skink, in Manitoba.

Skipper

Named for their abrupt, darting flight, skippers seem always to be in a hurry as they flit from flower to flower. Neither true butterflies nor moths, they exhibit characteristics of both. Like butterflies, skippers have clubbed antennae and are active by day. But their stout, hairy bodies, relatively small wings, and generally drab appearance are typical of moths. When at rest, many of the skippers show their dual allegiance by holding their forewings up, as butterflies do, and their hindwings down, like moths. Some 300 species of skippers are found throughout North America.

Striped skunks, our most common species, forage after dark for a variety of foods. They are frequently seen sniffing around lawns and gardens, where many a family pet has been doused with foul-smelling spray after ignoring the warnings of a startled skunk. A jet of skunk spray can accurately hit targets up to 12 feet away.

S

Skua *Catharacta skua*

Pirates of the high seas, great skuas are large, predatory seabirds that steal food from gulls and gannets. These close relatives of jaegers are dark, hawk-beaked marauders that watch patiently while other birds go after fish, then harass them in midair until they disgorge their catch. Great skuas (sometimes called bonxies or seahawks) also follow ships for scraps, kill and eat ducks, and prey on the eggs and young of neighbors that share their North Atlantic nesting grounds. Another species, the south polar skua, breeds in the Antarctic and is a rare summer visitor to both our East and West coasts.

Skullcap *Scutellaria*

Woods, meadows, and thickets in temperate parts of North America are home to nearly 100 species of skullcaps, which are named for the hoodlike upper lip on their flowers. Most are tall perennials with blue or violet blooms, branching stems, and oval, toothed leaves that grow in opposite pairs. One common species, mad-dog skullcap, was once touted as a cure for rabies; others, including downy skullcap, were believed to cure nervous disorders. While the rabies claim has been discredited, research has shown that the plants may have sedative effects.

Skunk

Our several skunks are short-legged, bushy-tailed members of the weasel family that are notorious for their foul-smelling defensive spray. Their conspicuous black-and-white patterns serve to scare off most potential foes. When necessary, however, a skunk will also stamp its feet and raise its tail. If all these warnings are ignored, the skunk then fires a jet of acrid fluid from its anal glands. The spray can cause temporary blindness, and the odor lingers for days.

Skunks spend the day in burrows, rock piles, or abandoned buildings and come out at night to feed on insects, rodents, birds' eggs, dead animals, grain, and fruit. Our most common species, the striped skunk, is found across most of North America. Spotted skunks live in the South and West, while hooded and hog-nosed skunks prefer the arid Southwest.

Skunk cabbage

Harbingers of spring in damp eastern woodlands, skunk cabbages often send up their hoodlike floral sheaths (or spathes) before the last snow has melted. The sheath, which encloses a knoblike structure (the spadix) studded with tiny flowers, has a foul odor and a brown to purple color that imitates rotting flesh. The fetid

Skunk cabbage sends up malodorous, fleshy brown to purple spathes in late winter. The heat generated by the developing plant is intense enough to thaw the frozen ground and melt the surrounding snow.

Sliders are brightly marked pond turtles that, if left undisturbed, will bask quietly in the sun for hours. Once commonly sold in pet shops, sliders are better observed among the weeds and pond lilies of their natural habitats.

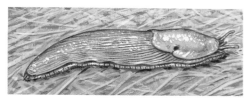

Banana slugs, wiener-size pests, are a bane of gardeners in the Pacific Northwest.

guise serves the plant well, however, for it attracts the flies that pollinate the blooms. Once the skunk cabbage has flowered, it unfurls bright green leaves up to two feet tall.

A similar species, called western or yellow skunk cabbage, has a skunky odor as well, but its floral sheath is yellow. It grows in the Far West from California to Alaska.

Slate

A metamorphic rock that can be split into durable sheets, slate is used for roofing, flagstones, and blackboards. Most slate originated as shale that was later altered in composition and structure by heat and pressure. Mica, quartz, and chlorite are the chief ingredients of slate, which is usually gray to black but can also be red or green if other minerals are present. In North America slate is quarried primarily in Pennsylvania and Vermont.

Slider *Chrysemys scripta*

A freshwater turtle that prefers the shallow, weedy areas of ponds and lakes, the slider gets its name from a reputation for slipping instantly into the water at the first sign of danger. Its shell is dark, with yellowish stripes, and behind the eyes is a red, orange, or yellow mark. One of the so-called basking turtles, sliders are exceptionally fond of sunbathing: they are often seen stacked two or three deep on logs as they laze in the sunshine.

Slug

Slimy, soft-bodied mollusks, slugs are simply snails without the protective spiral shells. Like other snails, they have two pairs of tentacles on the head, with eyes on the ends of the longer pair, and they glide along on a ribbon of mucus secreted by their own bodies. Slugs keep from drying out by hiding in crevices during the heat of the day; they venture out only at night and on damp or rainy days. Most are vegetarian and can cause considerable damage in gardens, but a few are carnivorous, preying on earthworms and other snails. Among the better-known species is the five-inch-long great slug, a European immigrant that has become a widespread garden pest throughout much of North America.

357

Snails live both on land and in water. Aquatic species, such as the apple snail, which lays its eggs on low branches or stems near the water (left), usually have gills, but land snails (above) all have lungs.

Smelt

Small relatives of salmon, most smelts are salt-water fish that spawn in freshwater lakes and streams. Pond smelts, however, live only in fresh water, and populations of several marine species have become permanent lake dwellers as well. Rainbow smelts, for example, native to the Atlantic, were introduced to the Great Lakes and Lake Champlain and now thrive in great numbers in their inland homes.

Like salmon, smelts are highly esteemed as food fish. Some are netted on spawning runs, while others are caught in lakes, especially by ice fishermen in winter. Eulachons, or candle-fish, a Pacific species, once served as more than food; they are so oily at spawning time that Indians dried them, added wicks, and burned the fish as candles.

Smog

As the name suggests, smog often is a mixture of smoke and fog. In industrial areas it is the hazy polluted air that results when smoke from burning fuels reacts with water droplets to produce sulfur compounds. Another kind of smog is formed when automobile exhaust fumes react with sunlight to produce ozone and other irritants. Both types of smog damage lungs, plant life, and even buildings. The ill effects are at their worst during temperature inversions, when a layer of warm air lies over cooler, polluted air and prevents the smog from dispersing.

Smokethorn *Psorothamnus spinosus*

These short, spiny trees of the arid Southwest usually grow in dry streambeds, or washes, where the occasional flash flood does not harm them. In fact, they benefit from the torrents: their seeds cannot germinate until their tough skins have been broken by tumbling along the stream bottom. The trees sprout a few leaves after it rains, but the fo-

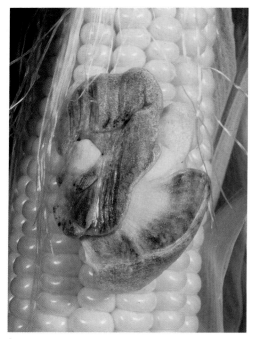

Smuts are parasites that get their name from the tiny black sootlike spores they produce.

liage soon drops away, leaving grayish twigs that look as insubstantial as puffs of smoke. In early June, however, smokethorns make a bolder show, covering themselves with purple flowers.

Smut

Serious agricultural pests, smuts are parasitic fungi that attack a variety of plants, especially corn, wheat, and other grains. When smuts infect plants, they sap the vitality of the host and produce a number of symptoms. Pustules form on the flowers, seeds, leaves, stems, or bulbs and become filled with dark, powdery spores. When the blisters rupture, the spores disperse, infecting nearby plants, or lie dormant in the soil, awaiting the next generation of hosts.

The schoolmaster, one of the smallest members of the snapper family, usually weighs less than a pound, a sharp contrast to the familiar red snapper, which can reach as much as 35 pounds.

Snakes grow continuously throughout their lives, though the rate slows as they age.

Snail

Soft-bodied mollusks that live coiled inside spiral shells, snails are found almost everywhere. The vast majority live in the ocean, but many others thrive in fresh water and on land. Snails move about by rhythmically contracting a strong, muscular foot that extends outside the shell. At the front of the foot is the head, which has paired tentacles and eyes and, in the mouth, a special "tongue" lined with tiny, rasping teeth that are used for scraping off bits of food. While most snails are vegetarians or scavengers, a few are predators. One kind, the oyster drill, for instance, is a serious pest in oyster beds. It bores holes right through oyster shells to get at the animals inside.

Snake

Long, slender, legless reptiles that slither about on their bellies, snakes have always fascinated humans, inspiring both curiosity and fear. While many people think of them as slimy, their skin (which is shed several times a year) is in fact dry and scaly. Living both in water and on the land, they are equally adept at swimming, gliding through grass or across rocks, and even climbing trees. Since snakes, like other reptiles, are cold-blooded, they regulate their body temperature by moving back and forth between sun and shade.

All snakes are predators, feeding on everything from insects and amphibians to birds and mammals. Poisonous kinds kill their prey with injections of venom, but constrictors suffocate their victims, and many others swallow live animals whole. Some snakes, such as the familiar garter snakes, bear live young, but most lay eggs. Our North American species range in size from the 9-inch Florida crowned snake to the indigo snake, which is nearly 10 feet long.

Snake bird See *Anhinga.*

Snapper

Most abundant along the Florida and Gulf of Mexico coasts, the snappers are a family of colorful fish prized by both anglers and lovers of seafood. They are large, sharp-toothed carnivores that average two to three feet in length and travel in dense schools, feeding on crabs, shrimp, and smaller fish.

The red snapper, named for its uniformly rosy hue, is the most popular and delectable of the family. It dwells in far deeper waters than the schoolmaster and yellowtail snappers, found among coral reefs, and the gray, or mangrove, snapper, which lives amid the tangled roots of mangrove thickets. While most species are edible, the dog snapper, named for its formidable fangs, is sometimes poisonous.

359

Snow, when it melts, is an important water source for streams and lakes in many regions.

S

The common snipe often builds its cup-shaped nest of moss and grass in a slight hollow at the edge of a marsh.

Snapping turtle

Quick to lunge at prey or passersby, snapping turtles are big, aggressive reptiles that use their strong jaws for defense. Much of the time, however, they lie quietly in the ooze of rivers, lakes, and ponds, where they feed on aquatic plants and small prey. They also relish an occasional duckling snatched from below. In early summer females leave the water to bury clutches of eggs on land. At home from Canada to the Gulf of Mexico, the common snapper grows up to 20 inches long and may weigh over 30 pounds. The 200-pound alligator snapper of the U.S. South and Midwest—the largest freshwater turtle in North America—has a pink wormlike growth on its tongue that it wiggles to lure fish into its gaping maw.

Snipe *Gallinago gallinago*

A long-billed shorebird found in marshes and wet meadows, the common snipe is a secretive creature that wears a concealing pattern of stripes and bars. It spends its time probing the damp soil with its bill, in search of earthworms, insects, and other prey. It is seldom seen until it suddenly takes to the air and zigzags off to safety.

On its breeding grounds in Canada and the northern United States, the male snipe performs a striking display flight that includes deep power dives, during which air rushing through the tail feathers produces a weird whinnying sound. Four speckled eggs are incubated by the female, but both adults tend the downy young, which leave the nest soon after hatching and begin finding their own food when only a few days old.

Snook *Centropomus*

Fine food and game fish with long, silvery bodies and protruding lower jaws, North America's four species of snooks live mainly where land meets sea and salt water mingles with fresh. They are found in shallow coastal seas and warm bays and lagoons along the south Atlantic and Gulf of Mexico coasts, but they also venture well inland in fresh water. Feeding mostly by night on fish and crustaceans, snooks, sometimes more than four feet long, put up a ferocious fight when hooked by anglers.

Snow

When temperatures in a cloud are below freezing, its moisture condenses directly into crystals of ice that grow into snowflakes. While all are six sided, the crystals are endlessly varied in detail:

Snow plants herald the arrival of spring by tinting forest floors of western mountains with their brilliant color.

Soapwort poultices were once used to treat skin problems.

Softshell turtles are distinguished by their long, tubelike snouts, which they often use as snorkels when they are underwater, buried in mud. The spiny softshell (right) is named for the spines or warts at the front of its dot-marked, leathery shell.

S

many look like stars, but others form columns, needles, or plates. Snow is far less dense than rain—when melted, 10 inches of snow equal 1 inch of rain—but in many areas snow is a major source of water. It also insulates plants and hibernating animals from winter's cold.

Snow plant *Sarcodes sanguinea*

Appearing in spring just after the snow melts, the fleshy red stems and blood-red flowers of snow plants are a startling sight on the barren forest floor. Because they lack chlorophyll, snow plants cannot manufacture their own food and instead draw nutrients from decaying organic matter in the soil. Seldom exceeding 12 inches in height, these wildflowers flourish only at elevations between 4,000 and 9,000 feet on the mountains of California and Oregon.

Soapwort *Saponaria officinalis*

An attractive wildflower that is common along roadsides and railway tracks, soapwort is named for the lather-producing substances in its sap. Weavers and textile mills once used the plant to clean and whiten cloth, but it was popular in the laundry and bath as well. Also known as bouncing bet, soapwort has straight, thick-jointed stems up to three feet tall and bears clusters of pink or white flowers from late spring through early autumn. The five-petaled blooms exude a spicy fragrance that is especially noticeable toward nightfall.

Softshell turtle *Trionyx*

Nicknamed "flapjacks" because of their flat, rounded form, softshell turtles have a leathery skin rather than horny plates on their carapaces. Three species—the spiny, smooth, and Florida softshells—inhabit lakes and rivers across much of North America. They often rest half-buried in mud in the shallows, where they can stretch their long necks toward the surface. Softshells also enjoy sunbathing on rocks and floating logs.

Fast-moving both in water and on land, softshells can strike with stunning speed to capture insects, fish, and other prey. They also have a well-deserved reputation for pugnacity: anyone who handles them is likely to come away quite badly scratched and bitten.

Soil must be protected in order for plants to grow properly. To keep it rich in nutrients, farmers often rotate crops, add various fertilizers, and even plow under whole fields of growing plants, which then decompose and enrich the soil.

S

Spadefoot toads call out to one another after spring storms and then mate in pools of rainwater.

Spadefish rarely grow more than 18 inches long, but some individuals have been known to reach a length of three feet and a weight of 20 pounds.

Soil

Most of the earth's land surface is covered by a mantle of soil, which varies from less than an inch to many feet in thickness. This complex substance consists mostly of weathered and eroded rock fragments (mainly clay, along with sand and silt), but these particles do not become soil until they are enriched with organic matter — the decomposed remains of plants and animals. Both the water that clings to the particles and the air in the spaces between them are also essential components of living soil. Depending on its composition, the color, texture, and other characteristics of soil vary from place to place and over time.

Because soil is the substance in which most land plants grow, it is essential to life on earth. Plants not only are anchored in soil but also rely on it for water and mineral nutrients. And the plants in turn serve directly or indirectly as food for all land animals. Slow to form but easily destroyed, soil is a vital natural resource that must be treated with utmost care.

Sole See *Flatfish.*

Solomon's seal *Polygonatum*

Some say the Solomon's seals are named for the scars on their rootstocks, which resemble the seals affixed to official documents; others claim that King Solomon used the roots to heal, or "seal," wounds. Whatever the case, Solomon's seals are most graceful plants, forming clumps of arching stems that rise in parallel curves up to six feet tall. Common in the U.S. East and parts of the Southwest, the plants are adorned in May and June with rows of white or yellowish flowers that dangle like little bells from their stems.

Sourwood *Oxydendrum arboreum*

Though the sourwood's sap is sour, its nectar is sweet; in midsummer, when its branches are arrayed with drooping clusters of creamy-white bell-shaped flowers, bees swarm to the tree and produce a honey that is prized by gourmets. Occasionally reaching a height of 60 feet, sour-

Chipping sparrows, unlike their relatives, often build nests high above the ground in vines, evergreens, or fruit trees.

Spanish moss, seen here with blooming crape myrtle, is not a moss at all but a relative of the pineapple. Its tough fibers were once used for stuffing mattresses.

S

wood is attractive in autumn as well, for its long oval leaves then take on a spectacular scarlet hue. Sourwood ranges from Pennsylvania to Florida and is also planted as an ornamental.

Southern pine forest See pp. 364–365.

Spadefish *Chaetodipterus*

Found near rocks, reefs, and pilings along the U.S. East Coast and off southern California, spadefish put up a respectable fight when hooked, and their tasty flesh is worth the struggle. Their bodies, usually one to two feet in length, are deep and flattened from side to side. On young fish the silvery sides are striped with dark vertical bars, but they tend to fade as the fish mature. Small mouths and teeth limit spadefish to a diet of plants, barnacles, and tiny crustaceans.

Spadefoot toad *Scaphiopus*

Equipped with a horny tubercle on each hind foot (their "spades"), spadefoot toads can burrow quickly, rear end first, into sandy or other loose soils. And there the secretive, seldom seen amphibians remain by day, emerging only after dark to feed and breed. The toads rely on temporary pools for reproduction and so must gather quickly after spring rains to mate and lay their eggs. Hatching almost at once, the tadpoles can become toads in less than two weeks, a record time for any North American frog or toad.

Spanish moss *Tillandsia usneoides*

A symbol of the South, Spanish moss hangs in graceful swags from trees, shrubs, and even fences and utility wires from southern Virginia to eastern Texas. The branching, gray-green strands, as long as 15 feet or more, do not harm the trees, for Spanish moss is an epiphyte, drawing its nutrients and moisture from air and rainwater. Producing inconspicuous flowers, it spreads by means of downy, windblown seeds.

Sparrow

Some 30 species of sparrows—small, streaked brown birds with stout, conical beaks—are native to North America. Many of them live in grasslands, but sparrows are found almost everywhere—from the tundra and spruce forests of the Far North to deserts and southern dunes.

Although most sparrows are seed eaters, they also feed on insects, and a few supplement their diets with snails and berries. They build tidy cup-shaped nests of grasses and twigs, usually hiding them on the ground or in shrubs. Both parents tend the nestlings, feeding them insects until they leave the nest at about 10 days old.

Among the most familiar species are the song sparrows, birds of gardens and thickets that are noted for their cheerful singing; the chipping sparrows, which have rusty caps and white eyebrows; and the field sparrows, whose sweet, whistled notes announce the courting season.

363

SOUTHERN PINE FOREST

Stretching along the coastal plain from eastern Texas to central Florida and north to Virginia is a wide belt of sandy soil dominated by pines. The most abundant species—longleaf, short-leaf, loblolly, and slash pines—often shelter an understory of young oaks and other hardwood saplings in their shade, but frequent fires (many of them deliberately set by woodsmen) serve to keep the broadleaf interlopers from taking over and, at the same time, restore the vigor of the commercially valuable pines.

The southern pine forests are home to a variety of creatures adapted for survival in this unique habitat. The sandy soil, easily excavated, is well suited to burrowers such as spadefoot toads, gopher tortoises, and pocket gophers. Ground level is occupied by animals as diverse as shrews and white-tailed deer. In the trees above, woodpeckers, warblers, and other birds probe the bark for insects and fill the forest with staccato drumming and melodious song.

In some forests the tall, stately pines tower over an understory of saplings and shrubs.

Bobcats are expert survivors that have successfully adapted to many different habitats. Common in the southeastern pine forests, these agile predators pursue birds, rodents, and even snakes but favor cottontail rabbits.

Short-tailed shrews have venomous saliva, which helps them subdue their diminutive prey.

Red-bellied woodpeckers eat huge numbers of insects destructive to trees.

Longleaf pines, named for their unusually long needles, begin life in a bushy, tufted "grass stage" (center) and assume a more treelike appearance as they mature (upper right).

The yellow-breasted chat, the largest warbler, is a loud and versatile vocalizer.

Gopher tortoises use their shovellike front feet to dig long tunnels in the sandy soil.

The gray fox, unlike most other members of the dog family, is adept at climbing trees.

Some speedwells are North American natives; the pioneers introduced others.

Sphagnum mosses vary in color, spanning the spectrum from pale green to deep red.

Cerisy's sphinx moth is marked with two distinct eyespots located on its hind wings. A close relative, lacking the black centers in its blue eyespots, is known as the blind sphinx.

Speedwell *Veronica*

No one knows just how the speedwells got their name. Some say that the bright flowers, which adorn roadsides well into summer, seem to cheer travelers on their way. Others trace the name to the speed with which the weedy kinds can spread. In fact, this adaptable clan flourishes in swamps, woodlands, mountain ravines, and lawns across most of North America. Whether upright or sprawling, all have pretty white, blue, or purplish four-petaled flowers. Some, such as water speedwell, bear the blooms in spikes; on other species they grow singly on slender stalks.

Sphagnum *Sphagnum*

Also known as peat moss, the sphagnums are aquatic mosses that are notable for their role in converting open water to dry land. The plants, up to a foot long and covered with tiny leaves just one cell thick, are most commonly found in bogs, where they form floating mats that, over time, can completely fill these wetlands. Because they secrete acids that retard decay, the mosses eventually accumulate in great spongy deposits that are gradually compacted into peat. Able to absorb up to 20 times their weight in water, sphagnums are often used as additives to garden soils and as packing material for shipping live plants. In Europe peat is also harvested and dried for use as fuel.

Sphinx moth

With wingspans of as much as six inches, sphinx moths, also known as hawk moths, are agile fliers that generally feed by hovering before flowers and sipping nectar with their long tongues. The majority are nocturnal and concealingly patterned in brown, but a few fly during the day. The larvae of most species have a horn or spine at the rear of the body and are called hornworms. Feeding on crop plants such as tobacco and tomatoes, some of the caterpillars are serious agricultural pests.

Spiderworts tint woodlands and prairies with brilliant colors, including various shades of purple.

A wolf spider—seen here with its young on its back— is one species that does not spin a web to snare its prey; instead, it hunts on foot.

Spicebush *Lindera benzoin*

A shrub that flourishes in moist eastern woodlands, spicebush bears tufts of tiny yellow flowers in early spring, long before the leaves appear. Wreathing the branches, the blooms exude the spicy perfume for which the plant is named. Its attractive oval leaves, also aromatic when crushed, turn bright yellow in the fall, then drop away to reveal the year's crop of little red berries. The fruits have been used since colonial times as a substitute for allspice, and the leaves for a fragrant tea.

Spider

Though spiders may look like insects, they in fact belong to a separate group of animals called arachnids, which also includes the daddy-long-legs, mites, ticks, and scorpions. In contrast to insects, which have six legs and a three-part body, spiders have eight legs and a two-part body. They range in size from the three-inch-long tarantulas of the Southwest to species that are practically microscopic. Most spiders have eight eyes, and all have poison fangs, used to subdue prey, as well as spinnerets, small organs at the tip of the abdomen that produce silk. Most spiders use their silk to spin webs for entangling insect prey, and some webs—especially those of the orb weavers—are complex and beautiful creations. But not all species make webs. Some hunt for prey on foot; jumping spiders pounce on their victims; and crab spiders hide in flowers to ambush unsuspecting insects looking

for nectar and pollen. Whether or not they spin webs, all spiders use silk to make cases for their eggs, and many spin strands for ballooning—drifting long distances on the wind.

Spiderwort *Tradescantia*

Natives of moist woodlands and prairies, some 60 species of spiderworts grow wild in North America. All have three-petaled blue, purple, pink, or white flowers, borne in loose clusters atop their stems. Producing long, narrow, grassy leaves, some spiderworts are erect and up to three feet tall, while others sprawl weakly across the ground. Pine spiderwort, found in parts of the Southwest, and western spiderwort, which ranges from Montana to Texas, were cooked as vegetables by aboriginal peoples. But the plants are more valued now as garden flowers, despite the fact that they sometimes develop into aggressive, persistent weeds.

Spirea *Spiraea*

Our several species of spirea are moisture-loving shrubs that thrive in damp places. A few are low or creeping evergreens, but most—including the attractive steeplebush, an eastern native and popular ornamental—are deciduous shrubs up to six feet tall. Spireas form thickets of erect stems clothed with oval, tooth-edged leaves; in summer they bear masses of five-petaled pink, white, or reddish blooms in dense clusters at the ends of the branches.

S

A cloud of spores, shot from a puffball, are scattered by the wind. These fungi form trillions of spores, increasing the odds for survival.

Roseate spoonbills were brought to the brink of extinction by plume hunters. Though they are now protected by U.S. law, their habitat along the Gulf Coast of Florida is steadily disappearing.

Spittlebug

Concealed by the masses of protective white foam that give these little insects their name, spittlebugs live in meadows and weedy places, where they feed by sucking the juices from plants. After molting several times, spittlebugs leave their bubbly hideaways as adults—now called froghoppers because they resemble tiny frogs and hop if disturbed. The foam makes the immature insects easy to find, but froghoppers usually slip away unnoticed.

Sponge

Best-known for some species' soft, absorbent skeletons, used for household cleaning and bathing, sponges are simple animals found in the sea and sometimes in fresh water. They live attached to rocks and other hard surfaces and are so plantlike in appearance that they were not recognized as animals until the 19th century.

A typical sponge has no mouth, stomach, gills, or heart. Its body consists, instead, of a chamber with many pores in its walls and a large opening at the top. Water, laden with food particles, flows in through the pores and is expelled through the top. Some species, such as the bath sponges, have skeletons of a fibrous material called spongin. Others have skeletons made up of limey or glassy spines, called spicules.

Sponges vary tremendously: they can be globular, branched, vase shaped, fingerlike, or simple, irregular crusts. Their colors range from drab browns to brilliant reds and yellows.

Spoonbill *Ajaia ajaja*

One of the most spectacularly beautiful of the large wading birds is the roseate spoonbill, a resident of the Gulf Coast from east Texas to southern Florida. Named for its bright pink plumage and long, flat, spoon-shaped bill, the bird feeds in a manner all its own. It swings its keenly sensitive bill from side to side in shallow water, snapping it shut on small fish, shrimp, and insects that it detects by touch.

Like other members of the ibis family, roseate spoonbills are usually found in flocks. The birds nest in colonies among shrubs and mangroves, often sharing island rookeries with herons, egrets, and other waders. Spoonbills are often seen flying in long lines at dusk, their slender necks extended, as they head to their roosts.

Tube sponges rise in fleshy clusters from a tropical seabed. Wastes leave through the tops of the tubes.

Spring beauties rush into bloom at the earliest possible moment.

Spore

Just as flowering plants rely on seeds for sexual reproduction, so others depend upon single-celled spores as a means of asexual reproduction. When ripe, spores are dispersed by wind and water, and if conditions are just right, they germinate. Spore-bearing structures dot the undersides of fern fronds, while the spores of mushrooms are visible as a telltale dust. Bacterial spores serve an additional function by providing protection during dormant periods; some are so resistant to harsh conditions that they can survive for hours in boiling water.

Spring

Whether freezing cold or boiling hot, mere trickles or gushing torrents, all springs are sources of water flowing from the ground. Most are found where the top of an aquifer comes in contact with the surface of the land, often on slopes or at the bases of cliffs. Springs also occur where fissures allow water under pressure to rise to the surface—sometimes forcefully, as in geysers and artesian springs. The largest springs, which can yield millions of gallons of water per day, pour from underground channels dissolved in limestone. Many are natural wonders; others are celebrated for the supposed curative properties of their mineral content, as are those in Banff National Park in Alberta.

Spring beauty *Claytonia*

Each year from March through May, spring beauties brighten damp woods and fields in both the East and West. Their slender 6- to 12-inch stems, each bearing a pair of long, narrow leaves, are topped with delicate, rose-veined pink or white flowers. The display is especially pretty where the plants grow in large patches.

Most species of spring beauty sprout from tubers that look like tiny new potatoes and taste

Spring peepers announce the arrival of the breeding season with calls so loud they can be heard up to a mile away. They cling to vegetation with their sticky toe pads.

like chestnuts. Aboriginal peoples gathered them for eating, and they are still prized by wild-foods enthusiasts. But the plants should be harvested only where they are plentiful.

Spring peeper *Hyla crucifer*

One of the best-loved signs of spring in the East is the chorus of spring peepers echoing from marshes and ponds. In the first warm days of the season, these tiny tree frogs gather to mate. Each male, just over an inch long, inflates his throat pouch to produce a high-pitched whistle; the calling of hundreds has been likened to the jingling of sleighbells. When mating is over, the adults return to the woods, leaving their eggs to hatch into tadpoles. Though the spring peeper is one of the most abundant frogs in the East, adults are seldom seen during the rest of the year. Equipped with adhesive discs on the tips of their toes, the little frogs easily climb high into the treetops in their quest for insect prey. On warm days in the fall, before they go into hibernation, lone males are sometimes heard calling deep in the woods.

Spruce trees, their silvery-blue foliage visible under a veil of snow, thrive in cool, mountainous areas.

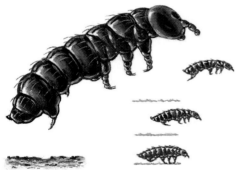

Springtails fly through the air, catapulted by hinged structures on their abdomens.

Springtail

Though primitive and wingless, springtails have a unique mechanism for becoming airborne: most species have a hingelike structure on the underside of the abdomen that, when released, catapults them several inches through space. Among our smallest insects, springtails make up for their size by sheer abundance; millions can often be found on a single acre of forest floor. While most are too small to be easily seen, some species gather in such masses that they are impossible to overlook. One of these, the tiny, dark-blue snow flea, often swarms on the snow in mild weather; another, the seashore springtail, is frequently found floating on tide pools. Most springtails feed on decaying plant matter, fungi, pollen, and even bacteria, but a few are pests in greenhouses and mushroom cellars.

Spruce *Picea*

Handsome evergreen trees that are most numerous in the North, spruces have the neatly tapered profiles of classic Christmas trees. So do firs, which the spruces resemble in many ways, but the two kinds of trees are easily distinguished. Spruce needles, which are stiff and prickly, leave peglike stubs when they fall from the twigs, while fir needles are softer and leave no stubs. Also, spruce cones hang down from the branches, while fir cones stand erect.

Our most abundant species are black spruce and white spruce, both of which range from British Columbia to Newfoundland. The tallest, the Sitka spruce of the Pacific Northwest, can exceed 200 feet and live for 800 years. Perhaps our loveliest species, admired for its silvery sheen and often planted as an ornamental, is the blue spruce of the Rockies. Spruce wood is used for everything from paper to pianos, and the twigs have even served as an ingredient in beer.

Spurge *Euphorbia*

Despite their immensely varied appearances, most spurges share one trait: the plants contain a bitter, often poisonous milky sap. As a result, cattle refuse to eat the acrid foliage of some of the spurges, which have overrun much western rangeland. Caper spurge, on the other hand, is cultivated by gardeners because it is said to repel moles and gophers. Snow-on-the-mountain, another common spurge, looks like a pale version of its subtropical relative the poinsettia.

Leafy spurges are persistent, troublesome weeds on western rangelands. Sheep, however, graze on the plants, helping to keep them under control.

Squawroots are parasites that take nutrients from other plants.

S

Squids, here seen off Catalina Island in California, gather in large schools to mate. The male fertilizes the fermale's eggs by placing a little packet of sperm in her mantle cavity. The eggs are then released and left to develop on floating weeds or on the ocean floor.

Squall line

A row of thunderstorms that may extend for hundreds of miles, a squall line is visible as a wall of storm clouds that advances well ahead of a cold front pushing into warm, humid air. Accompanied by gusty winds, thunder and lightning, rain, and sometimes hail and tornadoes, the squall line usually passes over quickly. Within a few hours, however, temperatures are likely to plummet with the arrival of the cold front.

Squawroot *Conopholis americana*

Like other members of the broomrape family, squawroot contains no chlorophyll and so cannot manufacture its own food. Instead, it takes nourishment from the roots of oaks and other trees in eastern U.S. woodlands. With its leaves reduced to small, brownish scales, squawroot looks like nothing more than clusters of pine cones lying on the forest floor. In late spring, however, it puts on a modest show, with small yellow, hooded flowers peeping out from between the scales.

Squid

The unlikely cousins of clams and snails, squids are marine mollusks whose shells have been reduced to internal remnants. They range from 2 inches to more than 50 feet in length, with eyes at the head end. Surrounding the mouth are 10 arms equipped with suction cups, including 2 longer tentacles used for seizing fish and other prey. Frequently found in large schools, squids swim by natural jet propulsion: by drawing water into their bodies and then expelling it through a funnellike tube, they shoot quickly backward. When threatened, squids release a cloud of inky fluid that serves as a smoke screen, allowing them to escape.

371

Naming the Numerous Squirrels

Most nonflying tree squirrels can be identified by size, color, and the area where they live. Fox squirrels are the exception; they vary in color from region to region. In the middle Atlantic region, where fox and eastern gray squirrels are nearly identical, the fox squirrels can be distinguished by their larger size and white noses. It should also be noted that individual squirrels of various species may be all white or all black.

Less than 15 inches long, including tail

Reddish above, white below

Red squirrel
(Alaska and Canada to southern Rockies and southern Appalachians)

Olive to rusty or gray above, reddish below

Douglas' squirrel
(British Columbia to central California)

More than 16 inches long, including tail

EARS WITH TUFTS

Gray above, white below

Abert's squirrel
(Southern Rockies and Colorado Plateau except north rim of Grand Canyon)

Gray above, black below, tail white

Kaibab squirrel
(North rim of Grand Canyon)

EARS WITHOUT TUFTS

Gray above, white below

Eastern gray squirrel
(East)

Western gray squirrel
(Washington to California)

Arizona gray squirrel
(Arizona and New Mexico)

Yellowish-rusty to dark gray above, yellow or orange below

Sometimes with white markings on head

No white markings on head

Fox squirrel
(East except Northeast)

Apache squirrel
(Southeastern Arizona)

Stalactites are formed over a long period of time by minerals deposited from water seeping through the ceilings of limestone caves. In the Luray Caverns of Virginia, an enchanting world is enhanced by the dramatic lighting.

Squirrel

Though chipmunks, prairie dogs, woodchucks, marmots, ground squirrels, and flying squirrels are all members of the squirrel family, the term *squirrel* means to most people the familiar non-flying, nut-gathering tree squirrels. Wherever there are trees, in fact—from the Great North Woods to the Mexican border—there is at least one kind of tree squirrel.

Bushy-tailed acrobats that leap from branch to branch and race up and down tree trunks (sometimes as if to play hide and seek), squirrels are not nearly so secretive as most other forest dwellers. All the more conspicuous because they are active during the day and around the year, the busy little rodents are usually searching for food. Opportunistic omnivores, squirrels feed on insects, birds' eggs, and even young birds, as well as mushrooms, fruit, bark, and the nuts and seeds they store for winter. While red, Douglas', and Abert's squirrels favor the seeds of pines and other conifers, gray and fox squirrels prefer acorns and hickory nuts. The various seeds and nuts are either buried singly (and later located by smell) or stored in large caches.

Squirrels sleep and raise their young in tree cavities, which they line with leaves and bark, or in bulky nests built high in the treetops. Made of leaves and sticks, the nests may seem flimsy and precarious, but they are sturdy enough to withstand wind, rain, and snow.

Stalactite

Among the most impressive features of limestone caves are the strange, often beautifully shaped stalactites, which hang like icicles from the ceiling. They are formed by the slow evaporation of mineral-laden water as it drips from the roof of the cave. Stalactites start out as tiny ring-shaped deposits on cave ceilings; bit by bit they lengthen into tubes and gradually become wider. Some grow an inch a year; others take 100 years to add that much. Stalactites consist of a

Stargazers are found along the southern Atlantic coast. When removed from the water, they are able to survive for several hours.

form of calcium carbonate. Naturally white, it is tinged red, yellow, or black by impurities.

When the flow of water is sufficient, it drips from the end of the stalactite to the floor of the cave, creating an upward-pointing formation called a stalagmite. If the two continue to grow, they may eventually meet and form a column. Stunning cave formations can be seen at such places as Luray Caverns in Virginia and Carlsbad Caverns in New Mexico.

Stalagmite See *Stalactite.*

Starfish See *Sea star.*

Stargazer

Homely fish with upward-slanting mouths and eyes on the top of their heads, stargazers habitually lie half-buried in sand or mud on the ocean floor with only their eyes and lips protruding. They wiggle a fleshy lure on their mouths, and when small fish, crustaceans, or other prey venture near to investigate, they leap up and snatch a meal. Stargazers also have special organs behind their eyes that can produce powerful electric shocks, perhaps to stun their prey, and some are equipped with venomous spines that help keep hungry predators at bay.

Sticklebacks lack true scales, but some species are protected by bony plates along their sides. All have sharp back spines.

The starling's feathers, tipped with white and buff in the fall (top), turn glossy black in spring as the tips wear off (above).

Starling *Sturnus vulgaris*

Introduced to New York City in 1890, the stocky, iridescent European starling promptly began to expand its range and is now found all across the continent. Well-adapted to agricultural lands in Europe, it had no trouble adjusting to farmlands in North America and has become one of our most abundant birds. Starlings generally feed in open country, probing in the soil for insects, larvae, seeds, and other food; but in the evening huge, noisy flocks often gather in cities to roost on buildings. Starlings build their nests in holes in trees, and in crevices in cliffs or on buildings; both parents incubate the clutch of four to six eggs. While starlings consume many harmful insects, these adaptable immigrants are a mixed blessing, not only because they damage crops but also because they compete with native song-birds for nesting sites.

Stickleback

These small fish of shallow lakes, coastal waters, and brackish estuaries are named for the stout spines that project from their backs. Numbering from two to nine, depending on the species, the spines are used as weapons against predators and, during the spawning season, against other sticklebacks. Normally dull-colored, the males don brighter hues when they are ready to breed. They build tubular nests of water plants, which they glue together with a sticky mucous secretion. Each male then gives chase to one or more females, nipping their fins to coax them into the nest to lay eggs. The pugnacious male carefully guards both eggs and young, using his stout spines to drive away intruders. Their unusual mating behavior, plus their generally aggressive temperament, make the sticklebacks popular aquarium fish.

Sticktight *Bidens*

Producing small, dry fruits armed with barbed prongs, the sticktights have earned such nick-names as beggar's ticks and devil's pitchforks. Because they attach themselves so easily to fur, feathers, or fabric, the fruits ensure wide dispersal of the weedy plants. Some of these members of the sunflower family have yellow ray flowers on their flower heads and are called bur marigolds, but most have only a drab central button of disc flowers.

Stilt *Himantopus mexicanus*

With 10-inch-long red legs that do indeed resemble stilts, these strikingly patterned black-and-white shorebirds are easy to spot as they stride through brackish lagoons and shallow lakes. Black-necked stilts sometimes wade belly-

S

A tall, slim stilt, elegantly attired in black and white, prepares to probe the shallows for small shrimp and other crustaceans, as well as the large variety of water insects on which it feeds. Stilts also eat the seeds of marsh and aquatic plants.

S

Many stink bugs are protectively camouflaged in shades of brown or green. But some other species—among them the crop-destroying harlequin bug (right)— are easy to spot because of their bright, distinctive patterns.

deep in the water, using their long, tapered bills to pluck insects nimbly from the surface. They also glean on nearby mudflats. Breeding in small colonies, black-necked stilts lay clutches of three or four spotted eggs, sometimes in shallow depressions in the sand and sometimes on islets in the water. Talented bluffs, nesting stilts are well-known for their very convincing distraction displays, which include both broken-wing and broken-leg acts.

Stingray

Like the skates and other rays, stingrays are flat-bodied kin of sharks that move through the water by undulating their winglike pectoral fins. From one to seven feet wide, they also spend much time buried in the sand in shallow water.

Bathers on both coasts should regard even the smaller kinds as armed and dangerous: when disturbed, stingrays lash out with their long whiplike tails, which, armed with venomous spines, can inflict painful injuries.

Stink bug

Protected from predators by the foul odors that have earned them their name, the stink bugs are shield-shaped insects that are usually about half an inch long. Most are green or brownish, but some are boldly patterned. The majority feed on plant juices, which they suck through their long flexible beaks, and a number of species are crop and garden pests. A few, however, are predators, using their beaks to drain the body fluids of caterpillars and other insects.

Stonecrops, such as the Sierra sedum of the Far West, use their leaves as water storage tanks.

S

Adult stoneflies, unlike the ravenous aquatic nymphs, eat next to nothing and soon die.

Storm-petrels feeding at sea sometimes are snatched from below by large fish.

Stinkpot See *Musk turtle.*

Stonecrop *Sedum*

Hardy plants, including many that live in dry, rocky places, the stonecrops have thick, succulent leaves in which they store water whenever it rains, and so are able to survive times of drought. Many are popular as rock garden plants, producing dense clusters of small flowers in shades of pink, purple, yellow, and white, on stems up to two feet tall. The yellow-flowered wallpepper, or mossy stonecrop, often planted as a groundcover, has escaped cultivation to spread mossy mats of thick, tiny leaves over rocks, cliffs, and dunes. Orpine, also known as live-forever, is another garden escape that enlivens roadsides and waste places with purplish blooms. The widespread, similar-looking roseroot thrives even in such forbidding habitats as high mountaintops and arctic tundra.

Stonefly

Poor fliers, stoneflies seldom venture far from the streams and rivers in which they spend their youth. With wings folded flat along the back, the adults are most often seen crawling over leaves or rocks near the water's edge. The aquatic nymphs, which creep about under stones and feed on algae or small animals, are themselves a major source of food for fish. While the nymphs take four years to mature, the adult insects mate and die within a few weeks.

Storm-petrel

Small, dark seabirds with white rumps, storm-petrels are swallow-size relatives of albatrosses and shearwaters. They are usually seen fluttering just above the waves, pattering the surface with their webbed feet as they search for small fish and other food. The birds nest in colonies,

376

Striped bass, smartly outfitted in pinstripes, are active predators. They cruise the waters along the Atlantic and Pacific coasts in search of small fish, crustaceans, and other prey. Prized by sport fishermen, they are often caught on their way upriver to spawn.

usually on remote islands, where each female lays a single white egg in a burrow. But even during the breeding season, storm-petrels spend the day at sea, returning to their nests only under the cover of darkness. Leach's and Wilson's storm-petrels are the most common species.

Storm surge

Driven by hurricane winds, storm surges are moving walls of water that can devastate low-lying coastal regions. They form as hurricanes move across the sea; howling winds drive seawater toward the shore and whip up the waves, causing them to swell to tremendous heights. By the time the storm reaches the coast, the sea level may have risen by 10 feet or more. If the storm surge strikes without warning, the results are likely to be calamitous, for its waters can wash away buildings, break levees, and flood the coastal lowlands for many miles inland.

Wild strawberries, a favorite of many birds, grow so close to the ground that turtles and small rodents can reach them as well.

Strawberry *Fragaria*

Living for several years and spreading by means of runners, each one tipped with a plantlet that soon takes root, a single wild strawberry plant can expand into a large bed, half-hidden in the grass of a meadow or under the trees in open woods. Clusters of white five-petaled flowers appear in late spring or early summer and are soon followed by the familiar strawberries.

Not a true berry at all, the juicy red, edible portion of a strawberry is actually a much enlarged stem end—what botanists call a receptacle—and each of the "seeds" on its surface is a separate, tiny, hard fruit. Though smaller than the cultivated kinds, wild strawberries are unrivaled for flavor and sweetness. Relished by humans for desserts and preserves, they also are avidly consumed by a wide range of wildlife, from birds to bears.

Striped bass *Morone saxatilis*

Nicknamed rockfish, stripers, and greenheads, striped bass have long been popular food and game fish. They are native to Atlantic waters but were introduced to the Pacific in 1886 and now thrive along the West Coast as well. The adults live in the sea but spawn in rivers and streams, where the females lay eggs by the millions and where the young remain until they are mature enough to head for the ocean. Some populations, especially in the Southeast, are landlocked in lakes and dammed rivers and so spend their entire lives in fresh water.

Olive to blackish above and silvery to white below, striped bass are marked from head to tail with bold horizontal lines. On the average, adults are two feet long and weigh about 10 pounds, but individuals occasionally exceed six feet and weigh over 100 pounds.

Lake sturgeons grow very slowly, often taking 20 years or longer to reach a mature weight of 70 or more pounds.

Plant succession in the years following a forest fire proceeds in an orderly, predictable fashion. A graceful aspen grove will soon be overshadowed by firs and other stately conifers, and these may well be replaced in time by other species.

S

Sturgeon

Giant, slow-moving fish armed from head to tail with rows of bony plates, sturgeons look as ancient and primitive as in fact they are. These bizarre-looking fish spend their time cruising ponderously along the bottom. Fleshy, sensitive barbels dangle from their flat, pointed snouts, helping them find small fish, crustaceans, and snails, which they suck into their mouths. Sturgeons mature slowly but are large and long-lived. The white sturgeon of the Pacific Coast, our biggest kind, sometimes grows to a length of 20 feet and lives for 75 years.

Some species, such as the lake sturgeon of the Great Lakes and Mississippi Valley, live in fresh water year-round. But most, such as the Atlantic sturgeon, are saltwater fish that migrate up rivers to spawn. Their eggs have long been prized for making the choicest caviar, and the smoked flesh is eaten as well. But because North American sturgeons have declined in number due to dam building, pollution, and overfishing, the United States enacted legislation that prohibits taking them for their roe. As a result, most of the caviar consumed in North America is imported.

Succession

Every habitat, whether pond, marsh, or meadow, changes over time in a predictable, orderly sequence known as succession. At each stage the reigning species of plants and animals alter the environment, making it suitable for new species to move in. Eventually, however, a point of equilibrium is reached, and no new species are introduced. This stage, known as the climax community, is self-sustaining and remains stable—sometimes for thousands of years—until an act of man or nature upsets the balance and the cycle starts anew.

A field laid bare by fire, for instance, is an open invitation to new plant life. Hardy pioneering weeds usually are first to arrive, enriching the soil and providing shelter for other seedlings. As conditions improve, shrubs begin to grow, shading out the sun-loving weeds. If conditions are right, pines may next appear, only to be replaced in time by a climax community of broadleaf trees. Ponds, too, undergo changes, as layers of debris accumulate and plants encroach from the shore. Inevitably all ponds fill in, becoming marshes and then dry land.

Some sundews (above) have clusters of broad leaves whose tiny gland-tipped hairs glisten with sticky fluid. Others, such as the dew thread (right), are efficient insect traps that ensnare prey on their long, narrow leaves.

Staghorn sumacs bear clusters of fuzzy fruits that persist through the winter.

S

Sucker

Thick-lipped freshwater fish found throughout North America, suckers have protruding, underslung mouths that are adapted for sucking worms, insect larvae, and other food off the bottoms of streams and lakes. Some, such as the chubsucker, are less than a foot long, while others, including the bigmouth buffalo (the largest member of the family), can exceed three feet in length and weigh over 70 pounds. In spring the abundant white sucker and many other species migrate to streams or to shallow areas in lakes for spawning. Each female sheds thousands of eggs, which hatch in about two weeks. Despite an abundance of tiny bones, suckers are often caught for their sweet, tasty flesh.

Sulfur

An abundant, yellow, nonmetallic element, sulfur is a highly reactive substance that combines to form hundreds of compounds. Coal, oil, and natural gas all contain sulfur compounds, as do ores such as pyrite and galena. Sulfur is also present in foods such as onions and cabbage. Important industrial compounds include sulfur dioxide, a preservative and bleaching agent, and sulfuric acid, a commercial chemical. Sulfa drugs, too, are made from sulfur compounds. Texas and Louisiana are our largest sulfur producers.

Sumac

Small trees or shrubs, sumacs are fast-growing plants with long, featherlike compound leaves that turn brilliant red, orange, or purple before dropping off in the fall. Their greenish flowers are borne in large, loose spikes that are followed by dense clusters of hairy red or smooth white fruits. The fruits are eaten by many kinds of wildlife, and those of the widespread staghorn sumac, named for its velvety twigs, and California's lemonade sumac can be brewed to make a refreshing tea. Other common species include smooth sumac, a pioneer plant that is quick to take root in abandoned fields and waste places, and shining sumac, which is sometimes planted as an ornamental. Although the sumacs are related to poison ivy, most are harmless. But one, poison sumac, contains a virulent sap that causes a severe rash.

Sundew *Drosera*

In the sunlight, inviting droplets glisten like nectar on the leaves of sundews. But insects lured to these carnivorous plants discover too late that they have been fooled: their bodies get stuck in the gluey fluid on the tips of fine surface hairs, then nearby hairs bend in upon them to complete the trap. The sundews, which thrive in bogs and damp sandy areas, then digest their victims and so obtain the nitrogen and other nutrients that are missing from the acid soils where they grow. The roundleaf sundew is our most widespread species.

S

The sunflower, a native North American plant, is the state flower of Kansas.

Banded sunfish, marked with dark vertical bars on their sides, are found in streams and ponds from New England to Florida.

A sunrise, mirrored in a tranquil lake, transforms a waterside grove into a striking silhouette.

Sunfish

Named for their iridescent colors, sunfish are a group of small lake and pond fish that are native to the East but have been transplanted to the West as well. Most are deep bodied, with a conspicuous flap at the rear of each gill cover. The bluegill and the common sunfish, or pumpkinseed, are favorites with children and beginning anglers because they are easily caught with simple equipment. Also included in the large and diverse sunfish family are crappies, black bass, and pygmy sunfish.

During the breeding season the males of all species use their tails to clear space on the bottom, making circular nests in which the females lay their eggs. The males then guard the eggs and fan them with their tails to keep them free of debris until they hatch.

Sunflower *Helianthus*

Beloved for their radiant yellow flower heads, sunflowers are also valued for their seeds, the oil they yield, and the tubers that some produce. A number of species are found across much of the continent, and most are easily recognized by their tall, stiff stems and showy, daisylike blooms. Three to 10 inches wide, the flower heads of the wild species are smaller than those of the cultivated sunflowers (up to 18 inches across) but are still dazzling. The common sunflower, grown by aboriginal peoples in the Southwest since about 3000 B.C., is one of the few North American natives that produce a major agricultural crop. Jerusalem artichokes, another common species, are as much as 10 feet tall and have flowers that are 2 to 4 inches wide. They are grown for their edible tubers.

The surgeonfish family includes the brightly colored blue tang, which changes from yellow (top) to blue (above) as it matures.

Barn swallows swoop gracefully down to drink water while on the wing.

Sunrise

The brilliant reds and yellows that tinge the sky at sunrise and sunset are easily explained. Red and yellow light, which have longer wavelengths than other colors, are less likely to be scattered by particles in the air (such as dust and water droplets). And since light must pass through more atmosphere—and more particles—when the sun is close to the horizon, it is the reds and yellows that we see.

Spectacular sunrises and sunsets often occur after volcanic eruptions because the volcanoes spew huge amounts of dust into the air. Ash from the gigantic eruption at Krakatoa in 1883, blown by the wind, created brilliant sunsets around the world for more than a year.

Surfperch

Common fish off the Pacific coast, most surfperch—true to their name—live in the surf zone. They are a great rarity among saltwater fish, for the females produce live young, giving birth to four or more offspring at a time. Remarkably, many of the tiny fry are able to mate within a day or two of their own birth. The barred surfperch, marked with golden stripes, and the walleye surfperch, steely blue with black-tipped fins, are the most abundant species.

Surgeonfish *Acanthurus*

Vegetarian reef-dwellers that look as gentle as they are beautiful, the surgeonfish nevertheless carry secret weapons: built-in switchblades. Scalpel-sharp spines, sheathed in folds near the tail, can be erected when the fish are disturbed; a swipe of the tail can then inflict deep cuts on a predator or a human diver.

Surgeonfish are found from the Gulf of Mexico and the Caribbean to Bermuda, and some range north along the Atlantic coast as far as New York. Also called tangs (German for "seaweed"), these thin, oval fish use their front teeth to scrape algae from rocks and coral reefs. Surgeonfish begin as colorless larvae, but many change dramatically in hue as they mature.

Swallow

Streamlined birds with long, pointed wings, swallows are swift flyers that nimbly snap up insects in midair. In cooler weather, when insects are unavailable, tree swallows sometimes feed on berries and seeds as well. All species are social, feeding in flocks and sometimes nesting in colonies. And all are migratory; some winter in the South, but most travel thousands of miles to the tropics.

Besides the purple martin, our largest swallow, seven other species breed in North America and display a variety of nesting styles. Tree holes are home to tree swallows and to the violet-green swallows of the West, while bank swallows dig tunnels in sand banks, often in large colonies. Rough-winged swallows nest in drainpipes under bridges and in tunnels abandoned by other birds. Cup-shaped nests of mud are built by cave swallows and by the familiar, fork-tailed barn swallows. Cliff swallows construct gourd-shaped nests out of mud pellets, cementing them to cliffs, culverts, or buildings, including the Mission of San Juan Capistrano in California, where the birds are famous for their predictable return each spring.

381

S

Swallowtail butterflies emerge from well-camouflaged brown or green cocoons that look like wood or curled-up leaves.

Swallowtail butterfly

Often large and dramatically patterned, swallowtail butterflies are named for the trailing extensions on their hindwings. Most of North America's two dozen or so species are black and yellow, black-and-white, or black and blue. Many of them look like other, foul-tasting species and so deceive predators. Their caterpillars also are protected in a number of ways. Some mimic vegetation or bird droppings, while others have large eyespots that make them appear far more fierce and formidable than they are. When disturbed, the caterpillars discharge an ill-smelling fluid from special glands near the back of the head. And those known as pipevine swallowtails feed on pungent roots that make them taste unpleasant to would-be predators who have not yet learned to avoid them by sight.

Swamp

In contrast to marshes, where grasses and reeds are the prevailing vegetation, swamps are wetlands that are dominated by trees. The constant supply of moisture in these wooded wetlands encourages the vigorous growth of many other plants as well, including shrubs, vines, epiphytes, and ferns.

The kinds of trees found in swamps vary from place to place. Near the Great Lakes, for example, the most common trees are spruces, white cedars, and other conifers, while red maple is typical of swamps in the U.S. Northeast. In the Southeast bald cypresses draped with Spanish moss tower over many inland swamps, but only mangroves can survive in saltwater swamps along the coast.

Thanks to the abundant moisture and lush vegetation, swamps are rich with wildlife. Insects proliferate and are consumed by countless fish, frogs, snakes, and turtles. Waterfowl of all kinds live there, and deer, raccoons, and other mammals are regular visitors.

Humans have not always looked kindly on swamps. Early settlers regarded them as hindrances to travel and as breeding grounds for disease and dangerous animals, while modern

Many freshwater swamps in the Southeast are dominated by bald cypresses, conifers that shed their needles in autumn.

developers often covet them as potential building sites. Such attitudes, however, are on the wane, and swamps are finally being appreciated as important habitats that deserve protection.

Swan *Cygnus*

Graceful birds with white plumage and long, sinuous necks, swans are our largest waterfowl. They live on lakes, ponds, and estuaries and feed both by dipping their heads underwater to browse on aquatic plants and by grazing on vegetation along the shore.

Bonded by noisy courtship rituals, swans, like geese, mate for life. They nest on huge mounds of dead plants, with both parents tending the eggs and young. Swans can be ferocious in defense of their offspring; they attack even dogs and humans who dare to venture near. The downy young, called cygnets, are brownish or gray and sometimes ride on the mother's back.

The tundra, or whistling, swan is the most abundant of the three species found in North America. It nests in the Far North and winters in marshes on the Atlantic and Pacific coasts. The trumpeter swan, named for its bugling call, lives on lakes in the Rocky Mountains and Alaska. Once endangered, it has increased in numbers in recent years. The mute swan, which, despite its name, can hiss and grunt, was introduced from Europe and is found on park ponds, especially along the East Coast and around the Great Lakes.

Trumpeter swans, the largest of our North American species, are also the loudest, delivering notes that are truly trumpetlike. Their nests are mounds of vegetation built on western lakes.

Sweet clover is often planted in fields because it enriches the soil with nitrogen.

Sweetgum wood is used for furniture and veneer, as well as for boxes and barrels.

Sweet clover *Melilotus*

On hot summer days sweet clovers fill the air with an unmistakable vanillalike aroma (it intensifies when the plants are dried). This scent alone distinguishes the sweet clovers from the true clovers. Found in waste places but also cultivated, sweet clovers produce tangles of branching stems up to 10 feet tall, covered with three-part compound leaves and topped from May to October with spires of white or yellow flowers. The plants are harvested for fodder, and a tea can be brewed from the fragrant blooms.

Sweet-fern *Comptonia peregrina*

Though its foliage is fernlike, sweet-fern is in fact a flowering shrub related to the bayberry. Growing up to four feet tall, it has long, narrow leaves—dark green above and downy below—that release a pleasant scent when crushed. Near the tips of the branching stems are clusters of small catkins that mature into brownish fruits that resemble burrs. Sweet-fern, found in poor soils from Nova Scotia to Georgia, has long been used for home remedies and sachets.

Sweetgum *Liquidambar styraciflua*

A native of moist bottomlands and swamps throughout much of the eastern United States, sweetgum is an important timber tree that yields a dark, attractive wood. It also exudes a fragrant resin that has been used for chewing gum and as an ingredient in perfumes and cosmetics. Growing as tall as 100 feet or more, the sweetgum is a handsome tree that is esteemed as an ornamental. It is easily recognized by its five- or seven-pointed, star-shaped leaves, which in autumn turn a brilliant red; the corky wings that form along its twigs; and the spiny, spherical fruits that dangle from the branches all winter long.

Swifts gather twigs and moss to build their nests, which are glued together with the same sticky saliva that cements them to the inside of a hollow tree, the interior of a chimney, or the rocky wall of a cave.

S

Sycamore trees are easily recognized by their mottled bark, maplelike leaves, and the globular fruits that hang from the branches.

Swift

Tireless, thoroughgoing aerialists, the fast-flying swifts spend more time on the wing than any other land birds—catching insects, drinking, courting, even mating while in the air. When not in flight, they cling to vertical surfaces with their sharp claws, since their tiny feet are not suited for perching. Widespread species include the chimney swift, a small, dark gray bird that nests in chimneys and hollow trees east of the Rockies. In the West the white-throated swift is often seen darting into rocky crevices, where large numbers roost at dusk. The black swift, also a westerner, often nests behind waterfalls.

Swordfish *Xiphias gladius*

A magnificent warrior of the open sea, the swordfish is enormous in size, spirit, and stamina. It is streamlined from the tip of its long, pointed snout to the sleek arc of its tail and easi-

ly gives chase to all manner of sea life. Up to 15 feet long and weighing as much as 1,000 pounds, swordfish have been clocked at speeds of 60 miles per hour. While they have been known to charge boats and occasionally puncture their hulls, they are more likely to use their strong, sharp-edged swords (which may be five feet long) for decimating schools of mackerel and other small fish. Swordfish bills have even been found embedded in whale blubber—another testament to the creature's pluck. Highly popular game and commercial fish, swordfish live in temperate to tropical waters of the Atlantic and Pacific oceans.

Sycamore *Platanus*

The most massive deciduous tree on the continent—the American sycamore—occasionally reaches heights of 170 feet or more, with a trunk 14 feet in diameter. Its western relatives, the California and Arizona sycamores, are more modest in size but, at up to 100 feet, are still among the tallest trees in the valleys and canyons that they favor.

Sycamores are easily distinguished by their unique bark—it flakes away in jigsaw-puzzle patterns, exposing the ghostly pale underbark and giving the trunks a mottled appearance. Also distinctive are the sycamores' fruits, which are tightly packed into balls that commonly hang from bare branches all winter long. In the wild the giant trees flourish beside streams, while in cities the species known as the London plane tree is often planted along streets.

Syzygy

The arrangement of three celestial bodies in a straight line in the heavens is known as syzygy. The sun, moon, and earth, for example, line up every two weeks during the new moon and the full moon. Since ancient times, many strange phenomena have been attributed to syzygy: astrologers place special significance on the alignment of planets, and a recent theory speculates that the syzygy of Jupiter, the earth, and the sun can cause volcanic eruptions and other cataclysms.

The taiga, where broadleaved trees sometimes mix with the evergreens, is the world's largest forest.

Taiga

Just south of the arctic tundra, a vast forest of spruces, firs, and other conifers encircles the globe. Known by its Russian name, *taiga,* the forest is also called the great north woods. It occupies an area that was scoured by glaciers during the last ice age and now is dotted with hundreds of bogs and lakes and crisscrossed by networks of streams. During the long, cold winters, the thin layer of surface soil is frozen solid, and summers are just warm enough to turn it into sodden muck. Despite such harsh conditions, the evergreens thrive; flocks of crossbills, grosbeaks, and other birds feast on the plentiful supply of conifer seeds; and lynx, moose, and other mammals eke out an existence in this wooded wilderness.

Talc

The softest mineral known, talc is also called soapstone. It ranges from whitish green to gray in color and is found in fibrous layers in certain metamorphic rocks. The basic ingredient in talcum powder, talc has been quarried since antiquity for a wide range of other uses. (The Assyrians and Egyptians carved talc into seals and amulets. Inuit still use block soapstone from Baffin Island and Quebec for their carvings.) Today talc is widely used in industry as a lubricant and an electrical insulator and is an ingredient in rubber and paper. Chemically unreactive, talc is also ground for filler in soap, crayons, paint, and other products. The United States is a leading talc producer. Madoc, Ontario, is a major Canadian producer.

Talus forms a dramatic, rocky slope in the Avalanche Canyon area of scenic Olympic National Park in Washington.

Talus

The accumulation of rock fragments that piles up at the foot of a cliff or, in some areas, a mountain slope is known as talus. The buildup of debris is slow but steady, often block by block, as pieces of rock break from outcrops near the top of the cliff or slope. While weathering and erosion start the process, gravity completes it, pulling loosened rocks from the faces of cliffs or down mountainsides. Since the rocks often break into smaller pieces along the way, talus ranges from gravel-size pebbles to enormous boulders. In certain places, particularly the arid areas of the West, rock slides produce much of the talus found at the base of mountain slopes, where it presents a daunting challenge to hikers.

Tamarack See *Larch.*

T

Scarlet tanagers (right) are as beneficial as they are beautiful, since they consume large numbers of destructive beetles and caterpillars. Western tanagers (below) are often sighted high in the mountains of the West, where they feed on insects and fruit. In spite of their different colors, these two tanagers are so closely related that they sometimes interbreed.

Tanager *Piranga*

Among the most brightly colored North American birds are the four species of tanagers, which, like their equally colorful tropical relatives, are creatures of the forest. The scarlet tanager, so brilliant that it is sometimes called the firebird, lives in deciduous forests in the East, while the summer tanager prefers oak and pine-oak woodlands in the U.S. South. Wooded areas in the mountainous Southwest are home to the hepatic tanager, and the western tanager—the only species in which the males are mainly yellow rather than red—nests in western forests of oaks or pines.

During the breeding season birds of all four species build cup-shaped nests of twigs and grass well out from the trunk on horizontal branches in trees. The greenish or yellowish females alone incubate their clutches of three to five eggs, but both parents share in the care and feeding of the young, with insects forming the bulk of the diet. As winter approaches, male scarlet and western tanagers acquire a duller plumage similar to that of the females, and all species migrate south.

Tanoak *Lithocarpus densiflorus*

Intermediate between chestnuts and oaks, the tanoak is a tree that produces erect spikes of flowers resembling those of the chestnuts, but bears acorns exactly like those of the oaks. On mountain slopes in California and southern Oregon, this handsome evergreen sometimes attains a height of 100 feet or more, though at high altitudes it commonly grows as a shrub. While the tanoak is seldom harvested for lumber—its reddish-brown wood tends to split and warp as it dries—leatherworkers at one time gathered its tannin-rich bark for tanning hides.

Tansy *Tanacetum vulgare*

A garden escape that thrives in fields and along roadsides throughout most of North America, tansy is a vigorous herb up to four feet tall with finely divided, dark green ferny foliage. It is sometimes known as bitter-buttons, an allusion both to its yellow buttonlike flower heads, which are borne in dense, flat-topped clusters, and to the intense aroma and bitter flavor of the entire plant. The strongly scented leaves were once used to flavor omelettes and sausages and, considered a natural insect repellent, were rubbed on meat to discourage flies. Tansy also has a long tradition of use in folk medicine, with its supposed powers ranging from the prevention of miscarriage to the cure of kidney disorders.

Tarantula

Big and hairy, with leg spans of five inches or more, tarantulas are North America's largest spiders. Most of them live in the U.S. Southwest, where they spend the daylight hours hiding in burrows and other dark places. At night, however, they roam about and hunt for insects or, in the case of the larger species, mice, lizards, and other small vertebrates. The tarantulas' eyesight is poor and they cannot hear, but their hairs are

Tarantulas, named after a large spider found near Taranto, Italy, can inflict bites that are about as painful as bee stings.

Tansy is a hardy and tenacious herb. Its stems and leaves are frost resistant, its bright yellow blossoms are long lasting, and a single patch may hold its ground for decades.

The tar pits at Rancho La Brea in California became a huge repository in which such ancient animals as giant ground sloths and the wolves that pursued them were preserved for all time.

T

sensitive and detect vibrations from prey and foe alike. Although the males have relatively short life spans, females have been known to live for 20 years or more. Basically reclusive and seldom aggressive, tarantulas can nevertheless deliver a mildly poisonous, though very painful, bite.

Tar pit

Commonly known as the La Brea Tar Pits, these unusual pools of thick natural asphalt located within the city limits of Los Angeles, California, are a treasure trove of animal fossils. The tar pits, formed by seepage from underground petroleum deposits some 20,000 years ago, served for millennia as wildlife death traps. Lured by inviting pools of water that collected on the surface, thirsty mammals, birds, and other creatures became mired in the deadly tar, sinking slowly to their deaths. Since 1906, when an ancient bear was exhumed, the remains of more than a million creatures—including mastodons, mammoths, saber-toothed cats, camels,

sloths, bison, and birds—have been recovered from this sticky mass grave. The tar pits are part of Hancock Park, and the fossils are on view in a nearby museum.

Tarpon *Megalops atlanticus*

A popular game fish along the Atlantic Coast, especially south of Cape Hatteras, and in the Gulf of Mexico, tarpons are well-known for their fighting qualities. When hooked, a tarpon immediately begins a series of spectacular twisting leaps, presenting a thrill and challenge to sport fishermen. Although these huge relatives of herrings can reach a length of eight feet and weigh 350 pounds, they are seldom taken for food: their coarse, oily flesh is considered poor eating. Their silvery scales, however, as big as silver dollars, are used in jewelry and other decorative work. Extremely prolific, the females lay as many as 12 million eggs at a time. The hatchlings begin life as transparent, ribbonlike larvae that look nothing like the adults.

T

The cinnamon teal, the largest of our three species, is seen most often on ponds and marshes in the West. Like other dabbling ducks, it finds its food by dipping its head under the water.

Termites are able to digest wood because of large populations of microorganisms in their intestines.

Teasels, prickly all over, have dense, durable flower heads that remain intact all winter.

Teal

The small, fast-flying teals are ducks that prefer the shallow water of marshes and weedy ponds, where they can easily dip down to feed on aquatic plants and, occasionally, snails and other small animals. Each year large numbers gather in the prairie pothole country of the West and build their nests in dense vegetation near shore. The males depart soon after mating, leaving the females to incubate the eggs and tend the ducklings on their own.

The green-winged teal, one of the commoner species, presents a spectacular show during migration: huge flocks fly in formation with the precision of well-trained drill teams as they head for the southern United States or Mexico. Often feeding on mudflats, the green-wing also forages in fields and woodlands. Its close relative, the blue-winged teal, flies farther south and is more aquatic. Aside from the colors of their wing patches, these two species can be identified by the males' head markings: green-wings have green ear patches, while white crescents mark the cheeks of blue-wings.

Teasel *Dipsacus*

The sharp spines that arm the leaves, stems, and flower heads of the teasels make them difficult to handle but extremely useful to weavers: the pincushionlike flower heads of one species, fuller's teasel, have been used since ancient times to tease, or to raise the nap on, newly woven woolens. Flourishing on wastelands, fields, and roadsides across much of North America, teasels grow up to six feet tall and produce lavender flowers. Their paired upper leaves are joined at their bases to form little cups around the stems. Early herbalists valued the rainwater that collects in these basins, using it to cool inflamed eyes and to "render the face fair."

Tent caterpillar *Malacosoma*

The larvae of medium-size brownish moths, tent caterpillars are destructive pests that cause serious damage to forest and orchard trees. In early spring, just as the leaves begin to unfurl, masses of voracious, hairy caterpillars hatch from egg masses that were laid on twigs the pre-

Terns are sometimes called sea swallows because of their forked tails. Arctic terns (above) breed in the Far North but travel all the way to Antarctic waters for the winter. Royal terns (right) can tolerate close quarters, nesting just inches from their neighbors; many thousands of pairs often manage to squeeze onto a small, sandy island.

vious summer. The larvae of many species spin communal silken nests in the crotches of branches and, on their forays from these protective tentlike structures, sometimes completely defoliate the trees in which they live.

Termite

Among the most destructive insects, termites are dreaded by home owners because of their remarkable ability to eat wood. Although they are more closely related to cockroaches, termites are sometimes called white ants because they look like pallid versions of those insects. They also resemble ants in behavior, for they are social creatures that live in huge, highly organized colonies. While some live in fallen logs or the wood of buildings, most live in the ground and tunnel to their food source. At the heart of each colony is the royal couple, a king and an oversize, egg-laying queen. Soldier termites defend the colony, and legions of blind workers gather food, build tunnels, and care for the young. In spring, swarms of winged termites leave their nests and fly off to start new colonies.

Tern

Graceful relatives of the gulls, terns are slender, long-winged birds that live along seacoasts and near inland waters. They are often seen hovering in midair, poised to plunge headfirst into the water to grasp fish and other prey in their long, pointed bills. Most terns have deeply forked tails and range from 8 to 22 inches in length. While many have white bodies and black caps, some, such as the black tern of inland marshes, are largely black.

Terns nest in crowded, noisy colonies, placing their eggs in shallow scrapes in the sand, or on flimsy platforms of marsh grass. Both parents incubate the eggs and feed the downy young.

Widespread species include the common tern, a swift, buoyant bird of inland lakes and coastal beaches, and Forster's tern, which looks similar but favors marshlands over seashores. Another, the arctic tern, is famous for its long-distance migrations of up to 22,000 miles a year. The least tern, our smallest species, nests on sandy beaches and is now endangered due to coastal development.

T

Claiming their territory, northern gannets, which spend most of their lives at sea, return to land at breeding time. They form huge nesting colonies and fiercely protect the areas they have staked out for themselves.

T

Terrapin *Malaclemys terrapin*

A turtle of salt marshes and estuaries along the East Coast from Cape Cod to the Gulf of Mexico, the diamondback terrapin is named for the deeply incised rings on its upper shell, which is four to seven inches long. The diamondback often floats just below the surface of the water with only the tip of its snout exposed. It feeds on snails, crabs, and plant shoots. Several times a year, females leave the water to dig nests in sandy banks or dunes and lay clutches of 4 to 18 eggs. When the young hatch, they immediately scramble down to the marsh to take cover in dense vegetation. Once hunted to near extinction for their tasty meat, terrapins are also threatened by foxes, gulls, and other predators.

Diamondback terrapins feed by day and bury themselves in the mud at night.

Territory

Animals of many kinds stake out and defend territories—areas of living space from which they exclude others of their kind as they vie for food or mates. These areas range in size from a few square inches to many square miles and may be used for feeding, mating, nesting, or all three. Pairs of golden eagles, for instance, lay claim to territories of 35 square miles or more and vigorously defend them against any other golden eagles that dare to venture in.

While most birds proclaim their territories with song, foxes, wolves, and other mammals use scent or urine to mark the boundaries of their private domains and discourage others from entering. Even bullfrogs compete for prime breeding territories: they sound loud warning notes when intruders approach and then, if necessary, launch an attack.

Thermal

When sunlight heats a patch of open ground, the air above it also becomes heated and begins to rise, creating a column of ascending warm air called a thermal. The air cools as it rises, and water vapor contained in the thermal eventually condenses, becoming visible as a puffy cumulus cloud. Hawks and other birds often take advantage of thermals to soar high in the sky in their search for prey.

Thistle

The tall thistle of the eastern and central United States, with stems up to 12 feet high, and the shorter pasture thistle, with fragrant magenta flower heads up to three inches across, are just

Prickly, pesty thistles include the Canada thistle (above) and the elk thistle (right), whose fleshy roots and stems were a source of food for Indian tribes.

T

The brown thrasher (left) and the curve-billed thrasher (right) are both skillful songsters.

two of our many native thistles. But the ones that most commonly infest fields and roadsides are a couple that arrived as stowaways in seeds shipped from Europe: the bull thistle and the misnamed Canada thistle. Both have spiny leaves and prickly flowers in shades of pink and purple. The tufts of silky threads on the fruits, which help them parachute to new areas, are avidly collected by goldfinches, who line their nests with thistledown. In the past, herbalists used thistles to treat intestinal and urinary problems, and thistle tonic was popularly used as a pick-me-up.

Thornapple See *Jimsonweed.*

Thrasher

Long-tailed birds that nest in low thickets and forage on the ground, thrashers nevertheless announce their presence with loud songs. Though they are less talented as mimics than their cousins the catbird and the mockingbird, their warbled melodies are just as sweet.

Ranging from the East Coast to the Rockies, the brown thrasher is the most widespread member of the group. Brown above with a pale, streaked breast, this secretive bird digs for worms and insects under the cover of dense shrubs but sings from the highest treetops.

The other thrashers are birds of the West. The curve-billed thrasher, for example, is common from Texas to Arizona and nests amid the protective spines of cholla cacti. The sage thrasher, a smaller version of the brown thrasher, builds its sturdy, cup-shaped nest in sagebrush thickets.

Thrips

Some 600 species of thrips are found in North America, but most of these insects are so tiny that they are visible only as little black specks moving about on leaves and flowers. The banded thrips are beneficial because they feed on such pests as mites and aphids. Most other kinds, however, are pests that suck the sap of garden flowers, grains, onions, pears, and other plants and often spread diseases.

391

Thunderstorms are punctuated by bolts of lightning that streak across the darkened sky.

Swainson's thrushes are daytime and nighttime singers. During their long migration they fly at night, filling the air with spiraling melodies as they head for summer nesting areas in the coniferous forests of Canada and the northern United States.

Thrush

Outstanding songsters, the thrushes produce clear, flutelike notes that carry long distances through the woodlands, their favored habitat. One species, the hermit thrush, is considered by many to have the loveliest song of any North American bird.

Mainly brown with spotted or speckled breasts, the thrushes are insect eaters that spend much of their time searching for food in the leaf litter on the forest floor. But all add fruit to their diet, especially during the fall migration and in winter. The females lay their distinctive blue eggs (spotted in some species, unspotted in others) in sturdy nests built of twigs, grass, and dead leaves and usually reinforced with mud.

Most spotted thrushes, including the familiar wood thrush, the veery, Swainson's thrush, and the gray-cheeked thrush, winter in the tropics.

The hermit thrush, however, nests in boreal and mountain forests and winters in the southern United States. The varied thrush, an orange-breasted bird, lives year-round in western coniferous forests.

Thunderstorm

It is hardly surprising that thunderstorms were once thought to be caused by angry gods, for their violent winds, torrential rains, flashes of lightning, and roaring thunder do indeed seem like celestial temper tantrums. Typically, however, a summer thunderstorm begins calmly enough, with a mass of warm, moist air rising skyward and cooling rapidly. The moisture condenses, forming huge, threatening clouds whose inner turbulence results in the buildup of electrical charges. When the charges become strong enough, they are released as bolts of lightning, and the blazing heat of the lightning causes the

Low tide (left) gives way to high tide (right) on the coast of British Columbia. Animals and plants of the intertidal area are adapted to the ebb and flow of their constantly changing environment.

A parasitic tick—here seen much larger than life—waits in ambush for a host to brush by.

Southern tickseeds, their petals resembling tiny rays of sunshine, brighten a Florida field.

surrounding air to expand with tremendous force, creating the racket that we call thunder. Drenching rain follows, and in some cases thunderstorms produce hail and tornadoes as well.

Tick

Relatives of mites and spiders, ticks are tiny parasites that attach themselves to the skin of animals or humans and gorge on their blood. They are found on shrubs and other vegetation, where they wait for prospective hosts to pass by. Once attached, a tick is tenacious and hard to remove because the entire head is embedded under the skin. Some species of these minuscule pests transmit serious illnesses, including Lyme disease, tularemia, and Rocky Mountain spotted fever.

Tickseed *Coreopsis*

Little flat fruits, each with two short bristles, give the tickseeds their name. (Even the scientific name means "buglike.") But the most distinctive feature of these plants is their bright, golden flowers. One to three inches across, they usually consist of eight petallike rays with notched tips, surrounding a brown or purplish center. North America is home to many tickseeds, including one, the giant coreopsis of coastal California, that grows as a small tree up to 10 feet tall.

Tidal wave See *Tsunami.*

Tide

As predictable as night and day, tides are the regular rising and falling of the surface of the sea caused by the gravitational pull of the moon and sun. The moon exerts the greater influence, pulling the water directly beneath it into a slight bulge; at the same time, it tugs at the earth beneath the water on the far side of the globe, creating a second bulge on the surface there. As the earth rotates, the two bulges move across its surface, raising and lowering water levels twice at any given place in the course of each rotation, so that two high and two low tides occur each day. When the sun, moon, and earth are all in a straight line, the gravity of the sun and moon reinforce each other to produce the highest tides.

Giant sea anemones grow like exotic flowers atop tidepool rocks. While they look harmless, their tentacles can inflict a painful sting.

Tidepools, revealed as the tide ebbs on the rocky shore, are filled with barnacle-covered rocks, lush growths of seaweed, sea stars, and other colorful creatures. These tranquil basins are natural aquariums that offer an intimate look at an array of sea life.

T

Tidepool

When the ocean's tide recedes, isolated pockets of water—tidepools—are left behind in natural basins among the rocks. These rich and picturesque habitats usually teem with an amazing array of sea life, from sponges and sea stars to periwinkles and rubbery-fronded algae.

Although their waters seem tranquil and protected, tidepools are in fact a demanding environment in which only the hardiest of creatures can survive. Alternately drenched by high tide and then partially drained when the tide goes out, they can be as warm as bathwater in summer and icy cold in winter. Beneath the hot sun evaporation sometimes makes their water unbearably salty, while sudden downpours can make it too dilute for most creatures to endure. Yet many of them do survive, making tidepools fascinating places to explore.

Tiger beetle

Slender, long-legged insects with bulging eyes, tiger beetles are named for their predaceous way of life. They are frequently spotted on sandy tracts as they await passing insects, which they seize in their sickle-shaped jaws. The larvae also are hunters; lurking at the top of deep vertical burrows, they are quick to snatch unwary passersby. Because many species are resplendent in iridescent blue or green, they are popular with collectors, but swift runners and fliers, tiger beetles are a challenge to catch.

Tiger beetles are active on hot, sunny days. Prized by collectors but a challenge to catch, they flee at the slightest provocation.

Tilefish

Deep-bodied fish with blunt snouts, tilefish have fleshy triangular flaps on top of their heads and dorsal fins that extend along almost the full length of the back. They live in deep, warm waters near the edge of the continental shelf and forage on the bottom for crabs, mollusks, and other invertebrates.

Our best-known species is the Atlantic tilefish, which can reach a length of three feet and weigh more than 30 pounds. First discovered in great numbers in 1879, the fish suddenly—and mysteriously—began dying by the millions three years later. Subsequently it staged a slow comeback, and the mild-flavored fish is now commercially harvested once more.

Toads, though oft maligned, are useful to gardeners. They use their sticky tongues to snap up insects and, because of their enormous appetites, provide a natural means of pest control. It has been estimated that a toad can eat 200 insects in a single night.

Titmouse

Small, stocky birds that are equally at home in woodlands or cultivated gardens, titmice frequently visit feeders and nest in birdhouses throughout the United States. Whether breeding in tree cavities or man-made shelters, the crested songsters raise broods of up to eight young. In winter these nonmigratory birds, relatives of chickadees, travel in small groups as they search for insects, fruit, and seeds.

The tufted titmouse, the most familiar species, prefers eastern forests, while the plain titmouse favors oak, pinyon, and juniper woodlands in the West. The Southwest is home to the bridled titmouse; the most distinctive of these predominantly gray birds, it has a black-and-white facial pattern that resembles a horse's bridle.

Toad

Unlike their mainly aquatic cousins the frogs, toads are amphibians that spend most of their lives on dry land. They are also stouter than frogs and can afford to be more sluggish as well, since their tough, warty skin secretes a poison that deters predators.

Toads have long, sticky tongues that can dart out and back instantly, zapping insects and other small prey. In spring males call out to females and mate with them in pools of rainwater. The eggs, contained in long strings of jelly, hatch into aquatic tadpoles that eventually metamorphose into adult toads.

North American species range in size from the one-inch-long oak toad of the Southeast to the nine-inch-long marine toad of Texas and South Florida, which is big enough to prey on mice. Much more widespread are the American toad and the common, or Woodhouse's, toad, both the size of a human fist. Smaller and more secretive are the spadefoot toads, which spend most of the daylight hours buried in the soil.

Tufted titmice, active, gregarious birds, are familiar visitors at feeders from Michigan to New England throughout the winter months.

Toadfish

At least as homely as their namesake, toadfish have broad, flattened heads and wide, gaping mouths and make occasional croaking sounds. Most are marine fish about one foot long that cruise the bottom in search of mollusks, crustaceans, and small fish, which they snap up in powerful jaws lined with sharp teeth. Some kinds, called midshipmen, are ornamented on their sides with rows of light-producing organs that suggest the portholes of ships lit up at night.

Toadstool See *Mushroom.*

A tornado's awesome funnel cloud sweeps capriciously across the prairies.

During a tornado trees are torn asunder and homes are reduced to rubble.

Tornado

As terrifying as they are short-lived, tornadoes are among the most destructive storms. No one knows exactly how these so-called twisters develop, but it is known that they occur only when a mass of cool, dry air overruns warm, humid air, producing thunderstorms and extremely turbulent wind conditions. A funnel of spinning air develops on the underside of a cloud, lengthening into a slender column that rises and falls in the air and threatens to touch ground—and once it does touch, the havoc begins.

Roaring like a freight train and whirling at up to 300 miles an hour, the deadly column of wind and debris becomes a violent engine of destruction that uproots trees, hurls huge objects through the air, and flattens entire towns. As the twister passes over buildings, low pressure inside the funnel causes them literally to explode.

Unlike hurricanes, which can last for days, tornadoes are usually over in a few minutes to an hour, and their paths of devastation are relatively short and narrow. One notable exception occurred in 1925, when a giant tornado roared some 220 miles through the U.S. Midwest, killing nearly 700 people. The Midwest is, in fact, the world's most tornado-prone area. Here enormous cold air masses from Canada collide with warm, moist air from the Gulf of Mexico, creating ideal conditions for major twisters.

Tortoise *Gopherus*

North America's three native tortoises are land-dwelling turtles adapted for digging in the soil. Equipped with stumpy, elephantine hind limbs and heavily scaled, flattened forelegs, they excavate long tunnels with large chambers at the end. These burrows may house one tortoise or many, and the turtles may even share their quarters with an assortment of other animals, including opossums, raccoons, and snakes. Tortoises also dig shorter, temporary tunnels, which provide refuge from heat, drought, or cold. Famous for their lumbering gait, tortoises emerge from their burrows by day to eat grass, leaves, and other vegetation. If threatened, they retreat into their high-domed shells—a defense that has not prevented one species, the desert tortoise of the U.S. Southwest, from becoming endangered. The gopher tortoise is found in the U.S. Southeast, and Berlandier's tortoise inhabits southern Texas.

Towhees, sometimes called ground robins, prefer the forest floor to the treetops. Not only do they find their food by scratching in the dirt like chickens, they even build their nests on or near the ground. Here a rufous-sided towhee tends to its gaping young.

Touch-me-not *Impatiens*

Touch the ripe seed capsules of these wild annuals and you will discover the secret of their name: the pods burst apart on contact and scatter their seeds far and wide. Common in moist woodlands and ravines throughout North America, touch-me-nots grow up to eight feet tall on thick, succulent stems. Also known as jewelweeds, they bear spurred orange or yellow flowers that dangle like little gems from the ends of delicate stalks. The seeds of the touch-me-nots have a pleasant nutty flavor, and the plants' juice, rubbed on the skin, is said to relieve the miseries of athlete's foot and poison ivy.

Towhee *Pipilo*

Long-tailed, sparrowlike birds, towhees are ground foragers that spend most of their time in the underbrush noisily scratching for insects and seeds and kicking up dirt and dry leaves in the process. They also conceal their cup-shaped nests close to the ground and lay clutches of two to six speckled eggs. Several towhees are native to North America, but only the rufous-sided towhee breeds in both the East and the West. Its song is unmistakable, for this rusty-flanked bird trills a distinct *drink-your-tea.* Common western species include the canyon and the California towhees, muted brown birds found in suburban shrubbery and chaparral in parts of the Southwest and along the coast of California; and the green-tailed towhee, a highly migratory bird of western mountains.

Tracks See pp. 398–399.

Trailing arbutus *Epigaea repens*

Nestled amid oval evergreen leaves, the nosegays of fragrant white or pink blooms on trailing arbutus make their first appearance in March and were traditional heralds of spring until over-

Desert tortoises feed on cacti and grasses by day and retire to their burrows at night.

Trailing arbutus, once abundant in the Northeast, is now difficult to find.

picking eliminated the plant in many areas. As its name suggests, trailing arbutus is a creeper that hugs the ground, especially on acid soils in northeastern and middle Atlantic woodlands. This diminutive relative of mountain laurel and rhododendron, also known as mayflower, is honored as the floral emblem of Nova Scotia and the state flower of Massachusetts.

Tracks

Hoofprints etched neatly in the mud beside a stream, or a dotted line of little round impressions in the snow—signs such as these are often all we see of the wild animals that live around us. Unlike birds, squirrels, and domestic animals, which are accustomed to humans and are active during the day, most of our wild neighbors are shy and nocturnal—the events of their lives hidden under the cover of darkness. When dawn arrives, these elusive creatures return to their hiding places. But they leave behind tracks and other signs that offer clues to what they are and what they have been doing.

Tales of mystery and suspense

For those who know how to read them, tracks tell tales—from the simple record of a deer walking to a pond for a drink, to dramatic evidence of life-and-death struggles between predator and prey. One might, for example, make a revealing series of discoveries while walking through a snowy field: first, a set of tracks left by a creature whose larger hind feet landed in front of the smaller forefeet—the sure sign of a bounding gait. Since the tracks in this case are too large for a squirrel, one might reasonably conclude that they were made by a cottontail.

Farther along, the tracks abruptly change direction and are spaced farther apart, indicating that the rabbit has reacted to something and increased its speed. Its tracks are then joined by others—the larger, four-toed footprints typical of a feline or canine predator. The presence of claw marks on the toes rules out a bobcat or other member of the cat family (their claws are retracted when they run), and the tracks are too large for a fox. So they must have been left by a dog, a wolf, or a coyote. At any rate, a chase was obviously in progress.

Some distance down the trail the suspense is ended at a patch of snow disturbed by a scuffle and reddened by drops of blood. From there the tracks of only one animal continue—those of the four-toed hunter.

Animal signatures

Just as the tracks of dogs, foxes, wolves, and coyotes—all canines—are similar to each other, those of other kinds of animals show resemblances as well. Deer, elk, moose, caribou, and

Polar bears have hairy feet that leave shapeless prints in loose, powdery snow. But impressions made in slush are unusually clear and detailed.

A squirrel's tracks record the animal's bounding gait, with the large hind feet landing in front of the smaller forefeet.

Grizzly bear tracks look like they could have been made by a barefoot human on tiptoe.

The several sets of tracks converging on a shrub suggest that something took place here, but exactly what is uncertain. In the foreground the parallel lines in the snow were left by the wing beats of a bird making a quick takeoff. Perhaps a ptarmigan feeding on tender buds was surprised by predators and barely escaped by taking flight.

mountain sheep, for example, all leave the two-part imprints of cloven hooves, and the tracks of most birds show three narrow toes in front and one in the rear. Muskrats, marmots, opossums, and raccoons leave tracks that look like little five-fingered handprints. Beavers do too, except that their hind feet are webbed, an unmistakable clue that distinguishes their tracks from the others. Bounding tracks, like those of rabbits and hares, with the footprints of the larger hind feet ahead of the smaller forefeet, are also typical of squirrels and several kinds of mice. In this case the size of the tracks is an important clue to the animal's identity.

Besides birds and mammals, a host of other creatures leave tracks. Snakes glide along the banks of streams or "side-wind" through desert sand, and sea turtles lumber across beaches to lay their eggs. Even invertebrates such as beetles and millipedes make methodical little trails in the sand, and marine snails trace unbroken lines through the mud at low tide.

Other signs of life

Tracks are not the only signs that animals leave behind. The shape and size of droppings, for example, often reveal what creature made them, as well as what was eaten. Feeding signs also tell tales: the heaps of pine-cone fragments left by red squirrels at their favorite dining sites, for example, or rotting logs torn open by skunks. Many other clues—a bed of flattened grass where a deer has spent the night, tender twigs nipped off by a rabbit, and a gnawed, pointed stump left by a beaver that has felled a tree—all

Raccoon tracks look uncannily like the handprints of a child—but one with claws.

tell us something about the kinds of creatures that visited a place, as well as what they did.

Because we see them so rarely, we are apt to assume that many animals—especially nocturnal mammals—are simply not there. But tracks remind us that these secretive creatures are indeed present, and often abundant, and that they are as much a part of the wildlife around us as the birds and squirrels we see by day.

399

A pair of treehoppers mimic the thorns of the plant on which they live. The stout spines on their backs and their remarkable coloration both account for the uncanny success of this camouflage.

T

Some trapdoor spiders make thick, corklike lids for their burrows, while others build wafer-thin doors of silk.

The queen triggerfish boasts long, graceful tail streamers.

Trapdoor spider

These close relatives of tarantulas live in vertical tunnels that they dig with toothlike spines on their jaws. Lining the burrow with waterproof silk and topping it with a silk-hinged lid, a trapdoor spider creates an ambush site, a nursery, and a fortress all in one. When it senses the vibrations of a passing insect, the spider rushes out to snatch its prey. The female's several hundred eggs hatch in the burrow, where the spiderlings spend most of the first year of their lives. When danger threatens—frequently in the form of parasitic wasps—the adult simply braces itself against the tunnel walls and holds the trapdoor shut.

Tree See pp. 402–403.

Treehopper

Small, agile jumping insects, treehoppers are noted for their strange, even bizarre, forms. Some, for example, are shaped like thorns, allowing them to blend in with spiny plants; an-other, the buffalo treehopper, has two pointed projections on its back that resemble the horns of a bison. Treehoppers live on plants, especially trees and shrubs, where the females lay their eggs in slits cut into the stems or twigs. After hatching, the nymphs mature quickly on a diet of plant juices, often to the detriment of the host. The nymphs of one kind, the locust treehopper, secrete honeydew, attracting ants that in turn protect them from predators.

Tree line

This marks the upper limit of arboreal growth. North of this line, which stretches across Alaska and northern Canada, trees cannot grow due to cold temperatures and the permanently frozen subsoil, called permafrost. This is the tundra, sometimes called The Barrens, a vast plain carpeted with mosses, lichens, shrubs and wildflowers. At and just below this line the few trees that manage to survive are stunted and contorted by the wind, often with branches growing only on their leeward sides.

Another kind of tree line—often called the tim-

Trilobite fossils, fairly widespread and quite common, reveal that these ancient creatures' many legs contained gills, which enabled the animals to breathe.

Triggerfish get their name from the stout life-saving spines on their dorsal fins. When danger threatens, a triggerfish darts into a rock crevice, where it wedges itself securely by snapping a spine upright. A second, shorter spine—the trigger—locks the first one into position, making it impossible for predators to extricate the fish from its hiding place.

Trillium

Among the most easily identified of all spring wildflowers, the trilliums, whose name derives from the Latin for "three," produce their parts in triplicate. A whorl of three leaves circles a stem that can rise to a height of two feet (though the dwarf species may reach only about six inches). Above this ring of leaves each stem is topped by a single flower with three green sepals and three pointed petals.

The blossom may be white, pink, maroon, or yellow. Appropriately, the yellow species usually smell pleasantly of lemons, while the purple-flowered stinking Benjamin, aptly named, has a foul odor. Particularly abundant in moist woodlands in the U.S. Southeast, trilliums range across most of eastern North America and the Far West. They are sometimes called wake-robins because they come into bloom just as robins are heading north in spring.

Large-flowered white trilliums (top), floral emblem of Ontario, and yellow members of the family (above) are among the loveliest harbingers of spring.

berline—and another kind of tundra are found on mountaintops. Above this boundary, the wind, cold, and short growing season make it impossible for trees to survive at all. In this zone, called alpine tundra, only the hardiest low-growing plants, such as sedges, grasses, and a few flowering perennials, can endure.

Triggerfish

The colorful triggerfish live among coral reefs in warm coastal seas. Up to two feet long, they have deep bodies that are flattened from side to side and small mouths with protruding teeth.

Trilobite

Creatures that lived in prehistoric seas from about 575 million years ago until their disappearance some 350 million years later, trilobites are among our most common fossils. Aptly described by Indians as "little water bugs in the rocks," the fossils reveal that trilobites, as their name implies, had bodies that were divided lengthwise into three distinct lobes. Most had large, compound eyes and numerous legs and lived by crawling or burrowing on the ocean floor. The smallest of these bottom dwellers were scarcely 1 inch long, while others ranged up to 18 inches in length.

Broad-leaved trees blaze with color in fall, a change triggered by shorter days and cool weather.

Tree

The trees of North America—whether the elegant and fragrant spruces; stately oaks, the very symbols of strength; or crab apples, their blossoms tinged with pink—are among the most impressive members of the plant kingdom. And with over 800 native species and millions of acres of forests, it is not surprising that some of those trees hold world records. The tallest trees on earth, for instance, are the California redwoods, which stretch to heights of 350 feet and more. This is 100 to 150 feet taller than Canada's giants, the 800-year-old Douglas firs on Vancouver Island. The world's oldest trees are also found on this continent: some of the gnarled bristlecone pines that grow on desolate mountaintops in the U.S. West are close to 5,000 years of age. But while these record holders boast superlatives, our lesser trees likewise are tremendously varied and intriguing.

Needles and leaves, cones and flowers

Trees are typically defined as woody perennial plants, at least 15 feet tall, that have a single main stem. They are further divided into two large groups: broad-leaved trees and conifers. Oaks, maples, and chestnuts are familiar examples of broad-leaved trees, which are also called deciduous since most drop their leaves in autumn. Some of the conifers, such as spruces and firs, have slender needlelike leaves, while others—cedars, for example—have scaly foliage. Because most conifers stay green all year, *ever-*

Crab apples are angiosperms, meaning that their blossoms mature into seed-filled fruits.

Sweet birch bears tassellike catkins, each composed of many inconspicuous flowers.

402

green is commonly used as a synonym—though a few drop their needles in the fall, just as hollies and some other broad-leaved trees retain their foliage year-round.

An additional difference is in reproduction: most broad-leaved trees reproduce by means of flowers, whereas conifers bear their seeds in woody cones. Some flowering trees, such as chestnuts and magnolias, produce conspicuous, showy blossoms that fill the air with fragrance. But on many others, such as oaks and elms, the flowers lack petals or sepals and are so tiny that they are easily overlooked.

The anatomy of trees

Even when a tree is growing most vigorously, the bulk of the wood in its trunk and branches is already dead. Nonetheless, a tree is a highly efficient pump, transporting many gallons of water from soil to leaves every day. At the center of the trunk is the heartwood, which supports the tree as it grows up toward the sun. Sapwood encircles this core and is filled with tiny tubes through which water and dissolved minerals travel up from the roots. Beneath the bark (the outer coat that protects the tree from injury) is a thin layer of living cells that produce the growth rings we see on cut trunks. Here too is another set of tubes that transport food from the leaves to all parts of the plant.

A tree's roots, of course, are fundamental to its survival, for they not only collect water and nutrients but also anchor the plant in the soil. Some penetrate deep into the earth—a mesquite's roots may reach depths of 80 feet—but as a rule, they run within the top few feet of soil. Tiny hairs near the growing tips of the roots take in the water that passes up through the trunk and into the leaves.

The leaves (including those of the conifers) are highly productive factories: they collect solar energy, using it to convert water and carbon dioxide into the energy-rich sugars that fuel the tree's growth. An important by-product of this process, known as photosynthesis, is oxygen—which all living things require.

Trees in our lives

Newsprint, turpentine, lumber, cherries, medicines, and more—life as we know it would be unthinkable without these and hundreds of other products from trees. But just as important is their environmental impact. Water evaporates from their leaves, cooling and humidifying the air. The leaves work as filters, too, helping to cleanse the air of pollutants. Trees also help conserve soil, prevent flooding, and—perhaps most important—play a crucial role in maintaining the balance of gases in the air. But quite simply, trees enrich our lives with their beauty.

Live oaks are among the few broad-leaved trees that are evergreen.

Spruces favor cool, northern climates; their stiff needles easily withstand fierce winter winds.

A conifer's small male cones bear pollen; its larger female cones bear seeds.

T

Rainbow trout are a favorite with sport fishermen because of the fight they wage on the line. Native to western lakes, these trout are so popular that they are now raised in hatcheries throughout North America.

Some tube worms, such as the two feather dusters pictured here, extend delicate, flowery tentacles.

Tripletail *Lobotes surinamensis*

So named because of the taillike lobes on their anal and dorsal fins, tripletails are fish of warm and temperate waters from Cape Cod to the Gulf of Mexico. The young, which live in bays and estuaries, rely on mimicry for protection: their flattened bodies, yellowish-brown color, and habit of swimming on their sides make them look like dead leaves floating on the water. The adults, which live farther offshore, can be up to three feet long and weigh as much as 50 pounds.

Trout *Salmo*

Considered by many to be the kings of freshwater game fish, trout thrive in cold, clear streams and lakes. (Some species spend part of their lives at sea but return to fresh water to spawn.) The demands of anglers have resulted in the spread of trout well beyond their original ranges, and various kinds are now found from the Arctic to mountainous regions in the South. Voracious carnivores, the fish eat everything from insects to small animals that fall into the water—and they can, of course, be tempted by artificial lures. Some grow to a length of 36 inches and weigh more than 30 pounds.

Trout are usually light colored, with black or brown spots. On brown trout, however, most spots are reddish orange, and the rainbow trout adds a red stripe to its sides during spawning season. For sheer drama, however, nothing surpasses the aptly named cutthroat, which has a bright red dash on each side of its lower jaw.

Trout-perch *Percopsis*

Though they share structural similarities with both trout and perch, the trout-perch in fact are closely related to neither. Our two species both are small freshwater fish of northern lakes and streams. The larger of the two, the six-inch-long trout-perch, has a silvery, translucent body covered with rough, saw-toothed scales. It is also the more widespread, ranging from Alaska to Quebec and south to Missouri and Kentucky. The smaller fish, known as the sandroller, is found only in the Columbia River basin in the Pacific Northwest. Both species feed by night on insects, crustaceans, and shellfish.

Truffle

Though European truffles are the ones famous among gourmets, the tasty subterranean fungi also grow in North America. (They are especially common in California and Oregon.) Ranging

Tufa cones ornament the shores and rise from the waters of Mono Lake in California. These limestone spires are deposited by mineral-rich springs flowing into the lake. As the water evaporates, tufa is left behind, eventually accumulating into calcareous mounds. Many tufa cones in and around Mono Lake were formed thousands of years ago when water levels were much higher.

T

from pea-size spheres to irregular balls several inches across, they are usually black, brown, or white. Truffles flourish near hardwood trees, taking nutrients from their hosts' roots and supplying minerals in return. Their pungent aroma attracts rodents, deer, and foxes, which eagerly unearth and devour these prizes.

Tsunami

Terrifying and often catastrophic, tsunamis are huge waves caused by volcanic eruptions, submarine landslides, or earthquakes on the ocean floor. These triggering events, which occur most often in the Pacific Ocean, send powerful shock waves through the water. On the open sea these waves appear as swells racing across the surface at speeds of up to 600 miles per hour. But when such a wave approaches the shallows near shore, drag on the bottom causes it to decrease in speed and increase dramatically in height— sometimes to 100 feet or more. Slamming the coast with horrifying force, a tsunami can demolish buildings, hurl ships ashore, and cause death and destruction far inland.

Tube worm

Marine relatives of earthworms, tube worms live in protective tubes built of sand, mucus, and other materials. Parchment worms, for instance, make U-shaped, papery tubes (open at both ends) in mud or sand and live by filtering food particles from seawater passing through the tube. Another kind, the feather dusters, extend brightly colored tufts of food-catching tentacles from one end of their tubes, attaching the other to shells or seaweed.

Tufa

A light, porous form of limestone, tufa is deposited when water rich in calcium carbonate flows into lakes or hot springs and begins to evaporate. Along the shores of Searles Lake in southern California, for example, eerie tufa cones rise some 75 feet into the air, while in other areas the mineral completely encrusts the surfaces of rocks. Though often beautifully colored by impurities, tufa is too soft and crumbly for ornamental or commercial use.

Russian thistle, a common tumbleweed, piles up along fences and other barriers on open plains. When young and green, the plant is eaten by cattle, but when mature, it is as spiny as a cactus.

T

The tuff cliffs in Big Bend National Park, Texas, etched by wind and water, were formed when layers of ash, ejected from a nearby volcano, consolidated into rock.

Tuff

A product of volcanic eruptions, tuff is a kind of rock made up of tiny particles of ash that have been compacted by pressure or fused together by intense heat. It sometimes contains fossils of animals that were overwhelmed by the ash. Large deposits of tuff are often sculpted by erosion into deep canyons, tall pillars, and other fanciful forms. At Frijoles Canyon, New Mexico, ancient Indians carved cliff dwellings into the soft tuff that makes up the canyon walls.

Tulip tree *Liriodendron tulipifera*

The stately tulip tree, also called the yellow poplar, is a North American native with only one close living relative, a species that grows in Asia. Although it thrives throughout most of the U.S. East, this giant among broad-leaved trees attains its greatest size in the Ohio River valley and the southern Appalachians. There tulip trees can exceed 150 feet in height, supported by magnificent, arrow-straight trunks up to 6 feet in diameter. The greenish cup-shaped blossoms that cover the trees in spring are splashed with orange and do indeed resemble tulips. In autumn oblong cones of winged seeds remain on the branches long after the leaves have fallen.

Tumbleweed

Forming globes the size of beachballs, the tangled stems of the various tumbleweeds roll and bounce across windswept plains. They begin as most other plants do—anchored in the soil. But after flowering, the tumbleweeds wither and snap free from their roots. What seems a frailty is actually a strength, however, for breaking loose in this way allows the plants to scatter their seed as they bounce along, sowing themselves far and wide. Two of the most common tumbleweeds are immigrants from the Old World: tumbling mustard, which has spread over much of the U.S. northern plains, and saltwort, or Russian thistle, which tumbles all across the West.

Tuna

The ultimate in streamlining, tunas have robust, torpedo-shaped bodies that taper dramatically and end in a deeply forked tail. Two rows of triangular finlets in front of the tail are a distinctive feature. Swift, powerful swimmers, tunas ply both warm and cool seas—in summer they are found as far north as Newfoundland in the Atlantic, and British Columbia in the Pacific. All

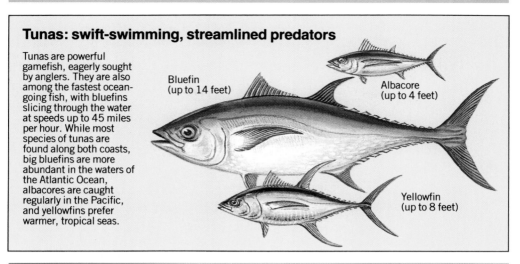

Tunas: swift-swimming, streamlined predators

Tunas are powerful gamefish, eagerly sought by anglers. They are also among the fastest ocean-going fish, with bluefins slicing through the water at speeds up to 45 miles per hour. While most species of tunas are found along both coasts, big bluefins are more abundant in the waters of the Atlantic Ocean, albacores are caught regularly in the Pacific, and yellowfins prefer warmer, tropical seas.

Bluefin (up to 14 feet)

Albacore (up to 4 feet)

Yellowfin (up to 8 feet)

The alpine tundra is a blaze of color for a few weeks each summer as wildflowers burst into bloom.

are able predators that swim long distances in large schools as they search for fish (especially the closely related mackerels), squid, and crustaceans. Female tunas lay eggs by the millions. The fry, about the size of houseflies upon hatching, take several years to reach maturity.

Tunas are among the most-prized commercial and sport fish. The largest, the massive bluefins, sometimes grow to 14 feet in length and weigh more than 1,500 pounds. Other popular species include the three-foot-long skipjacks; yellowfins, named for their black-bordered golden finlets; and albacores, which are sold as white meat tuna.

Tundra

In the Far North, beyond the evergreen forest that stretches from Alaska to Newfoundland, is a vast expanse of arctic tundra. Here no trees can grow and only the hardiest low-growing plants

are able to survive. In the dark, frigid winter, only a few animals—many of them outfitted in white—manage to find food: arctic foxes, for example, hunt lemmings, and snowy owls seek ptarmigan and other prey.

In spring and summer, when temperatures often rise above 50 degrees, the tundra wears a bright mosaic of lichens, sedges, shrubs, and wildflowers. While the subsoil (called permafrost) remains frozen, the surface is soggy and marshlike, attracting legions of clamoring waterfowl and shorebirds from points south. Here they nest and, in uninterrupted daylight, feed on an abundance of insects, seeds, and berries.

Another kind of tundra—one defined by altitude rather than latitude—is found above the tree line on our highest mountains. Here also, harsh conditions permit only a few small, tenacious plants to survive. They are grazed by elk and mountain goats, while golden eagles soar on high in search of marmots and ground squirrels.

Water tupelos thrive in wetland habitats; tupelo is, in fact, an Indian word for "swamp tree."

Tupelo *Nyssa*

Also known as black gums and sour gums, tupelos are trees that thrive in the moist soils of river bottoms and swamps throughout much of the eastern United States. In spring bees are attracted to their inconspicuous but nectar-rich greenish-white flowers and produce a crystal-clear honey that is prized for its purity. When fall arrives, the tupelos are among the first trees to change color; their oval, glossy green leaves turn to a vivid scarlet that contrasts dramatically with the year's crop of blue-black cherrylike fruits.

Turkey *Meleagris gallopavo*

Agile, swift, and wary, the wild turkey is about as comparable to the domestic variety as a nimble fox is to an overweight dog. Like their cousins the pheasants and grouse, wild turkeys are adept at making winged escapes but prefer to flee on foot. (They can nearly outrun a human.) The four-foot-long birds resemble their smaller relatives in courtship as well. Gobbling and strutting, the colorful males swell their bright red wattles and fan their tails to attract the attention of the females. When not courting, the birds forage by day for acorns, seeds, and insects and retire to the trees at dusk.

Wild turkeys once were plentiful in woods throughout eastern United States and south into Mexico. The birds also inhabited southwestern Ontario, which was the northern limit of their range. During the 19th century, land development destroyed their hardwood forest habitat, and unrestricted hunting reduced their numbers. By 1902, wild turkeys were completely wiped out in Canada. In recent decades, however, attempts have been made to restore the birds to their original and rightful domain. In Canada, they have been introduced locally in Ontario, Manitoba, Saskatchewan, and Alberta.

Wild turkey males put on colorful displays to attract females to their territory. Their gobbling can be heard up to a mile away.

Turnstone *Arenaria*

Stocky, robin-size shorebirds, our two turnstones are named for the way in which they forage near the water's edge: they search for snails, worms, crustaceans, and other fare by flipping stones, shells, and bits of debris with their short, stout bills. In spring the ruddy turnstone also digs in sand for horseshoe crab eggs.

The black turnstone nests only on the coast of Alaska, but the ruddy turnstone breeds in arctic regions. Females abandon the North before their young can fly, leaving the males to tend their offspring until they are ready to migrate. Winter finds the black turnstone along the Pacific Coast, while the ruddy turnstone heads for Atlantic, Pacific, and Gulf of Mexico shores.

Ruddy turnstones spend their summers on the soggy arctic tundra, arriving there in early June. In fall the birds head for beaches far to the south, where they feast on worms, insects, crabs, and other sea fare found by turning over shells and stones.

Box turtles are more at home on land than in water, but they sometimes cool off in puddles. A hinged lower shell allows them to close up more tightly than most other turtles. Some box turtles are reported to have lived for over a hundred years.

T

Turret shell

A widely distributed family of marine snails, turret shells typically have long, narrow, conical shells. Ranging from one to six inches in length, they look much like miniature dunce caps. But some members of the family, called worm shells, are less orderly in their growth. One end of the shell remains tightly twisted and turretlike. But after this normal start, the shell elongates in loose meanders that are suggestive of a worm. Some turret shells live on the seafloor; others live inside sponges.

Turtle

The only reptiles with shells, turtles have flourished for millions of years on land, in fresh water, and at sea. One secret of their success is their two-part suit of armor—the upper carapace and lower plastron—into which most can pull their heads and legs for protection. Turtles have no teeth but use their tough beaks to feast on a varied diet of plant and animal life. The females of all kinds, including even sea turtles, dig nests

in moist sand or soil. There they deposit their eggs, cover them, and leave them to be hatched by warmth from the sun.

Cold-blooded creatures, turtles are most abundant in temperate and tropical regions. Some 50 species inhabit North America, with the greatest variety found in the South. Freshwater species range from the diminutive mud turtles to the gigantic alligator snapper. The plodding, stout-legged gopher tortoises are among our several land turtles, while loggerheads are perhaps our best-known sea turtles.

Tusk shell

The curved and tapered shells of these marine mollusks are open at both ends but otherwise resemble tiny elephant tusks. The foot of the creature that inhabits the tusk protrudes from the wider opening and anchors the shell in sand or mud on the sea floor; the pointed end projects into the water. Tusk shells eat one-celled prey that they snare with threadlike tentacles. Indians in the Pacific Northwest used one species of these distinctive shells as wampum.

Ungulates, such as caribou, are fitted with natural running shoes—hooves that protect their feet.

Unicorn plants are also called devil's claws, since the dried, split fruit forms two hooks.

Umbrella sedge *Cyperus*

With stems that are triangular in cross section, the umbrella sedges resemble other members of the sedge family, but they are distinguished by their floral clusters. The flowers themselves are small and inconspicuous, but the clusters rise from a ring of long, leafy bracts that radiate from the top of the stem like the spokes of an umbrella. The most famous of these wetland plants is the papyrus, which supplied the ancient Egyptians with a paperlike material. Closer to home are the nutgrasses, persistent weeds of moist fields and meadows that grow up to three feet tall and produce tiny yellow or purple flowers.

Underwing *Catocala*

Widespread across North America, underwings are robust moths with drab forewings that conceal a colorful secret. Hidden beneath them are the smaller hind wings, which on most species are brightly banded with yellow, orange, and other hues. Dull though they are, the forewings provide excellent camouflage as the moths rest by day, pressed against the trunks of trees. And the patterned hind wings serve to startle predators when, with a flash, the moths take flight.

Ungulate

Many familiar farm animals, and their wild relatives as well, are ungulates—mammals with hooves. Made of a tough hornlike substance, hooves are, in effect, heavy-duty fingernails that cover and protect the toes. While horses have only one hoofed toe per foot, cattle have two, and pigs have four. Moose in the north woods, pronghorns on the prairie, and sheep and goats in the barnyard are other well-known examples of animals with hooves.

Unicorn plant *Proboscidea*

The long, gracefully curved seedpods of these plants—their unicorn "horns"—are curiosities today, but to aboriginal peoples they were a source of both food and fiber. When young and green, the pods were eaten fresh or pickled for later use; when mature and dried, they were split into strips and woven into baskets. Though once cultivated, the plants still survive in fields and waste places. Growing upright or in sprawling mats with sticky, hairy leaves, the unicorn plants bloom all summer long and bear clusters of trumpet-shaped pink or yellow flowers.

Urban wildlife is much more abundant and diverse than one would think. In coastal cities, for example, herring gulls (above left) routinely raid the fish markets for scraps. Even amid downtown bustle, robins (above right) take advantage of a Don't Walk sign, their nest kept warm by the electric lights. On the West Coast a busy harbor provides a sheltered winter home for sea lions (right).

U

Updraft

When wind meets an obstacle, it is deflected skyward, creating an updraft. Birds save energy by gliding on updrafts just as they do on the rising columns of warm air called thermals. Migrating hawks, for example, take advantage of updrafts along mountain ridges, while on seacoasts gulls soar effortlessly on those caused by buildings or cliffs. In high western mountains updrafts sometimes blow insects far above the tree line, where they are eaten by alpine birds.

Uranium

A silvery radioactive element, uranium is vital to the nuclear power industry and is used in manufacturing. Most uranium is derived from the ore uraninite, also known as pitchblende because of its coallike luster. It occurs as well in a few brilliantly colored (and sometimes fluorescent) minerals, such as carnotite and autunite. Canada is a world leader in uranium production.

Urban wildlife

Aside from pigeons, squirrels, and such all-too-familiar pests as rats, mice, flies, and cockroaches, one might reasonably ask what else in the way of "wildlife" our cities and towns have to

offer. In fact, a surprising array of creatures survive and even flourish in urban areas. But as is true in the country, many of them come and go under the cover of darkness and live in secret places—behind walls, in pipes and tunnels, on high ledges, or in abandoned buildings.

Raccoons and opossums, for instance, often hide out in parks during the day, sleeping in tree cavities or hollow logs, and emerge at night to raid garbage pails. In many areas such unlikely city critters as coyotes and red foxes are occasionally seen prowling the streets at night for rats, mice, and scraps of edible refuse. Roosting by day in tunnels or under the eaves of buildings, bats also come out at night to feast on the insects that swarm around streetlights.

Descendants of wild rock doves, which nest on cliffs, pigeons make their homes on the cliflike facades of buildings, while flat gravel roofs are preferred nesting sites for nighthawks, and chimneys are inhabited by chimney swifts. Both kestrels and barn owls roost in abandoned buildings, the former capturing sparrows by day and the latter hunting rats by night. Even the endangered peregrine falcon has been known to nest on the high ledges of skyscrapers. And such fragile tropical birds as parrots and parakeets—escapees from indoor cages—manage to thrive in southern cities. A few amazed onlookers have even spotted them in the urban Northeast.

A mountain valerian in full bloom captures the attention of a passing bee.

A little verdin stands guard at the entrance to its enormous nest, a round structure that also serves as a shelter in the wintertime.

V

The Venus flytrap's leaves can snap shut on unsuspecting insects in a split second.

Valerian *Valeriana*

Though several native species of these healing herbs live in moist places across the northern United States, it is an introduction from Europe, a garden escape, that is best known. Flourishing along roadsides, where it grows up to four feet tall, valerian has feathery leaves and produces sweetly scented clusters of tiny flowers. Belying the fragrance of its blooms are the plant's foul-smelling roots. Even so, valerian roots, whether native or naturalized, have traditionally been used as a sedative and are still sometimes prescribed for nervous disorders and insomnia.

Valley

Long depressions in the surface of the earth, valleys are erosional features formed by rivers or glaciers. The shape of a valley gives a clue to its origins. Deep, steep-sided, U-shaped valleys, like those seen in the mountains of the West, for example, were excavated by glaciers during the last ice age. In contrast, rapidly flowing rivers carve V-shaped valleys as their waters actively

scour the bed. In places such as the Grand Canyon where a river is cutting through solid rock, steep-sided canyons or gorges form. In low-lying areas, where a meandering river wends across a plain, the valley has a broad, relatively flat floor with gently sloping sides and is periodically inundated by floods.

Venus flytrap *Dionaea muscipula*

The only carnivorous plant of its kind in the world, the Venus flytrap thrives in sandy savannas near the coasts of North and South Carolina. The acidic soil there is deficient in nitrogen, but the flytrap overcomes this shortage by attracting insects to its hinged leaves. When an interloper touches the trigger hairs on a leaf, the trap snaps shut and the plant's digestive juices start flowing to extract nitrogen from the prey. In about 10 days the leaf reopens, set for its next victim.

The Venus flytrap bears clusters of small white or pinkish flowers at the top of 12-inch stems. Since each cluster produces an abundance of seeds, the plant has withstood the collection of millions of specimens that are sold each year as botanical oddities. Development of its native habitat, however, poses a real threat to the survival of this unique species.

Verdin *Auriparus flaviceps*

At home amid the drought and scrub vegetation of the American Southwest, this small, yellow-headed songbird is an expert at survival in the desert. It flits about in search of insects among

The vertebrate group includes a myriad of members, among them the powerfully built polar bear (above) foraging in northern Manitoba, and the foot-long collared lizard (left) that survives the searing heat of the southwestern states.

V

the paloverdes and mesquites, apparently getting all the moisture it needs from the insects and berries that it eats.

The verdin chooses a thorny cactus or shrub in which to build its large, globular nest. Constructed of hundreds of intertwined twigs, the nest is lined with feathers, spider silk, and soft plant fibers, making it well insulated for the comfort of the young. A small entryway and prickly surroundings discourage intruders.

Vertebrate

Mammals, birds, reptiles, amphibians, and fish are all vertebrates—animals with backbones. Made up of bone or cartilage, the backbone surrounds and protects the spinal cord, the main conduit of nerves that runs from brain to tail. To allow flexibility, the backbone is divided into segments called vertebrae (hence the word *vertebrate*). Among the other characteristics shared by vertebrates are skulls, internal skeletons, and bodies with right and left sides that are mirror images of each other. All other animals, such as insects, mollusks, and crustaceans, lack backbones and are called invertebrates.

Vervain *Verbena*

While the familiar garden flowers known as verbenas are mostly from South America, many of their equally colorful wild relatives, called vervains, are found all across North America. They were regarded as sacred by aboriginal peoples, whose medicine men used them to treat a variety of ailments. Most common is blue vervain, up to four feet tall with spikes of violet flowers that brighten meadows in the East and throughout much of the prairies. Hoary vervain, similar in appearance, is found mainly in the central United States, where it accents the wide open spaces with streaks of lavender.

Hairy vetch—sometimes called winter vetch—fills a West Virginia field with its sprays of delicate purple flowers.

The Upwardly Mobile Vines

Vines climb in several ways: English ivy has tiny, clinging rootlets; morning glories wind their entire stems around supports; grapes have twining tendrils; and Virginia creeper has tendrils that are tipped with sticky pads.

English ivy

Morning glory

Wild grape

Virginia creeper

The viceroy butterfly's black line across each hind wing, as well as its smaller size, differentiates it from a monarch butterfly.

V

Vetch *Vicia*

Though many are common roadside weeds, the vetches have earned a place in the farmer's field as well. Cow vetch is grown as fodder for livestock and is also planted as "green manure"—when plowed under, it restores nitrogen to the soil. Another vetch—the broad, or fava, bean—grown for its edible seeds, is one of the world's oldest cultivated crops.

The vetches have weak stems that either sprawl across the ground or climb other plants with the aid of tendrils growing from the tips of their feathery compound leaves. The dainty flowers, which have been compared to little butterflies, range from white to pink, purple, and blue. Members of the pea family, the vetches produce crops of distinctive pea-type pods that contain the plants' seeds.

Viburnum *Viburnum*

Elegant shrubs that beautify woodlands, especially in the East, the viburnums are prized by landscapers everywhere. Their showy, three- to five-inch clusters of white or pink flowers, often pleasantly scented, have the quaint look of old-fashioned lace caps. The berrylike fruits that follow—bright yellow, orange, red, or shiny blue or black—are truly eye-catching, inspiring such curious names as nannyberry, mooseberry, wild raisin, possumhaw, and highbush cranberry. The leaves, always in opposite pairs, vary in shape from species to species. Hobblebush, for example, has heart-shaped leaves; arrowwood's leaves are oval; and those of the highbush cranberry resemble maple leaves.

Viceroy *Basilarchia archippus*

Masterful mimicry protects this large, conspicuous butterfly from enemies. Brightly patterned with orange and black, the viceroy looks almost exactly like the monarch butterfly, an insect that is distasteful to birds. Though the viceroy is perfectly edible, the resemblance is enough to keep birds away from it. The butterfly is protected at other stages as well. Its eggs, laid on leaves, blend with the leaves' galls, and in autumn the caterpillars prepare for the cold of winter by wrapping themselves in bits of foliage attached to branches, where they remain until spring.

Nuttall violets are among the more than 60 species of violets that thrive in North America.

White-eyed vireo chicks, comfortably ensconced in a cup-shaped nest, hungrily stretch for their next meal.

Vine

In the competition for sunlight, vines have a distinct advantage over other plants. Their ability to climb—by using neighboring plants, cliffs, buildings, trellises, and other objects as supports—allows them to reach the sunlight quickly. Trees and shrubs, in contrast, need much more time for their stems to become sturdy enough to achieve any substantial height.

Vines climb in a number of ways. Ivies have tiny clinging rootlets or adhesive discs, which enable them to ascend flat surfaces such as cliffs or walls. Grapes and passionflowers hoist themselves up with coiling tendrils. Clematises use twining leaf stalks, and wisteria winds its entire snakelike stem around poles or tree trunks. Rambler roses use yet another technique: they hang onto their supports with sharp thorns.

Violet *Viola*

Each spring, these tiny wildflowers tint the land with blossoms of blue, white, yellow, and of course violet. The purple violet is New Brunswick's floral emblem. The blooms—five-petaled with a nectar-filled spur—are pollinated by bees. But many species have petalless, self-fertilizing flowers, often hidden underground. Some, like the common blue violet, have heart-shaped leaves, but on others they look like lances, arrowheads, or on the birdfoot violet, an avian foot. Rich, moist soils are the preferred habitat, but some adapt to dry grasslands (the prairie violet) or arid regions (the desert violet).

Viper's bugloss *Echium vulgare*

Called a wildflower by some and a weed by others, viper's bugloss brightens waste places all summer long. Also known as blueweed, it bears tubular blue flowers with long red stamens. The blooms grow on short curved spikes along the upper part of two-foot hairy stems.

The first part of the plant's common name refers to the shape of its fruits, which supposedly resemble a viper's head and gave the plant its reputation as a remedy for snakebite. The second part, *bugloss,* is from the Greek for "ox tongue," perhaps because of the leaves' rough texture.

V

Vireo *Vireo*

These little insect-eating birds resemble the warblers with whom they often migrate. Vireos, however, have somewhat thicker bills, search more slowly and carefully for food, and are not nearly as colorful. Eleven species breed in North American woodlands and thickets, where they construct cup-shaped nests that are suspended from the forks of tree branches.

Most of these songsters spend the winter in the tropics, but Hutton's vireo, a drab bird of the Pacific Coast and the Southwest, remains on its breeding grounds all year round. The most common species are the warbling vireo, whose drowsy song can be heard across most of the continent during the summer months, and the red-eyed vireo of southern Canada and the eastern United States, whose repetitive aria has earned it the nickname preacher bird.

Mount Hood, a dormant volcano in the Cascade Range, still emits an occasional puff of smoke.

Shiprock, a volcanic neck in northwestern New Mexico, rises to 1,700 feet over the featureless desert landscape. Exposed by erosion of the volcano that once surrounded it, Shiprock offers quiet testimony to dramatic events of the past.

V

Virginia creeper *Parthenocissus quinquefolia*

A widespread, vigorous vine, Virginia creeper flourishes in sun or shade, clambering up trees and walls or sprawling across the ground. The plant's twining tendrils are equipped with adhesive disks that release a gluey resin when they touch a potential prop. In fall the five-fingered leaves furnish one of the first signs of the season, turning from bright green to brilliant red. The fruits—dark blue berries with scarlet stalks—provide food for birds and other wildlife.

Volcanic neck

A volcanic neck is a plug of solidified lava that at one time filled the vent of a volcano. After volcanic activity ceased, the enclosing rock of the volcano's cone eroded, leaving the plug of rugged rock intact. Volcanic necks often stand as massive, craggy towers that loom over their surroundings. In Monument Valley, Utah, for example, Agathla Peak rises abruptly to a height of 1,400 feet. In some areas these imposing structures are the only clues to the existence of long-vanished volcanoes.

Volcano

Floods of molten magma; boulders hurled into the air; lethal clouds of fiery ash and caustic steam—all these and more can be part of a volcanic eruption. The mountains that result, known as volcanoes, owe their existence to huge subterranean reservoirs of magma, or molten rock. The gas-rich magma accumulates in chambers a mile or more beneath the surface, and when its pressure reaches a critical point, it bursts out through fissures in the earth's crust. Depending on the chemical makeup of the magma, it may emerge relatively quietly, producing rivers of red-hot lava, or it may erupt with ex-

Turkey vultures (above) and black vultures (right) are sometimes seen resting on lofty perches, often with their wings outspread. When they take to the air, they can spot dead animals from great distances. But while their senses are sharp, these strange-looking birds are voiceless, able to manage at most a weak but sinister hiss.

plosive force, sending ash, pumice, and boulders high into the sky.

Volcanic peaks build up gradually as a result of repeated eruptions. Explosive eruptions often produce the classic cone shape, while dome-shaped mountains (like those in Hawaii) are formed by gentler flows of viscous lava.

Most volcanoes occur at the boundaries of the earth's giant crustal plates. Such is the case along North America's Pacific Coast, where active volcanoes smolder from Alaska southward. In 1980 Mount St. Helens in Washington blew up with devastating force, causing dozens of deaths, denuding forests, and clogging lakes and rivers with debris. Nearby, Mount Rainier steams quietly beneath its ice cap, a reminder that it—and other seemingly dormant peaks in the vicinity—may erupt again one day.

Vole

Often called field mice, voles are rodents with shorter tails and smaller ears than true mice. Many, such as the widespread meadow vole, live in open fields, where they scoot from place to place along well-maintained pathways in the grass. Red-backed voles and woodland, or pine, voles live in forests, where they tunnel through leaf litter or burrow in the ground. Active day and night around the year, voles even tunnel

under snow in search of seeds, grass, roots, and bark. Like their close relatives the lemmings, they reproduce prolifically and from time to time experience population explosions that can increase their numbers tenfold. Because of their abundance, voles are a mainstay in the diets of foxes, owls, and a host of other predators.

Vulture

Big black, bald-headed birds that feed primarily on carrion, vultures are masters of the air. They often soar high in the sky for hours on end as they scan the countryside for food. Their beaks, though only slightly hooked, nevertheless serve well for tearing flesh, and their featherless heads are easily cleaned after probing inside large, messy carcasses.

Vultures do not build nests but lay their eggs on rock ledges, in hollow logs, or on the ground. Both parents care for the young, which are unable to fend for themselves until about three months old. The turkey vulture, often called the turkey buzzard, has a six-foot wingspan and is found in parts of Canada and from coast to coast in the United States. It has a red head and holds its wings in a V as it soars. The black vulture, a slightly smaller bird with a more southerly range, has a black head and soars with its wings held straight out, flapping them often.

Walkingsticks, which can be green, gray, or brown, are hard to see, even within the confines of a photograph (two are shown here). The insects make careless mothers; females simply scatter their eggs on the ground, where they are left to hatch on their own.

Alpine wallflowers brighten the cool tundra high in the Rocky Mountains.

Nut

Fruit

The black walnut's richly hued wood is esteemed by makers of fine furniture and musical instruments.

W

Walking catfish *Clarias batrachus*

Found in the muddy ponds and canals of south Florida, walking catfish not only walk but also breathe air. If their ponds dry up, these astonishing fish simply haul themselves out and use their stiff pectoral fins to wriggle overland in search of new homes. Breathing through lunglike sacs, the fish can stay out of water for hours or even days and are often seen crossing roads on rainy nights. Accidentally introduced from Asia, walking catfish are considered undesirable aliens because they compete with native fish for food and habitat.

Walkingstick

Remarkable mimics, the long, slim, wingless walkingsticks bear such a close resemblance to the twigs on which they live that the insects are virtually impossible to spot. Of the 20 or so species in North America, one kind reaches a length of six inches (our longest insect), but it, too, is

nearly invisible. These creatures feed only at night and are all but motionless by day, but in years when they are abundant, their voracious appetite for foliage can seriously damage trees.

Wallflower *Erysimum*

Far from inconspicuous, wallflowers are bold and showy, decorating dry hillsides, prairies, and mountain meadows with bright clusters of four-petaled, usually yellow or orange blossoms. Members of the mustard family, these sun lovers have strap-shaped leaves and, after flowering, bristle with long, slender seedpods. Western wallflower, a well-known species, is prized for its lovely pompoms of golden blooms.

Walnut *Juglans*

Tall, stately trees with spreading branches and feather-shaped compound leaves, walnuts of several species thrive on rich bottomlands in the U.S. East and along stream banks and ravines in

Walruses, contrary to popular belief, do not use their tusks to pry shellfish from the ocean floor.

parts of the West and Southwest. The largest, the black walnut, commonly reaches a height of 100 feet or more; it ensures itself adequate growing space by releasing a natural herbicide, juglone, from its roots. Its nuts, notoriously hard to crack, are nonetheless a popular ingredient in confections, and its wood makes fine furniture. Butternut, another common species, yields a yellow dye traditionally used by countryfolk.

Walrus *Odobenus rosmarus*

Long white tusks distinguish walruses from seals and sea lions, but otherwise, they have much in common with their smaller kin. Equipped with flippers and a thick layer of fat, walruses live in icy arctic seas, where they dive for clams and starfish. They also haul themselves out onto land and ice floes, where they move about with the help of their hind flippers. Male walruses are huge—some grow to a length of 12 feet, weigh more than a ton, and have tusks up to 3 feet long. The smaller females have tusks too, but theirs are thinner and shorter than the males'. While walruses sometimes use their tusks to defend themselves against polar bears, they use them more often to break through ice or haul themselves out of the water. Gregarious creatures, walruses congregate in herds of 100 or more and, like seals and sea lions, visit traditional breeding grounds to perpetuate their kind.

Wapiti *Cervus elaphus*

Also called elk, wapiti once roamed across much of North America but now are found mainly in the Rockies and along parts of the Pacific Coast. Except for moose, they are our largest deer;

Wapiti, an Indian word for "white," refers to the animal's buff-colored rump.

W

stags can reach a shoulder height of about five feet, weigh 1,000 pounds or more, and produce antlers with a span of five feet.

Traveling in herds between the high country in summer and sheltered valleys in winter, wapiti forage on grasses, twigs, and leaves. During the fall mating season, the males' loud bugling calls and antler-crashing fights echo through the countryside as they compete for harems. Wapiti fawns, born in the spring, are able to walk and travel with the herd only minutes after birth.

Yellow warbler

Our many warblers are brightly colored birds whose spring migrations attract considerable attention. During the breeding season warblers feed almost exclusively on protein-rich insects, which also nourish their young. Some species supplement their diets with occasional berries as well.

Chestnut-sided warbler

Blackburnian warbler

Warbler

Favorites among bird-watchers, the warblers are sometimes called butterflies of the bird world because of their small size, bright colors, and sprightly movements. Our 50-odd species, collectively called wood warblers to distinguish them from unrelated old-world warblers, winter mostly in tropical areas and nest in forests, swamps, and thickets all across North America.

Two of our loveliest species are also among the most commonly seen: the yellow warbler, a bright canary yellow, and the American redstart, strikingly patterned with black and orange, nest not only in wild places but also in city parks and gardens. Most warblers build cup-shaped nests in trees or shrubs, but the waterthrushes, ovenbird (named for its covered nest), and Wilson's warbler nest on the ground, while the prothonotary warbler makes its home in tree cavities.

With a few exceptions, warblers are undistinguished singers, but all are accomplished insect hunters. Many capture their prey on the wing, but others—among them the black-and-white and pine warblers—use their thin, sharply pointed bills to probe the crevices in tree bark. Since warblers dispatch vast numbers of harmful insects each year, their spring migrations are anticipated as eagerly by farmers and foresters as by bird-watchers.

Wasp

Of the more than 3,500 species of wasps found in North America, the best known are the social wasps, such as hornets, paper wasps, and yellow jackets. They live in colonies with strict social organizations and inhabit papery nests made of chewed plant fibers. But the majority of wasps lead solitary lives. While many nest in underground burrows, the more specialized mud dauber and potter wasps build nests of mud. Most solitary species are hunters that paralyze prey with their stings (only females have stingers), then leave the prey sealed in their nests as food for their developing larvae. Still other wasps are parasites that lay their eggs on caterpillars and other live hosts.

Watercress *Nasturtium officinale*

In the cool water of springs and gentle streams, watercress spreads like a ruffled green carpet. Though the plant can survive in damp soil, it also grows as a true aquatic, with its leaves wholly or partially submerged. Its clusters of small white flowers, however, are held well above the water's surface. Pioneers brought watercress to North America as a remedy for scurvy (the foliage is rich in vitamin C), but today it is popular as a peppery addition to salads and soups.

All waterfalls are products of erosion, whether a slender ribbon of water at Pictured Rocks National Lakeshore, Michigan (above left); a thundering torrent tumbling over rugged cliffs in Yosemite National Park, California (above right); or a splashing, steplike cascade in northern Washington (left). While many falls are appreciated for their awesome beauty, others are valued for the hydroelectric power they provide.

W

Waterdog See *Mudpuppy*.

Waterfall

From modest cascades along mountain streams to the thundering walls of water where rivers plunge over cliffs, waterfalls are almost always impressive. Some occur on the edges of high plateaus or along fault lines, while others are the legacy of glaciers that long ago carved their way down mountain slopes. After the ice melted, the shallow tributary glaciers that fed into far larger ones often left hanging valleys, from which rivers now empty into the deeper valley below. Yosemite Falls in California, among the loftiest in the world, for example, tumbles from a hanging valley for a total drop of nearly half a mile.

Ageless as they may seem, waterfalls undergo constant change. Some wear away their ledges grain by grain until they become gentle slopes, while others—those that plunge from hard cap rock to softer rock below—undermine their ledges chunk by chunk, gradually working their way upstream. Niagara Falls has been doing this for the last 10,000 years and, in that time, has traveled seven miles from its original site.

Water hyacinth *Eichhornia crassipes*

With clusters of lavender flowers perched atop rosettes of glossy green leaves, the water hyacinth is one of the prettiest aquatic plants. It is surely the most prolific, for in the warm waters of Louisiana, Florida, and Texas, 10 plants can multiply to smother an acre of lake or river in just eight months. This tropical transplant floats on air-filled bladders on its leafstalks, its dangling roots absorbing nutrients directly from the water. And it wanders freely, choking waterways and suffocating fish as it goes. Although the water hyacinth maintains its reputation as a pest, it has gained new ecological status in the South: planted in man-made lagoons, it now serves many cities as a wastewater purifier.

421

A green water snake, basking in the sunshine, is prepared to slither into the water the moment that it spots a fish or a frog. Using its teeth merely to grasp the prey, the snake swallows its victims whole.

Fragrant waterlilies are admired for their snowy beauty and delightful scent.

A waterspout's characteristic trunk-shaped funnel dips down into the Gulf of Mexico, creating a spectacular summer sight from the water's edge.

Waterlily *Nymphaea*

Like jewels adrift on the surfaces of ponds and slow-moving streams, waterlilies are among the best-loved aquatic plants. Anchored by thick rootstocks in the mud below, the underwater stems terminate in large oval leaves, or pads, and graceful blossoms that float on or project above the surface. Once the flowers fade, they sink underwater, where their seeds ripen, float away, and settle to the bottom to take root. Our most common species—the white, or fragrant, waterlily—opens its six-inch blooms only in the morning, while the pygmy waterlily opens its smaller, scentless white flowers only in the afternoon. White to pale pink in the North, waterlilies also come in yellow, blue, and violet in the South.

Water snake *Nerodia*

Often mistaken for the venomous cottonmouth, or water moccasin, which shares their aquatic habitat, water snakes look more dangerous than they are. Large and irritable, they strike if provoked, but their bite is not poisonous. Water snakes feed on fish and frogs and often bask on branches that overhang streams and ponds. The largest is the six-foot green water snake of the South. The four-foot northern, or common, water snake ranges from the Gulf Coast to Canada.

Waterspout

Whirling columns of water vapor and air, waterspouts develop beneath cumulus clouds as they pass over lakes and seas. As in tornadoes, a swirling funnel dips down from the base of the cloud and dances along the surface, sucking up water and disturbing anything in its path. Waterspouts are sometimes accompanied by strong winds, which can present a real hazard to boaters. Most, however, are short-lived and are no stronger than land-based dust devils.

Waves along the coast of California send spray skyward as they race toward the shore.

Water table

In most areas an underground reservoir of water (known as ground water) saturates soil and porous rock, percolating down until it reaches an impermeable layer. The uppermost level of this reservoir is called the water table, and its depth beneath the surface rises and falls depending on the season, the amount of precipitation, and how much water is being removed through wells. Where the water table intersects the surface of the land, springs and swamps—and sometimes lakes—can form.

Wave

The ripples produced by a frog jumping into a pond have much in common with the 20-foot swells stirred up by storms at sea, for all waves are caused by some form of energy disturbing the water's surface. Boats, animals, earthquakes, and even the gravity of the sun and moon can produce waves, but most are set in motion by the wind—the force and duration of which determines the size of the waves.

As waves move along the water's surface, the water itself does not move with them; it simply rises and falls as the waves pass by, as do objects floating on the water. Ocean waves change dramatically as they approach shore. The shallowness of the water forces them to rear up and form steep crests that spill over as breakers.

Waxwing *Bombycilla*

Named for the red tips, like bits of sealing wax, on some of their wing feathers, waxwings are sleek, crested birds clad in soft grayish brown. Both the sparrow-size cedar waxwing and the slightly larg-

Cedar waxwings are sociable birds that travel in flocks to seek out fruit-laden trees.

er Bohemian waxwing complete their attire with black masks and yellow-tipped tails.

Although waxwings eat some insects, they feed mainly on berries and other fruits. And like many other fruit-eating birds, they travel in flocks, roaming the countryside in a constant quest for edibles. The cedar waxwing, a bird named for its fondness for the berries of red cedars and other junipers, nests in midsummer or later, when fruit trees are heavy with morsels for the young. While cedar waxwings are widespread, Bohemian waxwings live mainly in the western mountains. In winters when food is scarce, however, they sometimes wander far to the south or east.

W

423

The ermine, or short-tailed weasel, like its kin the mink, is valued for its luxurious pelt.

Boll weevils feed on cotton seedpods, sometimes severely damaging the crop.

Weather can differ dramatically from climate. Every so often, for example, violent thunderstorms bring torrential rains and flash floods to this Arizona desert, where the overall climate is quite the opposite— hot and very dry.

W

Weasel *Mustela*

Agile and high-strung, our three weasels are small but deadly predators. The well-named least weasel is only 8 inches long, while the largest, the long-tailed weasel, rarely exceeds 16 inches. The third species, the ermine, or short-tailed weasel, is about a foot long. All are brown above and white below, but most ermines and northern populations of least and long-tailed weasels turn white in winter. The ermine and the long-tailed weasel keep their trademark—a black tip on the tail—year-round.

Weasels feed primarily on small mammals and birds, killing their prey with quick, well-placed bites on the back of the neck. Shy and mainly nocturnal, these long, slender, short-legged creatures are adept at snaking among boulders and into hollow logs; their prey, in fact, find few havens into which the fast-moving animals cannot follow. Although notorious as a menace to the chicken coop, weasels are appreciated for keeping rodents under control.

Weather

The condition of the atmosphere in a given place—hot or cold, calm or windy, rainy or clear—and how it changes from day to day are known as weather. Climate, in contrast, is the average condition of the atmosphere over years. Plants and animals, for the most part, are adapted to climate, but the daily changes in weather affect their lives as well. A cold snap in autumn, for example, can cause trees to drop their leaves prematurely, just as unseasonable warmth in February can stimulate early blooming. Wind storms can blow migrating birds far off course, and ice storms, by locking up seeds and other foods, sometimes cause animals to starve.

Weed

The nemesis of farmers and gardeners, weeds are usually defined as plants growing where they are not wanted. Weeds steal water, light, and nutrients from cultivated plants, harbor dis-

Wetlands with trees are called swamps. In a Florida swamp (above), alligators lurk beneath the towering bald cypresses. In contrast, marshes (right) have no trees. Dominated by grasses and sedges, they are important nurseries for birds, fish, and other wildlife.

eases and insect pests, and can be poisonous or just plain unsightly. On the plus side, weeds deter erosion, help enrich the soil, and provide food and shelter for wildlife. Some, such as clover and dandelions, considered weeds in lawns, are also cultivated as crops. Many of our most familiar weeds, such as crabgrass and purple loosestrife, were introduced from abroad.

Weevil

Sometimes called snout beetles because of their long, down-curved beaks, the weevils are a large, widespread group of insects that includes some of the worst agricultural pests. With sturdy mouthparts at the tip of the snout, the females bore into nuts, seeds, buds, and other plant parts to lay their eggs. The acorn weevil, for instance, deposits its eggs inside acorns while they are still on the oak tree. When the larvae hatch, they devour the inner meat of the acorns; then, after the nuts drop to the ground, the adult weevils leave the empty shells. Other weevils mature inside kernels of rice and grain. The granary weevil, for example, causes great damage by laying its eggs in harvested wheat.

Wentletrap

With their name derived from the Dutch for "spiral staircase," wentletraps are among the most beautiful of sea shells. Delicately ribbed and usually white, the whorls of the shells taper to graceful spires that have an elegantly sculptured look. The snails that dwell inside these handsome structures are carnivores that feed primarily on sea anemones. But wentletraps are not safe from predators themselves; fish sometimes swallow them whole. When danger threatens, the snails emit a pink-purple dye.

Wetland

From the soggy arctic tundra to the steamy Florida Everglades, North America is well endowed with wetlands—places where the land is soaked with water. Known more specifically as bogs, marshes, or swamps, wetlands can be freshwater or saltwater, smaller than an acre or hundreds of square miles in extent. All are rich and productive habitats that teem with birds, fish, insects, plants, and other wildlife and deserve to be carefully protected.

W

Humpback whales, up to 50 feet long, frequently leap headfirst out of the water (above) and slap the surface with their 16-foot-long flippers and powerful tails (left). In recent decades humpbacks have become famous for the sounds they make. Eerie and often beautiful, their vocalizations have been recorded and have inspired some unique compositions for orchestra.

W

Whale

Titans of the deep, whales include the largest creatures on earth. One, the 100-foot-long, 150-ton blue whale is the largest animal that has ever lived, surpassing even the colossal dinosaurs. But many other whales are not nearly so big: dolphins and porpoises, which are actually small whales, rarely exceed 10 feet.

Though they look like fish, whales are mammals—the descendants of ancient land animals that gradually adapted to life in the sea. The body became streamlined, the front legs were transformed into flippers, the hind legs virtually disappeared, and the tail came to resemble that of a fish. Whales breathe air through blowholes on top of the head, where a plume of vapor can sometimes be seen as they exhale. Highly intelligent, with a sense of hearing much more refined than our own, whales communicate with each other using a complex repertoire of sounds.

Whales fall into two broad categories. The toothed whales, equipped with peglike teeth, travel in groups called pods and feed on fish and squid. The largest is the 60-foot-long sperm whale, with a bulky square forehead and a disproportionately narrow lower jaw. Among the smaller toothed whales are the dolphins, porpoises, and killer whale, as well as the beluga, or white whale, and the narwhal, distinguished by its long, spearlike tusk.

The other group, called baleen whales, has no teeth. Instead, thin plates of baleen, or whalebone, in their mouths filter plankton from the water. The largest whales—the blue whale and the 80-foot fin whale—are baleen whales, as are the somewhat smaller humpback whale (which has no hump) and the gray whale, whose migrations along the Pacific Coast can be watched from shore.

Whelk

Among the many snails found in the waters off North America are the large, spindle-shaped whelks. They thrive in both cold and warm seas, where some kinds are active predators and others live as scavengers. Whelks lay their eggs in strings of papery capsules, which can be found stranded above the high-water mark on many

The **Sonora whipsnake** of Arizona and New Mexico often ventures into trees to search for young birds.

Whip scorpions, about three inches long, are rarely seen because they remain hidden in burrows or under debris during the daylight hours.

Western whiptails like to dash across open ground and are very hard to catch. Their sensitive noses can detect buried insects, which the lizards dig up and eat.

beaches. One of the most dramatic shells to wash up along the Gulf of Mexico and southern Atlantic coasts is the lightning whelk, a species that reaches a length of more than one foot.

Whip-poor-will See *Goatsucker.*

Whip scorpion *Mastigoproctus giganteus*

Named for their whiplike tails, these arachnids look as fearsome as real scorpions. When disturbed, they release a pungent vinegarlike spray that has earned them the alternate name of vinegaroons, but in fact whip scorpions are harmless to humans. They live in the South, where they hunt by night for slugs, insects, worms, and other small creatures. During the day, whip scorpions hide under logs or rocks and sometimes burrow into sand.

Whipsnake *Masticophis*

Slender and speedy, whipsnakes are hard to catch and harder to handle. They deliver a mean (though nonvenomous) bite, thrash around wildly when held, and zip away in a flash when released. Sometimes called coachwhips, whipsnakes are found all across the southern United States. They spend their days hunting for rodents, birds, frogs, and other snakes, often looping their bodies on top of prey to pin it down.

Whiptail *Cnemidophorus*

Slim-bodied and long-tailed, whiptails are lizards that flit along rapidly, jerking their heads from side to side. But while their nervous movements are distinctive, whiptails are of greatest interest because of their unusual reproduction. Some species consist entirely of females and reproduce by parthenogenesis—they lay fertile eggs without ever mating. Ranging from 6 to 15 inches in length, whiptails have patterned bodies, commonly marked with stripes or spots; large rectangular scales cover their bellies, while those on their backs are granular. Whiptails prefer deserts or dry woodlands and feed on insects, scorpions, and spiders.

Whitefish

Pale silvery relatives of salmon, trout, chars, and graylings, whitefish thrive in cool northern lakes and streams. The fine flavor and great abundance of these freshwater fish once made them popular and lucrative commercial catches. The lake whitefish population has decreased dramatically in recent years, however, especially in the Great Lakes, where overfishing and pollution have taken their toll. But in places where cool waters have remained pristine, summer anglers and ice fishermen alike still pursue these delicately flavored sport fish.

W

Greenhouse whiteflies, each no bigger than the head of a straight pin, appear as little white specks on the plants they infest. These sap-sucking pests of northern greenhouses and southern gardens die when exposed to the cold of winter.

Deer mice are the commonest of white-footed mice. In winter they live on stored seeds and keep warm by huddling together.

Wild ginger was used as a substitute for true ginger in the kitchens of early settlers.

W

Whitefly

Tiny insects with a waxy white powder covering their wings and bodies, whiteflies look a bit like miniature moths. Even the largest kinds are only one-eighth of an inch long, and so they appear as little more than specks on the leaves of the plants that they attack. Thriving outdoors in the warm climate of the South, whiteflies suck the sap from plants and often cause extensive damage to citrus and other trees. Indoors, the greenhouse whitefly—perhaps the most destructive species—is an unwelcome visitor to houseplants, which wither and die when they become infested with the insects.

White-footed mouse *Peromyscus*

These active, long-tailed little mice with brown backs and white feet and underparts are found throughout North America in forests, fields, and brushy deserts. Nocturnal in habit, white-footed mice venture out in the evening to gather seeds,

nuts, and berries, resting during the day in burrows, in crevices among rocks, in logs, or even in old birds' nests. Several kinds also invade houses, particularly in winter.

Of the many species found in North America, the deer mouse is the most common and, indeed, is one of the most widespread of all our mammals. Extremely prolific, it produces two to four litters of up to eight young each year. The pinyon mouse, a denizen of chaparral and dry woodlands in the West, is distinguished from other white-footed mice by its unusually large ears. The biggest species is the California mouse, whose length, including the tail, may exceed 10 inches.

Whooping crane See *Crane*.

Wildflower See pp. 430–431.

428

Wild lettuce's milky sap, though ineffectual, has been used as a drug since antiquity.

Weeping willows, though native to China, are common in the East and Far West, where they add a touch of elegance to the banks of ponds and lazy rivers.

Wild ginger *Asarum*

Though not related to the spice of the same name, wild ginger releases a similar fragrance when its leaves and roots are bruised. In spring dull brownish ground-hugging flowers appear beneath the large heart- or kidney-shaped leaves. The urn-shaped blooms, which flare at the mouth with three pointed lobes, emit a foul odor that offends humans but attracts pollinating flies. These woodland plants were used as a digestive remedy by aboriginal peoples, which explains one of their nicknames, Indian ginger.

Wild lettuce *Lactuca*

These coarse, weedy relatives of the familiar salad green bear sharply toothed, deeply lobed leaves and clusters of yellow, white, or blue flowers that look like little dandelions. Up to 10 feet tall, the wild lettuces are plants of roadsides, fields, waste places, and woodland clearings. Their milky sap, reminiscent of the juice of the opium poppy, was prescribed by generations of doctors as a sedative and painkiller until chemical analysis revealed that "lettuce opium" is, after all, not a narcotic.

Willow *Salix*

About 80 species of willows are native to North America. While a few are tall trees that reach heights of 100 feet or more, the majority are shrubs. Fast-growing plants with long, narrow, bladelike leaves, willows thrive in waterlogged soils, sending out networks of tangled, fibrous roots that help control erosion along streams and on riverbanks. Because willow wood is soft and pliable, the twigs have traditionally been used for baskets and wickerwork.

The black willow is the giant of the genus, sometimes growing to 125 feet in swamps and moist bottomlands in the South. The pussy willow, a well-known favorite, is admired for the furry gray catkins that adorn its branches in the early spring. Like many of the willows, its catkins are an important early-season nectar source for bees, while the buds and shoots are browsed by a variety of wildlife. The yewleaf willow, a shrubby species with needlelike leaves, manages to survive in desert grasslands, far from the cool, wet meadows most willows favor. Another anomaly is dwarf willow, a ground hugger that grows only an inch or two tall as it creeps across the tundra on high mountain slopes.

W

429

Blue columbine, the state flower of Colorado, graces western mountains.

Wildflower

Anyone who has admired the pink pouch-shaped blossoms of the showy lady's slipper—a wild orchid that grows on the forest floor—or who has driven through the Southwest when bluebonnets are drowning the countryside in a sea of color can attest to the surpassing beauty of wildflowers. While many think of them as shy and delicate plants of remote places, wildflowers are in fact as close at hand as the nearest roadside or vacant lot.

Indeed, wildflowers flourish in virtually every habitat all across the continent. Literally thousands of species are found in North America, with some 2,700 kinds of wildflowers living in the state of Texas alone. Some, such as buttercups and dandelions, grow like weeds in almost every dooryard, but others are vanishingly rare: the entire population of the Maguire daisy of central Utah, for example, is a mere five plants. But while the beauty of wildflowers is certainly alluring to us, their shapes, textures, colors, and scents are designed to ensure their perpetuation.

Survival strategies

Native wildflowers are exquisitely attuned to their environments, often adopting ingenious strategies for coping with less-than-ideal conditions. Carnivorous species, such as the pitcher plants and sundews, trap and digest insects, thereby flourishing in boggy, nutrient-poor soils that few other plants can tolerate. Beechdrops, pale parasitic wildflowers, survive in the shade of the forest floor by tapping into the roots of the overhanging trees.

Among the most spectacular—and successful—wildflower adaptations is that of the desert ephemerals. Their seeds sprout only after rain or snow has moistened the desert soil. But then they rush to maturity within a few weeks, flowering, dying, and leaving seed that lies dormant until the rains return.

Just as impressive is the summer show staged on the arctic tundra. In this harsh northern habitat, where the growing season lasts but weeks, many wildflowers sprawl across the ground in colorful mats. As delicate as they appear, however, these ground huggers are surprisingly hardy. The arctic forget-me-not, for instance, grows in dense pincushionlike clusters, an adaptation that protects the plant from fierce winds.

Equally successful are the many immigrants from foreign lands. A few, such as foxgloves, probably came as garden flowers and escaped into the wild. Many more arrived as impurities in agricultural seed or as hitchhikers in imported hay or in ballast that was dumped by visiting ships. Some were unable to compete with native wildflowers, but many gained a foothold, and a few—Canada thistle, for instance, and purple loosestrife—became aggressive pests, colonizing millions of acres.

Attracting pollinators

The intoxicating fragrance of honeysuckle on a summer evening, the slick yellow petals of buttercups, and the spurred blossoms of the columbines are all engineered to attract pollinators. Bees, the most common agents of pollination, are drawn to sweetly scented flowers, while carrion flies are attracted to early spring bloomers such as skunk cabbage, which waft an odor reminiscent of rotten meat. Moths, nocturnal fliers, visit heavily scented, usually white blooms that are easy to locate under the cover of darkness.

The color and shape of flowers also provide clues as to how they are pollinated. Honeybees

The yellow lady's slipper, a delicate orchid, lures pollinating insects into its pouch.

favor blue and yellow flowers that have petals modified into landing platforms. In addition, dark lines on petals, like the lights on an airport runway, tell the bees where to find nectar and pollen. Hummingbirds and butterflies visit long, tubular blossoms, many of which are bright red, a color that bees see as black.

The language of flowers

Wildflowers are a link with the lore of the past. Long used for medicines, folk remedies, dyes, and foods, they have, over centuries of familiarity, acquired common names that remind us of simpler times. Fleabane, a member of the sunflower family, for example, was used to repel fleas in the days when insecticides were unavailable, and the roots and leaves of soapwort were lathered into suds on many frontier laundry days. A syrup made from coughwort leaves was long a favorite remedy for colds, and Joe-pye weed preserves the name of a Massachusetts In-

dian who, in the late 18th century, used this wildflower to cure colonists of fevers. Round-leaved hepatica, a staple of herbal practitioners, was also known as liverleaf because of an old belief that a plant's outward appearance was a sign of its healing properties.

Though the use of wildflowers in home remedies and crafts is now largely a thing of the past, they still can be appreciated for their simple beauty. While a great number of species are accessible within a short walk of almost any front door, human activities have brought many others to the brink of extinction. The greatest threat is suburban development—1,000,000 acres of countryside is lost in this way every year. Fortunately, some cities and towns are trying to route development around sensitive habitats. Individuals can make a contribution by getting to know local varieties, learning the lore and legends they have inspired, and awakening others to the beauty and charm of wildflowers.

Purple trillium roots were given to women after childbirth, earning the plant the nickname birthroot.

A daisy's rays serve as landing pads for insect pollinators.

Sagebrush buttercups add a dazzling splash of color to western woodlands, meadows, and sagebrush country. Like other buttercups, its flowers and fleshy leaves are slightly toxic.

Winds along the Florida coast rarely cease and are often strong enough to bend palm trees and send clouds racing across the sky.

Wintergreen contains a chemical similar to aspirin that has been used for treating sore, swollen muscles.

Common witch hazel bears its wispy golden flowers in fall, just as the plant's leaves are beginning to drop. The fruits that follow were gathered by Indians, who toasted and ate the nutty black seeds. Herbalists have myriad uses for extracts of the bark and leaves.

W

Wind

Movements of air in the atmosphere—winds—are produced when air is heated by the sun, expands, and rises, permitting cooler, denser air to rush in and take its place. These movements can be as gentle as the breezes that rustle leaves or as powerful as gales that uproot entire trees.

While winds can blow in any direction, in our latitudes they generally travel from west to east. These prevailing westerlies help in predicting the weather. If it is raining a few hundred miles west of a place today, for instance, rain will probably fall in that place tomorrow.

Both wildlife and the environment are constantly affected by winds. They carry the seeds and pollen of plants, assist birds in their migrations, whip up waves at sea, and help sculpt the land through erosion.

Windflower See *Anemone.*

Wintergreen *Gaultheria procumbens*

A dwarf creeping shrub less than six inches tall, wintergreen spreads a carpet of oval, shiny evergreen leaves across sandy woodlands from Newfoundland to Alabama. In midsummer waxy, bell-shaped white flowers dangle among the leaves and are followed by tasty, bright red berries—a favorite winter food of grouse and other wildlife. The pungent oil that suffuses the plant is used as a flavoring in candies and chewing gum and in balms that soothe sore muscles.

Witches' broom

The clusters of spindly shoots that sometimes spring from the branches of forest trees and shrubs really do resemble the broomsticks that witches were supposed to mount and fly. And so it is not surprising that our ancestors believed that witches not only caused their growth but also used them as resting places during their

Timber wolves roam our northern woodlands night and day in pursuit of prey.

Witches' broom is a symptom of disease in plants; these unusual growths have inspired much folklore and legend.

travels. In fact, these abnormalities are a symptom of plant disease. The condition is caused by a number of agents, including viruses, fungi, and insects, and it appears on conifers as well as alders, birches, cherries, and other plants.

Witch hazel *Hamamelis*

Shrubs that are native to eastern woodlands and stream banks, both species of witch hazels are sometimes referred to as winterbloom. The nickname is appropriate, for common, or American, witch hazel unfurls its tassels of ribbonlike yellow petals as late as December, and vernal, or Ozark, witch hazel blooms in January or February. The woody fruits that follow are hard capsules that literally explode when they are ripe, shooting shiny black seeds more than 15 feet away. The familiar soothing lotion called witch hazel is made from the leaves and bark of the plant, and its forked branches have been used as divining rods.

Wolf *Canis*

Though the sound of wolves howling in the night is enough to send chills down the spine, their reputation as ferocious enemies of man owes more to fiction and folklore than to reality. Wolves, in fact, go out of their way to avoid humans. Even so, they have been hunted so persistently over the years that one of our two species, the red wolf of the Southeast, has virtually disappeared. The other—the gray, or timber, wolf—whose domain once included the South, now lives only in northern wilderness areas.

Resembling large, wide-faced German shepherd dogs, gray wolves vary in color from white on the arctic tundra to gray or black in forested regions. They travel in packs, working cooperatively to bring down such big game as deer, moose, and caribou. Though wolves are usually regarded as unbeatable in their quest for prey, they often fail to subdue their intended victims. Wolves are no match for a healthy adult moose, for example, and so must routinely select individuals that are old or sick.

Highly intelligent, wolves behave according to a complex set of social rules. The pack is led by a dominant male, and each member knows its place within the group. Wolves communicate by means of postures and scents, as well as an array of yelps, whines, and growls, and they all work together to rear the cubs, which are usually produced only by the dominant pair.

W

Woodchucks are able diggers that can excavate tunnels up to 30 feet long.

American woodcocks build leaf-lined nests on moist ground, where the females incubate three or four speckled eggs.

Wolverine *Gulo gulo*

Dark brown with dull yellow stripes on its forehead and sides, the wolverine, at up to 60 pounds, is one of the largest members of the weasel family. Though much smaller than any wolf or bear, it is nevertheless among the most formidable predators of the arctic tundra and far western mountains. A solitary hunter on the prowl both night and day, this tough, muscular creature plods relentlessly after prey. Incredibly strong for its size, the wolverine can bring down quarry as big as deer. Smaller animals are also fair game, and insects, birds' eggs, berries, and carrion supplement its diet. Despite its strength and prowess, the wolverine needs large wilderness areas in which to range and is intolerant of people; wherever humans modify the land, wolverines quickly disappear.

Woodchuck *Marmota monax*

Unlike most other marmots, which live in high mountains, woodchucks prefer lowland forests and meadows across Canada and the U.S. Northeast and Midwest. They have prospered in many farming areas and are often considered pests.

After fattening on tender plants—alfalfa and clover are favorites—woodchucks hibernate in their burrows in winter. Although they are the groundhogs of Groundhog Day, most remain underground long after February 2. The young, born in spring, are ready to venture into the outside world within a month. During the summer these stocky rodents can be seen standing in fields, ready to duck out of sight with a loud whistle at the first sign of danger.

Woodcock *Scolopax minor*

A stocky, snipelike bird of the East, the American woodcock is best known for the elaborate and unique aerial display that the male performs in early spring to attract a mate. He struts back and forth across his territory and then, with wings whistling, takes to the air. Flying in wide circles, he sings a bubbly song and, still singing, zigzags back to earth like a falling leaf. If successful, he is greeted by a suitably receptive female. Woodcocks build their nests on the ground, where the birds are camouflaged by streaked, brownish plumage that blends with the leaf litter. They use their unusually long, thin, sensitive bills to probe for earthworms in damp meadows and swampy woods.

Woodpecker

Famous for the *rat-a-tat* drumming with which they punctuate the peace and quiet of forests, woodpeckers are well equipped for life on tree trunks. Sharp claws and stiff, proplike tails hold the birds in place while muscular necks and stout bills work in concert to drill holes into bark.

Drilling is a way of life for these birds: it is used both for excavating nest holes and for finding insects, which are lapped up with a long, sticky tongue. Woodpeckers also drum on hollow branches to proclaim territory and communicate with mates. A few members of the family, however, are nonconformists. The northern flicker feeds on the ground, where its favorite food is ants; sapsuckers drill holes in bark to drink the sap that oozes out; and acorn woodpeckers drill holes in trees—and utility poles—as storage spaces for the acorns they eat.

Most of the 22 species are black-and-white with a dash of red on the males' heads. The smallest and one of the commonest is the six-inch downy woodpecker, found from coast to coast. Since the largest species, the 20-inch ivory-billed woodpecker of the Southeast, is probably extinct, the honor for top size now goes to the crow-size pileated woodpecker.

W

Getting Acquainted with the Woodpeckers

Easily recognized by the way they cling upright to tree trunks, with their tails serving as props, woodpeckers also call attention to themselves by hammering on wood with their chisellike bills. To sort out one kind from another, note the colors, patterns, and relative size. The adult males of our most familiar species are shown below.

Mostly brownish

Northern flicker (3 races)

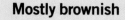

Yellow tinge on wings, black mustache
Yellow-shafted flicker
(East)

Yellow tinge on wings, red mustache
Gilded flicker
(Southwest)

Reddish tinge on wings, red mustache
Red-shafted flicker
(West)

Mostly black-and-white

LARGE AREAS OF BLACK AND WHITE

INTRICATE PATTERNS OF BLACK AND WHITE

Red crest, red mustache
Pileated woodpecker
(East and West)

Whole head red
Red-headed woodpecker
(East)

Red crown
Acorn woodpecker
(West)

Black-and-white bars across back

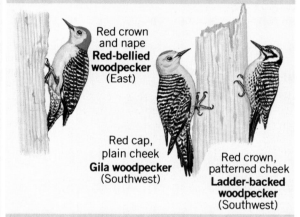

Red crown and nape
Red-bellied woodpecker
(East)

Red cap, plain cheek
Gila woodpecker
(Southwest)

Red crown, patterned cheek
Ladder-backed woodpecker
(Southwest)

White back, speckled wings

Small (6″), small bill
Downy woodpecker
(East and West)

Large (9″), large bill
Hairy woodpecker
(East and West)

Dark back, white wing spot

Red forehead and throat
Yellow-bellied sapsucker
(East and West)

Red head and breast
Red-breasted sapsucker
(West)

W

A wood stork stretches its long, graceful wings as it wades through the Florida Everglades.

Wood sorrel often forms a thick ground cover in the moist forests that it inhabits.

W

Wood rat *Neotoma*

Native to woodlands and other wild places, these furry rodents live up to their nickname, pack rats, for they nest in structures (sometimes huge) that are built of all sorts of odds and ends. (Desert-dwelling species ward off enemies by using plenty of cactus spines in their construction.) Wood rats often raid campsites at night, gathering coins and other shiny trinkets to incorporate into their fortresses. Leaving a twig or pebble in place of the purloined prize has earned them yet another nickname, trade rats.

Wood sorrel *Oxalis*

Delicate plants with cloverlike leaves, wood sorrels grow in moist, shady woodlands. The white blossoms of the common wood sorrel are striped with pink, but there are yellow- and purple-flowered species as well. Because of their pleasantly sour taste, the leaves are often added to salads. Herbalists have long used the plants for treating a variety of ills, but it is now known that overindulgence in the foliage inhibits the body's ability to absorb calcium.

Wood stork *Mycteria americana*

The large, long-legged wood stork is a wading bird that lives in the marshes and swamps of the Southeast. It feeds in shallow water, using its long, probing bill to catch fish, frogs, and other prey. Mostly white, the wood stork has a blackish, scaly-looking, unfeathered head that has earned it the nickname flinthead. Despite its homely face, it is graceful on the wing, soaring with its long neck and legs extended.

The gregarious wood stork breeds in large colonies, building a flimsy nest of sticks and twigs in a tree or other swamp vegetation. Since it depends on falling water levels to concentrate its prey in small pools, it does not nest at all in very wet years when prey is dispersed over a wide area. Because of habitat destruction, our only native stork is now listed as endangered.

Woolly bear *Isia isabella*

Black at both ends and brown in the middle, the familiar woolly bear is the caterpillar of the Isabella tiger moth. It is most often seen in autumn, crawling across the ground in search of a safe place to hibernate for the winter. Like the caterpillars of most other tiger moths, the woolly bear is covered with stiff bristles. When disturbed, it curls up quickly, and the bristles make it difficult for predators to pick up. Not at all fussy about its diet, the woolly bear feeds on the foliage of a wide variety of plants, including grasses, and is common from coast to coast.

A marsh wren sings among the reeds that—along with cattails and bulrushes—grow in the marshes where it lives. The male, for unknown reasons, builds several nests on the breeding grounds before the female arrives. They are never used, however, because the female constructs her own nest when she is ready to lay her eggs.

The woolly bear caterpillar (above) hibernates during the winter. In the spring it encloses itself in a cocoon of silk and caterpillar hairs, emerging two weeks later transformed into an Isabella tiger moth (right).

W

Wrasse

Found mainly in warmer waters, wrasses are a diverse group of brightly colored fish. Typically they have narrow bodies—from three inches to a few feet long—and pointed snouts; all have pharyngeal, or throat, teeth, used for crushing crabs, sea urchins, and other food. (Some of the smaller kinds pick parasites off other fish.)

The tautog, a common Atlantic wrasse, is popular with anglers: found from Nova Scotia to South Carolina, it lurks around breakwaters and other rocky areas. The California sheephead, with a distinctive hump on its head, favors the kelp beds and rocky shores of the Pacific.

Wren

Nine species of wrens—all of them small, stocky brownish birds that often perch with their tails cocked over their backs—are native to North America. The best known is the house wren, which nests in parks, farmyards, and orchards from coast to coast. Tenacious and ag-

gressive, it is a welcome springtime visitor that fills the air with bright, bubbly song. The Carolina wren, the largest eastern species, is a rusty brown bird that happily nests in baskets, mailboxes, and other man-made cavities, as do most other wrens. The starling-size cactus wren is a husky bird with a boldly spotted breast. Noisy and conspicuous, it flits along the desert floor, picking among rocks and brush for insects and other food, and builds its nest in the well-armed safety of a spiny cactus.

Wrentit *Chamaea fasciata*

These secretive West Coast songbirds are more easily heard than seen: the males sing year-round, but wrentits seldom venture from their home turf in dense scrub thickets or chaparral. Mated wrentits form devoted pairs, preening each other's feathers and foraging together for insects and berries. They also roost side by side, sometimes fluffing their plumage and leaning against each other so that they look like a single little gray-brown ball of feathers.

Yarrow blossoms have a spicy fragrance; when dried, they are popular in potpourris.

Yuccas have night-blooming flowers that are pollinated by just one kind of moth.

Xerophyte

Plants that are able to live in places where fresh water is in short supply—deserts and salt marshes, for example—are called xerophytes. Succulents such as cacti and agaves store water in their stems and leaves to weather times of drought. Other desert plants, known as ephemerals, germinate during the rainy season only, completing their entire life cycle—from seed to flower to seed—in a matter of weeks. Many xerophytes have waxy coatings or dense, feltlike coverings of hair that protect them from the sun and wind and slow down water loss. Others react to the blazing sun by folding their leaves, positioning them so that the sun's rays strike less surface area, or dropping them altogether during dry spells.

Yarrow *Achillea millefolium*

A tolerance for drought and an ability to thrive even on poor soils have made yarrow a common weed of waste places throughout North America. Growing up to three feet tall, it is clad with finely cut foliage that has a pungent aroma, as do the flat-topped clusters of small white—or sometimes pink—flowers that appear in summer.

Yarrow is said to have been used by the ancient Greek hero Achilles (hence the plant's generic name) to stanch the blood of warriors' wounds. Early settlers and aboriginal peoples used it as a healing herb: both drank yarrow tea to treat digestive ills and reduce fevers, and yarrow poultices were recommended for healing wounds, cuts, and burns.

Yellow rattle *Rhinanthus*

Flourishing as far north as the Arctic Circle, yellow rattle colors fields, moist alpine meadows, and thickets with spikes of bright golden blossoms. Each of the tubular flowers protrudes from a swollen green base, which matures into a bladderlike, seed-filled pod. When stirred by the wind, the dry, ripened pods do indeed make a rattling noise. Up to 24 inches tall, our most common species, also known as rattlebox, is in bloom from June to September.

Yellowwood *Cladrastis kentukea*

Named for its handsome timber, yellowwood is a slow-growing, long-lived tree that is found in isolated pockets in parts of the Southeast and Midwest and is nowhere abundant. It favors the rich soils of river valleys and streamsides, where it sometimes reaches a height of 60 feet. In early summer, yellowwood produces long, drooping clusters of fragrant, creamy white flowers, which are followed by papery seedpods two to three inches long. The featherlike compound leaves turn bright yellow before dropping from the tree in autumn. The durable wood, when available, is coveted for gunstocks.

Yew *Taxus*

Shade-tolerant trees and shrubs with flattened, evergreen needles, yews are easily distinguished from other conifers by their red berrylike fruits. Largest of the three species native to North

X

Y

Z

Yews bear colorful, juicy, berrylike fruits. The seeds are poisonous, but birds eat the succulent red flesh.

Zebra longwings have a bitter taste and smell that protects them from predators.

Little golden zinnias produce sunny yellow blossoms from May through October. Hardy wildflowers, they prefer the dry slopes, deserts, and prairies of the West and Southwest.

America is the Pacific yew; up to 60 feet tall, it is found in far western forests from southern Alaska to California. Its durable, reddish wood is used for archery bows, canoe paddles, and hand tools. Another northerner, Canada yew, is a low woodland shrub; though the foliage of all yews is poisonous, Canada yew is heavily browsed by moose and deer. Florida yew, a 30-foot tree, grows only in northwestern Florida.

Yucca

While yuccas are most common in the deserts of the U.S. Southwest, these dramatic plants range all across the southern states and even as far north as Montana. A few, including the renowned Joshua tree of California's deserts, are tall and branching. But most are shrubs with trunkless, ground-level clusters of daggerlike leaves that have inspired such names as Adam's needle and Spanish bayonet. The yuccas bear tall spikes of white to purplish, cup-shaped flowers. These open after dark and are pollinated by a type of moth that lays its eggs exclusively on yuccas.

Zebra longwing *Heliconius charitonius*

Our only member of a group of tropical butterflies called heliconians, the zebra longwing flies slowly, almost feebly, through wooded areas in the South. It seems to know that its bold black-and-yellow pattern warns predators that it is distasteful—the result of feeding on the poisonous leaves of passionflowers. Unlike most butterflies, the adults feed on pollen rather than nectar and gather at night in communal roosts.

X

Y

Z

Zinnia *Zinnia*

Though the cultivated zinnias that grace our gardens are all descended from a Mexican ancestor, several species of wild zinnias thrive on dry, rocky slopes and grassy plains in parts of the South and West. Like most members of the sunflower family, their blossoms are characterized by a ring of petallike ray flowers surrounding a central disk. The plants, which commonly grow from 4 to 20 inches tall, are in bloom from early spring through midfall.

ILLUSTRATION CREDITS

Art

Howard S. Friedman 12, 13, 18, 23, 30, 37, 41, 43, 45, 49, 52, 70, 72, 76, 83, 88, 103, 106, 109, 117, 118, 127, 128, 129, 135, 141, 143, 146, 150, 160, 164, 169, 174, 176, 196, 222, 223, 224, 227, 230, 231, 232, 240, 250, 257, 272, 279, 285, 297, 304, 328, 333, 339, 342, 343, 346, 350, 351, 352, 357, 361, 362, 370, 372, 373, 378, 383, 384, 407, 410, 418, 429, 433, 435 Dolores Santoliguido 414 Paul Singer 14, 21, 35 Wayne J. Trimm 64, 113, 167, 170, 387 Robert Villani 376, 381, 442

Photographs

Except for those in parentheses, all the photographers are represented by Bruce Coleman, Inc. The positions of photographs are identified as follows: *t = top; b = bottom; l = left; r = right; m = middle.*

Front cover: (*tl* Ron Sanford); (*tm* John H. Gerard from the Guetterman Collection); *tr* Gary Meszaros; (*b* David Muench). **Spine:** (Glenn Ellison/Stock Solution). **Back cover:** George Marler.

1 Gary Meszaros. **2–3** (R. Hamilton Smith). **4–5** (Richard W. Brown). **6** *l* James M. Cribb; *tr* Erwin & Peggy Bauer; *br* J. Fennell. **7** *l* M.P.L. Fogden; *r* William McPherson. **8** *t* Ken Sherman; *b* John Markham. **9** *t* Wolfgang Bayer; *m* Kim Taylor; *b* Robert P. Carr. **10** *t* Roy Morsch; *bl* E.R. Degginger; *br* Joy Spurr. **11** *t* Joy Spurr; *b* John Shaw. **12** *tr* Leonard Lee Rue III; *br* Jeff Foott. **13** *r* John Shaw; (*br* Albert Kuhnigk/Valan Photos). **14** *tr & br* E.R. Degginger. **15** *l* Jeff Foott; *r* Eric Crichton. **16** *t* Bob & Clara Calhoun; *bl* Jeff Foott; *br* Dwight R. Kuhn. **17** Ronald Thompson. **18** *l* Robert P. Carr; *br* Robert L. Dunne. **19** *tl & r* Alan Blank; *b* Dwight R. Kuhn. **20** Larry Ditto. **22** *l* Alan Blank; *r* Wayne Lankinen. **23** *t* Rosalie LaRue Faubion; *bl* Steve Solum. **24** *tl* E.R. Degginger; *r* Bob & Clara Calhoun; *bl* Joe & Carol McDonald. **25** John S. Flannery. **26** (*l* Wayne Lankinen/Valan Photos); *r* Bob & Clara Calhoun. **27** *l* Robert P. Carr; *r* E.R. Degginger. **28** Gary Withey. **29** *tl* Michael P. Gadomski; *ml* G.D. Ramsay; *top to bottom right:* Norman Owen Tomalin, Michael Gallagher, Jen & Des Bartlett, William H. Amos. **30** *b* Lois & George Cox. **31** *tl* S.L. Craig Jr.; *r* Phil Degginger; *b* Laura Riley. **32** *l* C.C. Lockwood; *tr* Charles G. Summers Jr.; *b* John Shaw. **33** *l* Kevin Byron; *r* Keith Gunnar. **34** *t* Jen & Des Bartlett; *bl* E.R. Degginger; *br* Kim Taylor. **35** *l* E.R. Degginger; *m* Steve Solum. **36** *tl* L. West; *r* Bob Gossington; *b* Norman Owen Tomalin. **37** *l* Gary Meszaros; *r* James H. Carmichael Jr. **38** *tl* John Shaw; *tr* James H. Carmichael Jr.; *b* Jeff Foott. **39** *l & r* Steve Solum. **40** *l* L. West; *tr* Edgar T. Jones; *b* Gordon Langsbury. **41** *bl* S. Nielsen. **42** *tl* Steven L. Hilty; *r* Martin W. Grosnick; *bl* Wayne Lankinen. **43** *r* Laura Riley. **44** *tl* Gary Meszaros; *tr* C.C. Lockwood; *bl* L. West; *br* Lynn M. Stone. **45** *t* Joy Spurr. **46** *l* Bob & Clara Calhoun; *tr* William Carter; *b* John Shaw. **47** *l* Bob & Clara Calhoun; *r* Laura Riley. **48** *l* D.R. Thompson/G.D. Dodge; *r* Jack Couffer. **49** *l* Robert L. Dunne; *mr* Timothy O'Keefe; *b* L.S. Stepanowicz. **50** *l* Robert L. Dunne; *tr* Jeff Foott; *b* Phil Degginger. **51** *tl* John Shaw; *tm* Wardene Weisser; *tr* Steve Solum; *bl* Bob Burch; *br* Wardene Weisser. **52** *tl* Wendell Metzen; *tr* Bob & Clara Calhoun; *bl* R.E. Pelham. **53** *l* Dwight R. Kuhn; *r* E.R. Degginger. **54** *l* Dwight R. Kuhn; *tr* John Shaw; *b* Barth Schorre. **55** *t* Edgar T. Jones; *b* Jack Dermid. **56** *l* Jeff Foott; *r* Leonard Lee Rue III. **57** *tl* R.L. Sefton; *r* C.C. Lockwood; *b* Steve Solum. **58** *tr* Robert L. Dunne; *b* L. West; *remainder* E.R. Degginger. **59** *all* L. West. **60** *t* Jen & Des Bartlett; *bl* Wayne Lankinen; *br* E.R. Degginger. **61** *tl & br* Jen & Des Bartlett; *tr* Wardene Weisser; *bl* Jeff Foott. **62** *tl* Edgar T. Jones; *tr* Bob & Clara Calhoun; *bl* S. Nielsen; *br* L. West. **63** *t* Marty Stouffer; *b* Gary R. Jones. **64** *tr* Laura Riley; *b* L. West. **65** *t* James Balog; *b* Jen & Des Bartlett. **66** *l* Alan Blank; *tr* D. Lyons; *b* Kenneth W. Fink. **67** *l* Laura Riley; *tr* Gary Meszaros; *b* Steve Solum. **68** *tl* Joe & Carol McDonald; *tr* James H. Carmichael Jr.; *bl* Robert L. Dunne; *br* Jeff Foott. **69** *l* Norman Owen Tomalin; *tr* D. Lyons; *b* Leonard Lee Rue III. **70** (*tl* Gerald Ferguson); *tr* E.R. Degginger. **71** *l* Bob & Clara Calhoun; *r* Hans Reinhard. **72** *tl & b* Kevin Byron. **73** *l* S. Nielsen; *r* Kevin Byron. **74** *l* Kenneth W. Fink; *tr* Jeff Foott; *b* Martin W. Grosnick. **75** *t* John Shaw; *b* J.M. Burnley. **76** *tr* Richard Mariscal; *b* Norman Owen Tomalin. **77** *l* Steve Solum; *r* L. West. **78** *l* Jack Dermid; *tr* Keith Gunnar; *b* Phil Degginger. **79** *l* John Shaw; *r* Dwight R. Kuhn. **80** *l & r* E.R. Degginger. **81** *l* Hans Reinhard; *r* L. West. **82** *t* Joseph Van Wormer; *b* Gary Meszaros. **84** *l* Joseph Van Wormer; *r* Kim Taylor. **85** *t* Joe McDonald; *bl* Larry Lipsky; *br* James H. Carmichael Jr. **86** *l* Jack Dermid; *r* Bill Ruth. **87** *l* Wayne Lankinen; *tr* Joe McDonald; *b* Rod Williams. **88** *l* Jen & Des Bartlett; *b* L. West. **89** *l* John S. Flannery; *r* Sullivan & Rogers. **90** Erwin & Peggy Bauer. **91** *tl* David Falconer; *tr* E.R. Degginger; *bl & br* Robert P. Carr. **92** *tl & b* E.R. Degginger; *r* Wayne Lankinen. **93** *t* Wayne Lankinen; *b* A. Kerstitch. **94** *t* C.C. Lockwood; *b* Martin W. Grosnick. **95** *tl* M.P. Kahl; *tr* James H. Carmichael Jr.; *ml* Wendell Metzen; *mr* R.E. Pelham; *bl* Wendell Metzen; *br* Erwin & Peggy Bauer. **96** *l* E.R. Degginger; *r* Barth Schorre. **97** *l* David Overcash; *tr* Adrian Davies; *b* Larry Lipsky. **98** *t* Hans Reinhard; *bl* John Shaw; *br* David Overcash. **99** *l* David Overcash; *tr* E.R. Degginger; *br* Bob Gossington. **100** *tl* Bob & Clara Calhoun; *tr* L. West; *bl* John Shaw; *br* S. Nielsen. **101** *tl* Robert P. Carr; *tr* Barth Schorre; *ml* L. West; *br* Leonard Lee Rue III; *bl* James Hanken. **102** *l* Erwin & Peggy Bauer; *r* Leonard Lee Rue III. **103** *tl & tr* Jack Dermid; *br* John Shaw. **104** *t* Robert P. Carr; *m & bl* Kenneth W. Fink; *br* Bob & Clara Calhoun. **105** *tl* Gordon Wiltsie; *tr* Jen & Des Bartlett; *ml* Jeff Foott; *mr* John Elk III; *b* Wardene Weisser. **106** *tl* E.R. Degginger; *r* Jeff Foott. **107** *l* David Overcash; *r* Bob & Clara Calhoun. **108** *tl* David Overcash; *tr* Kevin Byron; *m* Kenneth W. Fink; *b* Norman Owen Tomalin. **109** *t* E.R. Degginger. **110** *l* Larry Ditto; *tr* Joe McDonald; *b* Robert L. Dunne. **111** Jim Brandenburg. **112** *t* S. Nielsen; *b* Joe McDonald. **114** *t* G. Rockwin; *b* Glenn Short. **115** *t* John Hyde; *b* Bob Gossington. **116** (*t* U.S. Department of Commerce); (*b* The Bettmann Archive). **117** (*tl, bl & tr* AP/Wide World Photos). **118** *bl* Erwin & Peggy Bauer; *r* John Shaw. **119** *l* Bob & Clara Calhoun; *tr* Lynn M. Stone; *br* Jeff Foott. **120** *l* Wendell Metzen; *r* Wayne Lankinen. **121** *tl* John Elk III; *tr* Nancy A. Potter; *b* Jeff Foott. **122** *l* John E. Swedberg; *r* Phil Degginger. **123** *l* Wendell Metzen; *r* Sullivan & Rogers. **124** *tl* Bob & Clara Calhoun; *tr & m* Wayne Lankinen; *bl* Erwin & Peggy Bauer; *br* Leonard Lee Rue III. **125** *t* E.R. Degginger; *ml* W.E. Ruth; *mr* Barth Schorre; *bl* Gary Meszaros; *br* L. West. **126** *t* Kevin Byron; *b* George B. Schaller. **127** *tl* John Shaw; *tr* Lee Foster; *m* Kenneth W. Fink. **128** *tl & tr* John Shaw. **129** *l* Wayne Lankinen. **130** *l* E.R. Degginger; *tr* Gary Meszaros. **131** *l* Erwin & Peggy Bauer; *r* Tom Brakefield. **132** *t* Sullivan & Rogers; *b* Michael S. Renner. **133** *l* Thase Daniel; *tr* E.R. Degginger; *br* Gene Ahrens. **134** Jack W. Dykinga. **135** *tl* James H. Carmichael Jr.; *tr* Robert P. Carr; *ml* L. West; *mr* David Overcash; *bl* Robert P. Carr. **136** *l* E.R. Degginger; *r* Nicholas Conte. **137** *t* Cameron Davidson; *b* Richard Buettner. **138** *tl* Phil Degginger; *r* Norman Myers; *b* Kim Taylor. **139** *t* Dale & Marian Zimmerman; *b* Erwin & Peggy Bauer. **140** Gary R. Zahm. **141** *bl* Joe McDonald; *r* L. West. **142** *top to bottom left:* Michael P. Gadomski, Kevin Byron, Steve Solum, Joy Spurr; *top to bottom middle:* Joy Spurr, Joy Spurr, L. West, John Shaw; *top to bottom right:* Joy Spurr, Joy Spurr, Michael Gallagher, John Shaw. **144** *tl* Jane Burton; *r* J. Ehlers; *ml* David Overcash; *b* Robert P. Carr. **145** Gordon Langsbury. **146** *b* Leonard Lee Rue III. **147** *l & br* E.R. Degginger; *tr* Bob & Clara Calhoun. **148** *l* L. West; *r* Keith Gunnar. **149** *tl* E.R. Degginger; (*tr* James T. Vale, California Academy of Sciences); *b* Tom Brakefield. **150** *br* D. Lyons. **151** *tl* Tom Brakefield; *tr* C.C. Lockwood; *bl* Keith Gunnar; *br* Jack Dermid. **152** *tl* Edgar T. Jones; *tr* L. West; *ml & bl* Larry Lipsky; *br* Gene Ahrens. **153** *t* Robert P. Carr; *b* Jeff Foott. **154** *l* Robert P. Carr; *r* Wayne Lankinen. **155** *t* Robert P. Carr; *b* Wendell Metzen. **156** *l* C.C. Lockwood; *tr* S. Deiber; *mr* Lynn M. Stone; *br* Laura Riley. **157** *l* Bob & Clara Calhoun; *r* Charles G. Summers Jr. **158** *t* Jeff Foott; *m* Joe McDonald; *bl* M.P. Kahl; *br* John Shaw. **159** *tl* Jeff Foott; *ml* Lynn M. Stone; *tr, mr & b* John Shaw. **160** *l* L. West; *tr* Wayne Lankinen. **161** *tl* E.R. Degginger; *r* Erwin & Peggy Bauer; *b* Roger & Joy Spurr. **162** *tl* Jeff Foott; *tr* David Overcash; *bl* George Marler; *br* Chris P. Marsh. **163** *l* M.P.L. Fogden; *r* Joe McDonald. **164** *t* John Elk III; *bl* L. West. **165** *tl* David Madison; *tr* E.R. Degginger; *b* Wendell Metzen. **166** *l* John H. Hoffman; *r* Phil Degginger. **167** *tl* Jeff Foott; *r* Edgar T. Jones; *bl* Steve Solum. **168** Keith Gunnar. **169** *tr* Jeff Foott; *b* Larry Lipsky. **171** *t* Jeff Foott; *b* Mike Price. **172** *t* John Shaw; *bl* Phil Degginger; *br* Jane Burton; **173** James H. Carmichael Jr. **174** *r* Erwin & Peggy Bauer. **175** *t* Bob & Clara Calhoun; *bl* Kenneth W. Fink; *br* Robert P. Carr. **176** *t* Joseph Van Wormer. **177** *tl* E.R. Degginger; *r* John Shaw; *bl* Mike Price. **178** Jeff Foott. **179** *tl* Adrian Davies; *tr & b* E.R. Degginger. **180** *t & b* Bob & Clara Calhoun. **181** *tl & tr* Bob & Clara Calhoun; *b* Fred J. Alsop III. **182** (NASA). **182** *t* Jeff Foott; *b* James H. Carmichael Jr. **184** *tl* Jeff Foott; *tr* Richard Buettner; *b* Wendell Metzen. **185** *t* R.E. Pelham; *b* Jeff Foott. **186** *t* Bob Gossington; *b* Wayne Lankinen. **187** *l* Wayne Lankinen; *r* Robert P. Carr. **188** *l* Gary Meszaros; *r* David Overcash. **189** *tl & bl* Kjell B. Sandved; *tr* E.R. Degginger; *br* David Overcash. **190** *t* Bob & Clara Calhoun; *m* Robert P. Carr; *b* E.R. Degginger. **191** *tl* E.R. Degginger; *tr* John Ebeling; *bl* Timothy O'Keefe; *br* David Overcash. **192** *t* Gordon Langsbury; *bl* Wayne Lankinen; *br* Erwin & Peggy Bauer. **193** *tl* E.R. Degginger; *bl* William H. Amos; *r* L. West. **194** *tl* Gordon Wiltsie; *r* Erwin & Peggy Bauer; *b* David Overcash. **195** *tl* Harry N. Darrow; *r* Robert P. Carr; *b* Jeff Foott. **196** *t* Bob & Clara Calhoun; *bl* Laura Riley. **197** E.R. Degginger. **198** *t* Bob & Clara Calhoun; *bl* E.R. Degginger; *br* John Shaw. **199** *l* Bob & Clara Calhoun; *r* Edgar T. Jones. **200** *tl* Joe McDonald; *tr* Bob & Clara Calhoun; *b* Wendell Metzen. **201** *t* Keith Gunnar; *bl* Steve Solum; *br* Erwin & Peggy Bauer. **202** *t* James Blank; *ml* Charles G. Summers Jr.; *mr* Timothy O'Keefe; *b* S. Nielsen. **203** *tl* Bill Ruth; *ml* John Shaw; *bl* Bob & Clara Calhoun; *tr* William H. Amos; *mr* L. West; *mr* E.R. Degginger. **204** *tl* Phyllis A. Betow; *bl* Roger & Joy Spurr; *r* Norman Owen Tomalin. **205** *t* Alan Blank; *ml* William H. Amos; *mr* Dwight R. Kuhn; *b* David Overcash. **206** Keith Gunnar. **207** *tl* Ron Goor; *bl* E.R. Degginger;

A

INDEX

C

A dagger (†) following an index entry indicates that the entry is the title of a feature article.
Page numbers in **bold** type refer to illustrations.

443

A dagger (†) following an index entry indicates that the entry is the title of a feature article.
Page numbers in **bold** type refer to illustrations.

445

H

A dagger (†) following an index entry indicates that the entry is the title of a feature article.
Page numbers in **bold** type refer to illustrations.

447

M

A dagger (†) following an index entry indicates that the entry is the title of a feature article.
Page numbers in **bold** type refer to illustrations.

449

N

O

P

Pack rat. *See* Wood rat.
Paddlefish, 278†, **278**
Painted bolete, **255**
Painted bunting, **54**
Painted turtle, **228**, 278†
Painter. *See* Mountain lion.
Pallas's wallflower, **257**
Palm, 278†, **279**
　　cabbage palmetto, **123, 278**
　　saw palmetto, 337†, **337**
Palmetto bug, giant, 80
Paloverde, 280†, **280**
Panther
　　Florida, **119**
　　See also Mountain lion.
Paper wasp, **189**
Papyrus, 410
Paramecia, 308
Parasite, 280†
Parrot-bill, 64
Parrotfish, 280†, **281**
Parry's primrose, **248**
Parsley, 280–281†
Parsnip, 281
　　wild, 298
Partridgeberry, 281†, **281**
Pasqueflower, 13
Passenger pigeon, **123,** 290
Passerine (perching bird), 284†, **284**
Passionflower, 281†, **281,** 415
Patterned ground, 285
Pawpaw, 282†, **282**
Peacock flounder, 132
Pearly everlasting, 282†, **282**
Peat. *See* Sphagnum.
Pecan, 171
Peccary, 282†, **282**
Pelican, 283†, **283**
Peony, 14
Peppertree, 283†
Perch, 284†, 339
Perching bird, 284†, **284**
Peregrine falcon, 119
Perennial, 14
Peridot, 147
Periwinkle, 285†, **285,** 394
Permafrost, 285†, 401, 407
Persimmon, **29,** 285†, **285**
Petrel, 142, 285†
Petrified Forest National Park, 286
Petrified wood, 286†, **286**
Petroleum, 258, 267, 286†
Petunia, 263
Pewee, wood, 136
Peyote, 286–287†
Phacelia, 287†, **287**
Phainopepla, 287†, **287**
Phalarope, 287†, **287**
Pheasant, 288†, **288**
Philodendron, 299
Phlox, 288†, **288**
Phoebe, 69, 136, 288†, **289**
Photosynthesis, 8, 206, 208, 289†, 308
Phytoplankton, 294
Pickerel, chain, **290**
Pickerelweed, **229,** 289†, **289**
Pickle weed (glasswort), 151†, **151**
Pig, 410
　　hooves of, 173
Pigeon, 110, 290†

Pigeon (*contd.*)
　　passenger, **123,** 290
Pika, **249,** 290†, **290**
Pike, 290†, **290**
Pileated woodpecker, **260,** 290–291†, **290**
Pillow lava, 291†
Pilotfish, 191
Pimpernel, 281
Pincushion cactus, **60**
Pine, **83,** 291†, **291, 296**
　　bristlecone, **291**
　　ground, 79, **79**
　　longleaf, **365**
　　ponderosa, 29, **29**
Pine forest, southern, 364–365†, **364, 365**
Pine grosbeak, 129
Pine-hyacinth, 77
Pine nut (pinyon), 292†
Pinesap, 187
Pine siskin, 129
Pingo, 285
Pink, 292†, **292**
Pinkweed, 200
Pintail, northern, **113**
Pinxter, Florida, 26
Pinyon, 292†
Pioneer plant, 292†
Pipefish, 292†
Piping plover, **295**
Pipit, 284, 293†
Pipsissewa, **292,** 293†
Pitchblende, 411
Pitcher plant, 66, 293†, **293**
Pit viper, 84, 87, 294†, **296–297,** 316
Plankton, 106, 294†
Plant, 8, 164
　　aquatic. *See* Aquatic plant.
　　carnivorous. *See* Carnivorous plant.
　　endangered, 119
　　epiphytic. *See* Epiphyte.
　　extinction of, 123
　　mimicry in, 238–239
　　parasitic, 280
　　photosynthesis in, 8, 206, 208, 289†, 308
　　pioneer, 292†
　　poisonous. *See* Poisonous plant.
　　weed, 424–425†
　　xerophytic, 438†
Plant, flowering, 134†, 297
　　annual, 14†
　　See also Flower.
Plantain, 294†, **294**
Plant community
　　climax, 78†
　　succession in, 378, **378**
Plant louse. *See* Aphid.
Plateau, 294†
Playa, 295†
Plover, 62, 236, 295†, **295,** 352
Poacher, 295†
Pocket gopher, **169,** 296†, **296,** 325
Pocket mouse, 261, 296†
Pogonia, fringe-lipped rose, **271**
Poison hemlock, 168†, **169,** 298
Poison ivy, 298, **298**
Poisonous plant, 298–299†, **298, 299**
Poisonous snake, 296–297†
Poisonwood, 298
Pokeweed, 297†, **297,** 298
Polar bear, 338, **398, 413**
Pollen, 154, **172, 296,** 297†
　　ragweed, 313†

Pollination, 173, **212,** 239, **297,** 297†
　　bees and, 35, 430–431
　　hummingbird and, 181
Pollution, **300,** 300–301†
　　endangered species and, 119
　　eutrophication caused by, 122
　　of ground water, 161
　　See also Air pollution.
Polygala, fringed, 238, **238**
Polyp, 304, 341
Polyphemus moth, 301†
Pompano, 56, 191
Pond, **125,** 302–303†, **302, 303**
　　kettle, 197†
　　succession in, 378
Ponderosa pine, 29, **29**
Pond lily, 301†, **302**
Pondweed, 20, 301†
Poplar, yellow (tulip tree), 406†
Poppy, 301†
　　California, 62†, **104, 301**
　　desert, 102–103†
Porcupine, 16, 301†, **324,** 325
Porcupinefish, 301†
Porgy, 304†
Porpoise, 109, 304†, 426
　　echolocation of, 118
　　language of, 16
Portuguese man-of-war, 57, 304†, **304**
Possum. *See* Opossum.
Possumhaw, 172
Potato, hog, 172†
Potato-bug bird, 160
Pothole, 304†
Prairie. *See* Grassland.
Prairie chicken, 162, 208, 304–305†
　　greater, **159, 304**
Prairie crocus, 13
Prairie dog, 17, 128, **158,** 261, 305†, **305,** 373
　　black-tailed, **261**
Prairie dove, 163
Prairie pothole, 305†, **305**
Prairie wetland, 305
Praying mantis (mantid), 63, **222,** 223†
Precipitation, 306†
　　drought and, 111
Predator, 306†, **306**
Prickly ash, 306†
Prickly pear, **61, 104,** 307†, **307**
Primrose, 307†
　　evening, 122–123†, **122**
　　Parry's, **248**
Prince Edward Island, 114, 201, 270
Prince's plume, 307†, **307**
Promethea moth, 307†, **307**
Pronghorn, **158,** 308†, **308,** 410
Protozoan, 280, 294, 308†
Ptarmigan, **63,** 63, 162, 308†, 407
　　white-tailed, **309**
Puffball, **143,** 308†, **308,** 368
Puffer, 309†
Puffin, 309†, **309, 340**
Puma. *See* Mountain lion.
Pumice, 206, 319
Pumpkinseed, 380
Pupa, 234, 247
Pupfish, 198–199
Pussy willow, 68, **296,** 429
Pygmy mouse, 325
Pyrite, 309†, 379
Pyroxene, 144
Pyrrhuloxia, 64
Pyxie cup, **209**

A dagger (†) following an index entry indicates that the entry is the title of a feature article.
Page numbers in **bold** type refer to illustrations.

453

A dagger (†) following an index entry indicates that the entry is the title of a feature article.
Page numbers in **bold** type refer to illustrations.

455

Z